Contents

Chapter Nine Self-Determination and Self-Government: The Rights of Peoples   249

Chapter Ten The Inuit of the North: Nation Building in Practice   281

Chapter Twelve The Department of Indian and Northern Affairs Canada   349

Chapter Thirteen Aboriginal Economic Development: Local and Global Opportunities   377

Preface

When I started working on the first edition of this book, little did I know that I would continue this venture for more than a quarter of a century. Over this time the global environment has changed substantially and new people have occupied positions of power. Old political figures are no longer recognized by young Canadians, and new institutions and new ways of operating have been created. While the process of devolution has continued to advance, many of the attributes of colonialization still remain. This new edition chronicles the changes that have taken place over the past century and how they have impacted upon Canadians and Aboriginal peoples. Dr. René Gadacz, my co-author, is a social anthropologist and has made a substantive contribution to the breadth and scope of the material presented.

Aboriginal Peoples in Canada provides the reader with an understanding of Aboriginal rights within the context of the Canadian Constitution. We begin with a historical discussion of Aboriginal–non-Aboriginal relations and then trace the evolution of these relations over time. The primary task of this book is to provide the reader with an understanding of the place of Aboriginal people within Canadian society. We will provide this through a number of lenses. For example, the Supreme Court of Canada has dealt with Aboriginal rights and their links to British property law, and has clearly acknowledged that there is a new constitutional meaning and role for Aboriginal people. We also show how Aboriginal issues are viewed by politicians and representative Canadians. We have tried to maintain our objectivity in presenting the material in this volume. However, we are all human beings with values, and we admit that our personal experiences and points of view influence the approach taken in this book. Yet we have tried to state things as clearly as we can and not to let traditional or commonly accepted perspectives go unchallenged if they deserve to be challenged. We want readers to know that we do not have an "axe to grind," but we do have biases and we are sure they will show. Nevertheless, these are our personal views and should be assessed differently from those based upon solid social science research and careful public analysis.

The authors do not take a specific theoretical perspective in looking at Aboriginal–Euro-Canadian relations, although one could argue that the book is more focused on macro issues and looks at structural factors as shaping how Aboriginal people and the rest of Canada relate. We do not focus on micro (individual) factors although we understand that they operate in our society (e.g., prejudice, discrimination). But that is another story that deserves to be more fully articulated in another time and place. The book is steeped in an analysis of structural inter-group relations in which the two groups operate. We are convinced this approach is necessary for understanding the environment of Aboriginal–White relations and to make sense of the shifting landscape in which they take place.

For the first half of the 20th century, Canadians showed little interest in Aboriginal people. However, by the 1950s, government became embarrassed by international incidents that placed Canada and its treatment of Aboriginals on the global map. Through the commissioning of government reports, a small body of evidence emerged that suggested Aboriginal people were not benefiting from the growing economy and enhancing their quality of life. By the 1960s, academics began to write on the subject and to add to the growing knowledge base. However, it was not until the 1970s that an explosion of books, articles, movies, and other popular cultural and media representations occurred. By the mid-1980s, Aboriginal issues were dealt with by the mass media on a regular basis. Aboriginal issues are now commonplace in newspapers and magazines. Academics now routinely teach in Native Studies programs or courses concerned with Aboriginal people. In the past two decades, more and more material on Aboriginal people has been published in both scholarly journals and popular media outlets. These and other publications have a diversity of foci—legal, land claims, justice, deviance, health, housing, language—from a variety of theoretical perspectives (e.g., Eurocentric, Aboriginal, feminist, Marxist, structural-functional). Aboriginal Studies is now an accepted area of study, regardless of its lack of boundaries and central focus, and 12 different universities across Canada now offer academic programs in the area.

The seventh edition follows the general format of the original work. Nevertheless, the present volume comprises a considerable updating and revision of the last edition. While there have been many specific changes over the past five years, the overall position of Aboriginal people in our society has not appreciably changed. It is said that if you work on an enterprise long enough, you will eventually gain some perspective on it. But as noted elsewhere, failing eyesight sometimes offsets the gain in perspective. We have no doubt that as we write the seventh edition, both events have occurred. Nevertheless, even though our eyesight may have diminished, we are convinced that the perspective offered to the reader will illuminate his or her intellectual world and provide for a better under-standing of Aboriginal people in Canadian society. We hope we are able to give the reader a lens through which to view our complex and diverse society and, in the end, we hope the reader will be able to develop a better appreciation of how historical events influence contemporary issues and thus have the intellectual tools to better analyze Aboriginal–Euro-Canadian relations.

Novelists, academics, and politicians have been inspired for years to write about their observations of Aboriginal people. While many Canadians have some knowledge or con-ception about Aboriginal people, most of us have few encounters with Aboriginal people directly. Yet, at a more abstract level, we speak about their plight and treatment. As you, the reader, go through this book, sometimes you will be in agreement, on other occasions your perspective will differ. Our goal is to write a book that provides a critical interpreta-tion of the events that have shaped Aboriginal–Euro-Canadian relations and that thus have formed the structure of Canadian society. As we note in the text, many of the original works on Aboriginal people were written from the point of view of the dominant group. The material offered in this book tries to present ethnic relation from the position of "outsider," identifying both the majority and minority perspectives.

This seventh edition, like previous ones, has been written for individuals who are not experts in the area of Aboriginal Studies. It is primarily for the neophyte reader, but one who would like as panoramic a view as possible. More advanced readers will find it use-ful because it presents up-to-date statistical material, the latest court decisions, current leg-islation as it impacts Aboriginal people, and the most recent research on Aboriginal issues. The list of reference material presents the reader with a cornucopia of citations that span the last century and it will be a useful aid for covering the field.

Acknowledgements

Those who know the subject area will recognize that we owe a large debt to those who have already worked on and written about Aboriginal people. As such, regardless of what the copyright law says, this book is not the sole product of the co-authors. We have drawn heavily on the works of our colleagues across Canada and they have shared their thoughts and ideas with us—their understanding and criticism of old ideas made us search constantly for new conceptualizations and hopefully, new solutions. We thank them for their insightful and analytical comments. We would also like to thank those Aboriginal people who have, over the years, shared with us their views and interpretations of Aboriginal–Euro-Canadian relations in this country. The citations at the end of this volume should be regarded as further acknowledgments of a number of scholars who have written on the subject.

At Pearson Education we are grateful to our Acquisitions Editor, Jessica Mosher, and Marketing Coordinator, Erica Willer, for the strong support they have given this project. We owe special thanks to our Developmental Editor, Patti Altridge, for her endless good humour, patience, careful guidance, and outstanding contribution in preparing the manuscript for publication. Tara Tovell deserves accolades for her very fine copyediting. We also thank Charlotte Morrison-Reed and Anita Heyna for shepherding the text through production, as well as the team in Creative Services for their skillful design of the text. Lastly, we acknowledge Sandra Lonergan, Dennis H. McPherson, Rob Nester, Fred Shore, and John Steckley, whose critical review comments helped shape the earlier editions of *Aboriginal Peoples in Canada*.

Additional Thanks

I owe a great deal to Dr. Roy Bowles, whose intellectual influence on me began when I first took a course from him while in graduate school. Don Whiteside (sin-a-paw), Tony Lussier, and Katie Cook have, over the years, shared with me their philosophical perspectives as well as the materials I requested, some of which were provided at considerable cost to themselves. Other scholars such as Tony Hall, George Calliou, Shawna Cunningham, Rick Ponting, Terry Wotherspoon, William Reeves, Roger Gibbins, and Jim Webb have provided new interpretations to past events and given me the courage to challenge many previously accepted "truths."

J. S. Frideres
Calgary, Alberta

I would like to thank my students from the University of Northern British Columbia, Northern Lights College, Okanagan University College and the University of Victoria for participating in the very difficult task of nation-building by questioning (and sometimes revising!) their personal assumptions and philosophies in the field of Aboriginal Studies. A special thank-you to Ms. Leslie Fabriz, Nlaka'pumx Nation, for her very able research assistance on the seventh edition of this book. I am also grateful to Michael I. Asch, Bruce G. Trigger, and James S. Frideres for opportunities, advice, insights, and encouragements over three decades of scholarship. Finally, my thanks to you, Solange. Completing my various writing projects has been difficult, but without you, it would have been much harder.

René R. Gadacz
Kelowna, British Columbia

chapter one

The Legacy of Canadian Colonialism

INTRODUCTION

Questions concerning the rights of Aboriginal people in Canada have taken a curious prominence in Canadian politics. The federal government has, for the past half-century, conveyed a message to Canadians that it has, or is just about to, resolve the issues that Aboriginal people are bringing forth (Churchill, 1999). Thus it is not surprising that most Canadians find it difficult to understand the demands being made by Aboriginal people. Moreover, they will find that they are not prepared or able to link historical actions with contemporary events. In other words, it is difficult to see how historical events are causal agents of today's actions. Most people tend to see historical events as discrete events that have little or no bearing on today's events. One goal of this book is to show the reader how historical events, even though they may have happened one hundred years ago, have an impact on today's conditions. The analysis presented in this book reveals both an active interference and a benign neglect on the part of both the federal and provincial governments as they deal with Aboriginal people over time. The current marginalization that Aboriginal people experience today is no recent event but rather is rooted in historical circumstances. This political-economy approach will reveal the similarities among Aboriginal peoples around the world as they experienced similar fates in the past and face similar problems today. This suggests that there are similarities in settler societies with regard to the processes that affect Aboriginal peoples in historical times as well as in the present. These structural impacts began to affect Aboriginal people at the time of contact with Europeans and became increasingly influential as the immigrant population grew. As the world political economy began to integrate with the Canadian domestic economy, these structural effects relegated Aboriginal peoples in Canada and throughout the world to a peripheral position in society.

What are these processes? How have they impacted upon Aboriginal people? We begin our analysis of Aboriginal–non-Aboriginal relations and Aboriginal participation in society by moving from a micro (individual) analysis to a macro (structural) analysis. For too long, social scientists have viewed Aboriginal–non-Aboriginal relations through a micro model, focusing exclusively on individual actions, e.g., prejudice and discrimination. Not surprisingly, these models see solutions to the problems Aboriginal people face as being brought about through individual action, e.g., individual enhancement and individual entrepreneurship. We wish to approach the problems from a different perspective that involves social structural factors, e.g., the organization of the society, the alignment of social institutions, the change in demographic factors. While we will not deny that Aboriginal people are exposed to a great deal of prejudice and discrimination, their greatest obstacle is the very structure of our society itself, which prevents them from effectively participating in the social, economic, and political institutions of our society. Furthermore, we feel that there is a linkage between the structural effects (the institutional arrangements of our society) and the behaviour of individuals.

The analytical model presented here has as its forerunners those offered by P. Cumming (1967), Carstens (1971, 1991), and Patterson (1972). Drawing heavily on these authors, the macro model used here presents the Indian reserve as an internal colony that is exploited by the dominant group in Canada. Canadians are seen as the colonizing people, while Aboriginal persons are considered the colonized people. By conceptualizing the reserve as an internal colony of a larger nation, it is possible to see beyond the individual factors involved in inter-group behaviour. While the individualized approach has contributed much to the study of Aboriginal–non-Aboriginal relations, it has not produced any cogent explanation of those relations. Nor has it produced any meaningful improvement in the Aboriginal person's position in our society. Many social scientists have rejected the colonial analysis as misleading, claiming that our social and political patterns are significantly different from those in, for example, Africa or India. Although there have certainly been differences, these do not obscure the fact that the indigenous peoples of Canada were unquestionably colonized and that their position in Canada today is a direct result of the colonization process.

The colonization process can be considered in seven parts (Kennedy, 1945; Blauner, 1969). The first concerns the incursion of the colonizing group into a geographical area. This usually takes the form of forced-voluntary entry; acting in its own interests, the colonizing group forces its way into an area. In Canada, both French and English settlement followed this pattern. At present, many Northern Aboriginal people argue that forced-voluntary colonization is occurring in the North.

The second attribute of colonization is its destructive effect on the social and cultural structures of the indigenous group. In Canada's case, European colonizers destroyed the Native peoples' political, economic, kinship, and, in most cases, religious systems. The values and norms of Aboriginal peoples were either ignored or violated. For example, after the War of 1812, when a large number of European settlers arrived, the colonial government decided that Aboriginal persons should be forced to surrender their traditional lifestyles. Official programs were developed, and between 1830 and 1875 legislation was enacted to carry out this destructive policy (Surtees, 1969).

As Titley (1986) points out, the federal government's policies were in harmony with the demands of non-Aboriginal people. The creation of "trust authority" over Indian lands and assets demonstrates their commitment to dictate what resources will be exploited, in what quantities, and by whom. It also allows the government to determine for what purpose and at what cost. As Ward (1999) goes on to argue, it was important that the reserves be made to look "self-governing" so that they would be exempt from normal business practices and thus subject only to the unique rules established by Indian Affairs. The protests of Aboriginal people were futile, and when they took action to support their claims in the late 1860s, harsh repression followed, including the bombardment of coastal villages by British warships (Tobias, 1976). By the late 1890s, the federal government had amended the *Indian Act* (of 1876) so that "surplus" or "idle" Aboriginal land could be made available for the use of non-Indians. In 1911, amendments to the *Indian Act* gave even greater coercive powers to the federal government. For example, Section 46 allowed portions of reserves to be taken by municipalities or companies for roads or similar public purposes with the consent of the Governor-in-Council (today called the Cabinet), but without a surrender (Carter, 1990; Imai and Hawley, 1995).

Canadian officials have, since the early 19th century, viewed Aboriginal people as inferior. Education and religious groups actively engaged in strategies to bring about Aboriginal social change in order to "civilize" and "Christianize" them. During this time, a symbiotic relationship emerged between various churches and the state. The best example of this was when the churches were being frustrated in their efforts to Christianize Native people. Church officials felt that because certain Aboriginal cultural components were incompatible with Christianity, they should be eradicated. They therefore convinced the state to pass legislation outlawing a variety of dances and other ceremonies that were an integral component of the Aboriginal culture—for example, the potlatch.

The third and fourth aspects of colonization are the interrelated processes of external political control and Aboriginal economic dependence. In the standard practice of colonization, the mother country sends out representatives through which it indirectly rules the newly conquered land. In our model, the representative ruler is INAC (the Department of Indian and Northern Affairs Canada). Until 1940, Indian Affairs decided which Aboriginal people could and couldn't leave reserve lands. Aboriginal self-government has been effectively prevented. Until recently, band funds could not be used by Aboriginal people to develop social and political organizations of their own (Whiteside, 1972). In some cases, Aboriginal groups have been allowed to elect their own chiefs and band councils, but these are advisory only, with no real power. Council recommendations continue to be subject to acceptance or rejection by INAC.

The Minister of INAC can suspend almost any right set forth in the *Indian Act*. For example, Section 80 of the Act authorizes band councils to pass bylaws for public health and traffic regulation. However, to date, the Minister has granted less than two-thirds of band councils permission to do so.

Acting through Cabinet, INAC can also veto any decisions of band councils. For example, Section 82 of the *Indian Act* allows a band to enact money by-laws. However, Cabinet must first find that the band has reached a "high state of development." At present, fewer than 50 bands have been so defined, and these have mostly used their powers to build sewers, wells, and so on. Section 68 of the Act allows a band to "control, manage, and expand in whole or in part its revenue moneys." No band was actually permitted to do so until 1959, and to date fewer than 20 percent have received permission. Section 60 allows a band "the right to exercise such control and management over lands in the reserve occupied by that band as the Cabinet considers desirable." To date, Cabinet has found this desirable for less than 10 percent of the reserves. Section 35 of the Act explicitly states that reserve land can be expropriated by the federal government at any time. Unfortunately, this provision has been implemented many times over the past half-century.

In the initial stages of colonization, the colonized people generally accept their fate. Only later do they reject their powerless position. Aboriginal leaders on reserves today tend to be considerably more militant than those who initially signed treaties. But even if Aboriginal peoples no longer accept their subordinate status, there is little they can do to change it. Although, as Bolt (1980a) showed, many Aboriginal leaders view extra-legal activity as a viable method of pressing their claims, others have surrendered to a general apathy and dispiritedness that results in the long-term impact of colonialization. The process of acculturation and the demise of indigenous Aboriginal tribal associations have eroded Aboriginal self-identification. Communal bonds have broken down among individual Aboriginal persons and among bands, contributing to the continued failure of Aboriginal organizations. Leadership responsibilities on the reserves have become further divided and poorly defined, exacerbating the disorganization of Aboriginal groups. In the political arena, Aboriginal people have been ineffectual for several reasons. Most importantly, they have been prevented from voting or running for office until recent decades. Except in Nova Scotia, Aboriginal persons did not receive the right to vote in provincial elections until after World War II. They did not receive the federal franchise until 1960. Needless to say, this severely restricted their ability to make political demands. Those with no voice in the political structure that governs their lives have no means of influencing or sanctioning the policies that affect them. Even after receiving the vote, Aboriginal people continue to be skeptical of their rights, although this attitude is changing.

Aboriginal people remain economically dependent on the larger society because their reserves are treated as geographical and social hinterlands for Euro-Canadian exploitation. Euro-Canadian–controlled businesses exploit nonrenewable primary resources such as oil, minerals, water, and forest products, and ship them to urban industrial centres for processing. This practice has two important consequences for Aboriginal people on reserves: the development of Aboriginal-owned industries is pre-empted, and Aboriginal occupational activities remain at a primary level. As the treaties and the *Indian Act* show, federal policy has always tried to orient Aboriginal occupations toward agriculture and primary industries (Carter, 1990).

In the colonization process, a two-level system develops in which the colonizers own, direct, and profit from industries that depend upon exploitation of colonized peoples, who provide an unskilled, seasonal work force. On the reserves, the long-term result has been an Aboriginal population that lives at subsistence level, working at unskilled, seasonal jobs in primary industries, and practising subsistence agriculture to survive. Although the profits from raw material production are based on reserve resources and cheap Aboriginal labour, they disappear from the reserve into the pockets of non-Aboriginal entrepreneurs.

Reserve hinterlands are at a low level of economic development. Economic development is not the same as economic growth. Economic growth refers to an increase in the productive capacity of an area's economy, while economic development reflects a change in the structure of an area's economy, such as a movement from primary extractive or agricultural industries to secondary or processing industries. For example, some Alberta reserves and Métis colonies have experienced considerable short-term economic growth due to oil and mineral discoveries, but no real economic development. Most striking is the statistic relative to Aboriginal leaders who derive their influence from the economic sector. Not a single Aboriginal leader could be classified as exercising his influence in the economic sector. This provides evidence of the degree to which Aboriginal people generally have been excluded from the Canadian economic sector and hence the power structure.

The federal government had effectively discouraged the economic development of reserves, as the *Income Tax Act* and the *Indian Act* show. For example, many years ago Fields and Stanbury (1975) found that if Aboriginal people created a limited corporation to engage in business, they lost the benefit of exemption from taxation as individuals or as a band. As a result, income earned by a corporation wholly owned by Aboriginal people was subject to taxation the same as any corporation, even if the income was derived solely from activities on a reserve. While some provisions of the Income Tax Act have changed, the overall thrust remains the same today. The structural complexities involved in the payment of property taxes on reserve lands also prevent Aboriginal people from profitably leasing their lands. Imai (1999) has produced an annotated *Indian Act* and Aboriginal Constitutional provisions document to help band leaders and individual Aboriginal persons find their way through the complexities. To illustrate this, Fields and Stanbury posit an example in which a developer decides to build a warehouse on a piece of rented property. Two similarly suitable locations are available; one is on an Indian reserve, the other is not. The firm discovers that it can rent either the reserve or the off-reserve land for $3000 per year. When it approaches the band, however, it finds that it must agree to pay taxes to the municipality assessed at $1500 per year, as though it owned the land. In order then to compete with the owner of the off-reserve land, the band must reduce its rent to $1500 per year to absorb the taxes. Thus, by leasing its land instead of developing and occupying it itself, the band incurs an opportunity cost of $1500.

A fifth attribute of colonization is the provision of low-quality social services for the colonized Aboriginal persons in such areas as health and education. A survey by INAC confirms a desperate need for adequate social services. For example, the report points out a lower life expectancy than the general population, higher levels of support from social assistance organizations, and unhealthy lifestyles that are imposed by poverty. Although Aboriginal living conditions have improved in some material ways, social problems, including alcohol abuse and welfare dependency, have increased.

The sixth and seventh aspects of colonization relate to social interactions between Aboriginal and non-Aboriginal people and refer to racism and the establishment of a colour-line. Racism is a belief in the genetic or cultural superiority of the colonizers and the inferiority of the colonized people. With a colour-line, indicators such as skin pigmentation and body structure are established to become the basis for determining superiority and inferiority. Interaction then goes on only among members of the same group: non-Aboriginals interact with non-Aboriginals and Aboriginal people with Aboriginal people. In Canada, for example, Native people have the highest rate of marriage within their own ethnic group—almost 94 percent.

The ultimate consequence of colonization is to weaken the resistance of Aboriginal people to the point at which they can be controlled. Whether the motives for colonization are religious, economic, or political, the rewards are clearly economic. Non-Aboriginal Canada has gained far more than it has lost in colonizing its Aboriginal peoples. Currently, Aboriginal groups in Alberta are suing the federal government for more than $1.5 billion over non-payment of royalties on the extraction of natural resources from land set aside for them. These battles have long histories but, with long-term profits estimated at $1–2 billion, the state and private enterprise are not about to give up easily.

Like any model, the colonization approach has certain limitations. The world is complex: people, social structures, and cultures change with time. Of necessity, however, a model is frozen in time, a static recreation of what occurs around us. In order to construct a portrait that corresponds closely to the real world, we select and incorporate certain variables, discard others as unimportant, and make assumptions about how people behave.

If the resulting model produces accurate explanations and predictions, it can be considered successful. It may then become a useful tool in finding solutions to social problems and in developing social action programs. If, however, a model proves incapable of providing accurate predictions or explanations, it must be revised or discarded. Our model suggests that historical colonialism has shaped the organization of our society and set in motion a number of factors that propelled Aboriginal people to the margins of our society.

First of all, Aboriginal participation in the Canadian economy has become economically redundant over time because of changes in the structure and technology of the national economy. After the buffalo hunts ended and the fur trade all but ceased, Aboriginal people were largely unable to participate in the economy. As Canadian society moved to agriculture and then to an urban-industrial base, Aboriginal peoples did not possess, and were not in a position to acquire, new technologies or skills. The result is that Aboriginal people found themselves operating a subsistence economy parallel to that of the more modern economy. In other words, there are two economies in our society. The industrial and technologically based modern sector of the economy is dynamic: change promotes further change. The traditional, subsistence sector of the economy, however, resists change: it clings to the old ways and refuses to adopt new technology (Wien, 1986). This of course suggests that, as our economy becomes more knowledge based, barriers continue to be created that hinder or prevent entrance of Aboriginal people into the knowledge era. Certain technical and social skills are now prerequisites for entering the labour force. People without these skills will be kept from participating as full-time members in a modern national, as well as international, labour market.

As individuals are prevented from entering the modern economy, a cultural ethos emerges that is quite different from the one expressed in the social mainstream. Anthropologists have referred to this distinctive ethos as the "culture of poverty." When the goals of higher status are denied to people, other forms of adaptation are created—for example, withdrawal and rebellion (often self-destructive)—in order to deal with the despair and hopelessness that are central to the culture of poverty. This encourages individuals to develop a different perspective on life and on how to deal with everyday occurrences.

Once an individual is placed within the traditional culture of poverty, it is almost impossible for him or her to get out. As we have seen, the lack of certain technical and social skills keeps Aboriginal persons from entering the modern labour market. And as that market becomes increasingly segmented into a primary and a secondary market, there is greater difficulty in moving from the secondary to the primary market.[1] As a result, Aboriginal persons are increasingly shut out of the primary market.

Aboriginal peoples played an important role in the development of Canada. However, as the 20th century emerged, their lack of technological skills relegated Aboriginal people to second-class citizens. While many history books acknowledge the interaction of Aboriginal people and Europeans, they tend to characterize Aboriginal persons as passive, always responding to actions taken by Europeans. In short, the interaction between the two parties usually portrayed Europeans as the proactive agents, asserting their vision of Canada regardless of Aboriginal people. There are some exceptions to this general pattern (Miller, 2000), but the history of Aboriginal–Euro-Canadian relations in Canada has generally been told from the perspective of non-Aboriginal people. As Dickason (2002) points out, problems of interpretation become problematic when considering European accounts of their exploits in the new America. She notes, for example that there can be differences in connotations of words as used in the 16th or 17th century and today. She also points out that in the case of historical published accounts, what appears in print may not be what the author wrote. Historically, publishers were more interested in the saleability of material than in its veracity.

When Aboriginal people and Europeans first came into contact, two different cultures came into contact. Aboriginal people were hunters and gatherers (although there were some agricultural tribes) who lived in harmony with their physical environment. Their limited technological developments made few demands on the ecology, and the small numbers of people meant that population pressures were light (Miller, 2000). Europeans, on the other hand, were continually developing their technology to achieve control over nature. They were ethnocentric in outlook and had a mission to Christianize the world. The clash of these two cultures was resounding, and while there is no doubt that Native people have taken the brunt of this collision, they have, surprisingly, retained considerable elements of their culture. They have, when possible, taken a "controlled acculturation" perspective, adopting certain behaviours and actions of Euro-American culture while retaining other valued mental constructs from their own culture. Perhaps the creation of reserves and the resulting high level of isolation of many Aboriginal people has allowed this selective retention to be carried out (Brown, 1977, 1978).

The underlying basis characterizing Aboriginal–Euro-Canadian relations in our history is that Europeans have always assumed superiority over Aboriginal people. As was noted in the discussion of the characteristics of colonization, this is racism—the belief that one group is biologically inferior to another group.

As the British secretary of state for war and the colonies noted in 1830:

> It appears to me that the course which has hitherto been taken in dealing with these [Aboriginal] people has had reference to the advantages which might be derived from their friendship in times of war, rather than to any settled purpose of gradually reclaiming them from a state of barbarism, and of introducing amongst them the industrious and peaceful habits of civilized life. (Sir G. Murray, 1834)

Although some people may object to this claim, racism is undeniably the underlying ideology of the manifest policies regarding Aboriginal–European relations throughout the history of Canada.

Here is a statement by the Minister of the Interior nearly a century later in 1902:

> Our position with reference to the Indian is this: We have them with us, and we have to deal with them as wards of the country. There is no question that the method we have adopted [will bring] these people to an improved state.... There is a difference between the savage and a person who has become civilized, though perhaps not of a high type. (Debate of the House of Commons, 2nd sess., 9th Parl., 1902: 3046)

The reader may claim that these are isolated examples from a different era. However, a closer review of documents from the 17th to the 20th century reveal that these statements are representative of the prevailing legal, academic, and literary attitudes of the time. The reader might also claim that people are far more enlightened today. To be sure, most people today would not argue that one group of people are biologically inferior to another. However, this biological racism has been supplanted by a new form of social/cultural racism that focuses on the inferiority of a group's way of life, their ethos, and their assumptions about the world. In taking this view, people may escape being accused of racism: they are prepared to accept the biological similarities of different groups of people. However, they are not prepared to accept cultural equality. Individual racism has given way to structural racism. Examining structural racism allows one to focus on the way discrimination is built into systems of power and institutions in Canada (Nichols, 1998).

Over time, non-Aboriginal Canadians have revealed contradictory attitudes and behaviour toward Aboriginal people. They have publicly proclaimed respect for the rights of Aboriginal people while at the same time denying them such basic rights as voting and the right to choose their reserves (Anderson and Wright, 1971; Washburn, 1965). For those wishing to examine a more detailed historical review of Aboriginal–non-Aboriginal relations in Canada, the following sources should be consulted: *Report on the Affairs of the Indians in Canada,* 1844; Jenness, 1967; Stanley, 1952; Patterson, 1972; Miller, 2000; and Dickason, 2002.

Although it may never be possible to quantify the degree of racism that exists in a given society, the evidence unmistakably reveals that racism widely distorts the attitudes of Euro-Canadians toward Aboriginal peoples. Whether blatantly or covertly, many Canadians still believe that Aboriginal people are inferior; as a result, these people believe that there is a sound, rational basis for discrimination against Aboriginal persons at both the individual and institutional level.

The hostility and conflict established historically between Aboriginal people and political and legal enforcement bodies has contributed to the contemporary relationships between them, which are based on suspicion, disrespect, and mistrust on both sides. Through a history of enactments legislated through colonial Parliament, the institutions in this country have been used to segregate Aboriginal peoples from the dominant culture and to legitimize paternalistic control over all aspects of their lives. Having been excluded from recognition as human beings, Aboriginal persons were not granted a social identity as Canadians in the full sense of the word until after World War II. However, while being granted Aboriginal rights (in their own country) may have helped to alleviate some of the consequences that emanated from the horrific colonial era, no attempts were made by political or judicial quarters to address the discriminatory and biased legal provisions that were used to deny them parity and equality with their dominant counterparts. The historical situation provided the initial conditions, and by apathy and indifference, rather than intentional exploitation, those conditions have continued to exist. While the introduction of the *Charter of Rights and Freedoms* in 1982 was assessed as a significant step toward enacting a degree of reform in this area, the Aboriginal population found little comfort in it because of the inadequacies that were attached to its legislative jurisdictional powers.

The old ways of non-Aboriginal people looking at and relating to Aboriginal people have been reflected in the way government has treated them. However, some of these old views are now coming under scrutiny and being challenged. Weaver (1981) points out that the *Penner Report* on Aboriginal self-government (1983) and the *Coolican Report* on comprehensive land claims (1986) broke new ground in conceptualizing issues involving Aboriginal people. The Royal Commission on Aboriginal Peoples brought into focus what Aboriginal people were thinking and reflects their current view of how they should fit into Canadian society. What is this new conceptualization? First, a new idea about the relationship between Aboriginal and non-Aboriginal people is presented. Whereas non-Aboriginal people previously tended to view the linkages as eventually resulting in the "termination" of Aboriginal persons and/or their full integration into non-Aboriginal society (i.e., assimilation), these reports view the relationship as parallel over time, with the two cultures adjusting to each other as the time and context change. In other words, they see the relationship as equal, flexible, and evolving.

A second new conceptualization identified by Weaver (1981) is the notion of sanctioned rights, which she defines as those rights recognized by the state as justified claims against its actions toward a particular group. Related to this is a new political ethic developed in government with regard to how it deals with Aboriginal people. There is a new commitment to being direct, honest, and honourable in government dealings with Aboriginal people. This new ethic has been brought to the forefront as a result of a number of court decisions that have gone against the government. This also means that partnership is the relationship government will have with Aboriginal people. Out of this partnership, jointly formulated policies will emerge that will lead to some form of Aboriginal empowerment (Weaver, 1981).

All of the above reveal a new ethos regarding the relationship between Aboriginal people and the government. This is one of the major points that the recent Royal Commission on Aboriginal Peoples made. If it is to be accepted, then the relationship must be restructured. These new ideas have begun to challenge the old views, but before they become dominant in government thinking, old conceptualizations will have to be dropped. Therefore, during the current transitional period, the Department of Indian Affairs has undergone turbulent times in recent decades as proponents of each perspective try to make their position the basis for action. This is one reason why government seemingly takes contradictory stands in dealing with Aboriginal people. For example, Sanders (1993) points out that even the Supreme Court has not been consistent in its rulings with regard to Aboriginal people. In some cases the inconsistencies reflect the evolution of doctrine, while others defy explanation. Yet the changes seem to reflect the emergence of a new perspective and a new place for Aboriginal persons in Canadian society. However, whether or not this new view of Aboriginal people will become the dominant one remains to be seen.

Confrontations between Aboriginal and non-Aboriginal people noted in the press tend to focus on specific complaints, overlook broader issues, and reflect an old definition of Aboriginal people and their role in Canadian society. Hence, in many cases where conflict emerges, Aboriginal persons are labelled as malcontents, troublemakers, and opportunists—labels that can only be defended through a distorted and abbreviated view of history (Lambertus, 2004). As Weaver (1981) points out, the federal government's response to Oka was that the situation was a "law and order" problem which, when defined in this manner, required and justified the harsh and extraordinary measures that were taken.

As at Oka, the stage for clashes between Aboriginal and Euro-Canadian people has generally been set by historical facts and existing structural relations, though few people are interested in examining these. For example, the Lubicons in Alberta who have blockaded roads and shut down oil pumps have generally been depicted as irresponsible troublemakers. Yet surely the reasons for their protest were linked to the fact that the band has been fighting for land to be set aside for a reserve promised 50 years ago, for compensation for energy and forestry development that had taken well over $5 billion of natural resources from the area, for the Aboriginal children who die before their first birthday, for the Aboriginal people who are unable to get jobs, and for the large number of Native people who are unable to secure adequate housing. Nevertheless, when confrontations erupt, the implication is that the fault lies largely with Aboriginal people. This assumption reveals a biased and short-term perspective. Such an assumption ignores the subtle violence that has been perpetrated against Aboriginal people since the arrival of the European explorers. It also serves those who want to remain in power and maintain the status quo that excludes Aboriginal people from a share in their country's bounty and that allows them to remain hungry, uneducated, and inadequately housed in the midst of plenty.

Some readers will be angered by these statements and indignant that their society should be labelled racist. They will say that other history books do not make such claims. But history is humanity's way of recording past behaviour; historians are extremely susceptible to the political and social forces that govern while their histories are being written. What Aboriginal people have been encouraged to write histories? And when Aboriginal histories have been written, why have they been dismissed as fabrications?

An author's explanation of social events depends on an individual point of view. Because overt social behaviour can be interpreted in many different ways, the historian must always infer the actors' motives. Historians infer motives for groups as well as for individuals. Unfortunately, until recently, our historians have largely been Euro-Canadians; as a result, they have largely based their inferences on the same primary assumptions and therefore have presented similar views of social reality (Trudel and Jain, 1970).

Throughout recorded time, empowered groups have been able to define history and provide an explanation of the present. A good example is the portrayal of wars between Aboriginal and European peoples by Canadian historians. Euro-Canadian historians have concentrated on these wars partly because of the "enemy concept": as Pelletier (1970) has pointed out, non-Aboriginal endeavours are continually described in terms of fighting an enemy, whether the war is waged against crime, inflation, or cancer.

In the history books, when Aboriginal people attacked a non-Aboriginal village or fort and won, the result was called a massacre. If Europeans attacked an Aboriginal village and won, it was described as a victory. Because the dominant group was able to make these interpretations and definitions, it was also able to keep others from initiating alternative explanations or definitions. History gives credence and legitimacy to a society's normative structure; to legitimize its power, the dominant groups must reconstruct social history whenever necessary. The early reconstructions of Canadian history were effective: today, most Canadians continue to associate "savage" and "heinous" behaviour with Canadian Aboriginal people. As Churchill (1999) points out, the standard European/Canadian depiction of Aboriginals has been one of a small number of people who wandered about in scatter bands, grubbing out an existence through hunting and gathering, never developing writing or serious appreciation of art, science, or mathematics. It has been believed that aside from utilizing furs and hides for clothing and housing, there were few attributes that distinguished Aboriginal people from other higher orders of mammalian life.

Readers have reacted quite differently to books by Cardinal (1969), Pelletier (1970), and Waubageshig (1970) than they have to books by Morton (1963), McInnis (1959), and Lower (1957). The layperson typically rejects the conclusions of the first three authors as the products of bias. But the same person tends to accept the explanations provided by the second group of "established academic" authors. We are not suggesting that the first are right or the second wrong. But both groups deserve to be read and judged fairly.

As Patterson (1972) points out, alien history is pulled down and discredited, and national history replaces it. Continuity of tradition for any group is truncated when the communication channels are taken over by others who wish to transmit different information (Lindesmith and Strauss, 1968). How often have we known something to be true only to find out many years later that the government, or some other group, distorted information that might have led us to believe something quite different? Brown (1971) and Andrist (1964) have vividly portrayed American-Indian history from an alternative point of view. Their information concerning Aboriginal–non-Aboriginal relations is quite dissimilar to that provided by "established" historians. Recent histories by such authors as Miller (2000), Churchill (1999), Nichols (1998) and Dickason (1992) portray a more balanced perspective of historical events and reveal the Aboriginal side to Canadian history.

It is essential to realize that the history of Canada that is taught from Grade 5 through university has been written mainly by English-speaking Euro-Canadians, specifically of British ethnicity. The Ontario Education Commission, in a study of elementary Canadian history books, has discovered that many historical events involving Aboriginal peoples have not even been recorded. In fact, the commission found that many history books did not discuss the role of Aboriginal people in Canadian history at all. In a preliminary study, we have found the same omission from university history texts.

Walker (1971) characterized Canadian historians in their analysis of Aboriginal people in Canada as ignorant, prejudiced, and, in some cases, dishonest. But we do not have to attribute deliberate falsification to historians. In any reconstruction of the past, the author shapes an interpretation of events according to individual perceptions, memories, analytical preferences, and social background. Whether deliberately or unconsciously, a reshaping of the past occurs. No historian is free of bias; no history is capable of presenting only the facts.

HISTORY OF RELATIONS BETWEEN EURO-CANADIANS AND ABORIGINAL PEOPLES

The balance of this chapter will provide an overview of the history of the relations between the two dominant Canadian groups and Aboriginal peoples. First the French policy will be considered, then the British. Conclusions have been based on documents and histories written during the time of contact; this gathering of information through historical documents is known as a content analysis. Analysis has been limited to formal and informal documents relevant to the times, including personal correspondence between government officials.

Before discussing Aboriginal–non-Aboriginal relations, we should point out that Aboriginal–Aboriginal relations are also an important component in the way Canada has developed. For those concerned with this issue, we suggest reading the work of Trigger (1985) and Dickason (2002), who point out that Europeans were able to establish themselves in Canada partially due to the fact that a large number of Native people allowed them to and supported them in doing so. They make it very clear that, since Aboriginal people in the beginning controlled the fur trade and were militarily superior to the newcomers, European entry into the land could not have been accomplished without the cooperation of the Aboriginal groups (Coates, 1991).

In the study of Aboriginal–non-Aboriginal relations, there have been many critical historical periods that have shaped the structural linkages between them. These links determined the distribution of power, the opportunities to participate in the dominant structure, and the eventual position of subordination for the Aboriginal peoples (Nichols, 1998). In short, the actions of the government influenced the political development and incorporation of Aboriginal peoples. The most recent critical period was the 1960s, when the community development ideology began to emerge. At the turn of the century, the political links between Aboriginal and European peoples were extremely limited. Non-Indians had taken over Aboriginal communities and were accountable to other non-Indians. Power was unilateral in this relationship, which excluded Aboriginal people from participating in the larger socio-political structure. However, in the 1960s the federal government and other dominant agencies began to promote individualization as an antidote to what they saw as the problem of tribalism. This action would forever change the structure of the relationship between Aboriginal people and the government (Flanagan, 1983b).

Calls for reform in Aboriginal policy have been gaining momentum since after World War II. The new human rights awareness, the belief in social justice, and the interest in cultural diversity began to influence government policy. In the mid-1960s, the federal government commissioned a national study of the Aboriginal person's position in Canadian society—the *Hawthorn Report*. This document identified the appalling conditions under which Native people were forced to live. It suggested support for community development and promoted the implementation of major new initiatives in the areas of health and education. Nevertheless, the central assumption of the *Hawthorn Report* was that Aboriginal people should assimilate.

French-Aboriginal Relations

Initially, the French were interested in the New World as a source of wealth capable of financing wartime activities. It was hoped that the land would hold precious metals that would rival in worth those found in Spanish America (Trigger, 1985). Throughout the 16th century, fishing and whaling were the major economic activities that attracted more and more Europeans to North America. It was only at the end of the 16th century that the fur trade began to grow into an important economic activity (Brown, 1980a). The Canadian fur trade was important because, in 1583, the Swedes had captured the Baltic port of Narva through which Western Europe obtained furs from the Russians. Now that this port was closed, the French needed to find new sources.

French–Aboriginal relations must first be considered in the context of North America as a whole before we can turn specifically to Canada. A thorough review of the documents available on the attitudes of French settlers to the Aboriginal people reveals that no well-defined policy was established to govern French–Aboriginal relations. Generally, the French were attempting to exploit the land and to continue "pseudo-colonization" of North America. However, they did not initially intend to settle New France with any large stable population. Moreover, only a small number of French people wished to emigrate to New France; this fact, combined with France's mercantilistic philosophy[2] and the strong influence of Roman Catholicism, meant that no policy of cultural or physical genocide was invoked.

Initially, the French were totally dependent on the Aboriginal people, but the relationship between the two soon changed to a symbiotic one. Intermarriage, or "wintering in," between French trappers and Indian women soon became common practice, and was encouraged by French authorities who wanted to strengthen Aboriginal relations so that the fur trade would continue. These marriages between French men and Indian women were not meant to be exploitative; the relationships were stable, and the man was considered legally responsible for his wife and offspring (Brown, 1980b). However, the reader should understand that intermarriage was not a policy that originated in Canada. The French had used this technique when they colonized Brazil a century earlier. Moreover, as Dickason (1984) points out, intermixing was eased for the French by the belief that Aboriginals were really white, turning brown because of certain practices. The actual extent of intermarriage is only now being assessed. However, if one looks at formal records of intermarriage, the incidence would indicate a small number. However, other documents suggest that the rate was quite high, supported by the missionaries as a form of concubinage. Thus both economic and religious institutions supported intermarriage between Aboriginal women and French men.

In general, the French tried to expand their territories in North America by peaceful means (Francis, 1983). Usually they succeeded, because their agricultural style of life only minimally disrupted Aboriginal life.[3] After they had settled a territory, the French then asked the Indians to join in a treaty to acknowledge submission to the King of France. In this way, the French usually won territory without actually expropriating it. In 1611, Champlain sealed a pact of friendship with chief Anadabijou which allowed the French to establish themselves on Montagnais territory. In entering this alliance, the French were following a practice that they had developed a century earlier in Brazil and that was successful in establishing trade relations (Dickason, 2002). The French had long come to realize that diplomatic protocol and negotiations (by means of gift distributions) was the process by which alliances were built with Aboriginal people. However, the process was not always so peaceful, and the French were certainly prepared to use force when they found it expedient to do so. When the Marquis de Tracy was placed in charge of Canada in 1663, his commissions included a provision for the use of arms to subjugate the Aboriginal peoples if necessary.[4]

The two strongest ideological influences in 17th century New France were Roman Catholicism and mercantilism, which was popular as an economic theory. French policy, rather than treating Aboriginal people as distinct and inferior, tried to make them over into French citizens, at least in Canada.[5] This ideology of "Frenchification" is illustrated in various exchanges of letters between religious and state leaders of the day. For example, on April 6, 1666, Colbert wrote to Talon that:

> In order to strengthen the Colony in the manner you propose, by bringing the isolated settlements into parishes, it appears to me, without waiting to depend on the new colonists who may be sent from France, nothing would contribute more to it than to endeavour to civilize the Algonkians, the Hurons, and other Indians who have embraced Christianity, and to induce them to come and settle in common with the French, to live with them and raise their children according to our manners and customs. (O'Callaghan, 1856–1857: 184)

Talon replied, some seven months later, that he had tried to put Colbert's suggestions into practical operation under police regulations. Colbert then wrote, on April 9, 1667, as follows:

> Recommendation to mould the Indians, settled near us, after our manners and language.
>   I confess that I agreed with you that very little regard had been paid, up to the present time, in New France, to the police and civilization of the Algonkians and Hurons (who were a long time ago subjected to the King's domination) through our neglect to detach them from their savage customs and to obligate them to adopt ours, especially to become acquainted with our language. On the contrary, to carry on some traffic with them, our French have been necessitated to attract those people, especially such as have embraced Christianity, to the vicinity of our settlements, if possible to mingle there with them, in order that through course of time, having only but one law and one master, they might likewise constitute only one people and one race.

Another exchange of letters from the period demonstrates that this policy of assimilation was expressly favoured by the king. Duchesneau, in his letter to de Signelay, November, 10, 1679, writes:

I communicated to the Religious communities, both male and female, and even to private persons, the King's and your intentions regarding the Frenchification of the Indians. They all promised me to use their best efforts to execute them, and I hope to let you have some news thereof next year. I shall begin by setting the example and will take some young Indians to have them instructed. (Cole, 1939: 864)

In another letter to de Signelay, dated November 13, 1681, Duchesneau states:

Amidst all the plans presented to me to attract the Indians among us and to accustom them to our manners, that from which most success may be anticipated, without fearing the inconveniences common to all the others, is to establish villages of those people in our midst.

Thomas, commenting on this letter, says:

That the same policy was in vogue as late as 1704 is shown by the fact that at this time the Abnaki was taken under French protection and placed, as the records say, "in the centre of the colony." (1896: 544)

Through a policy, then, of assimilation rather than genocide, the French were able to maintain relatively amicable relations with the Aboriginal population for quite some time. Moreover, throughout the history of New France, the French adopted a policy that treated Aboriginals with every consideration, avoided violence when possible, and assimilated them when possible (Dickason, 2002). As O'Callaghan and Brodhead (1853) noted, the French had perfected the strategy of negotiation with Aboriginals through Indian diplomacy "first, by reasonable presents, secondly by choosing some of the more notable amongst them, to whom is given a constant pay as Lieutenant or Ensigne & thirdly by rewards upon all executions.... Fourthly by encouraging the youth of the Countrey (sic) in accompanying the Indians in all their expeditions." (vol. 4, 251)

When war broke out with England in the 18th century the demand for fur decreased, and the French mercantilistic philosophy came to an end. War also brought a change in the French policy toward the Aboriginal peoples (Jaenen, 1986). Aboriginal land rights began to be systematically ignored (Harper, 1947: 131). Letters signed by Louis XV at this time gave companies headed for New France full ownership of the land, coasts, ports, and havens of New France, and full right to dispose of these properties in any way they desired (French, 1851). Similar provisions can be found in the privileges, power, and requirements given to the Company of One Hundred Associates by Cardinal Richelieu nearly a century earlier.[6]

The King of France understood that if he was to colonize Canada, he would have to spend time, money, and energy in maintaining alliances with the Aboriginal peoples. He also realized that they were important allies in times of war, and that they would support the French if treated properly. Others have noted that the French used their Indian allies as "outposts" in the new world and thus reaped the benefits of low costs and accurate information. In the end, as Dickason (2002) points out, the French dealt with Aboriginal groups on a practical basis. It was a blend of give-and-take: giving when alliances were necessary, taking when the profits of the fur trade allowed.

British-Aboriginal Relations

The Aboriginal peoples' experience with the English was considerably more negative than that with the French. This was partly due to the operation of different structural variables when the English made a serious bid to control New France. Mercantilism as an economic theory had been discarded and the importance of the fur trade was dwindling; colonization in the true sense was now important. In addition, the religious ideology of the British had a very different basis than that of the French. Manifest destiny and the Hamite rationalization[7] pervaded the British secular way of life, exemplified in the Protestant ethic that hard work and no play would bring salvation.

A review of the documents relevant to the initial contact period between the English and the Indians in Canada reveals that Aboriginal concerns were completely ignored. Little control was exerted over the British settlers as they expanded westward. As Thomas points out, the Indians were not even mentioned in discussions when land was given to companies.

> For example, the letters patent of James I to Sir Thomas Gage and others for "two several colonies," dated April 10, 1606, although granting away two vast areas of territory greater than England, inhabited by thousands of Indians, in fact of which the King had knowledge both officially and unofficially, do not contain therein the slightest allusion to them. (1972: 550)

Although later charters recognized the existence of Aboriginal people, they did so in an extremely racist fashion. In the charters of Charles I, this statement, typical of several, authorizes the state to

> collect troops and wage wars on the barbarians, and to pursue them even beyond the limits of their province and if God shall grant it, to vanquish and captivate them; and the captive put to death.

Until 1755 the English followed a policy of expediency. At first they chose to ignore the Aboriginal population. When allies were required, Aboriginals were courted and provided with resources. When this was no longer necessary or feasible due to the need for westward expansion, the English chose to isolate Aboriginal people through the reserve system or to annihilate them, as they did the Beothuk of Newfoundland. In 1755 Indian agents, today called superintendents, were appointed, formally establishing Canada's policy of treating Aboriginal peoples as wards of the state. Significantly, the Indian agents initially placed in control of the reserves were always military men (Brown, 1996).

By 1830, the federal government was questioning the value of the Aboriginal person for Canada's future. Although it remained a concern for some, invasion from the south by the United States was no longer an immediate and direct threat. Because there were no other potential attackers, Aboriginal people were not likely to be needed for support in battle. Without their status as military allies, the Indians had no value for a "White Canada." Thus, in 1830, Indian Affairs was removed from military control and became a branch of the public service (Surtees, 1969). This change of jurisdiction allowed the British to adopt a more humanitarian attitude toward Aboriginal people (Doerr, 1974).

POST CONFEDERATION
ABORIGINAL-NON-ABORIGINAL RELATIONS

The first *Indian Act* after Canadian Confederation was passed in 1876. It was first revised in 1880, and received minor alterations in 1884 and 1885. For the next 65 years, the Act underwent annual minor changes. However, in 1951, a major revision left it essentially in its present form. Interestingly enough, the 1880 version of the Act and the present one are remarkably similar, indicating that Indian Affairs has not yet undergone any major ideological shifts in the past hundred years of dealing with the Aboriginal population.

Our analysis of Aboriginal–non-Aboriginal relations shows that explanations based on a "national character" are not only inadequate but highly suspect. As Trigger (1985) notes, one must go well beyond the old stereotypical trait analysis to explain why the French treated Aboriginal people differently than the English did. To adequately understand how Aboriginal–European relations unfolded over time, we must look at the activities and attitudes of different European social classes, the regions of Europe they represented, and the political factions that emerged. It is only then that we will have an adequate understanding of how an initial symbiotic relationship turned into one of overt hostility, leading to the genocidal policies that have been carried out against the Aboriginal peoples (Buckley, 1992).

In addition, Aboriginal affairs have long been thought of in terms of domestic affairs of little import in the operation of most of our institutional spheres, e.g., education, economics, and politics. Recently, it has become clear that they have taken on greater domestic importance and, as well, have entered the international scene. Furthermore, the impact of Aboriginal issues on Canadians is no longer limited to local areas. For example, in 1984, the Lubicon First Nation in Northern Alberta approached the United Nations, claiming they were being denied the right of self-determination. Six years later, the Human Rights Subcommittee of the United Nations concluded that the Canadian government had not respected the civil and political rights of the Lubicons. The committee noted that the historical inequities and more recent developments threaten the way of life and culture of the Lubicons and constitute a violation of Article 27 of the International Covenant on Civil and Political Rights. Canada had first tried to get the case dismissed, but it was not successful and now has found itself the centre of attention in the international arena. The U.N. committee's report, which is critical of a member country, is embarrassing to Canada. Furthermore, the government, arguing that its $45 million settlement is sufficient, sees the Lubicons' rejection of its offer as solely an issue of money.[8] Lubicons, on the other hand, argue that the federal government is haggling over a few dollars, while they are fighting over the matter of their own future for all time. From this example it is clear that as we move into the 21st century, Aboriginal issues can no longer be viewed as unique to one community or area of Canada. What happens in one part of this country has substantive impacts on Aboriginal affairs in other parts. It is also clear that Aboriginal issues are no longer the concern solely of Aboriginal people. All Canadians are affected by a variety of issues—both directly and indirectly. For example, the settlement of land claims bears directly upon non-Aboriginal people in the area where the claims are being dealt with. Indirectly, land claim decisions have an impact upon businesses and potential land users (Dunning, 1976).

ABORIGINAL IDENTITY

Aboriginal people are in an identity crisis situation. They are only beginning to have a clear vision of their own "heritage" culture, as distinguished from that of the "mainstream" society. As such, it is difficult to move from one to the other or resolve how to deal with the two seemingly different cultures. In addition, Aboriginal peoples are just beginning to build a strong collective identity. As Taylor (1993) points out, collective identity arises when a culture is able to provide to its members a clear compliance ideology upon which to build a strong identity. The strand that links Aboriginal peoples is the general sense of betrayal and injustice that they believe has been meted out over the past century. A sense of solidarity and identity is slowly bringing various factions together. The continued failure of the government to consult with Aboriginal people contributes to their sense of isolation within Canada. The inability of governments (federal or provincial) to act in a prudent manner to protect Aboriginal peoples continues to reinforce the belief that the achievement of any goals will have to come from within Aboriginal communities. Nevertheless, there remains an overall lack of Aboriginal identity, which has resulted in an inability to generate consensus on policy issues, chaos with various segmented groups constantly vying for popular legitimacy, and an impotency felt by many members living in First Nations communities (Wilkins, 1999; Sawchuck, 1998).

What do Aboriginal peoples want? What are they looking for? How do they plan to achieve their goals? Aboriginal peoples would like to see a power-sharing arrangement with the federal and provincial governments. Whether this sharing emerges out of the existing political structure or requires a new arrangement is irrelevant. They feel they must be able to participate in the power arrangements if they are to develop economically and become part of the larger economic system of Canada. They also feel that they must be in a position to protect what few rights they now have. There has been a continual erosion of Aboriginal rights, and there is a sense that these rights will become nonexistent if Aboriginal people themselves are not vigilant in protecting them. Therefore, there is a feeling that power sharing is a minimal condition that will allow Aboriginal peoples to integrate without assimilating.

Before continuing, we need to address the question: who is Aboriginal? Who is an Indian? And what are the differences? In other words, we must begin by addressing the age-old question of identity. There are two major ways of establishing identity: using objective or subjective criteria. In the objective approach, a number of attributes are established that identify the boundaries of identity. These attributes establish indicators that are "visible" to all observers. Then each individual under question is matched with these attributes. Thus, if skin pigmentation, hair texture, bone structure, language, and eye colour are used, one would assess each individual in terms of these attributes to determine whether or not he or she would fall into the category of "Aboriginal person" (or, similarly, "Native person," "Indian," "Inuit," or "Métis") (Campbell and Rew, 1999). The second approach, the subjective, is a more fluid one that flows from intrinsic self-definition. There are no measurable, objective criteria for "Indian," establishing the boundaries of inclusion and/or exclusion. In short, if others define you as an Aboriginal person and you agree (or in certain circumstances your agreement or disagreement is irrelevant), then you are Aboriginal. If you "feel" Aboriginal, then, under the subjective approach, you are Aboriginal. In other words, the identity of the individual lies in his/her conceptualization of self. We can attempt to measure this self-conceptualization in some form, but all it tells us is the degree to which an individual feels Aboriginal. It does not identify the defining attributes or the relative importance of each of these attributes (Dobbin, 1981).

We will not solve the problem of identity in this book because it is not solvable. It is a question that has two answers, depending upon the perspective used. Nor are the two perspectives independent of each other. How have these perspectives been used? The Department of Indian Affairs has chosen the former, while some Aboriginal people have chosen the latter. As a result, there has been considerable conflict over who is an Aboriginal person. In addition, government has, on occasion, allowed for the subjective approach in determining who is Aboriginal. Needless to say, this has generated considerable confusion for all Canadians in terms of trying to define who is Aboriginal, Indian, Métis, or Inuit (Foster, 1976, 1978).

A second issue regarding definitions centres on whose definition is used. Again, this is not to say that one definition is correct. It simply refers to a power relation that enables one party or another to employ a certain definition. The use of any definition also implies certain consequences. In the present case, the federal government has used its power to create a definition of Aboriginal people that has been incorporated into the legal structure of our political, social, and economic world. Thus, it should be clear that the dominant definition of Aboriginal people (or any subgroup definition) has been created by the federal government. Over time, many Aboriginal persons have come to accept this definition. It has come to be associated with certain rights and privileges. Hence it is important that we clarify the boundaries of the various terms and the social consequences that emanate from this definition.

CONCLUSION

Aboriginal policy of the French and English differed substantively. The French had a more practical approach, supported by an ideology that did not condemn Aboriginals to a position of subservience. Moreover, the French tried to understand the culture of Aboriginals and used that knowledge in negotiating with them. The results were positive and brought them benefits. English Canada, however, did not pursue the same policy. The English were more focused on domination and claiming the land for their expansion. In addition, they held religious and ideological perspectives that convinced them of the inferiority of Aboriginal people. Over time, we find that the policy governing Aboriginal–non-Aboriginal relations was administered differently throughout Canada. First of all, until 1830, Indians were viewed as military objects and were treated as such. If their presence would support the military campaign, they were given consideration. On the other hand, if their presence gave them no military advantage, Aboriginals were ignored. Later they would be defined as dangerous. In Ontario and Quebec, until 1860, the imperial government handled all the affairs and expenses of Aboriginal people. At that time, a Crown Lands Department was established and a commissioner appointed to assume the role of chief superintendent of Indian Affairs. In other areas of Canada, the Indian Affairs office was administered directly by the various provincial or colonial governments (Hawley, 1990).

Included in the *British North America Act* of 1867 was a special provision allowing for the administration of Indian Affairs to come under the control of the government of Canada. Initially, Indian Affairs was the responsibility of the Department of the Secretary of State, but in 1873 it was transferred to the Department of the Interior. In 1880, a separate Department of Indian Affairs was formed. In 1936, it was shifted to the jurisdiction of the Department of Mines and Resources, and in 1950 it was shifted again to the Department of Citizenship and Immigration. From 1953 to 1966, Indian Affairs was handled by the Northern Affairs and National Resources Department. Since 1966 this has been called the Department of Indian Affairs and Northern Development, or more recently Indian and Northern Affairs Canada. Hence, the administration of Indian Affairs has been shunted from one department to another and has never been allowed to develop consistent, humane policies. As the British began to settle Canada, they had to devise a strategy by which land would be taken away from the Aboriginals and opened for settlement. As a result, treaties and pieces of legislation of all kinds and shapes were passed to legitimize the takeover of land once occupied and settled on by Aboriginals.

NOTES

1. The primary labour market includes all those jobs that require skilled workers. The secondary market involves all unskilled labour.

2. Mercantilism was the economic theory that prevailed in Europe during the 18th century. Mercantilism held two basic tenets: the mother country was entitled to accumulate wealth in any form, and the mother country was entitled to exploit its colonies as a source for raw materials and a market for finished products, thereby maintaining a favourable balance of trade.

3. Because they used the seigneurial system of agriculture, the French always remained near major waterways and did not intrude into the interior of New France.

4. For a more thorough discussion of this issue, see Cumming and Mickenberg (1972).

5. Two additional factors contributed to the relatively peaceful relations between the French and the Indians: the military alliance of the Huron, the Algonkian, and the French; and the fact that the French settled in an area occupied by the Algonkian, who were migratory hunters (Jenness, 1937), who had no real tribal organization, and who were themselves recent arrivals in the area (Cumming, 1969).

6. See I.G. Shea, Charlevoix's *History of New France,* Vol. 2, 1879, p. 39.

7. Manifest destiny, though it varied considerably, was the belief that Europeans should control the world, or at least large parts of it. The Hamite rationalization was the belief, taken from the Bible, that Ham was cursed by God and turned into a non-White person so that "he and his descendants should remain cursed and be subservient to Whites from then on." To the British, the Indians were clearly descendants of Ham.

8. The two parties agreed in 1988 that a 246-square-kilometre reserve with full mineral rights would be established.

WEBLINKS

www.ukans.edu/history/VL/CANADA/canada2.html

This site is an excellent resource for a history and issues relating to the Aboriginal peoples in Canada. The site provides some 23 links to numerous topics, ranging from teaching First Nations history as Canadian history to a guide to the archival records of the government of Canada pertaining to Aboriginal peoples.

collections.ic.gc.ca/heirloom_series/volume2/volume2.htm

The Canada Heirloom Series, Volume 2, includes extensive information (much of it historical) about various regional Aboriginal peoples in its online exhibit, "Canada's Native Peoples."

www.inac.gc.ca

The Federal Department of Indian and Northern Affairs, discussed in this chapter, carries the institutional responsibility for "Aboriginal issues." Its website contains extensive resources, mostly from Ottawa's perspective.

Aboriginal Canada:

Identity and Consciousness

INTRODUCTION

Before we can discuss Aboriginal issues or Aboriginal–non-Aboriginal relations, we must first identify who is an Aboriginal person. In answering this question, it is important that the reader appreciate the plethora of terms now used in identifying the original inhabitants of North America. Moreover, we will find that the indigenous population has undergone name changes that are not universally accepted—by either the indigenous population or the non-indigenous peoples. For example, since the 1970s, Eskimos have been referred to as Inuit in Canada, while in the United States they are still called Eskimos. Indigenous people have been referred to as Aboriginal or Native people, and Native people worldwide often prefer the broader term "Aboriginal." The Métis are people of mixed ancestry—Indian and French, English, or Scottish background. Some Métis regard themselves as the only true Aboriginal or "original" peoples, since they alone emerged as a new group in North America. Aboriginal people may also consider themselves peoples of the "fourth world," defined as colonized populations living within developed and developing countries. Today, the term "First Nations" (a term not used by Aboriginal peoples outside Canada) has been used by a segment of Canada's indigenous population, and generally by status Indians as well as by the federal government. Finally, others prefer to use "Amerindian" as the most appropriate term. This chapter will define the various terms used to identify the growing number of indigenous peoples in our society (see Figure 2.1).

At the time when Europeans made first contact with the peoples of what is now Canada, they met Aboriginal peoples from a variety of cultural backgrounds, e.g., the Beothuk of Newfoundland and the Mi'kmaq of Nova Scotia, as well as a large number of peoples from the eastern regions of Quebec. There was a kaleidoscope of ethnic groups, each one unique in its economic organization as well as its language, religions, and values. Incoming Europeans found this ethnic diversity hard to deal with, and they quickly found a way to resolve the dilemma. Europeans quickly labelled all indigenous people as Indians. There would be some recognition of the different tribes, usually because of linguistic differences, but there was no real attempt to view Aboriginals as distinct cultural entities. When differences were acknowledged, they were considered minor attributes and were subsumed under the master trait of "Indian," which was a more meaningful and universal term from the Europeans' point of view (Hedican, 1995).

Having noted the extreme diversity among Aboriginal peoples, it must be pointed out that in a number of other ways there was some commonality. Aboriginal people interpreted life from a certain common perspective that was at variance with that of Europeans. For example, Europeans in the 16th and 17th centuries viewed science and religion as closely linked. They envisioned a rigid vertical hierarchical order of life with God on top; below God was a complex order of angels; below the angels, all other forms of life were ordered according to their descending levels of importance. These "natural" inequalities were fixed and ordained by God. Thus, poor people were not equal to rich people, and, it followed, ethical considerations appropriate for rich people did not need to be applied to the poor. Aboriginal people's view of their reality was quite different. They viewed all things (living and non-living) as having souls with a spiritual essence. Humans were no different than the trees, the lakes, or the bears. Humans did not have any predestined significance in the world; and while humans were different from other elements on earth, they were basically the same—having a spirit that gave them life. There were many other cultural differences between Aboriginal people and Europeans, such as attitudes toward animals, views of their environment, and approaches to time. Nevertheless, over time Europeans tended to homogenize the different indigenous groups (Jenness, 1967, n.d.) into the broad category of "Indians."

DEFINING AN ABORIGINAL PERSON

For the first 300 years after sustained contact was made with Aboriginal Canadians, there was little difficulty in determining who was or was not an Aboriginal person. Nor was there any real need to establish a legal definition. Residents living in a small community were aware of who was Aboriginal or not. Ancestry, physiology, and way of life were the determining factors. This is not to say the question never arose, but rather, when it did arise, the answer was clear from the local residents' perspective. And it should be noted that there was not always consensus on the answer. But for the most part, local community residents understood who was and who was not Aboriginal. However, as the population of Canada grew, and tension between Aboriginal people and the settlers intensified, it became apparent that a clearer demarcation as to who was an Aboriginal person would have to be established. It was not until 1850 that the first statutory definition of who was an Indian was enacted. This definition stated that an Indian was:

- First—All persons of Indian blood, reputed to belong to the particular body or tribe of Indians interested in such lands, and their descendants;
- Second—All persons intermarried with any such Indians and residing amongst them, and the descendants of all such persons;

FIGURE 2.1　Aboriginal Language and Cultural Divisions

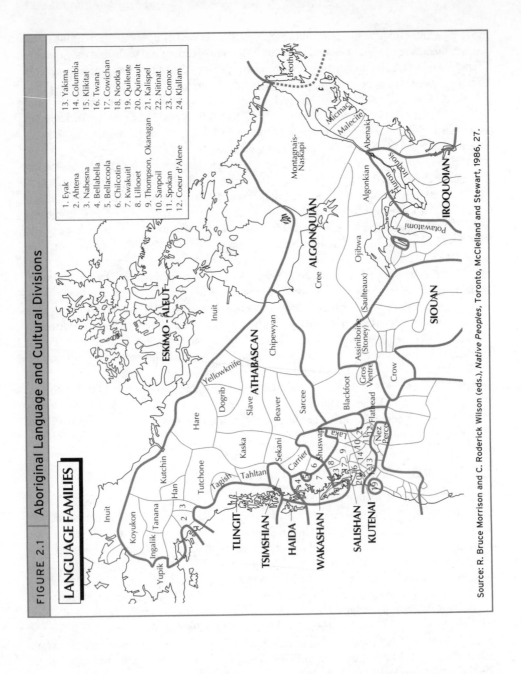

LANGUAGE FAMILIES

1. Eyak
2. Ahtena
3. Nabesna
4. Bellabella
5. Bellacoola
6. Chilcotin
7. Kwakuitl
8. Lillooet
9. Thompson, Okanagan
10. Sanpoil
11. Spokan
12. Coeur d'Alene
13. Yakima
14. Columbia
15. Klikitat
16. Twana
17. Cowichan
18. Nootka
19. Quileute
20. Quinault
21. Kalispel
22. Nitinat
23. Comox
24. Klallam

Source: R. Bruce Morrison and C. Roderick Wilson (eds.), *Native Peoples*, Toronto, McClelland and Stewart, 1986, 27.

- Third—All persons residing among such Indians, whose parents on either side were or are Indians of such Body or Tribe, or entitled to be considered as such; and
- Fourth—All persons adopted in infancy by any such Indian, and residing in the Village or upon the lands of such Tribe or Body of Indians, and their descendants.

It is clear that at this time the concept of Indian was a mixture of biology and culture. People of mixed ancestry were assigned either to Indian or Euro-Canadian society and did not constitute a separate category: only Indians and non-Indians existed (Hedican, 1991).

Once a legal/formal definition of an "Indian" was in place, criteria were established and would be used to categorize people. Nevertheless, changes to the definition of who is an Indian have been made over time, and one of the first changes was to drop the blood quantum factor—that is, having a certain proportion of Indian blood. While this is not part of a Canadian definition of who is an Indian, this has been one of the major attributes used in the United States to distinguish Indians from non-Indians.

After contact was sustained for some time, phenotypical, cultural, and linguistic attributes became the master traits associated with "Indianness" and "Whiteness." Thus, if a person evidenced a certain way of life, he or she was designated Indian or non-Indian, although in everyday life having evidence of visible biological traits of an Indian made it difficult to pass oneself off as a non-Indian, e.g., dark skin colour, straight black hair. Nevertheless, if the individual gave ample evidence of being "White," he or she would normally be treated as one. For example, if individuals lived in a house rather than a tipi, wore cotton or wool clothes rather than clothes made out of animal hides, and had short hair, they may have been treated as non-Aboriginal; i.e., because the individuals followed a White or European lifestyle. Métis were forced by the government to fall into one of these two categories. In some cases they were forcibly placed on the roll of Indians, while at other times they were considered non-Aboriginal. The result was that the early ethnic system was divided into two categories—Indians and non-Indians (Bartlett, 1980).

As the treaties were being established in the late 1800s, mixed ancestry people often were forced to "take treaty" and became Indians under the *Indian Act*. However, some declared themselves non-Indian and were treated accordingly. Both before and after Confederation, it was possible to treat people of mixed ancestry, either individually or in groups, as Indians or non-Indians.

British and Canadian law did not distinguish Métis from Indians as representing two different people; as we have seen, mixed ancestry groups were forced to assimilate into Euro-Canadian society or to become Indian. At the time of treaty signing, negotiators made it clear that Métis could become Indians and thus participate in the benefits granted to status Indians under the treaty, or live as non-Indians on the reserve—if the Indians agreed. However, they would not be acknowledged as a separate legal entity. Why was this distinction so important? Both legal and social factors forced the settlers to make these distinctions. If land was to be given to Aboriginals, then Euro-Canadians had to know who were the appropriate recipients. Social mores also demanded that an individual's ancestry be public so that the community could respond accordingly (Dunning, 1972; Kaye, 1981).

As negotiations with Aboriginal people began over treaties, it became increasingly clear that more refined definitions would have to be determined. With the establishment of the *Indian Act* (1876) and the subsequent creation of a roll—i.e., a list of all status (legal) Indians—it became possible to track and identify who was or was not Indian. By 1880, the federal government excluded Métis from falling under the provisions of the

Indian Act. And, as new legislation was passed, one could evaluate each person listed on the roll according to any new criteria that were enacted. Those who met the criteria remained on the roll, and they retained their Indian status. However, those who did not measure up to the new criteria were then dropped from the roll and by definition were no longer Indian. Whether their offspring retained their listing on the roll also varied according to the existing legislation. Nevertheless, it is important to remember that those struck from the roll were not necessarily considered Métis, although a large number began to define themselves by that term. If people struck from the roll were not Métis, how were they defined? Formally, they were classified as non-status Indians, which meant they were neither Indian nor Métis. At the social level it was clear they were not "White" (Laing, 1967). However, as Dickason (2002) points out, changes in definitions were continual, and the movement of large numbers of people in and out of categories is evident. Moreover, federal ministries in charge of keeping records were sloppy in documenting who was or was not Indian. Even when discrepancies were identified, federal ministries were more interested in reducing or limiting the number of people who would be labelled as Indian and were slow to change their records, if they ever did.

Thus, since the late 19th century, there have been four major Aboriginal subgroups—legal or status Indians, non-status Indians, Inuit, and Métis. However, these four groups are not recognized in all parts of Canada. The legal status of each of these categories also varies as one goes across the country; e.g., in Quebec, Métis are not recognized by government, while in Alberta, there are formal Métis settlements with official rolls denoting the membership. Nevertheless, there has been a social, if not legal, recognition of the four groups since the late 19th century. The category of non-status Indians became diffuse as we moved into the 20th century, although these people have long lobbied for some official recognition and legal rights. As the 20th century unfolded, more and more attention was given to the legal category of Indian. The label "Métis" also began to recede in importance with regard to the federal and provincial governments (Moore, 1978), although with the inclusion of "Métis" in the Constitution of Canada, 1982, their prominence has become greater and greater.

In censuses taken before 1941, ethnic origin was traced through the mother. Since eastern Indian tribes were matrilineal and matrilocal, this seemed a satisfactory means of distinguishing Indians from other ethnic groups. Before 1941, children whose mother was Indian were also defined as Indian. However, this was only true for those people who had been previously defined as Indian under the *British North America Act.*[1] Before 1941, Statistics Canada still made a distinction between Indian and "mixed origin." In 1941 the definition was changed so that, for off-reserve Indians, the father's ethnic status determined that of his children. For those who lived on the reserve, both the mother's and father's lineages were used to classify a person as Indian (Romaniuk and Piche, 1972).

In 1951 a more complex legal definition was introduced, stating that only those individuals who fell under the *Indian Act* would be classified as Indians. Today, while the federal government only recognizes any legal obligation to legal (registered) Indians, it recognizes the social existence of Inuit and Métis settlements (National Indian Brotherhood, 1977).

Culture and race no longer affect the definition of an Indian: today's definition is a legal one. If someone who exhibits all the racial and cultural attributes traditionally associated with "Indianness" does not come under the terms of the *Indian Act,* that person is not an Indian in the eyes of the federal and provincial governments. The following sections explain the categories in the government typology (Levine, 1970).

Registered Indians

The terms "legal," "registered," and "status" are generally used interchangeably to identify an Aboriginal person who is of federal concern. Registered Indians are defined in a legal manner and are different from other types of Aboriginal persons who do not have the same legal status. Because the original *Indian Act* (1876) has continually been changed by the federal government since Confederation, the legal definition of an Indian has been continually revised. In short, "Indian" refers to a person who, pursuant to the *Indian Act,* is registered as an Indian or is entitled to be registered as an Indian. Because of the complexity of such a definition, we reproduce Sections 11, 12, and 13 of the 1978 *Indian Act* in their entirety. We present this definition because it represents the federal government's thinking for nearly a century. It also allows us to make a comparison to the more recent changes that have been made to the *Indian Act.*

11. (1) Subject to Section 12, a person is entitled to be registered if that person

    (a) on the 26th day of May 1874 was, for the purposes of *An Act providing for the organization of the Department of the Secretary of State of Canada, and for the management of Indian and Ordnance Lands,* being chapter 42 of the *Statutes of Canada,* 1868, as amended by section 6 of the *Statutes of Canada,* 1869, and section 8 of chapter 21 of the *Statutes of Canada,* 1874, considered to be entitled to hold, use or enjoy the lands and other immovable property belonging to or appropriated to the use of the various tribes, bands or bodies of Indians in Canada;

    (b) is a member of a band

        (i) for whose use and benefit, in common, lands have been set apart or, since the 26th day of May 1874, have been agreed by treaty to be set apart, or

        (ii) that has been declared by the Governor in Council to be a band for the purpose of this Act.

    (c) is a male person who is a direct descendant in the male line of a male person described in paragraph (a) or (b);

    (d) is the legitimate child of

        (i) a male person described in paragraph (a) or (b), or

        (ii) a male person described in paragraph (c);

    (e) is the illegitimate child of a female person described in paragraph (a), (b), or (d); or

    (f) is the wife or widow of a person who is entitled to be registered by virtue of paragraph (a), (b), (c), (d), or (e).

  (2) Paragraph (1)(c) applies only to persons born after the 13th day of August 1956. R.S., c. 149, s. 11; 1956, c. 40, s. 3.

12. (1) The following persons are not entitled to be registered, namely,

    (a) a person who

        (i) has received or has been allotted half-breed lands or money scrip,

        (ii) is a descendant of a person described in sub-paragraph (i),

        (iii) is enfranchised, or

        (iv) is a person born of a marriage entered into after the 4th day of September 1951 and has attained the age of twenty-one years, whose mother and whose father's mother are not persons described in paragraph 11(1)(a),(b), or (d) or entitled to be registered by virtue of paragraph 11(1)(e), unless, being a woman, that person is the wife or widow of a person described in Section 11, and

(b) a woman who married a person who is not an Indian, unless that woman is subsequently the wife or widow of a person described in Section 11.

(2) The addition to the Band List of the name of an illegitimate child described in paragraph 11(1)(3) may be protested at any time within twelve months after the addition, and if upon the protest it is decided that the father of the child was not an Indian, the child is not entitled to be registered under that paragraph.

(3) The Minister may issue to any Indian to whom this Act ceases to apply, a certificate to that effect.

(4) Subparagraphs (1)(a)(i) and (ii) do not apply to a person who

(a) pursuant to this Act is registered as an Indian on the 13th day of August 1958, or

(b) is a descendant of a person described in paragraph (a) of this subsection. (5) Subsection (2) applies only to persons born after the 13th day of August 1956, R.S., c. 149, s. 12; 1956, c. 40, ss. 3, 4; 1958, c. 19, s. 1.

13. Subject to the approval of the Minister and, if the Minister so directs, to the consent of the admitting band,

(a) a person whose name appears on a General List may be admitted into membership of a band with the consent of the council of the band, and,

(b) a member of a band may be admitted into membership of another band with the consent of the council of the latter band.[2] (1956, c. 40, s. 5)

Registered Indians are under the legislative and administrative competence of the federal government, as spelled out in the *British North America Act,* and are regulated by the contents of the *Indian Act.* Today it is estimated that over 700 000 Canadians are defined as registered Indians. Being registered means that, with some exceptions, an individual is attached to a band and on the "roll" in Ottawa. Over the years, the federal government used a number of different criteria to decide who is and who isn't an Indian. For example, between 1868 and 1985 the following groups of people have been defined at times as Indians and at other times as non-Indian:

1. Indian women married to non-Indian men;

2. Children of non-Indian mothers whose father also had a non-Indian mother;

3. Indians residing outside Canada for over five years;

4. Indians with a university degree;

5. Half-breed persons outside Manitoba who accepted scrip.

As identified in Figure 2.2, there are subtypes of legal Indians. First of all, legal Indians can be categorized according to whether or not they have "taken treaty"—that is, whether or not they or their ancestors signed a treaty with the federal government. As Figure 2.3 shows, Indians in British Columbia (with the exception of Vancouver Island), Yukon, Quebec, and the Atlantic provinces did not sign any treaties involving land. Other groups, like the Iroquois of Brantford and Tyendingaga, who emigrated from the United States, are also considered non-treaty registered Indians.

Regardless of whether or not their ancestors signed a treaty, Indians are further subdivided into reserve and non-reserve, according to whether or not their ancestors were pro-

FIGURE 2.2 | Social-Legal Categories of Aboriginals Residing in Canada

Indians

Registered				Non-Registered
Band Membership			No Band Membership	Band Membership
Treaty		Non-Treaty		
Reserve	Non-Reserve	Reserve	Non-Reserve	
385 000	240 000	140 000	40 000	80 000	11 000

Métis

Off-settlement	On-settlement
190 000	23 000

Inuit

With disc number	Without disc number
15 000	41 000

Indian ancestry

over 1 000 000

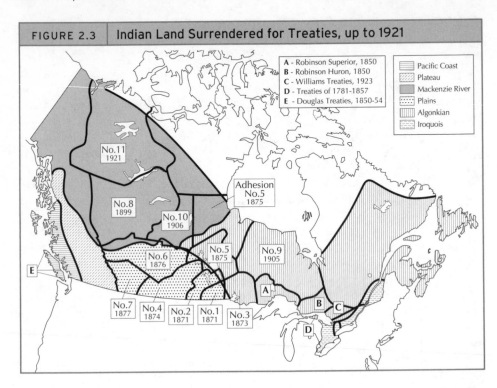

FIGURE 2.3   Indian Land Surrendered for Treaties, up to 1921

vided with reserve lands. For example, although a treaty (No. 11) was signed by Indians in the Northwest Territories, virtually no reserves exist. On the other hand, although British Columbian Indians have not taken treaty, most of them live on reserves.

In summary, the classification of a group of people as Indian arises from a legal definition. The concept "Indian" today does not solely reflect social, cultural, or racial attributes. The distinction between an Indian and a non-Indian is strictly a legal one.

Non-Status Indian

Although people in this group—i.e., people described as having some social or biological linkage to Indians—may exhibit all the social, cultural, and racial attributes of Indianness, they are not defined as Indians in the legal sense. Members of this group are not considered registered Indians because their ancestors refused, or were not allowed, to make agreements with the Crown. Included in this category are those Indians who have undergone "enfranchisement"—that is, who have lost their Indian status.

Enfranchisement can occur in several ways. For example, until 1960 an Indian had to give up legal status in order to vote in a federal election. Until recently, an Indian could choose to give up his or her Indian status by applying formally to Ottawa. In so doing, that person also surrendered status for all heirs (see Table 2.1). For years, one of the most common ways of losing Indian status was through intermarriage. Other ways of losing Indian status included obtaining the right to vote (up to 1960) or the title (fee simple) to land. Under Section 12(1)(b) of the old *Indian Act,* any legally Indian female who married a non-Indian male lost Indian status for herself and for her children. On the other hand, if an Indian male married a non-Indian female, the female became legally Indian as did any offspring that may have resulted.[3]

In general, a move from Indian to non-Indian status is made on the basis of legal criteria that are set forth by the *Indian Act*. However, informal changes to the Act also affect movement between categories; e.g., the Minister of Indian Affairs announced that, at the request of band councils, the government would suspend certain sections of the *Indian Act* that discriminated against Indian women who married non-Indians, as well as against their children. The Department of Indian Affairs has also empowered the government to declare that any portion of the Act may not apply to any Indian individuals, groups, or bands. These powers under Section 4(2) were recently invoked for members of certain bands in Quebec. Finally, as noted earlier, until the mid-20th century, Indian Affairs was notoriously lax in keeping accurate, up-to-date records about who was an Indian—using its own criteria. As Giokas and Chartrand (2002) point out, before the 1951 revision to the *Indian Act*, there was no well-organized or maintained manner of compiling a list of Indians who were to be on the Indian roll. The result was that many people who should have been on the list were omitted. Even when bands were provided with a "preliminary" list and people's names were provided by the band for inclusion, Indian Affairs did not add the names to the list. After the 1951 amendment, Indian Affairs did not exhibit "due diligence" in trying to establish an up-to-date and accurate list. Giokas and Chartrand (2002) suggest that there were several reasons: the very broad definition of "Indian," loose supervision of officials in the field, the pressures of trying to put a list together in a short time, and indifference to placing names on the roll. They also argue that irregular band members and non-treaty Indians were not considered by the registrar for inclusion in the roll at that time. The end result was the removal of many persons who would have legitimately been defined as Indian as well as the creation of the "non-status" Indian category.

Bill C-31

As noted above, until the late 20th century, the government focused on deleting Indians from the roll. However, in 1985, *Bill C-31 (An Act to Amend the Indian Act)* created new

TABLE 2.1	Accumulated Enfranchisements (1876–1985)
1876-1918	102
1918-1948	4000
1948-1968	13 670
1968-1969	785
1969-1970	714
1970-1971	652
1971-1972	304
1972-1975	467
1976-1985	94

Note: These figures include adult Indians enfranchised upon application together with their minor unmarried children as well as Indian women enfranchised following marriage to a non-Indian. Approximately 30 percent of the cases fall into the first category. The concept of enfranchisement is no longer considered operative since 1986, when further changes were made to the *Indian Act*.

Source: Department of Indian Affairs, 1980, 1987.

legislation that redefined who is and is not Indian. This amendment, for the first time, began to add people to the roll in a most peculiar fashion. The Bill was passed so that sexual discrimination would be eliminated, bringing the *Indian Act* into line with the *Canadian Charter of Rights and Freedoms* (Sections 15 and 28). It also abolished the concept of enfranchisement and provided for the partial reinstatement of those people who had lost their Indian status. Moreover, the Bill defined eligibility for various benefits that the federal government has provided for registered Indians.

The new Act identified four different types of Indians: (1) status with band membership; (2) status with no band membership; (3) non-status, but with band membership; and (4) non-status, non-band. As a result, one may hold legal status and be on the roll but not be a member of a band. Previously, no such distinction was made. In addition, those people who lost their Indian status through marriage or enfranchisement may now reapply for status as a legal Indian, and some may also apply for band membership. However, those individuals whose ancestors (more than one generation removed) lost their status are not eligible. Indian status is reviewed by Indian and Northern Affairs Canada (INAC), and a decision is made as to whether or not the individual has a legal right to claim Indian status. The almost 100 000 cases of adopted Indians were rejected by Indian Affairs on the grounds that the ethnic background of both the mother and father had to be known before approval would be given. In many cases this was not possible, or the mother was unprepared to name the father. On the other hand, band membership is determined by the band council. Bands were instructed by Indian Affairs to develop criteria for inclusion that had to be reviewed and approved by Indian Affairs officials. A deadline was given, and if the band had not completed its criteria the federal government would establish the criteria. However, there is no requirement that band membership rules be published or otherwise made available for inspection. Two different efforts to make the criteria public failed, and today it is difficult to obtain the membership rules. There is one exception to this rule. The approximately 20 000 women who lost their status through intermarriage automatically become band members if they are reinstated by the federal government through Indian and Northern Affairs Canada. The overall effect of the amendments is to ensure that no one would gain or lose status through marriage. Unfortunately this has not been the case, and even under the new amendments a person can still lose his or her Indian status.

Others who are reinstated must wait for two years to come under Sections 6(1) and 6(2) of the new *Indian Act*. Because acceptance into a band means that resources such as housing will have to be shared, many band councils are reluctant to accept reinstated Indians into their band membership lists. Bands were given until the middle of 1987 to enact a membership code. If they failed to do so, then all individuals who had been reinstated as Indians and had some historical basis for claiming membership to a particular band were automatically given band status. As a result, a new group of Indians (legal Indians with no band status) has been created.

At the time the Bill was passed, it was estimated that about 20 000 women would be eligible for reinstatement. In addition, somewhere between 60 000 and 100 000 children and enfranchised individuals would be eligible for reinstatement. Most of those who applied early were reinstated. However, these were the easiest cases to document, and preliminary results suggest that later applicants have had a much greater difficulty in "proving" their case. The Bill also addresses the issue of transmitting one's status (Section 6):

6. (1) Subject to Section 7, a person is entitled to be registered if

(a) that person was registered or entitled to be registered immediately prior to April 17, 1985.

(b) that person is a member of a body of persons that has been declared by the Governor in Council on or after April 17, 1985 to be a band for the purposes of this Act.

(c) the name of that person was omitted or deleted from the Indian Register, or from a band list prior to September 4, 1951, under subparagraph 12(2)(a)(iv), paragraph 12(2)(b) or subsection 22(2) or under subparagraph 22(2)(a)(iii) pursuant to an order made under subsection 109(2), as each provision read immediately prior to April 17, 1985, or under any former provision of this Act relating to the same subject-matter as any of those provisions.

(d) the name of that person was omitted or deleted from the Indian Register, or from a band list prior to September 4, 1951, under subparagraph 12(1)(a)(888) pursuant to an order made under subsection 109(1), as each provision read immediately prior to April 17, 1985, or under any former provision of this Act relating to the same subject-matter as any of those provisions.

(e) the name of that person was omitted or deleted from the Indian Register, or from a band list prior to September 4, 1951.

  (i) under section 13, as it read immediately prior to September 4, 1951, or under any former provision of this Act relating to the same subject-matter as that section or

  (ii) under section 111, as it read immediately prior to July 1, 1920 or under any former provision of this Act relating to the same subject matter as that section: or

(f) that person is a person both of whose parents are or, if no longer living, were at the time of death entitled to be registered under this section.

(2) Subject to Section 7, a person is entitled to be registered if that person is a person one of whose parents is or, if no longer living, was at the time of death entitled to be registered under subsection (1).

(3) For the purposes of paragraph (1)(f) and subsection (2).

(a) a person who was no longer living immediately prior to April 17, 1985 but who was at the time of death entitled to be registered shall be deemed to be entitled to be registered under paragraph (1)(a); and

(b) a person described in paragraph (1)(c), (d) or (e) who was no longer living on April 17, 1985 shall be deemed to be entitled to be registered under that paragraph.

7. (1) The following persons are entitled to be registered:

(a) a person who was registered under paragraph 11(1)(f), as it read immediately prior to April 17, 1985, or under any former provision of this Act relating to the same subject-matter as that paragraph, and whose name was subsequently omitted or deleted from the Indian Register under this Act; or

(b) a person who is the child of a person who was registered or entitled to be registered under paragraph 11(1)(f), as it read immediately prior to April 17, 1985, or under any former provision of this Act relating to the same subject-matter as that paragraph, and is also the child of a person who is not entitled to be registered.

(2) Paragraph (1)(a) does not apply in respect of a female person who was, at any time prior to being registered under paragraph 11(1)(f) entitled to be registered under any other provision of this Act.

(3) Paragraph (1)(b) does not apply in respect of a child of a female person who was, at any time prior to being registered under paragraph 11(1)(f), entitled to be registered under any other provision of this Act.

Thus, Sections 6(1) and 6(2) serve to define who will be a status Indian in the future and Section 6(1) identifies those who lost or were denied status as a result of the *Indian Act* prior to 1985. This includes such events as having married a non-Indian man, having been the child of a non-Indian man and a woman who was a status Indian at the time of birth, and enfranchisement. While at first reading it might seem as though the discriminatory aspects of the *Indian Act* have been removed, closer inspection will reveal that gender discrimination still remains, although it will not become evident for one generation. As Giokas and Groves (2002) point out, Section 6(1)(f) registers all those persons whose parents (living or dead) were registered or entitled to be registered under either Section 6(1) or 6(2). Section 6(2) registers only the child of one parent who was, or was entitled to be, registered under only Section 6(1). They go on to illustrate some examples.

A. If a 6(1) person marries a 6(1) person, the child becomes a 6(1).

B. If a 6(1) person marries a 6(2) person, the child becomes 6(1).

C. If a 6(1) person marries a non-Indian person, the child becomes 6(2).

D. If a 6(2) person marries a 6(2) person, the child becomes a 6(1).

E. If a 6(2) person marries a non-Indian person, the child becomes non-Indian.

As such, one can see that the children of a 6(2) parent are immediately penalized if that parent marries a non-Indian. At the same time, one can see that the penalty for a 6(1) person to marry a non-Indian does not have the same impact on the children of such a union. In summary, the changes to the *Indian Act* reveal that for 6(1) Indians, after two consecutive generations of marrying a non-Indian, Indian status will be lost. For 6(2) Indians, only one generation of marrying out will result in the children losing their Indian status. Similar issues arise when dealing with "illegitimate" Aboriginal children.

The above scenarios show that individuals who have obtained status through Section 6(2) and then marry a non-Indian will have children who are non-Indians. However, if they marry an Indian, then the child will be Indian. If those individuals who are registered under the conditions of Section 6(1) marry Indians, their children will be Indian. However, if they marry a non-Indian, the children will become Indians under Section 6(2) but will be unable to pass Indian status to their children. One final possibility would be to have two Indians under Section 6(2) marry. In this case, the children would be Indian under the provisions of Section 6(1). All children born "out of wedlock" will automatically be registered as Indians under Section 6(2) unless the mother can prove that the father was a status Indian, in which case they would be registered under Section 6(1).

Finally, the *Indian Act* also forces any enfranchised Indian who received more than $1000 of band funds (at the time of enfranchisement) to repay this money with interest before he or she can receive any band-fund disbursement or other band benefits (Joseph, 1991; Paul, 1990).

Figure 2.4 reveals the number of applicants for registration under *Bill C-31*. As of 2000, it is estimated that over 218 000 people had applied for registration. Data in Figure 2.4 show

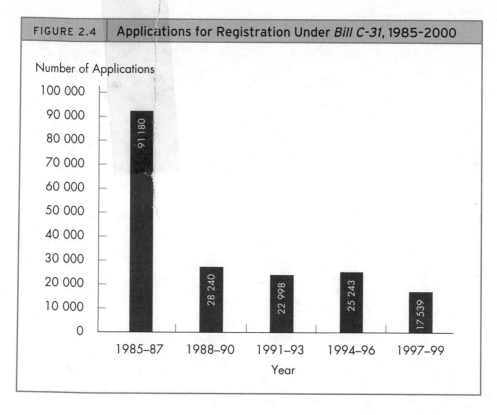

FIGURE 2.4 | Applications for Registration Under *Bill C-31*, 1985–2000

Number of Applications

(Bar chart: 1985–87: 91 180; 1988–90: 28 240; 1991–93: 22 998; 1994–96: 25 243; 1997–99: 17 539)

Year

that, over time, a decreasing number of individuals have applied for registration. Data from the Reinstatement of Status Information system has revealed that just over half of the applicants have been approved for registration (Joseph, 1991; Paul, 1990, INAC, 2002).

Table 2.2 shows that the total number of *Bill C-31* registrants who were added to the Indian roll between 1985 and 2001 was slightly more than 100 000, nearly 17 percent of the total registered Indian population. (Preliminary figures reveal that in 2002, approximately 115 000 people were added to the roll.) At this time we are unable to determine how many are registered because of Section 11 in the old *Indian Act*. Nevertheless, we know that 72 percent of the *Bill C-31* registrants under the new 6(1) are female. The data also show that the average annual growth rate between 1985 and 1991 was three to seven times higher than the overall Canadian growth rate. Today, the pool of potential applicants is exhausted, and today it is likely that *Bill C-31* will no longer have a substantial impact. Nevertheless, it does show that the growth rate for Aboriginals is about twice that of the overall Canadian population.

The addition of *Bill C-31* people to the Indian roll has created substantial social and political problems for reserve Indians as well as financial problems for the federal government. A serious rift now exists between Indians who have their roots on the reserve versus those who were enfranchised and forced to live in urban areas. The return of urban Indians to the reserves has brought about bitterness, jealousy, and factions within the reserve community. In many areas, such as in educational institutions, a great deal of animosity exists between "traditional" Indians and "*Bill C-31*" Indians.

TABLE 2.2	Registered Indians and Indians Registered Under *Bill C-31*, Average Annual Growth Rates, Canada 1981-2001

	Registered Indians			Average Annual Growth (%)	
Year	Excluding *Bill C-31*	*Bill C-31* Population	Total	Excluding *Bill C-31*	Including *Bill C-31*
1981	323 782	0	323 782	2.59	0.00
1982	332 178	0	332 178	2.95	0.00
1983	341 968	0	341 968	2.00	0.00
1984	348 809	0	348 809	2.82	3.28
1985[a]	358 636	1 605	360 241	3.16	7.66
1986	369 972	17 857	387 829	2.40	7.24
1987	378 842	37 056	415 898	2.71	6.73
1988	389 110	54 774	443 884	2.65	5.06
1989[b]	399 433	66 904	466 337	4.20	5.11
1991	429 178	92 282	521 460	3.55	4.23
1996	506 005	104 869	610 874	2.83	3.01
2001	517 226	105 675	622 901		

a. In 1985, the *Indian Act* was amended to allow, through *Bill C-31*, the restoration of Indian status to those who had lost it due to discriminatory clauses in the *Indian Act*.
b. The high annual growth rate between 1989 and 1991 is due in part to the upward adjustments of the Indian Register for the purposes of the projections and to the Department's estimate of 86 000 *Bill C-31* registrants in 1990-91 plus the growth due to natural increase.

Sources: In *Basic Departmental Data*-1990, pp. 7, Indian and Northern Affairs Canada.

Because enfranchisement meant that Indians had to leave the reserve, most migrated to urban areas. Thus, many *Bill C-31* Indians have lived and raised their children in urban areas, and, over a generation of absence from the reserve, have been assimilated, taking on the attributes of non-Aboriginal culture. Under the new legislation, these Aboriginals are allowed to be reinstated, to claim their Indian identity (or, what they have retained of it), and to benefit from the social and economic programs that are available to Indians. In some cases, this means access to a reserve and possible resettlement. Land allocation can be applied for and a share of the band profits will have to be allocated to these new Indians. In other cases, it means access to financial support to go to school. In still other cases, it provides an individual his or her birthright as an Indian. In these latter cases, the financial benefit is not at issue but rather the right to identify oneself with the group—Indians.

There are a number of complex problems involved in the implementation of *Bill C-31*. First of all, at a family level, it means that brothers and sisters may have different legal status. A second problem concerns band membership. Although some children (dependants—6[2]) have a right to reside on the reserve, it is not certain that independent 6(2) children and their non-Indian fathers are allowed to reside on the reserve. A further problem of *Bill C-31* centres on band membership for reinstated women and their children. Bands have been given control over their membership, and some of these bands have adopted the old *Indian Act* band membership system and thus are able to exclude reinstated Indians from their membership.

The impact of *Bill C-31* has been divisive and counter-productive for Aboriginals on and off the reserve. The inability (or, at least, the perceived inability) of urban Indians to appreciate the traditional way of life has been one focal point of discontent. The sharing of meagre resources has also brought about considerable factionalization within the Aboriginal community. Thus far, there has not been a serious attempt by any of the Native groups to deal with this problem.

Individuals reinstated through *Bill C-31* technically have the right to reside on a reserve. In the past, nearly all registered Indians were members of a band. However, because this new legislation allows for each Indian band to adopt its own rules governing membership, there are major differences between the number of people who are registered and the number who are members of bands. This difference may seem unimportant, but upon closer inspection several issues emerge. For example, if you are a band member, you are eligible to vote and to stand for band council membership. In addition, being a band member makes you eligible for a number of programs that are offered by the community, e.g., housing, social assistance, health. Moreover, if you are a band member you may be exempt from paying certain taxes. These are important considerations for any community, and they have not been taken lightly by First Nations.

However, the creation of membership criteria has been turned over to First Nations. Unfortunately, these criteria do not have to be made public, and anyone wishing to review the criteria must apply to the Band Council. White et al. (2003) have carried out a review of the membership rules of various First Nations and found four different types:

1. *Indian Act* rules as set out in Section 6 of *Bill C-31*;

2. Unlimited one-parent rules, where eligibility requires that at least one parent be a member;

3. Blood quantum rules where eligibility is determined by the amount of "Indian blood" the person has (typically 50 percent); and

4. Two-parent rules where eligibility requires that both parents be members of the band.

Their analysis shows that nearly 70 percent of the bands have chosen the "*Indian Act*" rule. Only about 15 percent have used a "one-parent" rule, and just over 11 percent have adopted the "two-parent" rule. The remainder (5 percent) are using the "blood quantum" rule.

The introduction of *Bill C-31* also has impacted the demography of the Aboriginal population. White et al. (2003) show that substantial age differences exist between *Bill C-31* and pre–*Bill C-31* populations. For on-reserve populations, the average age of the *Bill C-31* population registered under 6(1) was 43.5 years, or about 15 years older than its pre–*Bill C-31* population. For those registered under 6(2), the difference was 24 years older on average. They note that age differences for those off-reserve were even greater. While the immediate impact of *Bill C-31* was to increase the Indian population, the long-term impacts are also of great interest. Clatworthy (2000) has developed a projection methodology that explores the future impacts of *Bill C-31* on the population entitled to register under the *Indian Act*. His projections show that under the existing *Bill C-31* rules, the total population of survivors and descendants is projected to increase to slightly more than 2 million within four generations. However, the population entitled to be registered as "Indian" would grow for two generations to a peak of just over 1 million, and then an accelerating decline would take place over the next two generations. Thus, by the end of the fourth generation, only 750 000 would be registered as Indian, a number similar to today's population. When we look specifically at the *Bill C-31* population (and descendants who trace their ancestry entirely through this population), Clatworthy projects an increase for the next 10 years. After that, he projects a decrease in numbers such that by the end of the fourth generation, there would be less than 10 000 individuals classified as "Indian" (White et al, 2003).

When *Bill C-31* was passed, the federal government argued that it had addressed the issue of sex discrimination. However, as Giokas and Groves (2002) point out, injustices remain. First, they observe that not all persons of Indian ancestry were included in the new registry. Second, they note that sex discrimination has not been eliminated because the effects of the earlier sex discrimination fall harder on Indian women and their descendants than on Indian men. Third, band membership codes do not deal with every person who has Indian status. Fourth, even where bands have been unable to exclude the new band members that the bill added, other ways are found to exclude them from the benefits of band membership—e.g., per-capita disbursements under the *Indian Act* were stopped and the funds moved to a band-controlled account from which new members were not provided with per-capita disbursements. Finally there are problems in how children are defined.

In the end, *Bill C-31* has probably created as many problems as it tried to solve. First of all, while the bill certainly added a number of Indians to the official roll, in the long term it will decrease the number. It is estimated that substantial decreases will result in the Indian population by the end of the first generation. Second, intra-family discord will begin to take place. An example provided by Giokas and Groves (2002) illustrates the point. Assume that a status Indian brother and his status Indian sister both marry non-Indians. The children of the sister who married out prior to the 1985 amendments will be "new status" since they all fall into the 6(2) category at the outset because they will only have one parent who was registered under *Bill C-31*. The children of the brother who married out prior to the 1985 amendments will be "old status" because both their parents already had status. They will therefore be 6(1) and will start off with an advantage over their similarly situated 6(2) cousins in terms of status transmission. The reader will recognize that this has nothing to do with the actual Indian ancestry since the brother and sister have exactly the same degree of Indian ancestry. In the end, this new bill may sow the seeds of discontent between factions of a community and bring further tension and conflict within the reserve.

In the end, within one generation, there will be four different types of Indians. First, there will be the registered Indians who are eligible for band membership. A second class of citizen will be those individuals who are entitled to be registered as Indians but are not members of a band. The third type of Indian will be those who meet the criteria for band membership but are not eligible to register as Indians. Finally, there will be those who do not meet the criteria for either registration or band membership. As White et al. (2003) point out, the implications of such a structure, as well as how First Nations communities will deal with these different classes of citizens, will indeed be daunting challenges facing policy and program officials.

Métis

The question of "Who is a Métis?" has long gone unanswered. And, for the most part, the question was not really important. However, with constitutional recognition and affirmation of Métis as an Aboriginal people with rights, the question has taken on heightened importance. Métis are now recognized as an Aboriginal people, and we must therefore provide a definition that has clearly articulated criteria. To begin to generate such a definition, we need first to provide a brief historical journey.

In the end, a complex influence of the fur trade, the Hudson's Bay Company, the Roman Catholic Church, and Indian tribes all contributed to the development of Métis identity. They developed economic and social institutions and became a dominant economic force after 1750. By the 1820s many Métis had taken up residence at Red River, and thus it became their economic and social centre. It was at this time that they began to develop their own form of self-government. The Métis' sense of cohesiveness and political solidarity was evident by the late 1800s when they objected to the Hudson's Bay Company's decision to sell what is now Western Canada. Chartier (1988) notes that this same political consciousness was displayed in 1885 when the Métis fought the Canadian government. As Charlebois (1975) points out, the Métis developed a separate culture and took on the characteristics of a separate nation. Living in distinct communities, they developed their own local laws and attempted to implement their own form of government. It is estimated that by the end of the 19th century Métis made up nearly three-quarters of the Hudson's Bay Company's labour force (Adams, 1975; Thomas, 1985). Within the economy of the 19th century, the Métis of Red River and Rupert's Land began to develop their identity and culture. Nevertheless, over time, many Métis were forced to become "Indian" (just as many Indians were forced to become Métis) in order for the government to create definitional boundaries that would reduce its financial liability for Native people.

While we know a considerable amount about the history and culture of the Red River and Rupert's Land Métis, we know little about the identity and culture of people of mixed ancestry elsewhere in Canada. As a result of sporadic and inconsistent approaches by government to mixed ancestry people, there is little known about how they were defined and how they defined themselves in the 19th and early 20th centuries (Giokas and Chartrand, 2002). For example, in Ontario, a Half-breed group was included in Treaty No. 3 as "treaty Indian" while others were not. In other cases, mixed ancestry people were explicitly excluded from the Robinson Huron and Robinson Superior Treaties. In other areas, Half-breeds were excluded from Treaty No. 9 because they were not living the Indian way of life.

The crystallization of a Métis identity was probably born out of the large influx of European settlers in the District of Assiniboia (Manitoba) in the early 1800s. In 1816, the Métis, in opposition to the Pemmican Proclamation (limiting the export of Pemmican), raided a Hudson's Bay Company post, liberated the pemmican, and took it to the outskirts of Winnipeg. At a place called Seven Oaks, they were challenged by government forces. At the end of the battle, the government forces were killed and the Métis leader (Cuthbert Grant) was proclaimed the leader of Métis until the emergence of the new leader, Louis Riel senior, in the 1840s. The continued importance of the Métis in this region of the country can be seen in the figures obtained in the 1871 Census: there were nearly 10 000 Métis counted (out of a total population of 12 000). However, a decade later, the Métis made up less than 2 percent of the Winnipeg population, and by the early 20th century the proportion was 3 percent.

In the late 1800s, the Métis of the Red River area objected to the government of Canada sending out land surveyors without the consultation of the Métis living in the area. Louis Riel, the leader of the Métis, objected, and he argued that the Hudson's Bay Company's trade monopoly did not include rights over the land and the people, and that before any transfer could take place, the government of Canada would need to negotiate with the Métis. The creation of the Province of Manitoba in 1870 was largely the result of the demands of the Métis and, under the provisions of the *Manitoba Act*, 500 000 hectares of land were set aside for the children of the Métis. However, only 15–20 percent of the land was ever obtained by the Métis.

The continued influx of European settlers demanded that Métis and Indians be resettled to make way for the settlement of the newcomers. However, land title began to become a serious problem and there was no agreement between the Métis communities across the Prairies and the government as to how it should be resolved. As Dickason (2002) noted, "nothing seemed to work for the Métis, least of all getting Ottawa to listen"(p. 275). In the end, the conflict of 1885 between the Métis and the militia saw the Métis defeated at the battle of Batoche. The consequences were immediate and the Métis and Indians charged were imprisoned and, in nine cases (including Riel), hanged. The result was that the Métis, fearing for their lives, changed their names, fled to the United States or north to the Mackenzie River area, or declared themselves to be Indians and gained admittance to a reserve. In the end, a more dispersed Métis found themselves residing in an area between the Mackenzie and Red rivers.

Figure 2.5 locates the major belts of Métis and non-status Indians in Canada.

WHO ARE THE METIS?

The term "Métis" refers to "in-between people"—those who are neither Indian nor non-Indian. The English term "half-breed" is less semantically correct than the French term "métis" because it does not imply a biological mix of "races" (Giokas and Chartrand, 2002).

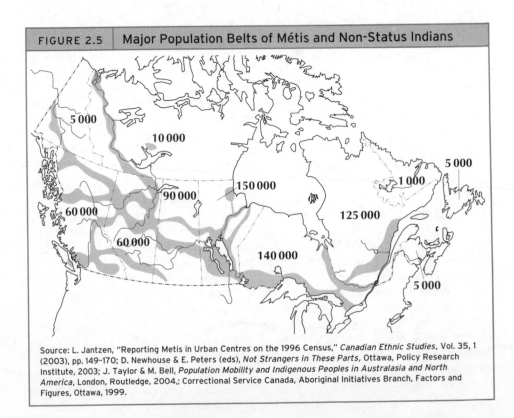

| FIGURE 2.5 | Major Population Belts of Métis and Non-Status Indians |

Source: L. Jantzen, "Reporting Metis in Urban Centres on the 1996 Census," *Canadian Ethnic Studies*, Vol. 35, 1 (2003), pp. 149-170; D. Newhouse & E. Peters (eds), *Not Strangers in These Parts*, Ottawa, Policy Research Institute, 2003; J. Taylor & M. Bell, *Population Mobility and Indigenous Peoples in Australasia and North America*, London, Routledge, 2004,; Correctional Service Canada, Aboriginal Initiatives Branch, Factors and Figures, Ottawa, 1999.

Over time, the concept "Métis" has become highly politicized and the definition reveals the fact that the term has been used in different ways at different times. For example:

1. Treating Métis of either English or French mixed ancestry groups (from Rupert's Land) as the same;

2. Including any person of mixed ancestry as "Métis" even though they have no connection with the Red River or Rupert's Land Métis Nation; and

3. Identifying as Métis any person of mixed ancestry who has no Indian ancestry or may have lost it. (Giokas and Chartrand, p. 85)

Giokas and Chartrand (2002) have addressed this question in an attempt to provide an answer. They point out that when the *Manitoba Act* (1870) was passed, it applied to all residents of the original province of Manitoba. And since the *Manitoba Act* was passed, references in Canadian legislation have not distinguished between the two distinct groups of mixed-ancestry people. One year later, when the *Constitution Act, 1871* was passed, it also began to treat the Red River people (French speaking, Catholic) and the Rupert's Land Métis/Half-breed (English speaking, Protestant) as the same. Thus began a confounding of the term "Métis" and all subsequent legislation (until recently) failed to distinguish between the two distinct groups. As a result of this merging of the two groups into one, today no terminological distinction is made between the two historical groups. The Ewing Commission in Alberta (1935) took an initial theoretical approach in defining a " Half-breed/Métis" as a person of mixed blood, European and Indian, who lives the life of an ordinary Indian. However, by 1940 Alberta took a more narrow and applied definition requiring all "Métis" to have one-quarter Indian blood.

Under the 1870 *Manitoba Act*, Métis were given statutory recognition for the first time. One motive behind this recognition was the search for peace—and the establishment of government control—in the Red River area (Ens, 1996). This Act extinguished Indian title to the lands in the province of Manitoba and appropriated a portion of ungranted lands, to the extent of 1 400 000 acres, for the benefit of the families of the Métis residents. Under the Act, the Governor General in Council would allow the Lieutenant-Governor to select lots or tracts of land in various parts of the province, as he deemed expedient, for Métis, and to divide the same lands among the children of the Half-breed heads of families residing in the province at the time of the transfer to Canada (Alberta Federation of Métis, 1978). In the end, the federal government allowed those who thought of themselves as Indian (and lived the Indian lifestyle) to be treated as Indians and allowed those who did not think of themselves as Indian to be treated as non-Indian. If a person accepted scrip (either land or money), they could not be considered Indian. This was formalized in the *Indian Act* that noted "no half-breed in Manitoba who has shared in the distribution of half-breed lands shall be accounted an Indian." If a person took scrip, they and their families and descendants could no longer be considered Indian. In short, not everyone who took scrip was a member of a Métis community. Nor was mixed ancestry an attribute that differentiated them from Indians. In all cases, Métis were offered the choice of taking treaty (as Indians) or taking scrip (as Métis/Half-breed.)

By the 1890s, the government began to implement its new policy of "civilizing" Indians. It began to promote individual enfranchisement and assimilation as well as to introduce and enforce the "out-marriage" provision in the *Indian Act*. The Half-breed/ Métis who had taken "treaty" with the Indians were approached and requested to "take scrip," thereby removing them and their descendants from the Indian roll and saving the Department money. Giokas and Chartrand (2002) point out that the 1885 Street Commission reported that one-third of the scrip claims allowed were issued to persons withdrawing from treaty. One year later, another Half-breed commission noted that nearly 90 percent of the individuals taking scrip were Half-breeds leaving treaty. They also point out that in the case of the treaty adhesion in the Lesser Slave Lake region, nearly 600 Indians were removed from the band list on the sole basis that they were of mixed ancestry. Although an inquiry was held and the presiding judge found that only about 200 people should have been removed from the roll, the Department only reinstated about one-third of those recommended to be put back onto the roll. In the end, it can be seen that Métis do not necessarily have to be part of the historic Red River or Rupert's Land Métis nation. Nor is there any real distinction between Métis and Indians or non-status Indians other than the fact that the two groups seem to have chosen different ways of addressing their land claims: Indians took treaty and lived on a reserve,while the Métis took scrip. Giokas and Chartrand (2002) conclude that if judicial rulings continue the way they have in the recent past, scrip-takers may have an actionable claim to the restoration of Indian and band status as well as treaty and reserve land rights (p. 94). In the early 1950s, several bands asked the Department of Indian Affairs to expel "mixed ancestry" residents from the reserve. Changes to the *Indian Act* in 1958 effectively ended this attempt to expel members from the reserve. However, in the end, it created two different types of scrip-takers—those who were band members and status Indians prior to that date (1958) and those who were not.

Estimates of the number of Métis range from less than 500 000 to more than 1 000 000, depending upon the source. The lack of accurate information resulted, in 1941, from the deletion of "Métis" from the census. By 1980 the Report of the Native Citizen Directorate of the Secretary of State showed the following figures:

- Métis and non-status Indian (core population)—300 000 to 435 000
- Métis and non-status Indian (self-identifying population)—400 000 to 600 000
- Métis and non-status Indian (noncore and nonself-identifying population)—1 to 2.5 million

However, after a lapse of several decades, the 1981 Census once again included Métis as a category of ethnic identification. The results were startling, since less than 100 000 people identified themselves as Métis. Today we find that, of persons who declared Aboriginal ancestry, nearly 175 000 identified themselves as Métis, with a further 26 000 status Indians identifying themselves as Métis.

Only Alberta has kept official records, and only for its Métis settlements. In 1980, approximately 4000 Métis resided on those settlements; estimates of Alberta's off-settlement Métis population range from 8000 to 15 000. Within the last decade, a number of government agencies have tried to determine more accurately the number of Métis and non-status Indians.

The Métis have argued for many years that, as a special people, they are entitled to Aboriginal rights. The federal government has maintained that those Métis whose ancestors signed treaties or received scrip and land have had their Aboriginal rights extinguished (Cumming, 1973a). Presumably, others have not. However, once the Riel Rebellion was crushed (1885), the implementation of the provisions of the *Manitoba Act* (as it related to Métis) was not seriously undertaken (Daniel, 1980).

Métis Claims Over the years, the federal government has often recognized the existence of Métis claims. Under the *Dominion Act* and the *Manitoba Act,* the government provided scrip and land to Métis to extinguish their Aboriginal rights. The 1889 Treaty Commission was instructed to treaty with the Indians and to investigate and extinguish any Half-breed titles (Cumming, 1973b). In the 1930s, the Ewing (Half-breed) Commission (1935) asserted the existence of Métis claims. As recently as 1969, the Indian Claims Commissioner also argued for the Aboriginal rights of Métis, stating that these were well established in Canadian law. According to the Commissioner, various actions of the federal government, such as scrip allocation in Western Canada and the Adhesions to Treaty No. 3, have granted special status to the Métis, both morally and legally.

Even while recognizing Métis claims, the federal and provincial governments have tried to wish them away. The rights of the Métis in the Northwest Territories were ignored until rebellion was threatened in 1885. In the 1940s, as was mentioned above, the federal government deleted "Métis" from the census as a separate ethnic category. In 1944, Indian Affairs removed the names of nearly 1000 Indians from the roll, arguing that they were really Métis. Although a subsequent judicial inquiry forced the department to replace most of the names, clearly the government was hoping that the Métis would simply assimilate into Euro-Canadian society and disappear, along with their claims (Barkwell et al., 1989).

In their attempts to retain their ethnic status and to receive compensation for Aboriginal rights, the Métis, like the Indians and Inuit, have created complex and highly political organizations. The Native Council of Canada (NCC) was established in 1970 and became the political arm of the Métis. The NCC became known as the Congress of Aboriginal Peoples (CAP) in 1994. By the mid-1970s, there were 10 Métis organizations representing Métis in all regions of Canada. The overall mandate of the congress and its many provincial affiliates for these groups is to seek improved social conditions and a land base, and to deal with historical grievances (Purich, 1988; Sawchuck, 1998). The Métis argue that those whose ancestors did not take treaty or receive scrip or land still have Aboriginal rights.

At present, the relationship between the Métis and the federal and provincial governments varies from province to province.[4] In the Yukon, Métis demands have gone relatively unnoticed, or at least are treated with less legitimacy than the Inuit or Dene demands (Coates and Morrison, 1986). On the other hand, in the Northwest Territories, the Métis are working alongside status Indians and Inuit to negotiate an agreement with the federal government. Until the 1990s, the British Columbia government refused to recognize the special rights of certain Aboriginal peoples in the province, including the Métis (Hatt, 1972).

Saskatchewan excludes Métis from any land claim registration now taking place with status Indians. In Saskatchewan, "farms" have been established for Métis, with land bases of less than four square kilometres each. Although Manitoba has historically recognized the Métis, it has recently refused to acknowledge their existence officially. The few monies that the Métis Association had been receiving from the provincial government for special education and cultural activities were cut off in 1982.

In Ontario, the Métis are recognized and are eligible to receive funds from a Native Community Branch. Although Quebec claims to define Métis and non-status Indians as Indians, it refuses to fund or implement programs for these special groups. In order to be officially recognized by the Quebec government, the Métis would have to reject the *Indian Act* and accept new terms outlined by the provincial government. Provincial policy with regard to Métis has been (with the exception of Alberta, which has accepted partial responsibility for Métis) one that claims that Métis fall under Section 94(21) of the Constitution and that they are thus a federal responsibility. Today there is no legislation in Canada that formally recognizes a group referred to as Métis prior to the acquisition of the Hudson's Bay Company in Rupert's Land in 1870. Nevertheless, Métis have been recognized as a

Métis Settlements in Alberta

By the turn of the 20th century, the Métis of Alberta had begun organizing, and two decades later they were recognized by the provincial government. In Alberta, the provincial government's *Métis Betterment Act*, 1938, outlines its relationships with the Métis. The Alberta government does not acknowledge the legal existence of Métis off what were then called the colonies. Therefore, all Métis individuals who do not reside on the colony are considered regular Albertans with no Aboriginal or special rights. While most provinces argued that mixed ancestry individuals with Aboriginal backgrounds should be reinstated to Indian, Alberta took the opposite approach. During the Ewing Commission hearings, they took the position that Half-breeds/Métis were really Indians and took as a definition of Half-breed/Métis "a person of mixed blood, White and Indian, who lives the life of the ordinary Indian...". This definition was used in the 1938 *Métis Betterment Act*, which eventually established Métis settlements. Later, Alberta would revert to a blood quantum theory—e.g., a person had to have at least one-quarter Indian blood to reside on the colonies. This blood requirement remained in the Act until 1990.

Métis settlements located across the northern part of Alberta include the settlements of Paddle Prairie, Peavine, Gift Lake, East Prairie, Buffalo Lake, Kikino, Elizabeth, and Fishing Lake. These eight settlements form the only constitutionally protected Métis land base in Canada. They consist of 505 102 hectares, much of it covered by forest, pasture, and farmland.

The Métis are the descendants of European fur traders and Indian women who emerged as a distinct group on the Prairies towards the early part of the 19th century. Following the Northwest Rebellion of 1885, many Métis moved to the north and west. After a period of political activism among landless Métis in Alberta during the Depression, the provincial government passed the original *Métis Population Betterment Act* in 1938. Lands were set aside for Métis Settlement Associations, though four of the original settlements (Touchwood, Marlboro, Cold Lake, and Wolf Lake) were later rescinded by order of the Alberta government.

A distinct Métis culture, combining Indian and Euro-Canadian values and modes of expression, is practised in the Métis settlements. For example, jigging, a favourite form of dance, mixes the reels of Scotland and France with the chicken dance of the Cree. A distinct Métis language called Michif (combining Cree, French, and some English words) is still spoken alongside English. Most residents of Métis settlements retain Indian spiritual beliefs and customs.

Education in most of the settlements is provided by the Northland School Division of the province's Department of Education. The settlements emphasize the need to make their children's schools responsive to the cultural values and history of the Métis people. Employment in the settlements is generated by commercial fishing, logging, farming, ranching, and energy projects. As in the past, the Métis people continue to emphasize the economic development of their land. A mixed economy combines traditional economic activities and new industrial and commercial ventures.

The later 1955 and 1970 *Métis Betterment Acts* provided for settlement associations for each of the eight communities and laid the foundation for self-government. In each settlement, councils of five members are elected by settlement members to deal with matters affecting the settlements. In 1975 the Alberta Federation of Métis Settlement Associations was officially established to act as the political voice of the settlements and to pursue such goals as land security, local self-government, and long-term economic self-reliance. In 1985 the Alberta government passed what was known as Motion 18, a resolution committing the province to transfer title of the settlements to the Métis people and to provide provincial constitutional protection of the lands by means of an amendment to the *Alberta Act*. This paved the way for the historic 1989 Alberta Settlements Accord, which passed into legislation with the 1990 *Métis Settlements Act*. Replacing the previous *Métis Betterment Acts,* the *Métis Settlements Act* provides for the legal transfer of land title to the Métis people, as well as local municipal and traditional style self-government, and establishes eight settlement corporations and the Métis Settlements General Council as legal entities. The new Act establishes the Métis Settlements Appeals Tribunal, which provides a dispute resolution mechanism dealing with membership, land use, and resource matters on settlements. Also part of the Act is the Subsurface Resources Co-Management Agreement, an agreement whereby the settlements and the province jointly manage oil, gas, and other subsurface resources on the settlements. Significantly, the constitution of Alberta was itself amended in 1990 to recognize and protect the Métis settlements' interest in their land and resources.

Source: René R. Gadacz, *The Canadian Encyclopedia 2000*, World Edition. Toronto: McClelland and Stewart. Reproduced with permission.

people through the *Manitoba Act* and other pieces of legislation. However, there has not been a consistent or coherent national policy on Métis (Morse and Grover, 2002). Early in the history of Canada there was a belief that the Métis (however defined) would become integrated either into the Indian or non-Indian population and would thus no longer be a people. As such, the country wouldn't need a long-term policy with regard to this group.

In the Atlantic provinces, most governments simply refuse to acknowledge the existence of the Métis. Although Prince Edward Island recognizes them, it has no special policy because there are so few of them.

At the federal level, the Métis have only in recent years received formal, legal, and constitutional recognition beyond that established in the *Manitoba Act* of 1870. The Métis argue that, under this Act, they were recognized as a separate people with certain rights. Furthermore, because the Act cannot be changed without Britain's consent, the Métis and non-status Indians continue to have separate legal status. The federal government has established a cabinet committee on Métis and non-status Indians to investigate more fully the claims and issues put forward by them. Currently there is considerable debate about the legal status of Métis and their rights.

In early 1981 the federal government recognized and affirmed the Aboriginal and treaty rights of Indians, Inuit, and Métis. These rights have been affirmed in the Constitution (1982, Sec. 35(1)), with the proviso that only "existing and treaty rights" are

Establishing Métis Rights

Recently, Métis have taken their case to the courts. In the recent case of *R.* v. *Powley*, the Supreme Court of Canada made its first ruling about Métis and their Aboriginal rights. In 1993, the Powleys (father and son) killed a moose and tagged it, "harvesting my meat for winter." One week later they were charged with hunting without a licence and unlawful possession of moose contrary to Ontario's *Game and Fish Act*. Five years later the trial judge ruled that the Powleys had the "Métis right" to hunt, which is protected by Section 35 of the *Constitution Act, 1982* and the charges were dismissed. The Crown appealed the decision, and in 2000 the Ontario Superior Court of Justice confirmed the trial decision and dismissed the Crown's appeal. The Ontario Court of Appeal heard the case in 2001 and upheld the earlier decisions. Nevertheless, the Crown appealed to the Supreme Court of Canada. On September 19, 2003, the Supreme Court of Canada, in a unanimous judgment, upheld the lower court decisions and said that the Powleys can exercise the Métis right to hunt that is protected by Section 35. In summary, the court confirmed the existence of Métis communities in Canada and the constitutional protection of their existing Aboriginal rights.

The reader should note that the Supreme Court did not define who the Métis people are. The Court set out three broad factors—self-identification, ancestral connection, and community acceptance—to be used in identifying who can exercise a Métis community's Section 35 right to hunt. This case is only about the Métis right to hunt and does not reflect on other rights Métis might have.

to be recognized. The Métis argue that their rights are a special case of Aboriginal rights, that they stem from the self-perception of the Métis people as an indigenous national minority (Daniels, 1981), and that they are derived from their Aboriginal ancestry and title—both of which constitute the national identity of the Métis.

In 1983, members of the Métis Nation created the Métis National Council, whose goal was to achieve a clear definition and defence of Métis rights. By the time the First Ministers' Conference on Aboriginal Affairs convened that same year, a separate invitation had been issued to the Métis National Council, thereby severing the formal relationship with the Native Council of Canada which had previously represented the Métis.

The Métis National Council has published material that identifies its criteria for determining whether a person is Métis:

The Métis are:

• an Aboriginal people distinct from Indian and Inuit;
• descendants of the historic Métis who evolved in what is now Western Canada as a people with a common political will; and
• descendants of those Aboriginal peoples who have been absorbed by the historic Métis.

The Council goes on to point out that the Métis community comprises members of the above groups who share a common cultural identity and political will (Métis National

Council, 1983). This is not to say that everyone accepts this definition. There is no single exclusive Métis people in Canada. Eastern Canadian Métis are different from Red River Métis. At a provincial level, the issue of who is or isn't Métis varies. In Alberta, recent changes to the *Métis Settlement Act* and the criteria set out by the Alberta Métis Nation Association have clarified the definition of a Métis. Both the government and the Association agree that a Métis is someone who declares himself or herself as a Métis, has traditionally held him- or herself as Métis, and is accepted by the Métis community as Métis.

In Manitoba, the Federation definition of a Métis remains a racial one that enables non-status Indians to join. The Saskatchewan Association of Métis and non-status Indians split in 1987, so the Métis Society of Saskatchewan defines a Métis in a manner similar to Alberta.

Today the term "Métis" has widespread usage. However, two different meanings have been given to the term. As the Métis National Council (1984) pointed out, written with a small *m,* "métis" is a racial term for anyone of mixed Indian and European ancestry. Nevertheless, the Métis National Council has objected to this distinction and argues that the acceptance of the latter (racial) definition undermines the rights of Métis people.

Today there is a distinction between the historical Métis and the Pan-Métis. "Pan-Métis" is a more inclusive term that includes historic Métis, people of mixed Indian-European ancestry, and non-status Indians. As Lussier (1979) points out, they gain their identity from a multitude of national roots.

The federal government has taken the position that Métis are a provincial responsibility, even though there are federal departments that provide funding for them—e.g., the Secretary of State. This position is based on the argument that Métis are not included in Section 91(24) of the *Constitution Act, 1867.* Provinces (except Alberta) contend that Métis are included under Section 91(24). The Métis National Council also maintains that Métis are a federal responsibility. Chartier (1988) claims that in 1984 the federal minister argued that, even if the Supreme Court ruled that Métis were a federal responsibility, the government could refuse to exercise its responsibility. Chartier holds that Métis are covered within the term "Indian" (as are the Inuit) in Section 91(24). Others, such as Schwartz (1985; see also Sawchuck, 1998), view Métis as a people distinct from Indians and thus side with the federal government. However, he does offer a compromise in suggesting that small-*m* métis would be covered by Section 91(24) while capital-*M* Métis would not. What is suggested is that Métis may be entitled to be governed by some federal laws; however, even if this were the case, substantial co-operation among all the provinces would be needed to generate a uniform regime of Métis control.

While the federal government treats Métis as a provincial responsibility, certain interpretations of general programs provided to Canadians have allowed the Métis to benefit. In other areas of concern—e.g., constitutional negotiations—an informal agreement has been made whereby the Minister of Justice is to act in a way that ensures that Métis interests are addressed and that the Métis have someone to listen to their concerns. Clearly, the inclusion of the Métis in Sections 35(1) and 35(2) of the Constitution is accorded legal significance. The recognition of the Métis as an Aboriginal people provides a constitutional base upon which negotiations for the recognition and compensation of their rights can fully begin. Finally, Section 25 also incorporates, by definition, a fiduciary relationship between the federal government and the Métis (Bell, 1991).

In 2002 the Métis Nation adopted a national definition of Métis and they have since been ratifying this national definition in the respective provincial jurisdictions. Their definition is that the Métis have a shared history, a common culture (song, dance, dress, national symbols), a unique language (Michif, with various regional dialects), extensive kinship connections from Ontario westward, a distinct way of life, a traditional territory, and a collective consciousness. The Métis Nation is represented through province-wide governance structures from Ontario westward; namely the Métis Nation of Ontario, the Manitoba Métis Federation, the Métis Nation-Saskatchewan, the Métis Nation of Alberta, and the Métis Provincial Council of British Columbia.

The question of who is a Métis will continue to be an issue as the boundary of inclusion and exclusion continues to shift. Aboriginal people also define themselves inconsistently and shift categories depending upon the situation and the changing definition of "who is an Indian" (Giokas and Chartrand, 2002). It is clear that the definition cannot be a biological one nor can it be dependent on kinship. The changing definition of who is or isn't an Indian also has clearly demonstrated that blood quantum is a fruitless strategy for defining the boundaries of a people. An equally fruitless strategy is kinship since out-marriage and enfranchisement have split families in may different ways. Self-identification is used by many Métis but this strategy has not had any political or legal support. Nevertheless, it is the only real choice people of mixed ancestry have in developing boundaries and political power. As Giokas and Chartrand (2002) have clearly noted, like much of our history, the basis for recognizing Aboriginal people is less a conscious policy and more of a shifting and haphazard strategy resulting from fiscal and political pressures over the years. As a result, no consistent basis for designating a person as Indian, Métis, or any other Aboriginal category has existed. In the end, there is no one single definition of the concept. As Peters et al. (1989) point out, the term Métis is widespread in usage. It appears to have a well-accepted general meaning, reflecting the social aspect of Métis identity, and a reality that cannot be denied.

Inuit

The category of "Inuit" also has undergone a number of redefinitions. Until Confederation, there was no legal definition of Inuit. At that time there was no real need to make a distinction. And, since the issue was limited to local concerns, the government did not see fit to enter the debate. Immediately after Confederation the Inuit were placed under the control of the *Indian Act*. However, after a short time they were placed, and continue to be, under the direct jurisdiction of the federal government under the Canadian *Constitution Act, 1982*.[5]

When Canada began to think of developing the North in the early 20th century, the government decided that a census was needed to establish the actual number of Inuit. As a result, a "disc" number was allotted to each Inuk; for a time, only those with numbers were officially defined as Inuit.[6] However, other definitions of Inuit have developed since and will continue to be used. For example, in the 1978 agreement between the Government of Canada and the Committee for Original Peoples Entitlement (COPE), an Inuk was defined as a member of those people known as Inuit, Eskimo, or Inuvialuit who claim traditional use and occupancy of the land. In the case of the 1975 James Bay Agreement, an Inuk was defined as any individual who possesses a disc number, or has one-quarter Inuit blood, or is considered an Inuk by the local community, and such other persons as may be agreed upon. Today it is estimated that about 50 000 Inuit reside in Canada, mostly north of the 49th parallel.

SOCIAL DIVISIONS AMONG ABORIGINAL PEOPLE

The definitions of "Indian," "non-status," "Métis," and "Inuit" are far from being settled. Many of the decisions will rest with the courts. Indeed, it is clear that no single definition of Aboriginal peoples has been agreed upon. However, as Mallea (1994) argues, whatever the definition of "Indians," the legislation in place led to the government strategy of "divide and conquer" as well as assimilation. She contends that it allowed the government to create an apartheid system by placing Aboriginal peoples on reserves. Moreover, the changing definition of who is an Indian has an impact on who is defined as Métis and/or Inuit. Why have these legal distinctions been inflicted upon Canadian Aboriginal people? Those in power have surely been aware that such nominal distinctions have a "divide and conquer" effect. Aboriginal people became easier to control as they began to fight among themselves. The distinctions between the non-treaty and the treaty Indians are particularly divisive; the two groups received different privileges, different amounts of money from different sources, and different rights.

Red Power advocates are now attempting to point out the divisive effects of legal distinctions and to suggest ways of counteracting their influence. According to these advocates, legal status is irrelevant in the face of discrimination. Because the distinction between registered and non-registered Indians cannot be made visually, Euro-Canadians cannot and do not distinguish between the two in daily interactions. All those who have an Indian appearance fall prey to the same stereotypes and find themselves treated as though they were lazy, drunk, or happy-go-lucky. Moreover, Aboriginal persons who fall under separate legal categories often lead similar lifestyles. Thus, the similarities among Aboriginal people frequently overshadow the legal differences (Burrell and Sanders, 1984).

Dyck (1980) has pointed out that the term "Native" is becoming increasingly popular with academics, laypersons, and politicians. This term, he argues, serves to cognitively combine peoples who, from a Euro-Canadian perspective, are similar. Yet the various categories into which the Aboriginal population is divided have since been shown not to be irrelevant; indeed, under specific circumstances, these "internal" differences can be very important. As Dyck suggests, these differences can be exaggerated or they can be ignored by the dominant group at will to suit its purpose. Distinctions can be emphasized to divide the Aboriginal population, or they can be ignored through stereotypes and generalizations that avoid individual issues.[7]

The Lavell and Bedard Cases

Two legal cases from the early 1970s involving the sex-discriminatory status regulations in the *Indian Act* clearly illustrate the issue of definitions, the process of developing social divisions among Aboriginal groups, and the complexity of the Aboriginal women's sexual equality problem. The *Lavell* and the *Bedard* cases also had a profound effect on the establishment of the Native Women's Association and the way it manifested itself vis-à-vis national male-dominated Aboriginal organizations (King, 1972).

Jeanette Corbiere Lavell, a status Ojibwa from the Wikwemikong reserve in Ontario who was to marry a non-Aboriginal man in December 1970, had already declared before the date of her marriage that she intended to contest Sections 12(1)b and 14 of the *Indian Act* in court.

A precedent had been set in 1967 by a court case involving a liquor infraction in the Northwest Territories. An Indian man named Drybones was convicted under Section 94(b) of the *Indian Act* for being intoxicated off-reserve. Drybones successfully challenged his conviction before the Supreme Court in 1969 on the basis that this particular section of the *Indian Act* contravened Section 1(b) of the *Canadian Bill of Rights* that prohibited racial discrimination. The *Drybones* case proved that it was possible for the *Indian Act* to be overruled by that Bill (Cardinal, 1979; Jamieson, 1978). The *Drybones* case and the report of the Royal Commission on the Status of Women, together with the withdrawal of the White Paper, resulted in renewed pride in Indian identity (Krosenbrink-Gelissen, 1983).

In June 1971, the Ontario County Court dismissed Lavell's case on grounds that, despite the loss of her Indian status, she had equal rights with all other married Canadian women. As such, it was found that she was not deprived of any human rights or freedoms contemplated in the *Bill of Rights.* The Court did not find her inequality within her own class of people contrary to that Bill and, thus, overlooked the fact that the *Indian Act* reinforced an inferior position of Indian women vis-à-vis other Canadian women (Chapman, 1972; INAC 1983; Jamieson, 1978; Krosenbrink-Gelissen, 1984).

In October 1971, Lavell made an appeal to the Federal Court of Appeals and won. The three judges concluded that the *Indian Act* resulted in different rights for Indian women than those of Indian men when women married non-status males or Indians from different bands. The Court decided that Sections 11(1)f, 12(1)b, and 14 of the *Indian Act* contravened the *Bill of Rights* and should therefore be repealed in due course. Right after the decision from the Federal Court of Appeals, the federal government declared that it would bring the *Lavell* case before the Supreme Court of Canada (House of Commons, 1982).

The second case concerns Yvonne Bedard, a non-status Iroquois woman from the Brantford reserve in Ontario. She had separated from her non-Aboriginal husband and returned to her reserve to live in the house that was willed to her by her parents. A year later, Bedard was evicted from the reserve by the band council, although DIAND had informed the council that on the basis of local control several other bands had decided not to implement that particular section of the *Indian Act.* Bedard successfully presented her case before the Supreme Court of Ontario on the same grounds that Lavell had used (Cheda, 1977; Jamieson, 1978; Weaver, 1978). Together with the *Lavell* case, the *Bedard* case was brought before the Supreme Court of Canada in 1973.

Both Lavell and Bedard received support from various women's groups, which recognized their cases as an opportunity to advance women's rights in general. Duclos argues that it was predominantly Euro-Canadian women who were spokespersons for the women's movement in Canada during the 1970s. They created "an image which constructs gender as the sole basis of women's oppression, cloaked in the privileges and power attached to being white" (1990: 38). Hence, feminist groups at that time focused on sex discrimination in the *Indian Act* as an example of the inequality of women, and did not recognize the dual discrimination operating in Indian women's situation. However, feminist groups were able to attract media attention. This way, Indian people across Canada were made aware of the significance of the *Lavell* and *Bedard* cases for the Indian movement (INAC, 1977, 1982).

The *Lavell* and *Bedard* cases led to considerable discussion among both Indian and non-Aboriginal people. Lobbying by both groups was complicated by a lack of consensus. Whereas non-Aboriginal groups focused on the matter of sexual equality per se, Aboriginal groups began raising the question of whether the federal government should continue determining Indian legal status and band membership. This awkward situation arose from the fact that Indian sexual equality rights were being discussed within the field of women's rights—a field which, as such, had nothing to do with the *Indian Act* (Roosens, 1986).

Over the years, the *Indian Act* created a friction between status and non-status Indians that became visible in the political arena. In 1968 the National Indian Council was abolished. Status and non-status Indians, as well as the Métis, had political priorities that were incompatible. Therefore, the National Indian Brotherhood was established to represent status Indians politically, while the Native Council of Canada was to represent non-status Indians and the Métis politically (Weaver, 1983; Whiteside, 1973b). Status was sometimes linked to biology and culture, meaning that women who had lost their status were not considered real Indians any more (Krosenbrink-Gelissen, 1983). Furthermore, being legally recognized as an Aboriginal person provided many Indians with a source of pride. And lastly, legal status had gradually become a gauge of "pure" Indian descent. It is within this framework that the motto "keep the Indian race pure" should be understood. Nevertheless, stigmatization by status persons created problems, in particular for non-status women. (See Table 2.3.)

Both the National Indian Brotherhood and the Native Council of Canada determined their membership in accordance with the status regulations of the *Indian Act.* It should not be forgotten that the *Indian Act* has profoundly affected Indian thinking over time. Other Indians, however, argued that legal status provided a person with official recognition by outsiders and, for that reason, it did not make a status Indian more Indian than a non-status Indian. The same objection was made with respect to Indians living off-reserve, who are for the most part non-status Indians. They argued that not living within an Indian community did not make a person less Indian (Goodwill, 1971).

A significant reason for the divisiveness among Indians regarding the legal status issue in the *Indian Act* was that most Indians did not know what the *Indian Act* entailed and what it could or could not enforce (Silman, 1987). Status Indians found it hard to comprehend the problems that non-status Indians were confronted with. At the same time, a fundamental change of the *Indian Act* seemed inconceivable to many status Indians (Wilson, 1974). A repeal of the *Indian Act,* according to them, would result in the loss of all Indian rights. Hence, those Indian persons who opposed Lavell and Bedard's actions in order to

TABLE 2.3	Indian Mixed Marriages* in Percentage				
Mixed Marriages	1966	1972	1976	1986	1996
Status male and non-status female	34.3	50.0	57.5	58.3	59.2
Status female and non-status male	65.7	50.0	42.5	41.7	40.8
Total in percentage	100.0	100.0	100.0	100.0	100.0

* Mixed marriage = marriage between non-status and status Indian persons, based on *Indian Act* regulations. Due to racial connotations, it is presumed that a non-status person is a non-Aboriginal person. However, the opposite may well be the case. Within this table, "Indian" should not be conceived as a social category but as a legal category. Intermarriage = marriage between two Indian persons from different bands or nations. There are no records on intermarriage. Between 1966 and 1976, mixed marriages remained continually around 50 percent of all Indian marriages.

Source: INAC, 1983: 5-12; Jamieson, 1978: 66; Krosenbrink-Gelissen, 1984: 53; Weaver, 1978: 7, 23a; Alberta Report, December 9, 1996, 9.

seek an *Indian Act* amendment were not necessarily in favour of sexual inequality, but feared the loss of all Indian rights.

In February 1973 the *Lavell* and *Bedard* cases appeared before the Supreme Court of Canada. The Attorney General of Canada had made the appeal in response to suggestions from government officials who were afraid of the far-reaching implications if previous decisions in the *Lavell* and *Bedard* cases should be upheld. Most important, the appeal was also made in response to pressure from the National Indian Brotherhood. The federal government did not want a revision of the *Indian Act,* in view of the previous negative reactions by Indians when change was suggested, and because the abolition of sex-discrimination in the *Indian Act* would bring about substantial financial liabilities. The number of status Indians would increase dramatically if non-status Indian persons were to regain status and corresponding government services.

According to the National Indian Brotherhood, sex discrimination against women in the *Indian Act* was wrong, but the organization was afraid that if previous court decisions were upheld, the federal government would be given the ultimate power to change or even to repeal the *Indian Act* without the consent of Indian people. The White Paper on Indian Policy of 1969 was still fresh in the memories of those involved. The National Indian Brotherhood considered Section 12(1)b of the *Indian Act* as a strong lever to force the federal government to negotiate an *Indian Act* revision. It wanted to sidetrack the issue of sexual equality for Indian men and women in the interests of preserving Indian rights, either through the *Indian Act* or through other legal guarantees. Therefore, the National Indian Brotherhood wanted Indian women to wait for a redress of their rights in the interest of preserving Indian rights for (status) Indians as a group. Women, therefore, were requested to subordinate their goal— Indian rights for Indian women—to that of Indian men; they were used as a political vehicle to pursue an *Indian Act* revision in the way that status Indian males saw fit.

While the National Indian Brotherhood's leading figures were against Lavell and Bedard primarily for political and strategic reasons, it appeared that the majority of its constituency—still not fully aware of the power and limitations of the *Indian Act*—was against these women's actions to regain their Indian rights for other and more far-reaching reasons. The constrained identity boundary mechanisms embedded in the status regulations of the *Indian Act* were largely internalized by Indian people and were therefore conceived of as Indian customary law. A good example of this is provided by the Association of Iroquois and Allied Tribes, of which Bedard's band was a member. The organization stated in a position paper of 1971 that the patrilineal and patrilocal status principles were in agreement with the traditional social organization of the Iroquois (Chapman, 1972). Anthropologists are aware that this claim is false. Furthermore, the National Indian Brotherhood's constituency in large part feared the influx of non-Aboriginal men on reserves if previous decisions in the *Lavell* and *Bedard* cases were upheld. This argument reflected an internalization of non-Aboriginal male sexism, since it indicated the Indian people's fear that non-Aboriginal men would take over political power. The presence of non-Aboriginal women on reserves (married, widowed, or separated from status Indian men) was not felt to be threatening, despite the increase in this trend. This argument also reveals a discrepancy between Indian ideology and practice. Although Indian males and females unanimously acknowledged Indian women's crucial and continuing roles as mothers in retaining and enhancing cultural patterns, non-Aboriginal women were not perceived as a threat to the cultural survival of Indians (Krosenbrink, 1989). Many non-status Indian people argued that sex discrimination in the *Indian Act* is not a women's issue per se. Since Indian women are removed from the centre of life through the *Indian Act* regulations, the survival of Indian communities was actually at stake. They claimed that "Indian motherhood" is vital to the continuation of Indian nationhood (Holmes, 1987; Krosenbrink-Gelissen, 1984; Meadows, 1981; Shkilnyk, 1985). Since the National Indian Brotherhood went so far as to determine Indian band membership in terms of cultural resourcefulness, the devaluation of women was perceived as detrimental to Indian cultural continuity (Weaver, 1978).

The Supreme Court decided, in a 5 to 4 vote, against Lavell and Bedard. The *Canadian Bill of Rights* was not considered effective to overrule the *Indian Act,* and the fact that Indian women were treated differently upon marriage to a non-status man or an Indian from another band was not considered relevant to the cases brought before the Court (Eberts, 1985; Jamieson, 1978; Kerr, 1975). Both the federal government and the National Indian Brotherhood saw the decision as a victory. The National Indian Brotherhood saw it as a victory for Indian rights. The fact that Indian women were denied Indian rights was ignored, since it was not relevant to their political mandate.

The *Lavell* and *Bedard* cases had awakened both the Canadian public and the Indian people. The cases presented a moral dilemma over which the women's movement and the Indian movement collided; the Indian ideology of special status was perceived as irreconcilable with the equality ideology of the women's movement. However, to Indian women the issue had never been as described above. They had never asked for equal rights with other Canadians, but for equal rights with other Indians: "We can't begin discussing universal women's rights because at this time we can't even get Indian rights for Indian women" (Indian Rights for Indian Women, n.d.: 15). Misinterpretations of Indian women's political goals on the part of both the Indian movement and the women's movement were due to a lack of understanding of the true character of the Indian or Aboriginal women's movement, as the Native Women's Association of Canada argued in the 1980s.

CONCLUSION

The organization of Indians into their present-day bands can be understood as a response to the draconian steps taken against Aboriginal people by government. The government, in a sense, forced Aboriginal persons to deal with them as a band, and, over time, this has become the basis upon which Aboriginal and non-Aboriginal people operate. Over time, Aboriginal people have accepted the band as the focus of their identity and organization. The indigenous institutional basis of the band is no longer evident. In other words, traditional forms of organization that were an integral part of Native culture have been replaced by a type of administrative structure designed primarily to serve the convenience of the federal and provincial governments. As Cornell (1988) points out, "Structures of authority and decision making, once embedded in the fabric of aboriginal society, are now attacked from the outside, institutionally separate from the culture of Natives" (pp. 101–102). Today the band no longer exhibits a sense of peoplehood but rather is a political–legal construct that has some legal relationship with other structures in our society.

Aboriginal identity has become complex and fragmented. For example, many people identify themselves as Bloods or Ojibwa, but this masks a multitude of meanings. For some it may mean a connection with the tradition of Bloods or Ojibwa, and for these people, maintenance of culture is of paramount importance. Others will identify with the local group experiences. Finally, some view their identity in terms of the legal definition of band membership. As a result, we find today that a sense of peoplehood is diverse, yet Aboriginal peoples are forced to act as a single political unit (Sealey, 1975).

Increasingly, for a large number of Aboriginal people, Native identity is becoming an important basis for action and thought. The number of local and national (as well as international) Native organizations reflects the importance of such an identity. This Native consciousness has allowed for pan-Indianism to emerge along with the social and political organizations. This pan-Indianism is a kind of cultural synthesis of a number of different but related cultures. The resultant new identity (Indian consciousness) has created a linkage among groups that previously were viewed by others (and themselves) as distinct. While Aboriginal people are beginning to develop a consciousness of band and group solidarity, the process of establishing themselves as an ethnic entity is not yet complete. There are still major divisions between the various groups (e.g., Indians, Métis, and Inuit) but it is clear that the process of Aboriginal self-definition and identification has begun.

From the turn of the century to World War II, a collective Native identity began to emerge. The development of this identity was gradual and intermittent, varying from region to region. At the same time, however, government actions reduced the amount of intertribal interaction as well as political action. As a result, networks (small at first) among various groups of Aboriginal people focused on social and cultural affairs. Nevertheless, these activities promoted a sense of shared Nativism. For example, pow-wows began to become public and they drew Aboriginal persons from other areas of the country for several days of socializing and learning cultural traditions.

NOTES

1. In 1982 the *British North America Act* was changed to the *Constitution Act, 1867.* An attempt is made in this book to distinguish between the two names by using the *British North America Act* when citing legislation passed under the Act or references made to it before 1982, and by using the *Constitution Act, 1867* for any references thereafter.

2. *Indian Act,* R.A., c. 1–6, amended by c. 10 (2nd Supp.) 1974–75–76, c. 1/8. 1978 (Hull: Minister of Supply and Services Canada: 6–8).

3. One of the major concerns that DIAND had with regard to the changes in Section 12(1)(b) of the *Indian Act* was the financial cost. In a once-secret document of DIAND entitled "Amendments to Remove Discriminatory Sections of the *Indian Act,*" the estimates ran from $312 to $557 million. These figures were based on estimates of the number of women who would be reinstated as Indian and the percentage who would return to the reserves; the low estimate allowed for a 30 percent reinstatement and a 30 percent return while the high estimate predicted a 100 percent reinstatement and a 70 percent return rate. In addition, approximately 57 000 children would be eligible for reinstatement.

    A Cabinet discussion paper released in 1982 showed that settling land claims in the next 15 years could cost the government as much as $4.1 billion. About $1.8 billion of these claims concerns land in British Columbia, where the fewest treaties were signed; most of the rest would be divided between Aboriginals in the two territories. The $4.1 billion includes reparation for hunting and fishing rights, payment for land, and the implementation of various programs and other benefits. In addition, another $500 million could be spent by the government in the next 20 years to settle specific claims (Indian News, Vol. 22, No. 7, October 1981:7).

4. For a more thorough statement regarding the status of the Métis in Canada, the reader should consult "Native Rights: Policy and Practices," *Perception,* 4, 2 (November/December 1981). Sawchuk (1998) provides an accessible and more contemporary account of Aboriginal—especially Métis—political organizing, lobbying, and activities. Much of the present information comes from this source.

5. In 1939 Duplessis was able to get Northern Quebec Inuit redefined as Indians so that they came under federal, instead of provincial, control (Richardson, 1972).

6. Numbers were stamped on small metal discs that Inuit could carry with them for identification.

7. However, other groups have now decided that this is a politically useful term and it now has symbolic uses that far exceed its original definition (Siggner, 1998). In addition to the above, the reader should be aware that different definitions are presented by agencies collecting data on the ethnic makeup of our population. Statistics Canada, for example, makes a distinction between ethnic identity and ethnic origin when it collects data. On the other hand, when the Department of Indian Affairs collects data, it is only interested in those individuals who have legal status. Finally, individuals can have more than one ethnic affiliation or origin. This means that allowances in the data collection must be aware of single and multiple ethnic affiliations. Thus, again, some data collection agencies will take these aspects into consideration when collecting data (Eschbach et al., 1998; Kreager, 1997).

WEBLINKS

www.bloorstreet.com/200block/sindact.htm

This website reproduces the entire *Indian Act*, with helpful notes explaining the provisions. It should be noted that this is the current version of the *Indian Act*, a piece of legislation that has been changed many times since its inception in 1876.

www.abo-peoples.org/programs/dnlsc-31.html

An argumentative essay by Harry Daniels of the Congress of Aboriginal Peoples on *Bill C-31* and its impact on Aboriginal identity. The author labels the legislation "the Abocide Bill."

www.metisnation.ca

The Canadian Métis National Council is a national organization representing Métis peoples across Canada. The site also provides current press releases, conferences, research, arts and culture, and links to regional and provincial councils.

chapter three

Profile of Aboriginal People I: Population and Health

INTRODUCTION

To fully understand the actions of a people, one must know not only the context and environment in which they live but also the attributes of the population. Are they wealthy? Are they an aging population? What is the birth rate? The answers to these questions will allow the reader to better understand the aspirations of Aboriginal people and will provide a basis for explaining their behaviour. This information also will provide the context in which the federal and provincial governments make policy and program decisions regarding Aboriginal people. To ensure up-to-date information, every five years the federal government undertakes a national survey in order to collect information about Canadians. Every 10 years a census is undertaken that collects data from every Canadian. This systematic collection of data allows governments (federal, provincial, and municipal) to assess their programs and policies as well as project into the future what programs will be required if they are to address the problems facing Aboriginal peoples. The Department of Indian and Northern Affairs also collects information on Aboriginal people. Thus, there are several agencies that collect data on Aboriginal people, including the Vital Statistics Section of the Health Division of Statistics Canada, the Decennial Censuses of Canada, and Indian Affairs. Unfortunately all three differ widely in their terms of reference, their definition of an Aboriginal, and their method of enumeration. As a result, statistics coming from one agency are not strictly comparable with statistics from the others. At present, no attempt has been made to reconcile the statistics produced by these major sources.

Needless to say, the lack of standardized data confuses policy makers and poses problems for short-term trend analyses while at the same time making future projections difficult.

Moreover, because the definition of an Indian has changed over time, statistics report-ed by different agencies show wide discrepancies and, in some cases, revised definitions of Indian status have meant that statistics related to a certain group are no longer appropriate.

Our profile of Aboriginal people in Canada will begin with a discussion of residential patterns and then move to population size and growth, including births and deaths. There is a third component to population growth and this is a form of migration. In the case of Aboriginal people, this does not refer to individuals who migrate into or out of Canada. Rather, this component acts like migration in that it identifies the number of people who take on the attribute of Aboriginal and those who lose it. In short, over the years, there have been many government policies that have defined non-Aboriginal individuals as Aboriginal, or redefined individuals having been initially defined as Aboriginal persons as not then being Aboriginal—a kind of surrogate "in" and "out" migration. While one policy (enfranchise-ment) was phased out in the 1980s, a new policy was introduced in the 1990s (*Bill C-31*) that has had immediate impacts and will have different effects 50 years into the future. We also will look at the health factors that impinge upon population growth and will conclude with an analysis of infrastructure related to health issues (LaChance-Brulotte, 1984).

RESIDENTIAL PATTERNS

Where do Aboriginal people live? They reside in all parts of Canada, although they are not evenly distributed. Tables 3.1, 3.2, and 3.3 reveal the regional dispersion of Aboriginal peo-ple over time. The data show that while the overall Indian population has increased all over Canada, the biggest gains were in Saskatchewan and Alberta. Approximately one-fourth live in Ontario, and another 16 percent in each of Saskatchewan and British Columbia. Western provinces show similar numbers, while much smaller numbers reside in Quebec and Atlantic Canada. Tables 3.2 and 3.3 identify the on- and off-reserve Indian population by region. In 1988, nearly 65 percent of status Indians lived on the reserve. While the number on the reserve has decreased over the years, nearly two-thirds of the population remain on lands set aside for Aboriginal people and held in trust by Ottawa. Less than half of the Yukon Indians live on reserves, Crown lands, or settlements, while in the Northwest Territories over 80 per-cent are "on-reserve." Within the provinces, Saskatchewan reveals the lowest percentage, while Quebec shows nearly three-fourths of its Indian population on-reserve. By the end of the 20th century it was estimated that there will be substantial increases in the on-reserve population for the Prairies. When we focus on the off-reserve population, we see that all regions have experienced increases. However, the largest increases were in Saskatchewan and Alberta, with Quebec having the lowest. As we predict the future, the data suggest that Alberta as well as Manitoba will continue to have substantial increases in off-reserve Indians. When we focus on the geographical distribution of Métis and non-status Indians in 1990, it shows that about 27 percent of the enumerated Métis live in Alberta while an addi-tional 40 percent live in the other two Prairie provinces. Focusing on non-status Indians, we find that 40 percent live in Ontario while an additional 30 percent are in British Columbia.

Reserves

Canada has some 2720 reserves, though this number, like the number of bands (614), varies over time according to the policy of the federal government. Reserves can vary in

TABLE 3.1	Registered Indian Population by Region, 1966–2001											
	1966		1976		1986		1996		2001			
Region	No.	%	No.	%	No.	%	No.	%	No.	%		
Atlantic	8 494	3.8	10 891	3.8	16 460	4.1	21 835	3.8	23 398	3.8		
Quebec	23 186	10.3	29 580	10.2	40 200	10.0	53 280	9.3	56 125	9.0		
Ontario	52 408	23.4	64 690	22.4	91 250	22.6	126 755	22.1	134 372	21.6		
Manitoba	31 000	13.8	42 311	14.6	59 064	14.7	84 684	14.8	93 020	14.9		
Saskatchewan	31 362	14.0	43 404	15.0	62 232	15.5	93 250	16.3	105 830	17.0		
Alberta	25 432	11.3	34 130	11.8	44 653	12.3	75 954	13.2	84 684	13.6		
B.C.	46 543	20.8	53 342	18.5	69 822	17.3	96 472	16.8	102 552	16.5		
Yukon	5 739	2.6	3 181	1.1	4 626	1.1	7 133	1.2	7 602	1.2		
N.W.T.			7 409	2.6	9 735	2.4	13 906	2.4	15 318	2.5		
Canada	224 164	100	288 938	100	403 042	100	573 269	100	622 901	100		

Sources: 1966–1989: Indian Register, DIAND; 1996–2001: *Population Projections of Registered Indians, 1986–2011*, DIAND, 1990.

TABLE 3.2 Registered Indian Population On-Reserve by Region, 1966-2001

Region	1966 No.	%	1976 No.	%	1986 No.	%	1996 No.	%	2001 No.	%
Atlantic	6 444	75.9	8 066	74.1	11 341	69.2	13 905	63.7	14 775	63.1
Quebec	18 720	80.7	24 198	81.8	32 137	79.9	38 238	71.8	40 223	71.7
Ontario	36 508	69.7	44 227	68.4	59 000	64.7	72 229	57.0	76 339	56.8
Manitoba	26 752	86.3	31 723	75.0	42 324	71.5	55 115	65.1	60 648	65.2
Saskatchewan	26 920	85.8	30 746	70.8	39 973	64.2	56 442	60.5	64 162	60.6
Alberta	22 573	88.8	26 841	78.6	35 798	72.1	48 656	64.1	54 630	64.5
B.C.	37 019	79.5	34 073	63.9	43 267	62.0	54 327	56.3	57 805	56.4
Yukon	5 482	95.5	2 620	82.4	3 023	65.3	3 905	54.7	4 182	55.0
N.W.T.			7 143	96.4	8 978	92.2	11 562	83.1	12 750	83.2
Canada	180 418	80.5	209 637	72.6	275 891	68.5	354 379	61.8	385 514	61.9

Note: On-reserve includes Crown lands and settlements. Percentages are based on regional totals shown in Table 3.1.

Sources: 1966-1989: Indian Register, DIAND; 1996-2001: *Population Projections of Registered Indians, 1986-2011*, DIAND, 1990.

TABLE 3.3	Registered Indian Population Off-Reserve by Region, 1966–2001										
	1966*		1976		1986		1996		2001	
Region	No.	%	No.	%	No.	%	No.	%	No.	%
Atlantic	2 050	24.1	2 825	25.9	5 069	30.8	7 930	36.3	8 623	36.9
Quebec	4 466	19.3	5 382	18.2	8 063	20.1	15 041	28.2	15 902	28.3
Ontario	15 900	30.3	20 463	31.6	32 250	35.3	54 526	43.0	58 032	43.2
Manitoba	4 248	13.7	10 588	25.0	16 740	28.3	29 570	34.9	32 372	34.8
Saskatchewan	4 442	14.2	12 658	29.2	22 259	35.8	36 809	39.5	41 669	39.4
Alberta	2 859	11.2	7 289	21.4	13 855	27.9	27 298	35.9	30 054	35.5
B.C.	9 524	20.5	19 269	36.1	26 555	38.0	42 145	43.7	44 747	43.6
Yukon	257	4.5	561	17.6	1 603	34.7	3 228	45.3	3 420	45.0
N.W.T.			266	3.6	757	7.7	2 343	16.8	2 568	16.8
Canada	43 746	19.5	79 301	27.4	127 151	31.5	218 890	38.2	237 387	38.1

Note: Percentages are based on regional totals shown in Table 3.1.
* In 1966, numbers include 274 individuals with unstated places of residence distributed as follows: Atlantic 5, Quebec 24, Ontario 51, Manitoba 12, Saskatchewan 33, Alberta 69, B.C. 56, Yukon and N.W.T. 24.

Sources: 1966–1989: Indian Register, DIAND; 1996–2001: *Population Projections of Registered Indians, 1986–2011*, DIAND, 1990.

size. Although there is no minimum area, 71.5 hectares per person is the maximum; some reserves in British Columbia cover only a few hectares, while the largest—at 900 square kilometres—is in Alberta. In Eastern Canada each band is generally limited to one reserve. In the West, one band may encompass several reserves; British Columbia has over 1600 reserves but fewer than 200 bands (Allan, 1943; Siggner and Locatelli, 1980).

Clearly, the reserve still provides security and roots for most Aboriginal people. The reserve is where the majority of Aboriginals have grown up among family and friends. Even for those who leave, it continues to provide a haven from the pressures of Euro-Canadian society. These factors, combined with the prejudicial attitudes of non-Aboriginal culture, create a strong internal pull and external push toward remaining on the reserve (Canada, 1984a). Even if an increasing number of Aboriginal people leave the reserve, the absolute population of those who remain will still show a sizeable increase. This could pose a number of problems for Canada. Reserves are potential hotbeds of political and social discontent. In addition, if Indians on reserves become economically developed, they could pose a competitive threat to some Canadian corporate structures. Already, in British Columbia and Alberta, Indians have angered local businesspeople by building housing developments or proposing casinos on reserve lands close to major cities.

Reserves are situated in a variety of geographical contexts that have significant implications for development potential, population mobility, and transportation routes. DIAND has characterized the reserves in four ways: urban, rural, remote, and special access. Reserves within 50 kilometres of a service centre are considered urban. Rural is a zone where the reserve is located between 50 and 350 kilometres from a service centre. A remote reserve is located beyond the 350-kilometre limit but is accessible by a year-round road. The special access designation is for any reserve that has no year-round road connecting it to a service centre (Siggner, 1980).

Table 3.4 shows the distribution and proportion of Aboriginal people in each of the designated zones. While a majority of people live in urban and rural zones, considerable numbers live in remote and special access reserves. The data shows that over one-third of the Aboriginal people in Manitoba and over one-quarter in Ontario live on reserves that have no road access to a service centre. A substantial number in Quebec and British Columbia reside in special access areas. On the other hand, fewer than 20 percent of Aboriginal persons in Alberta and Saskatchewan live in either remote or special access areas. Data gathered by Indian Affairs reveals that the pattern of residence has not changed substantially over the past two decades. The changes that are discernable reveal an increasing number of urban Indians (35 to 37 percent) and those living in rural areas (40 to 44 percent). At the same time there has been a decrease in the number living in remote and special access areas (5 to 2 percent and 21 to 18 percent respectively). These 2284 separate parcels of reserve land make up a little less than 3 million hectares of land. The total area of reserve lands per capita has decreased over the past 20 years. This per capita decrease has resulted despite the total increase in Indian lands over the past five years. One way in which Indian lands have increased recently is as a result of a number of court and other legal decisions whereby land has been given back to the Crown to be held in trust for Aboriginal people. For example, in 1991 the Department of Justice forced the Minister of Indian Affairs to return nearly 300 hectares of the Riding Mountain National Park in Manitoba to the Crown to hold in trust for the Keeseekoowenin Indian Band. Many other smaller land claims have been settled, and additional lands added to the existing inventory. However, because of the high population growth, per capita allocations are less today than they were previously. In 1959, across Canada, there were 13 hectares per capita; but by 1991, there were only 11.9 hectares per capita (see also Table 3.5). The exceptions to this are in the North and in recent comprehensive treaty settlements, where Aboriginals have signed agreements with the federal government that give them control over vast areas of land.

Indian Bands

Nearly all Indians are affiliated with one of the current 614 bands. A band is a group of Aboriginal people who share a common interest in land and money and whose historical connection is defined by the federal government. However, it is important to point out that the term "band" is also a political term; it is often arbitrarily imposed on Aboriginal groups, regardless of cultural differences, for the government's administrative purposes. The Ministry of Indian Affairs can create and do away with band designations, so that the number of bands often varies from year to year.

When the federal government first divided various Indian tribes into bands, it showed very little concern for the impact of these divisions on Aboriginal culture. For example, some tribes were matrilineal, tracing descent through the mother's side, while others were patrilineal. Yet, when the band system was established, tribes were arbitrarily thrown together, and all were treated as patrilineal. This produced serious social disorganization and a wide-ranging disruption of tribal culture.

Under the 1951 *Indian Act,* Section 2(1), "band" means simply a body of Indians. At present, nearly 400 000 Aboriginal people live on reserves and belong to over 600 dif-

TABLE 3.4	On-Reserve Registered Indians by Region and DIAND Geographic Zone, 2001			
	Geographic zone			
Region	Urban & Rural %	Remote %	Special Access %	Total Number
Atlantic	100%	0.0	0.0	17 412
Quebec	71.2	17.9	10.9	44 856
Ontario	73.2	0.0	26.8	79 574
Manitoba	70.2	0.0	29.8	69 689
Saskatchewan	92.9	1.7	5.5	55 340
Alberta	93.0	0.0	7.0	58 026
B.C.	78.4	6.4	15.2	56 895
Yukon	60.4	32.5	7.0	3 908
N.W.T.	54.5	8.5	37.0	10 871
CANADA	79.4	3.7	16.9	396 571

Note: On-reserve includes Crown lands and settlements. Excludes Cree and Naskapi bands in Quebec.

Sources: In *Basic Departmental Data*-2002, pp. 40, Indian and Northern Affairs Canada.

TABLE 3.5   Registered Indian Population and Indian Lands, by Region, 2002

	Atlantic Provinces	Quebec	Ontario	Manitoba	Sask.	Alberta	B.C.	N.W.T.	Yukon	Canada
Total Indian population	28 819	65 496	159 107	112 430	111 635	89 812	114 120	15 586	7 846	704 851
% of total Indian population	4.0	10.0	22.3	14.8	15.6	12.6	17.2	2.3	1.1	100.0
% of total provincial/ territorial population	0.6	0.5	0.9	4.9	5.4	1.9	2.2	17.2	16.5	1.4
% living off-reserve	28.8	20.3	36.1	28.3	36.0	28.1	38.6	7.7	42.0	31.9
Number of Indian bands	33	39	126	62	70	44	198	16	26	614
% of Indian bands	5.2	6.6	21.3	10.1	11.5	6.9	33.1	2.4	2.9	100.0
Number of reserves and settlements	67	33	185	103	142	90	1610	29	25	2284
% of reserves and settlements	2.9	1.4	8.1	4.5	6.2	3.9	70.5	1.3	1.1	100.0
Approximate area of reserves (hectares)	31 800	85 450	736 210	235 120	645 010	725 010	372 300	–	–	2 830 900

Source: *Registered Indian Population by Sex and Residence 2002*, Ottawa, 2003 (Ct. No. R31-3/2002E.)

ferent bands; the largest is the Six Nations band, near Brantford, Ontario, with a population of 8200. Each band is administered by one of 87 agencies across Canada; the Caughnawaga agency handles only one band, and the New Westminster agency handles 32. The average size of Indian bands in Canada has increased to approximately 500 people; in 1950 the average was 200. Most Aboriginal people currently live in bands of less than 500; the modal category (the single category with the greatest frequency) containing 43 percent, is 100–499 (see Table 3.6). Another 36 percent have a population of less than 100. Only 11 bands are very large, with over 2000 members, and most of these are located in Ontario and Alberta.

Band designations are not the only means of differentiating Indian peoples. Two further criteria are language and cultural lifestyle. Indians have been divided into 10 traditional linguistic groups: Algonkian, Iroquois, Sioux, Athapaska, Kootenay, Salish, Wakash, Tsimish, Haida, and Tlingit. Six major cultural areas have also been established: Algonkian, Iroquois, Plains, Plateaus, Pacific Coast, and Mackenzie River. There is, of course, a considerable overlap between the two categories. By 2002, the nomenclature had changed and data was provided by "registry groups" that are similar but not equivalent to bands. This data showed that for the total registered Indian population, only 4 percent were in groups of fewer than 100 people; 14 percent in groups of 100–200, 20 percent in groups of 250–499; 27 percent in groups of 500–999; 20 percent in groups of 1000–2000; and 16 percent in groups of more than 2000.

Bands

The band is a basic form of local residential group in traditional simple hunting and gathering societies all around the world. Before European colonization Canada had 26 band-organized societies: these included the Inuit, several Athapascan (Dene) societies, several northern Algonquian societies, and the Beothuk. The local bands were essentially several families, usually from about 20 to 50 people, who lived and worked together in a co-operative and egalitarian way with extensive sharing of food. The size and composition of these local groups fluctuated according to such factors as availability of game and movements related to marriages. In the annual round of hunting, fishing, and plant gathering, it was common for several of these local bands to get together once or twice a year for festivals such as the pow-wow and sundance, involving several hundred people. Today the Canadian government uses the term "band" to describe the local unit of administration by Indian and Northern Affairs Canada. These units include the dozens of more complex Native societies that were traditionally organized not as bands but as tribes or chiefdoms. There are over 600 of these modern administrative bands, which function as small Native municipalities and are managed by elected band councils according to the laws of the *Indian Act* of Canada. These bands do not always coincide with the cultural and linguistic groupings of Native people.

Source: René R. Gadacz, *The Canadian Encyclopedia 2000*, World Edition. McClelland and Stewart: Toronto. Reproduced with permission.

TABLE 3.6   Numerical and Percentage Distribution of Indian Bands by Size and Geographic Location, for Regions

Region	Distribution of Bands by Population Size						Distribution of Bands by Geographic Location							
							Remote		Rural		Semi-Urban		Urban	
	100	100–499	500–999	1000–1999	2000+	Total	No.	%	No.	%	No.	%	No.	%
Atlantic	11	17	3	2	–	33	–	–	13	45	10	34	6	21
Québec	15	16	5	7	1	44	14	36	5	13	15	38	5	13
Ontario	39	54	20	5	3	121	34	30	52	45	21	18	8	7
Manitoba	11	27	12	11	1	62	25	44	26	46	5	9	1	2
Saskatchewan	7	44	16	2	1	70	10	15	43	63	13	19	2	3
Alberta	9	13	11	3	5	41	7	17	19	46	12	29	3	7
B.C.	98	85	14	2	–	199	53	27	77	40	41	21	23	12
N.W.T.	17	–	–	–	–	17	8	–	7	–	1	–	–	–
Yukon	14	–	–	–	–	14	13	–	–	–	–	–	1	–
Canada	221	256	81	32	11	601	164	29	242	42	118	21	49	9

Sources: Statistics Division, *Registered Indian Population by Sex and Residence, 1977* (Ottawa: Program Reference Centre, IIAP, 1979); Ponting and Gibbins, 1980, 35; Perreault, J., L. Paquette and M. George, *Population of Registered Indians, 1981–1986* (Ottawa: INAC, 1985).

Over time, non-Aboriginal Canada has systematically obliterated many Aboriginal cultural and linguistic distinctions. The forced migration of some groups from one area to another has caused cultural and linguistic mixing. For example, the Ojibwa were originally from Southwest Quebec and Eastern Ontario. By 1750 they had moved into the area of the Great Lakes, and by 1805 they were established in Saskatchewan. Other groups, such as the Assiniboine and Chipewyan, have been split through migration, with some group members moving north, and others, south. We now move to identifying the Aboriginal population size and growth over the past.

Table 3.7 reveals the 20 largest bands in Canada and shows that while the size of the land base is remaining stable, the population base is increasing. These figures also demonstrate that managing bands has become a major activity for First Nations as their size increases and the complexity of operating is beginning to equal small towns.

TABLE 3.7	The Twenty Largest Bands in Canada, December 31, 2002	
Band	Region	Indian Register Population
Six Nations of the Grand River (479-121)[1]	Ontario	21 618
Mohawks of Akwesasne (470-159)	Ontario	9 771
Blood (700-435)	Alberta	9 358
Kahnawake (373-070)	Québec	9 092
Saddle Lake (731-462)	Alberta	7 941
Lac La Ronge (691-353)	Saskatchewan	7 459
Peguis (501-269)	Manitoba	7 338
Mohawks of the Bay of Quinte (479-164)	ONtario	7 270
Peter Ballantyne Cree Nation (691-355)	Saskatchewan	7 270
Wikwemikong (411-175)	Ontario	6 646
Fort Alexander (501-262)	Manitoba	6 123
Cross Lake First Nation (501-276)	Manitoba	5 978
Bigstone Cree Nation (700-458)	Alberta	5 975
Samson (700-444)	Alberta	5 970
Norway House Cree Nation (501-278)	Manitoba	5 704
Siksika Nation (700-430)	Alberta	5 576
Oneida Nation of the Thames (479-169)	Ontario	4 930
Sandy Bay (501-283)	Manitoba	4 775
Nisichawayasihk Cree Nation (501-313)	Manitoba	4 756
Montagnais du Lac St-Jean (377-076)	Québec	4 662

1 Six Nations of the Grand River consists of the following 13 Registry Groups: Bay of Quinte Mohawk, Bearfoot Onondaga, Delaware, Konadaha Seneca, Lower Cayuga, Lower Mohawk, Niharondasa Seneca, Oneida, Onondaga Clear Sky, Tuscarora, Upper Cayuga, Upper Mohawk, Walker Mohawk

Source: In *Registered Indian Population by Sex and Residence, 2002*, pp. xiv, Indian and Northern Affairs Canada.

POPULATION SIZE

We begin with a profile of the Aboriginal population size. It is crucial for policy and program analysts to have information regarding the size of the population they are dealing with. They must also be clear about the growth rate. The figures in Table 3.8 show a five-fold increase in the absolute size of the registered Indian population over the past century. During the same time period, however, the Indian population has come to constitute a smaller and smaller portion of the total population, decreasing from 2.5 percent in 1881 to 1.2 percent in 1990. During the 1950s the rate of increase for registered Indians was 3 percent. While this rate increased to 3.4 percent by the late 1960s, it once again decreased to 2.8 percent in the early 1970s, where it remained until the mid-1980s (Canada, 1985b).

POPULATION GROWTH

With the introduction of *Bill C-31,* the registered Indian growth rate increased to over 7 percent and averaged well in excess of 6 percent until the 1990s, when it decreased to about 2 percent. These growth rates must be compared to the general Canadian growth rate of about 1 percent over the past decade. The overall Aboriginal population (Indian, Métis, and Inuit) is growing very fast; it is estimated that in the near future, it will be in excess of 1 million. Figure 3.1 shows the proportion of the Canadian population constituted by Aboriginals

TABLE 3.8	Population of Aboriginal People in Canada, 1881–2001
Year	Registered Indian Population
1881	108 547
1901	127 941
1929	108 012
1939	118 378
1949	136 407
1954	151 558
1961	191 709
1971	257 619
1981	323 782
1986	403 042
1991	521 461
1992	531 981
1996	573 269
2001	622 901

Sources: Information Canada, *Perspective Canada I* (Ottawa: Queen's Printer, 1974), 240; *Perspective Canada II* (Ottawa: Queen's Printer, 1977), 282; Siggner (1986), 3; *Native Agenda News,* March, 1992; T. Courchene and L. Powell, *A First Nations Province,* Queens University, Institute of Intergovernmental Relations, Kingston, Ontario, 1995, 20; Registered Indian Population by Sex and Residence, 2002, Ottawa.

for 1981 to 2001. Projections show that from 1981 to 1991 on-reserve Indians increased their population by one-third. During this same period, off-reserve Indians more than doubled. Inuit increased their population by one-third during this time also (see Figure 3.2).

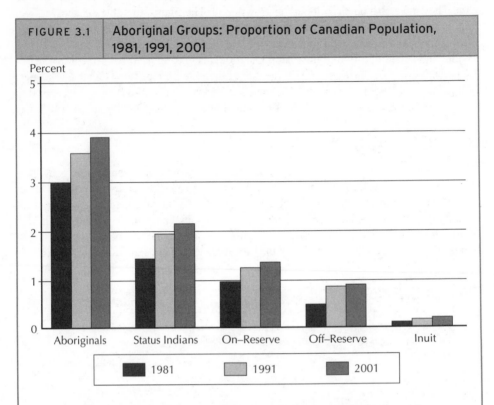

| FIGURE 3.1 | Aboriginal Groups: Proportion of Canadian Population, 1981, 1991, 2001 |

- Canada's Aboriginal populations are growing rapidly. Most Aboriginal groups will increase their proportion of the Canadian population by 2001, except non-status Indians.

- The percentage of all Aboriginal peoples in the Canadian population will have increased by one-fifth in the short term, from 3.0 percent in 1981 to 3.6 percent in 1991. The long-term increase will be more gradual, to 3.9 percent by 2001.

- The proportion of Canadians who are status Indians was 1.4 percent in 1981. This will have increased substantially by 1991. The long-term increase will be more gradual, to 3.9 percent by 2001.

- Growth in the proportion of Indians on-reserve is expect to be from 1.0 percent in 1981 to 1.2 percent in 1991 and 1.3 percent in 2001.

- The off-reserve Indian population will have doubled its share of the Canadian population by 1991, from 0.41 percent in 1981 to 0.77 percent. It will increase only marginally in the long term, to 0.81 percent by 2001.

- Population projections for the Inuit forecast that their percentage share of the Canadian population will not change substantially due to their small population size, from 0.11 percent in 1981 to 0.12 percent in 1991 and 0.14 percent in 2001.

Source: *Highlights of Aboriginal Conditions, 1981-2001, Part I, Demographic Trends*, p. 5, Indian and Northern Affairs Canada.

In summary, demographers predict that status Indians and Inuit will continue to have higher growth rates than the Canadian population for several decades. Table 3.9 identifies the registered Indian population and average annual growth rates for both on- and off-reserve.

Other data show that the growth rates are extremely high, as the population more than doubled in size since 1966. The estimated Indian population as we entered the 21st century

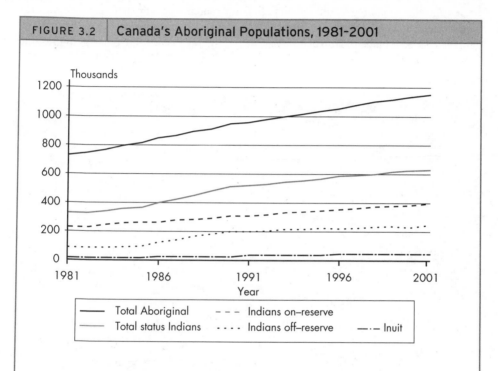

| FIGURE 3.2 | Canada's Aboriginal Populations, 1981–2001 |

- By 1991, the estimated population of Canadians with Aboriginal origins will increase nearly one-third, from 735 500 in 1981 to 958 500. In the long term, a further one-fifth increase to 1 145 100 is projected by 2001.

- The total status Indian population will have grown by one-half by 1991 to 521 500, up from 336 900 in 1981. By 2001, the number of status Indians will increase another one-fifth to 622 900, almost double the 1981 figure.

- By 1991, the number of Indians on-reserve will have increased one-third to 316 300, up from 237 600 in 1981. In the long term, the projections estimate a population of another one-fifth, to 385 500 in 2001.

- The number of Indians off-reserve will have more than doubled by 1991, from 99 300 in 1981 to 205 200. There will be little population growth between 1991 and 2001, when the off-reserve population is projected to be 237 400.

- The Inuit population has a projected growth to 1991 of nearly one-third, from 25 900 in 1981 to 33 400. By 2001 another one-fifth increase is projected to 40 900, over one and a half times the 1981 figure.

Source: *Highlights of Aboriginal Conditions, 1981–2001, Part I, Demographic Trends*, p. 4, Indian and Northern Affairs Canada.

was nearly 700 000. These data also show that in 1966, 80 percent of the Indians lived on a reserve; by 1990, this had decreased to 60 percent (Piche and George, 1973).

In June 1985 amendments were made to the *Indian Act* (*Bill C-31*) that restored Indian status and membership rights to individuals and their children who lost them because of discriminatory clauses—e.g., 12(1)(b)—in the previous *Indian Act*. Table 3.10 reveals the Indian population changes with and without *Bill C-31* additions. At the outset fewer than 2000 people were reinstated. However, by 1989 these new registrants represented nearly 15 percent of the total registered Indian population, and it was estimated that by 2001 they would make up nearly one-fifth. The data show that the annual growth rate has consistently exceeded 2 percent. However, when *Bill C-31* Indians are added to the figures, the growth rate increases to an astounding 6 percent (Paquette and Perreault, 1984).

TABLE 3.9	Population Growth of Status Indians: Total, On and Off Reserve, 1981–2001						
	Total Status Indians, Both sexes		On-Reserve Indians, Both Sexes		Off-Reserve Indians, Both Sexes		
Year	Total Population	Growth Rate	Total Population	Growth Rate	Total Population	Growth Rate	
1981	336 900	–	237 600	–	99 300	–	
1982	345 400	2.52	245 900	3.49	99 500	0.20	
1983	354 400	2.61	253 300	3.01	101 100	1.61	
1984	364 700	2.91	261 000	3.04	103 700	2.57	
1985	376 400	3.21	268 000	2.68	108 400	4.53	
1986	403 042	7.08	275 891	2.94	127 151	17.30	
1987	431 439	7.05	282 671	2.46	148 768	17.00	
1988	458 807	6.34	291 485	3.12	167 322	12.47	
1989	485 186	5.75	299 869	2.88	185 317	10.75	
1990	510 905	5.30	308 727	2.95	202 178	9.10	
1991	521 461	2.07	316 273	2.44	205 188	1.49	
1992	531 981	2.02	323 855	2.40	208 126	1.43	
1993	542 426	1.96	331 457	2.35	210 970	1.37	
1994	552 799	1.91	339 070	2.30	213 729	1.31	
1995	563 082	1.86	346 711	2.25	216 371	1.24	
1996	573 269	1.81	354 379	2.21	218 890	1.16	
1997	583 356	1.76	360 599	1.76	222 757	1.77	
1998	593 346	1.71	366 808	1.72	226 538	1.70	
1999	603 271	1.67	373 027	1.70	230 245	1.64	
2000	613 117	1.63	379 258	1.67	233 860	1.57	
2001	622 901	1.60	385 514	1.65	237 387	1.51	

Source: Adapted from the Statistics Canada "Aboriginal Peoples Survey," 2001.

Three factors affect the overall growth rate of the Aboriginal population: the birth rate, the death rate, and the rate at which people lose or gain Indian status. It is important that decision-makers have a clear picture of the impacts of each of these factors with a view to predicting long-term changes (Robitaille and Coiniere, 1984).

The natural increase (births minus deaths) for the Aboriginal population has been declining over the past 30 years because of a rapidly declining birth rate. For example, in 1921 the crude birth rate for Aboriginal people was over 50 per 1000 population. By the 1970s this rate had decreased to 28.5, and by 1991 was reduced further to 22.2, but was still nearly double the national average. Romaniuk (1984) has noted that the decline in the birth rate can be deduced from looking at the child:population ratio. The ratio of children under five years of age to the total Indian population fell from 19 percent in 1961 to 13 percent in 1991. Further evidence of fertility decline can be inferred from the average number of children born to never-married women 20–24 years of age. This was 2.3 in 1961 but fell to less than 1.5 in 1991. At the same time, the number of childless never-

TABLE 3.10	Registered Indians and Indians Registered Under *Bill C-31*: Average Annual Growth Rates, Canada, 1981–2001				
	Registered Indians			Average Annual Growth (%)	
Year	Excluding *Bill C-31*	*Bill C-31* Population	Total	Excluding *Bill C-31*	Including *Bill C-31*
1981	323 782[c]	0	323 782[c]	2.59	0.00
1982	332 178	0	332 178	2.95	0.00
1983	341 968	0	341 968	2.00	0.00
1984	348 809	0	348 809	2.82	3.28
1985[a]	358 636	1 605	360 241	3.16	7.66
1986	369 972	17 857	387 829	2.40	7.24
1987	378 842	37 056	415 898	2.71	6.73
1988	389 110	54 774	443 884	2.65	5.06
1989[b]	399 433	66 904	466 337	3.66[r]	5.75[r]
1991	429 178	92 282	521 461	1.99	1.91
1996	506 005[d]	104 869	610 874	2.83	3.01
2001	517 226	105 675	622 901		

a. In 1985 the *Indian Act* was amended through *Bill C-31* to allow the restoration of Indian status to those who had lost it due to discriminatory clauses in the *Indian Act*. The reinstatement process was expected to be largely completed in 1990/91.
b. The high annual growth rate between 1989 and 1991 is due in part to the upward adjustments of the Indian Register for the purposes of the projections and to the Department's estimate of 86 000 *Bill C-31* registrations in 1990/91 plus the growth due to natural increase.
c. Totals may not add up due to rounding.
d. Data taken from *Basic Departmental Data*, 1997, QS-3575-000-BB-A1, pg. 7. Growth rate of 96 over 1995.
r. Datum revised.

Sources: In *Basic Departmental Data-1990*, pp. 7, Indian and Northern Affairs Canada.

married women in the age category 20–24 went up from 11 percent in 1961 to 28 percent in 1991. When we compare fertility rates for on-reserve Indians and the general Canadian population for women aged 15–49, we find substantial differences. In 1986, on-reserve women had 3.2 children, while in the general Canadian population the number was 1.67. By 1993 Aboriginal women had decreased to 2.7 children while the overall Canadian number remained the same.

The birth rate is significantly influenced by the average age of marriage. Although, overall, the proportion of married Indians is lower than the national average, the proportion of married Indians in the highest-fertility age group of 20 to 24 exceeds that of non-Indians. Moreover, the fertility of Indians between 20 and 24 appears to be twice the Canadian average.

The average number of children by age group also reflects changes that have taken place in Aboriginal communities. In 1991 Aboriginal women had an average of 3.7 children, compared to 2.1 for non-Aboriginal women. When controlling for age, we find that the older Aboriginal women (65 and over) had 6.2 children during their child-bearing years (3.0 for non-Aboriginal women), with 6.0 children for Aboriginal women 45–64 (3.2 for non-Aboriginal women of this age). There are, however, considerable regional variations in Aboriginal birth rates. Aboriginal women living in Eastern Canada have similar fertility rates to those of non-Aboriginal women, while Aboriginal women in the Prairies have much higher rates.

The second factor in determining the growth rate of a population is the mortality rate. Traditionally, the mortality rates for Aboriginal people have been very high, with life expectancy less than half that for a non-Aboriginal person. By 1960, an Aboriginal's expected life span had increased to 60 years (while for a non-Aboriginal it was 69) and it remained there until the 1980s.

Figure 3.3 shows the life expectancies at birth for Indians and all Canadians by gender. It shows that the general trend of increasing life expectancy continues. It is estimated that, by the turn of the century, Indians had increased their life expectancy by eight years. Nevertheless, the data show that non-Indians still live longer than Indians. While the gap remains, it is narrowing; and the data show that by the 21st century the life expectancy for Indians was 70 versus 76 for non-Aboriginal men and, for women, 77 versus 83.

The average age at death is markedly lower for Aboriginal persons than the national average. As Table 3.11 shows, for Aboriginal persons the average age at death is 54 and for non-Aboriginal persons, 72. Recent data show that while Aboriginal life expectancy has increased to 69 for males and 76 for females, it still remains over six years less than that for the average Canadian (see Figure 3.4). Overall standardized death rates in 1981 show that for Indians it was 9.2 per 1000 compared to just 6 among the total Canadian population. Overall, Aboriginal people have mortality rates that were up to almost 1.5 times higher than the 1996 national rates. Infant mortality (deaths of babies before the age of one) is perhaps an even more important factor in determining the growth rate of the population. The number of Indian deaths per 1000 live births was nearly 80 in 1960. However, this decreased to 12.2 in 1993, while the Canadian rate was 6.8 (Latulippe-Skamoto, 1971). In 1999, Indian Affairs showed that the potential years of life lost by cause of death for First Nations and Canadians differed significantly. For example, it showed that in almost all causes of death, the rates for Aboriginals were much higher— e.g., mental disorders, injury and poisoning, congenital anomalies, musculoskeletal disorders. However there are some causes of death for which Canadians have higher rates than Aboriginals do—e.g., cancer, blood diseases, nervous system and sense organs, and circulatory system illnesses.

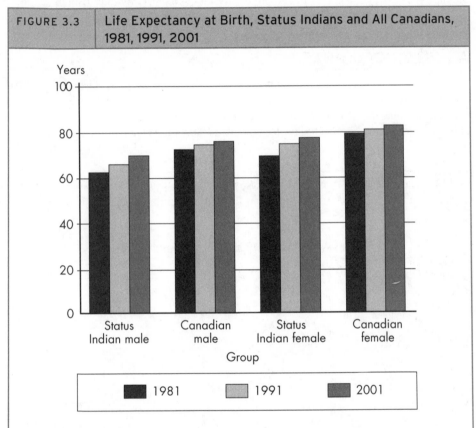

| FIGURE 3.3 | **Life Expectancy at Birth, Status Indians and All Canadians, 1981, 1991, 2001** |

- Life expectancy at birth for status Indians is increasing and will continue to increase. Between 1981 and 2001, the life expectancy at birth for status Indians is expected to have increased by 8 years for both sexes.

- Nonetheless, non-Indians live longer than status Indians. In 1981, the life expectancy at birth for status Indians was approximately 10 years less than that of the national population, the same as it had been 20 years earlier.

- While the life expectancy at birth will continue to increase for both status Indians and Canadians, there will still be a gap. The gap is narrowing, however. It is projected that by 2001 the life expectancy for status Indians will be 6 years less than that for Canadians, 70 versus 76 for men and 77 versus 83 for women.

- Nonetheless, the projected life expectancy for status Indians in 2001 will still be less than the 1981 Canadian figures for both sexes.

Sources: *Highlights of Aboriginal Conditions, 1981-2001, Part II, Social Conditions*, p. 5, Indian and Northern Affairs Canada.

The above discussion shows that Aboriginal people, since the turn of the century, have gone through three stages of birth–death trends. During the first half of the century the Aboriginal population was characterized by extremely high birth and death rates. Then, after World War II, the death rate decreased substantially (because of medical advances and increased sanitation and housing), although the birth rate remained high. Today we see the third phase, which is a decline in both the fertility and mortality rates (Siggner, 1986).

ENFRANCHISEMENT AND *BILL C-31:* A HISTORICAL NOTE

The number of Indians, as demonstrated earlier, is affected by external legislation that goes well beyond biology and health. As noted earlier, people have been removed from and placed on the Indian roll over the past century. Between 1955 and 1982 (when the general policy of enfranchisement was phased out), 13 502 adults and children (as well as all

TABLE 3.11	Specific Measures of Mortality Among Registered Canadian Indians and Among Canadians as Whole				
	A Crude Death Rate	B Infant Mortality Rate	C Average Age at Death	D Male Life Expectancy	E Female Life Expectancy
1960 Indians	10.9	79.0	–	59.7	63.5
All Canadians	8.0	27.3		68.5	74.3
1965 Indians	8.7	52.6	36.0	60.5	65.6
All Canadians	7.5	23.6	64.0	68.8	75.2
1970 Indians	7.5	43.2*	42.0	60.2	66.2
All Canadians	7.5	18.8	66.0	69.3	76.4
1976 Indians	7.5	32.1	43.0	–	–
All Canadians	7.4	16.0	67.0		
1981 Indians	9.5	22.0	45.2	62.0	69.0
All Canadians	6.1	10.0	69.0	72.0	78.0
1991 Indians	9.2	13.0	54.0	68.0	73.1
All Canadians	6.0	8.0	72.1	74.0	80.0
2001 Indians	8.0	–	70.4	75.5	–
All Canadians	5.3	6.5	82.1	–	–

Note: Due to the difficulty of obtaining data, the data in any given cell may be for a different year than for that shown. The difference is never more than two years and usually only one, and in any such cases of discrepancy the data are more recent than the date shown.
* This figure is an average of the rates for 1969 and 1971, since the 1970 data are unreliable due to incomplete reporting that year.
A Death per 1000 population.
B Deaths of children in first year of life per 1000 live births.
C Sum of the age at death of all persons dying in a given year divided by the number of people dying that year.
D & E Age to which a person can be expected to live, calculated at time of birth.
These figures are standardized death rates.

Sources: Medical Services Branch, *Health Data Book* (Ottawa: Department of National Health and Mortality Projections of Registered Indians, 1987 to 1996, INAC 1985); *Indian and Canadian Mortality Trends*, 1991, Ottawa, Health and Welfare Canada, Basic Departmental Data, 2002, pp.23, 26.

their descendants) were enfranchised (removed from the Indian roll and no longer defined as Indians under the *Indian Act*). Most of the enfranchisements were Indian women who married non-Indian men. Under the more recent *Bill C-31,* some of these people and their descendants have recovered their Indian status (IRIW, n.d.).

Both the enfranchisement rules and the "double mother" rule in the *Indian Act* have now been changed. As early as 1980, DIAND allowed bands that wanted to opt out of the conditions of 12(1)(b) and 12(1)(a)(iv) to do so. By 1984, 103 bands had opted out of the former section, while 309 acted on the latter. When *Bill C-31* was passed in 1985, new rules prevailed. This Bill was introduced in order to comply with Section 15(1) of the *Canadian Charter of Rights and Freedoms.* In short, any individual who was registered as an Indian and subsequently lost status due to discriminatory sections of the *Indian Act* could be reinstated. This included women who were deleted from the register upon marriage to a non-Indian (Sections 12(1)(b) and 14); individuals deleted at the age of majority because their mothers and paternal grandmothers were not Canadian Indian by birth (Sections 12(i)(a)(iv)); individuals deleted due to husbands'/fathers' enfranchisement (Sections 10 and 109); and any illegitimate children of Indian women who were deleted from the register upon proof of non-Indian paternity (Subsection 12(2)) (*Le Devoir,* 1985).

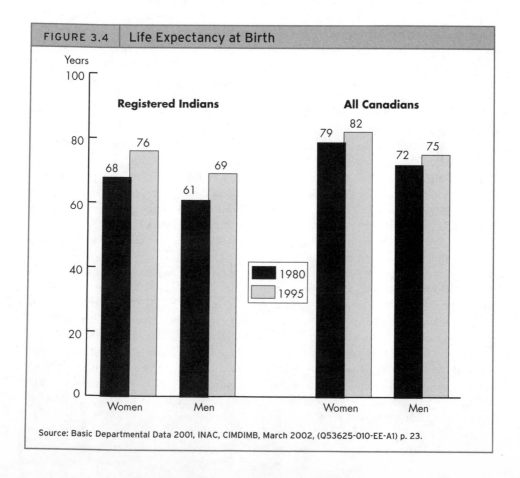

FIGURE 3.4 | Life Expectancy at Birth

Source: Basic Departmental Data 2001, INAC, CIMDIMB, March 2002, (Q53625-010-EE-A1) p. 23.

However, under this new change, only the first generation of those listed above are eligible for registration. Applications were to be accepted (one must apply) until the year 2003. This means that minors could achieve the age of majority and then apply. However, first-time registration is limited to first-generation children of a reinstated individual. If these children are themselves parents at the time of registration, their children cannot be registered. Once registered, however, these children have the capacity to transmit status to any children they have thereafter. In summary, projections for the Aboriginal population suggest that the overall registered Indian population will increase until 2041, at which time it will level off at around 1 million. After that time, it is expected to decrease, and the number of Indians will once again change because of a new definition that was established nearly 50 years earlier.

HEALTH

The size and growth of any modern population is due to health and health-related factors. While genocide was an important force during the 17th, 18th, and early 19th centuries, it has not played an important role in the 20th century population dynamics of Canadian Indians. However, health has been an important factor this past century. Nevertheless, the federal government believes that, with certain exceptions, it does not have any legal or fiduciary obligations with regard to health care for Aboriginal people. Aboriginals disagree and claim the right to special treatment. Disputes between the First Nations and the federal government revolve around three issues. First is the conflict in definitions of health. Second is how health policy is implemented for Aboriginal people. Third is the funding of First Nations health services, including the statutory, constitutional, or fiduciary obligations of the federal government regarding the provision of health services to Aboriginal people (Speck, 1989). Nevertheless, the federal government has accepted some responsibility for Aboriginal health. Under Health and Welfare Canada, approximately $600 million is spent on six major health programs: Community Health Services, Environmental Health and Surveillance, Non-Insured Health Benefits, National Native Alcohol and Drug Abuse Program, Hospital Services, and Capital Construction. While there is no direct federal government legislation for the provision of these services, custom and historical commitment provide the basis and rationale for covering the cost of these programs. There are some exceptions, such as the references to the provision of a "Medicine Chest" in Treaty No. 6.

Until 1945, the Department of Indian Affairs was the sole provider of health care services to Indians on the reserve. However, in that year these services were transferred to the Department of Health and Welfare, and they have remained there since that time. In 1962, Indian Health Services (a division in Health and Welfare) was merged with six other federal health programs to form a specific branch: Medical Services. In 1964, Treaty Indians were defined as insured persons under provincial medicare. By 1970, the present structure of Indian Health Services was in place, although the 1974 *Lalonde Report* for the federal government first set the stage for the transfer of health care away from the federal government. This policy document reiterated that no statutory or treaty obligations exist to provide health services to Indians. In 1979, a new Indian Health Policy was enacted and the Medical Services Branch started to work toward transferring control of health services to First Nations.

By 1981, a proposal to transfer responsibility for health care services to Indian communities was approved. In 1982, Indian Health Services standards were developed and introduced as a way of measuring the extent to which Aboriginal health needs were being met. The *Nielsen Report* was leaked in 1985 and focused on duplication of services as well as on determining the legal basis of federal government involvement with Aboriginal people (Legare, 1981).

In 1986 Health and Welfare (Medical Services Branch) announced a new policy initiative: The Indian Health Transfer Policy. This new policy, which was centred on the concept of self-determination, was to facilitate a developmental approach to transferring health care and services to Aboriginal communities. It was hoped that it would lead to First Nations autonomy and to community control of health care services (Speck, 1989). The Transfer Policy in health care is a continuation of the "devolution policy" developed by Indian and Northern Affairs Canada a decade earlier, in that it proposes that a larger share of the responsibility now allocated to the federal government be taken on by First Nations. In 2000, the Medical Services Branch was renamed the First Nations and Inuit Health Branch. Its mandate is to ensure the availability of and access to health services for First Aboriginal people. They also have agreed to help First Nations address local health issues and to build strong relationships between Health Canada and the First Nations' communities. There is considerable conflict between the two parties with regard to how and under what conditions the transfer of management will take place and what the nature of the relationship will be.

Speck (1989) points out that First Nations are denied self-determination, which in turn denies them the opportunity to create conditions whereby Aboriginal health could be improved. For example, she notes that the federal government continues to administer health services as an isolated service that is separate from the political, social, and economic dimensions of life—a fact that Aboriginal and other people have consistently identified as one of the major problems in health care for Aboriginal people.

Today, in all but three of the provinces, insurance premiums are paid for everyone by provincial governments, which take payments from tax revenue. A variety of arrangements exists in these provinces for payment of premiums by registered Indians, ranging from bulk payments to general means tests. As Speck (1989) points out, the specific features that differentiate Aboriginal from non-Aboriginal health services are the payment of medical and hospital insurance premiums by the federal government for three provinces, the provision of public health services by the federal government rather than the provincial, and the federal funding of additional non-insured services for Indians (p. 193). Regardless of the source of funding, a full range of medical services is provided to Indians, although these vary from one province to another depending upon the standards set by each province.

Medical Services Delivery

While the *Indian Act* itself says little about the specifics (see Section 73(1)) and its main focus is on the prevention of the spread of infectious diseases, there remains a strong financial commitment to Aboriginal health care through a variety of programs (Woodward, 1989). Health and Welfare Canada operates a number of programs that also provide health care to Aboriginal people throughout Canada. The first major program is Community Health Services, which focuses on communicable disease control, health education, mental health, nursing, and the provision of medical advice and assistance. The second is the non-insured health benefits program. Through this program, Aboriginal people are provided general health care through access to the provincial medicare systems and supplemental programs. In addition, the program includes the transportation of patients, dental services, and other medical appliances and services. The third major program is one in which funding is provided to train and employ local health care workers under the aegis of the Community Health Services.

In 1983 the National Native Alcohol and Drug Abuse Program was put in place. This experimental program still exists and has expanded its role as it deals with treatment, rehabilitation, and education (Canada, 1979a). Health Canada's National Native Alcohol and Drug Abuse Program encompasses 53 treatment centres and 7 solvent centres located in First Nations and Inuit communities across Canada. In-patient admissions have fluctuated between 4500 and 5000 patients a year. In 2000, the number of new admissions began to drop, although it is not clear if this is a trend. Over the past decade, the number of alcohol abuse admissions has decreased while, at the same time, the number of people being admitted for hallucinogens and other non-narcotic drugs has been on a upward trend. Research for the past quarter-century has noted that abuse of alcohol and other substances is a major problem in First Nations communities. In the recent Aboriginal Peoples Survey, nearly three-quarters of the respondents said that alcohol and drug abuse was a problem in their community. In this same survey, one in five Aboriginal youth reported having used solvents—and one in three solvent users is under the age of 15.

The provision of services for Aboriginal people is carried out through all three levels of government. Those services provided by provincial and municipal agencies are generally fully reimbursed by the federal government. At the federal level, the First Nations and Inuit Health Branch has over 200 doctors (less than 1 percent are Aboriginal) and over 1000 nurses (about 10 percent are Aboriginal). Over 500 community health workers are also contracted by Medical Services to provide health care for Aboriginal people. At the turn of the 21st century, there were almost 2000 Aboriginal health workers. Approximately 800 were Aboriginal nurses and 67 were Aboriginal physicians (with an additional 33 currently in medical school). Nearly all of the community health workers are Aboriginal. On a per capita basis, the First Nations and Inuit Health Branch spends about $600 per year per Aboriginal person, approximately the same spent on non-Aboriginal people. Overall, Health Canada spent about $1.7 billion on health services to First Nations in 2001, compared to just over $1 billion in 1995. Just under half of these funds were allocated to non-insured health benefits. The remainder was spent on transfer agreements, management and support, and community health programs and community-based health services.

Health services are also provided through contributions and contract arrangements with Aboriginal organizations, bands, and post-secondary educational institutions (Grescoe, 1981). Community Health Services carry out this program through four main activities: health care and treatment services, public health services, involvement of Indians in the health care system, and the provision of physical facilities (DIAND, 1984).

The overall structure for providing medical and health services to Aboriginal people is complex. At the national level, several government agencies interact to set policies, determine programs, and establish funding levels, e.g., Deputy Minister of Health and Welfare; Director General: Policy and Evaluation, Treasury Board; and the directors of Indian/Inuit Policy, Planning and Evaluation. At the provincial level, the regional director oversees implementation of the programs for each health zone, which involves doctors, nurses, and environmental health officers. At the local level, for those bands involved in health care delivery, band councils make decisions regarding training programs and who will be admitted to various health programs (Fernandez, 1983).

Aboriginal Health

Many of the statistics about disease and illness among Aboriginal people have been published and are well known. Illnesses resulting from poverty, overcrowding, and poor housing have led to chronic and acute respiratory diseases, which take a heavy toll among Aboriginal people (see Table 3.12). Overall, the crude mortality rate for First Nations is 354.2 deaths per 100 000. However, while the standardized death rate for the Aboriginal population was more than double that of the general Canadian population—15.9 versus 6.6 deaths per 1000 population (Nuttall, 1982; INAC, 1988), it is now similar to the general Canadian population (see Figure 3.5). The data reveal that the overall death rate among Aboriginal people has decreased by nearly one-half since 1978.

The data show that the First Nations' rate was similar to the national rate (662 versus 661 per 100 000 population). However, there is a gap between Aboriginals and the general Canadian population, particularly for ages 15 to 44; Aboriginals in this age group are more than two times likelier to die than the average Canadian. Moreover, the cause of death by age group varies. Figure 3.6 reveals the leading causes of death in First Nations by age group.

Infant mortality has a tremendous impact upon the population of all societies, since infants will (if they live) contribute to the growth of the population when they reach childbearing age. Over the years, there has been a substantial decrease in infant mortality rates (see Figure 3.7). The data show that the infant mortality rate among Indian people is now less than one-sixth of what it was in 1960. However, it should be noted that it is double that of the general Canadian population: the Canadian infant mortality rate is 7.9 per 1000 while the Aboriginal rate is 17.5 per 1000. Since 1988 a disturbing trend seems to have emerged. The data show that while the infant mortality rate for all Canadians continues to decrease, it is increasing for registered Indians. A closer look at the infant mortality rate shows that Aboriginal rates of perinatal deaths (stillbirths and under one week of age) are twice as high

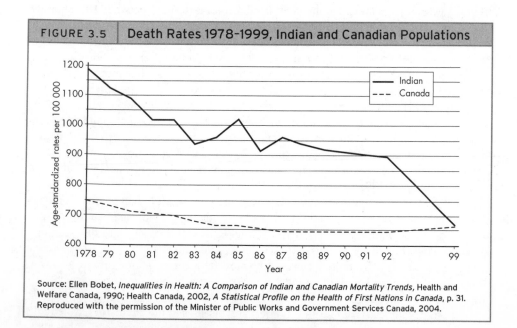

FIGURE 3.5 | **Death Rates 1978–1999, Indian and Canadian Populations**

Source: Ellen Bobet, *Inequalities in Health: A Comparison of Indian and Canadian Mortality Trends*, Health and Welfare Canada, 1990; Health Canada, 2002, *A Statistical Profile on the Health of First Nations in Canada*, p. 31. Reproduced with the permission of the Minister of Public Works and Government Services Canada, 2004.

TABLE 3.12	National Age-Standardized Rate of Tuberculosis in the First Nations. On-Reserve* and Overall Canadian Populations, and Standardized Morbidity Rations (SMR) (1990-2000)		
Year	First Nations	Canada	SMR (%)+
1990	69.4	7.2	960
1991	59.5	7.2	830
1992	74.8	7.4	1010
1993	54.3	7.0	780
1994	56.3	7.1	790
1995	53.4	6.5	820
1996	49.0	6.3	780
1997	53.3	6.6	810
1998	41.6	5.9	710
1999	61.5	5.9	1040
2000	34.0	n/a	n/a

* data includes reported TB cases in the First Nations, on-reserve populations of B.C., Alberta, Saskatchewan, Manitoba, Ontario, New Brunswick, and Nova Scotia
+ this figure represents the First Nations rate divided by the overall Canada rate, expressed as a percentage

Source: Tuberculosis in First Nations communities 2002, Health Canada, www.hc-sc.gc.ca/fnihb/phcph/ tuberculosis/tb_fni_communities.htm. Reproduced with the permission of the Minister of Public Works and Government Services Canada, 2004

as in the general population. On the other hand, neonatal (birth to one month) death rates for the two groups are very similar. Post-neonatal (one month to one year) death rates are more than three times higher for Indians. These rates reflect the poor housing and other environmental conditions that Aboriginal children are born into (Canada, 1980).

The effectiveness of the Native Health Care system is related as much to the environmental conditions in which Aboriginal Canadians live as to the treatment and facilities provided. Health care provided is sometimes countered by social and economic problems such as overcrowding, poor nutrition, chronic unemployment, and community and family violence. Thus, an Aboriginal person, after receiving effective medical treatment, finds himself or herself returning to the social conditions that created the problem in the first place. In short, the causes of poor mental and physical health are not dealt with (Canada, 1991).

What are the specific causes of death? Over one-third of all Indian deaths (compared to 8 percent in the general population) are due to accidents and violence. Aboriginal people are up to 6.5 times more likely than the total Canadian population to die of injuries and poisonings. For all age groups up to 63, Aboriginal people are four times as likely as other Canadians to die from these causes. The most frequent are motor vehicle accidents, drowning, and fire. Although these rates are extremely high, they have been reduced by over 40 percent since 1980.

The other major causes of death (in order) are: diseases of the circulatory system; diseases of the respiratory system; cancer; suicide; and chronic conditions, e.g., tuberculosis

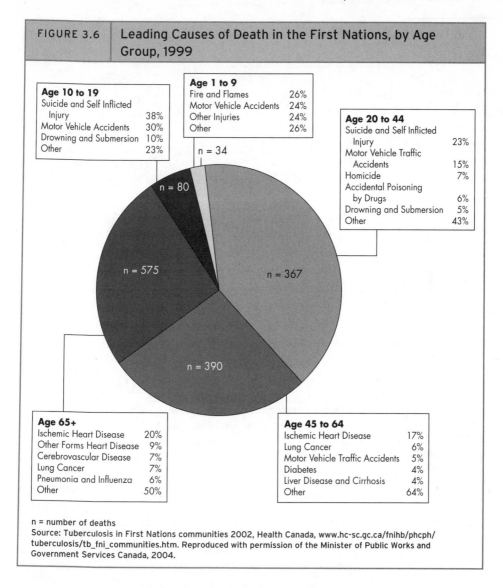

FIGURE 3.6 | Leading Causes of Death in the First Nations, by Age Group, 1999

Age 10 to 19
Suicide and Self Inflicted Injury	38%
Motor Vehicle Accidents	30%
Drowning and Submersion	10%
Other	23%

Age 1 to 9
Fire and Flames	26%
Motor Vehicle Accidents	24%
Other Injuries	24%
Other	26%

Age 20 to 44
Suicide and Self Inflicted Injury	23%
Motor Vehicle Traffic Accidents	15%
Homicide	7%
Accidental Poisoning by Drugs	6%
Drowning and Submersion	5%
Other	43%

n = 34
n = 80
n = 575
n = 367
n = 390

Age 65+
Ischemic Heart Disease	20%
Other Forms Heart Disease	9%
Cerebrovascular Disease	7%
Lung Cancer	7%
Pneumonia and Influenza	6%
Other	50%

Age 45 to 64
Ischemic Heart Disease	17%
Lung Cancer	6%
Motor Vehicle Traffic Accidents	5%
Diabetes	4%
Liver Disease and Cirrhosis	4%
Other	64%

n = number of deaths
Source: Tuberculosis in First Nations communities 2002, Health Canada, www.hc-sc.gc.ca/fnihb/phcph/ tuberculosis/tb_fni_communities.htm. Reproduced with permission of the Minister of Public Works and Government Services Canada, 2004.

and diabetes. Data in Table 3.13 reveal the major chronic diseases in Aboriginal people and the general Canadian population. Heart diseases and hypertension and AIDS are "new" diseases for Aboriginal people, although for each of the diseases listed, the incidence is much greater for Aboriginal people than for the general Canadian population. For example, the proportion of AIDS cases among Aboriginal persons climbed from 1 percent of all cases in Canada before 1990 to over 7 percent in 2001. From 1998 to 2001, over one-fourth of all reports of HIV positive tests were from Aboriginal people.

Case Studies in New Diseases

Tuberculosis   Tuberculosis (TB) began to return to First Nations communities in the mid-1980s, achieving near epidemic proportions. However, after a major tuberculosis

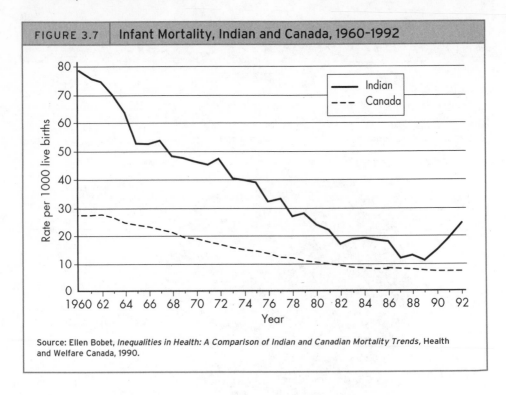

FIGURE 3.7 | Infant Mortality, Indian and Canada, 1960-1992

Source: Ellen Bobet, *Inequalities in Health: A Comparison of Indian and Canadian Mortality Trends*, Health and Welfare Canada, 1990.

elimination program that was implemented in 1992, the number of new and relapsed cases decreased until 1999, when they once again began to increase to 1990 levels. In 1992, the incidence per 100 000 people was 67.8, decreasing to 54.6 throughout much of the 1990s until 1999, when the rate went back up to nearly 64. As one can see in Table 3.12, these figures reveal a TB rate that was eight times that of the entire Canadian population. It is important to realize that TB is not uniformly distributed across Canada. Saskatchewan has the highest incidence (ranging from 155.7–104.3 per 100 000 over the past decade) over the past decade, but note that Alberta and Manitoba tend to experience higher rates than the national average. Mortality from TB is low due to aggressive case findings and effective treatment of the disease. In 1999 fewer than 50 individuals died from TB. However, what has emerged recently is the dramatic increase of HIV in First Nations communities and its primary and secondary (related to TB) contributions to death.

Diabetes Diabetes was virtually non-existent in the Aboriginal population before the 1940s. Today its incidence among Aboriginal people is estimated to be two to five times higher than in the non-Aboriginal population, and to be increasing rapidly (Wells, 1995). Its importance is heightened by the fact that it is increasingly showing early onset, greater severity at diagnosis, high rates of complications, lack of accessible services, increasing trends, and increasing prevalence of risk factors for a population already at risk (Young et al. 1998). Health care officials in British Columbia report increases of 22 to 190 percent between 1987 and 1992. A comparison of life tables (length of life) between the Aboriginal and non-Aboriginal populations over the past 20 years shows that there has

TABLE 3.13	Chronic Diseases			
		Age Adjusted Prevalence (%)		
Chronic Condition	Gender	First Nations and Labrador Inuit (FN&I)	General Canadian Population	FN&I/ Canadian Ratio
Heart Problems	Male	13	4	3.3
	Female	10	4	2.5
Hypertension	Male	22	8	2.8
	Female	25	10	2.5
Diabetes	Male	11	3	3.7
	Female	16	3	5.3
Arthritis/Rheumatism	Male	18	10	1.8
	Female	27	18	1.5

Sources: *A Second Diagnostic on the Health of First Nations and Inuit People in Canada*, 1999, p. 7, Health Canada, Ottawa.

been little improvement for Aboriginal people and even a deterioration in the past decade (Nuttall, 1982; Young, 1984; Bobet 1997).

Based upon Statistics Canada data collected in 1990, it is estimated that between 80 000 and 120 000 Aboriginal people 15 years of age and over have diabetes (generally type 2). A recent First Nations and Inuit regional Health Survey conducted by the National Steering Committee (1999) estimates that the above figures are underestimates by 20 percent. Recent figures show that among all First Nations people, the incidence of diabetes is 6.4 percent. For those living on reserves, the rate is 8.5 percent. Métis have reported a prevalence of 5.5 percent while Inuit report a 1.9 percent incidence. Age-standardized prevalence of diabetes for First Nations people is three to five times that of the general population, and this is true for all age categories. According to a regional health survey, 53 percent of the First Nations people with diabetes are 40 years old or younger and 65 percent are less than 45 years old. Bobet (1997) found that approximately two-thirds of the First Nations people diagnosed with diabetes are women—a pattern that is not reflected in the general Canadian population. Aboriginal women have over five times the rate of diabetes compared to women in the general population, and Aboriginal men have over three times the corresponding rate for men in the general population. Data from local research shows that there are wide differences among communities. For example, in Haida Gwaii, B.C., 17 percent of adults over the age of 35 had type 2 diabetes. In Sandy Lake, Ontario, one-quarter of the town's population over 10 years old has diabetes. And finally, in two Algonquin communities in Quebec, between 22 percent and 48 percent of women age 35 and older had the disease (Delisle and Ekoe, 1993; Grams et al, 1996; Harris et al, 1997). With the high rates of diabetes for Aboriginal people, it should not be surprising that health complications emerge. Secondary illnesses such as strokes, macro vascular disease, heart attacks, lower limb amputations, and high blood pressure are just some of the related health care issues for those who have diabetes. While national projections are not available, in Manitoba is has been estimated that the number of First Nations diabetes cases will increase three times over the next 20 years (Green et al, 1997). The impact of diabetes over the next decade is significant, and all kinds of resources will assume a high cost if this problem is not addressed today.

One of the changes that has been implemented is the limitation of non-insured health benefits. All registered Indians were previously eligible to receive prescription medication, medical supplies, dental services, medical transportation, optometry services, and mental health services. This program now exceeds $550 million per year and has become the target for fiscal restraint. Specifically, off-reserve Indians have been cut off from such benefits (Wells, 1995).

In summary, statistics show that the quality of life experienced by Aboriginal people is far inferior to that of non-Aboriginal people. How have they found themselves in this position? These conditions have come about as a result of the cultural imperialism of the Canadian government and the racist philosophy that promoted the dominant society's insistence on the inferiority of Aboriginal people (Cumming, 1967).

The pattern of unintentional injuries among Aboriginal people is similar to the general Canadian population, with the exception that the rates are much higher for Aboriginals. The most common death resulting from injury was related to motor vehicle accidents, with a rate of 40 per 100 000 population, which is four times the national rate. Accidental poisoning is the second highest cause of accidental death (17 per 100 000), followed by drowning (9 per 100 000), both of which are four times the national rate. Accidental falls and death by fire/flames were the least common types of death for Aboriginals, but comparable data for the general population show that the Aboriginal rates are nonetheless three times higher.

When we look at intentional injuries leading to death, a similar picture emerges. Suicide accounts for up to one-quarter of all injury deaths in First Nations people. A majority of suicides occur in 15–24-year-olds, although in recent times there has been a doubling of suicides in the 1–14 age group. In 1999, suicide accounted for nearly 40 percent of all deaths in youth (ages 10–19) and nearly one-quarter of all deaths in ages 20–44. Overall, the First Nations suicide rate in 1999 was 27.9 deaths per million, which suggests that a sustained decrease has not occurred in the past quarter-century. Data show that suicides occur in "clusters" of specific areas and time periods, and in some areas the rates of suicide are extremely high. While the overall rate for young people is high, in areas such as Sioux Lookout, it is 50 times higher than the general Canadian population for the 10–19 age group. Overall, at ages 15–24, the suicide rate in First Nations women is almost eight times that of the same age group for all of Canada, while for men it is five times higher. While completed suicides are typically much higher among males, in general, females attempt suicide far more often than males—a pattern also seen in the general Canadian population (Whitehead, et al., 1996). Homicide is the third most common cause of death by injury in First Nations communities: the rate is nearly five times higher than for the total population

In conclusion, Bobet (1990) shows that in First Nations communities, compared to the rest of the population, suicide and self-inflicted injuries are three times higher (six times higher for the 15–24 age group), homicide rates are twice as high, congenital anomalies are 1.5 times higher, and pneumonia more than three times higher. Aboriginal people have five times the rate of child welfare, four times the death rate, three times the violent death, juvenile delinquency, and suicide rate, and twice the rate of hospital admissions of the average Canadian population. Aboriginal people have three times the rate of heart problems and hypertension compared to the general Canadian population (see Figure 3.8 for an overall rate of death).

Off-Reserve Indian Health

Most of the research conducted on Aboriginal health has focused on those living on reserves. However, in 2000, a study was carried out to assess the health of the Aboriginal population living off-reserve in cities and towns across the country. As noted earlier, the off-reserve population is younger than the general population and is generally located in the north, west, and rural parts of Canada. One measure of health status is "self-perceived health." This measure examines the respondents' assessment of their own health. Overall, the off-reserve Aboriginal population reported better health than their non-Aboriginal counterparts and, as incomes increased, the proportion of people reporting fair or poor health decreased.

However, when chronic conditions were considered, over 60 percent of the off-reserve population reported at least one chronic condition, while less than half of the non-Aboriginal population reported this. Arthritis had the highest prevalence in the Aboriginal population (26 percent), followed by high blood pressure (15 percent) and diabetes (9 percent). When compared to the general Canadian population, these rates were much higher.

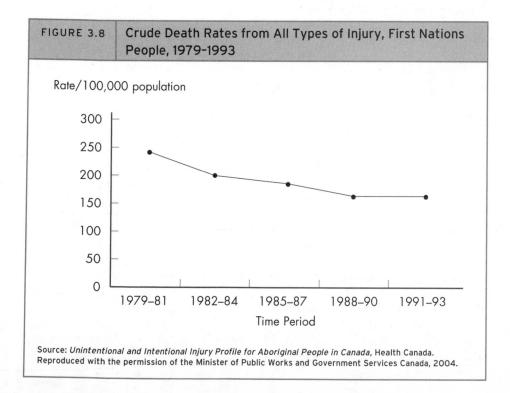

| FIGURE 3.8 | Crude Death Rates from All Types of Injury, First Nations People, 1979-1993 |

Source: *Unintentional and Intentional Injury Profile for Aboriginal People in Canada*, Health Canada. Reproduced with the permission of the Minister of Public Works and Government Services Canada, 2004.

For example, the diabetes rate was twice as high as that of the general population (Tjepkema, 2002). When long-term activity restrictions were assessed, over 16 percent of the off-reserve Aboriginal population reported such restriction, which was 1.6 times higher than in the non-Aboriginal population. When compared to Aboriginals living on-reserve, the residents reported similar levels of activity restriction. Surprisingly, middle-income off-reserve Aboriginals were more likely to report activity restrictions than other middle-income Canadians, while Aboriginals from high income groups report lower levels of restriction compared to high-income Canadians. The survey found that over 13 percent of the off-reserve Aboriginals had experienced a major depressive episode in the past year—nearly twice the level reported by the non-Aboriginal population. (Tjepkema, 2002).

An assessment was carried out to determine what caused these differences. Age, education, income, and various behaviours were identified as possible factors. Socio-economic status (income, education, job) are the major factors that determine the health status of both Aboriginals and non-Aboriginals. The second most important factor was physical activity, smoking status, and whether or not the individual was overweight or obese.

In terms of seeking health care services, over three-quarters of the off-reserve population had visited a general medical practitioner at least once in the previous year, and this was similar to the non-Aboriginal population. Contact with medical specialists was also similar between the two groups. However, when contact with dentists was assessed, Aboriginals were much less likely to see them than their non-Aboriginal counterparts.

Environmental Hazards

Aboriginal people are also exposed to severe environmental hazards: industrial and resource development have polluted water and disrupted fish and game stock for many reserve communities, seriously affecting quality of life. For example, residents of the White Dog and Grassy Narrows reserves in Ontario were found to have 40 to 150 times more mercury in their blood than the average Canadian (Bolaria, 1979). Various environmental disturbances have upset other Aboriginal communities, such as Cluff Lake (uranium pollution), Serpent River (acid discharge), and St. Regis (fluoride pollution). Obviously, Aboriginal lifestyles vary considerably from those of non-Aboriginal people (Ram and Romaniuk, 1984). In the second diagnostic study of the health of First Nations and Inuit people, researchers found that 60 percent of Inuit children under the age of 15, and 40 percent of Inuit women of childbearing age on Broughton Island, Nunavut, have polychorinated biphenyl (PCB) levels well above government definition of "tolerable." A similar study in Quebec found that concentrations of PCB in newborn children in Quebec Inuit and the Montagnais were four times higher than the concentrations in Southern Quebec infants. The concentrations of mercury in the Quebec and Northwest Territories Inuit were 6 to 14 times higher than the levels in the newborn Southern Quebec population. Another study in the James Bay area showed that although mercury levels exceeding the government levels had decreased over the past two decades, they were still higher than government standards.

In order to deal with escalating health care costs, the federal government placed a 6 percent cap on funding for Aboriginal health care for 1995–98. This cap can be better understood when one realizes that for the previous decade there had been an 8 percent yearly increase in health program spending.

HOUSING

The federal government has no legal or treaty obligation to provide housing units or to repair existing ones for Aboriginal people. However, it does have a historical commitment to provide housing for Indians, which, so far, it has chosen to continue. With a birth rate double the national average, there is an ever-increasing demand for housing. To support this activity, the Department of Indian Affairs provides support to First Nation Communities through the Capital Facilities and Maintenance Program.

Because of the geographical isolation and limited natural resources on reserves, most of them do not have the economic ability to meet the cost of various capital facilities. Therefore, funding by DIAND is critical for these communities. One of the more important types of community facility that is being subsidized by DIAND is housing. Support for individuals and bands in order to provide adequate housing takes place through subsidies for the construction and renovation of houses on reserves. The subsidy levels for new construction vary from $19 000 to $50 000. Today, about 46 000 (out of a total of 91 600) housing units have been built on reserves under the Indian and Inuit Housing Program, at a cost of well over $100 million in 1984–85. In addition to this, rural and Aboriginal housing programs have provided $88 million to subsidize housing for Inuit, Métis, and non-status Indians. Data relevant to the growth rate of the number of dwellings in relation to the growth rate of the population shows that between 1983–84 and 1989–90 an average of 3263 new dwelling units per year were built on reserves. In 1991 the number was slightly above 4000. However since this time, the number of new housing units each year has decreased, and by 2001 the number had decreased to fewer than 2000. Nearly 4000 homes per year since 1983 have been renovated, with an average subsidy of $8000 to $10 000. This activity also has decreased to fewer than 3000 homes per year. In the end, it is clear that these numbers are not keeping up with the demand. For example, the number of new housing units is approximately half the need.

The above figures must also be interpreted in the context of public housing standards. Aboriginal housing units, because of the standards employed by DIAND, have a life span of 15 to 20 years—less than half the national average life span. Thus, even though there has been an increased number of housing units built on reserves, the poor quality of the houses and the increase in the number of people living on the reserves through *Bill C-31* intensifies the competition for good housing. In the end, we find that the number of units in need of replacement has remained at about 5000 for the past five years, and the number of units in need of renovations has remained at about 30 000 over the past decade.

Figure 3.9 shows that the number of Aboriginal homes with more than one person per room is 200–300 times that of the overall Canadian population. The average number of Aboriginal persons per dwelling is 3.5, while for all of Canada, it is less than 2. The average Canadian dwelling has 7.2 rooms, while the Aboriginal dwelling has 5.8. This overcrowding decreases the lifespan of a house and it worsens social problems in communities.

A more recent evaluation of the on-reserve housing program estimated that about three-quarters of all existing housing was inadequate in that it failed to meet some of the basic standards of safe and decent living. For example, while only 2 percent of the Canadian population live in crowded conditions, more than one-third of the Aboriginal houses were found to be overcrowded. In addition, the number of Aboriginal houses requiring major repairs nearly doubled between 1985 and 1991. By rating housing conditions as requiring regular maintenance, minor repairs, or major repairs, government officials determine the state of Aboriginal housing stock and provide an overview of housing conditions on reserves. Generally, slightly more than half the houses require major repairs.

Much of the housing on reserves is provided by the federal government, and because individual title is severely limited, most homes are not owned by individuals but by the band. The band councils "rent" the houses at a break-even point to keep the costs down. As a result, the absence of individual ownership reduces the chances that the occupant will maintain the unit in good repair. Houses on the reserves are also single-family units.

The above-mentioned program and philosophy have been unnecessarily restrictive and have partially contributed to the lack of Aboriginal housing. Some reserves in Ontario and Quebec have tried to combat the official rules and methods by investigating the feasibility of providing multi-unit buildings. A recent study carried out by DIAND shows that nearly $1 billion would be needed to bring Aboriginal housing up to average Canadian standards. Despite this ongoing crisis in Aboriginal communities, the Canada Mortgage and Housing Corporation cut its funding in half for new Indian housing, which means that the number of new houses will be reduced to 600 per year. This exacerbates the housing budget problem, as it has been frozen since 1988, when housing programs for off-reserve Indians were also eliminated.

The federal government has tried to deal with the problem of housing. By 1996, the total number of houses on reserves had increased to nearly 80 000 and, of these, about half were considered "adequate." In addition, over the past decade, nearly 20 000 additional houses were renovated. In 1996 the government introduced a new housing policy. This new approach gives Aboriginals control of their housing design, construction, and placement. Under this new First Nations Innovative Housing Initiative, new housing designs and types of construction—e.g., log houses—are being built in Aboriginal communities. In addition to the $138 million provided annually to support First Nations housing on-reserve, Indian Affairs has committed another $220 million to support the 1996 policy. Through this initiative, housing on-reserve has improved. Between 1996 and 2002, the total number of houses on-reserve increased by more than 17 percent. During the same period, the number of houses considered to be in adequate condition increased by nearly 25 percent. In addition, the Innovative Housing Fund introduced in 1998 provides $2 million in annual funding for new building technology, alternative house designs, and energy sources. Finally Indian Affairs provides Ministerial Loan Guarantees and has increased the department's guarantee authority for these housing loans from $1.2 to–1.7 billion.

Infrastructure Services

The number and extent of government services available to Aboriginal people has a considerable impact on their quality of life. A major factor in the provision of services is accessibility by road or rail; without good transportation access, services are difficult and costly to provide. Yet only about one-third of the reserves even have year-round road access. Nearly half of all reserves and settlements are accessible only by water. And only 18 percent are accessible by both rail and road.

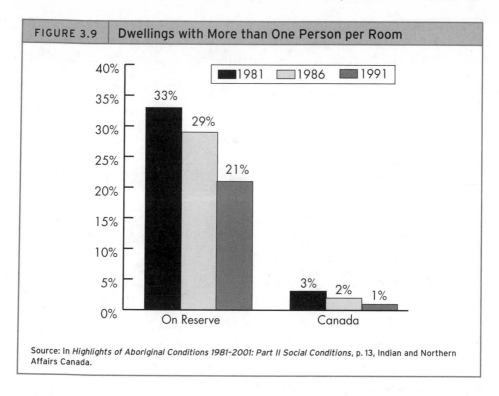

FIGURE 3.9 | Dwellings with More than One Person per Room

Source: In *Highlights of Aboriginal Conditions 1981-2001: Part II Social Conditions*, p. 13, Indian and Northern Affairs Canada.

Figure 3.10 shows the average percentage of housing on Indian reserves with a sewer (or septic tank), and with running water. The data show that, on average, over 95 percent of reserve houses have an adequate water supply and sewage disposal. These figures show remarkable improvement when you consider that in 1963, just over 10 percent of the Indian reserve population had adequate water supply and sewage disposal. Other data show that over 90 percent now have electricity. Recent statistics show continual improvement. However, just over one-quarter of the housing units on a reserve are now covered by fire protection services and this figure reveals a slight decrease from a decade ago.

While the infrastructure picture on reserves is better than it was in the past, when we compare these figures with the overall Canadian rate we find that Aboriginal dwellings are still far behind in having the basic necessities that most Canadians take for granted.

While these data show improvements, there can be little doubt that housing for Aboriginal people is inferior to that for the non-Aboriginal population. Less than three-quarters of Aboriginal homes have central heating, in contrast to over 90 percent of non-Aboriginal homes. As we have seen, crowding is also a problem for Aboriginal people. One in 43 non-Aboriginal homes was crowded, compared to the one-in-six proportion of Aboriginal homes. More than 15 percent of Aboriginal homes require major repairs. Overall, Aboriginal people have the least favourable housing conditions of any ethnic group in Canada.

The housing data released from Indian Affairs reveals a growing Aboriginal population with an almost static number of adequate houses now on the reserve. This reflects the aging housing stock, the slow construction (upgrading) of new housing, and the growing population.

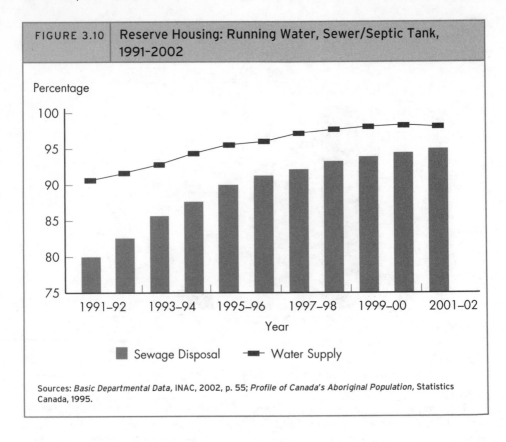

FIGURE 3.10 | Reserve Housing: Running Water, Sewer/Septic Tank, 1991–2002

Sources: *Basic Departmental Data*, INAC, 2002, p. 55; *Profile of Canada's Aboriginal Population*, Statistics Canada, 1995.

Overall, the funded capital assets (excluding houses) across the reserves show that the average number of new assets was about 1300 per year for the past decade. Utilities accounted for 41 percent of new assets, buildings for 29 percent, and transport for 26 percent over the past decade. One specific facility that has increased over the past 10 years has been educational space. The total educational space on reserves has increased by 25 percent, and similar increases have been noted for increases in space allocated for schools.

CONCLUSION

The above data reveals a profile that is unique in Canadian history. The number of Aboriginal people rapidly declined in the late 19th and early 20th centuries. However, since that time they have exhibited exceptionally high birth rates, decreasing death rates, and unprecedented "in-migration" rates, particularly during the past two decades. These changes have brought about phenomenal growth of the Aboriginal population. However, this has been moderated by the overall growth of the Canadian population. As a result, the proportion of the Aboriginal population in Canada has decreased slightly over the past half-century.

WEBLINKS

www.anac.on.ca

Founded in 1974, *The Aboriginal Nurses of Canada* recognizes that Aboriginal people's health needs are best met and understood by health professionals of similar cultural background. This site lists publications as well as a schedule of seminars and conferences on Aboriginal health issues and care.

www.inac.gc.ca/pr/sts/index_e.html

Despite the absence of an authoritative source for information about Aboriginal demographics, a good starting point is the Statistics page of the federal Department of Indian and Northern Affairs, which includes recent census data on Aboriginal people, information about social conditions, and more.

www.ainc-inac.gc.ca/ch/rcap/index_e.html

The 1996 Royal Commission on Aboriginal Peoples Final Report contains a wealth of information about living conditions of Aboriginal peoples across Canada. It includes information on demography and discusses Aboriginal relocation, housing, health, and other issues.

chapter four

Profile of Aboriginal People II: Social Attributes

INTRODUCTION

We now move to looking at the more general social profile of the Aboriginal population. While much of the data presented is from the Department of Indian Affairs and thus focuses solely on First Nations, data from other sources reveals that the profile is similar to that of other Aboriginal groups, e.g., Inuit, Métis. These statistics provide a mental image of the Aboriginal population and, when possible, comparisons with the average Canadian population are given. This will allow the reader to place the Aboriginal population in context within Canadian society. The profile will also allow policy analysts to better see the differences between Aboriginal and non-Aboriginal peoples and to understand the kinds of programs that need to be put in place to deal with the problems facing Aboriginal people. We will begin with a basic age–sex profile.

AGE

Figures 4.1, 4.2, and 4.3 show the distribution of Aboriginal Canadians by age, relative to the total Canadian population. The data reveal a very young population: well over one-third of the Aboriginal population is younger than 15 and over half is younger than 25. Of the total Canadian population, only about one-fifth of the population is under 15 and about one-third is under 25. When on-reserve Indians and Inuit are singled out of the status Indian population, greater discrepancies are evident. Thirty-seven percent of on-reserve Indians and Inuit are under age 15, while nearly two-thirds of them are under 25 (see Figure 4.4). Over 70 percent of the Aboriginal population is under 40 years of age, evenly divided between males and females.

| FIGURE 4.1 | Age Structure of the Populations: Total Canadian and Indians Off-Reserve |

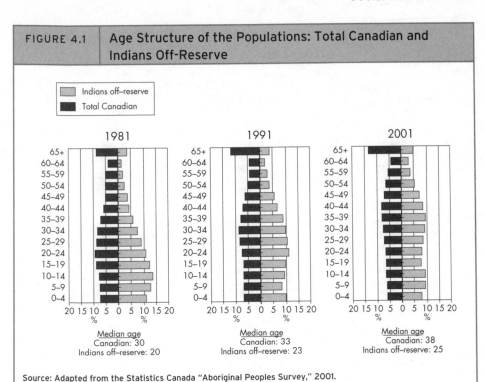

Source: Adapted from the Statistics Canada "Aboriginal Peoples Survey," 2001.

| FIGURE 4.2 | Age Structure of the Populations: Total Canadian and Inuit |

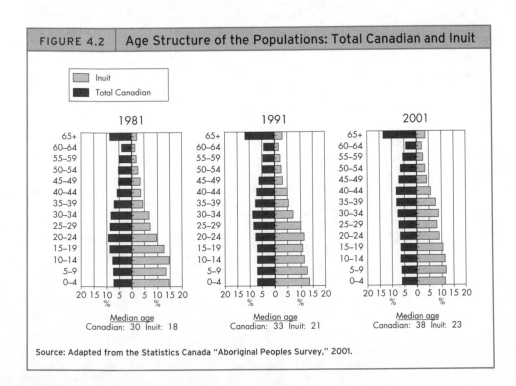

Source: Adapted from the Statistics Canada "Aboriginal Peoples Survey," 2001.

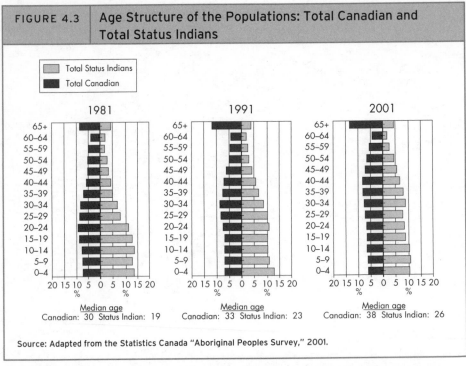

FIGURE 4.3 | Age Structure of the Populations: Total Canadian and Total Status Indians

Source: Adapted from the Statistics Canada "Aboriginal Peoples Survey," 2001.

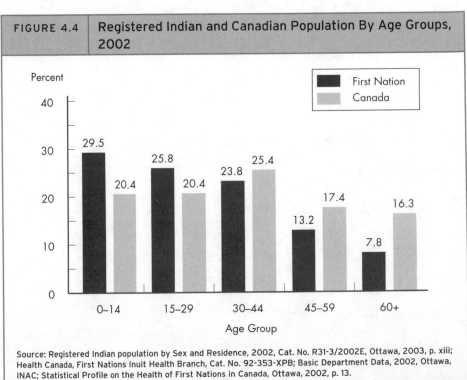

FIGURE 4.4 | Registered Indian and Canadian Population By Age Groups, 2002

Source: Registered Indian population by Sex and Residence, 2002, Cat. No. R31-3/2002E, Ottawa, 2003, p. xiii; Health Canada, First Nations Inuit Health Branch, Cat. No. 92-353-XPB; Basic Department Data, 2002, Ottawa, INAC; Statistical Profile on the Health of First Nations in Canada, Ottawa, 2002, p. 13.

Thus far the evidence reveals that the proportion of young people in the overall Aboriginal population is growing. However, the growth is slowing down as the Aboriginal population ages. For example, in 1981 the median age for Aboriginal people was 19, while for the overall population it was 32. Today we find that the Aboriginal median age is 23, while the overall population has only increased to 33. Nonetheless, the proportion of Aboriginal people in the ages between 15 and 44 is similar to that found in the non-Aboriginal population. In the 45 to 65 age category there are nearly twice as many non-Aboriginal as Aboriginal persons. A similar profile is evident in the age category of 65 and over.

The dependency ratio is one way of assessing the burden of care placed on the working age population. The dependency ratios are outlined in Table 4.1. They show that, again, while the Aboriginal young dependency ratio is falling, it is substantially larger than that of non-Aboriginal people. At the same time, the aged dependency ratios have remained the same over the past decade. The overall dependency ratio for the Canadian population has remained stable over the past decade and will continue at this level (47 percent) into the 21st century. On the other hand, the dependency ratio for Aboriginal people declined from 77 percent (1981) to 66 percent in 1999. In the case of Inuit, the overall dependency ratio declined from 84 percent (1981) to 61 percent in 2001.

As both the Aboriginal and Canadian populations continue to age, the starting points are different: in the case of the general population, they are aging into retirement, while Aboriginal people are aging from youth to the working age group. The aging patterns of Inuit mirror those of status Indians.

The above figures carry a number of implications. Clearly, there is a stable Aboriginal population-growth rate, meaning continued high growth, as well as a decreasing death rate. Unless birth rates also decrease, more and more Aboriginal people will belong to the prime employment category of 15–40, and the demand for jobs will increase. As Table 4.1 shows, the dependency ratios are already over twice as high for Aboriginal people as for the general population; this means that the working-age population must support a large number of non-productive people. Unemployment is already rampant among Aboriginal Canadians, and, as more and more Aboriginals move into the prime employment category, fewer and fewer jobs are likely to become available. The data from Census Canada show that the number of people in the labour-force age range (15–64) has been increasing—from 46 percent in 1966 to nearly 65 percent by 2001. This is likely to add more than 75 000 Aboriginal people to the labour force.

LANGUAGE USE AND RETENTION

The language of any group is the repository of concepts, images, and history that allows individuals to organize their social environment. As such, language shapes the thoughts of those who use it. Reitz (1974) has argued that languages are an expression of collective identity and an important element in the survival of an ethnic group. Thus it is important to know the extent to which Aboriginal people use and retain their Aboriginal languages. Price (1981) and Norris (1998) have investigated the potential for the survival of Aboriginal languages in Canada. There are approximately 50 languages of Canada's Indigenous peoples belonging to eleven major language families (Norris, 1998). Norris found that some language families are large and strong, others small and endangered. However, the three largest families are Algonquian (147 000),

TABLE 4.1 | Age Distribution and Dependency Ratio of Aboriginal and Non-Aboriginal Population

| | Age Group | | | | | Dependency Ratio[a] | | | |
| | 0-14 years (%) | 15-64 years (%) | 65 years and over (%) | No age given (%) | Population | Young | | Aged | |
						Indian	Non-Indian[b]	Indian	Non-Indian[b]
1924	32.2	51.2	5.9	10.7	104 894	62.9	56.5	11.5	7.9
1934	34.7	55.4	6.2	3.7	112 510	62.7	50.3	11.1	8.8
1944	37.5	55.9	6.6	–	125 686	67.0	42.4	11.8	10.2
1954	41.7	53.2	5.1	–	151 558	78.5	49.0	9.6	12.5
1964	46.7	49.1	4.2	–	211 389	95.0	58.1	8.6	13.1
1974	43.2	52.4	4.2	0.2	276 436	82.4	47.5	8.1	13.0
1981	39.0	57.0	4.0	–	323 000	68.4	48.8	7.0	12.8
1991	35.0	60.0	4.0	–	521 500	65.2	46.3	7.0	13.6
1999	29.5	65.3	5.2	–	604 400	59.5	29.4	6.3	17.9

a. The dependency ratios reflect the relationship between the groups least likely to be involved in the workforce (i.e., the young and the elderly), and the working-age population.
b. Data were not available for the corresponding year; the years represented are: 1921, 1931, 1941, 1951, 1961, 1971.

Sources: Information Canada, *Perspective Canada II*, (Ottawa: Queen's Printer, 1977), 287; *Census of Canada*, 1981; Indian and Northern Affairs Canada, *Quantitative Analysis and Socio-Demographic Research*, 1992; Registered Indian Population by Sex and Residence, 2002, INAC, Ottawa, 2003, Cat. No. R31-3/2002E; Health Canada, A Statistical Profile on The Health of First Nations in Canada, Ottawa, 2002.

Inuktitut (28 000), and Athapaskan (20 000). Estimates are that long-term future viability has been secured for at least 18 Aboriginal languages (the three largest are
Inuktitut, Cree, and Ojibway) for which there are a minimum of 1000 speakers. An
additional 16 languages are spoken by an estimated 100 to 1000 Aboriginal people and
could be considered "endangered." The remaining 16 languages have less than 100
speakers and these are considered "near extinction," meaning that they are beyond the
possibility of revival.

While Aboriginal people still maintain a relatively high degree of adherence to their
mother tongue,[1] this is diminishing. In 1941, fewer than 10 percent of Aboriginal people claimed English as their mother tongue. The figure reached 15 percent in 1951 and
over 25 percent in 1961; another 2 percent claimed French. By 1991, 67 percent claimed
English and fewer than 5 percent were bilingual (i.e., spoke an Aboriginal language as
well as either English or French). At the turn of the new millennium, this had increased
to over 70 percent. Of those who claimed Aboriginal dialects as their mother tongues,
more than 40 percent were "somewhat" bilingual.

Home language reveals an equally skewed distribution, with almost 80 percent
claiming English as the home language. However 20 percent state that an Aboriginal
language is used in their home. The data also show that 80 percent of Aboriginal people
claimed to have a working knowledge of one official language.

In reviewing various surveys from the 1970s, Price (1981) found that the percentage
of Aboriginal-language speakers within different Aboriginal populations varied from a
low of 62 percent in Toronto and Vancouver, to 73 percent in Winnipeg, and up to 100
percent on many reserves. He also found Saskatchewan to be the most conservative in the
retention of Aboriginal languages. Earlier, Stanbury and Fields (1975) had found that only
18 percent of Vancouver Indians used their Aboriginal languages in their homes. Overall,
22 percent of the nearly 1.5 million Natives in Canada speak an Aboriginal language at
home. Of those who listed an Aboriginal language as their first language, 43 percent speak
Cree, 14 percent speak Inuktitut, 13 percent speak Ojibwa, 3 percent speak Athapaskan,
and 1 percent speak Sioux. Of those claiming to speak an Aboriginal language, we find
that the average age is well in excess of 40. This suggests that it is the older segment of
the population that still retains the language and not the younger generation (Siggner,
1986). Norris (1998) found that the index of continuity had decreased for all Aboriginal
languages over the past two decades. She found that the index of continuity was at 76 percent in 1981 but that 15 years later this had decreased to just below 65 percent. This means
that for every 100 people with an Aboriginal mother tongue, the number who used an
indigenous language most often at home declined from 76 to just under 65.

The overall diminishing of Aboriginal-language use is somewhat mediated by special
schools and language instruction programs. Almost 34 000 students (or 42 percent of
Aboriginal enrolment) received some Aboriginal language instruction in school during
the year. In addition, the number of students taking courses in which an Aboriginal language is the medium of instruction over half the time increased by more than 60 percent
during the 1980–84 period. However, like other ethnic minorities, Aboriginal people
have learned that, to integrate into the larger society, they must learn to speak English or
French. Thus, to a certain extent, the decreasing number of Aboriginal-language speakers reflects an increasing move away from the reserves and an increasing contact with
non-Aboriginal persons. For example, 57 percent of on-reserve and 87 percent of off-reserve

Indians have English as their home language. For mother tongue, even greater differences are evident: only 47 percent of on-reserve Indians compared to 76 percent of off-reserve Indians had English as their mother tongue. Of course, the educational process had also increased the number of English/French-language speakers, though the high Aboriginal drop-out rate at elementary levels has minimized its impact on English/French-language retention and use. However, as Aboriginal people increasingly recognize the value of English/French-language education, their languages and dialects may disappear even more rapidly (Priest, 1984).

Jarvis and Heaton (1989) used census data to examine Aboriginal language shifts for all the provinces and territories of Canada, with the exception of P.E.I. They found that nearly all Aboriginal people who change language shift to English (96.8 percent). They also found that fewer than 30 percent of Aboriginal persons began with an Aboriginal mother tongue. However, of those individuals, nearly three-fourths are still using their Aboriginal language as their principal language in the home. Aboriginal people living in the north of Canada were reluctant to change languages, while Métis were most likely and Inuit were least likely to do so. The authors found that gender had little to do with linguistic shifts. When age was investigated as a possible determinant of linguistic changes, the authors found that the young (under 14) and the old (65+) were least likely to take on English as their operating language. Younger children will, as they grow older, be more fully exposed to the larger society and will begin the process of linguistic shift. Thus, the fact that young people still retain their Aboriginal tongue is no indication that they will be fluent in that language as they enter the labour force. The lack of shift in the older generation is due to the fact that they have spent their lives speaking an Aboriginal language and have been least exposed to the modern industrial society outside their community (Jarvis and Heaton, 1989).

Even though the number of persons reporting an Aboriginal mother tongue has increased by 25 percent over the last 15 years, proportionately fewer of these individuals used this indigenous language at home. As Norris (1998) points out, Aboriginal language vitality is decreasing at an alarming rate. At the same time, the link between the respondents' perceptions regarding children's grasp of Native culture and language is clear. Data show that the ability to speak an Aboriginal language is directly related to increasing age, and the last census shows that the number of children possessing an Aboriginal mother tongue has decreased substantially. As such, the lack of or inability to communicate in their Native language suggests they will be unlikely to sustain their traditional culture.

RELIGION

According to present statistics, 46 percent of Indians in Canada are Catholics. This, of course, reflects the early Jesuit and Oblate missionary work among the Aboriginal people. Protestants make up an additional 36 percent, while "no religion" adds another 17 percent. The second-largest Indian religious denomination is Anglican, with 18 percent. Another 10 percent of Indians belong to the United Church, and the remaining 8 percent are evenly distributed among the other Christian churches in Canada. This information is based on official government statistics. However, no information has been gathered regarding the extent to which Aboriginal people still adhere to pre-Christian religious beliefs. Apparently, a significant percentage of Aboriginal persons have retained their indigenous religious beliefs. Nonetheless, Christianity has had a definite impact on Aboriginal culture during the past few centuries. Its ideology of acceptance and obedience has contributed significantly to a widespread conservatism and fatalism among Aboriginal peoples.

MARITAL STATUS

Figures on the marital status of Aboriginal people do not support the stereotype of the broken Aboriginal family. The percentage of divorced Aboriginal persons is very similar to that of the general Canadian population. There are, however, a number of explanations for this statistic. Because Aboriginal people are frequently poor, they often avoid the court costs and alimony payments that accompany formal divorces by simply separating from or deserting their families. Moreover, many women, even though they live with a man and bear children, never officially get married. Instead, they live common-law or marry according to tribal ritual, which has not been recognized by the federal government since 1957. Aboriginal women may choose not to marry for various reasons. Unmarried women with children receive a fairly substantial income through the federal child tax benefit: an unmarried Aboriginal woman with three children receives greater financial compensation than a married-but-separated woman with three children. Unmarried Indian women are also eligible for various educational and vocational-training programs not available to married women. Finally, unmarried women, until recently, did not risk losing their Indian status.

The low official divorce rate of Aboriginal people, then, should not be used as an indicator of family stability. In addition, some anthropologists have argued convincingly that non-Aboriginal North American standards of family stability should be used only for the non-Aboriginal population and not for members of other cultures. The definition of stability is so open to various culturally-based interpretations that no attempt to apply it to another culture can be free of ethnocentric bias.

Other statistics suggest that Aboriginal family patterns depart from non-Aboriginal norms. About 60 percent of Aboriginal people living together are officially married, as compared to 67 percent of the overall Canadian population. Husband–wife families make up about 80 percent of the Aboriginal families (86 percent for non-Aboriginal), with 16 percent consisting of female lone-parent families (12 percent for non-Aboriginal) and the remainder being male lone-parent families. These figures are similar for all subtypes of Aboriginals—e.g., Inuit, Métis, other Aboriginal. The proportion of families headed by a single mother rose from 20 percent in 1981 to nearly 25 percent in 1996. Approximately one in three Aboriginal mothers in 1996 was a lone parent, compared with one in six in the overall Canadian population. Non-Aboriginal families have respective figures of 85 and 13 percent. Young Aboriginals between 15 and 19 are much more likely to marry than are other Canadian teenagers (Anderson, 1978), although these young people are three times more likely to be single mothers than Canadian women of the same age. By the end of the 20th century, we found that lone-parent families headed by a single father were twice as common among on-reserve Registered Indians as among the Canadian population. All of these statistics have implications for the high illegitimacy rate characteristic of the Aboriginal population (IRIW, 1979).

Related to marital status is the number and growth rate of Aboriginal families. In 1996 there were 137 500 families, a major increase from 1986. There is no question that

Bill C-31 had a significant impact on this growth rate: in 1987 the growth rate for families was 9 percent, six times that of the general Canadian family. However, even when the impact of this legislation is removed, the growth rate of Aboriginal families continues to be considerably higher than for the general Canadian population. The data show that the Aboriginal family is larger than the Canadian family, although there has been a decrease in family size from 1981 to 2001.

The total fertility rate for Aboriginal people over the next 20 years is a crucial demographic factor. The data show that the fertility rates are much higher than those for non-Aboriginal people. The projected fertility rate for Registered Indians in 1996 was 2.7, while for all Canadian women the rate was 1.6. In 1999, the projected fertility rate on-reserve was 3.2, while the off-reserve rate was 2.4 (Statistics Canada, 1999). The data also show that while the rates will decrease over the next decade, they will still remain nearly twice the overall Canadian rate. Finally, the data show wide variations in the fertility rate as one moves from region to region; for example, Yukon will have a rate of 2.5, while in Saskatchewan it is expected to be 3.12 in 2005. Census families with no children were twice as common among non-Aboriginal families than among Inuit families. However, for all groups of Aboriginals and non-Aboriginals, families with one or two children generally accounted for one-quarter to one-third of families. (See Figure 4.5.)

SOCIO-ECONOMIC STATUS

The quality of life experienced by Canadians is a function of their position in the stratified social system. Those who rank high are able to enjoy the benefits of a modern industrial society with its enhanced educational, medical, and leisure activities. On the other hand, those who place low in our hierarchical system will not be able to benefit from the increased technological innovations to enhance their quality of life. In our social system, four factors influence one's ability to participate in modern industrial society: income, labour force participation, occupational status, and education.

Income

In 1966 Hawthorn et al. established that the per capita income per year for Aboriginal persons was about $300, and for other Canadians, about $1400. On a yearly earnings basis, Aboriginal workers received $1361, while Canadian workers received $4000. In 1997 the average Aboriginal income, for those in the labour force, had increased to over $9000. While these figures represent a substantial increase in income, the overall average Canadian income had increased to nearly $20 000, representing twice the income received by Aboriginal people. Four years later, in 2001, the average income for the general population was just over $24 000 per year, while for Indians it was nearly $17 000.

Before discussing income further, it is important that the reader fully appreciate that income can be generated from a number of sources. The most general categories used in this review are those of wage (earned) and non-wage (unearned or transfer).

The data in Figure 4.6 show that earned income was the major source of income for all groups. It reveals that employment income makes up at least 60 percent of income for all groups. However, for on-reserve Aboriginals, 35–40 percent is from government transfer payments, in comparison to the 10–13 percent for non-Aboriginals. We also see

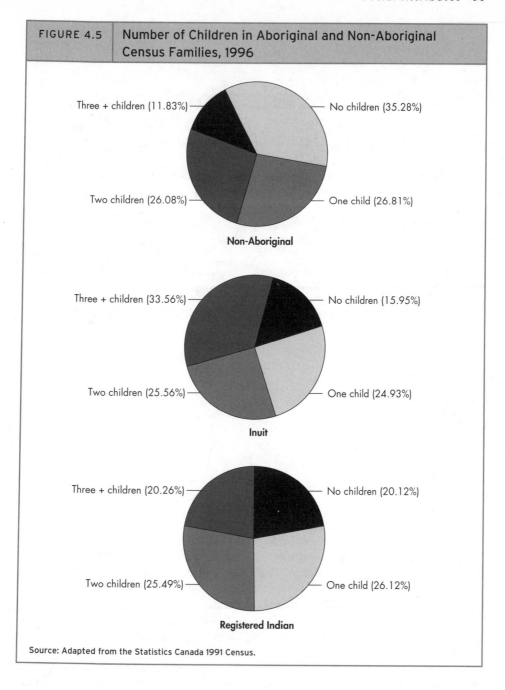

FIGURE 4.5	Number of Children in Aboriginal and Non-Aboriginal Census Families, 1996

Three + children (11.83%) — No children (35.28%)

Two children (26.08%) — One child (26.81%)

Non-Aboriginal

Three + children (33.56%) — No children (15.95%)

Two children (25.56%) — One child (24.93%)

Inuit

Three + children (20.26%) — No children (20.12%)

Two children (25.49%) — One child (26.12%)

Registered Indian

Source: Adapted from the Statistics Canada 1991 Census.

that only non-Aboriginals have a substantial proportion of "other" income. Figure 4.7 reveals the total family income (regardless of source) for Canadians, compared to Aboriginal families. We see that well over one-third of Aboriginal families make less than $20 000 per year, compared to only 17 percent of non-Aboriginals. At the other end

FIGURE 4.6	Population Ages 15+ Not Attending School Full Time, by Income Composition and Sex, 1995

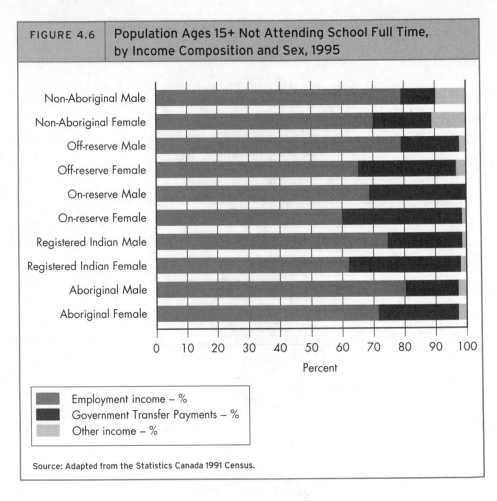

Employment income – %
Government Transfer Payments – %
Other income – %

Source: Adapted from the Statistics Canada 1991 Census.

of the continuum, we find that 30 percent of non-Aboriginal people are making more than $70 000, while just over 10 percent of Aboriginal families have that high an income.

We now move to the question of how many Aboriginal and non-Aboriginal people have an income. At least 75 percent of the total Canadian population (over the age of 15) has some income. However, nearly one-fourth of the Aboriginal population reported no income, while nearly 90 percent of the Canadian population reported income. (See Figure 4.8.)

In all cases, the data show that between 1980 and 1990 more non-Aboriginal Canadians reported receiving an income than did Aboriginal Canadians.

The data show that the disparity between non-Aboriginal Canadian and Aboriginal individual income remained the same during the 1980–90 period. In 1980 the average income for Indians was 70 percent of that for all Canadians, and by 1990 this had not changed. However, by 1995, this had decreased to just over 50 percent of the average Canadian yearly earnings. Family incomes show a similar pattern. Status Indian families have an average income of $21 800, which is about half that of the average Canadian family of $38 000. Like individual incomes, family income disparity has increased, and recent information suggests that the increase continues.

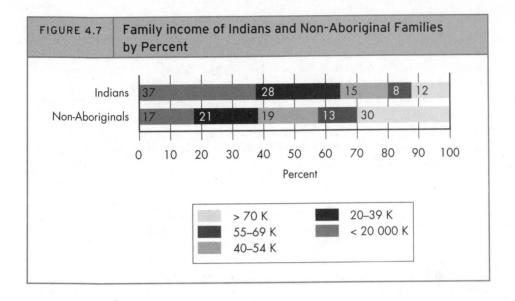

FIGURE 4.7 | Family income of Indians and Non-Aboriginal Families by Percent

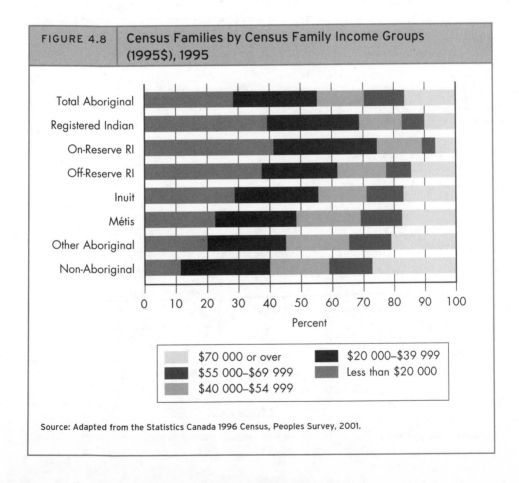

FIGURE 4.8 | Census Families by Census Family Income Groups (1995$), 1995

Source: Adapted from the Statistics Canada 1996 Census, Peoples Survey, 2001.

Figure 4.9 shows the average Aboriginal earnings in 1995. It shows that the on-reserve population made one-fourth less than the off-reserve population and nearly 50 percent less than the general Canadian population. Even the Inuit made more than the on-reserve population. Much of this difference can be explained by the lower participation rate in the labour force under the age of 35.

When we compare 1980 with 1990, we find that "all Canadian" average income increased from $23 119 to $24 001. However, Aboriginals' average income dropped from $15 303 to $14 561. These data show that in 1981 Aboriginal people made about 67 percent of the "all Canadian" average income. But, 10 years later they made only 60 percent of the average Canadian income.

In summary, we find that the disparity of income between Aboriginal and non-Aboriginal Canadians noted by Hawthorn in the 1960s still exists. In addition, the data suggest that the gap between the two groups is getting larger. This startling fact emerges despite the large and complex structure we have put in place to help Aboriginal people find a niche in our society and integrate into the economic structure.

Income Polarity   While the data presented above reveal that, as a group, Aboriginal people are economically disadvantaged (consistent with the data presented by George et al, 1996; Junkwski and Moazzami, 1994), the question arises as to whether or not these disparities are increasing or decreasing. Little and Stinson (2000) noted that the Canadian population experienced the greatest increase in family income during the 1990s than ever before. Maxim et al. (2003) note that, on average, Canadian incomes increased 1.7 percent

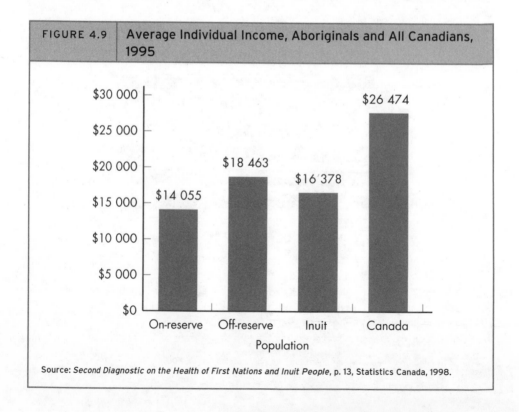

| FIGURE 4.9 | Average Individual Income, Aboriginals and All Canadians, 1995 |

Source: *Second Diagnostic on the Health of First Nations and Inuit People*, p. 13, Statistics Canada, 1998.

in the last decade. We now ask whether or not Aboriginal people have followed that trend. Data from Maxim et al. show that while the overall increase was just under 2 percent, the top quintile of Canadian families experienced a 6.6 percent increase, while the lowest quintile experienced a 5.2 percent decrease in income. Given that we know that most Aboriginals have incomes in the lowest quintile, we can conclude that they have experienced a decrease in income over the past decade, thus exacerbating the income polarity that existed a decade ago. When transfer payments—e.g., old age pension, disability, interest, dividends—are added to the total income of individuals, we find that there is no decrease in the income polarity but in fact an increase in disparity. In other words, wealthy people are making more in government transfers than poor people are.

Labour Force Participation

The extent to which Aboriginal people have been over- or underrepresented in various occupational categories has been well established.[2] To make the data more meaningful through comparison, similar "over–under" statistics will be noted for the ethnic category of British Canadians. The data show that there has been an increasing underrepresentation of Aboriginals in professional and financial occupations; that is, a smaller proportion of Aboriginal persons is in these occupations. Simultaneously, there has been an increasing overrepresentation over time in primary and unskilled jobs. Statistics for the British "charter" group show an opposite trend. British underrepresentation between 1931 and 1961 increased only for low-prestige jobs. Moreover, British overrepresentation in the professional and financial category increased from 1931 to 2001.

Darroch (1980) has examined the over–under occupational representations of various ethnic groups. Using an index to measure the discrepancy between an ethnic group's occupational distribution and that of the entire labour force, Darroch determined the ethnic job distribution for 1971, and compared his findings with previous data. He found that, for most ethnic categories, occupational differentiation had been substantially reduced. However, for Aboriginal people, comparison of the 1951 index (23.9) with the 1971 index (29.0) showed a considerable increase. More recent data suggest that this disparity is continuing to increase.

The participation in the labour force is highly differentiated as we look at comparisons between Canadians and Aboriginal Canadians (see Figure 4.10). Data from Indian and Northern Affairs Canada (INAC) show that the gap between Aboriginal and Canadian labour force participation decreased between 1980 and 1990. Furthermore, since this time, the gap has not changed as we have entered the 21st century. One might argue that since many Aboriginal communities are small and isolated it would be inappropriate to compare them to the overall Canadian statistics. However, as the Royal Commission on Aboriginal Peoples points out, even when Aboriginals are compared to similar rural, isolated non-Aboriginal communities, their economic performance falls short.

While more Aboriginal people entered the labour force over the past two decades, their percentage of unemployed doubled, while for Canadians, the increase was minor. In 1997–98 the unemployment rate on the reserves was about 29 percent, a rate that was triple the official national rate of 10 percent. The 1996 labour force participation rate for the total Canadian population was 68 percent—1.2 times higher than it was for First Nations. This disparity was larger on an age-specific basis. The gap between the First Nations and Canada was widest among the 15–24 age group, with a difference of 30 percent. We also found that

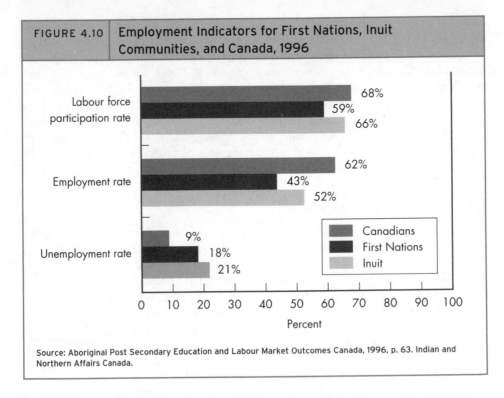

| FIGURE 4.10 | Employment Indicators for First Nations, Inuit Communities, and Canada, 1996 |

Source: Aboriginal Post Secondary Education and Labour Market Outcomes Canada, 1996, p. 63. Indian and Northern Affairs Canada.

the gap between the employment rates of First Nations people (43 percent) and Canadians (62 percent) was widening. In 1996, the unemployment rate for First Nations was three times higher than the Canadian rate (see Figure 4.10). For all age groups and sexes, the First Nations rates were at least two times higher, and the highest unemployment rate was in the 15–24 age group, at 41 percent (Health Canada, 2002). These figures illustrate the degree of exclusion of Aboriginal communities from the Canadian economy. To achieve parity with all Canadians, nearly 100 000 more Aboriginal people would have to be employed.

Participation in the labour force may be full-time or part-time/seasonal work. Today, about one-fifth of the Aboriginal population is involved in full-time, full-year jobs, while for all Canadians the average is approaching 40 percent (or double that of the Aboriginal rate). (See Table 4.2.) Only in the full-time (less than half-year) jobs do Aboriginal people have a greater involvement in the labour force than the average Canadian. If we look at part-time employment levels, we also find more Aboriginal people participating in jobs for less than half a year. However, as the length of the job increases, the rate of participation for Aboriginals decreases.

When we look at the earnings from these jobs we find great discrepancies between Aboriginal persons and other Canadians. For example, the earnings from employment per person (age 15+) for Aboriginal people is almost half that of all other Canadians ($9140 compared to $17 020). Looking at the data slightly differently, we find that the earnings from employment per employed person were $21 270 for Aboriginal persons and $27 880 for the Canadian rate.

Turning now to the type of labour force participation, focusing first on males, the data show that over half of the jobs held by Aboriginal men were made up of skilled, semi-

TABLE 4.2	Labour Force Participation Rate of the Registered Indian Population 15+ Not Attending School Full Time, by Highest Level of Schooling and Age Group, Canada, 1996

	Labour force participation rate (percent)				
	Age Group				
	15-24	25-44	45-64	65+	Total
Registered Indian					
Less than grade 9	29.9	47	36.3	5.6	32.6
Secondary school	49.1	64.3	56.3	12.4	57.2
Trades/other non U.	77.3	81.5	73.2	21.1	78
University	80.6	86.2	82.4	26.1	84
TOTAL	51.4	70.1	55.2	8.2	59
Other Canadians					
Less than grade 9	56.2	62.9	46.8	5.1	30
Secondary school	76	81.4	65	7.5	63.5
Trades/other non U.	90.8	89.6	76.6	10.5	77.9
University	91.2	91.9	83.3	13.3	83.2
TOTAL	81.3	86.5	69.4	8.2	67.7

Source: Hull, 2000, *Aboriginal Post-Secondary Education and Labour Market Outcomes, 1996, Canada.* Winnipeg: Prologica Research Inc. pp. 39 & 41.

skilled, and other manual occupations (see Table 4.3). In fact, over one-fourth of the jobs held by Aboriginal males were in manual labour. Ten percent fewer of the Canadian population were in the above three types of occupations. When we look at the upper scale of the occupational list (upper- and middle-level managers and professionals), we find nearly 25 percent of the total Canadian population, but less than half that percentage of Aboriginal people. Overall, compared to the total population, there are fewer Aboriginal persons in upper-status occupations and more Aboriginal persons in lower-status occupations.

When we look at females in the labour force, we find a different distribution than evidenced by the male population. At the upper ends of the occupational scale we find Aboriginal women and all women to have similar distributions, even though Aboriginal women are slightly underrepresented when compared to all females. The major differences between Aboriginal and all females is in two occupational categories—clerical and services. Nearly 30 percent of all female Canadians in the labour force hold jobs as clerks. For Aboriginal people it is less than 23 percent. On the other hand, one-fifth of the Aboriginal females are in service occupations, compared to just over 10 percent of the total female population in the labour force (see Table 4.3) (Public Affairs, 1990).

In summary, Aboriginal people are participating more in the labour force over time. At present, 43 percent are employed, while a similar number (over the age of 15) are not part of the labour force. The remainder (14 percent) are officially considered unemployed.

TABLE 4.3	Total Aboriginal Female and Male Experienced Labour Force by Occupation, 1996 (Percent)	
	Female	Male
Occupation unique to processing manufacturing & utilities	3.55	9.20
Occupation unique to primary industry	2.08	10.92
Trade, transportation, & equipment operators & related	2.85	32.10
Sales & service occupations	39.80	20.91
Occupation in art, culture, recreation & sport	3.17	2.51
Occupation in social science, education, government services & religion	10.46	4.91
Health occupations	6.20	1.06
Natural & applied sciences & related	1.31	4.38
Business, finance & administration	25.35	7.13
Management occupations	5.24	6.87

Source: Adapted from the Statistics Canada 1996 Census Peoples Survey, 2001.

However, their participation continues to be at the margins and is not representative of the jobs that characterize a modern industrial society. In an attempt to further integrate Aboriginal people into the labour force, the federal government has introduced a number of programs to help Aboriginal people find jobs and relocate if necessary. These federal programs are attempting to raise Aboriginal people to the average Canadian standard of living. Unfortunately, the programs offer too little to be more than band-aid measures. They also operate only for short periods of time as pilot projects, which ensures that there is no commitment of funds beyond a one- or two-year period. In addition, the programs are generally designed only to meet the needs of middle-class Aboriginal people. Finally, the independent structure of programs reflects a lack of wide-ranging, integrated federal policy (Knight, 1978).

The Aboriginal participation rate in the labour force is about 20 percent lower than the national rate. And it has been estimated that, of those who do participate, over 12 percent will remain permanently unemployed. However, these figures should be approached warily. The criteria that determine the active labour force are largely based upon White, middle-class values and include only those Aboriginal persons who have worked or looked for work during the past week. Moreover, because primary and unskilled jobs are extremely susceptible to seasonal factors, the time of year has a disproportionate impact on the Aboriginal employment rate. Nevertheless, even taking these factors into account, Aboriginal unemployment is still three times higher than the national average.

Because Aboriginal people usually work at seasonal or part-time jobs, they have little job security. And even in seasonal jobs, they are often discriminated against. La Rusic (1968) found that highly skilled Indian men employed by mining-exploration companies as line-cutters and stakers never received the same high pay or good working conditions that non-Indians received. Thus, the low income of Aboriginal workers reflects both the seasonal nature of their jobs and discrimination. The results show that once Aboriginal persons are able to enter the labour force they do quite well, although less so than the general population (Siggner, 1986). In 1995, almost one-third of the working Aboriginal population worked in sales and service, compared to one-quarter of the non-Aboriginal population. As the Second Diagnostic on the Health of First Nations and Inuit report pointed out, occupations in sales and service accounted for a little over two-thirds of the 25 lowest-paying occupations in Canada. Management, on the other hand, accounted for almost half of the top-paying fields, and the proportion of Aboriginal workers in that field was about 1.5 times lower than the non-Aboriginal workforce. Health occupations and jobs in natural and applied sciences are the next two most frequent occupations in the 25 highest-paying occupations (see Table 4.3). The Aboriginal labour force in those two categories was half of the non-Aboriginal workforce.

EDUCATION

Canadian culture places a great emphasis on the value of education. Education is generally seen as essential to success; young people who do not show academic potential are usually regarded as early failures. Certainly, education has a great impact on lifestyle and life chances. Yet, for a variety of reasons, not all Canadians are able to use the educational system as effectively as possible. Aboriginal people in particular are excluded by several factors from the benefits of Euro-Canadian education. The *Indian Act* allows the minister to provide educational services to Indian students from ages 6 to 18 who are living on-reserve or on Crown land. In addition, post-secondary education is encouraged through grants made to eligible Aboriginal students (Knight, 1985).

The federal government does appear to have fulfilled its responsibility to Aboriginal people in the area of financing for education (Frideres, 1972). Federal expenditures for Aboriginal education were $13.5 million in 1956 and $52 million in 1967; by 1980 they reached well over $270 million, or 39 percent of the total Indian–Inuit Affairs budget. The total education budget in 1991 was estimated to be nearly $900 million and, in 2002, the Department spent $1.068 billion in elementary/secondary education and an additional $300 million on post-secondary education. Today this represents less than 20 percent of the Department's total budget. During the 1970s, the number of students increased nearly 2 percent annually, to almost 100 000 students. (Today there are about 120 000.) In 2003, the government committed $35 million to deal with recommendations that were presented by the Indian Affairs National Working Group on Education. These figures demonstrate that expenditures per student more than doubled between 1981 and 1993. In 1993 the per capita expenditure was $7212, representing an average annual growth rate of 7.1 percent. By 2002, the per capita average had increased to over $11 000 per year.

In comparison, over the past five years the federal government contributed over $7 billion to the education of non-Aboriginals, for activities that are not within the federal jurisdiction (i.e., education).

Because of the increased number of high school graduates, more and more Aboriginal students are attending post-secondary educational institutions. In 1988, just over 14 000 students were registered in a post-secondary institution. By 2002 this number had increased to approximately 26 000. From a modest $2.5 million budget in 1981, the post-secondary budget increased to over $298 million in 2002. Bands, or their educational authorities, administer more than 80 percent of the primary/secondary education budget. The number of Aboriginal students receiving assistance more than quadrupled since 1981 to an estimated 25 000 in 2000. In addition to helping individual students, the post-secondary education program funds the Indian Studies Support Program and special institutions such as the Saskatchewan Indian Federated College (now called the First Nations University of Canada, in Regina). Recognizing the importance of post-secondary education, the federal government committed an additional $1.2 billion for a five-year (1991–1996) period. In 2003, the government created a $12 million endowment for scholarships for Aboriginals who want to go on to post-secondary schools.

However, less than 5 percent of this money has gone directly to Aboriginal communities to be controlled by Aboriginal people themselves. Most has been spent on the creation of various federal administrative and bureaucratic positions, or on capital grants to provincial and local governments to purchase "seats" in non-Aboriginal schools. In each province, the curriculum used in Aboriginal schools is regulated by the province's government and is the same as that designed for White middle-class students in all the other public schools (Waubageshig, 1970; Ward, 1988). This process is now undergoing scrutiny.

Educational Curriculum

People see and make sense of the world in many different ways; they also see their relationship to the environment in different ways. Since this is so, they approach problems looking for different solutions, and they may process information differently in arriving at those solutions. Hence, the educational process has an important impact on people exposed to it. For those who accept and are able to utilize the process to its fullest, the results are positive. However, there are others who do not accept it or are otherwise unable to take maximum advantage of conventional educational methods. This suggests that some people who are exposed to our particular type of educational system may be mismatched with the teaching process. Any discrepancy between learning style and instructional methods will lead to inefficiency and possibly to failure on the student's part (Pask and Scott, 1971).

The present school system has been established on the premise that all members of our society are field-independent thinkers. To some extent, this may indeed be the predominant mode of thinking in our culture. However, some cultural groups do not promote this type of thinking and consequently find the present school system useless. Our best evidence suggests that Indian culture promotes a relational type of thinking (Weitz, 1971; see also the work of O'Meara and West, *From Our Eyes: Learning from Indigenous Peoples*). If such a statement is true, then the dismal educational record of Indian people should not come as a surprise.

Other experts in the field feel that the poor performance of Aboriginal students in formal education settings is a result of substandard schools and lack of reinforcement of education in the families. In addition, until recently the Aboriginal community did not place a high value on obtaining an education. Thus, these structural conditions make it extremely difficult for many Aboriginal people to achieve success in the educational system.

History of Aboriginal Education

For many years after Britain took control of Canada, Aboriginal education was controlled by the military, acting for the Crown. Then, legislation was passed in 1830 transferring the responsibility to the provincial or local governments (Special Senate Hearing on Poverty, 1970: 14, 59).

In general, European settlers were indifferent to Aboriginal education: a public fund was not established for this purpose until 1848. In some cases, European settlers encouraged the school enrolment of Aboriginal children in order to pressure the province to establish more schools. As the density of the non-Aboriginal population increased, however, Aboriginal education was increasingly ignored. Later, the federal government was reluctant to operate schools for Indians, and passed the responsibility to other, mainly religious, agencies. With the passage of the *British North America Act, 1867* Canada's Parliament was given the power to administer Aboriginal affairs, including education. In 1876 the *Indian Act* was passed, providing the legal basis for federal administration of Aboriginal education. In addition, most treaties signed after 1871 contained an educational commitment to maintain schools on the reserve and provide educational services when required.

Federal and provincial government policy on Aboriginal education can be considered in two phases. The first, from 1867 to 1945, has been labelled the "paternalistic ideology." Until 1945, Native schooling was "education in isolation." During this period, schools and hostels for Indian children were established, but scant attention was paid to developing a curriculum geared to either their language difficulties or their sociological needs. A few Indian bands established schools for their children on the reserves, but the majority of them had neither the financial resources nor the leadership to establish and operate their own schools. Provincial governments were too preoccupied with their own priorities to become involved in Indian education. Missionaries provided a modicum of services, but their "noble savage" philosophy effectively insulated the Indians from the mainstream of society (Special Senate Hearing on Poverty, 1970: 14, 59).

The second phase, from 1945 to the present, has been called the "democratic ideology" (Hawthorn et al., 1967). The second phase simply refers to the "open door policy" that enabled Aboriginal students to attend school off the reserve.

The paternalistic policy, whereby Aboriginal students were considered backward children, was adopted and perpetuated by various religious orders in Canada. After Confederation, the first schools for Aboriginal children were quasi-educational institutions set up by religious orders. Under Sections 113 to 122 of the *Indian Act*, the federal government could legally arrange for provincial governments and religious organizations to provide Aboriginal education. Four churches—Roman Catholic, Anglican, United, and Presbyterian—began to educate Aboriginal children in denominational or residential schools.[3] Of these, the Catholics and Anglicans have had the greatest impact on Aboriginal people in Canada, and continue to do so.

Education has traditionally been viewed by churches as the best way to acculturate Aboriginal people. The religious missionaries, who up until recently controlled Aboriginal education, were far more concerned with teaching useful, practical knowledge and skills. Because they felt that Aboriginal people would always live in isolation, the missionaries made no attempt to prepare them for successful careers in modern Canadian society. Instead, they concentrated on eradicating all traces of Aboriginal languages, traditions, and beliefs (Fuchs, 1970).

Because religious ideologies are fundamentally conservative, they discouraged protest and revolt on the part of the Aboriginal people. For example, Roman Catholicism holds that poverty is not a social evil, but is God's will. Instead of struggling against God's will, Catholics are encouraged to humbly accept their fates in order to ensure a place in heaven. Thus Roman Catholicism discourages social change, particularly that which involves force: in heaven "the first shall be last and the last shall be first" (Matt. 19:30).

Churches that operated schools were given land, per capita grants, and other material rewards for their efforts.[4] Often these grants resulted in the material exploitation of the Aboriginal peoples as churches pursued property and profits (McCullum and McCullum, 1975; Grant, 1996). Even today, the churches' continuing opposition to integrated joint schools, Aboriginal teachers, Aboriginal language use, and so on suggests a greater concern for their vested financial interests than for the quality of Aboriginal education. As Hawthorn et al. point out:

> We note that the greater the educational resources possessed by a church or the greater its investment in Indian education, the greater its anxiety to maintain the status quo. On the contrary, the faiths having the least material interests in Indian education are much more open to innovation. (1967: 61)

Well over half of Aboriginal Canadians today are Roman Catholic. A special joint Senate–House of Commons committee (1946–48) interpreted Sections 113 to 122 of the *Indian Act* to stipulate that, when the majority of Aboriginal band members belong to a given religion, members of that religion must be in charge of education in that school. This suggests that religious groups will continue to control many Aboriginal schools despite their proven antipathy to Aboriginal independence.

Residential schools were almost all built in rural locations, far from non-Aboriginal settlements. Contact between Aboriginal children and their parents was minimized. The schools were highly regimented and insisted on strict conformity. There were few adults and most of these were non-Aboriginal persons; as a result, normal adult–child relations could not develop. Few of the teachers were well qualified; they neither stimulated the children nor acted as positive role models. The average annual staff turnover was never less than 21 percent and often higher, particularly in later years.

In 1945, the "open door policy" was introduced, which allowed students to travel off the reserve to receive an education. This was a radical departure from the earlier policy of isolation, and residential schools began to decline in enrolment. Particularly since the early 1960s, the number of Aboriginal children attending residential schools has been drastically reduced. The unpopularity of these schools should come as a surprise to no one.[5]

Types of Indian Schools

Federal Traditionally, Aboriginal students could attend either federal schools or integrated (provincially/federally funded) joint schools. There were four types of federal schools: day schools; denominational (also called residential or religious) schools; boarding and hospital schools; and band schools. Day schools were the largest group under federal control. They were located on the reserve and provided education only for those who lived there, including the non-Aboriginal children of teachers.

Denominational schools were those operated by religious groups. Since the late 1930s DIAND (now INAC) has also operated residential schools, at first through the churches and then more directly. When day schools were established in 1950 for elementary education, residential schools began to provide secondary education only. Since the late 1960s the residential schools have been systematically shut down; as of 1987, there were only two operating in Canada.

Hospital schools provide classes for Aboriginal students in government hospitals, from the pre-school level through to adult education. Boarding schools are for Aboriginal orphans or children from broken homes, and may or may not be on the reserve.[6] All boarding schools are currently under government-financed church control, mainly Roman Catholic. Although these schools are technically integrated, they have a majority of Aboriginal students. At present, only eight federal schools remain in operation. Thus, for practical purposes, federal schools have been phased out of existence.

In 1961, over two-thirds of the Indian elementary and high school students went to federal schools. By 1966 this had dwindled to 52 percent, and by 1980 it had further decreased to 44 percent. Today, less than 2 percent of Aboriginal students attend federal schools. If we look at the current Aboriginal population, we find that nearly 14 percent of those aged 55 years or older attended federal residential schools. This percent decreases to 11 percent for the 45–54 year category; and for the 15–34 age group, the number who attended federal residential schools is just over 2 percent.

Band The creation of band schools emerged out of the political lobbying that Aboriginals participated in during the late 1960s and early 1970s. While these are technically federal schools, they have taken on an air of independence and largely manage themselves even though they receive federal dollars to operate. By 1973 the National Indian Brotherhood produced a document, *Indian Control of Indian Education,* which was later accepted by the federal government and adopted as official educational policy for Aboriginal education. This policy explicitly incorporated the principles of parental responsibility and local control. It was, for Indians, a time when they believed that they would become active participants in affecting their own educational experiences. The educational branch of Indian Affairs established guidelines and procedures for school transfers to bands and introduced a national formula-funding system for the allocation of resources for the band-operated schools.

By 1980, well over 100 band-operated schools were educating students. By 1990 the number had increased to 300. On average, the number of band-operated schools has increased by 15 each year. Today, there are 494 band-controlled schools. Band-operated schools make up an increasingly larger portion of the total Aboriginal student enrolment. Figure 4.11 shows the growth rate of First Nations schools. Table 4.4 shows the number of registered Indians enrolled in Kindergarten to Grades 12/13 by type of school. The information in Table 4.4 shows that over 60 percent of the primary and secondary school population attend First Nations (band) schools. Just over one-third attend provincial joint-integrated schools.

Provincial Integrated joint schools are not controlled by the federal government. Essentially, these are provincial schools that allow Aboriginal students to attend. The structure and curricula of these schools are not significantly different from those controlled by the federal government. The difference lies in the administration and financing. Although education is a provincial responsibility, the federal government pays each local school board a per diem fee for each Aboriginal child enrolled there.[7]

In 1963–64 approximately 55 000 Indians were enrolled in elementary and secondary schools. Of these, 59 percent were in federal day schools, 13 percent were in residential schools, and 1 percent were in hospital schools. The remaining 27 percent were attending integrated joint schools.

FIGURE 4.11 Number of First Nation Schools, Canada, 1992–93 to 2001–02

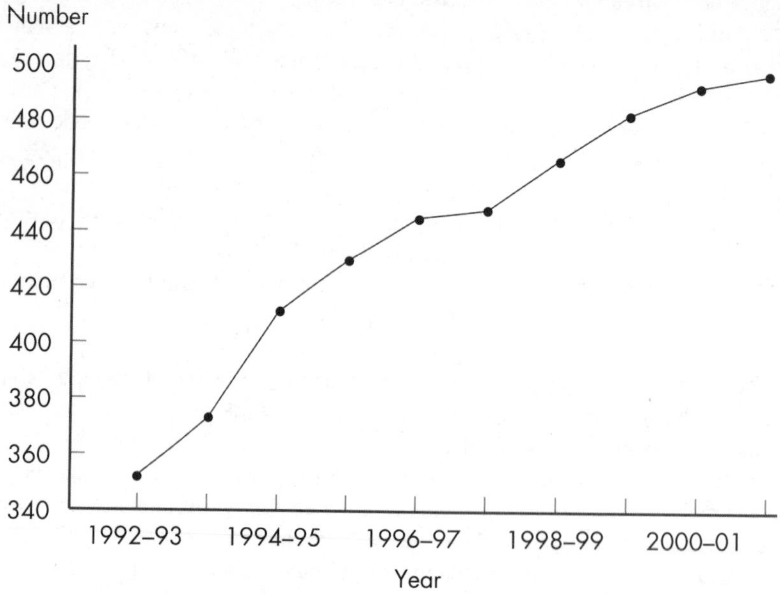

Source: In *Basic Departmental Data*, p. 40. Indian and Northern Affairs Canada, 2002.

Data from the Indian–Inuit Affairs Program (IIAP) show that from 1964 to 1981, over 800 agreements were made between local school boards and the Department of Indian Affairs in order to secure positions for Aboriginal children in provincial schools. Table 4.4 shows the relative trends for Aboriginal enrolment by all types of schools.

The data provided in Table 4.5 shows the historical increase in Indian enrolment from 1961 to 1991. The data also show that the percentage of school-age children attending school has increased. In the early 1960s less than three-quarters of the potential student population was attending school. This increased to a high of 93.5 percent in 1980/81, but decreased over the following decades. The decrease noted from 1980 to 1989 was a result of the government's change in policy regarding the funding of off-reserve Indians and the elimination of funds for off-reserve urban students to buy books and supplies. The decrease from 1991 to 2001 is a result of the number of registered Indians through *Bill C-31*. These young Indians do not attend a federal, band, or provincial integrated school but rather attend a regular provincial urban school. Thus, while the rate looks low, if these additional students are counted, the school participation rate is about 87 percent.

School Attendance: Primary and Secondary

Most Indian children used to attend federal schools until Grade 6 and then switch to provincial schools for their secondary education. Fewer than 10 percent continue in the

TABLE 4.4	Enrolment by School Type, On-Reserve Population, Canada, 1975/76-2001/02				
Year	Federal	Provincial	Band-Operated	Private	Total
1975/76	29 581	38 079	2 842	1 315	71 817
1977/78	29 412	41 358	5 639	1 679	78 088
1979/80	27 742	45 742	6 311	1 442	81 237
1981/82	22 525	43 652	13 133	1 156	80 466
1983/84	21 893	39 474	16 715	n/a	78 082
1985/86	19 943	39 712	20 968	n/a	80 623
1987/88	17 322	40 520	26 429	n/a	84 271
1989/90	11 764	41 720	34 674	n/a	88 158
1991/92	6 180	43 092	45 665	1 657	96 594
1993/94	3 453	44 331	53 747	2 548	104 079
1995/96	1 794	43 787	63 000	2 534	111 115
1997/98	1 773	43 943	68 250	2 340	116 306
1999/00	1 708	43 775	71 823	2 064	119 370
2001/02	1 656	43 420	72 457	2 041	119 574

Sources: In *Basic Departmental Data-1990*. p. 43, Indian and Northern Affairs Canada.

federal school system; this is partially due to a lack of federal secondary schools. In the 1950s and 1960s the federal government embarked upon a policy to phase out federal schools, and began by closing federal secondary institutions.

The switch from one school system to another has a serious disruptive influence on the educational and social development of Aboriginal children. The change in social milieu has the greatest negative impact. Initially, Aboriginal children enter federal schools as a distinct cultural group with a minimal knowledge of English or French. However, because they all share a similar social status, no one is at a disadvantage. When these students transfer as a group, the group is usually broken up and the individuals are sent to different provincial schools, where they become outsiders among Euro-Canadian students for whom English or French is the mother tongue.

Aboriginal students at provincial schools face considerable discrimination. On the reserve these students have already met indirect, institutionalized racism; however, as Lyon et al. (1970) have shown, Aboriginal students in integrated schools are exposed daily to direct discrimination from teachers and other students. In the long term, racism results in a serious and permanent distortion of the Aboriginal children's self-image. The more short-term effects of discrimination include lower marks and a tendency to drop out at an early age.

The competition for achievement is also greater in integrated schools than in federal schools. Aboriginal children, not used to the intense competition that exists among non-Aboriginal, middle-class students, may become psychologically uncomfortable and

TABLE 4.5	Enrolment in Kindergarten, Elementary, and Secondary Schools On-Reserve, Canada, 1960/61-2000/01		
Year	Enrolment[a]	Population 4-18 Years	Enrolment Rate
1960/61[b]	41 671	57 550	72.4%
1965/66[b]	54 670	73 632	74.2%
1970/71	68 449	81 531	84.0%
1975/76	71 817	88 660	81.0%
1980/81	82 801	88 581	93.5%
1985/86	80 623	92 080	87.6%
1986/87	82 271	94 169	87.4%
1987/88	84 271	95 336	88.4%
1988/89	85 582	96 606	88.6%
1989/90	88 158	97 751	90.2%
1990/91[c]	94 501	102 605	92.2%
2000/01	119 574	215 101	55.6%

Note: On-reserve includes Crown lands and settlements.
a. Total enrolment includes registered and non-registered Indians and Inuit in Kindergarten to Grade 13.
b. A breakdown of on/off-reserve Indian population was not available in 1960/61 and 1965/66. Based on 1975 Indian Register data, off-reserve was estimated to be 26 percent of the total population. Data also were not available for the 4-18 age population for 1960/61, estimated to be 42 percent of the total Indian population.
c. Data are based on population age 5-14, single response.

Sources: In *Basic Departmental Data-1990*, pp. 35, Indian and Northern Affairs Canada. And in *Basic Departmental Data-2002*, p. 36, Indian and Northern Affairs Canada.

begin to lose academic ground. Usually they do not receive adequate counselling prior to or following placement in integrated schools. Not surprisingly, these social disruptions eventually result in a high drop-out rate among Aboriginal students.

The rate of Aboriginal students attending school has shown a general increase over the past two decades. This is particularly true for the younger ages. For example, in the late 1960s only about 43 percent of Aboriginal children aged four to five went to Kindergarten. By the early 1990s this figure had increased to nearly 70 percent. Total enrolment in elementary/secondary school has increased by over 8 percent during the past seven years and, as noted earlier, about 85 percent of the youth now attend school. Table 4.6 reveals the total enrolment by level and sex. Similar increases are evident for older groups, but not at nearly so dramatic a rate. Overall, about 39 percent of Indians aged 15 to 24 are attending school full time, while over 44 percent of the general population is doing so. Looking at the issue from another perspective, the differences are clearer. More than half the Aboriginal students 15 years and older with less than a Grade 9 education are not attending school. The corresponding figure for the general population is 22 percent.

TABLE 4.6	Total Enrolment[1] by Level[2] and Sex				
School Year		Total	Kindergarten	Elementary	Secondary
1993/94	Total	103 644	14 545	59 070	30 029
	Male	53 084	7 472	30 428	15 184
	Female	50 560	7 073	28 642	14 845
1994/95	Total	107 091	14 945	61 178	30 968
	Male	54 852	7 657	31 724	15 471
	Female	52 239	7 288	29 454	15 497
1995/96	Total	110 642	15 441	62 676	32 525
	Male	56 583	7 943	32 460	16 180
	Female	54 059	7 498	30 216	16 345
1996/97	Total	108 914	15 237	62 653	31 024
	Male	55 834	7 776	32 602	15 456
	Female	53 080	7 461	30 051	15 568
1997/98	Total	109 542	15 262	62 547	31 733
	Male	56 032	7 969	32 466	15 597
	Female	53 510	7 293	30 081	16 136
1998/99	Total	110 687	15 048	63 519	32 120
	Male	56 423	7 792	32 968	15 663
	Female	54 564	7 256	30 551	16 457
1999/2000	Total	112 471	14 682	64 729	33 060
	Male	57 448	7 641	33 615	16 192
	Female	55 023	7 041	31 114	18 868

[1] Includes Registered Indians and Non-Registered (as approved by the Minister) individuals living on-reserve and Inuit students in Kindergarten 4 to Grade 13 (where applicable), inclusively.

Detailed information on students under the James Bay and Northern Quebec Agreement attending school in 1996/97 and 1997/98 are not available. In 1996/97 there were 3146 students without details not included in the above data, therefore the total enrolment was 112 060. In 1997/98 there were 6254 students without details not included in the above data, therefore the total enrolment was 115 796. In 1998/99, 6355 Inuit, Cree, and Nasapi students were not counted; therefore the total enrolment was 117 042. These numbers have been reported inclusively in Basic Departmental Data. The Nuu-Chah-Nulth Tribal Council in B.C. has negotiated a separate agreement with DIAND and therefore is not included in any total funded counts found in these tables. In 1999/2000, there were 380 Nuu-Chah-Nulth students not included in the above data. As well, 1999/2000, 6519 Inuit, Cree, and Naskapi students were not included; therefore the total enrolment was 119 370. These numbers have been reported inclusively in Basic Departmental Data. Excludes N.W.T from 1997 to 2000, Nunavut after 1999 and a portion of various Nisga'a.

[2] Grade breakdowns vary across regions. Kindergarten–K4 & K5 in all regions; Elementary–Grades 1-8, except Quebec (Grades 1-6); and Secondary–Grades 9-12 & Special Students, except Quebec (Secondaire 1-5) and Ontario (Grades 9-13).

Sources: Indian and Northern Affairs Canada, *Basic Departmental Data*, 1990, 37; 1960/61-1977/78: Statistics Division, Program Services Branch, DIAND; 1978/79-1989/90: Nominal Roll, Education Branch, DIAND; Overview of DIAND Education Program Data, 2001.

Successful school completion to Grades 12 or 13 is still much lower among Aboriginal students than among Canadians as a whole. In 1966 fewer than 5 percent of Indian students remained in school throughout the full 12 or 13 years. Although dramatic increases had occurred, the retention rates levelled off during the 1980s. However, since the mid-1990s the percentage of on-reserve students remaining until Grade 12 for consecutive years of school increased to 74 percent in 1997–98. When we compare these retention rates for the general population, we find that the rate is about 30 percent less.

Nevertheless, the trend shows a steady increase in the number of Indian students remaining in school, although in the past 10 years (when large numbers of band schools were established) the retention rate has doubled. While these figures reflect a positive impact of education, the data do not provide information on the number of successful graduates. Furthermore, there is some information that casts doubt on the above figures. While Indian students remain in school, they often do not receive a diploma or matriculation degree. The province of Alberta, for example, has had few Indian graduates from the regular provincial school system over the past decade. Nevertheless, an increasing number of students are attending high school and graduating (see Table 4. 7) although this rate is less than half the rate of graduation for non-Aboriginal population.

The reasons for the high drop-out rate among Aboriginal students are complex but at the same time straightforward. According to Castellano:

[T]he distorted reflection of himself which is presented to the Indian child is not even the chief source of the sense of incongruity which most Indian children experience in the White school system. Far more significant and handicapping is the fact that the verbal symbols and the theoretical constructions which the Indian child is [being asked] to manipulate bear little or no relation to the social environment with which he is most familiar. (1970: 53)

The Canadian educational system has been developed and refined by and for a White, urban, middle-class culture. This system becomes alien and meaningless in the context of life on a reserve (Fisher, 1969). The subject matter is largely irrelevant to the Aboriginal child's everyday life. And the curriculum is set firmly within a White, middle-class system of values, which bears little relation to local Aboriginal concerns. Classes are taught by teachers who are almost always non-Aboriginal and who seldom become involved with the local Aboriginal community. Furthermore, the competitive hierarchical structure of the schools is foreign to Aboriginal values. Not surprisingly, Aboriginal students are alienated from their educational system at a very young age.

Aboriginal students also have to contend with the poor image of themselves projected by the mass media, including films and books used in the schools. A study of social studies texts for Grades 1 through 8 revealed that Aboriginals were generally portrayed, if at all, as nonentities, evil-doers, or savages (Vanderburgh, 1968). These portraits have a serious impact on the personal development of Aboriginal children. As Kardiner and Ovesey (1951) have pointed out, people to whom negative traits are continually assigned will eventually begin to incorporate them into their identities. Someone who is continually called inferior will eventually believe it to be true.

Hawthorn et al. (1967), Elliott (1970), and others have argued that lack of parental support is an additional factor in the drop-out rate. However, there are many structural reasons for this. Not surprisingly, because Aboriginal parents have had no control over curriculum, textbooks, or staff, until recently they have come to regard the educational system as an "outside," racist institution, to be tolerated but not supported. In some provinces, Indians still cannot be school board members.[8]

Active adult community support for education will only develop when Aboriginal people who live on the reserve are allowed to hold teaching and administrative positions. To blame parental neglect for the high drop-out rate is naive: when all the structural variables are considered, the reaction of Aboriginal parents to the educational system is not apathetic but actively and understandably hostile (Battiste and Barman, 1995).

Quality of Aboriginal Education

The quality of Aboriginal education is determined by a variety of factors, including operation and maintenance costs, pupil–teacher ratios, the proportion of Aboriginal teachers, educational expenditures, and overall per-student education costs.

The pupil–teacher ratio provides some evidence as to the amount of time teachers can spend with individual students. Teachers in charge of a class of 27 have less time to deal with students than those operating in a class of 17. Federal schools have pupil–teacher ratios that are higher than in provincial schools. In addition, the educational qualifications of teachers in federal schools are lower than those evidenced in provincial schools. This partially reflects an unwillingness of teachers to teach on reserves and the ability of outstanding teachers to move to large urban areas. In the end, while all teachers have to meet minimum standards, many teachers on the reserves are considered unable to secure jobs elsewhere in the school system. In addition, since the creation of the band schools, teachers and the curriculum have been increasingly subjected to political battles that take place in the community. The proportion of Aboriginal administrators and teachers in federal schools more than tripled between 1966 and 2001, to over 36 percent. However, even though 90 percent of the teachers in Aboriginal schools have formal teaching credentials, only about 23 percent of the teachers are university graduates. In addition, reserve schools do not have the professional backup resources—for example, curriculum development specialists and language consultants—which are present in most provincial schools (Elliott, 1970).

In some fiscal years, additional monies are added to the educational budget. In 1984–85, for example, $7 million was used to deliver special education programs to those

TABLE 4.7	Percentage of High School Graduates Who Were Enrolled in Grade 12 or 13, On-Reserve Population, Canada, 1994-95 to 2000-01		
School Year	Enrolment	Graduates	Graduate Rate
1994-95	5743	1662	28.9
1995-96	5909	2001	33.9
1996-97	5618	1785	31.8
1997-98	5948	1975	33.2
1998-99	6036	1939	32.1
1999-00	6463	2072	32.1
2000-01	7063	2168	30.7

Sources: In *Basic Departmental Data*-2002, p. 38. Indian and Northern Affairs Canada.

Indian students identified as "hard to serve." This group of students includes those with some form of disability, including physical handicaps and perceptual difficulties. These funds enabled Indian and federal education authorities to develop and provide more appropriate programs for these students. This is an area that was identified as a high priority for Indian communities at the time, but it has since been deleted as priorities have changed. Five million dollars were spent in 1998–2000 to carry out urgently needed renovations to ensure that school facilities meet recognized health, safety, and energy conservation standards.

More recently, Indian Affairs commissioned a National Working Group on Education to look at ways to improve education for First Nations children and youth. The report *Our Children—Keepers of the Sacred Knowledge* made several major recommendations, and the Department has set aside funds to implement the recommendations. The question remains as to whether the funds set aside will be allocated to implement the recommendations or whether other priorities will take precedence.

Educational Attainment

In terms of financial aid, INAC appears to be providing adequate educational opportunities to Aboriginal students. Yet most Aboriginals attain only a low level of educational achievement. The following section presents data on the educational attainments of Aboriginal Canadians.

In 1981 (when systematic data was first collected), there was evidence of a major gap between Aboriginals and non-Aboriginals in every level of educational attainment. For example, 17 percent more non-Aboriginals graduated from elementary school than Aboriginals. Ten years later, this gap had been reduced to 10 percent. However, since this time, the gap has remained unchanged. An even larger gap existed between Aboriginal and non-Aboriginal people for high school graduation. In 1981 the gap was 23 percent, and by 2001 was reduced to just under 20 percent. Gaps between the two groups for successful completion of post-secondary education remain, although not as large as those above. These data show the changes (or lack thereof) that are taking place within both the Aboriginal community and all of Canada. Unfortunately, data from 2001 reveals a gap that is equal to that evidenced 20 years ago. Current data for the total population's highest level of schooling is shown in Table 4.8.

The data show that when compared to the overall Canadian rate, the educational attainment of Aboriginals is substantially less. In 1996, over half of the Aboriginal population aged 15 and over did not have a high school diploma, compared to one-third of the non-Aboriginal population. Less than 5 percent of Aboriginal people have a university degree, compared to 16 percent of non-Aboriginal people. Nevertheless, the current figures reveal an increasing trend for Aboriginal people to improve their educational attainments. For example, when comparing 1991 with 2001 the proportion of Aboriginal people in their twenties with a post-secondary degree or diploma increased from 19 percent to 23 percent. Those with a university degree or certificate increased from 3 to 5 percent. And during the period of 1981 to 1996, the proportion of Aboriginal people with less than a high school education decreased from 59 to 45 percent.

The highest level of education for Aboriginal Canadians and all Canadians is presented in Table 4.9. It shows the educational attainment for those above 15 years of age, as well as their income. The data show that Aboriginals have entered the educational arena,

TABLE 4.8

Female and Male Population 15+ Not Attending School Full-Time by Highest Level of Schooling, 1996

Female	Total Aboriginal	Registered Indians			Inuit	Métis	Other Aboriginal	Non-Aboriginal
		Total	On-Reserve	Off-Reserve				
Total – Highest level of schooling	333 990	135 805	60,035	75 770	9 400	51 320	137 465	9 860 985
Subtotal – Less than Grade 9	56 895	33 510	19 680	13 830	3 890	7 895	11 600	1 357 990
No schooling or kindergarten only	6 735	4 310	3 265	1 045	1 165	575	685	117 110
Grades 1–4	7 445	4 315	2 675	1 640	485	1 150	1 495	182 180
Grades 5–8	42 710	24 890	13 735	11 150	2 245	6 170	9 410	1 058 700
Subtotal – Grade 9–13	129 400	52 190	21 250	30 940	2 795	21 300	53 115	3 615 600
(%) With secondary school graduation certificate	29.4	20.4	17.2	22.6	18.4	29.0	38.9	45.2
Subtotal – Trades and/or other non-university only	99 655	35 425	13 805	21 620	2 275	15 600	46 350	2 774 280
(%) With certificate or diploma	70.5	67.6	69.0	66.7	62.6	69.7	73.4	77.6
Subtotal – University	48 040	14 675	5 300	9 380	440	6 520	26 405	2 113 110
(%) With university degree	42.5	34.0	30.3	36.0	30.7	37.2	48.7	59.2
Subtotal – Post-secondary education	147 695	50 105	19 105	31 000	2 715	22 120	72 755	4 887 395
(%) Incomplete – without degree/ certificate/diploma	38.6	42.2	41.7	42.5	42.7	39.9	35.6	30.4
(%) Complete – with degree/ certificate/diploma	61.4	57.8	58.3	57.5	57.3	60.2	64.4	69.6

(continues)

TABLE 4.8 Continued

Female	Total Aboriginal	Registered Indians			Inuit	Métis	Other Aboriginal	Non-Aboriginal
		Total	On-Reserve	Off-Reserve				
Total – Highest level of schooling	305 650	120 020	64 880	55 140	9 550	51 800	124 280	9 327 020
Subtotal – Less than Grade 9	56 135	30770	21 640	9 130	3 520	9 320	12 525	1 202 115
No schooling or kindergarten only	6 665	4 165	3 260	910	1 060	670	770	78 285
Grades 1-4	8 915	4 875	3 455	1 415	470	1 715	1 860	169 895
Grades 5-8	40 550	21 735	14 925	6 805	1 990	6 935	9 885	953 935
Subtotal – Grade 9-13	121 350	47 885	23 600	24 280	2 570	22 265	48 630	3 135 930
(%) With secondary school graduation certificate	27.0	19.8	15.5	23.9	16.5	26.2	35.1	40.2
Subtotal – Trades and/or other non-university only	92 380	31 880	16 170	15 705	3 115	15 455	41 930	2 787 690
(%) With certificate or diploma	75.6	71.1	71.3	70.8	73.4	77.9	78.4	81.5
Subtotal – University	35 785	9 480	3 465	6 020	345	4 765	21 190	2 201 285
(%) With university degree	43.9	28.1	20.3	32.5	30.4	37.6	52.6	64.7
Subtotal – Post-secondary education	128 165	41 360	19 635	21 725	3 460	20 220	63 130	4 988 970
(%) Incomplete – without degree/ certificate/diploma	33.3	38.8	37.7	39.8	30.9	31.6	30.3	25.9
(%) Complete – with degree/ certificate/diploma	66.7	61.2	62.4	60.2	68.9	68.3	69.7	74.1

Source: Adapted from the Statistics Canada "Aboriginal Survey," 2001.

although there is still a sizeable proportion of the population with less than a Grade 9 education. However, looking at the category of high school, Aboriginal people show a higher rate than other Canadians. But as the educational attainment level rises, the gap between Aboriginal and all Canadians increases.

Post-Secondary School Attendance

Indian Affairs also promotes post-secondary education for Aboriginals. It provides financial assistance and instructional support services. All Indians and Inuit who have been accepted in a post-secondary school qualify for financial support that covers tuition, tutorial assistance, books, supplies, and transportation. The cost of providing these services is just under $8000 per student.

Since the mid-1970s, the Aboriginal post-secondary enrolment has increased nationwide from 2500 to over 25 000. This reflects an increase from less than 1 percent to about 6 percent in the past two decades (for those in the 17–34 age group). Nevertheless, this is still considerably lower than the overall national rate of over 12 percent.

The data (see Table 4.10) show that, until recently, there has been a steady increase in the number of Aboriginal students receiving INAC funding and attending post-secondary institutions. The 1985–86 year shows a substantial increase because this was the first year in which *Bill C-31* Aboriginal people were redefined as Indians. These major increases provided the impetus for change in education policy regarding Aboriginal people, as well as for budgetary increases. More recent data show that the increase continues as the number of Aboriginal high school graduates continues to rise. INAC estimates that in 2000 there were over 40 000 Aboriginal students attending a post-secondary educational institution either full- or part-time (not including the northern territories). Roughly half of these students are taking non-university courses, while the other half are undergraduate students in a degree program. Less than 5 percent of the Aboriginal student population is seeking a graduate degree. In the late 1990s, the federal government cut back its financing program, and the number receiving INAC funding has therefore has decreased since that time.

TABLE 4.9	Education and Employment Income, Ages 15+, 2001		
INCOME			EDUCATION
	Percent	Percent	
Less than $10 000	10	31	Less than Grade 8
$10 000-$19 000	21	32	Some high school
$20 000-$29 000	20	6	High school graduate
$30 000-$39,000	19	24	Tech/vocational diploma
$40 000+	34	8	University degree

Note: The importance of education is seen by the nearly linear relationship between education and income. With one exception (college without a certificate), the average income increases with additional educational attainment.

| TABLE 4.10 | Full-Time Post-Secondary Enrolment Rates for Registered Indian Population Receiving INAC Funding, Compared to All Canadians, 1996–97 to 2000–01 |

	1996–97	1997–98	1998–99	1999–2000	2000–01
Registered Indians					
Enrolled full-time 17–34[1,3,4,5]	12 725	13 230	12 506	12 470	12 055
Population aged 17–34	196 290	198 114	199 098	201 229	204 740
Enrolment Rate	6.5	6.7	6.3	6.2	5.9
All Canadian Population[6]					
Enrolled full-time, aged 17–34[1,2]	884 123	912 200	921 068	N/A	N/A
Population aged 17–34	7 956 843	7 903 114	7 823 526	N/A	N/A
Enrolment Rate	11.1	11.5	11.8	N/A	N/A

Note:
1. Includes university and community college full-time enrolment for the Fall snapshot date. The age group 17–34 was selected because most students enrolled in post-secondary institutions fall within this age group. However, Indian students tend to be older than other Canadians when they enrol in post-secondary institutions.
2. Data from the University Student Information System (USIS) and the Community College Student Information System (CCSIS) of Statistics Canada.
3. Excludes N.W.T. (except UCEP) as they are funded by the territorial government. The University and College Entrance Program (UCEP) is a preparatory program and does not qualify as a post-secondary program.
4. Excludes Nunavut as they are also funded by the territorial government.
5. Estimates were used to calculate the enrolled Registered Indian population due to inconsistent reporting.
6. The enrolment rate for the Canadian Population has not been updated by Statistics Canada for 1999–2000 and 2000–2001.

Sources: Adapted from the Statistics Canada CANSIM database, http://cansim2.statcan.ca/cgi-win/CNSMCGLEXE, Table 510001, and the Statistics Canada "Aboriginal Survey," 2001.

With regard to supporting post-secondary education, INAC allocated $304 million in the 2002–03 budget. While this reflects a major increase in expenditures from 1990 ($170 million) and 1984 (only $50 million), the data shows that this represents about 6 percent of the total INAC budget, and this proportion has not changed for the past two decades (see Figure 4.12). Beyond the elementary school level, and particularly beyond the secondary level, the pattern of Aboriginal student enrolment diverges sharply from the Canadian norm. In 1981, fewer than 1 percent of Aboriginal persons attended university, as compared with nearly 7 percent of the general Canadian population. It seems clear that nearly all Aboriginal people who enrol in post-secondary training were being prepared for jobs at the semi-skilled level or lower (DIAND, 1978–79 Annual Report).

Figure 4.13 shows a dramatic increase since the early 1960s in the number of Aboriginal students attending college and/or university. A number of universities have tailored special programs to meet the interests and needs of Aboriginal students, while others have provided remedial services to assist Aboriginal persons who are entering university. However, even though the increase in Aboriginal enrolment has been rapid, the Aboriginal participation rate is still less than half the national level. For example, in 1975,

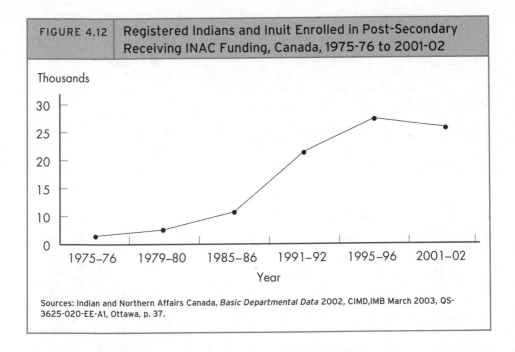

| FIGURE 4.12 | Registered Indians and Inuit Enrolled in Post-Secondary Receiving INAC Funding, Canada, 1975-76 to 2001-02 |

Sources: Indian and Northern Affairs Canada, *Basic Departmental Data* 2002, CIMD,IMB March 2003, QS-3625-020-EE-A1, Ottawa, p. 37.

20 percent of the Canadian population between the ages of 18 and 24 was enrolled in universities, while only 8 percent of the same-aged Aboriginal population was. Today we find that 6.6 percent of the Indian population aged 17–34 is enrolled in a post-secondary program, while for the non-Aboriginal group this rate is 11.4 percent.

Even more dismal than the enrolment figures are the statistics that reflect the rate of graduation from post-secondary educational institutions. In the 1967–68 academic year, 156 Aboriginal students were enrolled in universities in Canada. Of these, 17 percent withdrew voluntarily during the year, and 15 percent failed one or more courses, generally resulting in automatic exclusion under the terms of their special-entry program. The rest passed all their courses, but at the end of the program only 6 percent remained to graduate. These figures remained constant for the next decade. In 1970, 432 students were enrolled in universities and only 12 percent graduated. When we look at all Aboriginal students enrolled in post-secondary educational institutions, only 9 percent graduate, compared to a graduation rate of well over 18 percent for non-Aboriginal students (see Figure 4.14 for current graduate numbers). Clearly, an Aboriginal student's chances of finishing university are still quite small. For individuals having attended university, non-Indians are about 2.4 times as likely as Indians to earn a degree. However, while the success rate for Indians is lower than that of the general population, it is increasing. Language and cultural differences, as well as the effects of discrimination, have not been adequately addressed and continue to place Aboriginal students at a serious disadvantage in the university system.

While the participation rate in post-secondary education shows small increases, registered Indians' participation rate still lags behind the average Canadian rate. Aboriginal organizations have recently entered the arena of post-secondary education. Several major agreements have been signed in Western provinces. For example, the Nisga'a

FIGURE 4.13	University and College Enrolment of Aboriginals Between 1957 and 1995

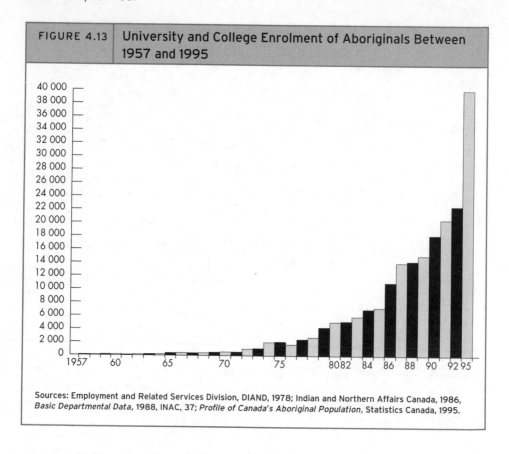

Sources: Employment and Related Services Division, DIAND, 1978; Indian and Northern Affairs Canada, 1986, *Basic Departmental Data*, 1988, INAC, 37; *Profile of Canada's Aboriginal Population*, Statistics Canada, 1995.

have contributed $250 000 to the University of Northern British Columbia to offer courses in the Nass Valley, the traditional home of the Nisga'a. To implement the program, the Wilxo'oskwhl Nisga'a post-secondary institute was created. The University of Manitoba also began offering social work classes to isolated First Nations communities. The University of Calgary's Virtual Circles Program is a similar arrangement that has been established for distance education in Alberta. In this program, instructors go to various First Nations communities to teach social work.

In Hobbema, Alberta, the community is investing $7.5 million in an attempt to provide Aboriginal people the first two years of a degree program. This move replaces the existing Maskwachees Cultural College and expands the course offerings. Red Crow College, in Cardston, Alberta, has linked with the University of Lethbridge to provide students with courses in the community and to offer the college's own courses that can be transferred to the university for credit.

The challenge facing Aboriginal communities today is to take control of the formal education process; however, there is nothing in the *Indian Act* that would give them any leverage in doing this. The minister of INAC has complete control over which schools students attend and over the nature of the contents of any education agreement. Aboriginal people have no right of appeal or review. Any change to the *Indian Act* would require action by Parliament, and the federal government has taken the position that it will not

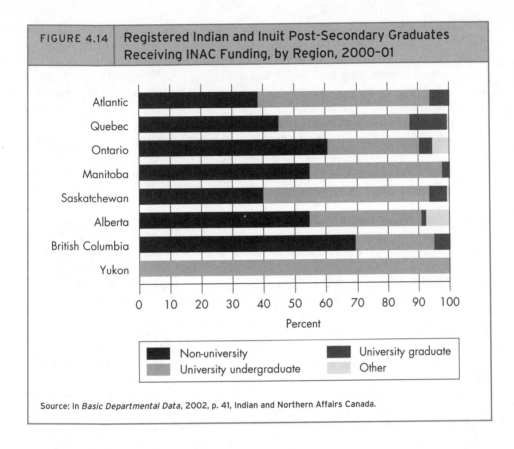

FIGURE 4.14 | Registered Indian and Inuit Post-Secondary Graduates Receiving INAC Funding, by Region, 2000-01

Source: In *Basic Departmental Data*, 2002, p. 41, Indian and Northern Affairs Canada.

amend the Act piecemeal, even though there might admittedly be some need for change. Hence, it is unlikely that the Act will be changed in the near future to allow for greater Indian control in matters of education (Barman, Hebert, McCaskill, 1987).

Even if the Act were changed, it is unlikely that Aboriginal people could take control of the education process. In the first place, the federal government has more trust in provincial school authorities (with regard to finances) than in Aboriginal people. Second, because the federal government does not operate an educational system, it relies on the provincial curricula and standards. Thus it is not interested in developing new approaches to education that would be appropriate or relevant to the diversity of Aboriginal communities (Longboat, 1987). Finally, INAC's education policy is developed and carried out by department officials; it is not a cooperative effort between Aboriginal people and the government. For example, even though the government adopted a stance acknowledging Indians' right to control education in the early 1970s, it added an important condition: any agreement that had been signed with provincial officials would be honoured until its term expired. In other words, local control of education would not be discussed until the terms of the agreement had concluded. Because most of the capital agreements (agreements to pay a percentage of the school board's capital and building costs) are 20- to 25-year contracts, Aboriginal communities will have to wait an entire generation before they can begin to discuss local control of their schools (Longboat, 1987).

From 1980 until today, there have been some major policy developments. Changes were made to the K–12 guidelines in 1987,[9] and the publication in 1988 of the Assembly of First Nations' National Review of First Nations Education brought about substantial changes in government programs. Earlier changes (1983) made it possible for Aboriginal students to obtain preparatory study prior to full-time entry into university. Aboriginal studies programs were created in the 1980s at various universities, which allowed Aboriginals to gain entrance to the schools under conditions different from those of non-Aboriginal students. These programs started small but they have grown in size over the years. Nevertheless, as universities continue to experience budget cuts, they are currently under review as "untraditional programs." Their vulnerability is exacerbated by the fact that few academic administrators are prepared to lobby for their continuance.

Overall, the educational attainment of Aboriginal people has increased over the past 20 years. These increases are a result of several factors. First, they are due in part to the increased number of band-operated schools. In 1997, almost all of the schools on reserves were administered by First Nations themselves, and many of these schools were secondary. Second, there has been an increase in federal funding for post-secondary education (from $109 million in 1987 to $274 million in 1997). Third, there has been a major expansion of Aboriginal Studies programs in 14 Canadian universities.

LIVING CONDITIONS AND QUALITY OF LIFE

"Living conditions" refers to specific objective factors that affect an Aboriginal person's ability to maintain a quality of life commensurate with that of other Canadians. This includes such considerations as the availability and quality of housing, and the provision of community services such as health care and welfare. As pointed out previously, the life expectancy of Aboriginal people is still much lower than the national average. Other indicators, such as the rates of suicide, violent death, and alcohol abuse, demonstrate a general increase in social problems and a lowering of the quality of life, especially among reserve Indians.

SOCIAL ASSISTANCE

Aboriginal people rely upon social assistance more than any other ethno-cultural group in Canada. Participation in social assistance programs is just one indicator of poverty. The data examined show that this reliance is increasing, even though a variety of economic development projects have been implemented. The extent of social assistance indicates both the quality of life of Aboriginal people and how well the economic programs are working. Table 4.11 shows the total social assistance expenditures for Indians from 1973 to 2003. The results show that the amount of expenditures has doubled over this time. In the past decade, the expenditures have nearly doubled again. However, even though the budget has doubled, the expenditure per recipient increased only by one-third. The average annual number of recipients per month has increased by nearly 30 percent over the past 10 years, and is now nearly three-quarters of a million people. When dependants of these recipients are added to the figures, we find that over 146 000 Indian people are receiving social assistance, at a cost of over $600 million per year. This expenditure represents a 30 percent increase over the 1990 level and is about 3 percent of the overall total Canadian social assistance budget. In addition, $570 million is allocated for social support services and an additional $205 million is earmarked for Aboriginal welfare services. Child and Family Services (78 percent) and Adult Care (22 percent) make up this program's budget. Expenditures per child in care increased at an annual average rate of 17 percent over the past decade ($28 138 in 1991). During the same period, adult care increased annually at 10 percent, from $12 000 to $28 250. Recently a Family Violence initiative was created, with a budget of $36 million. The funds are to be used to provide services to families on the reserve and for training of health and social service personnel.

TABLE 4.11	Social Assistance Expenditures, Registered Indian Population, Canada, 1973/74–2000/01				
Fiscal year	Number of Recipients[a] (current $)	Total Expenditures (current $)	Per Recipient (current $)	Total Expenditures[b] (81 constant $)	Per Recipients (81 constant $)
1973/74	n/a	53 319 000	n/a	112 014 706	n/a
1974/75	n/a	64 105 000	n/a	121 410 985	n/a
1975/76	n/a	73 023 000	n/a	124 825 641	n/a
1976/77	n/a	78 660 000	n/a	125 055 644	n/a
1977/78	n/a	85 753 000	n/a	126 293 078	n/a
1978/79	n/a	105 983 000	n/a	143 414 073	n/a
1979/80	n/a	122 004 400	n/a	151 182 652	n/a
1980/81	n/a	141 985 300	n/a	159 713 498	n/a
1981/82	39 146	165 030 100	4 216	165 030 100	4 216
1982/83	42 101	196 241 700	4 661	177 113 448	4 207
1983/84	43 750	216 157 600	4 941	184 434 812	4 216
1984/85	45 408	235 433 500	5 185	192 504 906	4 239
1985/86	48 494	255 288 200	5 264	200 698 270	4 139
1986/87	50 879	278 070 900	5 465	210 023 338	4 128
1987/88	54 170	314 446 000	5 805	227 529 667	4 200
1988/89	56 573	351 706 500	6 217	244 580 320[r]	4 323[r]
1989/90	59 680	390 017 600	6 535	258 289 801	4 328
1997/98	70 927	–	–	–	–
2000/01	72 465	–	–	–	–
2002/03	73 975	624 000 000	8 432	–	–

a. Excludes Indians residing in N.W.T. and Newfoundland.
b. The expenditures in constant dollars have been calculated using the Consumer Price Index based on the year 1981 from Statistics Canada.
r. Datum revised.

Source: *Basic Departmental Data*, 1990, Indian and Northern Affairs Canada, p. 57.

In addition to the above, in 2001–02, nearly 700 adult Indians were in institutional care, with a cost of over $17 million per year. This represents a ratio of 3.1 per 1000, which has decreased only slightly from 1971, when the ratio was 3.7 per 1000.

Since the mid-1970s, when the number of Indian children in care peaked at 6.5 percent of the total child population (age 16 and under), there was a decrease until the mid-1990s, when dramatic increases were evident. Nevertheless, today, just under 6 percent of the total Aboriginal children are under state care. As Table 4.12 shows, this represents about 9000 children in care facilities. The cost of child care has risen from just under $2 million in the mid-1960s to well over $100 million today—a sevenfold increase.

The number of Indians receiving social assistance has increased since the early 1980s. While the increase between 1981 and 1986 was from 16.5 to 17.8 percent, a similar increase for non-Aboriginal people was 6.2 to 7.9 percent. Nevertheless, these figures show that the rate of poverty for Indians is twice as high as for the general population.

The funds provided through social assistance enable Aboriginal people to maintain basic levels of health, safety, and family unity. They provide Aboriginal recipients with food, clothing, and shelter, as well as counselling to enable them to achieve independence and self-sufficiency. In addition to the social assistance program, Indian Affairs also offers welfare services to ensure that Aboriginals who need protection from neglect or who need help with personal problems have access to a variety of services (Canada, 1979b).

Overall, over half of the total Aboriginal population received social assistance or welfare payments in 2000. An even more astounding fact is that nearly 90 percent of Indians, at one time in their lives, have received social assistance/social support. These figures compare with 14 percent for non-Aboriginal people in 1999, and a lifetime non-Aboriginal experience with social assistance of 22 percent. There are regional variations in the numbers of social-assistance recipients. Both Aboriginal and non-Aboriginal people in the Maritimes have required social assistance and social welfare at much higher rates than elsewhere in Canada. Finally, it should be pointed out that most of the Aboriginals who have received welfare payments were employable. These facts suggest that social assistance to Aboriginal people is offered as an alternative to employment, not as a measure to help them enter the labour force and obtain wage labour. As the data show, there is an increasing number of Aboriginal people who seek social assistance and social welfare. These conditions have not reversed, which suggests that economic dependency will continue well into the 21st century.

Unemployment creates a need for social assistance that goes beyond simply providing funds for food and housing. A considerable number of studies have shown that an indirect effect of unemployment is its negative impact upon interpersonal relationships. Unemployment places considerable strain on individual relationships, including relations within the family. These interpersonal problems do not appear immediately, but develop slowly and come into full play when a person feels emotionally battered and unable to cope with other stresses (Lauer, 1989).

In summary, social assistance is a far more serious problem for Aboriginal people than for other social groups in our society. Structural factors have produced the problems that have forced Aboriginal people to become dependent on social assistance; yet most Canadians engage in a form of personal attack, implying or asserting that Aboriginal people themselves are the cause of their need for social assistance. Maintaining that Aboriginal people, as a group, have brought on their own problems

TABLE 4.12	On-Reserve Children in Care, Registered Indian Population, Canada, 1966/67–2001/02						
Fiscal Year	Children in Care*	Children aged 6 and under	Percent	Fiscal Year	Children in Care*	Children Aged 16 and Under	Percent
1966/67	3 201	93 101	3.4%	1978/79	6 177	94 866	6.5%
1967/68	3 946	93 484	4.2%	1979/80	5 820	94 414	6.2%
1968/69	4 310	94 616	4.6%	1980/81	5 716	94 916	6.0%
1969/70	4 861	94 698	5.1%	1981/82	5 144	94 608	5.4%
1970/71	5 156	95 048	5.4%	1982/83	4 577	96 105	4.8%
1971/72	5 336	94 777	5.6%	1983/84	4 105	98 379	4.2%
1972/73	5 336	94 906	5.6%	1984/85	3 887	97 586	4.0%
1973/74	5 582	94 634	5.9%	1985/86	4 000	99 213	4.0%
1974/75	5 817	96 960	6.0%	1986/87	3 603	101 841	3.5%
1975/76	6 078	96 493	6.3%	1987/88	3 836	101 537	3.8%
1976/77	6 247	96 417	6.5%	1988/89	3 989	102 529	3.9%
1977/78	6 017	96 780	6.2%	1989/90	4 178	105 992	3.9%
				1990/91	4 352	109 165	4.0%
				1991/92	4 504	111 050	4.1%
				1995/96	5 299	135 704	3.9%
				1997/98	6 220	139 564	4.5%
				1999/00	7 762	148 664	5.2%
				2001/02	8 828	150 646	5.9%

* The total number of children in care calculated by Social Development Branch is obtained by dividing the total number of case-days by 365. Child care cases do not include preventive and alternate approaches to child and family services (e.g., homemakers). Excludes Indians residing in the N.W.T. and Newfoundland.

Sources: Adapted from the Statistics Canada publication, "Social Security, national programs," Catalogue 86-201, 1978, and Catalogue 86-511, 1981/82, 1989/90, and the Statistics Canada "Aboriginal Peoples Survey," 2001.

draws our attention away from dealing with the structural problems preventing them from fully participating in Canadian society.

At the same time, Canadians appear to be largely in agreement that our "social charter" requires that we provide assistance to people unable to attain an adequate quality of life. Yet we provide that assistance grudgingly and not without comment, while failing to try to solve the underlying conditions that brought about the problem.

CONCLUSION

As we have seen, Aboriginal people in Canada reside in scattered communities and are divided by geographical boundaries, cultural differences, and legal distinctions. However, Aboriginal Canadians do share one common feature: across Canada, they lead marginal lives characterized by poverty and dependence. Indeed, many people argue that Aboriginal people are members of a culture of poverty. They are alienated from middle-class Canadian society not only through Euro-Canadian racism but also through the destructive mechanisms whereby one class profits at the expense of another.

The position of Aboriginal Canadians in today's society is not the result of any single factor but of complex historical and contemporary events. The alienation of Aboriginal Canadians began with historical subjugation and subsequent economic displacement. This was followed by a failure to recognize and guarantee certain inalienable Aboriginal rights.

The subjugation and control of Aboriginal Canadians has been continued through a process of individual and institutional racism. The federal government has neglected to consult with Aboriginal peoples concerning their welfare, has failed to develop and finance effective programs to assist Aboriginal persons, and, at times, has actively prevented Aboriginal people from becoming organized in pursuit of their rights. The political organization of Aboriginal people has also been hindered by the factionalism that has developed within different segments of Aboriginal society. All these factors, and others, have led to the marginality of Aboriginal people in Canada.

Both Aboriginal people and government officials decry the poverty and associated ills that currently face Aboriginal people. Since 1960 considerable efforts have been made to raise the social and economic status of Aboriginal Canadians. INAC has substantially increased its expenditures and attempted to develop a new philosophical perspective through which to solve the "Indian Problem." But, as the data presented in this chapter have illustrated, the efforts of INAC have not been successful. Although Aboriginals have achieved some absolute gains in income, education, and occupational level, they continue to fall further and further behind other ethnic groups in Canada.

Despite the statistics provided above, little seems to have been done to redress or correct the problem in any significant manner. It should not come as a surprise then that Aboriginals feel hostile toward our justice system. Aboriginal people's contact with the legal system has brought about an experience that not only denies them their self-esteem but also contributes to their dysfunctional state, leaving them unable to cope with the legal system in particular and with mainstream Canadian society in general.

NOTES

1. Statistics Canada defines "mother tongue" as the language a person first learns in childhood and still understands.

2. The data show how many percentage points each group is over or under its representation in the general labour force. That is, if ethnicity were not a factor in occupational placement, the proportion of each ethnic group in every occupational category would be the same proportion of that group to the total population. For example, if Aboriginals made up 1.2 percent of the total population, they would make up a similar percentage in each occupational category. Ideally, the over-/underrepresentation should hover around zero.

3. Denominational schools are founded and operated by a particular religious group. Residential schools are also denominational.

4. Religious schools receive a fixed amount, proportional to the number of pupils, for the administration, maintenance, and repair of their buildings.

5. See Caldwell (1967) and the Canadian Superintendent (1965).

6. All of these schools were funded by the federal government but operated by religious orders.

7. In certain provinces, such as Nova Scotia, the Department of Indian Affairs has a master agreement with the province concerning payment for Aboriginal students in provincial schools.

8. This policy of exclusion is now under review. Aboriginals now use school committees to communicate their desires and objections. These committees are set up by the band council and authorized to act on behalf of the Aboriginal community, but under regulations drawn up by Indian Affairs.

9. These are written documents produced by the government of Canada outlining the policy and programs designed to deal with Indian educational issues, such as funding, building of schools, eligibility of students, etc. (for Kindergarten to Grade 12/13).

WEBLINKS

www.ayn.ca/band_home.asp

The Aboriginal Youth Network is an organization dedicated to the creation of a dynamic community nationwide.

afn.ca/Programs/Residential%20School%20Issues/Default.htm

The legacy of residential schools for Aboriginal students is documented on a special part of the Assembly of First Nations' website. It includes discussion of ongoing court cases and an analysis of the needs of victims of abuse.

chapter five

The Canadian Justice System:
The Tragedy and the Travesty

INTRODUCTION

Aboriginal people find themselves in conflict with Canadian law in many different contexts. One result of such conflict is that, while Aboriginal people make up less than 3 percent of the total Canadian population, they make up nearly 40 percent of the prison population. At the same time, approximately 35 percent of the Aboriginal population report having been the victim of at least one crime in the preceding year. Once they come into contact with the justice system, they are disproportionately represented on the court dockets, disproportionately represented in the jails, and less likely to obtain parole than their non-Aboriginal counterparts. This chapter will focus on the justice system in Canada and how it deals with Aboriginal people.

While we will focus on the legal consequences of this conflict, it should be noted that not all conflict is dysfunctional for society. As social scientists have pointed out, conflict can also play an important positive function for society. It can teach us where the boundaries are between right and wrong and thereby establish what is acceptable behaviour. It also allows minorities to take on roles that they normally would not be able to assume and thus formalizes the process by which they are able to publicly articulate their concerns, i.e., they can interact with the dominant group as equals. Finally, conflict situations bring social issues to the public foreground and force people to address them (Schmeiser, 1974).

The conclusion of this chapter is that many Aboriginal people are losing confidence in the courts and the justice system, which are unable to respond to their needs and goals. They are also finding it difficult to support a system that seems to disenfranchise them each step of the way. They argue that law is unresponsive to their needs, and that the remedies prescribed do not deal with the issues as experienced by their people.

CONFLICT

As Black (1998) points out, conflict emerges whenever anyone provokes or expresses a grievance—whenever someone engages in conduct that another individual or group defines as inappropriate and requires an agent of society to respond. This relational concept reveals that conflict is not the opposite of order, nor should these two concepts be viewed as opposite ends of a continuum. Moreover, the responses to conflict may vary from polite admonishments to more harsh responses, such as prison or death. Finally, the issue of who responds and under what conditions needs to be assessed (Nielsen and Silverman, 1991).

With their domination of Aboriginal peoples in the 18th century, Euro-Canadians began to define right and wrong behaviour. As they solidified their control over the social character of Canadian society, some of their definitions became paramount and took on the status of "law." In short, conceptions and discussions of right and wrong were based upon a Euro-Canadian perspective, and all other behaviour would be defined and dealt with in terms of this definition. Moreover, those conceptions also would define the responses toward "correct" and "wrong" behaviour. Once a social issue was characterized in one particular way, the institutional order of the dominant culture established appropriate organizations and structures to maintain and legitimize that characterization. For example, as the Law Commission (1999) points out, once the police define behaviour as a criminal offence, the individuals involved in the action are powerless to change that definition. The decision on how to proceed to resolve the "conflict" is built into the structure of society, and rules are established as to how to deal with the resolution. For many years, the definition of right and wrong was a fixed assessment by Canadians, as they took their Euro-Canadian perspective as the only one to be used in judging people's behaviour. It has only been in the recent past that Canadians have begun to accept the idea that definitions of right and wrong are not fixed, and that other cultural perspectives may have some validity (Robertson, 1988).

From an Aboriginal perspective, the current definitions of deviance are a means by which the relationships of unequal power are maintained by Euro-Canadians (Canada, 1999). Moreover, Aboriginal people believe that the law has been ineffective in controlling or reducing the amount of crime committed by Aboriginal people. They believe both that once Aboriginal people are defined as criminals or charged with an offence they will re-offend, and that the justice system will fail to deter or rehabilitate offenders. In fact, some would argue that prisons make some offenders more prone to commit crimes when they are released (Canada, 1999).

EURO-CANADIAN VIEW OF JUSTICE

When Europeans first set foot on what is now Canadian soil, they found a rich and complex Indian culture. While social and formal norms were part of this society, the intruders refused to acknowledge or act upon indigenous values or social structures. As Jefferson (1978) points out in his history of legal concepts among Aboriginal peoples, most Aboriginal societies had well-developed rules with regard to "deviant" behaviour in their community. While the definition would vary from one group to the next and the penalties for violating social norms varied, the concept was in force. Children were instructed in the customs and rules of their society, and violations were dealt with in an appropriate manner. Justice was most refined in the Iroquois Confederacy (Five Nations) and was formalized by a constitution recorded on wampum belts to preserve the social relations over generations. If this society had such a well-developed system of justice, how was it that the early immigrants were unable to see it or to understand it? As noted earlier, with predetermined definitions, the settlers were simply able to define Aboriginal values and organizations as inappropriate or irrelevant. Moreover, with the lack of understanding of the culture or the language, it is unlikely that many settlers fully understood the full range of the Aboriginal justice system.

From the earliest contact between the settlers and the Aboriginal people, it was clear that settlers' rule would prevail (Jefferson, 1978). As such, representatives of the government such as Indian Agents, Superintendents, and Commissaries were given power to act as legal magistrates in dealing with Aboriginal issues. By the late 1800s, the North West Mounted Police were created to maintain law and order. To effectively enforce the dominant view of reality, the police were given the right to arrest, prosecute, judge, sentence, and confine persons residing in the Northwest Territories. While the police implemented these actions, they had not created the laws or regulations. Nevertheless, by this time, it was evident that no other view of reality mattered, as only actions condoned by the dominant society could be defined as acceptable behaviour. In short, the social transformation had occurred!

ABORIGINAL INVOLVEMENT

While there were virtually no differences between Aboriginal and non-Aboriginal people with regard to their contact with the police for things such as seeking information or traffic violation, Aboriginal people were more likely than non-Aboriginals to have had contact with the police for what are considered to be more serious reasons. For example, they were more likely to come into contact with the police as victims of crime (17 percent vs. 13 percent), as witnesses to a crime (11 percent vs. 6 percent), and by being arrested (4 percent vs. 1 percent).

It has been suggested that when Aboriginal peoples of Canada were given the unconditional right to vote (1960), this created a climate of cultural and political revival, a renaissance in Aboriginal culture (Jefferson, 1978). One year later the National Indian Council (representing all Aboriginal peoples) was formed to give a united and uniform voice to Aboriginal issues. Later in that decade, the federal government introduced the White Paper (1969) that would have shut down the Department of Indian Affairs and done away with the *Indian Act* if it had been enacted. This White Paper brought a degree of solidarity among Aboriginal groups and fostered the notion of Aboriginal self-help. It is ironic that the first Aboriginal self-help social movements in Canada were developed within prisons. Prisoners of Aboriginal descent were acutely aware of their minority status, and they realized that the only people who would help them were other Native inmates. The development of these social organizations drew inspiration from the American Indian Movement as well as the Black organizations that were so evident in the United States.

The First Indian Brotherhood was formed in Stoney Mountain Penitentiary in Manitoba and comprised status Indians (later, all inmates of Aboriginal ancestry could join). While this first organization was recognized by the Commissioner of Penitentiaries, it was not until 1975 that the Commissioner of Penitentiaries officially recognized it as a viable self-help program. The central focus of activities for this and other groups was on cultural awareness and pride in Aboriginal identity. As Jefferson (1978) points out, the Brotherhood focused on leadership training, public speaking, cultural pride, and self-awareness. It also provided Aboriginal inmates with some protection against discriminatory treatment, either by other inmates or by the staff of the institution. While the role of alcohol has been a major force in Aboriginal people coming into contact with the law, it was not until the mid-1970s that alcohol counselling programs were supported by the government.

Today, almost every federal and provincial correctional institution has Aboriginal Brother/Sisterhood organizations operating. While these organizations work within the correctional system, there is little outside the system to help Aboriginal people integrate into the larger society once they leave the correctional system. This problem arises due to jurisdictional wrangling as to who has responsibility—federal or provincial governments.

It has been argued for many years that Aboriginal people need to be involved in the administration of justice. Today, after more than a quarter-century since the first self-help program was implemented, the dominant bureaucracy maintains control of the policy, direction, and staff of the justice system (Canada, 1969a).

Early programs such as the Band Constable policing system lasted only a few years. Less than 1 percent of the police force is Aboriginal. While a small program to encourage Aboriginal people to join the Royal Canadian Mounted Police was implemented, it was phased out by the late 1980s. Although national data are unavailable, detailed information about Alberta was made public in The Report on the Task Force on the Criminal Justice System and Its Impact on the Indian and Métis People of Alberta, 1991. This report showed that only 2.5 percent of the RCMP employees were Aboriginal. The representation of Aboriginal people in municipal police forces was even less—1 percent. In provincial jails, only 2.7 percent of the employees were Aboriginal, while at the federal level Aboriginals made up only about 4 percent of Correctional Services of Canada employees. Today, 10 years later, the profile has not changed significantly. The Special Indian Constables (as part of the RCMP) are the only major vehicle by which Aboriginal persons come into contact with other Aboriginal persons in the context of justice. However, even under such a program, Band Councils are not involved in the operation of the program. Governments and Native organizations have failed to show interest in incarcerated Aboriginal people or in dealing with them once they are released (Canada, 1973).

ABORIGINAL-EURO-CANADIAN CONCEPTIONS OF JUSTICE

The differences in the principles involved in the administration of justice between Canadians and Aboriginal society are vast. The dominant society bases its laws upon a modified version of the British tradition of Common Law and principles. Aboriginal society reveals that the exercise of power was tempered by the expression of public opinion and that the family was the basic social, economic, and political unit for inspiring and restoring peace. Table 5.1 identifies the highlights of the two systems. Aboriginal people have a desire for community harmony, and they avoid confrontation and adversarial positions. They are reluctant to show emotions and are generous in sharing. They have traditionally used ridicule, avoidance, shaming, and teasing to maintain order and community harmony. Conflicts arise when Aboriginal values mix with the Canadian justice system. Judge Murray Sinclair claims that the legal concept of innocence/guilt is not granted the same importance by Aboriginal culture as it is in the Canadian criminal justice system. In an Aboriginal community, guilt is usually secondary to the central issue that something is wrong and has to be fixed. The main concern in Aboriginal communities is not to punish a wrongdoer but to restore the harmony that existed before the violation of the norm.

TABLE 5.1	Canadian vs. Traditional Native Justice	
Anglo-Canadian Justice	**Traditional Indian Justice**	
• laws formulated by elected representatives	• laws formulated by the community through tradition and consensus	
• laws tied to man-made economy	• laws tied to the natural environment, only a few universally condemned actions	
• Protestant Ethic and Christianity the moral foundation of the law	• traditional Indian religions the foundation of Indian codes of behaviour	
• personal offences seen as transgressions against the state as represented by the monarch	• personal offences seen as transgressions against the victim and his/her family; community involved only when the public peace threatened	
• law administered by representatives of the state in the form of officially recognized or operated social institutions	• law usually administered by the offended party, e.g., the family, the clan	
• force and punishment used as methods of social control	• arbitration and ostracism usual peacekeeping methods	
• individualistic basis for society and the use of the law to protect private property	• communal basis for society, no legal protection for private property. Land held in trust by an individual and protected by the group	

While not all of the above cultural elements have continued today, there are still enough differences in the two cultures that pose problems for Aboriginals who come into conflict with the law. The legal philosophy, the offences, and the court procedures are often the root of the problem, and this is compounded when Aboriginals find themselves in an urban context. In addition, language difficulties, ignorance of the law, poverty (particularly the inability to pay fines), and lack of education add to the disadvantage of Aboriginal people when facing the justice system (Hylton, 1981). When the laws have benefited the dominant society, they have been relentlessly applied; when the laws have not been to the advantage of the dominant group, they have been openly defied. Such is the case when one group has power (Hagan, 1974).

ABORIGINAL VICTIMIZATION AND JUSTICE ASSESSMENT

While over one-third of Aboriginals surveyed in the 1999 General Social Survey of Canada claimed to be a victim of crime during the past year, only about one-quarter of the non-Aboriginal population made such a claim. Moreover, Aboriginal people are twice as likely to be victimized more than once in a year (19 percent) than their non-Aboriginal counterparts are (10 percent). In addition, Aboriginal people are more likely to be victims of violent crime, as identified in Figure 5.1.

What is surprising is that the fear levels of crime and violence among Aboriginal people are relatively low. When asked whether or not they felt safe walking alone in their neighbourhood after dark, almost 90 percent of Aboriginal people said that they did. Sixty percent were not worried when using public transportation alone in the evening.

When asked how they evaluated the behaviour of the police, the courts, and prisons, Aboriginal people were less satisfied and more critical of police than their non-Aboriginal counterparts. They were less likely to rate the police at doing a good job in a number of areas: being approachable and easy to talk to, ensuring the safety of citizens, enforcing the laws, supplying information on ways to reduce crime, and responding promptly to calls. On the other hand, they were more likely than non-Aboriginals to assess the courts positively. With regard to the prison and parole system, there were virtually no differences in the opinions of Aboriginal and non-Aboriginal people, although they both were generally not very positive in their assessment. For example, approximately one-quarter of the sample felt that the prison system was doing a good job of supervising and controlling prisoners and only 14 percent felt that the system was doing a good job at helping prisoners become law-abiding citizens. Again, Aboriginals and non-Aboriginals were similar in their assessment of the parole system. Only 16 percent felt that it was doing a good job at releasing offenders who are not likely to re-offend.

INCARCERATION

Canada is one of the most frequent users of imprisonment as a means of punishment, compared to other Western, Asian, and Pacific countries. In Canada, members of minority groups

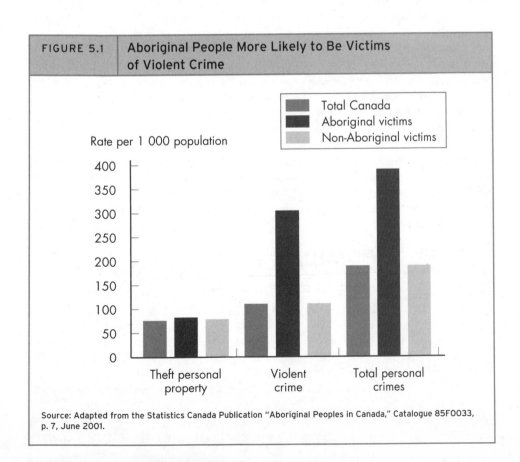

FIGURE 5.1 **Aboriginal People More Likely to Be Victims of Violent Crime**

Source: Adapted from the Statistics Canada Publication "Aboriginal Peoples in Canada," Catalogue 85F0033, p. 7, June 2001.

are 7 to 16 times more likely than non-Aboriginals to be imprisoned. One explanation is that these groups commit more imprisonable crimes than members of the dominant group. An alternative explanation, offered by Frideres and Robertson (1994), is that the justice system is racially discriminatory. Their data clearly show that Aboriginals are disproportionately suspects for homicides in every major city in Canada. At the same time, Aboriginals are victims of homicides well beyond their national representation within each of the cities.

The incarceration of individuals within a society emerges from two competing explanations. On the one hand, it is suggested that the agents involved in the administration of justice are the responsible forces. For example, if police bring fewer charges against individuals, the courts will have fewer individuals to deal with. And, if the courts are not content to send people to jail, there will be fewer individuals incarcerated. An alternative explanation is that social structural factors produce variations in the crime rate. For example, economic recessions are linked to the increased rate of crimes committed. Thus, this explanation argues that when there are structural changes in the society, more or fewer crimes will be committed. We suggest that both explanations form a more complete explanation as to why individuals commit crimes and why they are (or are not) sent to jail. It is important to point out that, for those Aboriginals sentenced to a federal jail, over half of the Aboriginal population have had at least one previous sentence to jail. In comparison, only 25 percent of non-Aboriginal offenders have had one or more previous sentences and less than half of the non-Aboriginal male population has had more than one previous jail sentence.

Aboriginal people are placed in prison at levels higher than their proportion in the general population. In Canada, 17 percent of the prison population is Aboriginal even though they represent less than 3 percent of the population. Within federal prisons, Aboriginal people make up between 10 and 13 percent, while in provincial institutions the rate is much higher. The data show that Aboriginal overrepresentation in prisons is greatest in the Prairies for both federal and provincial correctional institutions.

Table 5.2 reveals the 2001 inmate population in Canada, classified according to prison security level.

When the Aboriginal–non-Aboriginal ratio of sentenced admissions in provincial jails is reviewed, we find that Saskatchewan is nearly 25 times higher than the overall average; Manitoba is nearly 10 times higher, and Alberta is more than 7 times higher (see Tables 5.3 and 5.4). Aboriginal women are also disproportionately represented in admissions in comparison to non-Aboriginal women in all provinces. In a 1996 study it was found that females accounted for 5 percent of inmates on-register in Canadian correctional facilities.

TABLE 5.2	Level of Security of Prison Inmates by Sex, 2001		
Security	Men %	Women %	Aboriginals %
Maximum	14	9	16
Medium	59	40	62
Minimum	21	44	17
Not yet classified	6	7	5

Source: ©Her Majesty the Queen in Right of Canada. All rights reserved. www.csc.gc.ca/text/facts/facts07-content05.shtml, Correctional Service of Canada, 2003. Reproduced with the permission of the Minister of Public Works and Government Services Canada, 2004.

In provincial/territorial facilities, 7 percent of the inmates were women, and in federal facilities, less than 2 percent of the inmates were women. Nevertheless, Aboriginal female inmates accounted for nearly one-quarter of the female inmate population. In contrast, Aboriginal males accounted for 18 percent of the male inmate population. In the specific case of fine defaults, we find that Aboriginal offenders are disproportionately more likely than non-Aboriginal offenders to serve time. This simply reflects the poverty of Aboriginal people and their inability to pay fines imposed by the courts. Table 5.5 reveals the percentage of Aboriginal intake for both provincial and federal prisons. These numbers are to be compared to the overall population of Aboriginal people, which now stands at less than 3 percent.

We can debate the values of prisons and the appropriate amount of jail time for an offence. However, the data today do not show an association between prison time and deterrence. In other words, a greater reliance on imprisonment does not reduce crime rates. The results of today's research suggest that prisons are merely warehouses for the socially undesirable and that they focus on punishing the disadvantaged and marginalized.

Aboriginal Inmates

Aboriginal inmates are younger; have less education (48 percent in provincial correctional institutions and 56 percent in federal ones had less than Grade 9); are more likely to be unemployed (50–70 percent for Aboriginals compared to 40–47 percent for non-Aboriginals); and are from more dysfunctional families than non-Aboriginal inmates. The median age of Aboriginal provincial inmates is three years less than non-Aboriginal inmates (29 vs. 32) while in federal prisons, they are four years younger (31 vs. 35). On the other hand, Aboriginal inmates are similar to non-Aboriginal offenders in that they all have drug and alcohol addiction problems, poor upbringing/poverty, abuse and violence in their lives, as well as a lack of education, and are similar in the types of offences committed. Aboriginal offenders reflect the "revolving door" syndrome. Many are admitted to a

TABLE 5.3	Ratio of Aboriginal and Non-Aboriginal Sentenced Admissions		
Provinces	Aboriginal Sentenced Admissions Rate/10 000	Non-Aboriginal Sentenced Admissions Rate/10 000	Ratio of Aboriginal to Non-Aboriginal Sentenced Admissions
British Columbia	106	25	4.24
Alberta	681	94	7.24
Saskatchewan	522	21	24.85
Manitoba	194	20	9.7
Ontario	115	37	3.1
Average Rate	323	39	8.28

Sources: Population source 1991 Census; Sentenced Admission data taken from 1991 Provincial Data Sets, except for Saskatchewan 1993 data was used.

TABLE 5.4	Percent Remand and Sentenced Admissions and Total Aboriginal Population		
Province	Total Number of Offenders	Percent of Total Population that is of Aboriginal Descent	Total number of Provincial Offenders that are of Aboriginal Descent
Newfoundland	890	10%	89
Prince Edward Island	650	3%	20
Nova Scotia	1 507	7%	105
New Brunswick	1 555	7%	109
Quebec	14 372	2%	287
Ontario	31 980	9%	2 878
Manitoba	3 025	69%	2 087
Saskatchewan	3 410	77%	2 626
Alberta	15 164	38%	5 762
British Columbia	9 263	21%	1 945
Yukon	280	76%	213
Northwest Territories	562	90%	506
Nunavut	217	98%	213
Total Incarcerated population	82 875		16 840

Source: "Breakdown of Provincial Aboriginal Offenders (Admissions for 2001/2002)" adapted from the Statistics Canada publication, "Juristat," Catalogue 85-002, Vol. 23, No. 11, Adult Correctional Services in Canada, 2001-2002.

prison several times a year and it is estimated that 90 percent of all adult male Indians have been in jail at least once. Jackson (1992) found three kinds of Aboriginal inmates: traditional, bi-cultural, and assimilated. These groups differed in terms of their facility with the English language, time spent on the reserve/in the city, mobility, Aboriginal identity, and beliefs and practices (Métis and Non-Status, 1977). Table 5.6 reveals the attributes of the Aboriginal and non-Aboriginal inmate population in 2000–2001.

Table 5.7 reveals the admissions to custody over a 10-year time period. What is particularly disturbing is that the pattern of the percentage of Aboriginals in custody shows an increase over time. The data show that the problem of Aboriginal overrepresentation in correctional institutions and the criminal justice system seems unlikely to disappear.

Types of Offences   Given the social and economic position of Aboriginal people, it is not surprising to find that they are overrepresented in offences involving fine defaults, failure to appear for court, and breaches of probation. Table 5.8 shows the actual incidence as well as the percentage distribution for specific offences of Aboriginal and non-Aboriginal offenders. These data reveal remarkable similarities in types of offences, although there are some crimes unique to each group. With their lack of monetary resources, it is not surprising to find that Aboriginal offenders would run the risk of defaulting on their fines. With cultural differences and lack of resources, it also is no surprise that Aboriginal persons would find it difficult to deal with the urban courts. How does a poor person find his or her way from a reserve to an urban centre for a precise appointment the court has set without consulting the accused? On the more "serious" side of offences, we find that about 14 percent of Aboriginal people were charged with some form of murder, and 16 percent of non-Aboriginal people were similarly charged. However, when comparing the two groups on the crime "assault causing injury," we find that nearly twice as many Aboriginals have been found guilty as non-Aboriginals. The 1999 General Social Survey study found that Aboriginal inmates were incarcerated more often than non-Aboriginal inmates for crimes against a person (42 percent compared to 31 percent in provincial facilities and 79 percent vs. 72 percent in federal ones). On the other hand, the percentage of Aboriginal people charged with a "firearms" offence is about half that for non-Aboriginal people. Hann and Harman (1992) found that the charge against an Aboriginal person was most likely to be for a crime against a person, while for non-Aboriginal suspects the charge would involve a property offence. Table 5.9 reveals the major offences for Aboriginal and non-Aboriginal prisoners in 1998.

Sentence Length   In both federal and provincial cases, Aboriginal sentences are less severe than those of non-Aboriginals. This difference comes about due to the types of crimes committed and the seriousness of them as viewed by the courts. We find that the average federal sentence (excluding life sentences) for Aboriginal offenders is 3.57 years, while for non-Aboriginal offenders it is 3.72. What is more pronounced is the range of sentences exhibited in the two groups. Aboriginal people receive shorter sentences (average 3.4 years), but the range is 33 years. For non-Aboriginal persons the average is 4.3, with a range of 75 years. Thus, the variability of sentences for

TABLE 5.5	Aboriginal Inmates in Correctional Institutions by Region		
Region	Aboriginal Inmates in Provincial Institutions (% of all inmates)	Aboriginal Inmates in Federal Institutions (% of all inmates)	Off-Reserve Registered Indians (% of all Registered Indians)
Atlantic Provinces	3	3	33
Quebec	2	1	22
Ontario	8	4	46
Manitoba	49	39	34
Saskatchewan	68	52	46
Alberta	34	31	34
British Columbia	18	14	47
N.W.T.	91	37	21
Yukon	63	94	54

Sources: R. Boe, "Aboriginal Inmates: Demographic Trends and Projections, *Forum*, 2000, 12,1, p. 7.

TABLE 5.6	Profile of Prison Inmate Population, 2000-2001			
	Aboriginal		Non-Aboriginal	
	Male %	Female %	Male %	Female %
Age 20-34	58	66	47	56
Serving a first sentence	57	72	62	82
Length of Sentence				
< 3 years	21	39	19	36
3-6 years	33	22	31	27
6-10	17	17	15	12
10+	9	7	13	5
Life	20	16	21	19
Offence				
Murder-1st	4	1	5	4
Murder-2nd	13	13	13	15
1 (no sex)[a]	67	56	59	44
1 (sex)[b]	21	1	16	2
2 (drugs)	4	22	9	24
Non-violent	12	8	14	14

Note:
a. Schedule 1 excluding sexual offences
b. Schedule 1 including sexual offences

Source: ©Her Majesty the Queen in Right of Canada. All rights reserved. www.csc.gc.ca/text/facts/facts07-content05. shtml, Correctional Service of Canada, 2003. Reproduced with the permission of the Minister of Public Works and Government Services Canada, 2004.

non-Aboriginal offenders is nearly twice that of Aboriginal persons charged with a crime. The data also reveal a pattern that shows a larger percentage of Aboriginal people receiving short-term sentences (nearly always greater than non-Aboriginal persons), and this trend reverses as we move to the 10-year and longer sentences (Solicitor General, 1985). The data in Table 5.10 reveals the average sentences under different conditions. Motiuk and Nafekh (2000) show that the average sentence length of Aboriginal offenders was found to be shorter than for non-Aboriginal offenders at admission and release, in institutions, and on conditional release.

Provincial data show that Aboriginal persons receive sentences marginally shorter than their non-Aboriginal counterparts, but this is partly due to the less serious nature of their crimes. For federal cases, on the other hand, the seriousness of Aboriginal crimes may be considered high; however, their sentences are substantially shorter than for similar crimes committed by non-Aboriginal people (Solicitor General, 1989).

Aboriginal Youth and the Law Aboriginal youth face many obstacles as they grow up. They live below the poverty line, and their families have experienced violence, illness,

TABLE 5.7	Adult Correctional Services Survey, 1989–1999. Admissions to Custody by Aboriginal Status, by Selected Province					
	% Aboriginal					
Province	1989	1992	1994	1996	1998	1999
Newfoundland	11	6	7	9	6	6
Nova Scotia	5	4	3	4	5	4
Quebec	3	4	5	5	6	8
Ontario	4	3	5	7	7	7
Manitoba	43	43	55	47	47	n/a
Saskatchewan	56	58	58	56	61	63
Alberta	21	24	23	22	24	20
B.C.	15	17	15	16	16	17
Yukon	60	71	79	69	96	80
N.W.T.	91	93	n/a	n/a	n/a	n/a
Total Canada	13	12	13	14	14	13

Source: Adapted from the Statistics Canada publication, "Aboriginal Peoples in Canada," Catalogue 85F0033, June 2001.

and substance abuse. They have limited access to education or recreational facilities and they have limited occupational choices. On top of all this, they have to adapt to mainstream Canadian society while at the same time trying to learn and retain their traditional culture (Mount Pleasant-Jette, 1993).

Young Aboriginal offenders have a history of offences. Nearly 60 percent of the males and 40 percent of the females admitted to correctional facilities have had at least one prior offence. Nearly half of the males and one-quarter of the females have been under community supervision when admitted to correctional facilities. This leads us to question to what extent young Aboriginals are exposed to the justice system. Are young Aboriginals who come into contact with the police diverted to alternative measures of a non-judicial type? Alternative programs include such actions as financial compensation to a victim, community service, educational programs, and apologies that are related to the offence. In 1999, 4 percent of the youth population were Aboriginal, but they contributed to 15 percent of the alternative measures that were implemented—an increase of 3 percent from the preceding year. Aboriginal youth participation in alternative measures was particularly noticeable in Saskatchewan (making up nearly half of the cases involving alternative measures), and in Alberta and the Yukon. Nevertheless, as the Cawsey Task Force pointed out, between 1986 and 1989 only 11 percent of Aboriginal young offenders were referred to the alternative measures program, compared with 3 times that percentage of non-Aboriginal offenders. In addition, they found that Aboriginal youth offenders spend, on average, longer periods of time in custody than non-Aboriginal young offenders for the same offences.

TABLE 5.8	Specific Offence Type for Aboriginal and Non-Aboriginal Offenders, 1995				
	Aboriginal			Non-Aboriginal	
Offence	Percent of Aboriginal Offender Population*	N		Percent of Non-Aboriginal Offender Population*	N
1st Degree Murder	1.9%	46		3.1%	609
2nd Degree Murder	10.4%	259		10.8%	2 142
Schedule I					
Attempted Murder	1.6%	39		3.2%	640
Assault Causing Injury	28.4%	706		16.7%	3 296
Kidnapping	5.0%	125		7.3%	1 435
Sexual Assault	8.1%	202		7.3%	1 444
Sex Involving a Child	3.1%	78		3.7%	735
Firearms Offence	5.5%	136		10.4%	2 051
Robbery	25.3%	627		30.5%	6 042
Arson	0.6%	14		0.9%	185
Prison Breach	1.1%	28		1.4%	283
Schedule II					
Trafficking	4.6%	114		16.1%	3 176
Import/Export	0.2%	5		3.2%	635
Cultivation		0		0.4%	75
Money Laundering	0.04%	1		0.6%	121
Total Offences		2 630			23 860
Total Offenders		2 483			19 784
Percent of offenders that fit into more than one offence category	5.6%			17.1%	

* Percents are based upon the number of Aboriginal or non-Aboriginal offenders in each offence category divided by the total number of offenders in the specific column. Column percents will not total 100 because offenders can be in more than one offence category. For example, 16 Aboriginal and 359 non-Aboriginal offenders in the first degree murder category are also serving the same sentence for offences ranging from second degree murder to prison breach and cultivation.

Aboriginal youth admissions made up over one-quarter of the total admissions to remand although they made up only about 7 percent of the youth. This is particularly noticeable in Western Canada. For example, in Manitoba, nearly 70 percent of youth admissions into remand were identified as being Aboriginal, while these youth make up only 16 percent of the total population. In Alberta, one-third of the admissions were Aboriginal, while they make up only 6 percent of the total youth population.

TABLE 5.9	Main Offence Categories for Aboriginals and Non-Aboriginals, 1998

Population	North American Indian	Métis	Inuit	Non-Aboriginal
Institutional	11.6	4.2	1.0	83.2
Homicide	12.9	3.8	0.7	86.6
Sex	15.7	3.6	3.4	77.3
Robbery	9.8	4	0.2	96.1
Drug	6.1	3.3	0.2	90.0
Conditional Release				
Homicide	7.3	2.5	0.6	89.6
Sex	13.4	2.6	0.4	83.6
Robbery	6.7	3.6	0.2	89.5
Drug	4.7	2.6	0.2	92.5

Source: ©Her Majesty the Queen in Right of Canada. Motiuk and Nafekh, 2000, p. 13, Correctional Service of Canada, 2000. Reproduced with the permission of the Minister of Public Works and Government Services Canada, 2004.

We also find that Aboriginal youth are overrepresented in sentenced custody admissions. The data from the General Social Survey (1999) revealed that Aboriginal youth admissions accounted for nearly one-quarter of the total admissions to sentenced custody. In almost every province in the country (P.E.I. being the exception), Aboriginal youth were overrepresented. For example, in Manitoba, where 16 percent of the youth are Aboriginal, over 75 percent of the sentenced custody admissions were Aboriginal. A similar situation exists for Saskatchewan. When we look at probation, we find that Aboriginal people account for 14 percent of youth on probation.

Today, governments have recognized the importance of proactive approaches to crime, and they have tried to develop new policy designs and programs to meet the needs of First Nations youth. For example, diversion programs, bush camps, and Aboriginal youth justice

TABLE 5.10	Average Sentence Length by Aboriginal and Non-Aboriginal

Population	North American Indian	Métis	Inuit	Non-Aboriginal
Admissions	3.57	3.24	3.92	3.72
Releases	3.94	4.11	4.12	4.41
Institutional	5.06	5.16	4.95	5.75
Conditional Release	4.07	4.43	4.28	5.47

Source: ©Her Majesty the Queen in Right of Canada. Motiuk and Nafekh, 2000, p. 13, Correctional Service of Canada, 2000. Reproduced with the permission of the Minister of Public Works and Government Services Canada, 2004.

committees have been established to deal with Aboriginal youth offenders as an alternative to their entering the criminal justice system.

Explanations   Why are Aboriginal people overrepresented in our prisons? Early theories claimed that they were genetically prone to commit crimes. Later, cultural theories emerged that linked the disparity between Aboriginal culture and the dominant society as the basis for Aboriginal people committing more "crimes." Today, Braithwaite (1990, 1993) argues that social integration is the best explanation for why Aboriginal people seem to violate the law. He notes that the degree to which an individual is linked to significant people and institutions, such as schools, jobs, and family, will determine the extent of deviant behaviour exhibited. These structural factors impinge upon an individual's social conscience and are an external source of direction in regulating an individual's behaviour. Since individuals of lower socio-economic status or those operating in an anomic state are not as linked to the middle-class structures, they have less control. In addition, lower-class individuals or those experiencing anomie are more likely to experience dysfunctional families, lack steady employment, and be more marginalized than any other group. Aboriginal people living in the inner core of large major urban centres are characterized by these structural linkages (Canada, 1978b).

Braithwaite notes that the greater the degree of interdependency and integrativeness of people, the lower the levels of deviant behaviour. His argument is that "shaming" is a reintegrative process that allows for the criminal to seek forgiveness and be accepted back into the community. As Aboriginal people continue to be marginalized and anomic, their level of integrativeness with either their own community or that of the dominant society has decreased over time and continues to block the effects of integration. The result is that the Aboriginal offender is unable to find a community into which he or she can integrate. Aboriginal people have lost their social sense of community; even reserves reflect trends of the dominant society in that they are becoming communities that reveal extreme social and economic cleavages preventing the development of a caring, integrative social unit. This social dislocation and economic stratification within Aboriginal communities does not allow for either formal or informal social control mechanisms to be effectively implemented. In addition, the diminishment of the family and group authority on the reserve has created social and economic divisions between individuals and families, and has had a profound impact on the socialization of the young (LaPrairie, 1996).

Is there a difference in the number of urban and rural Aboriginal people committing criminal offences? The Cawsey Inquiry (1991) showed that about 6 percent of the Aboriginal persons charged with a criminal offence in Alberta were living on a reserve at the time they were charged even though two-thirds of the Aboriginal population reside on reserves. McCaskill (1985) found that over two-thirds of the federal and provincial prisoners from Manitoba lived in urban areas when they were charged with an offence. Johnston (1997) found that at the time of offence for federal prisoners, about one-quarter were originally from a reserve or remote rural area, 44 percent were from a rural area, and 30 percent were from urban areas. Why? It may be as simple as the level of police coverage. In rural areas there is far less coverage than in urban centres and thus offenders are more likely to be caught in urban areas. Other explanations are that crimes in urban areas are more likely to be reported or detected, e.g., public disturbance (Nuffield, 1998).

The propensity of Aboriginal people to participate in crime in urban areas is partially a response to different social structures. On the reserve, because everyone knows everyone intimately, there is a built-up tolerance for each individual. An individual's behaviour is always judged in the historical context in which the individual grew up, as well as the contemporary conditions in which he or she operates. Thus, if an individual engages in deviant behaviour, the community will tolerate it if it is widely known that the individual came from a particular background and is experiencing a set of conditions that are judged as temporary. While this tolerance has limits, over time the rationale and boundaries of acceptable—as well as unacceptable—behaviour widens. In the urban context, this tolerance is considerably reduced and others are unwilling to judge the individual's behaviour in any historical or contemporary context.

Nevertheless, LaPrairie (1998) points out that reserves are not the peaceful and cohesive communities that are sometimes portrayed. Many reserves are characterized as high crime areas that have high unemployment and demonstrate many other indicators of social disorganization. In some cases, interpersonal violence has become accepted behaviour if the circumstances are understood by the community. When the individual moves into an urban centre, there is a radical change in the level of tolerance, and thus many Aboriginal persons who exhibit normative behaviour on the reserve are called to the attention of the police in urban areas.

REHABILITATION

What happens to the individual once he or she is placed in jail? Are Aboriginal and non-Aboriginal inmates treated differently? Are there differential rates of correctional rehabilitation? Overall, the impact of rehabilitation in prison seems minimal, irrespective of the individual's ethnicity. Antonowicz and Ross (1994) point out that their research finds only 20 effective programs implemented over the past two decades. Others argue that methodological issues such as measuring "success" are problematic and need to be reconceptualized. For example, if recidivism is a measure of success (or lack thereof), it does not measure any other increases in the individual's "well-being" that might have been brought about through the program, e.g., community reintegration, family interaction. In addition, others who continue to commit crimes but are not caught are not accounted for in the statistics.

Overall, correctional institutions are notoriously poor in implementing rehabilitation programs for any inmates, Aboriginal or not. Why is this so? Correctional officials are security conscious, so any program that compromises or potentially compromises this issue will be viewed negatively. Other reasons include a general distrust of the inmates by the prison officials, a disbelief that the program will help inmates, and a lack of resources to implement the program of rehabilitation. Bonta et al. (1992) argue that other factors, such as the nature of the programs and the population identified to be part of the program, are responsible for low success rates.

On the other hand, there have been some successes, and these seem to have focused on linking the prisoner with his or her community, e.g., school, family, social service agency, neighbourhood organization. This involves significant community input and participation in the programs directed toward the inmates. LaPrairie (1996) points out that successful programs are properly administered and implemented. She also finds that program efficacy is an important element in a successful program. Her research concludes that programs taking a social cognitive approach are the most effective. It has only been since the 1970s that correctional institutions have come to accept the claim that

Aboriginal people in prison need special attention. Prior to this time, they were considered similar to the general inmate population and were provided programs and therapy similar to those offered other prisoners. However, as the overrepresentation of Aboriginal people in jails became increasingly evident and a general acceptance took hold among the Canadian population that Aboriginal people were "different," correctional institutional officials began to develop special programs to deal with them. Because of the politics of sovereignty, self-government, and the acceptance of "cultural differences," Aboriginal people have been partially successful in getting institutional officials to develop special Aboriginal programs for inmates.

As noted previously, the Native Liaison Support System was the precursor of today's Native Liaison Program, which operates in both the provincial and federal correctional institutions. Now evident in prisons are programs that are cultural and/or spiritual in nature, with a focus on reintegrating the offender into the home community. In 1987 a federal policy on "Native Offender Programs" was instituted and it also established the Task Force on Aboriginal Peoples in Federal Corrections to examine how an Aboriginal person is processed through the correctional institution. Today, the policy objectives related to Aboriginal offenders in prison focus on each institution developing Aboriginal-specific programs to replace "regular" programs for Aboriginal inmates and take into account both the culture and language of the Aboriginal people. The *Corrections and Conditional Release Act* notes that all prisons should provide a range of programs to deal with the needs of Aboriginal prisoners and contribute to their successful reintegration into the community. Under the new policy, Correctional Services Canada can transfer care and custody of Aboriginal offenders to an Aboriginal community or organization. Advisory committees that counsel federal bodies on Aboriginal issues have also been created. Finally, the Act established the office of the Corporate Advisor, Aboriginal Correctional Programs, to act as a catalyst for Aboriginal programs and to liaise with Aboriginal communities (LaPrairie, 1996).

While most provincial correctional institutions have the same programs and policies as noted above, Ontario, Alberta, and British Columbia have gone one step further by identifying Aboriginal justice branches to support provincial correctional institutions. Programs such as Traditional Spiritual Practices, Aboriginal Literacy, Aboriginal Cultural Skills, Sacred Circles, Native Awareness, Sweat Lodge Ceremonies, and Aboriginal Language programs are evident as one moves from one institution to another. In this respect, provincial jails do not have the consistency that is found in federal jails, but they do consider regional variations in developing specific programs for Aboriginal people. In addition, provincial correctional institutions have hired Aboriginal people and required staff to take courses on cross-cultural training. Specific programs that have been developed include the Search of Your Warrior Program, developed by the Native Counselling Services of Alberta. This program focuses on violent criminal behaviour and is implemented in the Prairie, Pacific, and Quebec regions. The Mama Wi Program is a family violence treatment program that is currently being implemented in the Prairie region. A national Aboriginal offender pre-orientation program has been developed to increase inmates' preparedness to benefit from other programs offered by Correctional Services Canada and to determine cultural and criminogenic needs and start the education of Aboriginal offenders about corrections, Aboriginal heritage, and healing opportunities. Finally, a national Aboriginal healing program that identifies traditional cultural methods of living in balance is being developed in collaboration with Native Court Workers and the

Aboriginal Healing Foundation. Thus far, 23 Aboriginal specific programs have been identified (13 federal, 10 provincial) (Epprecht, 2000).

Correctional Services Canada has now taken a position that it is committed to providing reintegration programs that are responsive to the needs of Aboriginal offenders. However, it is agreed that while the Aboriginal-specific programs are successful, there are many other social and economic factors that need to be dealt with if the prisoner is to successfully integrate into his or her community or larger society. Solving a specific problem is the outcome of the program, but securing the total "well-being" of the individual once released from prison is more than the specific program deals with. The results of evaluations of this program also demonstrated that Aboriginal inmates have fewer personal and social skills than non-Aboriginal inmates on a number of dimensions (Ellerby, 1995).

RETURNING TO SOCIETY

We now turn to the issue of what happens when the inmate is being considered for release. First of all, prison officials need to carry out a risk assessment if the inmate is not up for statutory release. Parole officers generally carry out risk assessments to determine if an individual can be released into community supervision. The data show a difference between Aboriginal and non-Aboriginal offenders applying for release on full parole. Twelve percent more Aboriginal offenders who were released on parole were defined as high-risk, compared to non-Aboriginal offenders released on parole. A similar assessment was evident for offenders on statutory release. As a result, fewer Aboriginal offenders are eligible to be released to community supervision than non-Aboriginal offenders.

Who actually gets released or paroled? It has been argued that the reason for the high rate of Aboriginal incarceration is that Aboriginal offenders do not get early release from prison. The Task Force on Aboriginal Peoples in Federal Corrections assessed data from the early to late 1980s, and found that Aboriginal inmates are indeed less likely to be released on parole than non-Aboriginal inmates are. The difference was substantial: the rate of release by the late 1980s showed that non-Aboriginals were twice as likely as Aboriginal inmates to be given parole. This assessment still holds true in the early years of the 21st century. Nevertheless, a more detailed analysis by LaPrairie (1996) shows that the difference arises because of the type of crime committed. The fact that Aboriginal offenders are more likely to have committed violent person-type crimes seems to explain the difference—and not racial bias in the system. In the end, Aboriginal people tend to spend more time in prison even though they may have received shorter sentences than non-Aboriginal offenders. Welsh (2000) carried out a study comparing Aboriginal and non-Aboriginal offenders at two stages of the full parole review process. He found that 6.3 percent of Aboriginals were given day parole, compared to 4.8 percent of non-Aboriginal inmates. On the other hand, only 18.3 percent of Aboriginals were given full parole, in comparison with 44.7 percent of non-Aboriginal inmates. Finally, nearly three-quarters of Aboriginal inmates were given statutory release, while only 50 percent of non-Aboriginals received such paroles. Welsh (2000) found that Aboriginal offenders are far less likely to apply for full parole than non-Aboriginal offenders are. This probably reflects Aboriginal distrust of the correctional system. Second, he found that when Aboriginal offenders apply for full parole, they are less likely to be granted release.

Nevertheless, it is important to point out that Aboriginal inmates are considered to be at higher risk to re-offend than non-Aboriginal prisoners and to have higher needs than non-Aboriginal inmates. Nearly 60 percent of Aboriginal inmates in provincial facilities were classified as a high risk to re-offend, as compared to only 44 percent of non-Aboriginal inmates. In federal facilities, almost 70 percent of Aboriginal inmates were classified as high-risk, as compared to less than 60 percent of non-Aboriginal inmates. As for needs, each prisoner is assessed in terms of his or her needs when released. Seven needs are assessed in the conditional releases that take place. Overall, about half of the Aboriginal inmates are shown to have employment, personal/emotional, and marital/family needs. In addition, about one-quarter to one-third of these inmates have substance abuse, unsavoury associates, and lack of community functioning needs (see Table 5.11).

What happens to the offender once he or she is released into the community? The answer depends upon how well the individual has been integrated into his or her community. Risk factors associated with re-offending are unemployment, negative attitude toward probation, lack of permanent address, age, number and type of prior convictions, use of drugs, and family relations. Do recidivism rates between Aboriginal and non-Aboriginal people differ? A growing body of evidence suggests that Aboriginal recidivism tends to be higher than for non-Aboriginal groups. The answer seems to lie in the fact that Aboriginal people are higher in the risk category and thus tend to recommit crimes. Hann and Harman (1993) showed that the recidivism rate for Aboriginal people in federal jails (66 percent) was about one-third higher than for non-Aboriginal people. However, such a trend was not evident in a limited study of Ontario provincial jails.

The last step in the justice process is reintegration. How do offenders reintegrate into the community? In looking at the reintegrative process, we must note that there are two components to the equation: the offender and the community. Unless the community is prepared to accept the offender into the community, it is clear that the process will be difficult. At the same time, the offender must be prepared to take on the necessary skills in order to achieve reintegration. This, of course, is complicated by the type and nature of the crime

TABLE 5.11	Risk and Need Levels of Aboriginal/Non-Aboriginal Inmates	
	Aboriginal	Non-Aboriginal
Risk level		
Low	37.5	54.6
Medium	34.7	23.7
High	27.7	20
Need level		
Low	20.7	39.6
Medium	47	37.7
High	32.3	20.9

committed by the offender. Less serious crimes are less problematic for community members, while serious crimes leave the community members apprehensive and concerned about their own and their family's safety and security. In the end, a lack of reintegration assures that the offender will become a repeat offender, and the process spirals upward.

ALTERNATIVES TO IMPRISONMENT

Is there an alternative? What is the value of imprisonment? What are the costs to society? Many Canadians are uneasy with the tendency of our state to impose prison sentences on more and more people, particularly young offenders. Three possible strategies have been offered to deal with the growing prison population and the increasing tendency to deal with offenders by placing them in prison. The first is the use of alternative sanctions. These include fines, community service, home detention and electronic monitoring, close supervision, and boot camps. It has been argued (Junger-Tas, 1994) that these alternative sanctions ensure that the offender faces real punishment and retribution while, at the same time, society is attempting to keep the individual from repeating his or her crime. While such alternative sanctions have their supporters, there are many who are critical. They argue that these new sanctions widen the net of correctional controls over an increasing number of people. In the end, more people will be captured in the "net" and be labelled criminals. In addition, the cost of administration will far outpace the costs of maintaining prisons. They also argue that the fact that these types of social control mechanisms exist does not mean the courts will use them.

The second alternative to prisons is to increase the use of the existing community-based correctional resources. There are a number of different types of resources that are now being used: attendance centres, bush camps, home detention, and community correctional centres. Today, there are only two Aboriginal-specific community correctional centres in Canada: the Stan Daniels Centre in Edmonton and the Wasekun House in Montreal. However, Aboriginal people may use the services of other centres that are not Aboriginal-specific.

A third and highly controversial alternative is the use of local justice systems. While there is some acceptance of the community's role in the criminal justice process, there is no consensus as to what this role might be. Focusing specifically on Aboriginal systems, there are several examples across the country. Sentencing circles in the North, the Western provinces, and Quebec have proven to be highly controversial (LaPrairie and Roberts, 1997). This community-based program is a good example of a culturally sensitive approach to justice. Sentencing circles, which are Aboriginal forms of dispensing justice, gained the attention of the Canadian criminal justice system in the early 1900s within the Yukon Territorial Court. The concept involves the community hearing the evidence of an alleged crime and seeking input from all sectors of the community (defendant, perpetrator, and others in the community who have been affected by the alleged crime), after which the community decides on the appropriate sentence. This method is used only when the community requests such "court proceedings," the Crown gives permission, and the presiding judge gives permission to invoke this form of justice. At the same time, the entire process is monitored by a Canadian judge. The Community Holistic Circle Healing project in Hollow Water, Manitoba has been defined by both Aboriginal and non-Aboriginal people as a success. Other examples of local justice in Aboriginal communities are the Indian Brook Diversion project in Nova Scotia, the Toronto Aboriginal Legal Services project, and the Family Group Conferencing in Newfoundland (Jackson, 1992).

While most Canadians hold the court system in high regard, Aboriginal people tend to see the courts as a tool of oppression. Aboriginal people do not experience the courts as being accountable to their communities, nor do they see them as resolving disputes between parties. For Aboriginal people, justice can only be obtained thorough the establishment of day courts and justices of the peace. These courts would be staffed by Aboriginal people and would be a suitable compromise, allowing justice to be more equitably distributed. This arrangement would allow Aboriginal people to become more involved in the system. It is argued that in the adjudication of criminal offences, the involvement of elders and laypersons (as members of the Aboriginal community) would lend greater legitimacy to the process. And, in the end, their involvement would be more effective in resolving problems in the community (Indigenous Bar Association, 1990). As noted above, the Canadian criminal justice system is viewed by Aboriginal people as a foreign system not compatible with their way of life. Because of the difference in worldview, the Aboriginal cannot fully comprehend our dominant society's court process, nor can the courts fully understand the Aboriginal. For example, the difficulties of language incompatibility have been included in many Aboriginal claims that the court system does not adequately represent Aboriginal people. As the Alexander Tribal Government pointed out in its submission to the Task Force on the Criminal Justice System and Its Impact on the Indian and Métis People of Alberta, some members of the courts suffer from "cultural blindness." They are unable to see and hear the Aboriginal victims, the accused, and the witnesses who appear before them; Aboriginals lack a voice in the process (Cawsey, 1991).

Furthermore, Aboriginal people have pointed out that, because of the isolation of many Aboriginal communities, the provision of justice by our courts is viewed by them as serving the convenience of the judges and lawyers while inconveniencing community people. Aboriginal people have argued that, in isolated communities, the courts rush the process of justice so officials can return to their homes. Postponements of court appearances are also based upon convenience to the courts, not to the community. In short, few court hearings are held in Aboriginal communities, which supports the Aboriginal view that the courts are foreign institutions (Elias, 1976).

The right to counsel upon arrest is another issue of concern for Aboriginal people. For many Aboriginal people in remote communities, this right is meaningless because counsel is not easy to obtain. And, although police have the duty to advise people of their rights to silence and to consult a lawyer, they do not have to make counsel available. A 1989 study in an urban Canadian centre noted that over 60 percent of the Aboriginal defendants were with legal counsel. Thus, in urban areas, legal counsel is widely available and used, while in rural areas it is almost nonexistent. And, when legal aid is available for Aboriginals in these isolated communities, it doesn't begin until the actual court appearance. Our research has also found that, regardless of his or her criminal record or the type of offence with which he or she has been charged, an Aboriginal is more likely to be held in custody than to be released with a summons to appear.

Through persistent dialogue with various levels of government, Aboriginal communities across Canada have gradually begun to explore the possibility of administering various components of the criminal justice system. While this has been a slow process and many problems still exist within the current relationship between Aboriginal offenders and the judicial system, some progress is being made. The divergence between Aboriginal and Euro-Canadian values also has contributed to the high proportion of Aboriginals who are incarcerated.

Community Policing Guided by Traditional Teachings of the Medicine Wheel

By Jean Sayers

In our culture the medicine wheel teaches us that we have four aspects to our nature: the physical, the mental, the emotional, and the spiritual. Each of these aspects must be equally developed in a healthy, well-balanced individual through awareness and healing. As one aspect of a person's personality is changed in a positive way, the lives of everyone around that person are changed as well. This is also true when the changes in an individual's behaviour are negative. In many cases, negative behaviour is passed on, from generation to generation. To break this cycle, it is imperative that police officers and all social service agencies work together towards a common goal—the wellness of the individual and the community in which they live.

The Anishnabek Police Services (APS) adopted this philosophy as the foundation for an effective community-based peacekeeping that is holistic in nature. It differs in many ways from the traditional, strict law enforcement–policing model, historically in use in North America. The focus is to provide a peacekeeping service where our police officers can maintain visibility and communication, participate in community events and organize educational activities for the children and members. A police officer who stops during his shift to visit an elder or who has an opportunity to stop and chat with the kids in the playground can do much to improve the image of the police in the eyes of the community.

First Nations Justice

First Nations Policing Policy (page 2)
www.sgc.gc.ca/abor_policing/fir_nat_policing_e.asp

In June 1991, after extensive consultation with the provinces and territories and First Nations across Canada, the federal government announced a new First Nations Policing Policy. The Policy and Program are based on partnership between the federal government, the provinces and territories and First Nations working together to develop police services for First Nation communities. The goals of the program and policy are: to provide First Nations with professional, effective and culturally responsive First Nations police services; to improve safety and security in on-reserve communities; to give First Nations communities a strong voice in the administration of justice as they assume greater control and responsibility for matters that affect their communities; and to ensure that First Nations police services are accountable to the communities they serve.

The First Nations Policing Policy provides for a range of policing options to be available to First Nations communities including: stand-alone police services, developmental policing arrangements designed to smooth the transition from one type of policing to another, and special contingents of First Nations officers within an existing provincial or municipal police service.

Aboriginal Policing Directorate

The Aboriginal Policing Directorate is responsible for administering the First Nations Policing Policy and providing national leadership regarding the delivery of policing services for Aboriginal people off reserve. The mission of the Directorate is:

- to contribute to the development, implementation and maintenance of First Nations and Inuit policing services that are professional, effective, efficient and responsive to the unique needs of these communities; and
- to support the Solicitor General and the Deputy Solicitor General in the exercise of their respective responsibilities regarding First Nations policing and law enforcement.

The federal government pays 52 percent and the provincial governments 48 percent of the government contribution toward the cost of establishing and maintaining First Nations police services maintained pursuant to agreements under the First Nations Policing Policy. Today over 80 policing agreements have been implemented.

An independent review of the first five years of operation of the First Nations Policing Policy found the policy framework to be "relevant, sound and on-track." The review also found that provincial, territorial and most First Nations partners believe the tripartite process is the most effective way to address First Nations policing at this time.

On the strength of this review, the federal government reaffirmed its ongoing commitment to the First Nations Policing Policy, and approved minor changes to the Policy in the spring of 1996. The changes are intended to address suggestions raised in implementing the Policy and by the policy review.

WEBLINKS

www.usask.ca/nativelaw/jah_scircle.html

Often hailed as the example par excellence of adapting the conventional European model of justice to an Aboriginal context, "sentencing circles" often involve the offender, victim, and members of the community in determining the penalty for a crime. This is an excellent collection of information about sentencing circles.

www.usask.ca/nativelaw/jah.html

Justice as Healing is a newsletter that focuses on Aboriginal concepts of justice based upon Aboriginal knowledge and languages, and rooted in Aboriginal experiences and feelings of wrongs and indignities. It is published in an online format by the University of Saskatchewan Native Law Program.

www.soonet.ca/fncpa

For some Aboriginal communities, the face of justice is literally changing. Policing is, increasingly, managed by Aboriginal peoples. The First Nations Chiefs of Police Association website promotes First Nations police services.

chapter six

The New Crucible of Aboriginal Revitalization: Urban Centres

INTRODUCTION

The urban Aboriginal population is growing rapidly and has doubled in the past 10 years. Nearly half of the Aboriginal population currently reside in urban areas across Canada. As the presence of Aboriginals in urban areas becomes increasingly visible, new relationships between Aboriginals and non-Aboriginals are emerging. While this visibility has been evident for some time in some Western cities, it is now increasingly evident across the country. The increase in visibility is not just due to increasing numbers but is a result of the emergence of Aboriginal communities, businesses, institutions, and networks in urban centres. It also is a "relay point" between Aboriginal communities on the one hand and different First Nations on the other (Levesque, 2003). As a result, new ties are being forged between cities and rural Aboriginal communities. The growth in the numbers of Aboriginal people now living in urban centres has produced a major crisis for federal, provincial, and municipal level governments. Aboriginal people today are a visible presence in every city in Canada and their numbers continue to increase (Hanselmann and Gibbins, 2002). The Aboriginal presence in Western urban centres is particularly important as it is estimated that in 10 years, one-sixth of the labour force in Winnipeg, Saskatoon, and Regina will be Aboriginal (Mendelson and Battle, 1999).

The settlement patterns of Aboriginal people have come to be a major concern to all levels of government, social and non-government agencies, and Aboriginal leaders. However, governments at all levels have been hesitant to develop policy with regard to urban Aboriginal people. The central reason for this reluctance is that that there has been and continues to be a jurisdictional debate as to which level of government has legislative authority and responsibility for urban Aboriginal people. The federal government is quick to agree that it is responsible for all Indians who live on reserve or Crown land. However, the authority and responsibility for other Aboriginal people is subject to dis- agreement, and the federal government argues that the provinces have a primary (but not exclusive) responsibility for other Aboriginal people. The provinces in turn, have argued that all Aboriginal people are the primary responsibility of the federal government and that provincial responsibility is limited to serving Aboriginal people as part of the larger provin- cial population. The provincial governments have therefore not developed inclusive policy with regard to urban Indians (Hanselmann, 2001). The consequence is a "policy vacuum" that has resulted in urban Aboriginals being ignored. As the Royal Commission on Aboriginal People noted:

> First, urban Aboriginal people do not receive the same level of services and benefits that First Nations people living on the reserve or Inuit living in their communities obtain from the feder- al government.... Second, urban Aboriginal people often have difficulty gaining access to provincial programs available to other residents.... Third,... they would like access to cultural- appropriate programs that would meet their needs more effectively (RCAP, 1996,538).

The effects of urbanization on Aboriginal Canadians have not been adequately stud- ied, despite the concern expressed by various levels of government. This is due in part to a lack of data to support the claims of Aboriginal leaders and municipal and provincial government officials as to the issue's importance. Because urban Aboriginals are hyper- mobile and tend to blend into the general population of the urban poor, statistics are par- ticularly difficult to obtain; politicians, as well as academics, tend to concentrate their efforts elsewhere. However, the issue of urbanization has recently been brought to the attention of municipal, provincial, and federal governments by indirectly related issues such as social services, unemployment, and urban crime (Manuel and Poslums, 1974). In addition, the Royal Commission on Aboriginal Peoples did not forcefully address the issue of urbanization of Aboriginal peoples and thus further marginalized their participation in the political and legal processes now being employed by more traditional "land based" Aboriginal communities (Anderson and Denis, 2003).

When Hawthorn carried out his study of Aboriginal people in the 1960s, he predicted a major influx of reserve Aboriginals into major urban centres. He also went on to point out that when this happened, special facilities would be needed to deal with the process of social adjustment. This migration has been as massive as Hawthorn predicted, and as Figure 6.1 identifies, the proportion of on-reserve registered Indians has decreased from 71 percent in 1960 to only 58 percent in 2001. This "hyper-mobile" population has posed considerable problems for city planners and urban programs. By the mid-1980s this migration movement began to slow down and Siggner (1986) noted that, at the time, the mobility patterns of Aboriginals and non-Aboriginals were almost identical; nearly one-fifth of both groups lived at a different location than the one they had lived at 10 years previously. However, more recent data shows that the Aboriginal population is more mobile than the non- Aboriginal population. For example, Norris et al. (2002) observe that between 1991 and 1996, well over half of the Aboriginal population moved (compared to just 40 percent of the non-Aboriginal population. They note that the Aboriginal population living in urban centres is particularly mobile, and between 1991 and 1996, 70 percent of Aboriginal resi- dents moved, compared to just under 50 percent of the non-Aboriginal population.

As Aboriginal people were forced onto reserves, their social and economic structures became incapable of supporting a growing population. In addition, the process of enfran-

FIGURE 6.1	Distribution of Registered Indian Population On- and Off-Reserve

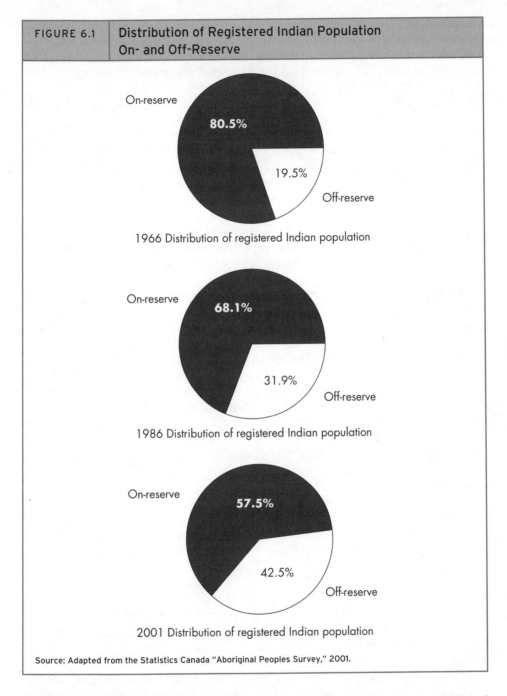

On-reserve

80.5%

19.5%

Off-reserve

1966 Distribution of registered Indian population

On-reserve

68.1%

31.9%

Off-reserve

1986 Distribution of registered Indian population

On-reserve

57.5%

42.5%

Off-reserve

2001 Distribution of registered Indian population

Source: Adapted from the Statistics Canada "Aboriginal Peoples Survey," 2001.

chisement moved individuals off the reserve and into urban centres. As the Aboriginal population continued to increase, greater demands on scarce resources emerged. Moreover, lack of job skills and low educational achievement kept Aboriginal people on the reserve. Unemployment was high and temporary farm labour was the only alternative form of work they found. However, after World War II, Canada shifted from a rural, agricultural economic system to an industrialized, urban society. As a result of this transition, Aboriginal people found themselves migrating to urban centres in larger numbers than before. For example, in Manitoba the urban Aboriginal population jumped over 300 percent between 1966 and 1986.

Before World War II, nearly all Aboriginal people lived in rural areas of Canada (Waddell and Watson, 1971). However, by 1960 about 15 percent had moved to urban areas. By 1986 this percentage increased to nearly one-third (see Figure 6.2). Later data from the 2001 Census show that the percentage of Aboriginal people living off-reserve continues to increase. As can be seen in Figure 6.2, in some provinces the proportion was then nearing half the population. While these figures show a dramatic increase in the proportion of Aboriginal people living in urban centres, they vary considerably from the statistics for the general population, which show 80 percent of the population living in urban centres. Table 6.1 reveals the off-reserve population by age group from 1981 to 2001. The results show that the off-reserve population is aging and will continue to get older; e.g., in 1981 about 3.5 percent were in the 45–49 age group; by 2001 that number will have doubled.

Nearly 80 percent of off-reserve Aboriginal people are living in large metropolitan centres. Table 6.2 shows the rate of growth in the Aboriginal population for selected cities between 1951 and 1996. Clearly, rapid growth has taken place in the number of Aboriginals moving to the city. However, Table 6.2 does not reflect the number of Aboriginals who have entered the city as other than full-time residents, or whose lifestyles have frustrated the attempts of an enumeration agency to count them. Only a few cities in Canada have tried to gather up-to-date and dependable data, with often surprising results: on the basis of its own figures, Regina predicts that by 2011, over one-third of its population will be Aboriginal. Table 6.2 also shows a dramatic increase in the urban Aboriginal population since 1951. At present, there is some debate as to whether the urbanization process has peaked or will continue to increase. So far the evidence suggests that the rate of Aboriginal urbanization has stabilized and will only increase marginally over the next few years.

The number of off-reserve Aboriginal people varies widely from province to province. Data from 1966 show that most areas of Canada had surprisingly low numbers (see Figure 6.2). Today, three provinces—British Columbia, Saskatchewan, and Ontario—have nearly 50 percent of their Aboriginal population living off-reserve. The most dramatic increases from 1966 to 2001 have been in the West and North, where off-reserve rates have doubled and, in the case of Saskatchewan, have quadrupled.

Migration is a reciprocal process, referring to the movement of Aboriginal people both into and out of the city. In some cases, Aboriginal people who move off the reserve settle permanently in the city; others only sojourn in the city, remaining for a while, then moving back to their reserves. Nevertheless, urban areas continue to be the destination of Aboriginal migrants. Even though urban areas are the recipients of large numbers of Aboriginal people, they also contribute to the total number of out-migrants among Aboriginal people. The end result in the past few decades was that for the period of 1976–81, compared to 1966–71, urban areas showed a 6 percent increase in the influx of Aboriginal migrants but a net loss of 2 percent in the Aboriginal population. Focusing just on registered Indians, we find that the five year net migration flow between 1991 and 1996 reveals an important pattern. The results show that on-reserve communities have had an

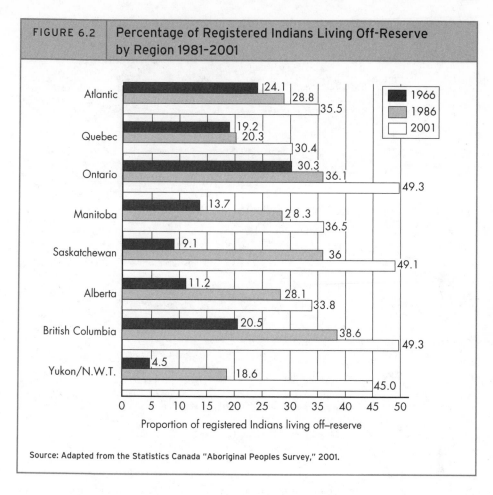

FIGURE 6.2 — Percentage of Registered Indians Living Off-Reserve by Region 1981–2001

Atlantic
24.1 (1966)
28.8 (1986)
35.5 (2001)

Quebec
19.2 (1966)
20.3 (1986)
30.4 (2001)

Ontario
30.3 (1966)
36.1 (1986)
49.3 (2001)

Manitoba
13.7 (1966)
28.3 (1986)
36.5 (2001)

Saskatchewan
9.1 (1966)
36 (1986)
49.1 (2001)

Alberta
11.2 (1966)
28.1 (1986)
33.8 (2001)

British Columbia
20.5 (1966)
38.6 (1986)
49.3 (2001)

Yukon/N.W.T.
4.5 (1966)
18.6 (1986)
45.0 (2001)

Proportion of registered Indians living off–reserve

Source: Adapted from the Statistics Canada "Aboriginal Peoples Survey," 2001.

increase of nearly 15 000 people (coming from rural and urban areas). This influx is partially due to the changes in definition of an Indian, but it also demonstrates that there is considerable migration between rural, urban, and reserve contexts. Figure 6.3 elucidates this flow.

Before examining the process of migration in detail, a brief characterization of the Aboriginal people who currently live in Canadian cities will be useful.

URBAN ABORIGINAL PROFILE

Table 6.1 shows that in 1981 more than one-fourth of the Aboriginal population who lived off the reserve were between the ages of 25 and 44. However, this proportion of off-reserve Aboriginal people increased substantially from the early 1950s until the early 1970s, when it began to decrease. By 1991 well over one-third of the urban Aboriginal population was in this age category. These figures support the observation that urban migration is slowing down as the urban migrants age and fewer Aboriginal people enter the urban setting. When age groups are compared, however, no substantial difference

TABLE 6.1	Population by Age Group, Aboriginals Off-Reserve, 1981, 1991, 2001					
Age	1981 Population	% Total Pop.	1991 Population	% Total Pop.	2001 Population	% Total Pop.
0-4	10 908	10.99	19 252	9.38	18 934	7.98
5-9	12 651	12.74	16 535	8.06	22 320	9.40
10-14	13 294	13.39	18 701	9.11	22 116	9.32
15-19	12 205	12.29	19 791	9.65	17 261	7.27
20-24	10 559	10.64	21 395	10.43	17 632	7.43
25-29	8 751	8.81	21 083	10.27	19 399	8.17
30-34	7 491	7.55	19 902	9.70	21 827	9.19
35-39	5 985	6.03	17 313	8.44	22 282	9.39
40-44	4 401	4.43	13 781	6.72	20 079	8.46
45-49	3 407	3.43	10 650	5.19	15 997	6.74
50-54	2 599	2.62	7 994	3.90	12 136	5.11
55-59	2 079	2.09	6 046	2.95	9 042	3.81
60-64	1 428	1.44	4 373	2.13	6 590	2.78
65+	3 523	3.55	8 373	4.08	11 772	4.96
Total	99 281	100.00	205 188	100.00	237 387	100.00

Source: *Highlights of Aboriginal Conditions*, 1981-2001, *Part I, Demographic Trends* p. 27, Indian and Northern Affairs Canada.

emerges in migration patterns. This suggests that members of all age groups migrate in almost equal numbers to urban centres, although somewhat fewer Aboriginals over 50 migrate. The high proportion of children up to 14 years old shows that many Aboriginals bring their children with them as they enter the city. For example, as early as 1970 Vincent found that in Winnipeg over half the Aboriginal people were younger than 30; other studies have since supported this finding, with slightly different figures (Indian Association of Alberta, 1971; Denton, 1972; Nagey et al., 1989). Vincent also found that 60 percent of urban Aboriginal people were married, though not necessarily living with their spouses. According to the male–female ratio, there are about 10 percent more Aboriginal women in urban centres than men. This figure does not include women who have been forced off the reserves through marriage to non-Aboriginal men.

Levels of education for off-reserve Aboriginal people are significantly lower than the national average (Stanbury and Fields, 1975; Federation of Saskatchewan Indians, 1978; Hanselmann, 2001). However, when compared to the educational levels of on-reserve Aboriginal people, the difference is not significant. In other words, there is no "brain drain" operating on the reserves. Nevertheless, Table 6.3 reveals major differences in educational achievement between urban Aboriginals and urban non-Aboriginals. The data in Table 6.3 reveal that Aboriginal adults without a high school diploma are not as employable and are at more significant risk than non-Aboriginals.

TABLE 6.2   Educational Attainment of Aboriginals and Non-Aboriginals, Selected Urban Areas, 1996 (percent)

	Vancouver		Calgary		Saskatoon		Winnipeg	
	Aboriginal	Non-Aboriginal	Aboriginal	Non-Aboriginal	Aboriginal	Non-Aboriginal	Aboriginal	Non-Aboriginal
Less than Grade 12	40	28	40	27	48	32	54	34
High school diploma	32	33	33	32	31	31	28	31
Trades/certificate	3	3	2	3	2	3	2	3
Other post-secondary	20	19	19	20	12	18	13	17
University	5	18	19	20	7	16	4	15

TABLE 6.3	Growth of Aboriginal and Métis Population in Urban Centres, 1951–1996		
	1951	1971*	1996
Calgary	62	2 265	23 450
Edmonton	616	4 260	44 150
Halifax	–	–	7 795
Hamilton	493	1 470	11 020
London	133	1 015	8 200
Montreal	296	3 215	43 875
Ottawa-Hull	–	–	29 915
Regina	160	2 860	14 570
Saskatoon	48	1 070	18 160
Toronto	805	2 990	39 380
Vancouver	239	3 000	48 805
Winnipeg	210	4 940	52 525

Note: The cities chosen were those that had the largest number of Aboriginal residents. The numbers are probably understated since many arrivals in a city are itinerant and are, therefore, very difficult to count in a census.
* Does not include Inuit.

Source: Information Canada, *Perspective Canada I* (Ottawa: Queens Printer, 1974), 244; Canadian Metropolitan Areas, *Dimensions*, Statistics Canada, Table 9, 1986; Newhouse and Peters, 2003; INAC, Registered Indian Population Projections, 1998-2008.

A number of surveys over the past two decades have been undertaken to assess the labour force involvement of urban Aboriginals (Stanbury and Fields, 1975; United Native Nations Manpower Survey, 1976; Bob Ward Associates, 1978, DIAND, 1980; Frideres and Ryan, 1980). More recent surveys confirm the earlier findings (Wotherspoon, 2003). All the data show that the unemployment rate for off-reserve Aboriginals is five to six times higher than for non-Aboriginal people living in the urban area. Not only are unemployment rates higher but the length of time that Aboriginals have held jobs is also much shorter than for non-Aboriginal people. Only about one-fifth of the urban Aboriginal population have held jobs for more than a month. Hanselmann (2001) demonstrates that in Western Canada, participation rates in 1996 for Aboriginal people in urban areas were significantly less than for non-Aboriginals. For example he found that the percentage participation rates in Vancouver were 67.3 vs. 63.1; in Calgary 74.1 vs. 69.8; in Edmonton 71.4 vs. 61.4; in Saskatoon 70.6 vs. 52.3; and in Winnipeg 67.7 vs. 57.7. Unemployment rates reveal the same differences, as outlined in Table 6.4, for selected urban centres.

The surveys attributed unemployment among off-reserve Aboriginal people to a lack of training and a need to attend to family responsibilities. However, Stanbury and Fields (1975) also found that discrimination in employment contributed significantly. Because of the low labour-force participation rate, high unemployment, and low educational attainment, the income levels of urban Aboriginal people were very low. Well over half of the

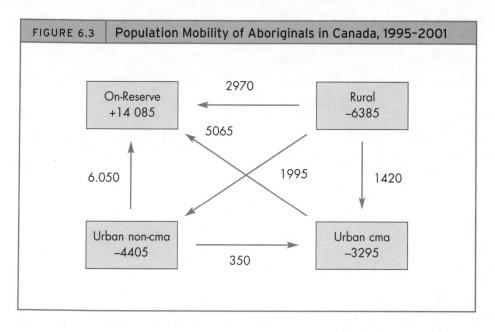

FIGURE 6.3 | Population Mobility of Aboriginals in Canada, 1995-2001

Aboriginal people in urban centres had incomes well below the poverty level. This number is to be compared with less than one-fourth of the non-Aboriginal population. Twenty-five years later, Hanselmann (2001) reviewed the percentage of the population 15 years and older with total yearly incomes below $10 000. The results of his research (shown in Table 6.5) show that the picture has not changed.

Because of their difficulty in obtaining employment and their low incomes, many Aboriginal people in urban centres have a lower standard of living than their non-Aboriginal counterparts. As a result, their lives require extensive social assistance, e.g., housing, child care, and food. Their lower standard of living also leads to an increased risk in family and social problems and an increased risk of homelessness. We find that Aboriginal people who live in urban centres are exposed to many more services than those living on reserves. However, because of legal disputes between the federal and provincial governments, they are not able to gain access to this multitude of services. Their lack of access is also a result of their poor understanding of their rights as Canadians and their unwillingness to press for services that they might need. As a result, urban Aboriginal people continue to live in poverty, as they did on the reserve. Jantzen (2003) has carried out an analysis of Métis residing in urban areas, and her work confirms the above. She concludes that Métis—especially those reporting a single Métis origin—are not faring as well as the non-Aboriginal population.

In summary, our analysis of urban Aboriginals reveals a profile that is different from non-Aboriginals living in major urban centres. The data confirm that Aboriginal people (1) are more likely to have low levels of education, (2) have low labour force participation rates, (3) have higher unemployment rates, (4) have low income levels, (5) have high rates of homelessness and greater housing needs, (6) are overrepresented in the criminal justice system (both as victims and offenders), (7) have poor health status (particularly in areas such as diabetes, HIV and AIDS, suicide, and substance abuse), and (8) are over twice as

TABLE 6.4	Unemployment Rate	
	Aboriginal	Non-Aboriginal
Montreal	21.0	9.8
Toronto	15.7	9.3
Ottawa-Hull	16.3	8.7
Vancouver	20.4	8.4
Calgary	14.3	6.5
Edmonton	22.5	7.8
Saskatoon	25.1	6.6
Regina	26.8	6.4
Winnipeg	25.1	7.1

Source: Hanselmann, 2001. © Copyright Canada West Foundation.

likely to be lone parent families and experience domestic violence. These results portray a sub-population in the urban context that needs special attention as they try to integrate into the larger social and economic structure of the industrial economy. (See Table 6.6 for an identification of the number of Aboriginals living in major urban areas.)

Decision to Migrate

Most studies of Aboriginal migration have focused on the individual, i.e., on the factors that lead individuals to migrate to the urban centres from their reserves. The effects of the reserve community upon migration have seldom been investigated. The work of Gerber (1977, 1980) is an exception to this and merits an extended discussion in any analysis of Aboriginal urbanization, since both levels of variables need to be discussed if we are to clearly understand the process of Aboriginal urbanization (Neils, 1971).

TABLE 6.5	Annual Income Less than $10 000	
	Aboriginal	Non-Aboriginal
Vancouver	40.9	25.9
Calgary	40.0	25.2
Edmonton	47.3	26.5
Saskatoon	51.3	27.3
Regina	47.6	24.3
Winnipeg	45.9	25.9

Source: Hanselmann, 2001. © Copyright Canada West Foundation.

TABLE 6.6	Estimated Urban Concentration of Aboriginal People, 1996	
Province	City	Indians and other Aboriginal People
British Columbia	Vancouver	46 805
	Victoria	10 000–15 000
	Prince George	2000–3000
	Prince Rupert	4000–5000
Alberta	Calgary	23 850
	Edmonton	44 130
Saskatchewan	Regina	14 570
	Saskatoon	18 160
	Prince Albert	2000–3000
	North Battleford	1000–2000
Manitoba	Winnipeg	52 525
Ontario	Ottawa–Hull	29 415
	Toronto	39 380
	Thunder Bay	8 600
	Kitchener	6000–10 000
	Oshawa	5000–6000
	St. Catharines-Niagara	9000–10 000
	Windsor	7000–10 000
Quebec	Montreal	43 675
	Chicoutimi-Jonquière	2000–3000
	Sherbrooke	9000–10 000
	Trois Rivières	2000–3000
	Quebec City	6000–10 000
Atlantic Canada	Halifax	7 795
	St. John's	1000–2000
	Saint John	2000–3000

The structures of particular reserves have an important influence on Aboriginal migration patterns. Gerber found that Prairie reserves are very communally oriented, while Eastern reserves tend to be much more individualistic. For example, Eastern Aboriginal people are more likely to hold location tickets (a legal document entitling an individual to the right to occupy and use a piece of land), that they can will or sell to other Aboriginals. This cultural variable has considerable impact on an individual's decision to migrate (Reeves and Frideres, 1981).

The specific structural factors of reserves that Gerber found important in affecting Aboriginal urbanization were proximity of the reserve to an urban centre, road access, the size of the band, the degree of community development, and the retained use of Aboriginal languages. As Gerber's research shows, high-migration bands were small, not present in the Prairies, and largely English-speaking. In addition, the sex ratio of high-migration bands was, on average, 141 men to 100 women.

Gerber also found that the development of personal and group resources was particularly important in determining migration patterns. Table 6.7 shows the typology she developed to indicate potential migration patterns. Bands in cell 1 are inert in that they are not adapting to the larger dominant culture or attempting to develop internally. Those in cell 2 are "pluralistic." They are high in community development yet low in personal resources; even though considerable economic and social development has taken place, individuals have not participated in the education system or labour force to any great degree. In contrast, the bands in cell 3 are "integrative." Through education and job experience they have prepared individuals to enter the dominant culture, but they have not created opportunities within the community. As a result individuals must move to the outside world. Finally, the "municipal" Aboriginals have a high rate of migration, but opportunities exist on the reserve for those who choose to remain.

In short, as one moves counter-clockwise from cell 1 in Table 6.7 the likelihood of urbanization increases. Apparently the band itself provides the basic structural context that determines the rates of and reasons for urban migration. Those bands with high community development provide opportunities for their members to remain on the reserve. Those communities with high personal-resource development encourage their members to migrate to the city; when, in addition, community development is low, individuals are forced off the reserve but can compete successfully in the urban context. However, as Gerber argues, an increase in off-reserve residence also results when community development stimulates out-migration to compensate for a lack of personal-resource development (Ryan, 1978).

Clearly, the structural conditions that govern life determine, more or less, the decisions of individual Aboriginal people to migrate off the reserve. Denton (1972) also points out that, in addition to social factors, cultural factors come into play. According to Denton, reserves are governed by strong "village norms and social control mechanics which encourage work, independence, and earning one's own money" (1972: 55). Thus, from an early age, children are socialized into work roles and, as they grow older, make increasing contributions to family maintenance (Honigman, 1967). Often conflicts result between children and parents; children are taught to be self-reliant and independent, but at the same time must bend to the will of their families (Vincent, 1970).

These structural, social, and cultural conditions, then, are instrumental in pushing the young Aboriginal off the reserve and into the urban context. Moreover, a decision to return to the reserve is also influenced by these factors; community development must be such as to easily absorb the returnee (Ablon, 1965).

A number of academics have divided Aboriginal city-dwellers into transients, migrants, commuters, and residents. The transient moves continually from one place to another without establishing full residence in any urban area (Nagler, 1971). The migrant simply transfers a social network from a rural base to an urban one, moving to the city but only interacting with other Aboriginal people. The commuter lives close enough to an urban centre to spend large amounts of time there, yet retains residence on the reserve. The resident has been born in the city and spends most of his or her time in an urban context (Brody, 1971).

Many researchers have assumed that the longer an individual Aboriginal resides in an urban area, the more likely integration into the dominant society becomes. This assumption is true only for a certain segment of the urban Aboriginal population. Some Aboriginal peo-

TABLE 6.7	Gerber's Typology for Migration Patterns		
		Level of Community Development	
		Low	High
Level of personal resources	Low	1ª	2
	High	3	4

a. Numbers are for identifying the cell, i.e., the type of band.

Source: Based on Gerber, 1979.

ple, in order to become socially and politically integrated into Euro-Canadian society, terminate most social and family ties with their band. But most Aboriginal people are unable to integrate into the larger society, whether they desire to or not (City of Edmonton, 1976).

Although social factors undoubtedly play a part, most Aboriginal people tell investigators that they have come to the city to participate in the labour force. This provides a legitimate explanation to non-Aboriginal people and allows Aboriginal people to apply for welfare aid more easily. However, Aboriginal people are very much aware of the poor opportunities for steady employment in the city. What, then, are the real reasons for urban migration? First of all, as pointed out previously, an increase in population has created overcrowding on the reserve, specifically in the areas of housing and employment. Most reserves are rural-based and can only provide jobs for a limited population. As Deprez and Sigurdson (1969) point out, because the economic base of most reserves is incapable of supporting the existing Aboriginal population, out-migration is essential.

Each Aboriginal person must assess the chances of obtaining work and housing on the reserve. Because both are scarce, a great deal of competition exists among reserve residents. As in most social organizations, access to housing and employment is partially controlled by a relatively affluent social elite. The housing needs of young, single males and females are not considered high priority; young singles are seen as capable of entering the world outside the reserve and they generally lack a social network on the reserve, which is required if Aboriginal officials are asked for help. In particular, unmarried females, with or without children, receive low priority in housing allocation. This partly accounts for the high ratio of males to females on certain reserves, as well as for the high proportion of children under 15 who have moved off the reserve.

Migration away from the reserve is much more the result of push factors than of pull factors. The urban setting is attractive only to those who are qualified to participate actively in it; few Aboriginals are able to do so. Most Aboriginals decide to leave the reserve only when they are forced to by an absence of housing and employment opportunities.

Entering the City

In the early stages of urban migration, the first Aboriginal institutions to emerge in a city are bars with large Aboriginal clienteles. From these first interactions, cliques then emerge and create a social network for Aboriginal people to enter and leave at will. Through these cliques, the second stage of urbanization evolves; Aboriginal social and cultural centres develop, along with more extended social networks. J. Price (1979) calls these centres "second-stage institutions." The centres inhibit integration into the city, yet increase the odds for urban survival. In addition, they promote and facilitate a chain migration of Aboriginals to the cities (Johnson, 1976).

The third stage of urbanization, institutional completeness, has not yet been reached. Institutional completeness is the creation and maintenance of a set of institutions, such as schools, churches, and employment agencies, that meet most social, cultural, and economic needs of the ethnic group. Aboriginal institutional completeness has failed to develop in the urban centres for a number of reasons. The leaders of Aboriginal bands generally remain on the reserve, even though regional, provincial, and national government offices are located in urban areas. Aboriginal political organizations continue to focus on rural issues, such as band claims and treaty rights. Due to internal rivalries between Aboriginal factions, urban Aboriginal leaders have failed to gain political momentum. Moreover, because urban Aboriginal organizations, such as friendship centres, are continually preoccupied with crisis situations, they have not been able to address the general social and economic needs of urban Aboriginal people.

Clearly, few Aboriginal persons enjoy the stable social networks in cities that would permit institutional completeness to develop. Aboriginal urbanization will not be complete until agencies are developed and staffed by Aboriginals to provide employment and services to the Aboriginal community. At this time, Aboriginal people have become heavily involved in social and cultural centres, provincial political associations, and local and Aboriginal political organizations. Each urban area is developing somewhat differently, however, and according to varying schedules.

Progressive urbanization is producing more and more urban Aboriginal people. What happens after the Aboriginal enters the city? What kinds of experience take place? The answers to these questions largely depend on the lifestyle of the individual. For the purposes of this discussion, urban Aboriginal people can be divided into transients and residents.

Transients are those individuals who are unable or unwilling to integrate into non-Aboriginal society because of their high mobility patterns. Because they retain a rural orientation and possess few skills, transients are not able to participate in the social or economic fabric of Canadian society. As a result, they become more and more dependent on the same social-service organizations that, ironically, encouraged them to migrate in the first place.

Table 6.8 lists some of the value differences that exist between Aboriginal and non-Aboriginal people. Of course, both value systems are in a state of flux and neither is as straightforward as it appears. For example, the introduction of social welfare, combined with Aboriginal people's lack of control over their destiny, has led to a dependency ethos that did not exist before contact with European culture.

A basis for some of the differences that exist between Aboriginal and non-Aboriginal people lies in the philosophical assumptions made about human beings and society. The basis of present Western thought can be found in the liberal political philosophy of Rousseau, Locke, and Hobbes, which stressed that individual self-interest should take precedence over group rights. However, it was argued, individuals must operate in a collective unit so that all individuals can survive. To further this aim, a state apparatus was created in which individuals voluntarily agreed to subordinate their self-interest to the common good. Nevertheless, the individual is considered to be morally prior to any group, and the individuals within a state are to be viewed as acting for themselves, not as members of any collectivity (Boldt and Long, 1985a).

TABLE 6.8	Cultural Differences Between Non-Aboriginals and Aboriginals
Aboriginal Values	**White Values**
Group emphasis	Individual emphasis
Cooperation (group concern)	Competition (self-concern)
Present-oriented	Future-oriented
Non-awareness of time	Awareness of time
Age	Youth
Harmony with nature	Conquest of nature
Giving	Saving
Practical	Theoretical
Patience	Impatience
Extended family	Immediate family
Non-materialistic	Materialistic
Modest	Overstates (over-confident)
Silent	Noisy
Low self-value	Strong self-value
Respects other religions	Converts others to own religion
Religion a way of life	Religion a segment of life
Land, water, forests and other resources belong to all, and are used reasonably	Land, water, forests and other resources belong to the private domain, and are used in a greedy manner
Equality	Wealth
Face-to-face government	Representative democracy

Source: Based on Tanner, 1983.

Contrary to this Western philosophical position (which emerged out of feudalism), Aboriginal people were not grounded in state institutions or in relationships that supported vertical hierarchical arrangements. Vachon (1982) argues that Aboriginal people have a cosmocentric view of the universe (in contrast to homocentric) that focuses not on the individual but on the "whole." Individuals, then, are to be subordinate to the whole. Human beings are just part of the whole, which also includes animals, plants, and inanimate objects. All of these parts must exist in harmony, and the parts as well as the whole can only survive if each works in harmony with the others. Therefore, all the parts are forced to interact with each other and to take the others into consideration. Human beings, in Aboriginal culture, are viewed as just another limb in the body of life, but a limb with certain additional responsibilities. As a result, individual self-interest is defined as group-interest and the group and the individual are seen to share a common identity. Laslett (1963) uses the onion-skin analogy to illustrate the relationship of the individual to the whole. The entire onion represents group-orientation attributes. Each person has more or fewer of these group attributes as he or she moves through society over time. However, if all oriented attributes are removed, there is no core of self or individual remaining. While not all Aboriginal people fully subscribe to this perspective, there are remnants of this philosophy present today in varying degrees.

In summary, non-Aboriginal society can be characterized as using "linear and singular" thinking. A good example of this is the concept of time as defined by non-Aboriginal Canadians. First, time is conceptualized as a straight line. What is immediate in time is present; what is behind is the past and the future is yet to be achieved. Time can be viewed as a row of similar units that can be divided into separate and different units. Thus, for example, Europeans think in terms of minutes, hours, and days and implicit in this linear thinking is the view that time flows one way and you cannot recapture time from the past. Linear thinking also lends itself to singular thinking; that is, linear thinking propels individuals toward values that imply "one answer," "one way." Linear thinking can be either horizontal or vertical, but the general principle remains the same. This linear worldview also leads to specialist activity in that one moves toward "one thing." You can only be good at one thing, not a number of things.

In contrast to the linear worldview, the Aboriginal worldview can be characterized as cyclical or holistic. This view begins with the premise that everything is interrelated. It is a generalist perspective rather than the specialist one that characterizes Canadian non-Aboriginal culture. As many Aboriginal people note, their view of the world is more circular; there is no beginning, no end. There are phases and patterns to the world, but they are repetitive and cyclical. Since all parts are interrelated, each part is equal to all others. The system could not continue with a missing part. In addition, when the world is viewed as a whole there is a tendency to see the whole or group as more important than the individual. Being part of the group is better than being alone. The interrelated whole results in harmony and balance (Cawsey, 1991).

Aboriginal Canadians find a great deal of discontinuity between life on the reserve and life in the city. As they reach the city they enter a world that is generally alien, frightening, frustrating, and hostile. Many Aboriginal people express total confusion as to "how Whites work." Of course, the reaction of individual Aboriginal people to Euro-Canadian society varies: some find it extremely bizarre and hostile, while others quickly adapt to the Euro-Canadian ethos. The extent to which Aboriginal people can reconcile the "two solitudes" of reserve life and city life depends on early socialization experiences and past interactions with non-Aboriginal society. Insofar as the structure of Canadian society plays a large role in socialization experiences, it has a profound effect on the ability of Aboriginal people to integrate into urban life. We now turn to examining the processes that affect and influence the Aboriginal's foray into urban life. We will show how the various organizations impinge upon the Aboriginal's attempts to deal with life in an urban area.

Social Organizations and Aboriginal Urbanization

In Canada, state-funded social services have been used to expand the rights of citizenship and to encourage members of the lower classes to participate politically (Bendix, 1964). Mass education has been developed to raise literacy levels and to provide the formal qualifications necessary for employment in urbanized settings. In addition, social welfare organizations have been expanded to ensure an educated population and to provide support for an urbanized labour force. These social services pulled people from peripheral areas into the mainstream of modern economy and, by so doing, played a part in the urbanization of Canadian society.

The federal government has tried to repeat this process through the urbanization of Aboriginal people, but this policy is highly suspect. The government is trying to encourage Aboriginal people to abandon their reserves and treaty rights, mobilizing them as Canadian citizens but not as "citizens plus" (White Paper, 1969; Weaver, 1980). "Citizens plus" refers to the view that, since Aboriginal people were the first inhabitants of Canada, they should be afforded special status and rights. By curtailing services on the reserves, most noticeably in the area of housing, the government has tried to push Aboriginal people into the city, especially during winter. In addition, by transferring the provision of services from the federal to the provincial system, the federal government has attempted to reduce its treaty obligations.

However, the federal government does not have jurisdiction over many of these social services, particularly education and social welfare, that have been used to expand citizens' rights and to urbanize members of the lower classes. In Canada, these services are generally provided by provincial agencies. While the provincial educational system has made some effort to increase Aboriginal levels of literacy and formal certification, the welfare system has not been expanded to incorporate Aboriginal people into urban society. Although the number of Aboriginal persons on welfare has increased in cities, they generally receive only short-term services that relieve temporary problems of urban subsistence (Stymeist, 1975).

The lack of educational qualifications continues to prevent full urban integration for most Aboriginal people. As stated earlier, Aboriginal people who claim a desire for employment as the primary reason for moving to the city generally do so because of the requirements of the welfare system, rather than because they perceive actual employment opportunities for themselves. For some, such as single mothers with children, provincial welfare services allow a higher standard of life in the city than on a reserve or in a Métis colony. For most, however, government social services are not sufficient to encourage Aboriginal people to remain in cities. As a result, an increasing number of urban Aboriginal persons can be classed as transient.

More and more young Aboriginal people are moving back and forth between urban and rural residences, generally on a seasonal basis. Faced with an inability to secure employment, or even to understand and use various government and private agencies, they commute into the city for short periods of time and then leave, their frustrations intact (Frideres and Ryan, 1980). Even though these Aboriginal people may spend large amounts of time in the urban context, they retain their social ties in the rural area.

A second group of Aboriginal people has succeeded in establishing residence, if not employment, in the cities. This group is predominantly female with young dependants (Gerber, 1977). In lieu of employment, these Aboriginal people rely on the support of relatives and friends in addition to government services. For example, from an Edmonton sample, 76 percent of urban Aboriginal persons had relatives in the city when they first entered and 65 percent had friends (City of Edmonton, 1976).

A third, much smaller, group of Aboriginal people appears to have successfully settled into urban society. Members of this group most closely approximate the White, middle-class, urban family: they live in single-family units as married adults with children; they have full-time employment; and they live in acceptable housing. Successful entry into urban society appears to be contingent upon attaining a level of education, health, and well-being possessed by the vast majority of non-Aboriginal citizens of Canada.

The Transition

Aboriginal people move into the urban context in a series of stages.[1] Although these stages are serial, they are not necessarily "step-wise sequential"; that is, all of the steps are not essential in order to achieve the final stage. Also, progression through the stages is usually not completed in one continuous sequence.[2] As Figure 6.4 indicates, Aboriginal people are exposed to a funnelling effect: although most have some contact with service organizations, few become independent of the organizations, and even fewer are successfully placed in the city.

Aboriginal people move from Stage 1 to Stage 2 largely as a result of the recruitment procedures of service organizations. The type of service organization and its policy plays an important role in determining the rate of rural-to-urban transition (see Table 6.9). Service organizations have a great influence on the degree to which Aboriginal people can successfully adapt to the urban centre.

The issue of whether government or voluntary agencies should deal with Aboriginal problems has long been debated in Canada. Although the provincial governments recognize a partnership between the two sectors, they have tried to maintain the primacy of government both in policy formation and in program maintenance. Private agencies do not have the complex network of contacts and services that government programs can provide. Nonetheless, a policy of subsidiarity, whereby governments refuse to duplicate the services offered by private citizens, has taken precedence. As a result, the government has become essentially a financier, relying upon the private sector to provide primary services to those in need.

Aboriginal Policy

The development of policy provides a guide for governments as to how to spend money, develop programs, and set priorities in terms of action. In another sense, policy is a statement of responsibility on the part of government. As Hanselmann (2001) points out, a policy reflects an overarching public written statement that sets out a government's approach to an issue. In the case of Aboriginals, most policy related to them emanates from the federal Department of Indian and Northern Affairs Canada. Unfortunately, there are few government-wide policies with regard to urban Aboriginals. The reader should note that policy is quite different from programs that are specific actions taken by a department. While programs

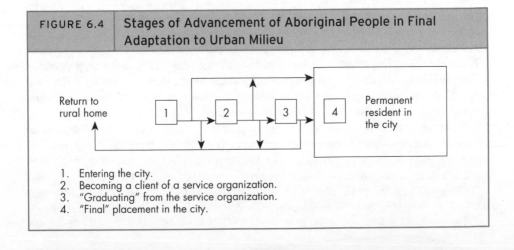

FIGURE 6.4	Stages of Advancement of Aboriginal People in Final Adaptation to Urban Milieu

1. Entering the city.
2. Becoming a client of a service organization.
3. "Graduating" from the service organization.
4. "Final" placement in the city.

generally implement the policy, they may also be unique and "one off" in design. In addition, just because there is no policy with regard to a field, this does not mean that there are no programs. In fact, this has been one of the problems that urban Aboriginals have faced. Various levels of government have funded programs but have no policy to link them to. As a result, within short periods of time, these programs are stopped and other "ad hoc" programs emerge. The chart in Figure 6.5, developed by Hanselmann for Western Canada, shows the comparative policy landscape for 6 urban areas with regard to urban Aboriginal policies across 17 fields of action.

Hanselmann's results reveal that both the federal and provincial governments are engaged in policy making and programming for urban Aboriginal people. However, the data show that the issues are not systematically being addressed. Rather, as Hanselmann (2001) points out, the responses to the challenges facing urban Aboriginal people are taking place in a "differentiated policy environment". His analysis shows that the urban Aboriginal–specific policy landscape ranges from comprehensive government-wide strategies to specific departmental programs. Governments are not responding in a consistent manner, although all levels of government seem to have implemented some urban Aboriginal policy. The existing policy environment (disagreement between the federal and provincial governments as to who has primary responsibility for urban Indians) continues to thwart any system of policy development with regard to urban Aboriginals. Moreover the analysis shows that there are major gaps in the policy fields. For example, there are no policies in the areas of child care and family violence, and only partial coverage in areas such as income support, housing, and human rights. Finally, it should be noted that the policies that exist are not well linked to the everyday experiences of urban Aboriginals. For example, housing is a major concern for urban Aboriginals and yet only half of the cities surveyed have a policy with regard to urban Aboriginals. Finally, the data reveal considerable overlap in policies among the three levels of government. While some of the overlap may be complementary, some is simply duplicative. While this multiple-level policy suggests that different levels of government agree that this field is important, these different levels have yet to coordinate their activities to ensure efficiency and effectiveness.

Models of how urban Aboriginals might organize and meet the needs and aspirations of their constituency have not been well developed. These models need to understand that Aboriginal people in urban areas may participate fully in the local, provincial, and federal arenas, but in other matters—such as those related to cultural survival—Aboriginal people may develop their own services and institutions (Wherrett and Brown, 1994). The problems faced by Aboriginal people in Canadian urban centres have led them to try to develop services and institutions to suit their unique needs. The forms of organization and scope of services provided by existing institutions reveal the weaknesses and strengths of the current political and institutional framework. For example, the institutions in place today have been limited by a lack of autonomy and inadequate and inconsistent funding. Aboriginal organizations also have to align their activities with the municipal, provincial, and federal programs that are in place but not specifically directed toward Aboriginal people (Wherrett and Brown, 1994).

Aboriginal Organization Contact

Aboriginal people entering the city usually find the process difficult and problematic. Most find that they must utilize the services of a variety of organizations in order to remain. Although some Aboriginal people on reserves or in Métis colonies find that some

FIGURE 6.5	Comparative Policy Landscape

	Vancouver	Calgary	Edmonton	Saskatoon	Regina	Winnipeg
Education	P	P	P	P	P	M
Training	F P	F	F	F P M	F P	F M
Employment	F M	F P	F P	F P M	F P	F M
Income Support					M	
Econ. Development		P	P	P	P	M
Family Violence						
Childcare						
Health	P	P	P	P	P	M
Addictions						
Suicide						
Homelessness	F	F P M	F P	F M	F	F
Housing				P M	P	M
Justice	F	F P	F P	F P	F P	F
Human Rights				M		
Urban Transition	P	P	P			
Cultural Support		P	P	P M	P	M
Other	F P	F P M	F P M	F P M	F P	F

F   Federal policy   P   Provincial policy   M   Municipal policy

Urban Aboriginal policy

Source: Hanselmann, 2001, p. 18. © Copyright Canada West Foundation.

form of sponsorship is necessary to remain in an urban centre, most of them are poorly prepared for urban life. Educational standards on the reserves and colonies have been considerably below those in other Canadian schools. The quality of social services, particularly for housing and health, has been well below national norms. Not surprisingly, the lifestyle of the rural Aboriginal person has adapted to inferior levels of education, work experience, housing, and health.

Even disregarding social and cultural factors, the vast majority of Aboriginal people entering cities do not have the qualifications necessary to get work, obtain social services, or succeed in school. Most cannot even qualify for employment insurance. Their poverty, combined with their unconventional lifestyles, exposes them to much higher than average levels of detention and arrest by the police. In the end, most Aboriginal people are not successful in adapting to city life.

Because of their unique position, urban Aboriginal people are much more likely than non-Aboriginals to come into direct contact with service organizations that regulate and monitor social behaviour. Aboriginal people have consistently posed problems to those organizations in their attempts to establish public order and provide various services. Organizations that attempt to deal with Aboriginal urban problems can be broken down into four categories: public service, acculturating service, accommodating service, and member organizations. Table 6.9 outlines the attributes of each type.

PUBLIC SERVICE ORGANIZATIONS

Public service organizations provide a single, specific service, such as justice, education, or welfare, to the general public. They work within the prevailing Canadian system of values and beliefs and are typically staffed by middle-class executives, clerical workers, and members of service-oriented occupations. From one perspective, public service organizations are designed to provide certain minimum levels of service to the general public. As a citizen, each individual has the right to a basic education, a basic standard of living, and equal treatment before the law. From another perspective, public service organizations, especially education and justice systems, are important mechanisms for encouraging the participation of individuals in society. For example, educational achievement draws individuals out of their immediate locales and moves them into a socio-economic framework through entry into the labour force. Similarly, the basic requirements of public health and order encourage normative social behaviour.

In Canada, public services have failed to integrate Aboriginal people into urban society. Aboriginal persons who have come into contact with these organizations have tended to become virtually permanent clients, as evidenced by recurrent patterns of detention and arrest, high rates of hospitalization and premature death, and the inability of most Aboriginal people to leave the welfare rolls. In the educational system, where permanent subsistence is not permitted, Aboriginal students tend to drop out before achieving the minimum standards of attainment for success in the labour force.

Public service organizations do not assist most Aboriginal people to live in the city as competent citizens. Indeed, as currently constituted, these organizations more often present a barrier that denies Aboriginal citizens entry into the mainstream of urban Canadian life.

ACCULTURATING SERVICE ORGANIZATIONS

Like the public service, acculturating service organizations draw their staff from the middle class and act to promote or maintain the assimilation of Aboriginal people into Euro-Canadian culture. Acculturating service organizations include post-secondary institutions, such as colleges and universities, provincial apprenticeship branches, the Central Mortgage and Housing Corporation, and the Alberta Opportunity Fund (a source of credit for small business). The agencies share many characteristics with regard to Aboriginal people. They usually obtain many, if not most, of their clients through a system of referrals. Whenever possible, they exercise discretion when accepting prospective clients, taking only those who

TABLE 6.9   Attributes of Types of Service Organizations

Organizational Type	Organizational Effectiveness	Value Representative	Selected Attributes of Organizations			
			Membership Recruitment	Extent of Services	Ethnic Comp. of Staff	Ability to Place Clients
Public Service	High	Middle-class	Mass[a]	Singular	Middle-class; White	High
Acculturating Service	High	Middle-class	Very[b] selective	Multiple; integrated	Middle-class; White	High
Accommodating Service	Low	Aboriginal	Mass	Singular	Mixed-Aboriginal; middle-class; White	Low
Member	Moderate	Aboriginal	Mass; Aboriginal	Singular	Aboriginal	Low

a. Recruitment is selective, yet the services offered are considered the right of all citizens.
b. Recruitment is usually on a sponsorship basis.

Source: J. Frideres and W. Reeves, Native Urbanization in Canadian Society (Calgary, Alberta, mimeo, 1984).

have a good chance of succeeding in their programs. Once accepted, their clients typically do succeed: formal and informal counselling services, along with other sources of support, minimize the drop-out rates. For example, a few Aboriginal people on Aboriginal reserves or Métis colonies who display a potential for academic achievement are maintained through secondary school and then referred to a post-secondary institution, usually a college or a university. Once sponsored, these people have a high incidence of success in the system.

Acculturating service agencies are also similar in that their clientele includes very few Aboriginal people. Most simply do not have the minimal qualifications necessary to be referred to or accepted into such programs. Furthermore, Aboriginal people have found it difficult to obtain services from these organizations because they have difficulty understanding and coping with non-Aboriginal rules and procedures.

ACCOMMODATING SERVICE ORGANIZATIONS

Accommodating service organizations attempt to compensate for the lack of preparation revealed by certain visible-minority groups in their contacts with Euro-Canadian society. These agencies are often funded by public service organizations to deal with problematic clients. For example, the Special Constables Program of the RCMP, the Courtworkers' Program, and the race relations units of municipal police forces all attempt to handle the problems that have arisen among Aboriginal citizens, the public, and the courts. These agencies try to protect the rights of Aboriginal people and, at the same time, render the legal system more efficient. Also, several acculturating service organizations support the work of accommodating service organizations; examples include the Aboriginal counselling and Aboriginal studies programs on the campuses of various universities.

The ability of an accommodating service organization to actually alter the fate of its clients is extremely limited. These agencies support the work of public and acculturating service organizations and generally operate within a White, middle-class value system. They have managed to attract Aboriginal clients by hiring a greater proportion of Aboriginal staff members and by modifying some operating procedures to reflect their clients' cultural background. However, because funding often depends on enrolment figures, this "accommodation" of Aboriginal interests is not entirely altruistic.

Because funding is almost always limited to support for a particular project for a limited time, programs offered by these organizations usually lack scope and continuity. Accommodating agencies are generally expected to simply direct their clients to existing services provided elsewhere. Indeed, accommodating service organizations are often limited simply to registering, screening, and referring their clients to other organizations. Moreover, they are unable to offer any real assistance to Aboriginal people in their dealings with those other organizations.

MEMBER ORGANIZATIONS

Unlike the other three types of service organizations, member organizations tend to work against the assimilation of Aboriginal people into the mainstream of Canadian society. Member organizations represent the interests of Aboriginal people as members of a distinct ethnic group. They provide some employment for Aboriginal persons, promote the revitalization of Aboriginal culture, and attempt to provide the broad range of social support necessary to allow people to lead an Aboriginal lifestyle. Some organizations, like provincial Aboriginal associations, are working to develop and document a case for entrenched Aboriginal economic and political rights. Others, like the Aboriginal friendship centres, are attempting to promote an Aboriginal lifestyle in the cities. These organizations also function to encourage the emergence of a Aboriginal elite that has not been co-opted into the staff of public service organizations.

Although member organizations successfully provide services to urban Aboriginal people, their effectiveness is weakened by a virtual absence of employment for Aboriginal people as Aboriginal people. Member organizations have tried to promote the institutional completeness needed for in-group cohesiveness and solidarity. However, this institutional completeness cannot be achieved without the creation of jobs for their members. To remedy this problem, Aboriginal people, like Hutterites, need to establish and run their own businesses; at present, there are few urban Aboriginal enterprises. And, like Roman Catholics, Aboriginal people need to control the beliefs, values, and skills taught in government-supported schools.

At present, an inability to establish jobs for their memberships stymies the success of Aboriginal organizations. Like those who rely on public service organizations, Aboriginal persons who belong to member organizations continue to be excluded and stigmatized by non-Aboriginal, urban society. Unlike the clients of public service organizations, however, Aboriginal people in member organizations are less likely to regard themselves and their fellows as failures (McCaskill, 1981).

PROBLEMS FACING SERVICE ORGANIZATIONS

As more and more Aboriginal people moved to the city in the late 1960s, public and acculturating service organizations came under increasing pressure. In coping with this influx, public service organizations experienced a disproportionate decrease in effectiveness and a disproportionate increase in costs. Although the schools experienced some problems in assimilating Aboriginal children, the brunt of this problem was felt by the police and courts. Young Aboriginal people who migrated to the cities lacked the prerequisite skills for employment and were unable to cope in a conventional fashion with the demands of urban society. Frustration and unemployment combined with divergent values to produce a style of life that frequently deviated from the social norms and laws in the cities. While greater expenditures on law enforcement increased the number of Aboriginal persons being processed (and reprocessed) in the system, they did not reduce the threat to public order. This simultaneous decrease of effectiveness and increase in costs was underscored by social scientists, who pointed out that nearly half the inmates in provincial jails were Aboriginal.

Managers of acculturative service programs were also faced with escalating costs accompanied by decreased effectiveness. Their programs were sporadic, unevenly implemented, and made little attempt to find standardized solutions to Aboriginal problems. In addition, they were under pressure to debureaucratize existing legitimate programs.

Acculturating service organizations were also criticized on a different ground. Because Aboriginal people as a group were systematically undercertified, exceedingly few of them enrolled in university, entered unionized occupations, or qualified for credit assistance in purchasing a home or establishing a business. With greater urbanization Aboriginal people became a more visible minority, demonstrably denied access to many of the avenues to success in Canadian society. Aboriginal member organizations publicly questioned the legitimacy of training programs and assistance agencies that failed to recruit proportionate numbers of Aboriginal people into their publicly funded programs.

Like the public service organizations, then, the acculturative service agencies were faced with a legitimate problem: those Aboriginal people most in need of their services were clearly not receiving them. Both in public and acculturative service organizations, middle-level managers, who were responsible for day-to-day internal administration, funding, personnel, and clientele, felt that some action was necessary. Although the issue of legitimacy did not actually threaten their budgets, it did increase public scrutiny of funding and internal administration, reducing managerial discretion and hindering the management of day-to-day operations. However, it is important to point out that this legitimacy crisis did not become a political issue; e.g., government did not become involved in determining policy or setting standards.

In order to reach a greater number of Aboriginal people, middle-level management in public and acculturating service organizations began to fund new projects proposed by accommodating service organizations.[3] In some cases, existing Aboriginal member organizations were co-opted to run these programs, e.g., Plains Indian Cultural Survival School, Native Counselling Services, Native Employment Transitional Services, and Native Alcoholism. In other cases, funding was provided for the formation of new Aboriginal-oriented service organizations. In yet other cases, such as the Aboriginal Outreach Program, existing organizations created a new branch to deal with a specific type of client.[4]

Whatever their origins, accommodating service organizations tend to enhance the legitimacy of existing service organizations. Accommodating service programs essentially deal with the problem clients of public service organizations, and leave other operations intact. For example, Aboriginal students unable to complete their secondary education in the public high schools are referred to an "alternative" public school run by Aboriginal personnel.

By registering, screening, and referring problematic clients, accommodating organizations can forecast or even regulate the number of clients they deal with, and accommodating agencies can tailor specific projects to particular problematic groups. These special programs justified their high costs and provided a rationale by which public service organizations could offer special treatment to, and acculturating service organizations could relax entry and performance standards for, certain preferred groups such as Aboriginal people. Over the years, as Newhouse (2003) points out, a number of member institutions have been established by urban Aboriginals. However, over time, these institutions have evolved into accommodating service organizations and are not distinguishable from other non-Aboriginal accommodating service organizations.

Essentially, by offering a bicultural program, the middle-level managers of service organizations shifted some of the responsibility for problem clients onto the shoulders of those operating the accommodating organizations. The bicultural program could accommodate both non-Aboriginal and Aboriginal values. Moreover, accommodating service organizations could attract increasing numbers of clients without seriously affecting either the service standards of acculturating organizations or the cost-effectiveness of public service organizations.

Ironically, the accommodating organizations inherited the same problems of legitimacy that plagued the public and acculturating service organizations. Accommodating organizations are generally small, independent, voluntary associations that undergo major program and staff transformations every few years. Their instability is partly due to the nature of their financial support. They face serious problems establishing a permanent source of funding and, therefore, a clearly defined mandate. Usually their budgets are mostly made up of grants from public service organizations. These grants are generally earmarked for specific projects designed to last for a limited period of time, often one to three years. In addition, they are aimed at protecting the rights of individual clients, and do not attempt to address the general problems of Aboriginals. As a result, accommodating service agencies generally offer services for Aboriginals that are far too restricted in focus to address adequately the low qualifications, marginal living standards, low incomes, and high crime rates of Aboriginal Canadians.

The accommodating service organizations have inherited many of the criticisms once aimed at the public service and acculturative service organizations. To get funding, the accommodating organizations orient their programs toward Aboriginal culture in hopes of attracting Aboriginal clients. However, the placement of these clients then becomes problematic. Because non-Aboriginal businesses generally refuse to hire them, Aboriginal people become perpetual clients of the agencies and are locked into a limbo between the reserve and the city. As a result, a large number of them enter these accommodating organizations, but few graduate. Accommodating service organizations are particularly effective at placing those clients who no longer need their services. Also, because the organizations to some extent encourage Aboriginal values and lifestyles, they do not prepare Aboriginal people for White, middle-class society; at best, they produce marginal Aboriginals.

Because the federal and provincial governments desire to provide social services on an equal basis to individual members of the general public, they have been unwilling to address the problems of particular groups or communities. The current political climate exacerbates this problem. At the constitutional level, the provincial government has refused to accept sole legal responsibility for the social support of status Indians off the reserve. To avoid giving even *de facto* recognition to the collective rights of Aboriginal people, these governments have restricted their support of organizations for Aboriginal persons to narrow-range, small-scale, temporary projects.

The precarious status of accommodating agencies undermines their effectiveness. Overly specific short-term programs discourage the regular, full-time participation of Aboriginal people. Moreover, remedial programs are often too narrow to ensure continued Aboriginal participation without a broad range of additional social support to counteract the effects of poverty and unemployment. To obtain this support, accommodating organizations must refer their clients to the system of social services offered by public and acculturating organizations, despite the fact that their own projects often run counter to and are not integrated with these social services. Clearly, whatever the efficiency of accommodating organizations under ideal conditions, the absence of wider social support sabotages their effectiveness and undermines what few gains they manage to achieve.

URBAN RESERVES

Before we draw this chapter to a close, we need to introduce the concept of "urban reserve" that has recently become part of the public policy dialogue now underway. With increasing numbers of Aboriginals living in urban areas, many are beginning to push for the creation of an urban reserve. Today, we find that Aboriginals make up a sizeable portion of urban centres. When we add the number of sojourners (coming and going), the total Aboriginal population in many large urban areas is significant. For these individuals, city life is now an integral attribute of "urban" Indians. Moreover, this urban migration was brought about because of an aggressive federal policy started over half a century ago.

As such, Aboriginal people now make up a part of the urban landscape and will remain there for a long time. However, rather than assimilating into the larger society, these residents maintain close ties to their communities of origin and desire a quality of life that maintains a distinctive culture as well as exercising self-governance. Peters (2003) points out that, for Aboriginal people in the city, maintaining their identity is an essential and self-validating pursuit. Contemporary urban Aboriginal people see their communities in urban centres as real and as no different than rural reserve communities. These residents have a growing interest in self-determination and self-government in cities, and there are attempts to coordinate all levels of government to support their urban communities. This new view sees urban Aboriginals as part of their communities, with goals and needs that they want to attain within an urban landscape (Peters 2001). The Royal Commission on Aboriginal Peoples addressed this issue, and the federal government is reviewing its traditional stance on considering urban Indians a provincial responsibility. This new concern has yet to be systematically addressed, but as the Aboriginal presence in our cities continues to grow, the challenge will have to be addressed.

CONCLUSION

The number of Aboriginal people entering urban centres, either as transients or permanent residents, will continue to increase over time. Nevertheless, a sizeable proportion of the population will remain on the reserves. This split population, along with the hyper-mobility they exhibit, makes it difficult to develop policy to deal with the urban sector of the population. The consequence of this increased urbanization will be greater demands placed on service organizations to deal with Aboriginal people, demands which most urban service organizations are unable to fulfil. As a result, few urban Aboriginal persons are fully participating members of the modern industrial society. They are marginal in their own country.

In recent years, some urban areas have attempted to develop strategies to circumvent the policy vacuum and jurisdictional dispute. Hanselmann and Gibbins (2002) have shown that several urban centres have been able to develop programs without a macro policy framework. They have identified the development of multilateral agreements (memoranda of understanding) as an instrument through which federal and provincial governments work together, and with third parties (Wong, 2002). An example of this is the city of Winnipeg, which has formal agreements with Aboriginal organizations and two levels of government. These agreements have resulted in significant investments by the three levels of government in partnership with Aboriginal organizations. Another example of informal partnerships is the Saskatoon Community Partnership Table, in which the Aboriginal community identifies certain social issues as a priority (e.g., housing and homelessness) and the three levels of government and the First Nations and Métis come to the table for discussion of the issues as equal partners. All participants have equal voice regardless of the resources they bring to the table. This approach has required the federal and provincial governments to modify their practices in dealing with Aboriginal communities. These and other strategies are being developed to address the lack of impact that traditional organizational structures have had with regard to urban Aboriginals. The slow acceptance of an intergovernmentalist approach has opened new ways of dealing with urban Aboriginal issues.

Others (Wherrett and Brown, 1994) have identified alternative strategies for exercising self-government within an urban context. If the traditional reserve exists within the urban area, governing would simply become an extension of how governance is applied on any reserve. Examples here are the Micmacs in Halifax, the Algonquians in Ottawa–Hull, and the Sarcee in Calgary. Another way in which urban Aboriginals might exercise governance would be to use Section 35 of the *Constitution Act, 1982* to develop a National Treaty that covers all Aboriginal people, no matter where they live. In developing models, Aboriginals will need to explore alternatives. For example, some may wish to use a "community of interest" model in instances where Aboriginals are dispersed throughout an urban area. In this case, the "territory" would be cultural rather than geographic. In this instance, they would need to develop their own school system as the Catholic and charter schools have done. Wherrett and Brown (1994) point out that another possibility exists where there is a concentration of Aboriginals in a particular area of the city: here, a "neighbourhood" model might be more appropriate. This is not a new idea, as Dosman (1972) proposed this type of model well over a quarter-century ago. This model would see a community take over various institutions in the neighbourhood to provide support for Aboriginals attempting to integrate into the urban setting and to help meet their economic, political, and psychological needs.

NOTES

1. Some of the material presented has been previously published by Reeves and Frideres in *Canadian Public Policy* (1981).

2. The length of time between stages varies and should not be seen as equal. Movement to the next stage is not automatic and several starts may be needed before it takes place.

3. At the same time, Aboriginals on the reserves and in the city lacked an elite to promote a rediscovery and resurgence of Aboriginal culture. They also lacked service organizations to encourage participation in the larger society. The end result was the creation of a very passive and apathetic population that remained on the reserve or in rural areas. Those who became "active" were generally co-opted and acculturated out of Aboriginal culture and into mainstream society.

4. These organizations screen potential clients and sort them into appropriate homogeneous streams before providing services. In essence, accommodating service programs stream special problems away from the general program. The bicultural program can accommodate Euro-Canadian and Aboriginal values, thereby rendering acculturating service organizations more effective while increasing the clientele of accommodating service organizations. This new composite organization has allowed an increasing number of Aboriginal people to stay in urban areas.

WEBLINKS

www.nafc-aboriginal.com

The National Association of Friendship Centres site provides valuable links to provincial and territorial centres and their websites, press releases on various topics of interest, history, and links to aboriginal urban youth centres across Canada.

www.ainc-inac.gc.ca/ch/rcap/sg/sj1_e.html#perspectivesandrealities

Volume 4 of the Royal Commission on Aboriginal Peoples Final Report discusses urban Aboriginal issues, including identity in an urban context, governance, and urban Aboriginal women, elders, and youth. Click on each of the seven chapters and two appendices listed for Volume 4 at this site.

www.lexum.umontreal.ca/csc-scc/en/pub/1999/vol2/html/1999scr2_0203.html

The Supreme Court of Canada, in the *Corbiere* case, recently ruled that off-reserve band members must be allowed to vote in band council elections. The decision may have political implications both for bands and urban Aboriginal people. This link takes you directly to the high court's decision, which is based on the equality guarantee in the Charter of Rights and Freedoms.

chapter seven

Indian Treaties and Métis Scrip: Old Promises and New Struggles

INTRODUCTION

When William Robinson was sent to deal with Indian complaints about the intrusion of Whites looking for minerals on land along the eastern and northern shores of Lake Superior, a new era in Indian–White relations emerged. Robinson met with the Ojibwa leaders, and the first land-based treaties (Robinson–Superior and Robinson–Huron treaties of 1850) were established. These treaties provided a template that would be used by Robinson's successors and would forever change the social landscape of Canada. Later treaties negotiated were intended to give recognition to Indian interests in the land, to provide compensation, and to establish an orderly transition of land ownership from one group to another. The treaties also established the rules of relationship between the two parties (Indians and the federal government) after the transfer of land (Daniel, 1980).

While the land rights of Aboriginal peoples in Canada have by no means been treated uniformly, there did develop in British North America a consistent body of precedent and tradition that was utilized on new frontiers where fairly rapid settlement or resource exploitation was being promoted. This involved the making of treaties under which Aboriginal peoples surrendered most of their territorial rights and gained various forms of compensation. Although numerous land surrender treaties had already been made in the Thirteen Colonies, it was not until after the American Revolution that the system was first systematically used in Canada (Ray, 1974).

Nevertheless, many Canadians feel that treaties are no more than outdated contracts between a group of Indians and the federal government. There is also a belief that, since the treaties are old, the agreements within them can be breached. However, in a recent Supreme Court decision (*Simon* v. *The Queen*), the Court held that treaties were neither contracts nor international instruments. They are to be regarded as agreements *sui generis*.

ORIGIN OF THE TREATIES

Some of the earliest agreements between the Indians and government have been called "Peace and Friendship" treaties, and were carried out primarily in the Maritime area.[1] These pre-Confederation treaties generally dealt with military and political relations, and did not involve specific land transfers, annuities, trading rights, or compensation for rights limited or taken away (Sanders, 1983a). Yet by no means are these early treaties unimportant even today. A good example of "Peace and Friendship" treaties are those signed between the Mi'kmaq and the Governor of Nova Scotia in 1760–61. It was these treaties, and specifically the right within them to catch and sell fish for profit (including lobster), that were at the centre of the controversial and highly publicized Marshall case, argued in the Supreme Court of Canada (*R.* v. *Marshall,* 1999; Coates, 2000). Pre-Confederation agreements continue to be reinterpreted and to generate new court rulings over access to different resources, as the example in the box, below, shows.

By the Treaty of Utrecht (1713), France ceded Acadia (excepting Cape Breton Island) to Great Britain, recognized the British sovereign's suzerainty over the Iroquois people, relinquished all claims to Newfoundland, and recognized British rights to Rupert's Land. When the charter for exploitation of Rupert's Land was granted by Charles II to the Hudson's Bay Company in 1670, it is doubtful that even the claimants were aware of the vast territory involved: all the land draining into Hudson's Bay from Baffin Island on the northeast to the headwaters of the Saskatchewan River in the southwest. For the next cen-

---

Natives Win Right to Log on Crown Land

Court gives bands and New Brunswick government a year to negotiate a deal

By David Stonehouse

Natives in New Brunswick are hailing a court victory that grants them the inherent right to harvest wood on Crown lands, but the decision could mean chaos for the provincial forestry industry. Yesterday's ruling throws out existing logging agreements between the government and native bands....

In a 283-page decision, the Appeal Court ruled 2–1 that Joshua Bernard, a Mi'kmaq from the Eel Ground First Nation near Miramichi, has a treaty right to harvest and sell trees on Crown lands traditionally occupied by the Mi'kmaq. It threw out a conviction that Mr. Bernard unlawfully possessed timber and declared existing laws an unjustified infringement of his treaty rights. His lawyer, Bruce Wildsmith, hailed the decision as a "milestone" for New Brunswick natives. It is expected to open doors for other aboriginal loggers in the Maritimes.

Source: Material reprinted with the express permission of Pacific Newspaper Group Inc., a CanWest Partnership.

tury and a quarter, the western boundaries of Rupert's Land were to remain the firmest delineation of British America's western extent.

With the fall of the French fortress at Louisbourg, Cape Breton, and by the Treaty of Paris in 1763, which ended hostilities, France ceded all its North American possessions to Great Britain, with the exception of St. Pierre and Miquelon Islands (which it still retains) and Louisiana (which it later ceded to Spain). In the spring of that year the crystallization of Indian misgivings gained expression through the activities of Chief Pontiac,[2] although particular provisions in the *Royal Proclamation* concerning the protection of Indian-occupied lands were designed to allay such fears. The *Royal Proclamation* of 1763 did indeed define lands that were to remain, at the sovereign's pleasure, with the Indians as their hunting grounds, but Rupert's Land and the old colony of Quebec were specifically exempted. In what was to become Canada, the hunting grounds in the east comprised a relatively narrow strip between the northern bounds of Quebec and Rupert's Land, along with all of what was to become Upper Canada; in the northwest, they comprised an amorphous area bounded by Rupert's Land, the Beaufort Sea, and the Russian and Spanish claims to the west and south.

In 1769, St. John's Island (renamed Prince Edward Island in 1798) became a separate government. By the *Quebec Act, 1774,* in what has been described as a statutory repudiation of *Royal Proclamation* policy, Quebec's boundaries were extended to encompass all the land described in the preceding paragraph as the eastern Indian hunting grounds.

With the Revolutionary War of 1775 to 1783, the emphasis in the colonies of Nova Scotia and Quebec changed irrevocably to settlement, development, lumbering, fishing, and trade; dissolution of the 200-year-old partnership between Indian and fur trader was well on the way. The most immediate effect was a 50 percent increase in population in the two colonies occasioned by the influx of United Empire Loyalists, who were primarily interested in farming, homesteading, and business. These were followed, particularly in Upper Canada after 1791, by a steady stream of settlers with like interests from the south. They brought with them the desire for peace, law, good order, and the other concomitants of settled living.

The Treaty of Paris, 1783, signed between Great Britain and the United States, established the boundary from the Atlantic to the Lake of the Woods. At one stroke Canada lost the entire southwestern half of the vast inland domain that French and British adventurers had discovered, explored, and exploited with the help of the Indian people. Along with it went that portion of the Indian hunting grounds, established in 1763, that was bounded by the Great Lakes and the Ohio and Mississippi Rivers. A natural point of departure for the future boundary at the 49th parallel of latitude was also ensured. The inevitable dissension with the Indian people that followed, however, was reaped by the United States rather than Great Britain.

In 1784, as a result of the large-scale influx of United Empire Loyalists into the Saint John River area the year before, New Brunswick was separated from Nova Scotia. Cape Breton Island also became a separate entity.

By the *Constitutional* (or *Canada*) *Act* of 1791, the Imperial Parliament divided Quebec into the provinces of Upper Canada and Lower Canada, abolished the conciliar form of government that had existed in Quebec for two centuries, and established representative government in both provinces. Land was to be granted in freehold tenure in Upper Canada and could be so granted in Lower Canada, if desired.

In 1796, by the Jay Treaty, the fur-trading posts of Niagara, Detroit, Michilimackinac, and Grand Portage—which were still in British hands—were handed over to the United States in accordance with the boundary provisions agreed to in 1783. In order to facilitate what remained of the fur trade, an article in the Jay Treaty provided for the free passage of Indian trappers back and forth across the boundary with "their ordinary goods and peltries"; it is on the basis of this provision that the present-day Iroquois claim duty-free passage across the international boundary (Innis, 1970).

In 1803, by the Louisiana Purchase, the United States acquired that vast, vaguely defined territory west of the Mississippi that had been ceded back to France by Spain in 1800. The consequent push westward, and the inevitable rivalries arising, would once again raise the contentious question of the boundary between British America and the United States.

On the Pacific coast, the leading protagonists changed over the course of time from Russia, Britain, and Spain to Russia, Britain, and the United States, but it was not from the sea that this contest was to be settled. Indeed, Captain Cook had made his landfall at Nootka Sound in 1778, but the traders who followed him lost their vessels and furs to the Spanish who were engaged in a last endeavour to enforce their claims to the northwest coast. In 1791, Captain George Vancouver arrived to officially acknowledge the restoration of British rights after the Nootka Convention; the Russians were concurrently pushing down from the north, following the seal and the sea otter.

The only firm and lasting links with the Pacific coast, however, would have to be established by land, and these were provided through Alexander Mackenzie in 1793, by way of the Peace River canyon to Dean Channel; Simon Fraser in 1808, by the tumultuous river that bears his name; and David Thompson in 1811, down the Columbia to its mouth. These Canadian Scots were all members of the North-West Company, and they were rivals, not only of the Spanish, Russians, and Americans, but also of the Hudson's Bay Company. With their exploits the chain of discovery and exploration, whose initial links were forged in the quest for furs along the Atlantic coast over the preceding two centuries, was complete from ocean to ocean—all in the name of the fur trade. In each instance, the ubiquitous Scot was accompanied, guided, and sustained by Indian companions (Wildsmith, 1985).

For the United States, Lewis and Clarke had, of course, paced the Canadians, reaching the Columbia River in 1805. John Jacob Astor established the western headquarters of his fur company at the mouth of the Columbia in 1810. In 1809, by the *Labrador Act,* Anticosti Island and the coast of Labrador from the St. Jean River to Hudson Strait were transferred from Lower Canada to Newfoundland. Not even the eastern provinces, however, were to be allowed to engage in such peaceful organizational exercises much longer. The improvement in relations that the Jay Treaty appeared to herald had not resolved the border ambiguities at the centre of the continent, and the animosities of the American Revolution were by no means exhausted.

The outbreak of war in 1812 saw 500 000 British Americans (of whom less than 5000 were regular troops) confronted by a population of 8 million in the United States. Great Britain was not only at war with the United States but had its strength committed to the struggle with Napoleon. Through a combination of dogged determination on the part of the British Americans (aided by several hundred Indians under Chief Tecumseh) in throwing back invasion forces and ineffective planning on the part of the enemy, Canada managed to hold out until the defeat of Napoleon in 1814 allowed Britain to bring all its forces to bear in America. Having thus gained the initiative in no uncertain manner, it is hard to understand why the British did not seek more equitable boundary terms by the

Treaty of Ghent in 1814, but both parties appeared content to settle the controversy through a mutual return of conquered territories. Thus were Canadian interests sacrificed to ensure American cordiality.

The United States considered the Jay Treaty of 1796 to be abrogated by the War of 1812–14; but the Convention of 1818 settled the outstanding boundary matters by confirming the border to the Lake of the Woods and extending it along the 49th parallel to the Rocky Mountains. The Treaty of Ghent reinstated the provisions of the Jay Treaty affecting Indian people, but, as the conditions of the former were not considered to be self-executing, it became the individual responsibility of each of the governments concerned to give effect to the relevant provisions by appropriate legislation (Leslie and Maguire, 1978).

In terminating the international boundary at the Rocky Mountains, the Convention of 1818 left one major area subject to contention with the growing neighbour to the south— the so-called Oregon Territory jointly occupied by Britain and the United States. The first large-scale movement of American settlers into Oregon in 1842 naturally created a clamour for annexation to the United States. Fortunately, the contention was resolved through the Treaty of Washington in 1846, by which the boundary was continued to the sea along the 49th parallel and Vancouver Island confirmed as a British possession. With the agreement of 1825 between Britain and Russia on a description of the Alaska boundary, to all intents and purposes Canada's external boundaries now were fixed and its attention could be concentrated on consolidation.

POST-CONFEDERATION

The pre-Confederation treaties were made with the Crown through representatives of the British government. Later, after Confederation, the treaties would be made through the Canadian government. All the terms of the pre-Confederation treaties were turned over to the Canadian government, either at the time of Confederation or since then. When the *Royal Proclamation* of 1763 was issued, Indian rights were, for the first time in Canadian history, specifically referred to. The *Royal Proclamation* confirmed that Aboriginal rights existed. However, the question still remains as to how much of what is now Canada is covered by the Proclamation. Driben (1983), for one, points out that it is difficult today to determine the boundaries of what the Proclamation referred to as "Indian territory."

When the Hudson's Bay Company (HBC) surrendered Rupert's Land in 1869, Canada inherited the responsibility for negotiating with the resident Aboriginal tribes. Prior to the transfer, the *Royal Proclamation* had established the "equitable principles" governing the purchase and surrender of Aboriginal lands. The Imperial Order in Council that transferred this responsibility is stipulated in Article 14:

> Any claim of Indians to compensation for lands required for the purposes of settlement shall be disposed of by the Canadian government in communications with the Imperial government; and the Company shall be relieved of all responsibility in respect of them.

The administrators who were subsequently appointed to negotiate federal treaties with the Indians were inexperienced and unfamiliar with Aboriginal customs. Lacking firsthand knowledge, these administrators fell back on the legacy of the Hudson's Bay Company's treatment of Aboriginal people as well as on some sketchy reports of the negotiations behind the Robinson Treaties of 1850 and 1862 and the Manitoulin Island Treaty, also in 1862.

Preliminary negotiations between the Indians in Manitoba and the representatives of the government began in 1870. By 1871, Treaties Nos. 1 and 2 were signed, and in 1873 the lands between Manitoba and Lake Superior were ceded in Treaty No. 3. Northern Manitoba and the remainder of the southern prairies were surrendered by the Aboriginal peoples between 1874 and 1877 in Treaties Nos. 4, 5, 6, and 7.

The land taken by the Canadian government under Treaties Nos. 1 through 7 provided sufficient land for the mass settlement of immigrants entering Canada. However, by 1899 the pressures of settlement and mineral development again caused the government to negotiate for new lands from the Aboriginal peoples. Although these later treaties, Nos. 8 through 11, differed in many respects from the earlier ones, they were clearly modelled upon earlier treaties. Subsequent modern agreements may, in turn, be modelled upon and indeed even replace these numbered treaties, as is the case for Treaty 11 (see below for details on the 2003 Tlicho [Dene/Dogrib] Agreement).

The federal government decided to negotiate with the Aboriginal peoples largely because its own agents foresaw violence against European settlers if treaties were not established. However, this perception was not based on particular threats or claims on the part of the Aboriginal peoples, who simply wished to carry out direct negotiations with the government to recompense them for the lands they occupied prior to European settlement. After the first treaty was signed, neither the government nor the Aboriginal people attempted to find alternative means to deal with "Indian claims." Government officials based future treaties on prior ones and Aboriginal groups insisted on treatment similar to that received by those who had signed earlier treaties.

Despite specific differences, the contents of all the treaties are remarkably similar. Treaties Nos. 1 and 2 set the stage. They created reserve lands granting 160 acres per family of five. Annuities of $3 per person, a gratuity of $3 per person, and a school on each reserve were agreed upon. Other promises were also made orally during the negotiations; some of these were later given formal recognition by an order in council.[3] Treaty No. 3 contained the same provisions as Treaties Nos. 1 and 2, except that its reserve allotment was increased to 640 acres per family of five.[4]

The federal government desired treaties that were brief, simple, and uniform in content. Nonetheless, although constrained by these government limitations, negotiators were often forced to make minor additions to a treaty; sometimes these took the form of verbal promises, presumably to avoid deviations from the standard written form. For example, the government negotiators for Treaty No. 6 were forced to add several benefits such as medicine chests and provisions for relief in times of famine.

In general, however, the government negotiators had by far the best of the bargaining. Indeed, most treaties were written by the government and simply presented to the Indians for signing. The terms, for example, of Treaty No. 9 were determined by the Ontario and Canadian governments well in advance of discussions with Aboriginal people. Moreover, there is evidence that, in many cases, hard-won oral promises have never been recognized nor acted upon by the government.

In their negotiations with the Aboriginal people, treaty commissioners always avoided discussing the nature or extent of Aboriginal land rights. Although the commissioners obscured the issue, the Aboriginal people clearly surrendered land claims by signing the treaties. In many cases, the commissioners argued that the Indians had no land rights at all; if the Aboriginal negotiators objected to this argument, the commissioners would enlist support from missionaries or traders whom the Aboriginal people trusted. In the end, however, no Indian treaty was ever brought before Parliament. Instead, the treaties were presented to Cabinet and ratified by an order in council. This suggests that they were accepted by the Government of Canada, both as a recognition of Aboriginal land claims and as a means of their negotiation and resolution.

British Columbia: A Special Case

British Columbia was a special case in its handling of treaties. Between 1849 and 1854, James Douglas, the governor of the colony, negotiated a series of treaties with the Indians on Vancouver Island. After 1854 this policy was discontinued: although the colonial office in England supported the treaties, it would not provide Douglas with monies to continue them. British Columbia settlers refused responsibility for negotiations with the Indians and would not release public funds to settle land claims.

As Berger (1981: 222–23) points out, British Columbia's House of Assembly had initially recognized Aboriginal land titles. However, when told by London that it would have to provide the funds to settle those titles, the House of Assembly withdrew recognition of Indian land claims. This meant that, technically, the Aboriginal peoples were not entitled to any compensation.

No further treaties were ever made in British Columbia, although Treaty No. 8 covers the northeastern part of the province. With the entry of British Columbia into Confederation in 1871, the administration of Indians and Indian lands in the province fell under the jurisdiction of the federal government. However, the federal government's interpretation of this jurisdiction has remained controversial up to the present (see also Duff, 1997).

When British Columbia entered Confederation, the actual terms concerning the treatment of Aboriginal people were unclear. The terms of union clearly stated that all public lands were to be the property of the provincial government; this meant that the federal government owned no land outright in the province to give to the Aboriginal people. Some provision was made, however, for Aboriginal lands. The province agreed to relinquish to the federal government "tracts of land of such extent as it had hitherto been the practice of the British Columbian government to appropriate for that purpose" (Berger, 1981: 224).

Unfortunately, the practice of the British Columbian government was to supply considerably less land than did the federal government. When allotting land, the province had simply set aside a number of acres per family. Although non-Aboriginal settlers had received 320 acres of land per homestead, Aboriginal people had been granted considerably less. In 1887 the federal government asked the province to determine the size of the reserves by relinquishing 80 acres per Indian family. The province set aside only 20 acres per family, a much lower acreage than that set aside for other Aboriginal peoples by the Canadian government. Understandably, Indians in British Columbia objected strongly and insisted on their Aboriginal rights.

The British Columbian Aboriginal peoples continued to oppose the establishment of reserves and to argue title to their own lands. The federal government dissolved its commission in 1910 after the provincial government refused to sanction any more reserves. In the early 1900s, Indians sent delegations to Victoria and to England in an attempt to argue their claims for Aboriginal rights. The federal government partly supported these claims and tried unsuccessfully for a hearing before the Supreme Court of Canada. The province refused to comply.

In 1913 a royal commission was established, partly to adjust the acreage of the reserves in British Columbia. In 1916 the commission produced a report detailing lands to be added to and removed from existing reserves. The added land was to be twice the size of the land taken away; however, the land to be taken away was, at that time, worth twice as much money.

As the federal government tried to implement this report it met increased opposition from the provincial government and from the Aboriginal peoples. The province finally confirmed an amended version of the report in 1923, but the Aboriginal peoples never accepted it. The Allied Indian Tribes of British Columbia emerged to become a powerful political force uniting Aboriginal opposition to the decision. In 1923 the Allied Indian Tribes of British Columbia presented a list of far-reaching demands to the federal government and agreed to relinquish their Aboriginal title claim only if the demands were met. These demands were remarkably similar to those met by previous treaties in other provinces, namely 160 acres per capita, hunting rights, and the establishment of reserves.

The Allied Indian Tribes of British Columbia demanded that either a treaty be negotiated or that their Aboriginal title claim be submitted to the judicial committee of the Privy Council. In essence, they argued that, contrary to the beliefs of the federal and provincial governments, there had been no final settlement of their claims. As a result of the Indians' petition, a special joint committee of the House and Senate was convened to hear evidence and make a decision. This committee decided that the Indians had not established any claims to land based on Aboriginal title; however, it did recommend that an annual sum of $100 000 be spent for the good of Indians in British Columbia.

In order to prevent an appeal of this decision, the federal government passed an amendment to the *Indian Act* that prohibited the collection of funds from Aboriginal people for the advancement of a land claim. This amendment remained law until the middle of the 20th century. As a result, Aboriginal groups became powerless to press their claims and were successfully ignored by the federal government throughout the Depression and World War II. Of necessity, local issues replaced larger concerns during this time: the Native Brotherhood of British Columbia was established in 1931 and, in 1942, became prominent in its fight against income tax for Aboriginal fishermen. But Aboriginal claims in British Columbia (McGhee, 1996) did not emerge again as an issue until the 1960s, when they played an important role in, amongst other things, the creation of the Indian Land Commission. Chapter 9 will detail more recent developments in British Columbia, including the 2002 Referendum on Aboriginal Treaties.

Early Ontario Treaties

Algonkian-speaking peoples formed the Indian population of Southern Ontario when the European claim to territorial sovereignty passed from the French to the British in 1763, but European settlement did not occur there to any degree until 20 years later. In these post-Revolutionary years, the separation of the Thirteen Colonies from British North America created an urgent need for land on which to settle disbanded soldiers and other Loyalists. The unsettled areas of British North America provided a ready solution to the problem.

About 10 000 United Empire Loyalists moved into the area of the St. Lawrence–Lower Great Lakes. In presiding over this settlement, the Imperial government did not simply grant land to these newcomers without regard for the Indian inhabitants. As has been seen, the *Royal Proclamation* of 1763 declared that Indian land rights could only be alienated at a public meeting or assembly of the Indians called for the purpose, and then only to the Crown. Although often honoured only in the breach, the Proclamation's principles were respected through a complicated series of formal treaties and surrenders in what became Southern Ontario.

To the government, treaties were little more than territorial cessions in return for once-for-all grants, usually in goods. However, there is evidence that some of the Indians involved felt that the government was assuming broader trusteeship responsibilities as part of the bargain. Annuities, or annual payments for the ceded land rights, first appeared in a treaty in 1818 and thereafter became routine. At this stage, the provision of land for Indian reserves only occasionally formed part of the surrender terms. Similarly, the right to continue hunting and fishing over ceded territories was very rarely mentioned in the written terms of surrender. Not until 1850, when cessions of land rights were taken by William Robinson along the northern shores of Lakes Huron and Superior, were treaties made that granted to the Indians all four items: once-for-all expenditures, annuities, reserves, and guarantees concerning hunting and fishing. It was for this reason that Alexander Morris, the most widely known of the government's negotiators, wrote of the Robinson Treaties as constituting the "forerunners of the future treaties" to be made by the recently created Dominion.

The provisions of many of the Southern Ontario treaties and surrenders are quite discordant with more recent agreements conveying far greater benefits to Aboriginal peoples elsewhere. Most cessions made in Ontario after 1830 were concluded in trust. The government assumed responsibility for disposing of the ceded lands on the Indians' behalf, with the proceeds of sales usually going to the particular Indians involved. As with land cessions made earlier, which were at times outright surrenders with the government as purchaser, there are strong arguments that inadequate compensation was given. Surrenders concluded prior to 1818 provided for a lump-sum payment along with a nominal yearly rent; in one 1816 surrender of Thurlow Township, for instance, the yearly rent was fixed at one peppercorn. In an 1836 surrender, it was considered sufficient to promise the Chippewa claimants agricultural and educational aid in exchange for their surrender of 1.5 million acres south of Owen Sound. The Robinson–Huron and Robinson–Superior Treaties also supplied only minimal payments to the Indians, although they contained provisions for a limited augmentation of annuities in the future. One oversight in the Huron Treaty presumably left Aboriginal rights intact at Temagami.

The Numbered Treaties

Treaties Nos. 1 to 7 were made during the 1870s in the territory between the watershed west of Lake Superior and the Rocky Mountains in what was then Canada's newly acquired Northwest. These treaties utilized many features of the earlier transactions, but were far more comprehensive in their provisions and more uniform and consistent with one another. Their characteristics and relative similarities were not due to a broad policy worked out in advance by the federal government. Indeed, immediately before the first of these treaties was made, the government had little information about the Indians of its new territory, let alone a policy. It proceeded to deal with the Aboriginal occupants in an ad hoc fashion as necessity dictated. Almost inevitably the patterns of earlier Canadian experience were adapted to a new time and place. The seven treaties that emerged were partly shaped by the Indians themselves and were indirectly influenced by United States practice.

The government's purpose in negotiating treaties in the Northwest was to free land for settlement and development. A corollary of this was the urgent desire to satisfy the Indians sufficiently so that they would remain peaceful. The nature and extent of Indian rights to the territory were not discussed at the negotiations, nor were they defined in the treaties themselves. It is evident from the texts, nevertheless, that the government intended that whatever title the Indians might possess should be extinguished, since the opening clauses of all seven agreements deal with land cession. This emphasis was not reflected in the preliminary treaty negotiations. There the stress was on what the Indians would receive rather than on what they were giving up. The commissioners gave them assurances that the Queen understood their problems and was anxious to help them (Henderson et al., 2000).

The loss of control over land use and the diminishing game supply threatened the traditional Aboriginal way of life. While the Indians attempted to retain as much control as possible over their own territory and future, a secondary desire was the attempt to gain sufficient compensation and support to ensure their survival amidst rapidly changing conditions. As a result of hard bargaining, Indians did manage to have some additional provisions included in the treaties beyond those the government had originally intended. These included agricultural aid and certain liberties to hunt and fish (Rotman, 1996).

Aboriginal people today make several points in relation to these treaties. The major one is that the treaty texts do not reflect the verbal promises made during the negotiations and accepted by a people accustomed to an oral tradition. They state that their ancestors understood the treaties to be specifically designed to protect them and help them adapt to the new realities by developing an alternative agricultural base to complement their traditional livelihood of hunting and fishing. An excellent discussion of the Aboriginal view of treaties, their intent, expectations, and interpretation is presented in a study by Treaty 7 Elders and Tribal Council (1996).

Aboriginal associations strongly deny that the treaties obligate the government only to fulfil their terms as they appear in the bare texts. They uniformly insist that the written versions must be taken together with the words spoken by the government's agents during the negotiations. In a submission to the Commissioner on Indian Claims, the Federation of Saskatchewan Indians states that:

> In his various addresses to Chiefs and Headmen at treaty meetings, Commissioner Morris had a single message for the Indians: The Queen was not approaching the Indians to barter for their lands, but to help them, to alleviate their distress and assist them in obtaining security for the future. "We are not here as traders, I do not come as to buy or sell horses or goods, I come to you, children of the Queen, to try to help you. The Queen knows that you are poor: the Queen knows that it is hard to find food for yourselves and children: she knows that the winters are cold, and you(r) children are often hungry: she has always cared for her Red children as much as for her White. Out of her generous heart and liberal hand she wants to do something for you...."
>
> These verbal assurances and statement of Crown intent, and the many others like them given by Morris in his address to Chiefs and Headmen, cannot be separated from treaty documents because they were accepted as truth by the assembled Indians (*Saskatchewan Indian*, 1982: 30).

The nature and extent of the implementation of treaty provisions are another source of grievance in this area. The government's open policy of detribalization, which held as its goal the assimilation of Indian people into the dominant society, motivated a number of specific policies that were destructive of Indian efforts to develop within the context of their own cultures. The field of education is one of the most conspicuous examples of this process, since it is easy to appreciate the effects of isolating children in residential schools where they were taught that their parents' language and culture were inferior, and where were instilled in them a set of alien customs and values (Pennekeok, 1976).

In the Aboriginal peoples' view, during the late 19th and early 20th centuries the government failed to provide the expected agricultural assistance and unduly restricted Indian agricultural development. It encouraged the surrender of some of the best agricultural land from the reserves when its efforts failed to turn the Indians into farmers.

All of the Prairie Aboriginal organizations, along with the Grand Council of Treaty No. 3 in Northern Ontario, think the treaties should be reworded in terms that will embody their original spirit and intent. As in Aboriginal title areas, the results of such settlements could, they say, provide the basis for revolutionizing the future development of Aboriginal peoples and reserves on Aboriginal terms. The treaty Indians' organizations have outlined some specific objectives and proposals for an approach to development. A primary characteristic of these is their rejection of the concept of assimilation or detribalization, and, stemming from this, the conviction that the Aboriginal people must initiate and control the development effort themselves. Only at the turn of the century, when mineral exploitation provided the impetus, were treaties made to the north of the areas surrendered during the 1870s. Treaty No. 8 was concluded in the Athabasca District, Treaty No. 9 in Northern Ontario, and Treaty No. 10 in Northern Saskatchewan. In addition, adhesions to Treaty No. 5 were taken in Northern Manitoba to extend the limit of ceded territory to the northern boundary of the province. Finally, in 1921, following the discovery of oil at Norman Wells, Treaty No. 11 was made in the Northwest Territories.

The "contract" treaties between the Indians and the Dominion began in the mid-1800s (in Southern Ontario) and moved westward, eventually encompassing all of Manitoba, Saskatchewan, and Alberta. The treaty period ended in 1921 with the signing of Treaty No. 11, which encompasses almost all of the Mackenzie Valley of the Northwest Territories. Today, only British Columbia, the Yukon, parts of Quebec, and Newfoundland have not "treatied" out with the Indians. It should be noted that where treaties have not been made, Aboriginal title is said to still exist, thus providing the basis for subsequent land claims and the modern-day treaty making process (McKee, 1996).

CLAIMS REGARDING TREATIES

As we pointed out earlier, the treaties have been the focal point for specific claims that have been pursued by Indians. Their claims with regard to treaties focus on several aspects. First of all, Indians argue that the treaty texts were not the same as the verbal promises made by the government during the negotiation period prior to the actual signing. Hence, they argue that the treaties oblige the government to keep promises made in both verbal and written contexts—for example, Treaties Nos. 8 and 11 (Melville, 1981). Secondly, inequality among the various treaties' land provisions has provoked specific claims—for example, Treaty No. 5 provides for 71 hectares per family while other treaties provide 285 hectares.

One example of a modern settlement involving a treaty concerns the Peter Ballantyne Band in Saskatchewan. To fulfil its remaining outstanding land entitlement claim, the Peter Ballantyne Band has selected approximately 81 000 hectares of land, including the site of the Prince Albert student residence. With the exception of the residence land, the rest is provincial Crown land. Remaining transfer settlements are now to be made between the province and the band. Under the terms of the Saskatchewan Formula of 1976, which is the federal–provincial agreement under which outstanding treaty land entitlements in

Saskatchewan are being settled, the Peter Ballantyne Band's outstanding entitlement is 92 860 hectares. The selection of these lands must deal satisfactorily with the interests of affected third parties. The transfer to reserve status means that the land will continue to be federal Crown land; however, it will be set aside as a reserve for the use and benefit of the Peter Ballantyne Band. The minister has approved the band's request that the land be set aside under the authority of Section 18(2) of the *Indian Act* for Aboriginal educational use. The band has stated that the current use of the land will not change in the foreseeable future.

The Prince Albert School is the only parcel of federal Crown land in Saskatchewan within a major urban area that has historically been administered by Canada, through the Department of Indian Affairs, for the benefit of the Aboriginal people. In this respect the selection is unique and its transfer to reserve status is now viewed as a precedent for future land selections.

The 1991 settlement between the Alberta Stoney Indian tribe and the federal government is the second-largest specific claim ever settled in Alberta. It provides nearly $20 million in compensation to the tribe for loss of mineral rights on land surrendered in 1929 for hydro development. In 1999, Canada's oldest Indian person (aged 106) launched a suit against the federal government for $1.5 billion and access to a few square kilometres of land in Alberta's tar-sands country. Mr. Raphael Cree and others have been pressing their claim to the little Clearwater River Reserve for decades (first in 1921) without success. The claim stems from the signing of Treaty 8 and the failure to include all Indian groups in the area.

Treaties have three possible interpretations. In one sense they can be viewed as agreements between two or more nations. Most Aboriginal people claim this interpretation when they refer to the various treaties with the federal government. On the other hand, it is clear that the Canadian government (as evidenced through certain legislation and court decisions) does not interpret the treaties in the same manner (Weaver, 1983).

Secondly, treaties have at times been interpreted as contracts. While there is some legal support for this interpretation, the nature of the court cases dealing with this issue is so specific that one must be cautious in interpreting treaties from this perspective. Nevertheless, former prime minister Pierre Trudeau publicly stated that treaties are analogous to contracts.

Finally, treaties can be viewed as pieces of legislation. This interpretation is plausible since many Indian treaties were made before such legislation as the *Indian Act.* Hence, any legal means that attempts to establish an orderly relationship between people could be viewed as analogous to legislation (Marule, 1977).

To date, it is unclear which interpretation will prevail. In addition, the courts have tended to rule that the provisions of the treaties can be overridden by federal, but not provincial, legislation. Nevertheless, they have also viewed treaties as enforceable obligations and have in the past forced the federal government to live up to those obligations.

Treaties are legal arrangements between Aboriginal peoples and the Government of Canada. Moreover, treaties confer benefits upon successors even though at times it is difficult to identify who those successors are. The Supreme Court of Canada has recently identified a number of conditions to determine if a document is a treaty. It listed five considerations:

1. continuous exercise of a right in the past and at present;

2. the reasons that the Crown made a commitment;

3. the situation prevailing at the time the document was signed;

4. evidence of relations of mutual respect and esteem between the negotiators; and

5. the subsequent conduct of the parties.

If, after reviewing the above, ambiguity still remains, the Court decided that one could look at extrinsic evidence, such as the historical context, information about what went on at the time the document was signed, and the subsequent conduct of the parties. In all instances regarding the interpretation of treaties, the Supreme Court encourages and supports interpretations in favour of, and for the benefit of, Indian people as part of fiduciary doctrine. The Court's and the federal government's reasoning extends even to the "Peace and Friendship" treaties of the 18th century, as shown by the Marshall decision in September 1999.

"Scope of Aboriginal Ruling in Dispute"

Natives, federal minister say forestry and mining, as well as fishing rights must be discussed

By Heather Scoffield

Indian Affairs Minister Robert Nault says he would be able to resolve the Mi'kmaq fishing dispute on the East coast if only the provinces would cooperate....

The federal government has appointed a chief negotiator to lead talks between the Aboriginal groups, the maritime provinces and the federal government. The object is to settle on how to interpret the Sept. 17 Supreme Court decision, which ruled that maritime Natives have the right to fish, hunt and gather for a "moderate livelihood."...

Mr. Nault says the negotiations must involve more than fish. The Supreme Court decision that set off the dispute between Native and non-Native fishermen on the East coast, applied broadly to Aboriginal rights in all natural resources, he said.

But the Maritime provinces, which met with Mr. Nault earlier this week, say the negotiations with the Natives of the East coast should be limited to dealing with the lobster fishery.

Nova Scotia's Minister of Aboriginal Affairs said the lobster dispute must be settled before there can be any discussion of extending the treaty right.

"People here are extremely frustrated that more than one month after the Supreme Court of Canada ruling there is still too much uncertainty over management of the lobster fishery," Michael Baker said in a statement. "We've said it before, but what we need here is some real leadership."

New Brunswick Aboriginal Affairs Brad Green has insisted that his province does not accept the federal view that the treaty right extends to logging.

But since the decision, several loggers in the northern New Brunswick Bands of Big Cove and Red Bank have resumed logging operations....

On Thursday, the Mi'kmaq of Nova Scotia won another court battle over natural resources. The federal court of appeal ruled that the National Energy Board did not deal adequately with Aboriginal people when it granted construction rights for a $1.7 billion pipeline for the Sable Island project.

And another key case about Aboriginal rights over natural resources is expected soon.

"We keep going back to the whole theme of Aboriginal people having the right to share in resources," Mr. Nault said.

Source: Excerpted from *The Globe and Mail*, October 23, 1999, p. A5.

MÉTIS SCRIP

Related to the issue of treaties are the concerns Métis people have regarding their Aboriginal and/or land rights. While not called treaties, several acts were passed by the federal government that provided land for Métis, e.g., the *Manitoba Act* and *Dominion Lands Act*. The conditions for the transfer of land to Métis are outlined in these various acts. In the case of the Métis, the allocation of land (or money) was through the process of scrip. Scrip is a certificate giving the holder the right to receive payment later in the form of cash, goods, or land (Sawchuk et al., 1981). This process differed from Indian treaties in that it involved grants to individuals as individuals; it did not purport to set up the Métis as a continuing corporate entity. For over 30 years (1885–1923) there was a series of scrip allotments to Métis. Each time that a new part of the prairie provinces or the Mackenzie Valley was ceded by Indians, persons of mixed blood who did not participate were allocated scrip redeemable in land (Flanagan, 1983a).

Prior to 1870, Métis had not been dealt with as a separate group. However, expediency or perhaps humanitarian reasons led to a change; under Section 31 of the *Manitoba Act, 1870,* a proportion of 623 000 hectares originally calculated as unoccupied land was set aside for the children of Métis families in Manitoba. This land was reserved for "the benefits of the families of the half-breed residents." It was to be divided "among the children of the half-breed heads of families" residing in the province at the time of its transfer to Canada. Initially, the amount of land set aside was thought to provide each child with 290 acres (116 hectares). However, due to miscalculations, the government also had to issue money scrip in lieu of land. In 1874 the heads of Métis families were also provided with scrip (71 hectares or $160). Under the *Dominion Lands Act* in 1885, all Métis resident in the Northwest Territories outside the limits of Manitoba in 1870 were granted 107 hectares. By this time, the government had allotted 579 264 hectares of land and $509 760 to Métis in Manitoba. Four years later this would be extended to Métis resident in the area ceded by the adhesion to Treaty No. 6 (Taylor, 1983). In 1899 Métis in the Athabasca and Peace River areas were given scrip, and in 1906 all Métis permanently residing in the territory ceded at the time of making Treaty No. 10 were provided with 107 hectares. Finally, in 1921 each Métis of the Mackenzie River district received $240 to extinguish their Aboriginal rights (Sealey and Lussier, 1975). In all, the government handled more than 24 000 Métis claims (14 000 in the Northwest Territories, Saskatchewan, and Alberta, and 10 000 in Manitoba). These claims involved over one million hectares of land and in excess of $3.6 million.

The use of scrip was not confined to Métis. Non-Aboriginal settlers in 1873, and later (1885) veterans of the Boer War and officers of the North West Mounted Police, were also given land scrip. The scrip were in two forms and looked as follows.[5]

A typical land scrip certificate read:

Dominion of Canada

Department of the Interior

This Scrip note is receivable as payment in full for ONE HUNDRED and SIXTY ACRES of Dominion Lands, open for ordinary Homestead only if presented by _____ at the office of Dominion Lands of the District within which such lands are situated in conformity with Scrip Certificate form _____ granted by the North West Half Breed Commission this _____ day of _____, 18 _____.

A typical money scrip certificate read:

Dominion of Canada

Department of the Interior

In conformity with Certificate form No. _____ granted by the North West Half Breed Commission, it is Hereby Certified that under the authority of an order of the Honorable the Privy Council dated _____ day of _____, 18 _____ as amended by the order of _____ of _____, 18 _____, and in accordance with the provisions of subsec. (e), Sec. 81, 46 Vic. Cap. 17 _____, a Half-Breed is entitled to TWO HUNDRED AND FORTY DOLLARS IN SCRIP. The coupons attached to this will be accepted in payment of Dominion Lands on presentation at the office of Dominion Lands of the District within which such lands are situated.

Issued at the Department of the Interior, Ottawa, this _____ day of _____, 18 _____.

After passage of the *Manitoba Act* of 1870, which set aside lands for Métis, the government began a systematic process of amending the Act so that land set aside would not actually be allotted. From 1873 to 1884, 11 amendments were passed, referred to as Manitoba Supplementary Provisions. Nearly half of these amendments altered substantive portions of the original law. The effect of all of the amendments was the dispersal of the original Métis people in Manitoba. Only about 20 percent of the claimants received and made use of their land allotments. A similar percentage of river-lot occupants obtained patents and remained on the land they occupied in 1870. Over half the potential recipients were denied their land through a number of government manoeuvres (Sawchuk, 1978, 1998).

Perhaps the single most important factor that prevented Métis from reaping the potential benefits of land claim settlements was the 1874 amendment to the 1870 Act, which restricted eligibility for the initial allotment. It should be noted that even in the original allotment many children were omitted from participating in the benefits of the Act. The 1874 amendment, which declared that heads of families were entitled to the same benefits as children, excluded the heads from receiving any part of the original 1.4 million acres set aside. Instead they were awarded $160 in scrip that could be used to purchase Crown land (Dickason, 1992). As Dickason points out, "Fortunes were made at the expense of the Métis—half-breed scrip millionaires" were created (1992, p. 317). Scrip was sold to land speculators (bankers and wealthy individuals) for as little as half its face value. In some cases, accepting scrip left Métis poorer than before.

Children who received an allotment were not adequately protected. For example, their allotments were subject to payment of local taxes from the moment the allotment was drawn. Thus, even if they were minors and had no way of paying the tax, they were expected to do so. Failure of tax payment meant the loss of the property.

Finally, Métis river-lot claimants were not compensated by the government for railway or other public expropriation. However, homesteaders were. The federal government acted in many other ways that placed the Métis in a disadvantageous position (Peterson and Brown, 1985).

Some writers, such as Flanagan (1983a), claim that Métis only wanted money scrip and thus were not interested in obtaining land scrip. He also notes that some Métis insisted on receiving their entitlements in as liquid a form as possible. He points to the Métis of Lesser Slave Lake, who refused to accept scrip until it was rewritten "payable to the bearer." He also argues that Métis were good negotiators and that they operated in a "willing buyer–willing seller" market. We would acknowledge that some Métis preferred money scrip and we would concur that some were skilful negotiators. However, the structural conditions under which Métis operated did not allow for the exercise of choice, nor did they fully understand the implications of not having land deeded to them. For example, nearly 60 percent of the Métis were illiterate, a definite liability when dealing with banks and lawyers. The Métis Association of Alberta also pointed out in its study, *Métis Land Rights in Alberta: A Political History* (1981), that the use of land scrip came about because Métis opposed money scrip and wanted land grants. Métis of the Qu'Appelle Lakes refused to accept money scrip. Thus, land scrip was considered a compromise. There is also no doubt that most of the land scrip issued to Métis was eventually owned by banks and financial agents.

Evidence today is clear that when fraud was committed in obtaining these certificates, the government did little or nothing about it. For example, in 1900 two federal commissioners found that many powers of attorney were signed without the forms being completed. In other cases, Métis who anticipated receiving scrip were asked to sign power of attorney to brokers hoping to make money out of scrip settlements (Purich, 1988). Other evidence shows that land owned by minors was not safeguarded and was lost to non-Aboriginal land speculators for much less than it was worth. It is clear that large-scale land transfer from Métis to land agents and banks took place. What remains to be seen is how the government deals with these fraudulent transfers (Pelletier, 1974, 1975).

The scrip claims being pursued today by the Métis centre on several charges: (1) that scrip was unjustly and inefficiently administered, (2) that the compensation was inadequate, (3) that Métis in British Columbia, Southern Alberta, and the Yukon received no compensation, and (4) that in certain areas most of the scrip issued was in the form of cash, not land (Hatt, 1983). Driben (1983) argues that since the government agreed to make scrip available to Métis in Western Canada, it was a *de facto* admission that they held Aboriginal title. Furthermore, he argues that the legal definition until just after Confederation did not distinguish between Métis and Indians; they were both considered "Aboriginal." Scrip takers and their descendants are now challenging the legality of the issuance of scrip to many people, which forced them to lose their Indian status and treaty rights. Giokas and Chartrand (2002) note that court cases filed focus on "Canada's breach of their treaty rights as well as instances of duress, undue influence, fraud, bribery, and *non-es factum*" (p. 94). Finally, Driben points out that Métis were, on occasion, included in the treaties, and he cites Treaty No. 3 as an example. Indeed, a Supreme Court landmark decision September 19, 2003, finally recognized Métis peoples as Aboriginal peoples under the Canadian Constitution, granting them status on par with Native Indians and Inuit.

TREATIES TODAY

Are treaties signed years ago still valid? Canadians woke up on September 17, 1999, to find they are indeed. A Supreme Court decision on that day upheld a 240-year-old treaty between the King of England and the Mi'kmaq Indians. The Supreme Court ruled that the treaty gave Mi'kmaq the right to fishing for daily needs and/or to obtain a moderate livelihood, including food, clothing, and housing, supplemented by a few amenities. This decision has forced the federal government to reassess its position on the 334 outstanding treaty cases now before the Department of Indian Affairs. The impact of this decision is far reaching and Aboriginal people on the West Coast have argued that they also have fishing and hunting rights under the 150-year-old Douglas Treaty. Russel Barsh has noted that the high court's ruling includes a "way of life" provision that will have a dramatic effect on provincial hunting and fishing regulations in Canada. For example, he noted that members of Treaty 7 could hunt legally in the national parks and on unoccupied Crown land.

As a result of the treaties, the government of Canada received millions of acres of land from the surrender of First Nations while, in return, 0.32 percent of Canada's land mass was set aside for reserves. Many irregularities emerged in the allocation of this land and, in many cases, treaty land entitlements could be claimed. While these entitlements are complex and complicated, they are legal obligations, recognized in the Constitution of Canada, that must be dealt with by the Government of Canada. The term *treaty land enti-*

Métis Win Landmark Ruling

Supreme Court decision grants status on par with native Indians and Inuit

By Kirk Makin

The Métis people are a distinct aboriginal group with a constitutional right to hunt for food, the Supreme Court of Canada said in a landmark ruling yesterday.

The unanimous judgment vaulted the approximately 300,000 Métis across the country from their lowly station in Canadian constitutional limbo to a rank that equates them with native Indians and Inuit.

If their overtures are rejected, the Métis would be in a position to return to court clutching the court's powerful ruling as ammunition.

A jubilant roar filled the Supreme Court's vast marble lobby as the ruling was released. Dozens of Métis people wearing colourful traditional sashes hugged and wept. The decision caps a 130-year battle dating back to the rebellions led by Louis Riel.

The court's judgment stressed that the existence in the Constitution of the Métis—of mixed native and European descent—"protects practices that were historically important features of these distinctive communities, and that persist in the present day as integral elements of their Métis culture."

Highlights of the Supreme Court ruling on the Métis:

- The development of a more systematic method of identifying Métis rights-holders for the purpose of enforcing hunting regulations is an urgent priority.
- In addition to demographic evidence, proof of shared customs, traditions and a collective identity is required to demonstrate the existence of a Métis community that can support a claim to site-specific aboriginal rights.
- As Métis communities continue to organize themselves more formally and to assert their constitutional rights, it is imperative that membership requirements become more standardized so that legitimate rights-holders can be identified.

Source: Excerpted from *The Globe and Mail*, September 20, 2003, pp. A1, A4. Reprinted with permission from the Globe and Mail.

tlement is used to document land claims that flow from Treaty Nos. 1–11. There are two forms. The first is called initial or "late" entitlement, which reflects the fact that the First Nations did not receive the land promised under the treaty. The second is a shortfall, which refers to the situation in which a calculation for the amount of land to be set aside did not include all the eligible population. To resolve these claims requires considerable time and money to ensure that all factors are taken into consideration when evaluating the claim.

One of the major recommendations presented by the Royal Commission on Aboriginal Peoples was that the federal government develop a trilateral relationship with regard to establishing new treaties. These new treaties would establish integrated processes on a regional level to deal with governance and jurisdictional issues. This recommendation has been accepted and is now in force in several provinces. With a new federal policy emphasizing a renewed partnership with Aboriginal peoples and an agreement that land claims need to be settled, it comes as no surprise that considerable activity has focused on land and land compensation. British Columbia is by far the most active in establishing new treaties and, by mid-2003, 51 Aboriginal groups, representing over 70 percent of B.C.'s First Nations, were active in treaty negotiation through the tripartite lands commission. Setting the stage, the province established a Treaty Negotiation Advisory Committee in 1996 to provide input and advice to the government with regard to establishing treaties in the province and settling outstanding claims by Aboriginal peoples. Progress is equally dramatic in other jurisdictions, as shown by the example of the Tlicho final agreement (August 25, 2003), which effectively replaces the 82-year-old Treaty No. 11 from the Northwest Territories (see box on p. 201).

One of the most important settlements that has taken place over the past five years is the 2000 Nisga'a Treaty. This treaty is the first British Columbia treaty since 1899 and is the fourteenth modern day treaty in Canada. This settlement was approved amid considerable political controversy and over 500 public events and consultations have taken place in the negotiations between the Nisga'a and the provincial Treaty Negotiation Advisory Committee, composed of 31 individuals representing various third-party interests. The treaty has been accepted by the Nisga'a Council and the B.C. Legislature and once Parliament ratifies the treaty, it cannot be amended by Parliament according to the provisions of the treaty itself.

The Nisga'a treaty took 111 years to be settled and represents a milestone in treaty settlements in British Columbia. It will also give the Nisga'a a central government with the authority to make laws concerning social services (including child and family issues), adoption and health services, as well as tribal jurisdiction over education. While laws can be established by the Nisga'a, they must be in agreement with the existing provincial and federal statutes. Laws established by the Nisga'a will have standing in any court dispute. In addition, the Nisga'a will administer and deliver federal and provincial social services. How this will take place has not yet been determined and, once formulated, will have to be agreed to by both the provincial and federal governments. Under the treaty, the Nisga'a will continue to provide the services they have been taking over and will then have full jurisdiction over them. These services will be funded through a federal transfer of funds. However, as soon as the Nisga'a begin to generate their own income, perhaps through taxation, the transfer funds will be reduced commensurately. On the face of it, the treaty seems to give the Nisga'a municipal status. However, the fact that they will be in control of their social services, health, and education makes their system different from a municipal structure. For example, the treaty notes (Section 27) that in the event of an inconsis-

N.W.T. Natives Granted Control of 39,000 sq. km

PM signs land claim the size of Belgium

By Nathan Vanderklippe

About 3000 aborginal residents of the Northwest Territories entered a new era of self-determination yesterday as federal, territorial and aboriginal leaders signed the Tlicho [Dogrib] final agreement....

The Tlicho final agreement creates the first aboriginal government in the N.W.T. It gives the Tlicho $152-million over 15 years, year-round hunting and fishing rights and control over 39 000 square kilometres....

Negotiations on the Tlicho final agreement began in 1992, 17 years after the N.W.T. Indian Brotherhood issued a controversial statement saying that the government of the Northwest Territories was not the government of the Dene.

The new agreement creates two new land and water management boards, giving the Tlicho regulatory authority over their land. It also gives the Tlicho the ability to assess royalties on any mining or oil and gas activity within the newly created region....

The Treaty 11 Council has already developed an extensive network of band-owned companies that build roads and houses, operate an airport, run a sporting-goods store, haul diamond ore, fight forest fires and match southern companies with northern workers.

The agreement leaves administration of key programs such as health care and education with the territorial government for the next 10 years, while the Tlicho prepare to run programs.

Source: Material reprinted with the express permission of Pacific Newspaper Group Inc., a CanWest Partnership.

tency between the Nisga'a laws and federal and provincial laws of general application, Nisga'a law will prevail. Finally, the treaty stipulates that voting rights on Native territory will be restricted to people of Nisga'a descent.

Several criticisms of the treaty have been identified. First of all, critics claim that the treaty is "race based" and thus it gives the Nisga'a rights that other "races" do not have. A closer look at the treaty characterizes the Nisga'a as a linguistically and culturally identified group, not a race. Others claim that the treaty is an example of modern day apartheid. As Foster (1998–99) points out, there is something hypocritical about stripping a people of their resources in one generation and then describing a complex and careful attempt by the next generation to restore some of those resources as "apartheid" or as a violation of equality before the law. A second criticism is that the government "gave it all away." In truth, the Nisga'a will only be getting about 10 percent of the land they are able to demonstrate as their traditional territories. In British Columbia, Indian reserves make up about 0.35 percent of the province and the treaty will add little to this figure. Surely this cannot be viewed as an exorbitant land settlement. Other critics claim that the treaty amends the Constitution because it requires a referendum by both the provincial legislature and the federal House of Commons. On the contrary, the treaty does not amend the Constitution but rather ensures that both levels of government confirm the treaty and take it seriously. Finally, it is argued that it is not prudent for Canada and British Columbia to sign a final agreement with the Nisga'a when it is still not clear whether or not the *Delgamuukw* decision has given them more rights than the Nisga'a will get. According to federal and provincial authorities, they, along with the Nisga'a, reviewed the decision before deciding to carry on negotiations and they have agreed that the treaty is a final settlement of the Nisga'a land claims. Behind these criticisms, one suspects that the real reason for objecting to the Nisga'a treaty is that it sets a "benchmark" for all others now being negotiated. No Aboriginal negotiator will take less than the Nisga'a, and that might be a real problem—or one that simply leads to unrealistic expectations. Whichever the case, the treaty has implications for future negotiations (Gibson, 1998–99).

In addition to non-Aboriginal people criticizing the treaty, other Aboriginal groups have raised questions (Sterritt, 1998–99). They argue that the Nisga'a do not have a claim to the entire Nass watershed (based upon the critics' own evidence) and thus the treaty violates the rights of other nearby Aboriginal groups. They go on to point out that the failure of the provincial and federal governments' response to the claims made by the Gitksan and Gitanyow submissions has serious consequences for their "overlapping" claims (Rotman, 1997).

CONCLUSION

From the time the first European set foot on what was to become Canada until the current limits were fixed by the inclusion of Newfoundland in 1949, European sovereignty over the land was essentially a matter of effective occupation. On the East Coast, the Vikings barely established a toehold and disappeared almost without a trace; the bitter contests between the French and first the English, then the British after the Union of the Crowns, were finally resolved by force of arms in 1756–63, following three centuries of contention. On the West Coast, despite the claim said to have been established by Drake at the 38th parallel in the 16th century, Spain held the coast well north of the 40th parallel until pushed out of contention. The Russian claim to the entire coast from the 55th parallel north was never seriously contested by Britain, yet Russian America passed rapidly to the United States by purchase in 1867.

With the extension of international rivalries on the North American continent, traditional inter-tribal conflicts were often intensified. Group movements became more frequent and were subject to manipulation by the competing European factions, both in colonial wars and through the fur trade. The fur trader needed the Indian collector, and from this need grew esteem and understanding. As fur resources were depleted and large-scale settlement became a factor, the Indian could not escape the unappreciative attention of the incoming developers and homesteaders.

Indian treaty activity in Canada began with the Maritime "Peace and Friendship" agreements during colonial struggles, in which the principals agreed to aid each other in conflict or to remain neutral. There was no mention of land title, and, invariably, the Indian people were assured that they would not be disturbed in their traditional pursuits (hunting, fishing, and trapping). Between 1725 and 1779 there were as many as eight agreements of this type; the Mi'kmaq treaties of 1760–61 are examples of these that have become the basis for modern-day treaty interpretations and negotiations.

The most significant date in Canadian Indian treaty matters is October 7, 1763, when, by *Royal Proclamation*, the British Sovereign directed that all endeavours to clear the Indian title must be by Crown purchase. In effect, the Proclamation applied to lands then west of the settled areas, Old Quebec and the Maritimes having been passed over as if they had been adequately dealt with. The anticipated influx of settlers was accelerated by the Revolutionary War (1775–83) and then by the War of 1812; hence, the half-century between 1775 and 1825 witnessed a comprehensive land surrender scheme to extinguish Indian title, involving most of what is now Southern Ontario. Compensation to the Indian groups deemed to be *in situ* was sometimes in cash, sometimes in goods. The land so cleared or ceded was considered freed of all encumbrance, with plenty of room for Indians and non-Indians alike.

Thereafter, the exigencies of Canada's growth westward and northward dictated the pace and direction of treaty activity. The discovery of minerals north of Lakes Superior and Huron precipitated the negotiation of the Robinson Treaties in 1850 with the Ojibwa. Plans to settle the region of the Fertile Belt in the Prairies exerted similar pressures as the Indian peoples and the Crown in right of Canada signed Treaties Nos. 1 through 7 between 1871 and 1877. Subsequent treaty activity continued ad hoc—the discovery of gold at the Klondike River (1897) led to Treaty No. 8 in 1899, thus clearing the access route from Edmonton to the Pelly River; plans for construction of roads and railways precipitated the signing of Treaty No. 9 in 1905; Treaty No. 10 in 1906 immediately followed the attainment of provincial status for Saskatchewan and Alberta; the discovery of oil at Norman Wells in 1920 preceded Treaty No. 11 by one year.

The Commissioners saw the treaties in one way; the Indians in quite another. A reading of the reports of the Commissioners and of Lieutenant-Governor Morris's book (1880, 1971) shows that the two groups came together with radically different expectations. The Indians sought to be protected from land-grabbing settlers and from the evils they sensed. Buffalo herds were diminishing—the railway was projected; they sought wide ranges that they could call their own and over which they could live much as they had in the past. The Commissioners saw Indian reserves as places where Indians could learn to be settlers and farmers. Some Indian spokesmen appeared to accept the idea of farming, but it is unlikely that they fully understood all that was entailed (Maybury-Lewis, 1997).

There has been little treaty activity in Canada since the 1923 Chippewa and Mississauga Agreements in Ontario (agreements that involved compensation for surrender of Indian hunting, fishing, and trapping rights).

In the 1970s, loss of "traditional livelihood" through hydroelectric power development (James Bay) and oil-producing schemes (Northern pipelines) precipitated a strong dialogue between Aboriginal groups and government. By combining a higher degree of research with consultation and negotiations on both sides, compensatory agreements have been or are being worked out in many non-treaty areas of Canada. In those areas already covered by treaties, the federal government has stated that it will honour its "lawful obligations"; to this effect it has provided research funding for Aboriginal bands and organizations in order to investigate claims or grievances relating to the fulfilment or interpretation of Indian treaties.

Aboriginal people see more advantages than disadvantages in the treaty process, and consider it the preferred manner in which to handle future negotiated settlements. The disadvantages stem from issues of interpretation that have led to disagreements between the two parties. When trying to resolve treaty issues, governments have insisted on looking only at the written documentation without reflecting on the oral arrangements that led up to and included the written document. On the other hand, when the courts have been asked to render an interpretation, the more recent cases (but not all) have favoured the Indian position. This has raised some concerns about using treaties as the strategy for resolving land/treaty claims for Aboriginal groups (Perry, 1996).

Aboriginal people feel that the terms set out in each treaty need to be fulfilled and dealt with immediately. They also feel that there must be reconciliation between the spirit and intent of the treaties and the rights of Canadians as a whole.

NOTES

1. Portions of this chapter are from *Indian Claims in Canada and Indian Treaties in Historical Perspective* (Ottawa: Minister of Supply and Services, 1981). Permission has been received from the Minister of Supply and Services Canada to reproduce the material.

2. Pontiac was an early leader of a Nativistic movement directed against the intrusion of missionaries in the area. He was also a firm believer in uniting Indian tribes and had led several successful engagements against the English, including such unorthodox Indian war strategies as laying siege to Fort Detroit.

3. In 1981, the Ontario Supreme Court decided that Aboriginal peoples who have treaty rights can legally hunt and fish out of season on Crown land in Eastern Ontario. The decision, involving the 1818 treaty with the Mississauga Indians, was partially based upon oral records of the day. The decision states that the minutes of a council meeting between the deputy superintendent of Indian Affairs and the Indians in 1818 recorded the oral portion of the 1818 treaty and are as much a part of the treaty as the written articles of the provincial agreement.

4. The increased allotment of 640 acres (260 hectares) in Treaty No. 3 became standard for all future treaties except for Treaty No. 5, which reverted to the 160-acre (65 hectares) allotment. Other changes that became standard included assurances of continued hunting, fishing, and trapping rights, an annual budget for ammunitions, and the provision of agricultural supplies, such as cattle, seed, and farm implements.

5. Over time the specific words were changed, but the overall structure and legal effect remained the same.

WEBLINKS

www.bloorstreet.com/200block/brintro.htm

"A Brief Introduction into Aboriginal Law in Canada," by Bill Henderson, is an ideal point of departure for learning about various historical treaties between Aboriginal peoples and European-settler governments.

www.bloorstreet.com/200block/rp1763.htm

The *Royal Proclamation* of 1763 is reproduced in full, with an annotation giving some context and interpretive assistance. The treaty is known as the "Magna Carta of Indian Rights."

www.inac.gc.ca

This link is to the Indian and Northern Affairs site, which provides current highlights, access to regional offices, programs and services, publications and research, and important internal links to news releases and information on Aboriginal status and treaties. A related site is www.inac.gc.ca/bc/ftno which is the Federal Treaty Negotiation Office; this site provides information on progress in treaty negotiations, FAQs, and links to many treaty-related sites across Canada.

chapter eight

Contesting Title and Ownership: The Modern Claims and Treaty Process

INTRODUCTION

Aboriginal land claims today involve much more than legal questions about the collective title and property rights of Aboriginal peoples. They are also not simply concerned with determining an appropriate amount of financial compensation (Moss and Niemczak, 1991). Land claims are a balance between negotiation and litigation, and government action and inaction, as well as being subject to passive and active resistance by both Aboriginal people and governments (Hodgins et al., 1992). They are perhaps the most sensitive and volatile issues now confronting Aboriginal peoples and government (Mallea, 1994).

In the 19th century, Aboriginal land fuelled Canadian and American economic growth. However, dispossession had an opposite effect on the Indian Nations. It contributed to their underdevelopment to the extent that Aboriginal peoples were unable to sustain themselves. Within a century this process had destroyed the Aboriginal economic base. In addition, the land base was unequally distributed: the most fertile land was taken for European settlers, control over water went to the government, and the environment was altered to the disadvantage of Aboriginal people. As Cornell (1988) points out, they struggled to adapt, but their economies were falling apart and they had no way of entering the new emerging capitalist structure. The result was the beginning of economic marginalization and dependency. Today Aboriginals remain among the most marginalized and poorest communities, discriminated against and often exposed to grave abuses of their fundamental rights. While the Canadian government has publicly stated that it wants to make indigenous rights a reality, as demonstrated by its actions and failure to act, the results have not changed First Nations' status in over a century. This lack of commitment is most clearly demonstrated by the way government has been dragging its feet with regard to land claims. Large-scale projects for the construction of infrastructure or the extraction of natural resources on indigenous lands are pursued without consultation or thought as to how they will impact the lives and health of Aboriginal people.

The reactive stance that Aboriginal people have typically adopted can be seen in a variety of institutional settings—religious, economic, and educational. The inability to coordinate their actions, the lack of funding, and the lack of understanding of the political process have led to this failure to control the agenda when dealing with the federal/provincial governments. The emergence of various factions within the Aboriginal community has also hindered their planning and political strategies. Attempts to establish any sense of community and/or compromise amongst Aboriginal groups have been lacking—a situation ostensibly at odds with the traditional Aboriginal "consensus" model of decision making.

This lack of consensus has been exploited by agencies and organizations dealing with Aboriginal people. It has allowed them to act in any way they felt, justifying their actions through the inability of Aboriginal people to agree. However, conditions have changed over the past two decades and Aboriginal people are beginning to act in a concerted, proactive manner. They have come to realize that if they do not, decisions will be enacted that will seal the fate of Aboriginal peoples as peoples relegated to a marginal position in the political economy of Canada (Cultural Survival Quarterly, n.d.).

Aboriginal people have over the past several decades begun to think in proactive terms, not constrained by existing bureaucratic rules. However, a century of control and marginalization has had its impact; a dependency mentality has been created, and it is this sense of limited capacity to act that must be dealt with. Nevertheless, Aboriginal people are beginning to become proactive in their dealings with provincial and federal governments. They are also establishing a priority of goals that they are prepared to pursue. Boundaries are being established in order to determine when and how they will take action through either reaction or proaction. Agendas are being clearly spelled out and strategies planned. Community divisiveness is being dealt with and ranks are being closed to ensure a unified response to government. Finally, fiscal issues are being considered as only one component in the highly complex matrix of decision making. If decisions are always based on financial considerations, then the process of consultation and negotiation is reduced to economic choices, a substantial handicap for any group trying to advance its agenda (Sanders, 1983a, 1983b).

One issue about which Aboriginal people have become more proactive is their concern over land. They have, after many years, realized that they can pursue land claims even though results are not easily achieved. The early, disappointing outcome of their land claims slowed their initiatives. However, as they have become more skilled at legal confrontation, their successes have increased. They have also fully appreciated the connectedness of land and their culture. As Altman and Nieuwenhuysen (1979) point out, the special relationship that Aboriginal people have with the land seems best described by the word "spiritual." Having fully reclaimed this perspective, Aboriginal people have now taken on the challenge of reclaiming land that they feel rightly belongs to them. As Mallea (1994) and Issac (1995) have pointed out, the law on this subject has developed rapidly in the last four years, and concepts and precedents have travelled across international borders.

THE EARLY LAND CONFLICTS

Aboriginal peoples of Canada have come under European influence in various ways, to differing degrees, and at different historical periods. For example, little impact was made on Aboriginal peoples in the Arctic until this century, and most of that has occurred since

World War II. On the other hand, the Indians of the Atlantic coast and along the shores of the St. Lawrence River encountered Europeans early in the 16th century. As a result of this contact, the Beothuk of Newfoundland were obliterated. Overall, Aboriginal people in the more southerly parts of the country have, since contact, moved toward a Euro-Canadian way of life, while in northern areas more continuity has been preserved with traditional patterns of living. However, nowhere has Aboriginal life been entirely unaffected by the advent of the European settlers and the domination of territory that was once the exclusive domain of Aboriginal peoples (DIAND, 1978, 1981a).

Early relationships between Aboriginal peoples and Europeans were both helpful and destructive, sought after and rejected, rewarding and penalizing. However, for Aboriginal peoples, the positive outcomes of contact were outweighed by the negative. The acquisition of metal tools allowed them to hunt and gather in a more efficient manner, which probably improved the quality of their lives. However, at the same time, this acceptance of "modern" technology meant the destruction of their habitat, their way of life, and eventually their ideology—i.e., the belief system that structures the relationships among Aboriginal people and their relationship with the cosmos. On the other side, as Miller (2000) points out, Europeans benefited from the contact through profit and expansion; the fur trade was the most obvious advantage.

European–Aboriginal interaction has taken many forms. As noted above, the fur trade significantly altered the way of life of a large segment of the Indian population, economically, politically, and socially. While the fur trade introduced European goods and commercial values, it also brought with it Western moral and religious persuasions. At the same time, social interaction brought into being the people of mixed ancestry often referred to as Métis. The later occupation of land for settlement was further instrumental in modifying the economic and socio-cultural bases of Aboriginal societies. Resource exploitation in almost every part of the country also disturbed the lives of Aboriginal peoples both directly and indirectly through its environmental effects. Such activity continues today, with similarly disruptive results.

From an early period, the government of the colonizing society made itself specifically responsible for the relationship between the immigrants and the Aboriginal people. In law, the Aboriginal interest in land and other natural resources could not be acquired directly by the newcomers, but only through the agency of their government. In addition, the government assumed much of the direction of Aboriginal societies, particularly those whose traditional way of life was most disrupted. The historical relationship of the government to Aboriginal groups accounts for Aboriginal insistence on their continuing special status as the original people of Canada (Shewell, 2004). As a result, the federal government has become the target of Aboriginal grievances in regard to land, natural resources, and the management of Aboriginal affairs. These claims are based on Aboriginal rights or on agreements made with the government that were based on the Indians' position as unconquered indigenous occupants of the land.

TYPES OF CLAIMS

There are three general categories of claims: Aboriginal rights (including "title"), treaty and scrip settlement grievances, and land claims. Chapter 7 focused specifically on treaty and scrip issues, so this chapter will deal specifically with Aboriginal rights and land claims. The notion of Aboriginal rights underlies all Aboriginal claims in Canada.

Aboriginal people assert that their rights to land derive from their original occupancy, and they point out that Aboriginal title has been recognized by the dominant society through various judicial decrees and actions of the government. It is important to note that no treaties were ever made for about half the territory in Canada where Aboriginal people ceded their lands. On this basis alone, both status and non-status Indians, as well as Inuit, are now developing or negotiating terms.

Treaty Indians have a number of claims that relate to the agreement for the cession of their lands through treaty. Some of these rest on an insistence that specific treaty terms have not been fulfilled and that the broader spirit of the treaties has not been assumed by the government. A frequent claim is that verbal promises made at the time of the negotiations were not included in the written texts. In some areas, Indian people also emphasize in their treaty claims that these transactions constituted inadequate settlements, even if all their terms were fulfilled. (See discussion of treaty land entitlement claims, in Chapter 7.) These claims involve assertions about the way in which treaties were negotiated, the disparities between the two contracting parties, and the alleged unfairness of the terms.

Most status Indians belong to bands, which have rights to reserve lands held in common. Most bands, whether in treaty or non-treaty areas, usually have specific claims to make. The most numerous and widespread are those stemming from reserve land losses. Reserve lands were sometimes lost through squatting by non-Aboriginal people or being re-surveyed. Most typically they were lost as a result of formal surrenders and expropriations by the federal or provincial governments. Claims may be based on the specific nature and legality of these occurrences or on the general propriety of such forms of land alienation. Management of band funds and reserve resources and the administration of band affairs, particularly with regard to economic development, are also central features of many potential band claims.

Land is an extremely important element in Aboriginal claims in general. As mentioned above, Aboriginal peoples are becoming more articulate about their unique relationship to the land, both past and present, and about the meaning it has for them. They are also aware that the material standard of living that has been achieved generally in Canada derives ultimately from the land and its resources. As a consequence, they seek not only a role in determining the way in which the land and other resources are used but also a just portion of the benefits derived from their exploitation. This theme is basic in the Aboriginal rights claims, but it also appears in treaty claims, where the original land agreements may be in question, and in band claims concerning lost reserve land or other natural resources.

For the Aboriginal people, *trusteeship,* a fundamental element in their claims, involves both protection and assistance. When the federal government assumed political control over Aboriginal people it undertook responsibilities for reserve land and band finances, and it imposed special limitations on Indians as a feature of Indian status. It adopted a protective role over Indians and their affairs analogous to that of a guardian or trustee toward a ward or beneficiary (Rotman 1996). From this fiduciary relationship flow grievances and claims that pertain to the government's management of Indian resources (DIAND, 1982a, 1985).

ABORIGINAL-GOVERNMENT RELATIONS

Canadian jurisprudence has taken the position that Canada was acquired by discovery or settlement (Bartlett, 1984) and, although the concept of "existing Aboriginal rights" (from which it is assumed that Aboriginal title flows) is now entrenched in the Canadian

Constitution (see Sections 25, 35, and 37), no one is able to say precisely what those words mean (Henderson, 1983; Sanders, 1985b, 1990).

One of the first legal rulings on this issue was handed down in 1885 (*St. Catherines Milling and Lumber Company* v. *The Queen*). This ruling characterized Aboriginal title as a possessory right, a right to use and occupancy similar to a usufructuary right—i.e., right based on traditional use and occupancy (Thompson, 1982). The Privy Council in 1888 changed this interpretation slightly when it characterized Aboriginal title as a personal usufructuary right, dependent upon the goodwill of the sovereign. Unfortunately, since that time few legal cases in Canada have pursued this issue. It would not be until nearly a century later, when in 1973 the *Calder et al.* v. *Attorney General of British Columbia* case came before the Supreme Court of Canada, that this concern was re-examined. Even though the Nisga'a Indians did not win this case, three of the seven Supreme Court justices ruled that Aboriginal title did exist in common law irrespective of any formal recognition—that is, independent of the *Royal Proclamation* of 1763. These justices argued that once Aboriginal title has been established it is presumed to continue until the contrary is proven, and that the onus is upon the government to prove that it intended to extinguish Indian title through various legislation ordinances. Since no specific legislation was enacted that provided for Indian title to be extinguished, these judges concluded that the Indians may indeed still be in possession of Aboriginal title.

Prior to the Nisga'a case, the federal government held that Aboriginal land rights were so general and undefined that it was not realistic to view them as claims capable of remedy through a policy. However, after this Nisga'a case, the government announced a change in its policy with regard to legal obligations to legitimate claims being pursued by Indians. The government indicated that it was willing to negotiate settlements with Native groups where Native rights based upon usufruct had not been extinguished by treaty or superseded by law (Bankes, 1983; Asch, 1993).

Other writers, such as Driben (1983), Cumming and Mickenberg (1972), Clark (1994) and Asch (1993, 1997), have gone beyond the Supreme Court's ruling and have suggested that Aboriginal interest rests on a solid legal foundation. They point to the *Royal Proclamation* of 1763, which pledged, in a legal context, that Aboriginal title would be respected. Land title extinguishment could only take place if Indians approved of the action at a public meeting with public officials. When the extinguishment took place, the land could only be ceded to the Crown. Today, according to the courts, Aboriginal rights are vested in Native people by virtue of both the *Royal Proclamation* of 1763 and by the fact that they were the sovereign inhabitants in Canada before the land was considered French or English property (Indian Claims Commission, 1975).

Land Claims Before 1969

The modern Specific Claims process traces its roots to 1947, when the federal government struck a special joint committee of the House and Senate to investigate matters relating to Indian Affairs. This committee operated for one year and heard presentations from Aboriginals across the country. The committee recommended the creation of an independent administrative tribunal to adjudicate claims, but this did not come to pass. Ten years later another joint committee was created. It made the same recommendation as the previous committee but, as before, nothing came of the recommendation (Prentice and Bellegarde, 2001). Similar recommendations were made for the next 20 years, but a "lack of political will" was demonstrated in that no such tribunal was ever established. As such, prior to the establishment of the Indian Lands Commissioner (1969) and the Office of Aboriginal Claims (1974), Indian claims were handled on an individual basis. The processing of a claim was dealt with either by the Department of Indian Affairs and Northern Development or by the Department of Justice. There was a dual filing system utilized by DIAND through which all claims were sorted. One was labelled "petitions and complaints," the other "claims and disputes." The former label was interpreted by government officials as representing grievances and as such did not require any legal action on their part. However, the claims in the latter file were interpreted as legitimate and thus required the department to respond (Daniel, 1980; Wright, 1995).

By 1969, the federal government decided to take a different course and it offered its infamous White Paper to deal with such thorny issues as land claims, Aboriginal rights, and other disputes between Aboriginal and non-Aboriginal peoples. This, of course, would have solved the issue of Indian claims in that Indians would have, in a legal sense, no basis upon which to bring claims forward (McNab, 1999).

As Daniel (1980) points out, the 1969 White Paper on Indian Policies was vigorously repudiated by Indian leaders. They were joined in their opposition by a number of non-Indian social and political organizations, and the policy soon became the *bête noire* of government–Indian relations. However, one recommendation of the White Paper was for the appointment of an Indian Claims Commissioner. In late 1969 Dr. Lloyd Barber was appointed Canada's first and only Indian Claims Commissioner, a position he would hold until 1977 when the office was terminated. The Commissioner's mandate was to receive and study grievances and to recommend measures to adjudicate any claims. He himself did not have powers of adjudication since his role was only advisory. Nevertheless, he played an important role in educating government officials and the public at large (Morse, 1991). The Indian Claims Commission and the Indian Claims Commissioner's office had divergent aims, and this was partially a result of the government's insistence that Indians had no legal basis on which to make claims. The creation of the Commissioner's office was an interim structure developed by the government that was meant to be phased out once a new policy could be drafted (Sanders, 1983c, 1985a).

The government also established funding programs to help defray the costs to Aboriginal groups of researching and presenting their claims. Funds were provided by the Privy Council from 1970 to 1973, by the Indian Claims Commissioner from 1972 to 1973, and mainly by the Rights and Treaty Research Program (DIAND) from 1972 to 1976. In 1974 the federal government created the Office of Native Claims (within DIAND) to deal with specific grievances. While the Indian Claims Commissioner and the Office of Native Claims (ONC) overlapped between 1974 and 1977, their roles were very different. The Indian Claims Commission was established to receive and study grievances presented by Indians as well as to suggest the process by which particular claims could be adjudicated. On the other hand, the Office of Native Claims accepted the legitimacy of Aboriginal land rights. Thus, its function was to coordinate federal negotiations regarding claims that Indians presented to the federal government.

GOVERNMENT LAND NEGOTIATIONS

Since Confederation, the Canadian government has shown a reluctance to negotiate with Aboriginal people over land issues. Each time the federal government has developed a land claims policy, Aboriginal people have denounced the content. As Mallea (1994) points out, on the whole, Aboriginal people have found negotiating with the government to be a frustrating exercise. In most cases the government has been viewed as an obstruction to achieving justice.

In approaching land claims, Aboriginal groups have been required by the courts to meet four conditions to establish proof of Aboriginal title. This is referred to as the "Baker Lake Test" (*Baker Lake* v. *Minister of Indian Affairs and Northern Development,* 1980) The requirements are

1. that they and their ancestors were members of an organized society;
2. that the organized society occupied the specific territory over which they assert the Aboriginal title;
3. that the occupation was to the exclusion of other organized societies; and
4. that the occupation was an established fact at the time sovereignty was asserted by England.

In 1990 the Supreme Court of Canada set specific guidelines for determining Aboriginal rights in general in a landmark decision. This decision (*R.* v. *Sparrow* [1990]— see below) held that an Aboriginal right could be claimed even though it was not otherwise supported by a treaty. The Court also noted that existing Aboriginal rights were not subject to Section 35(1) of the Charter, which allows for the implementation of the "notwithstanding" clause. Finally, the *Sparrow* decision goes on to say that legislation negatively affecting Aboriginal people may only be enacted if it meets the test for justifying such an interference.

Sparrow and *Delgamuukw:* A Turning Point

Aboriginal land rights were given a serious blow in the *Delgamuukw* v. *British Columbia* (1991) case when the B.C. Supreme Court judge, A. McEachern, ruled that the 8000 Gitksan and Wet'suwet'en British Columbian Indians do not hold Aboriginal rights to the land. He stated that the *Royal Proclamation* of 1763 has never applied to the province of British Columbia and that Aboriginal interest in the land did not include ownership of or jurisdiction over the territory. He also ruled that pre-Confederation colonial laws, construed in their historical setting, show a clear intention to extinguish Aboriginal interests in order to give unburdened titles to the settlers, and, thus, the Crown extinguished all Aboriginal rights even though no specific extinguishment act was passed, even before the province entered Confederation in 1871. Therefore, he argued, since Confederation the province has had title to the soil of the province and the right to dispose of Crown lands unburdened by Aboriginal title. However, the judge did acknowledge that the Indians could use vacant Crown land, but this is not an exclusive right. Furthermore, their use is subject to the general laws of the province.

The trial took more than four years, during which communities and forestry and mining companies fought the Aboriginal land claims. Their $1 billion investments were at risk until the judgment was made. Uncharacteristically, the judgment ended with a stern lecture from the judge. He urged that only political negotiations could solve the land issue and questioned the focus on legal and constitutional matters such as ownership, sovereignty, and rights. He also noted that the issues now facing Aboriginal people cannot be solved by continuing the reserve system, which, he argued, has created "fishing footholds and ethnic enclaves." He concluded his judgment by arguing that enlarging the reserves is not in the best interest of anyone and suggested that Indians must leave the reserve and enter the urban centres of Canada so that they can participate in the economic activities found there. The Gitksan-Wet'suwet'en nation appealed the decision and the case eventually went to the B.C. Supreme Court.

Before discussing the appeal, it might prove instructive to discuss the original court's decision. First of all, the judge (Alan McEachern) assesses Aboriginal society using a very ethnocentric perspective, e.g., since Aboriginal people did not use the wheel, have a written language, or use domesticated animals for food production, he claims that they did not have an organized, integrated society. In fact, he argues that early Aboriginal life was "nasty, brutish and short." He concludes that "many of the badges of civilization, as we of European culture understand them, were indeed absent" (p. 31). In short, the judge introduces highly ethnocentric and biased perspectives about what constitutes "civilization" and/or "development" and concludes that since Aboriginal people did not have many of the cultural artifacts of Europeans, they can only be considered "primitive."

The findings of McEachern are also puzzling and without precedent. He rejects testimony from certain experts out of hand and without adequate justification, while allowing testimony from others. For example, he rejects anthropological testimony but accepts that from historians and linguists. Furthermore, there are well-accepted principles that the judge did not follow. For example, all testimony must be understood by the judge (since he/she must make a ruling); otherwise, the judge must simply accept the conclusions of the experts unless those are successfully challenged by information from other experts. Nevertheless, the transcripts of the trial show that the judge openly acknowledges that he does not understand the logic or the argument of certain witnesses, yet he accepts their conclusions unquestioningly, even when the illogical and uninterpretable arguments are questioned by others. The judge's insistence on seeing himself as a social scientist is without precedent. Much of the data presented to him by anthropologists were rejected with no good explanation. He then proceeded to develop his own biased and ethnocentric explanation about Aboriginal people, totally devoid of evidence or logic (Elliott, 1991).

The *Delgamuukw* Appeal

In 1993 an appeal of the *Delgamuukw* decision was heard by the British Columbia Court of Appeal. A majority of the judges agreed with the trial judge that certain Aboriginal rights were in force when British sovereignty was established. Moreover, the Appeal Court agreed that these rights were *not* ownership rights. However, it disagreed with the trial judge in finding that the Aboriginal rights had not been extinguished, basing its decision on a test much less stringent than that adopted by the *Sparrow* court (see below).

This B.C. Court of Appeal decision modified the meaning of the *Sparrow* decision in that it redefined what it thought the Supreme Court meant when it delivered its judgment. There have been few cases since the *Delgamuukw* appeal, so it is difficult to interpret the impact of this case. Subsequent well-known cases that have variously expanded upon *Sparrow* mostly in favour of Aboriginal people and that have served as important precedents for the final 1997 *Delgamuukw* Supreme Court of Canada decision (1997) include *R.* v. *VanDerPeet* (1996), *R.* v. *NTC Smokehouse* (1996), *R.* v. *Gladstone* (1996), and *R.* v. *Côté* (1996), among others.

In the *Guerin* v. *Regina* (1984) and *Sparrow* (1990) cases, the Supreme Court acknowledged and reinforced the fiduciary relationship between the Crown and Aboriginal people. These precedent-setting judgments forcefully noted that the government has a responsibility to act in a fiduciary capacity with respect to Aboriginal people.

Delgamuukw–"We Are All Here to Stay"

The claim by Gitksan and Wet'suwet'en was originally for "ownership" and "jurisdiction" over separate portions of 58 000 square kilometres of northern British Columbia. The following are some of the significant finds from the decision (Supreme Court of Canada, December 11, 1997):

- The court found that Aboriginal title is an exclusive communal interest or a right to the land itself, encompassing more than hunting and fishing rights.
- The court emphasized that Aboriginal title encompasses the right to choose what happens on traditional lands. First Nations can now expect to be included in decisions involving the allocation of such lands and resources.
- The court found that Aboriginal title can be held jointly by more than one First Nation—two or more First Nations may jointly hold title if their joint use of the land meets a test of exclusive possession (i.e., an ability to exclude others).
- The court sent a strong message to trial courts to be more open to evidence in the form of oral histories and other forms of traditional knowledge used in establishing First Nations' use and occupancy of their traditional territories.
- The province does not have the authority to extinguish Aboriginal title. Only the federal government has that power and authority.
- First Nations wishing to use lands under Aboriginal title in ways that conflict with that title must first surrender their title and convert the lands into non-title lands. Maintaining title requires that use of land and resources does not destroy the unique value of the land.

The court identified Aboriginal title at one end of the spectrum of Aboriginal Rights protected under Section 35(1) of the *Constitution Act*. At the other end are activities integral to their culture, as well as their right to engage in traditional activities such as hunting and fishing. The rights First Nations have over lands in their traditional territories will therefore vary from a right to the land itself to the right to use the land for traditional practices. With this decision, the Supreme Court of Canada sent a message that Aboriginal title requires a process of good faith negotiation and reconciliation between the Crown and First Nations. Aboriginal rights and title can no longer be ignored in the general economic development of the province. The resolution of this case and other outstanding issues and competing interests is, as the court suggested, best achieved by negotiation and not litigation. As the chief justice observed, "Let us face it, we are all here to stay."

They went on to point out that the relationship between the government and Aboriginal people is trust-like rather than adversarial, and contemporary recognition and affirmation of Aboriginal rights, as reflected in the (1997) *Delgamuukw* decision, must continue to be defined in light of this historic relationship.

Beyond its fiduciary obligation toward Aboriginal people, the federal government is also required to guarantee the rights and freedoms found in the Charter. Actions by government toward Aboriginal people reveal that there are numerous violations of Aboriginal civil liberties. For example, the presentation by the Indigenous Bar Association to the

Standing Committee on Aboriginal Affairs regarding the events of Kanesatake and Kahnawake during the summer of 1990 noted that the most serious violation of Aboriginal civil liberties was the Minister of Indian Affairs signing an agreement on preconditions to negotiations with Aboriginal peoples!

The pivotal *Sparrow* (1990) case in B.C. has attracted the attention of all individuals interested in Aboriginal–non-Aboriginal affairs. The case involves an Indian who was fishing at the mouth of the Fraser River. In 1987, in what amounted to a sting operation, agents working on behalf of the Fisheries Department acted as individual Canadians who wanted to buy fish illegally from band members. While the "sting" resulted in 25 Indians being charged, none were convicted of illegally fishing. It was at this time that the Fisheries Department implemented another procedure to reduce the number of fish caught by Aboriginal people; i.e., they reduced the net from 38 to 25 fathoms so that the Indians would not catch as many fish.

After the new regulations were in place, Sparrow, an Indian fisherman, was caught fishing with a net over 25 fathoms and was subsequently charged under the new regulations. Even though historical data showed that Indians had fished this area since time immemorial, the provincial court found Sparrow guilty. The court ruled that Aboriginal rights had been extinguished at the beginning of the century. This was appealed to the county court, then to the Court of Appeal of British Columbia and eventually to the Supreme Court of Canada. The Supreme Court ruled that while the provincial regulations were legal and forced Indians out of their fishing activities, the province could not extinguish Aboriginal rights through the application of provincial or federal regulations. The regulations would have to specifically state that Aboriginal rights were to be extinguished. The Supreme Court ruled that in cases where there are ambiguous or vague regulations, the interpretation would be in favour of Aboriginal people. This reasoning was upheld specifically in such cases as *Gladstone* (1996) and *NTC Smokehouse* (1996).

Comprehensive Claims

There are two major categories of claims now being pursued by Aboriginal peoples in Canada. The first is referred to as a comprehensive claim or Aboriginal title claim, while the second is called specific and will be discussed later. Progress in some jurisdictions has been significant, as examples in the previous chapter show. In British Columbia, for example, these claims make up nearly 75 percent of the province.

These claims take two different forms which are, to some extent, regionally based. In the North, the claims focus on a demand for formal legal recognition of Aboriginal land title and all the rights that are derived from it. In the South, comprehensive claims place more emphasis on the cooperation between Aboriginal peoples and the government for the extinguishment of Aboriginal title and the restitution of specific rights—e.g., hunting and fishing rights (Government of Canada, n.d.).

The map in Figure 8.1 identifies the major areas in Canada that are under comprehensive claims processing at the present time. As one can see, almost the entire Canadian North is claimed by Aboriginal groups, and various Aboriginal associations are actively pursuing their cases. Areas in the Arctic are being pursued by the Inuit, while the Métis and Indians in the Mackenzie Valley area of the Northwest Territories and in the Yukon have filed several claims.

Comprehensive claims are not negotiations about grievances related to the interpretation and the shortcomings of previous treaties. Rather, they are land claims that deal with areas of the country where various Aboriginal people continue to live and where treaties were never entered into. A partial exception to this is the Dene/Métis claim in the Northwest Territories. The policy of establishing comprehensive land claims began in 1973, and has subsequently been revised and updated several times. As Harry Swain, then Deputy Minister of Indian Affairs, pointed out in 1988, comprehensive claims are a unique arrangement in which Aboriginal people can finally settle outstanding land issues.

The process is one through which Aboriginal groups agree to exchange their Aboriginal title over all or most of the land covered in return for land, money, certain rights, and other conditions designed to protect and enhance their social, cultural, and economic well-being.

The comprehensive land claims agreements that emerge from these negotiations are formal, legal, and binding documents. Also known as modern-day treaties, they have to be ratified by the Aboriginal groups and communities concerned and by the federal government, and are then enacted into law by Parliament. They now constitute a substantial body of law and have helped to redefine the relationship between the Government of Canada and many of its Aboriginal citizens. Since 1982 these agreements have also been protected constitutionally.

The first of these landmark comprehensive land claims agreements was the James Bay and Northern Quebec Agreement, which was reached between the federal and provincial governments and the Cree and Inuit communities of Northern Quebec in 1975 (Niezen, 1998).

This was followed by the Northeastern Quebec Agreement in 1978 and by an agreement with the Inuvialuit of the Mackenzie Delta and the Beaufort Sea region in 1984.

As of March 2002, 53 First Nations were participating in modern land claim negotiations. There were also 18 other comprehensive land claims taking place throughout Canada involving 78 communities. Since the inception of the Program (1973), 15 Final Land Claim Agreements have been completed (Indian and Northern Affairs Canada website, July 17, 2003).

Each of these land claims is distinctive and has taken into consideration the unique conditions of history, geography, culture, and economic circumstances that exist in the particular region and communities concerned. Still, there is a similar pattern to all of these claims—a pattern set initially in 1973 and reinforced in the government's revised comprehensive land claims policy of 1986. As a result, while there are individual differences, a considerable body of precedent has been established in the terms and conditions provided in these settlements.

When faced with the decision to cede, or surrender, in whole or in part their Aboriginal title to certain areas, Aboriginal Canadians are naturally concerned that in return they receive benefits that will enable them to prosper as distinct and definable groups. The most basic concern is of course for land. All the agreements are, at heart, land settlements. All designate specific lands that the claimant group will own outright, as well as land-related rights in areas where they have certain interests in perpetuity. But Aboriginal concerns go beyond mere ownership of land. Essentially they seek, through these agreements, terms and conditions that will allow them to:

- continue to maintain to the greatest degree possible their traditional lifestyle and culture;

FIGURE 8.1 Comprehensive Claims: Areas Claimed by Aboriginal Associations

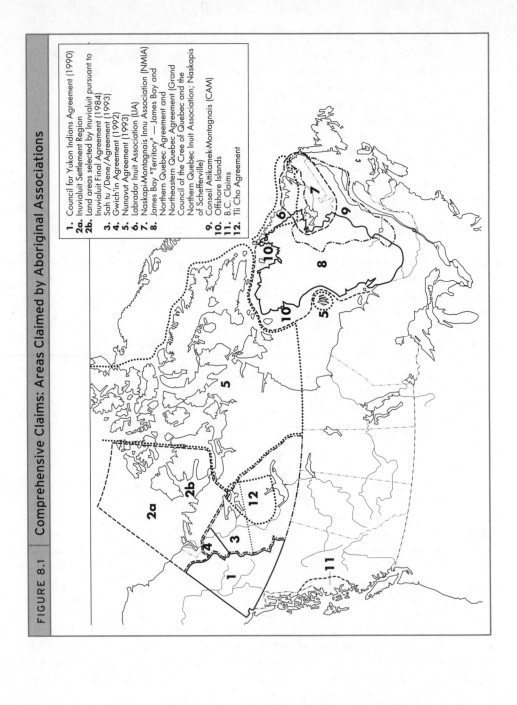

1. Council for Yukon Indians Agreement (1990)
2a. Inuvialuit Settlement Region
2b. Land areas selected by Inuvialuit pursuant to Inuvialuit Final Agreement (1984)
3. Sah tu /Dene/ Agreement (1993)
4. Gwich'in Agreement (1992)
5. Nunavut Agreement (1993)
6. Labrador Inuit Association (LIA)
7. Naskapi-Montagnais Innu Association (NMIA) James Bay "Territory" — James Bay and Northern Quebec Agreement and Northeastern Quebec Agreement [Grand Council of the Cree of Quebec and the Northern Quebec Inuit Association; Naskapis of Schefferville)
8.
9. Conseil Attikamek-Montagnais (CAM)
10. Offshore Islands
11. B.C. Claims
12. Tli Cho Agreement

- participate in the decision-making process regarding land and resource management within their claim area; and
- receive a fair share of the economic opportunities and economic benefits that may exist in the claim area.

As a result, these comprehensive claims agreements cover a range of issues besides land and basic compensation. The issues include surface and sub-surface resource provisions, guaranteed rights for wildlife harvesting and fishing, resource revenue sharing, participation in renewable resource management, and environmental protection measures. An excellent example of a modern-day treaty, or comprehensive claim, wherein these issues are paramount, is the 2000 Nisga'a Treaty (see page 200). Six major issues are present in comprehensive claims resolved to date. They include:

- *Land:* "All agreements confer on the beneficiaries primary interest over extensive areas of land."
- *Cash:* "In consideration for certainty of title over their settlement regions, all signed agreements provide significant financial compensation packages. These are considered payments in exchange for rights."
- *Wildlife:* "Wildlife management and Aboriginal control over wildlife harvesting are usually negotiated. These are an important part of traditional Aboriginal lifestyles. The agreements in principle or sub-agreements also provide for harvesting rights, priorities, and privileges. For instance, some provide for the right to harvest all species up to the full level of economic, social, and cultural needs. And, if there are residual surpluses, Aboriginal organizations have harvesting priority. Should surpluses still exist, a limited entry system gives preference to local residents in the allocation of commercial licences. Various rights and privileges under these agreements include permit or tax exemptions; the right to sell, barter, exchange, and give freely the harvested wildlife; the right of first refusal for new hunting, fishing, and tourism lodges over settlement regions; and the right of first refusal for the marketing of wildlife, and wildlife parts and products."
- *Environmental protection:* All agreements have provisions for the protection of the environment and the Aboriginal societies in the settlement areas that spell out the terms and conditions of any future development. These regimes subject all developers to specific duties and responsibilities. For instance, before approval of a project, a developer may be required to conduct prior consultation with local communities, offer compensation, and negotiate employment of contractual opportunities."[1]
- *Economic participation:* "The agreements recognize the necessity to preserve Aboriginal cultural identity and values, in part through enabling Aboriginal people to become more equal participants in Canada's economy. The comprehensive claims policy provides for resource royalty sharing. For example, the Dene/Métis agreement in principle provides that the Aboriginal claimants will annually receive 50 percent of the first $2 million and 10 percent of the balance of resource royalties from the settlement area.

  All agreements in principle and sub-agreements contain various similar provisions to support the beneficiaries and businesses under their control. These cover such items as access to information relating to business ventures and opportunities, tax exemptions, incentive measures, contract splitting, and financial and technical support measures."

- *Interim protection:* The present policy permits the negotiation of interim measures to protect Aboriginal interests while the claim is being negotiated. They are identified in the initial negotiating mandate. These measures operate over the claimed territory and remain in effect until a final agreement has been signed. They can impose general or specific obligations on the parties that relate to land and its future development; the protection of traditional hunting, fishing, and trapping activities, and the other rights that are generally negotiated in a comprehensive claim.

  The measures enable negotiations to proceed in good faith, thus lessening the need for court intervention that could have the effect of freezing any type of development in a claimed area. It must be said, however, that the agreement on interim measures does not affect the rights of any party to seek judicial recourse should they consider their interests to be endangered."

- *Other provisions:* There is a whole range of other provisions in the agreements, covering in substantial detail areas such as access to Aboriginal lands, establishment of protected areas, fisheries, social protection, and the incorporation and management of local governments. These are positive measures intended to provide a genuine opportunity for Aboriginal economic and cultural progress.

  The terms and conditions of the agreements are established in Canadian law and, under the Constitution, cannot be unilaterally changed. They are not subject to override by other existing laws nor by any future legislation that may be enacted. The comprehensive claims process has resulted in long-term agreements between Canadian governments and Aboriginal peoples' agreements that have in fact redefined in a truly unique way the relationship between Aboriginal people, the Canadian government and other Canadians.

  By 1990 the government came under attack because of its handling of comprehensive claims. Aboriginal people accused the government of pursuing a goal of extinguishing the "burden" of Aboriginal rights and minimizing its legal obligation. A working group composed of Indian leaders representing Aboriginal interests across Canada was established to identify problem areas and recommend change. Later in the year, the policy of restructuring the number of comprehensive claims being investigated to six was removed. Recent amendments to the comprehensive claims policy remove the idea of "blanket extinguishment" of all Aboriginal rights, including title, and allow for the retention of Aboriginal land rights, provided these rights do not conflict with the negotiated settlement agreement.

  Aboriginal groups have also been critical of the land management powers accruing to Aboriginal communities under comprehensive claim settlements. While the evidence is not clear, it would seem that the management powers provided in settlements exceed the authority under the *Indian Act*, and settlement agreements are constitutionally protected under Section 35 of the *Constitution Act, 1982*. In summary, it has been suggested that the powers given to Aboriginal groups in comprehensive claim settlements supersede the limits set by the *Indian Act* (Clark, 1994).

  The Assembly of First Nations (1990a) has claimed that the existing comprehensive claims policy excludes self-government provisions. The federal government has argued that this claim is untrue. Yet when the *Delgamuukw* case was appealed to the Supreme Court of Canada after 1993, Chief Justice Lamer rejected "The Respondents' submission with respect to the substitution of Aboriginal title and self-government for the original claim of ownership and jurisdiction." But so far a legal case has not been brought before the courts for resolution. Aboriginal negotiators have consistently sought to settle their land claims and to establish the right of self-determination through the process of self-government. The government is prepared to give "advanced" bands some legal powers similar to those of a municipality, but not additional powers.

Specific Claims

A specific claim deals with treaties and scrip (discussed in Chapter 7) and band claims. It is, as the term implies, specific to a particular concern; for example, a clause in a treaty or land withdrawn from a reserve. Between 1970 and 1981, 250 specific claims were presented to the Office of Native Claims for adjudication. During this 11-year period, only 12 were settled, for a total cost of $2.3 million. As of March 2002, 117 specific claims were under negotiation, with a further 491 under assessment.

Table 8.1 identifies the number of specific claims that have been submitted. As is clear from the paucity of claims that have been settled, the Office of Native Claims and subsequent agencies did not substantiate all of the Native claims.

During the late 1980s and until the turn of the century, the government spent less than $5 million per year on the Indian Claims Commission for mediation services, public education, and ongoing inquiries with regard to Aboriginal land claims. Since then, there has been a slight increase to nearly $6 million per year. During the decade that the Indian Claims Commission existed, it facilitated the process by which First Nations would enter negotiations with the federal government. For example, in 2002/03 the Claims Commission handled nearly 60 cases. They recommended that the government accept 42 of these for negotiation. At the present time, the government has accepted most of these recommendations. On the other hand, the Commission did not recommend that seven of these be sent to negotiation. The remainder of the cases considered by the Commission were dealt with in different ways. Some were sent back to the First Nations community for additional work, others were actually settled, and still others are under further review by the Commission.

The history of Aboriginal claims shows that that there has been sustained pressure on the Government of Canada to reform the Specific Claims process and establish an independent claims body. Yet this would not happen until 2003. It takes the Government of Canada five to eight years to complete its validation process in assessing a First Nations' claim. Then, it takes another five to seven years to negotiate the resolution of a claim. On average, since 1973, the Government of Canada has resolved only 7.5 claims per year. This means it will take the next 50 years to settle existing claims without adding the new ones that emerge. From 1991 to 1999, Canada settled 23 specific claims, totalling nearly $33 million and involving the return of nearly 15 000 acres of land back to Aboriginal people.

In 2003, the Government of Canada passed the *Specific Claims Resolution Act* that will create the Canadian Centre for the Independent Resolution of First Nations Specific Claims. It will replace the Indian Claims Commission, which was created in 1991 as an interim structure to deal with Aboriginal land claims. The new Centre will have two separate components: a commission and a tribunal. In addition, the commission will facilitate negotiated settlements using mediation, negotiation, and other means of dispute resolution. It will provide these services for all claims, regardless of the potential amount of a claim, although there is a $10 million ceiling on settlements. The tribunal will be a quasi-judicial

TABLE 8.1	Specific Claims in Canada, 2001
Specific claims are concerned with unfulfilled or disputed treaty obligations. The specific claims that have been submitted can be subdivided into the following statuses.	
Under review[a]	408
Resolved	251
Rejected	89
In negotiation	115
Before the ICC	61
In active litigation	47
Total	1071

a Includes 56 treaty land entitlements in the Prairie provinces.

body able to make final decisions on the validity of claims that were not reached through a negotiated settlement.

Band Claims

A special type of specific claim encompassing the multifarious, scattered claims of individual Indian bands is called a band claim. Several categories of these can be identified at present, including claims relating to the loss of land and other natural resources from established reserves, as well as issues pertaining to the government's stewardship of various bands' financial assets over the years. Underlying all these claims is the difficult question of trusteeship.

The full story of the government's management of reserve resources and band funds across Canada is only gradually being pieced together from the files of DIAND, from the accounts of missionaries and other Euro-Canadian sources, and from the oral testimony of Indian people themselves. Reserve resources include not only land but also minerals, timber, and water. Band funds in most cases derive from land and other resource sales. Where land was surrendered and sold off from reserves, the capital went into band funds to be administered by the federal government.

Land losses from established Indian reserves account for by far the majority of band claims brought forward to date. Groups of them are probably sufficiently similar to be classified on a regional and historical basis. Grievances arising in New France have certain elements in common, as do Indian claims in the Maritimes, in Ontario, in the southern Prairies, and in British Columbia. The problem of pressure for reserve-land acquisition by speculators and settlers is central to all.

The French, who were the first European power to control the northern half of North America, were the first to establish any sort of Canadian Indian policy. Their approach was dictated by several factors, including geographical distance from the mother country, overwhelming Aboriginal military strength, a fur trade economy, and negligible European settlement. They sought, if unsuccessfully, the Indians' assimilation into French-Canadian society and saw the converted Aboriginal people as equal in civil and legal status to France's European subjects.

There are conflicting interpretations of whether Indian territorial rights were affirmed or extinguished under the French regime; treaties were never concluded for territory either in New France or in Acadia. Land was given to Indians through imperial grace, just as it was to European colonists. However, the Crown, instead of granting such tracts directly to the Aboriginal people, handed them in trust to the religious orders: the most efficient civilizing and Christianizing agencies then known. Six Indian reserves were formed in this manner.

At the time of the British takeover in 1760, France's Indian allies had been given land for their exclusive use. By 1851, 230 000 acres (92 000 hectares) were set aside as Indian reserves and a further 330 000 acres (132 000 hectares) similarly appropriated by the Quebec *Lands and Forests Act* of 1922. Additional reserves were created through the transfer of land from the provincial to the federal government by letters patent issued by Quebec, through direct purchase by the Dominion from a private party, or through private leases.

The Aboriginal peoples of Quebec have, over the years, sought increased compensation for land lost from these reserves; settlement of disputes between bands and tribes over reserve ownership; restitution for damages done through logging, fishing, and canal construction; and compensation for questionable band-fund management. The existence of these grievances suggests a basic difference in perspective on the part of the Indians and the federal government, which has historically tended to judge the issues solely on their legal merits as determined by the Department of Justice.

In the 19th century, for instance, the complaints of the Hurons of Lorette and the Montagnais of Pointe-Bleur against European squatters went unnoticed. Charges that the municipality near the Iroquois Oka reserve had unjustly taken over land to allow for the construction of three roads were only briefly considered, as was the Caughnawaga claim for land sold as a clergy reserve. The St. Regis Iroquois protests against the Quebec government's unilateral renewal of leases to, and sale of, islands in the St. Lawrence, along with their claim to compensation for the flooding of additional islands by the Cornwall Canal, were to no avail. Dozens of claims to islands, first voiced in the 18th and 19th centuries, remained unsettled, and many of the current disputes over expropriation, whether by settlers, clergy, or the Crown, go back to these earlier years. At the root of most of this lack of responsiveness is the government's and the courts' persistent denial of the Indians' contention that they owned the land initially granted to the religious orders. The denial is based on the grounds that title thereto had been given directly to those orders and not to the Indians themselves.

The arrival of the British in New France, so far as the Indian people were concerned, did not favourably alter their condition. The same could be said for the Maritimes. As British settlement and power increased, large tracts were set apart for Indian use and occupation. Although these lands were called Indian reserves, they were not guaranteed to the Indians through treaties and were subsequently reduced as the land was required for settlement. Further pressures on these reserves in the Maritimes in the early 19th century, coupled with problems in dealing with flagrant non-Aboriginal squatting, motivated the colonial governments to appoint commissioners to deal with and supervise reserves. These officers apparently had and certainly exercised the right to sell reserve lands without Indian consent. With Confederation, the existing reserves were transferred to the jurisdiction of the federal government, though for a long time the underlying title lay with the respective provinces.

Several claims have been presented to the federal government for past reserve-land losses. Within this category several main types of claims are emerging. A large number contest the legal status of surrenders of reserve lands. These include submissions on surrenders processed without proper Indian consent, uncompleted sales of surrendered land, sales of lands prior to their being surrendered, lack of letters patent for completed sales, and forged Indian signatures or identifying marks on surrenders. In Nova Scotia, a general claim has also been presented contesting the legality of all land surrenders between 1867 and 1960. This is based on the argument that the Mi'kmaq Indians of that province constituted one band; and that under the *Indian Act* and its subsequent amendments throughout the period, surrenders could only be obtained at a meeting of a majority of all band members of the requisite sex and age. Another group of Maritime band claims against the federal government arises from the contention that several reserves transferred to the federal government after Confederation were subsequently listed or surveyed by the Department of Indian Affairs as containing smaller areas than the original acreages listed, or were simply never surveyed and registered as reserves at all.

There are also Maritime Indian claims against the federal government's handling of its trusteeship role. The Union of Nova Scotia Indians has put forth a number of claims concerning mismanagement by the government of its obligation to ensure adequate and proper compensation for reserve lands surrendered or expropriated for highway rights-of-way, utility easements, and other public purposes.

The sources of Aboriginal claims in Southern Ontario are similar to those in Quebec and the Maritimes. Probably the bulk of them have not yet been disclosed; at any rate, no formal comprehensive claims statement has emerged. In common with Quebec, though, past cases or recorded claims for such losses abound. Some have been rejected by the departments of Indian Affairs and Justice or by the courts; many, however, lie dormant. It would not be unreasonable to expect these cases, and new contentions based on them, to be advanced in greater numbers in the near future.

Indian people have claimed that unjust cessions and legally questionable government expropriations of reserve lands were common. Government initiatives, along with pressure from non-Aboriginal speculators and settlers, were, as usual, dominant factors. The Six Nations' Grand River surrender in 1841, the Mohawks' cession of Tyendinaga Township in 1843, the Moore Township surrender made by the Chippewa later that year, and the 1847 cession by the St. Regis Iroquois of Glengarry County are prime examples of cases where surrenders were attained under pressure. All these lands were ceded in trust, although there is evidence that the trust provisions were not always upheld. Similar grievances pertain to the government's acquisition of unceded islands. Equally familiar was the variety of expropriation that allowed the sale of individual lots from Indian reserves for clergy and state purposes. Disputes over the status of territory were also prevalent. These were generally related to squatter infiltration and occasionally extended into inter-tribal conflicts for reserve lands and, accordingly, for annuities.

The social and economic factors underlying the loss of Indian reserve lands in central and eastern Canada soon found expression on the Prairies. In the years following the making of the treaties and the setting aside of the reserves, the southern Prairies were gradually settled. Towns and cities sometimes grew on the very edges of reserves or even around them, and railways ran through them or along their boundaries. As in Ontario, Prairie reserves located on good farming land were coveted by settlers. For all these reasons, political pressure frequently developed for the surrender of all or a portion of a reserve. In many cases the Indian Department responded by obtaining a surrender of the reserve land in question; proceeds from the sales of such land were credited to the particular band's fund and administered under the terms of the *Indian Act* (Hall, 1991).

In the last few decades of the 20th century, the bands and Aboriginal associations of the Prairies have clearly articulated several claims arising from previous government policies in relation to land surrenders. They have re-examined both the justification for these surrenders in general, and the legality and propriety of specific cessions, such as those involving Enoch's Band near Edmonton. In this case, three surrenders took place. The entire Passpasschase Reserve was ceded shortly after most of the band members left treaty and took Métis scrip. The remaining members moved elsewhere and subsequently the band and its assets were amalgamated with Enoch's Band, residing on the Stony Plain reserve. In 1902 and 1908, political forces largely supported, if not generated, by the minister responsible for Indian Affairs compelled the surrender of portions of this reserve. In taking the surrenders, government officials used approaches that appear to have been morally and legally dubious. Such questions surround many other surrenders in the Prairie region and also in Northern Ontario (Sanders, 1983b).

At the heart of many Indian grievances in the Prairies is the issue of unfulfilled treaty entitlements to land. Complex in themselves, such claims have been further complicated by the need for provincial assent to any proposed transfer of lands to Indian reserve status. Under the 1930 Natural Resources Transfer agreements, the three Prairie provinces obliged themselves to transfer to the federal government, out of the unoccupied Crown lands, sufficient area to meet unfulfilled treaty obligations. Aboriginal people have felt that there has been provincial reluctance to comply with this, and disputes have arisen over the exact nature of the commitments. The Island Lake bands in Manitoba, for instance, have raised the matter of what population base should be utilized in the granting of unfulfilled treaty entitlements. A substantial proportion of the bands' allotments under Treaty No. 5 were made in 1924, but the land assigned was approximately 1200 hectares short, if based on the populations at the date and on the treaty terms. The bands maintain that their total entitlement should be computed using a recent population total, with the 1924 allotment simply subtracted from the new allocation.

In addition, this case points to the inequality among the various treaties' land provisions throughout the West. In common with other treaties in Manitoba, Treaty No. 5 provides for 160 acres (65 hectares) per family of five, compared with the 640-acre (260-hectare) figure for treaties elsewhere. Since the land in this region of Canada cannot be farmed, an additional inequity is present relative to more southerly fertile regions. The bands contend that a fair solution, satisfying the twin criteria of population data and uniform treaty terms, would be an allocation of almost 120 000 hectares.

In British Columbia the history of Indian reserves is substantially different from those recorded in the other provinces. During the 1850s, when Vancouver Island was still provisionally governed by the Hudson's Bay Company, certain minor surrenders were concluded by the company's chief factor, James Douglas, for several parcels of land there. But these, along with the territory in the northeastern corner of the mainland included in Treaty No. 8, are the only areas covered by treaty. The dual governorship of the two colonies of Vancouver Island and British Columbia under Douglas in 1858 was soon accompanied by the establishment of comparatively liberal reserves both within and outside the treaty areas. But then, expanding European settlement motivated Douglas's successors to reverse his policy of allowing the tribes as much land as the Indians themselves judged necessary and, accordingly, to reduce the reserves wherever possible. Only with great reluctance did the colonial government allot new reserves in areas opening to settlement (Flanagan, 1983a).

By 1871, when the colony entered Confederation, Indian complaints concerning the failure to allot adequate reserves and reserve land reductions were already numerous. The Terms of Union that year did nothing to allay these grievances. Fundamentally, the Terms provided for the transfer of responsibility for reserves to the Dominion, and for the conveyance of land for new reserves from the province to the Dominion. Since no amounts were agreed upon, a dispute immediately arose between the two governments over the appropriate acreage to be allotted per family. The province declared 10 acres sufficient; the federal government proposed 80. An agreement establishing an Indian Reserve Commission was concluded in 1875 to review the matter, but there continued to be provincial resistance against attempts to liberalize reserve allotments.

This is just one more source of Indian claims in British Columbia. A report by the Union of British Columbia Indian Chiefs, entitled *The Lands We Lost* (1974), details others. They include the by-now familiar pattern of encroachment by non-Indian people, together with questions about various government surveys and commissions, federal orders in council, and reserve land surrenders. The primary cause of such losses and the major grievance expressed in this regard were the work of the federal–provincial McKenna–McBride Commission, set up in 1912 to resolve the outstanding differences between the two governments respecting Indian land in British Columbia. The Commissioners were appointed to determine the land needs of the Indians and to recommend appropriate alterations to the boundaries of Indian reserves. All reductions were to require the consent of the bands involved, but in practice this stipulation was not followed. The recommendations were subsequently ratified by both governments under legislation that authorized these reductions irrespective of the provisions of the *Indian Act* controlling the surrender of reserve lands. Eventually, some 35 cut-offs totalling 36 000 acres were made, while lands of far less value, although of larger area, were added to the reserves.

In summary, most of the band claims now being dealt with by the federal government have come primarily from the Maritime provinces and the Prairies, with a lesser number from Quebec, Ontario, and British Columbia. Some of these claims have been submitted to DIAND, while others have been channelled through the Claims Commission.

CLAIMS POLICY TODAY

After the 1973 Supreme Court decision with regard to the Nisga'a Indians in British Columbia, the federal government developed new land claims policy. The new policies on comprehensive and specific claims identified the procedures and limitations of negotiating. The policies also provided the philosophical assumptions (on the part of the government) underlying these policies. These new policies divided land claims into the two types discussed above—comprehensive and specific. Furthermore, it suggested that the comprehensive claims (British Columbia, Northern Quebec, the Yukon, and parts of the Northwest Territories) would receive more favourable treatment than comprehensive claims from Southern Quebec and the Atlantic provinces. However, this policy also specified that Aboriginal claims would be dealt with through direct negotiations between DIAND and the Aboriginal claimants. The government felt that, in Southern Quebec and the Atlantic provinces, historical negotiations had taken place between the government and the Indians, however imperfect those negotiations had been. There was some evidence that the government had taken treaty with these Indians. However, in British Columbia, Northern Quebec, the Yukon, and areas of the Northwest Territories, it was clear that no negotiations had ever taken place.

The comprehensive claims policy was adopted in 1981 with the publication of the document *In All Fairness: A Native Claims Policy, Comprehensive Claims.* The policy stated that the federal government was willing "to exchange undefined Aboriginal land rights for concrete rights and benefits" (1981: 19). Some of these benefits would entail land, wildlife, sub-surface rights, and monetary compensation. With regard to land rights, the document stated that lands to be selected by Aboriginal peoples would be limited to traditional lands that they currently use and occupy. It also stated that "third parties" would be fairly dealt with on the issue of sub-surface rights and that the government was prepared to grant some sub-surface rights in certain areas. Finally, the compensation (in whatever form) was to be "specific and final." However, the policy paper adopted the use of the term Aboriginal "interests" rather than "rights" (Iverson, 1990; Swain, 1988).

The process for resolving these comprehensive claims is to follow a negotiating procedure culminating in a compromise settlement. In summary, Aboriginal people are limited in (1) the scope of what they can negotiate, (2) their standing in relation to other "interests," and (3) the extent of their involvement in trying to settle their claim (Hatt, 1982). The actors involved in the process usually consist of the federal government, the Aboriginal group, and a provincial/territorial government. Because of the scope of such undertakings, the federal government, until recently, has limited to six the number of negotiations that may proceed at any time. For example, it currently is negotiating with the Council for Yukon Indians, the Dene/Métis of the Northwest Territories, the Tungavik Federation of Nunavut, the Conseil Attikamek–Montagnais, and the Labrador Inuit Association.

In 1982 the government published its policy with regard to specific claims in a document titled *Outstanding Business.* This policy reaffirmed the government's commitment to resolving specific claims and in some respects expanded on the previous role it played in settling claims. As noted previously, specific claims relate to the administration of land or other Indian assets under the *Indian Act* and to the fulfilment of treaties or other agreements. Under the terms of the policy for specific claims, the process of handling the claims is a combination of adjudication and negotiation. Claims are first submitted to the minister of INAC, acting on behalf of the Government of Canada. After the claim is submitted, the Office of Native Claims (ONC) reviews the case and analyzes the material. The claim and supporting materials (both *for* or *against*) are referred to the Department of Justice for advice. On the basis of the Department of Justice's advice, the ONC (1) negotiates a settlement with the claimant, (2) rejects the claim, or (3) returns the claim for additional documentation. If the claim is accepted, the ONC and the claimant negotiate the terms of settlement; for example, land, cash, or other benefits. Once the claim has been settled it represents final redress, and a form release is obtained from the claimant so that it cannot be reopened at some later time.

Because Aboriginal peoples do not have their own financial resources to carry out research in order to document their claims, the federal government has made substantial contributions to various Aboriginal organizations that are engaged in this research process. Since 1973 the federal government spent in excess of $100 million on negotiations, but has produced only three agreements. For example, between 1972 and 1982, more than $22 million in contributions were made for research into Aboriginal rights, treaties, and claims, plus an additional $94 million in loans between 1974 and 1982. Since the creation of the ONC in 1974, more than $26 million has been spent on the operation and management of the claim process (both specific and comprehensive). If the claim being submitted by the Indians is substantiated and compensation paid, part of the "contribution" portion given to the Indians is repaid. Thus far about $15 million has been repaid by Aboriginal groups who have signed final agreements. On the other hand, if the claim is dismissed, no repayment is necessary. This infusion of money into Aboriginal organizations has enabled them to pursue vigorously many claims which, without the funds, would never have been researched and brought forward.

Research contributions and loans are provided to Aboriginal people for both specific and comprehensive claims. Funding for both specific and comprehensive claims in the late 1970s was about $8 million. However, in the early 1980s this was increased to about $14 million, where it remained until 1989. However, as we entered the 1990s, major expenditures were provided to settle a growing backlog of both comprehensive and specific claims.

In 1985 a task force that had been struck to review comprehensive claims policy reported to the minister of DIAND. The report noted that the negotiating process used up till then to resolve Aboriginal claims had tried to incorporate two principles: (1) to encourage the cultural development of Aboriginal people, and (2) to provide a climate for the overall economic growth of Canada. The government, in dealing with Aboriginal peoples, had argued that Aboriginal goals could be best pursued by settling claims through an extinguishment of all Aboriginal claims once and for all. Aboriginal peoples had not accepted this philosophy. As a result, negotiations had stalled and settlements of various Aboriginal claims had been few. The task force recommended that a blanket extinguishment of all Aboriginal rights now no longer be an objective. Furthermore, it made the following noteworthy recommendations:

1. Agreements should recognize and affirm Aboriginal rights.

2. The policy should allow for the negotiation of Aboriginal self-government.

3. Agreements should be flexible enough to ensure that their objectives are being achieved. They should provide sufficient certainty to protect the rights of all parties in relation to land and resources, and to facilitate investment and development.

4. The process should be open to all Aboriginal peoples who continue to use and to occupy traditional lands and whose Aboriginal title to such lands has not been dealt with either by a land-cession treaty or by explicit legislation.

5. The policy should allow for variations between and within regions based on historical, political, economic, and cultural differences.

6. Parity among agreements should not necessarily mean that their contents are identical.

7. Given the comprehensive nature of agreements and the division of powers between governments under the Canadian Constitution, the provincial and territorial governments should be encouraged to participate in negotiations. The participation of the provinces will be necessary in the negotiation of matters directly affecting the exercise of their jurisdiction.

8. The scope of negotiations should include all issues that will facilitate the achievement of the objectives of the claims policy.

9. Agreements should enable Aboriginal peoples and the government to share both the responsibility for the management of land and resources and the benefits from their use.

10. Existing third-party interests should be dealt with equitably.

11. Settlements should be reached through negotiated agreements.

12. The claims process should be fair and expeditious.

13. An authority independent of the negotiating parties should be established to monitor the process for fairness and progress, and to ensure its accountability to the public.

14. The process should be supported by government structures that separate the functions of facilitating the process and negotiating the terms of agreement.

15. The policy should provide for effective implementation of agreements. (DIAND, 1985: 31–32)

Previous claims were settled through one of two options: (1) by the signing of a final agreement extinguishing all Aboriginal rights, or (2) by doing nothing and maintaining the status quo. The present policy does not see a settlement as a final agreement but rather as an agreement that will settle immediate issues and define the context for issues that emerge later on. It argues that there is no need to insist on extinguishment of Aboriginal rights when a voluntary surrender of rights has been obtained from the Aboriginal peoples. This procedure has been made more acceptable by all parties because of the difficulties that emerged after the signing of the James Bay Agreement, when DIAND found that there were problems of implementation, unresolved disputes, and in some cases a failure to fully implement the agreement in both its spirit and intent (DIAND, 1982a; Mendes and Bendin, n.d.).

The task force suggested several alternatives to the present claims process. Each of the recommendations presented has some shortcomings and will, of course, be subject to interpretation as they are implemented. In addition, the implications of each approach are somewhat unclear at this time. One alternative is to return to the legal technicalities used in pre-Confederation treaties. Specific rights such as land and wildlife harvestry would be subjected to extinguishment or retention. However, the loss or retention of one right would not affect other rights; each would have to be subjected to a court of law (Dyck, 1990).

A second option is to separate land rights from all other rights. Thus, land rights could be dealt with by negotiations or through the courts but would be separate from other Aboriginal rights such as culture and religion. Finally, a third option would be to set aside the issue of Aboriginal rights altogether when discussing land rights. Although this would not produce an answer with regard to the existence of Aboriginal rights, it would allow Aboriginal groups and other parties to continue to carry out economic activities. An example of this approach in another area is that of the federal and Nova Scotia governments' approach to the ownership of offshore rights: the issue of ownership of offshore oil has been set aside so that development of the natural resource can proceed.

Regardless of the option pursued there will have to be some flexibility in its application since Aboriginal groups come from different regions, have different interests, and operate in different political contexts. The task force has recommended that negotiations continue to be the major mode of settling claims. The force's members felt that litigation fosters an adversarial approach that is not conducive to settling claims and to developing a true social contract between Aboriginal and non-Aboriginal people. The task force's report goes on to suggest that, prior to negotiations, the process of "scoping" be undertaken. This process, in which important issues and alternatives are dealt with by both parties prior to actual negotiations, is now used in social impact assessments. The task force also felt that negotiations must deal more expeditiously with Aboriginal claims and that Aboriginal interests should be protected during the negotiations.

In summary, the task force felt that new approaches to settling Aboriginal claims must be undertaken. Contemporary policies have not really been effective, either in social or economic terms. If Canada is to continue to develop as a nation these issues must be resolved. At the same time, if Aboriginal people are to retain their identity and self-worth by developing communities that will actively participate in Canadian society, settlements must be negotiated. As the members of the task force so eloquently stated in their report:

Much is at stake in working towards consensual settlements with those Aboriginal peoples who have never entered into agreements concerning the destiny of their traditional lands within Canada. In the deepest sense, what is at stake is our identity as a nation that resolves its internal differences not through coercion or domination by the majority, but through agreements based on mutual consent. (Task Force, 1985: 101)

In April 1991 the prime minister announced plans to establish a royal commission on Aboriginal affairs. There was also a promise by the federal government to ensure Aboriginal participation in the constitutional process and to put more money toward resolving the land claims disputes. Specifically, the government made a commitment to spend $355 million on resolving land claims between 1991 and 1995, four times the amount spent in the late 1980s. The government also developed "streamlined" procedures to deal with land claims under a half-million dollars. In addition, DIAND was given complete authority to approve settlements of up to $7 million without the Treasury Board having to review and accept the proposal. There is a belief that the 250 outstanding claims can be settled within the first few years of the new millennium.

Defining a Claim

One of the first tasks of the government is to determine the validity of the claim. There must be a determination as to whether the claim is simply a difference of opinion held by one party with regard to another, or whether it is a bona fide claim. A claim is a grievance with a legal basis that is communicated to the second party, either directly or through a third party. When the complaint is communicated to the third party and there is a difference of opinion concerning a right or supposed right, then this is transformed into a dispute (Colvin, 1981).

The use of advocates in pursuing a claim and entering into a dispute with the federal government has proven beneficial to Aboriginal groups. At times, however, it has been a liability; for example, occasionally the government, rather than attacking the claim, will discredit the advocate and thus weaken both the formal intent of the claim and the willingness of the Indians to continue their case (Daniel, 1980). Nevertheless, advocates have been able to offer Aboriginal groups a wealth of information (both technical and political) that has helped them in pursuing their claims. At other times, they have even carried the dispute without cost to the Aboriginal group. As Daniel (1980) points out:

... our research found many instances in which the federal government's disposition towards a claim had the appearance of having been altered to a significant degree by a change in personnel associated with the case.... [The] policy with respect to the comprehensive claims of the Chippewas and the Mississaugas seems to have been more liberal after the appointment of R.V. Sinclair, a man known to have been an advocate of several claims and an occasional critic of Indian Affairs Policy. (216, 146)

There have been a number of other impediments that have prevented Indians from proceeding with a claim. For example, until passage of the 1951 *Indian Act*, the government had to give its approval before another party could take it to court. There also was a time when the government forbade the use of Indian money to support a lawyer to pursue a claims case for them (Lang, 1974).

In the past, the federal government held the view that the Department of Indian Affairs was alone responsible for Indians. The idea that Indians have the right to take independent action against the government was a new concept that Indian Affairs officials were slow to accept. Because of the impediments mentioned above, we find that Aboriginal claims tend to be viewed by most Canadians as a recent activity. However, upon closer inspection, we find that Aboriginal groups have tried to pursue claims since well before the beginning of the 20th century. Because of the structure of the bureaucracy and its governing legislation, these claims were either suppressed or simply not defined as bona fide claims. It is only recently that these structural barriers have been lifted to allow the various claims to be presented.

In summary, the federal government, early in the history of Canada, was clear in its policy. The *Royal Proclamation* of 1763 outlined the policy for comprehensive claims, and it codified the process of land surrender. The subsequent treaties, beginning with the Robinson–Huron, 1850, and lasting until the 1920s, suggested that the federal government's policy for dealing with comprehensive claims was well defined. In return for giving up their land rights and pledging to keep the peace, Indians were given compensation, annuities, reserves, and "other considerations"—even though the contents of the treaties are remarkably similar and generally reflect the fact that they were drafted long before the treaty commissioner was sent into the field to "negotiate" with the Indians. What remains contentious even today is whether or not the terms of the treaties have been upheld and, if they haven't been, what type and amount of compensation should be provided.

Courts and Claims Commissions

Only occasionally have the courts in Canada been asked to adjudicate issues concerning the rights of Indian people. Although there have been exceptions, in general the judicial system has not responded positively or adequately to Aboriginal claims issues.[2] In regard to Aboriginal rights, the judiciary decreed that any European colonial power, simply by landing on and laying claim to lands previously undiscovered by European explorers, became automatically the sovereign of this "newly discovered land." Occupation was taken to confirm that right. The government and the courts both considered Aboriginal rights to be matters of prerogative grace rather than obligations that came with the assumption of sovereignty.

Aboriginal people have clearly faced social and cultural obstacles in becoming litigants in a legal system largely foreign to their experience. And even if some might have considered taking action through this forum, they had until very recently little or no capacity to pay the necessary legal fees. As a result, most of the early but significant decisions in the area of fundamental Indian rights have been handed down in cases where the Indian people affected were not directly represented. Many of these cases involved disputes between the federal and provincial governments over questions of land and resources. Aboriginal rights became material to the cases only because the federal government sought to rely upon them to reinforce its own position by citing its exclusive constitutional responsibility for Aboriginal people and lands (Weaver, 1986).

As noted previously, what was, until very recently, the only significant case on the question of Aboriginal title in Canada was decided by the Judicial Committee of the Privy Council in 1888. This, the *St. Catherines Milling* case, involved litigation between the federal government and the province of Ontario over the question of whether the former could issue a timber licence covering land obtained from the Indians and eventually declared to lie within Ontario. The Indians themselves were not represented. The federal government, for its part, argued that it had properly acquired the title to the land from the Indian people; the Judicial Committee of the Privy Council denied that the Aboriginal people, at any time, had "ownership" of their land in the sense that Europeans understood the term, and stated "that the tenure of the Indians, was a personal and usufructuary right, dependent upon the good will of the Sovereign." The Law Lords went on to say that the effect of signing treaties with Indian peoples was to extinguish this "personal and usufructuary right," and to transfer all beneficial interest in the land covered by the treaty immediately to the province. Nearly a century was to pass before the nature of Aboriginal title would receive further consideration by Canada's highest court of appeal.

As has been mentioned, a number of interpretations of the Indian treaties have been put forward by the courts. Some treaties have been regarded as transactions between separate and independent nations; such has been the traditional claim of many Six Nations Indians. Some have been characterized as special protective agreements in which Indian people surrendered their rights to land in return for irrevocable rights conferred upon them by the government. Others have been interpreted as analogous to any commercial contract made at the time with the government. A judgment written by the Judicial Committee in 1867 opted for this last interpretation in a dispute among the attorneys-general of Canada, Ontario, and Quebec. Indian people thus found themselves constrained by adverse precedent before they could begin to make their own arguments in court.

In addition to the rights at stake, the courts have also dealt with the promise of continued hunting and fishing rights. Their decisions have affirmed the federal government's right to break express promises made by treaty. On occasion, however, the judiciary has questioned the morality of such legislative action. Many of the most fundamental treaty promises regarding social and economic development have not yet reached the courts. It would require a radical departure from established precedent for the courts to give treaties the character granted them by the Indians.

Cases touching the many Aboriginal land-loss grievances have, on occasion, come before the courts. Little can be learned about which direction the courts might take in future land-loss claims from a reading of these judgments, since they disclose no clear pattern of judicial thought. Decisions on claims concerning the mishandling of Indian monies have been equally rare and uninstructive. The fundamental question of the relationship between the federal government and Aboriginal people in the areas of land- and monies-management remains legally undefined. Aboriginal people regard this relationship as one of trust, and the federal government has also often referred to it in these terms. This fiduciary obligation places a very heavy burden on the federal government to act in good faith and always to consider the best interests of Indian people as the paramount concern.

As an avenue for Indian claims, the Canadian legal system can only have been seen in Aboriginal eyes as an incomprehensible gamble. As Fudge (1983) points out, Indians are risk-averse and tend to look at "loss avoidance" as the preferred option when dealing with the federal government. Only in recent years have the courts responded more favourably to these claims, not by fully and satisfactorily resolving them, but by providing a basis from which the Indian people can negotiate with the government. The realization on the part of both Aboriginal and non-Aboriginal people in the United States that the ordinary courts were unsuitable forums for the presentation and resolution of Aboriginal grievances and claims brought forth a response that has increasingly preoccupied Canadian governmental and Aboriginal thought. Efforts that began in the 1930s in the United States to establish a special adjuratory body with powers to hear and determine Indian claims culminated in 1946 with the creation of an Indian Claims Commission. In Canada, the joint committees of the Senate and House of Commons on the *Indian Act* and on Indian affairs, which sat in 1946–48 and 1959–61 respectively, recommended establishing a similar, though more limited, body. As a result, enabling legislation received first reading in the

Commons in December 1963, and the draft bill was sent to Indian organizations, band councils, and other interested groups for comment. A slightly amended version of the proposal was introduced in June 1965.

The terms of the bill provided for a five-person Indian claims commission and the jurisdiction of the commission would have been limited to acts or omissions of the Crown in right of Canada or of the United Kingdom, but not in right of a province. The suggested Canadian commission would have lacked jurisdiction to hear just those classes of cases which, in the United States, formed the bulk of those heard. They included claims for the government's failure to act "fairly or honourably" where land was involved, as well as others requiring that treaties be reopened on grounds such as "unconscionable consideration." The Canadian legislation, on the other hand, would have permitted the commission to consider only failure to fulfill treaty provisions, not the general question of reopening treaties. The bill also ignored the Aboriginal organizations that were emerging as a force at that time. Instead, the proposed commission was to be authorized to hear claims only on behalf of bands as defined by the *Indian Act*. Regional Aboriginal organizations, however, might not have been recognized as claimants. Furthermore, the commission would have been given authority only to make money awards, not to restore land (Haysom, 1992).

Because of these and other inadequacies, this proposal for an adjudicatory commission met with Indian opposition. It was allowed to die following the dissolution of Parliament later in 1965. This appears to have been the government's last public discussion of the projected commission before the announcement of a new Indian policy in June 1969. This demise was attributed to consultations with Indian representatives and the review of Indian policy that preceded the drafting of the new White Paper.

The White Paper and the Indian Claims Commissioner: A History Lesson

The first of a series of contemporary responses to Indian claims started with the 1969 White Paper on Indian Policy. This event marked the beginning of a new era of unprecedented claims activity. The government proposed an approach that it said would lead to equality of opportunity. This was described as "... an equality which preserves and enriches Indian identity and distinction; an equality which stresses Indian participation in its creation and which manifests itself in all aspects of Indian life" (Canada, 1969b). To this end, the *British North America Act* would be amended to terminate the legal distinction between Indians and other Canadians, the *Indian Act* would be repealed, and Indians would gradually take control of their lands. The operations of the Indian Affairs Branch would be discontinued, and services that had previously been provided on a special basis would be taken over by the federal or provincial agencies that serve other Canadians. Economic development funds would be provided as an interim measure. In short, Indians would come to be treated like all other Canadians: special status would cease. In laying out these proposals the government continued to recognize the existence of Indian claims, and proposed the establishment of an Indian claims commission, but solely as an advisory body. It was made clear that the government was not prepared to accept Aboriginal rights claims: "These," the paper said, "are so general and undefined that it is not realistic to think of them as specific claims capable of remedy except through a policy and program that will end injustice to Indians as members of the Canadian community. This is the policy that the government is proposing for discussion." Treaty claims, while acknowledged, were also placed in a dubious light:

The terms and effects of the treaties between Indian people and the government are widely mis-understood. A plain reading of the words used in the treaties reveals the limited and minimal promises which were included in them.... The significance of the treaties in meeting the eco-nomic, educational, health, and welfare needs of the Indian people has always been limited and will continue to decline.... Once Indian lands are securely within Indian control, the anomaly of treaties between groups within society and the government of that society will require that these treaties be reviewed to see how they can be equitably ended.

The government apparently felt that while the central Aboriginal and treaty claims had little virtue and were directly at odds with the proposed policy, there were instances where claims might be accepted. Lawful obligations would be recognized.

Rather than proceeding with the kind of commission discussed in the 1960s, it was decided that further study and research were required by both the Indians and the federal government. Accordingly, the contemporary form of commission was established under the *Public Inquiries Act* to consult with the Indian people and to inquire into claims aris-ing out of treaties, formal agreements, and legislation. The commissioner would then indi-cate to the government what classes of claims were judged worthy of special treatment and would recommend means for their resolution.

Given the nature of Indian views on their rights and claims as we understand them, it is not surprising that their reaction to the 1969 White Paper was strongly negative. The National Indian Brotherhood (NIB) immediately issued a statement declaring that

the policy proposals put forward by the Minister of Indian Affairs are not acceptable to the Indian people of Canada.... We view this as a policy designed to divest us of our Aboriginal, residual and statutory rights. If we accept this policy, and in the process lose our rights and our lands, we become willing partners in cultural genocide. This we cannot do.

In the following months, Aboriginal groups across the country forcefully and repeat-edly echoed this response. When the Commissioner, Dr. Lloyd Barber, was appointed in December 1969, the National Brotherhood rejected his office as an outgrowth of the unac-ceptable White Paper, viewing it as an attempt to force the policy on Aboriginal people. Indians saw the White Paper as the new articulation of a long-resisted policy of assimila-tion. The proposal was denounced as a powerful, threatening extension of traditional Indian policy in Canada.

In rallying to oppose this apparent challenge to their rights, the Aboriginal peoples in turn produced extensive statements of their own positions. While difficulties were encountered in arranging for research funding, sufficient government monies were made available to finance some of this work. The resulting statements, together with concerted legal and political action on the part of Indians, led to significant changes in the govern-ment's approach.

An early response occurred in August 1971, when, in reply to submissions from the Commissioner and Indian leaders, then Prime Minister Trudeau agreed that the Commissioner would not be exceeding his terms of reference if he were to "hear such argu-ments as the Indians may wish to bring forward on these matters in order that the govern-ment may consider whether there is any course that should be adopted or any procedure suggested that was not considered previously." The Commissioner took this to mean that he was free to look at all types of grievances and claims, including Aboriginal rights issues.

In August 1973, the government made a substantial change in its position on Aboriginal rights by announcing that it was prepared to negotiate settlements in many areas where these had not been dealt with. Then in April 1975, on the basis of proposals developed through consultations between Indian leaders and the Commissioner, the government accepted an approach to the resolution of Indian claims based upon negotiation.

This new policy would take the issue of land claims out of the legal arena and provide an alternative forum to solve problems. This also meant that there could be greater flexibility in introducing and using certain documents—for example, historical and anthropological ones—in the negotiating process. In addition, the government felt that this process would also provide a forum that would take into account the interests of non-claimant groups who reside (or have an interest) in an area that could be affected by a settlement. Finally, and perhaps most importantly, it was believed that the process would allow for transforming the Aboriginal-rights concept into concrete and lasting benefits. In addition, the process would be final and not subject to being reopened at some later time.

This procedure had been attempted in 1890–91 when a three-person board of arbitrators was appointed to settle disputes between the Dominion and the provinces of Ontario and Quebec. Claims were presented by the Department of Indian Affairs on behalf of the Indians. Twenty cases were heard by the board, but few were resolved since the cases generally became embedded in federal–provincial conflicts. In addition, because the board had no final adjudicator, its power, by the turn of the century, waned into insignificance. With few exceptions, the Indians derived no benefit from this board of arbitrators.

To facilitate the process of negotiation and to stem the tide of Aboriginal opposition to DIAND, the government formed a joint NIB–Cabinet committee in 1974. Its role was to identify and address issues that Indian people felt had to be resolved. As Morse (1989) explains, in order to facilitate this, the Canadian Indian Rights Council was established as an independent body to act as a secretariat for the joint committee. Four years later, the joint committee was dissolved because of lack of progress.

Not all Indians, however, were prepared to give up this process. The four Ontario Indian associations approached DIAND with a proposal to create a new structure that would be applicable to Ontario. As a result, new tripartite councils have been created. The Indian Commission of Ontario, for example, assists the three parties (federal, provincial, and Indians) in resolving Indian claims. As Daniel (1980) points out, the functions of the commissioner include arranging mediation to resolve issues that have been authorized by the tripartite councils. However, the commission lacks the institutional structure that could facilitate the processing of a large number of claims; for example, it has neither the authority to bring legal pressure to bear on recalcitrant parties nor the legal powers necessary to provide an incentive for compromise.

While coercion was widely used in the late 18th and 19th centuries, the process of resolution of Aboriginal claims has changed over time. Negotiation has become the accepted strategy, even though it presupposes that the two disputants are of equal power. But since Aboriginal peoples are not equal in power to the government, it has become clear that this important precondition for negotiation has not been met (Dyck, 1981). In certain cases the government has tried to equalize that power—for example, through the provision of loans to Aboriginal groups so that they can research their claims. Nevertheless, a new strategy for resolving Aboriginal claims, one of mediation, is slowly emerging. Modern-day claims, therefore, are not to be viewed solely in a legal context. Many legal experts and politicians are beginning to agree that the issues are more of a political than a legal nature. As former Justice Minister Otto Lang stated:

> We have legal questions raised about [claims] and non-lawyers particularly love the legal questions; love to think that the caveat of the court will decide the issue. But probably it is not so. The important questions are political ones. (From personal correspondence with the author, 1974)

As Watson (1979, 1981) points out, each group (non-Aboriginal and Aboriginal) attributes to the other a failure to redeem debts. Aboriginal tradition states unequivocally that non-Aboriginal people owe them for the land they provided, which permitted European settlement to proceed unhindered. Non-Aboriginal people, on the other hand, view treaties as a thing of the past and of small consequence. As a result, they do not acknowledge a debt to Aboriginal people. However, these positions are not inflexible, and they are modified and abandoned when opportune. The negotiating of claims, then, is not carried out by a strictly reasoned legal argument, but by public bargaining over symbolic provisions.

Differing Perceptions

We have identified the changes that have taken place over time in the way that Aboriginal claims are regarded and approached. And we have described the process by which claims are dealt with. It is clear that even when the procedures are carefully identified, substantial differences between the government and the Aboriginal peoples remain. It is important to identify the perception and definition of treaty claims (both comprehensive and specific) held by the Crown on the one hand and First Nations on the other. The Crown views comprehensive claims as a strategy that addresses Aboriginal rights claims. They feel that this policy will sort out land and resource rights among the various stakeholders in Canada and ensure that Aboriginal claims are upheld. To achieve these goals, they have outlined a process whereby the claim is prepared, data is collected to support the claim, and a format is established by which the claim is reviewed (Starblanket, 1979).

From a First Nations perspective, the policy on claims does not provide any recognition or affirmation of Aboriginal rights, a position they find untenable. They feel that the sole objective of the policy is to extinguish Aboriginal rights for all time. They note that the process for submitting a claim has become increasingly complex, and requires extensive research, time, and financial resources. There is the feeling that, because of these factors, Aboriginal people are becoming less and less involved in the process. Furthermore, they feel that the final settlements established thus far have been biased in the interests of the federal government, developers, and multinational companies, while Aboriginal peoples' benefits are minimized.

The process of settling a claim is also seen differently by the two parties. The federal government has adapted, for all practical purposes, the criteria outlined for example in the *Baker Lake* case. Developments in case law—e.g., *Sparrow, Sioui, and Simon*—that bear directly upon Aboriginal rights are not always accounted for in the current policy. This lacuna is the focus of a major dispute between the Crown and First Nations. Furthermore, the process of settling claims has, until recently, been limited to six comprehensive cases. This means that there will likely always be a large backlog of claimants (as of 1996 it is estimated that the number is 25). These claimants have no protection of their interests as they wait for the negotiations to proceed or the courts to hear their cases. This has meant, in some cases, that the Aboriginal interests were prejudiced before the negotiations began.

Once the process begins, the Crown requires both a detailed agenda that negotiations will follow and a statement limiting the issues to be negotiated. Aboriginal people claim that these frameworks are imposed unilaterally by the federal government, and limit the scope of issues to be negotiated as well as the substantive issues to be included in the negotiation process. While the federal government takes the position that Aboriginal people do not have to negotiate, if they do not negotiate their only recourse is through the courts. Alternatively, the federal government may unilaterally take action. Furthermore, Aboriginal people feel that, although they are not forced to negotiate, many pressure tactics such as funding allocations are used by the federal government to ensure that they do negotiate. The scope of negotiations is also perceived very differently by the two parties. The Crown, in carrying out negotiations, argues that it is prepared to give Aboriginal people rights and benefits on such issues as land ownership, participation on management boards, resource revenue sharing, hunting and trapping, as well as financial compensation. Aboriginal people argue that their rights regarding the issues identified by the federal government are exchanged for legislated benefits.

They further point out that not only are their rights redefined as "benefits," but the nature and scope of those benefits are limited. For example, there is often little recognition of Aboriginal ownership of sub-surface resources; also, participation on management boards is restricted and subject to ministerial veto. This redefinition of issues also means that Aboriginal concern with self-government is not negotiated because it is simply defined as being outside the scope of the negotiations (Harrison, 1972).

The process of settling comprehensive claims is viewed by the federal government as extinguishment of all Aboriginal land rights. Although the federal government correctly points out that the current policy does not require surrender of all lands, in practice the policy does not allow retention of Aboriginal title and does not confirm it. Aboriginal people are also concerned that provisions in the claims may prejudice the future clarification of other Aboriginal rights (Hermann and O'Connor, 1996).

There is also concern by Aboriginal people that, when a settlement is made, the cost of carrying out the extended process means that payments must be made to the Crown for loans and interest on those loans. Their concern is at two levels. First, when negotiations are being carried out, the federal government monitors the loan funds to ensure that the funds be used only as it (the federal government) says. Any attempts to use the funds in a manner not prescribed by the federal government will result in the funds being withdrawn. Second, Aboriginal people find the principle of loan funding to be offensive. They are expected to pay from their compensation the costs of negotiation, which were brought about by the illegal actions of the Crown. Furthermore, in the settlements the federal and provincial governments benefit.

This last point is also a source of dissatisfaction for Aboriginal people. The federal government has allowed the provinces to enter the negotiation process when they think it is necessary. Aboriginal people, on the other hand, argue that provincial involvement is a violation of federal fiduciary responsibility. Furthermore, provincial governments are often a major obstruction in the negotiation process and have, in many cases, vetoed negotiated settlements.

Specific claims are also seen differently by the two parties. Differences between the two stakeholders begin with the historical bases of the claim: the Crown chooses to talk about assuming responsibility for Indians and lands reserved for Indians at the time of Confederation; Indians argue that the First Nation–Crown relationship was confirmed by the *Royal Proclamation* of 1763. And, Aboriginal people argue, the federal government's responsibility toward them goes well beyond the *Indian Act,* a claim that has support in several decisions by the Supreme Court. Finally, Aboriginal people are concerned that many issues such as taxation, fishing, and water rights cannot be dealt with under the process of specific claims.

Funding is another source of friction between the two parties. The federal government notes that bands are funded to research their specific claims. Indians acknowledge this but point out that the funding is inadequate, and too many restrictions are placed on how the funds can be used. In other words, because the funds can only be used the way the federal government dictates, many claims are inadequately researched and therefore are not accepted by the Crown as legitimate.

Once the claims are researched, documentation is submitted to the federal government and analyzed by the Specific Claims Branch of DIAND. While this description of the procedure is correct, it is also deceptive, claim the Aboriginal people: the description hides (or, at least, fails to make clear) the protracted debate over the potential legal merit of the case—what is referred to as the clarification process. This process usually takes years and requires time, money, and effort on behalf of the claimants. Usually the Specific Claims Branch simply refuses to submit the claim to the Justice Department (which rules on the claim) until the Aboriginal group submitting the claim agrees to make it conform to the government's policy. In short, justice is obtained, but only under the rules as defined by the federal government. Perhaps even more disconcerting is the federal government's use of "discounting" in negotiating with the specific group that has submitted the claim. Discounting is the process whereby one party offers compensation to another party on the basis of the degree of probability that the case could be successfully fought in the court system. In other words, if the Specific Claims office feels that the Aboriginal claim has a good chance of winning in the courts, the offer of compensation is high. Conversely, if it feels that the case does not stand a good chance in the courts, offered compensation is low. This, of course, runs counter to the generally accepted practices of law, and forces Aboriginal people to accept something less than justice (Tennant, 1985).

Aboriginal people also point out that in the negotiation process the definition of the claim itself undergoes changes. Thus, Aboriginal groups might submit one type of claim, but by the time the Specific Claims Branch and the Justice Department review and accept the case the specifics of the claim may be very different than when first submitted.

The Department of Justice then rules on the claim and takes action accordingly. Aboriginal people point out that the Minister of Indian and Northern Affairs has the right to deal with claims in ways that go beyond strict legal obligations. However, thus far the minister has never done so. Furthermore, when a claim is rejected, Aboriginal people are not allowed to see the legal opinion that rejected their claim. They only receive a notice with a vague, general rationale as to why the claim was not accepted. Once the rejection has taken place, there is no mechanism for appeal. Aboriginal people have long argued that some sort of independent mediation or arbitration process should be put in place to deal with claims that are rejected on questionable criteria (Frideres, 1986).

Interestingly, the Assembly of First Nations has argued in the past that there should be an elimination of the distinction between comprehensive and specific claims. In their submission to the Coolican Task Force, they called for a First Nations rights policy which would take away the artificial distinction of claims and allow for other issues to be dealt with. No other situation in the recent history of Aboriginal–non-Aboriginal relations has brought the complexity of the issue of comprehensive and specific claims into sharper relief than the Oka stand-off of the summer of 1990, as the following section explains.

The Oka Crisis of 1990: Another History Lesson

For 78 days the Oka stand-off kept Canadians wondering how this armed conflict would be resolved. The events of Oka have remained fresh in our minds as we remember the barricades, the tanks, the low-flying aircraft, and the nightly interviews with municipal, provincial, or federal officials recounting the events of the day. After watching these events Canadians were convinced that this conflict would produce substantive changes in our treatment of Aboriginal people.

There are seven Mohawk communities in Canada— Kanesatake, Kahnawake, Akwesasne, Tyendinaga, Wahta, Six Nations at Ohsweken, and Oneida of the Thames— totalling about 40 000 persons. The following discussion focuses on Kanesatake since it was central to the events at Oka. Other groups in the Six Nations were involved in the resolution of the Oka dispute, but they played a more supportive role in the events.

In the 17th century the Mohawks were located in the northern part of New York State (from the Adirondacks in the east to the Five Finger Lakes in the west). By the middle of the 17th century, following the arrival of the Europeans, a number of Mohawks converted to Catholicism and joined settlements of New France. The origin of land disputes between Aboriginal and non-Aboriginal people in the region of Kanesatake and Oka can be traced to the 1717 land grant by the King of France to the Ecclesiastics of the Seminary of St. Sulpice of Montreal. Around 1721, the Sulpicians established a settlement of religious converts, composed of Iroquois (Mohawk), Nipissing, and Algonquin people within the 1717 seigniorial grant at Lac-des-Deux-Montagnes. The original grant was subsequently enlarged by the King of France in 1735. It is generally acknowledged that these tracts of land were granted to the Sulpicians for the purpose of protecting and instructing the indigenous people (a policy reflecting the ethnocentrism and paternalism of that time). However, the precise nature of the obligations of the Sulpicians to the Aboriginal people has remained a point of controversy ever since. Later, seigneuries were granted to the Jesuits and the Sulpicians for the benefit of the Indians living in the Montreal area, at Kahnawake and Oka. By the mid-18th century, a portion of the Mohawks of Kahnawake settled in St. Regis, where the Akwesasne reserve was later created.

Although the *Royal Proclamation* of 1763 recognized that Indian lands had to be purchased by the Crown before settlement could occur, it was not applied in the St. Lawrence Valley or Atlantic colonies. Nevertheless, the Sulpicians' claim was accepted, even though the claim made by the Mohawks in neighbouring Kahnawake against the Jesuits of Sault St. Louis had been recognized. After 1787, the Mohawks publicly protested the Sulpicians' claim several times, but to no avail. They continued their protest well after the mid-19th century.

Conflicts between the Aboriginal people and the Sulpicians over the land were frequent, particularly over the issue of sale of the land to third parties. In response to petitions from Indians of Oka during the 1800s for title to the land granted to the seminary, the Legislature of Lower Canada enacted a statute confirming the full proprietary title of the seminary to the disputed land while retaining the somewhat vaguely defined obligations to the Aboriginal population. *An Act Respecting the Seminary of St. Sulpice* incorporated the members of the Seminary and provided that the corporation shall have, hold, and possess the "fief and seigniory" of Lac-des-Deux-Montagnes as proprietors in the same manner and to the same extent as the seminary did under the original land grant. Local Mohawks continued to dispute the right of the seminary to sell the land and complained about the manner in which the land was managed.

In the early part of this century, the federal government attempted to resolve this issue by initiating a court action on behalf of the indigenous people at Lac-des-Deux-Montagnes to determine the respective legal rights and obligations of the seminary and the Aboriginal population. In determining the nature of the land rights of the seminary, its ability to sell the land unencumbered to third parties would also be clarified. This legal action culminated in the 1912 decision of the Judicial Committee of the Privy Council (then the final court of appeal for Canada). The Court stated that the effect of the 1841 legislation "was to place beyond question the title of the respondents [the seminary] to the Seigniory; and to make it impossible for the appellants to establish an independent title to possession or control in the administration." The Privy Council also said that the Mohawks could not assert title over the land because they had not been in the area from time immemorial. Furthermore, it was accepted that the French had extinguished whatever title the Indians might have had. The Indians had not taken treaty, nor had the land been set aside for them in trust. The Privy Council went on to suggest that there might be the possibility of a charitable trust, but that the issue was not argued in this case. In essence, the Court held that the Mohawk people had a right to occupy and use the land until the Sulpicians exercised their unfettered right to sell it.

The conflict between the seminary, which continued to sell off parts of the original grant, and the Aboriginal people continued. In 1945, in another attempt to end this controversy, the federal government purchased what was left of the Sulpician lands and assumed whatever obligations the Sulpicians had toward the Mohawks, but without consulting the Mohawks about this agreement. This was the beginning of a process that continues today of assembling land under federal jurisdiction for a reserve at Kanesatake.

In the 1960s, further legal action was pursued. However, resistance at the departmental level prevented the claim from being acted upon. One of the obstacles to creating a reserve base under the *Indian Act,* or any future legislation, is that the land purchased in 1945 consists of a series of blocks interspersed with privately held lands within the Municipality of Oka. Both the community of Kanesatake and the Municipality of Oka are faced with the dual problems of making decisions regarding land use and management that may affect the other community and dealing with the effects of decisions made by the other community. The question of coordinating land-use policies has been a source of friction between the two communities for some time.

In 1975 the Mohawks of Kanesatake presented a joint claim under the federal comprehensive land claims policy with the Mohawk people of Kahnawake and Akwesasne, asserting Aboriginal title to lands along the St. Lawrence and Ottawa Rivers in Southern Quebec. Comprehensive claims, as we have seen, involve claims to an existing Aboriginal title and presume the need to negotiate a range of matters such as land to be held under Aboriginal control, lands to be ceded, compensation, and future legislative regimes to be applied to the territory in question (see Figure 8.2). The Mohawk comprehensive claim includes the southwestern part of the province of Quebec, encompassing the area along and adjacent to the St. Lawrence and Ottawa Rivers stretching south and east to the U.S. border and north to a point near the Saguenay River, and including areas to the north and west of the St. Lawrence and Ottawa Rivers.

The federal government rejected the Mohawk 1975 comprehensive claim on the following grounds:

1. The Mohawks could not assert Aboriginal title as they had not maintained possession of the land since time immemorial. The land had been alternately and concurrently occupied by the Nipissing, Algonquin, and Iroquois.

2. Any Aboriginal title that may have existed had been extinguished first by the Kings of France with respect to the land grants made by them, including the seigniorial grant to the Seminary of St. Sulpice, and by the British Crown through the granting of title to others when lands were opened to settlement.

3. Mohawk presence in the region did not pre-date European presence; the Mohawks came to settle at Oka only after the Mission was established in 1721.

The Department of Indian Affairs restated its view that the fundamental weakness of the Mohawk land claim in the area of Oka is that the historical record, as the Department views it, fails to demonstrate exclusive Mohawk use of the territory since time immemorial—relative to both other Aboriginal peoples, and non-Aboriginal people such as the Sulpicians. From the Mohawk perspective, the claims of Canadian governments and non-Aboriginal settlers are at least equally flawed.

The Mohawk claim has also been expressed another way. Since the Department has described the Mohawks at Oka as descendants of the Iroquois, Algonquins, and Nipissings (Information Sheet, "Mohawk Band Government," July 1990), then the indigenous people of Kanesatake could demonstrate traditional use and occupancy of the land not just as Mohawks but also as descendants of all Aboriginal peoples who used that territory prior to and since the arrival of Europeans.

As an alternative argument to the comprehensive claim, Mohawks say that the Sulpician land grant was intended for the benefit of the indigenous people. Accordingly, the Sulpician Order was not free to sell any of this land without the consent of the Aboriginal people concerned. If this argument is used, then this is regarded as a specific claims issue, since specific claims arise from allegations of government mismanagement of particular Indian lands. With respect to any specific claim in this region, the federal government has taken the position that the 1912 Privy Council decision fully answered the question of any outstanding legal obligation of the federal government. The answer was *none*.

The Mohawks also submitted a specific claim in June 1977, which was ultimately rejected in October 1986. The Department of Justice advised that a lawful obligation on the part of the federal government did not exist. However, in a letter to the band informing them that no outstanding lawful obligation on the part of Canada existed, then minister of Indian Affairs, Bill McKnight, expressed the federal government's willingness to consider proposals for alternative means of redress of the Kanesatake band's grievance.

In summary, Mohawk claims to land have been advanced on a number of grounds, each representing a separate legal argument but also related to one another:

1. territorial sovereignty flowing from status as a sovereign nation;
2. treaty rights;
3. the *Royal Proclamation* of 1763;
4. unextinguished Aboriginal title under common law;
5. land rights flowing from the obligations imposed on the Sulpician Order in the 18th century land grants to the Order by the King of France.

From the viewpoints of the federal, provincial, and municipal governments, these issues were decided against the Mohawks as a result of the 1912 decision of the Judicial Committee of the Privy Council in *Corinthe* v. *Seminary of St. Sulpice*. However, it is important to note that the issue of Mohawk sovereignty was not directly before that court.

Mohawk land rights issues at Kanesatake are distinct from many other indigenous land rights issues because they are one of a handful of Aboriginal title cases to have reached a

FIGURE 8.2	Mohawk Reserves in the St. Lawrence Valley

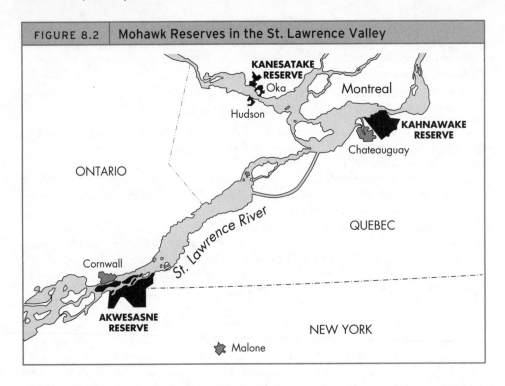

final court of appeal (this is not to suggest that there are not other legal issues relating to land that could be litigated); and the Mohawks are one of a few groups to have worked their way through both the specific and comprehensive claims processes. Both claims have been rejected by the federal government. Despite these setbacks, Mohawks continue to argue that they have land rights based on all the grounds set out above. The Mohawk people today argue that, independent of the arrival of Mohawk religious converts in 1721 at the Sulpician Mission at Lac-des-Deux-Montagnes, the Mohawk Nation used and occupied that territory and exercised sovereignty over it long before the land grants by the King of France. The Mohawk people make reference to a number of treaties with European powers (Holland, France, and England), which they say acknowledge the sovereign status of the Mohawk people throughout their territory in Canada and the United States. They also question the legality, under international law, of the land grants. For example, if these lands were unoccupied by non-Aboriginal people before 1717 but were occupied and used by indigenous people (whether Mohawk, Nipissing, or Algonquin), by what international legal principle could a European power assert sovereignty over the territory in the absence of conquest or cession?

Contrary to this position, the Municipality of Oka, the federal and provincial governments, and persons claiming a clear title through the seminary argue that the Aboriginal people have no proprietary rights outside the federally purchased lands and that this issue has been conclusively settled by legislation and litigation. In 1936 the Sulpician order sold nearly all of the land to a Belgian real estate company. The company began to sell the land in parcels for agricultural development. In 1945 the Department of Indian Affairs purchased the seminary's unsold lands plus some additional surrounding land. The seminary retained a small parcel, which is used for religious purposes. The land question continued to be important to the Mohawks, but the government felt that the issue had been resolved. Lacking funds and legal expertise, the Mohawks were unable to pursue their claims. It would not be until the 1990s, in the face of the Oka affair, that the federal government would act on the claim.

The conflict was over 39 hectares of land. The municipality wanted to use this land to expand an existing nine-hole golf course. This land included an Aboriginal cemetery and parts of a pine forest that the Mohawks consider theirs. Ottawa has since purchased the land for $5.2 million and has plans to turn it over to the Mohawks.

In early 1991, one year after the Oka crisis, a Quebec judge ruled that the federal government could hold a referendum to determine the method of local government in the Kahnesatake community at Oka. The chief and council at Kahnesatake are not elected but instead selected, by Mohawk custom, by clan mothers of the Turtle, Wolf, and Bear clans. In June of 1991 the community elected an interim chief and band council. The new interim band developed a Kahnesatake Mohawk election code that was acceptable to the community.

In 1992 the Grand Chief of the Mohawk Council of Kahnawake and the Minister of State for Indian Affairs and Northern Development signed a framework agreement to start negotiations on a new relationship between the government and the Kahnawake. In the long term, the Mohawks are proposing to revive the structures, institutions, and principles of the Great Law of the Iroquois of Six Nations. In the meantime, they intend to change their existing relationship with the federal government in order to get recognition of their jurisdiction in a variety of areas—e.g., policing. Negotiations include the nature and scope of Mohawk government, justice, land management, land control, environment, social services, health, education, and cultural matters.

LATE 20TH- AND EARLY 21ST-CENTURY CLAIMS

Since the establishment of a federal policy for the settlement of Aboriginal land claims in 1973, 12 major comprehensive claims agreements have come into effect in Canada (to 2000). An American claim in Alaska (1971) became the model for subsequent Canadian settlements—e.g., in James Bay (1975) and the Western Arctic (1984). These include the Northeastern Quebec agreement (1978), the Inuvialuit final agreement (1984), the Nunavut land claims agreement (1993), the Sahtu Dene and Métis agreement (1993), the Selkirk First Nation (1997), and the Nisga'a Treaty (2000), among others. These settlements involve three major components: land cession to the Aboriginal groups, financial payment for cession, and the creation of corporate structures to deal with land, money, or environmental issues. Aboriginal corporate and political structures were also established. A more detailed description of these settlements can be seen in the "Case Studies" section.

In British Columbia, direct action by Aboriginal people in the 1970s and 1980s prompted the federal government to re-evaluate its policy and programs. Although the provincial government has continued to deny the existence of Aboriginal title, by the late 1980s it became more responsive to Aboriginal concerns. The Ministry of Native Affairs and The Premier's Council on Native Affairs were created to meet with Aboriginal groups regarding a range of Aboriginal issues. In 1990 the British Columbia government agreed to establish a process by which Aboriginal land claims could be received and placed on the negotiating table. In August 1990, the province of British Columbia agreed to join Aboriginal groups and the federal government in negotiating land claims settlements. This meeting resulted in the creation of a tripartite task force to develop a process for negotiations. By late 1990 this task force was created, and in June 1991 it submitted its report.

The British Columbia Claims Task Force was established in the early 1990s to provide advice to parties involved in negotiating a land claim. Members of the Task Force include provincial and federal authorities as well as members from the First Nations community. In addition the province created a Land Claims registry, which receives and provides an initial assessment of a claim once it has been accepted for negotiation by the federal government. Finally, a Land Claims Implementation Group was established in an attempt to help coordinate the activities of general inter-ministry committees and other groups involved in data collection with regard to land claims being pursued by Aboriginal groups.

There are currently over 50 comprehensive land claims being negotiated in British Columbia by various Aboriginal groups. The total land area being contested represents almost the entire land area (nearly three-quarters of the total land area) of the province. In addition to the claims under negotiation, three other major land claims have been presented (Sechelt, Musqueam, and Homalco), representing an additional 10 000 square kilometres, but have not been accepted for negotiation by the federal government. Thus far, only one of the claims has been settled. In early 1996, the Nisga'a in the B.C. Nass River Valley settled a land claim over 100 years old. The 2400 people, living in four communities, received $200 million and over 2000 square kilometres of land.

It is estimated that B.C. land claims (both specific and comprehensive) will cost in excess of $10 billion, when they are all settled. Under provincial–federal agreements, land claims are equally shared by both parties. The federal government will contribute most of its share in cash while the province will pay most of its share in land. As shown in the previous chapter, British Columbia is indeed a special case in that Aboriginal title in all of the province still exists except in the northeast (where title was extinguished by virtue of Treaty No. 8). There has thus been pressure on the provincial government to accelerate the treaty process and settle claims quickly. In 2002 the British Columbia government proposed a province-wide referendum to determine both support for and direction of treaty negotiations, perhaps in the hopes of ending the process entirely. Ultimately the referendum and its results were rejected on the basis that the process itself constituted an attack on the agreements between the Crown and Aboriginal people, and on decisions of the courts that have established Aboriginal rights (in addition to significant lack of voter support). The referendum was considered a shameful act for the B.C. government by First Nations and their supporters (including the Canadian Jewish Congress, B.C. Federation of Labour, and the David Suzuki Foundation), who argued that the rights of a minority should not be determined by a vote of the majority. Voters were asked to consider and vote "yes" or "no" to some eight principles, including the following:

1. Private property should not be expropriated for treaty settlements.
2. Hunting, fishing, and recreational opportunities on Crown land should be ensured for all British Columbians.
3. Parks and protected areas should be maintained for the use and benefit of all British Columbians.
4. Province-wide standards of resource management and environmental protection should continue to apply.
5. The existing tax exemptions for Aboriginal people should be phased out.

Notwithstanding the fact that these were "loaded" statements in the first place, it was the potential precedent of specifically targeting minority group rights that angered First Nations and most citizens. The 2002 B.C. referendum provides a clear example of how strong feelings are in relation to treaties and claims, and how far some governments are willing to go to deal with them.

In 1991 the federal government formed the Indian Claims Commission to examine claims rejected by the federal government, to review compensation awards, and to help mediate disputes between government and Aboriginal claimants. This board can only recommend actions to the federal government, and there have been several occasions when the government has rejected the board's advice. In 1996 the members of the board resigned after the federal government refused to act upon their recommendations. However, today the board still operates and continues to mediate claims brought forward by Aboriginal groups.

An argument to reopen the treaties might be made for Canada. The White Paper introduced by the government in 1969 brought to the collective attention of Canadians the problems of Aboriginal groups and their claims. This was buttressed by the Supreme Court decision in 1973 (*Calder* case) and the Berger Commission (1974), which both gave some credence to Aboriginal claims.[3] However, by the late 20th century public interest and support had waned somewhat (Ponting, 1987). The issue of land claims is still being overshadowed by other concerns such as employment, the environment, constitutional reform, health care, energy policies, and Quebec secession. Settling land claims has faded somewhat into the background (except perhaps in British Columbia and in parts of Northern Canada), and this means reduced interest in and support of Aboriginal claims on the part of Canadians. National surveys carried out in the late 1990s show that less than 5 percent of the people questioned felt that Aboriginal–Non-Aboriginal problems should be the first of our national priorities. The environment, senior-citizen issues, "Quebec independence," and women's issues were cited as having higher priority. It would seem, then, that the government's commitment to settling claims is a one-time deal. Aboriginal people are consequently well aware that failure to achieve a settlement now may mean that the issue will be shifted to an even lower priority and require a heavier investment of time, money, and energy sometime in the future. On the other hand, to settle now, under existing conditions, may mean that their land and culture might be lost.

COMPREHENSIVE LAND CLAIMS: CASE STUDIES

1. James Bay

The James Bay and Northern Quebec Agreement (1975) and the Northeastern Quebec Agreement (1978) required the federal and Quebec governments to enact special legislation in respect to local government and land administration for Aboriginal people in the area. Between 1976 and 1979 a number of bills were passed to enact the agreements. Thirty-one boards, committees, commissions, and councils were established in order to deal with the organizational structure that resulted from the agreements; for example, the Cree School Board, the Income Security Board, and the Cree Trappers Association (see Figure 8.3). The agreements also required that the traditional financial arrangements between Aboriginal groups in the area and the federal government be changed as bands began to take on more and more political control and accountability. The new agreements (confirmed in the *Cree/Naskapi Act, 1984*) provided for:

1. funding for local government, safeguarding of community infrastructure and delivery of essential services;

2. the determination of funding needs;

3. the principle of local autonomy and the elimination of unnecessary central administration;

4. unconditional grant funding; and

5. grants that will be submitted to Parliament annually based on five-year agreements. (Indian and Aboriginal Program, 1985; 261–262)

In return for the Cree allowing Phase I to proceed, they received $136 million from the Quebec and federal governments. This money was invested in the Cree Regional Economic Enterprises (CREECO) and the Cree Regional Authority Board of Compensation. CREECO dominates the Aboriginal economy, by means of its $36 million in revenues and through its control of the airways and housing projects. Both companies have expanded and created hundreds of jobs. However, profit is slow to come, and CREECO registered a $5.2 million deficit in 1989. In addition to the above revenues, CREECO obtained over $30 million in Hydro-Quebec contracts in 1989 and over $50 million in 1990. This has created permanent jobs for the Cree and changed their lifestyle considerably. With assets of over $140 million, the Cree have invested in Quebec government bonds, debentures, and blue chip stocks (they were required under the terms of the Agreement), thus generating over $11 million revenue. Other monies received were used by communities to build infrastructure and develop creative investments; e.g., Waskaganish Enterprises Development Corporation entered into a joint venture with Yamaha Motors Canada to build fibreglass freighter canoes.

Proponents of Hydro-Quebec's James Bay development, which will divert and store the waters that flow into James Bay and Hudson Bay, feel that the production of 26 000 megawatts of power is reason enough for its existence. The original project altered the flow of several rivers in the region. When the water from the Caniapiscau River was first diverted to a reservoir, the volume (19 billion cubic metres) was so great that a minor tremor was felt.

The battle over this $50 billion project has once again come to the foreground, now that the first phase has been completed (in 1984) and the provincial government is moving into the second stage. Over two decades the Cree (10 000 of them) fought against development, but eventually agreed to allow the project to proceed after the provincial and federal governments agreed to compensate them (Raunet, 1984).

Today, as Phase II continues, the Cree have asked the court to declare the original settlement "null and void" because the agreement was based upon the assumption that hydroelectric power development was compatible with the Cree way of life and this, the Cree argue, is not true. In Phase I Hydro-Quebec erected 215 dams and dikes, and more than 10 000 square kilometres of new lake was created. Some consequences were not anticipated; for example, flooding released mercury from the bedrock and thus contaminated certain fish. But the more dramatic and significant consequences are the social impacts. The sudden modernization and urbanization of a previously nomadic society will have immediate and long-term effects (Wertman, 1983).

The Quebec government is now beginning to assess La Grande Phase II (completed in 1995), Great Whale (still not completed at the end of the 20th century), and the Nottaway-Broadback-Rupert project (slated for completion in 2007). Estimated construction costs for these three projects are over $35 billion (1991 dollars). However, there has been substantial Aboriginal resistance to the proposed project, as Phase II will involve five claims and will affect an additional 10 000 square kilometres of land (almost 2 percent of the total area of Quebec). Preliminary negotiations are now going on with the Inuit, who are the major group to be affected by Phase II (unlike Phase I, which affected the Cree).

Almost 50 percent of the people in Northern Quebec, including the Cree, remain unemployed. The tradition of community food is no longer part of their customs. Alcoholism, substance abuse, and spouse abuse are rampant, as are suicide attempts. On the other hand, the villages established now have water, sewage, electricity, and schools. Children no longer have to be sent to Southern schools to be educated in English.

2. Council of Yukon Indians (CYI) Claim

The Yukon Indians had pressed to settle their land claims for nearly a quarter-century. And, while the federal government accepted their claim for negotiation in 1973, no final agreement has been put in place. An initial agreement was signed in 1984, but this agreement was eventually rejected by the Council of Yukon Indians General Assembly. Two years later a new federal comprehensive claims policy was announced that dealt with many of the concerns raised by the Council. In 1988 a new agreement in principle was accepted.

In 1989 the federal government approved the negotiation of self-government agreements for the Yukon First Nations Final (land claim) Agreements. Four Yukon First Nations have signed self-government agreements and no longer have to function under the *Indian Act*. Each group will exercise law-making powers on settlement lands with regard to land use, hunting, trapping, fishing, licensing, and the regulation of businesses. They

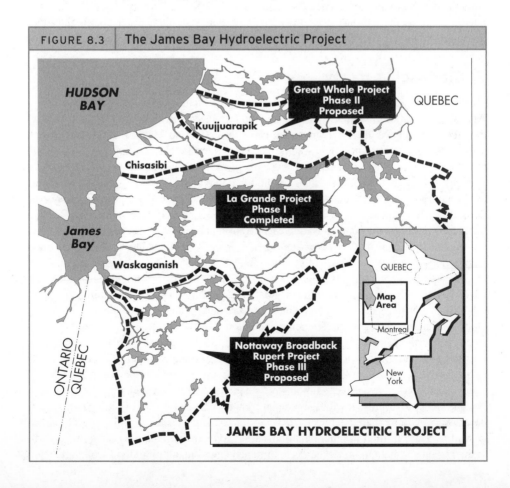

FIGURE 8.3 | The James Bay Hydroelectric Project

will also have the right to pass laws in the areas of language, culture, health care and services, social and welfare services, training programs, care and placement of children, educational programs, and licences to raise revenue. These self-government agreements will not affect any Aboriginal claim or right and will still allow them to participate in government programs for status Indians.

In 1993 a comprehensive settlement was made with the Yukon First Nations. The Council of Yukon Indians Umbrella Final Agreement is a framework agreement that sets out the terms for final land claim settlements and self-government agreements with each of the Yukon's 14 First Nations. Ten other Yukon First Nations are to be included in the agreement.

The umbrella agreement is composed of two parts. First is the land claim agreements, and second is the self-government agreements. These agreements involve about 8000 Yukon Indians. Under the Umbrella Final Agreement, each of the 14 First Nations will conclude their final claim settlement agreement. Overall, the agreement provides for over 41 000 square kilometres of land, including category A land (which is controlled solely by Aboriginal people, while category B land is controlled by the federal government subject to input by Aboriginal communities) with surface and sub-surface rights, and category B land with surface rights only, but including rights to materials such as sand and gravel. In addition, $243 million will be divided among the 14 First Nations and paid over 15 years. Yukon First Nations will also receive full rental revenues from surface leases and royalties from the development of nonrenewable resources. First Nations will be guaranteed at least one-third representation on the land use planning bodies, Yukon water board, and other agencies. Individual First Nations in Yukon continue to pursue final land claim agreements.

3. The Nisga'a Treaty

Canadian history was made on August 4, 1998, at the initialling of the Nisga'a Final Treaty Agreement. Ratified first by the Nisga'a and the province of British Columbia and then by Parliament in Ottawa, the final agreement came into effect on May 11, 2000. It is British Columbia's first treaty since 1899—some 112 years after the Nisga'a first went to Victoria to attempt to settle the land issue. By this agreement, the Nisga'a Aboriginal rights under Sections 25 and 35 of the Constitution are modified into both treaty rights and a land claims agreement. To the extent that any Aboriginal rights or title that the Nisga'a have, or may ever have, differ from those set out in the treaty, those rights are released by the Nisga'a. The treaty also reaffirms the Nisga'a Nation as an Aboriginal people of Canada, while acknowledging that the Canadian *Charter of Rights and Freedoms*, the Canadian Criminal Code, and other federal and provincial laws of general application apply to Nisga'a government.

The Final Agreement sets aside approximately 2000 square kilometres of the Nass River Valley as Nisga'a lands (of the original land claim of 24 000 square kilometres) and establishes a Nisga'a central government with jurisdiction and powers similar to those of other local municipal-style governments, including law making, policing, corrections services, and establishment of a Nisga'a Court. The 56 Indian reserves will cease to be reserves and become instead Nisga'a communal and fee simple property. Under the terms of the treaty, the Nisga'a will own surface and subsurface resources on Nisga'a lands and have a share in the Nass River salmon stocks and Nass area wildlife harvests.

The treaty also provides for a financial transfer of $190 million (with a formula for how the cost will be shared between British Columbia and Canada), payable over 15 years, as well as $21.5 million in other benefits. These payments will support economic growth in the region and help to break the cycle of dependency. In addition, the Final Agreement specifies that personal tax exemptions for Nisga'a citizens will be phased out. Other provisions in the treaty specify that, after a transition period of 12 years, the Nisga'a will cease to be administered under the *Indian Act*, will become subject to all provincial and federal taxes, and will become responsible for an increasing share of the cost of public services as the Nisga'a develop their own sources of revenue.

Despite continued opposition and criticism from some federal and provincial political parties, some resource companies, and some non-Aboriginal people, the Nisga'a treaty has set a new precedent for settling the approximately 100 outstanding Aboriginal land and rights claims in British Columbia. The treaty is considered a milestone, particularly considering that between 1890 and the 1960s Nisga'a negotiators were banned from the legislature in Victoria and prohibited from publicly raising their claims.

4. Tli Cho Agreement

In 2003, the Tli Cho Agreement transferred control of the largest block of land in Canada to the Dogrib First Nation, covering an area from the Great Slave lake to the Great Bear lake and into Nunavut (39 000 square kilometres). The transfer includes both surface and sub-surface rights. Three levels of government are involved as this land covers the Northwest Territories and Nunavut and includes the Tli Cho First Nation government. Highlights of the Agreement include a public government for each of the four communities in the area—Behcho Ko (Rae-Edzo), Wha Ti (Lac La Martre), Gameti (Rae Lakes), and Wekweti (Snare Lake). The new Dogrib government will have the power to tax Dogrib citizens on Dogrib land but also be tax exempt regarding its government activities, as is other government in Canada. A Dogrib community government will comprise an elected chief and an even number of councillors, and no more than half of the council seats can be filled by persons who are not Dogrib citizens. The Dogrib Nation will control hunting and fishing as well as industrial development. This new government also will have entitlement to royalties on resources from its land and waters.

CONCLUSION

Land and other title claims continue to be a major focal point between Aboriginal groups and government. They also represent a growing crisis for both Aboriginal and non-Aboriginal people. Aboriginal groups continue to press for compensation, whether it be through a reinterpretation of treaties, errors in land transfers, or comprehensive land claims. The Mi'kmaq of Nova Scotia and Prince Edward Island illustrate the first case, whereby they are trying to force the government to compensate them for land taken under the Treaty of Utrecht (1713, 1725, and 1752). They are also seeking other Aboriginal rights under this treaty that they feel have been taken away. The Mississauga First Nations claim is a good example of "error" compensation. In the mid-1990s they signed a compensation package for $13.7 million plus 16 000 hectares of land because of an error made in 1852. The Cree of James Bay have taken the federal and provincial governments to court in an attempt to get them to implement the agreement they signed over two decades ago. Interpretation of the agreement has been under question and a second generation of court cases aimed at both renegotiating the original agreement and implementing aspects of the agreement has emerged.

Given the large number of claims now before the courts and the slow pace at which they are resolved, land issues will remain an important "flash point" between Aboriginal and non-Aboriginal Canadians for some time to come.

NOTES

1. The Canada–U.S. free trade agreement does not change the negotiated rights of Indian and Inuit people. The responsibility for determining the pace and conditions of exploration and development remains in Canada.

2. Judges taking this stance narrowly define concepts and words. For example, a positivistic judge would interpret the term "medicine chest" (as used in a treaty) as "a small wooden box with an assortment of medicines and bandages for injuries." A more liberal interpretation would be to define the term in the context in which it was being used as well as within that of the 20th century. As a result, some judges have defined the concept as "universal health care" because Indians were trading their land for health services available at that time. Now that health services have expanded and become more comprehensive, it does not mean that Indians are not eligible because they agreed to a "medicine chest."

3. In 1974 the federal government appointed Mr. Justice Thomas Berger to conduct a social and environmental impact assessment on the proposed pipelines that would cut across the Mackenzie Valley, where they would eventually connect with the existing pipeline system. Soon after his appointment, Berger declared that he would visit all communities in the North that were likely to be affected and solicit their assessments and recommendations. He also held hearings in major urban areas in Southern Canada. After more than two years of hearings, he submitted the first of two volumes of his report to the minister of DIAND—*Northern Frontier, Northern Homeland*.

   His recommendations were straightforward. He did not recommend against building the pipeline, but rather concluded that a ten-year moratorium be placed on its construction in order for the Aboriginal people to prepare themselves for such a project, to settle the land claims they had with the federal government, and to allow further testing of some "state of the art" technology being proposed in the construction of the pipeline.

   In the end, the federal government accepted Justice Berger's recommendation not to build the pipeline at that time and chose an alternative route. However, due to hydrocarbon finds in British Columbia and Alberta, the decline in the price of oil and gas, as well as other social, economic, and political factors, the entire idea of transporting hydrocarbons from the North to the South was dropped.

WEBLINKS

www.bctreaty.net

The British Columbia Treaty Commission has been at the heart of the recent treaty process in that province, discussed in this chapter. Its website explains its work and offers updates on recent developments.

www.bloorstreet.com/300block/ablawleg.htm

This is an excellent general website on issues in Aboriginal and First Nations law. It includes a discussion of major cases in the area, including a number dealing with treaty and Aboriginal rights like *Delgamuukw* and *Sparrow*. It also includes links to those decisions (at the Supreme Court's website).

www.gcc.ca/Political-Issues/jbnqa/jbnqa_menu.htm

The Grand Council of Cree website on the James Bay and Northern Quebec Agreement, including the text of the Agreement.

chapter nine

Self-Determination
and Self-Government:
The Rights of Peoples

INTRODUCTION

The quest for self-determination by Aboriginal peoples has gone on for many years. It would not be until the 1973 *Calder* case, when the judges ruled that Aboriginal title existed prior to Confederation, that self-government would be put back onto the negotiation table and a new era of discussions would take place between Aboriginal groups and the government (Dyck, 1997). Aboriginal peoples continue to make choices that maximize economic and social activities while, at the same time, maintaining their group identity and political self-sufficiency. Aboriginal groups across Canada agree that the right to self-determination requires control over one's life individually and collectively (Fontaine, 1998).

All of this takes place in the ethos of Canadian society, which seems to accept the premise that Aboriginal cultures are doomed and that no human efforts can save them from extinction. This philosophy was put in action over the past two centuries as vigorous measures were designed to undermine tribal authority and extinguish tribal ways of life (Laselva, 1998–99). Aboriginal people are victims of colonialism and are treated as an inferior culture in their own homeland. As Laselva points out, when equality has been offered to them, the condition for it was a renouncement of their identity. In the end they have rejected assimilation, exhibited the will to survive, and insisted on their right to self-government (Bell, 1998).

After World War II, many Canadians believed that we had become a "class-based" society, and that ethnicity was no longer important as a basis for identifying oneself or defining social relationships. Canadians felt sure that as Aboriginal people became exposed to modern society and the industrial technological complex, Aboriginal identity (both individual and collective) would wane. The fact that more and more

Aboriginal people were migrating to the city seemed to underscore this belief. However, a series of political and legal events occurred in the 1960s and early '70s that gave impetus to a growth in Aboriginal identity. The publication of the *Hawthorn Report,* the establishment of the Bilingual and Bicultural Commission, and the Supreme Court's ruling that Aboriginal rights existed, all contributed to a re-emergence of Aboriginal self-determination (Chretien, 1969).

Ideologically and practically, governments argue against Indian self-determination. From an ideological perspective, Canadians argue that all legal responsibility has been delegated to either the federal or provincial government and that there is nothing left to delegate. Furthermore, there is a belief (evidenced by the support of the *Indian Act*) that Aboriginal people have not yet become sufficiently "developed" to make major political and economic decisions. Finally, it is argued that Aboriginal people are Canadian and thus subject to the two levels of government. From a practical standpoint, few people could envisage over 600 mini-governments (even the Royal Commission on Aboriginal Peoples suggested there might be as many as 60 First Nations); the economic implications of such an arrangement were staggering (Mickenberg, 1971).

On the other hand, Indians began to demand the right to be recognized as a distinct culture with all the rights afforded to a sovereign nation. They argued that when the existing Constitution was put in place Aboriginal people were excluded and treated as a racial minority, rather than as a political community with full collective rights (Chartrand, 1993). They demanded that the two levels of government recognize them as a "distinct society" with political rights (Deloria and Lytle, 1984). Aboriginal people began to demand policies and programs that would support indigenous institutions, and they wanted the freedom to adopt whatever non-Aboriginal institutions they thought were compatible with Aboriginal values. Aboriginal people have not merely asserted their right or claimed that their goal was to "oust" the colonizers but have pushed for what they see as their legitimate entitlement of self-government.

Nevertheless, Aboriginal people want a new order of government that would be set within the Canadian Constitution and that would guarantee the inherent right of Aboriginal people to self-determination and self-government (Bell, 1998). This new fourth order of government would have the right to opt out of parts of the Canadian *Charter of Rights and Freedoms* under certain conditions. In the end, Aboriginal people want to be assured that they have the authority to make their own choices as to how they are governed (Hutchins, Hilling and Schulze, 1999). For example, *Bill C-49* gives signatory bands the power to expropriate land for community use and draft land codes. Aboriginal people argue that the Supreme Court has supported their basic objective of self-government. In the *Delgamuukw* case, the Chief Justice noted that the Crown is under a moral, if not a legal, duty to enter negotiations with Aboriginal people in good faith with the objective to achieve reconciliation of the pre-existence of Aboriginal societies with the sovereignty of the Crown (Laselva, 1998–99).

The use of ethnic exclusiveness has become an increasingly important means of differentiating people and of establishing ethnic organizations that are region- or nation-wide (Shaw, 1985). Various ethnic symbols and connections have been created to enhance the social and political positions of Aboriginal people. Aboriginal party leadership has sought support and solidarity on ethnic grounds. It remains to be seen if old divisions—for example, treaty–non-treaty, status–non-status, Blood–Blackfoot—can be set aside and issues can be dealt with solely from an ethnic perspective. Since the beginning of the 1980s the various levels of government have once again characterized Nativeness (ethnicity) as a problem for Canadian society, saying that it undermines the existing political order. This sort of pronouncement was very evident at two most recent first ministers' constitutional conferences on Aboriginal affairs. Whether this stance will successfully divide Aboriginal people, or whether they can maintain their ethnicity in the face of modernization, also remains to be seen.

The cultural resurgence and the defence of territory are but two overt expressions of Aboriginal self-determination. The concept of self-determination was born during the French Revolution, although it had certainly been developing long before. Our use of the term refers to the right of Aboriginal people to determine their political future and to freely pursue their cultural and economic development (Umozurike, 1972). Politically, this idea is expressed through independence, self-government, local autonomy, or some other form of increased participation in the governing process. In Canada, federalism and minority rights are fundamental constitutional principles and have acquired increased importance over the past two decades. Aboriginal people seek independence in order to ensure democratic government and the absence of external domination. Unfortunately, the concept of self-determination has been variously defined and interpreted over the last decade. This has exacerbated the problem of cross-cultural communication between Aboriginal people and those non-Aboriginal people who discuss the issue. Whatever unifying factors are used to define a people—e.g., ethnic, national, class, or racial—are arbitrary symbols, but they are profoundly meaningful to the people using them. The basis for unifying people may change over time or may contain more than one of the components identified above. It may also lead to different strategies being employed by different Aboriginal people to achieve the common goal of self-determination (Miller, 1991).

Self-determination involves a new respect for Aboriginal culture and a commitment to its survival. This, in turn, will enhance self-concepts and validate the positive aspects of Aboriginal culture (Elliott, 1980).

Aboriginal peoples have taken a seemingly contradictory stance regarding federal trust. They feel that the federal government has a "trust relationship" with them that must be honoured. As Cornell (1988) points out, the demands for self-determination and a continued relationship of entrustment—i.e., independence and paternalism—seem contradictory. Closer inspection of this ideological position reveals that most Aboriginal people feel that they will be better able to achieve self-determination if they deal with the federal government rather than provincial officials. They are clearly aware that linkages with the federal government mean that they are dependent upon it both politically and economically. However, Aboriginal people believe that through this linkage they will be able to obtain some long-term base financial support that will allow them to become economically independent.

The actions Aboriginal people take in the future will depend upon how they choose to develop a sense of identity and cohesion. For example, if solidarity were to be solely class-based, then their goal would be to change the political system. On the other hand, if the basis were ethnic, then they would demand a separate state or, at least, a relationship of autonomy within the state (Rohen, 1967).

As the issues confronting Aboriginal people have increased in number and scope, policy-making (for both Aboriginal people and the government) has become more and more complex. Many more government departments (besides INAC) have become active participants in the process. As Weaver (1985) notes, this has led to central government agencies playing the role of referee when different departments disagree over policy creation, change, or implementation. Overall, this has reduced the ability of INAC to carry through with its own policies. In short, Aboriginal policy is no longer the exclusive role of one department, but results from a collaboration by a number of departments and agencies.

CONSTITUTIONAL PATRIATION

Before we begin discussing sovereignty and self-determination, we need to place these ideas in their philosophical and political context. The federal government's desire to patriate the Constitution facilitated the efforts of Aboriginal people to discuss their concerns and bring several new issues to the foreground. The discussion of constitutional issues provided a national and international forum for Aboriginal people to air their concerns about their inability to participate in Canadian society. The average Canadian could no longer claim to be ignorant of the issues, nor could the elected representatives hide behind such a facade. The issues became public and were forcefully articulated by the Aboriginal leaders, who also managed to convey a sense of urgency (Morse, 1991).

Until the late 1970s, the federal government's attempts to patriate our Constitution were vague and episodic. Eventually, however, constitutional reform won national attention because of (1) Quebec's threats to secede from Confederation, (2) the increasing alienation of the West, and (3) conflict between the federal and provincial governments (Gibbins, 1986b). Constitutional reform was not initiated by Aboriginal people's concerns or by lobbying efforts exerted by Aboriginal organizations. Nevertheless, Aboriginal people had become interested in the constitutional issue and had been active in the arena since the mid-1970s, when northern Aboriginal people developed and presented the *Dene Declaration*. This was followed by the Inuit's *Nunavut Proposal* and the Federation of Saskatchewan Indians' *Indian Government*. In line with these new political philosophies, Indian organizations adapted to the new realities of the time; for example, the National Indian Brotherhood reorganized during the 1980–82 period and created the Assembly of First Nations. These political activities by Aboriginal groups were made possible through increased government funding and by the 1973 Supreme Court ruling in the Nisga'a land-claims case, which acknowledged (albeit indirectly) the existence of Aboriginal rights.

When the first constitutional amendment bill was introduced in 1978, only vague references were made to Aboriginal issues. This suggested that Aboriginal people were not considered an important element in Canadian society by the federal and provincial governments. It also seemed to imply that the 1969 White Paper (which would have done away with the legal concept of Indian) was being implemented through the back door. Because of pressure brought to bear by a variety of non-Aboriginal groups, the federal government agreed to allow the three major Aboriginal organizations to attend the first ministers' meetings as observers. Aboriginal people responded by claiming that this was exclusion in disguise. They preferred to sit at the conference as equals and be given voting privileges when matters pertaining to Aboriginal people were discussed.

Late in 1979 the Continuing Committee for Ministers on the Constitution (CCMC) met to decide how to handle further challenges and protests from Aboriginal people. They created a steering committee to meet formally with the three Aboriginal organizations representing the status Indians, Inuit, and non-status Indians and Métis—the National Indian

Brotherhood (NIB), the Inuit Committee on National Issues (ICNI), and the Native Council of Canada (NCC). The Federal–Provincial Relations Office (the federal body dealing with Aboriginal people on this issue) met both formally and informally with Aboriginal groups through the remaining months of 1979 (Barlett, 1984).

When the 1980 First Ministers' Conference was held, Aboriginal issues were not on the agenda and Aboriginal peoples were invited only as observers. The Aboriginal people, feeling completely left out when issues directly affecting them were being discussed, chose to act in a more visible political manner both nationally and internationally (Sanders, 1983b). This increased international activity on the part of Aboriginal people and produced some coalitions among the three major Aboriginal groups, as well as among non-Aboriginal organizations. By early 1981, the federal government relented and added two sections to the constitutional proposals that (1) protected the rights of Aboriginal peoples, and (2) required that future first ministers' meetings be held to deal with Aboriginal issues. However, further amendments were introduced by the government that would have permitted it and any provincial government to come to a bilateral agreement nullifying the protection of Aboriginal peoples (Zlotkin, 1983). As a result, Aboriginal people, with the exception of the Inuit, withdrew their short-lived support of the first constitutional conference.

In late 1981, the Supreme Court ruled that a unilateral request to amend the Constitution by the federal government was legal but not in keeping with tradition. But since the federal government wanted the provinces' support, it agreed to delete the clause affording protection to Aboriginal people from the final form of the November Accord of 1982. When it was announced, the Accord did not contain any clause recognizing or affirming Aboriginal or treaty rights. The Aboriginal groups strongly objected to this and created the Aboriginal Rights Coalition. In addition, they began to intensify their international lobbying (Sanders, 1983a). It was also at this time that media support began to materialize on behalf of the Aboriginal people; for example, *The Globe and Mail* supported the entrenchment of Aboriginal rights. As a result of both domestic and international concern, the premiers agreed to reinstate the Aboriginal-rights clause with one change: "rights" was changed to "existing rights."

Aboriginal rights were entrenched in Section 35 of the *Constitution Act,* which came into force April 17, 1982. In addition, Section 25 of this Act ensures that Aboriginal rights are not adversely affected by the *Charter of Rights and Freedoms.* Finally, Section 32 required that the federal government convene additional constitutional conferences to deal with Aboriginal peoples. The first conference, held in 1983, resulted in minor changes to Sections 25(b), 35, and 37 of the Constitution. Since then, three additional first ministers' meetings have been held to deal with Aboriginal issues. None of these meetings produced any substantive results. (For a thorough review of the first two conferences, see Schwartz, 1986.)

Between the first conference in 1983 and the last one in 1987, the *Penner Report* was released, *Bill C-31* was passed,[1] the task force reviewing comprehensive claims policy released its report, and *Bill C-43* (the *Sechelt Indian Band Self-Government Act*) was introduced. A new political climate was evident as the participants prepared for the last conference, but internal discord emerged on the Aboriginal side, and a lack of political will was apparent in the preliminary statements released by the premiers. The talks, therefore, were doomed to failure before they began.

Provincial officials had quietly agreed among themselves to take a stand against the form of Indian self-government being promoted by the Assembly of First Nations. The premiers were not prepared to be innovative in their approach to Aboriginal issues, nor were they in any mood to propose new policy directions themselves. In short, their chief concern was to maintain the status quo while still fulfilling the requirement to hold this conference, as set out in the Charter in 1982 (Assembly of Manitoba Chiefs, 1994).

Aboriginal involvement in the constitutional patriation process was based on several premises. First, Aboriginal people saw the Constitution as a symbolic statement about what is important in Canadian society. They also viewed the document as a potential lever for use in future political action. As Gibbins (1986a) points out, the inclusion of Aboriginal people and their concerns in such important documents legitimizes the group's interests and claims. In short, Aboriginal people felt that if they could be recognized as an important group in Canadian society, they could use this as a stepping stone to further such aspirations as settling land claims. They also wanted to influence the government in regard to Aboriginal and treaty rights. Finally, they hoped that through their involvement in the patriation of the Constitution, they would be able to exert pressure on the federal government to discuss issues of sovereignty and self-government (Indian Tribes of Manitoba, 1972).

The initial involvement in the constitutional talks by Aboriginal groups was minimal because of a lack of organization and funds. Also, they did not offer any stance of their own in regard to Aboriginal rights, but merely reacted to the federal and provincial governments' vague pronouncements. It was only after debate had been initiated that Aboriginal groups put forth proposals with regard to Aboriginal, treaty, and land rights. Federal and provincial officials reacted to these proposals by asking for more information and clarification. The governments did not put forth any new proposals, but simply used this strategy of stalling to maintain a benevolent image by never having to say "no" (Schwartz, 1986). It was also during this time that Aboriginal people began to discuss the issues of sovereignty and self-government. Although their concerns were initially dismissed by government officials, their persistence paid off. Slowly these issues entered the public arena of discussion, and when the *Constitution Act, 1982,* was finally enacted, Aboriginal rights had been entrenched.

The preamble to the *Constitution Act, 1982,* makes a significant statement on the nature of Canadian culture: "Canada is founded upon principles that recognize the supremacy of God and the rule of law." This assumption is insensitive to cultural differences and inaccurate for Aboriginal groups. Furthermore, the Charter does not support a collectivist idea of rights for culturally distinct (non-European) peoples. Turpel (1990) notes that the Charter expresses the values of a liberal democracy on the European model. It favours individualism and assumes a highly organized and impersonal industrial society. The paradigm of rights, based on the prototypical right of individual ownership of property, is antithetical to the understanding of the individual's relationship to society that is widely shared by First Nations peoples.

SOVEREIGNTY AND ABORIGINAL RIGHTS

The concept of sovereignty[2] as defined by Indians implies that they have the right of self-determination. This right, they argue, arises not only out of the various treaties, the *Constitution Act, 1867,* the *Royal Proclamation* of 1763, and assorted other federal acts, but also (and perhaps more importantly) as a gift from the Creator. This gift has never been, nor can it ever be, surrendered (Nadeau, 1979). Aboriginal people also argue that there are certain federal statutes (or documents that have the force of statutes) that specify that the federal government has a special trust relationship with them and is responsible for providing the resources that will enable them to achieve their goal of self-sufficiency.

Some Indian organizations have recently formally established their positions on this issue; but, partially because the various Aboriginal groups cannot agree and partially because the issue has not been fully analyzed, no precise statement on sovereignty, self-determination, or self-government has been articulated by Aboriginal groups or organizations. The Royal Commission on Aboriginal Peoples has presented some options but concludes that the specific form will vary from one First Nation to the next (Fleras and Elliott, 1992).

Contesting the Concept: Different Interpretations

Prior to the arrival of the Europeans, Aboriginal peoples occupied and controlled the area that is now called Canada. The question of sovereignty, however, remains unresolved and the Government of Canada has taken the position that Indians, Inuit, and Métis were never nations in the legal sense and are not now to be treated as such. Needless to say, Aboriginal people disagree with this interpretation and argue that they have always been nations and should be accorded all the rights, privileges, and responsibilities pertaining to nations.

On the basis of certain historical documents, the Crown, until the 20th century, recognized the inherent sovereignty of Indians. In this century, however, recognition has been less overt and consistent. More recently, there has been a formal rejection of Aboriginal claims to sovereignty. How has this come about? The initial relations of the Crown with Aboriginal people were heavily influenced by pragmatic factors, and this led directly to the recognition of Aboriginal sovereignty. But over time this necessity passed, and the Crown could afford to take the position to which it now subscribes. As a result, various political and legislative acts have been put in place that have, at least to the government's satisfaction, phased out any recognition of Aboriginal sovereignty. To illustrate this, we will briefly look at some of the major acts that have a bearing on such a claim. Ironically, these acts have been interpreted by both Aboriginal people and government officials as substantiating their opposing positions. We will start with assessing the Aboriginal interpretation.

Historically, royal charters (including the Hudson's Bay Company Charter of 1670) were used to establish political relationships between peoples. Many of the early charters recognized the autonomous status of Indian peoples and their ownership of land. For example, the HBC Charter states that the Company was to make peace or war "with any Prince or people whatsoever that are not Christians." Also during the early history of Canada, various royal instructions from the British Crown could be interpreted as being based on the premise that Indians existed as nations. For example, the instructions sent to the governor of Nova Scotia (after the signing of the Treaty of Utrecht, 1713) stated that Indians were a nation. The signing of various treaties in 1725 by Indians and the British suggest that the agreements were between two independent, sovereign nations. In other words, these actions imply that Indians were viewed as an organized body of people with their own distinct government systems (Lyon, 1985).

Treaties between Indians and Euro-Canadians were made as legalistic, written documents. Aboriginal people have viewed these documents as sacred and as representing agreements between two sovereign nations. Euro-Canadians, on the other hand, view them as having a status similar to that of a contract, although they are not contracts. In a sense, treaties were procedures used by Euro-Canadians to expedite a political process ensuring economic and military inroads. As Turpel (1990) points out, it is interesting that treaties with Aboriginal peoples are not considered equal to treaties carried out with other sovereign international peoples or nations. If you raise the question why, the answer is that Aboriginal people were not sufficiently "civilized" to qualify as sovereign people, or that they had already lost their sovereignty through some predestined and mysterious process. But both these myths have been challenged successfully. Why then are these arguments perpetuated? Why do we continue to pretend that Aboriginal people lack distinct cultures, or have inferior cultures, or had no political structure? The answer is clear. To accept the opposite view would require substantial changes in Aboriginal/non-Aboriginal relations, with all the attendant costs.

The *Royal Proclamation* of 1763 is further evidence that the Crown explicitly recognized Indians as sovereign nations. In addition to this, and consistent with it, over 80 treaties were concluded between various Indian groups and the Crown. These treaties seem to recognize the sovereignty of Indian nations (Assembly of First Nations, 1990b).

The *Constitution Act, 1867* (*British North America Act*) and the *Rupert's Land Transfer* are two additional pieces of evidence used by Indians to argue their sovereign status. Specifically, they cite Sections 109, 91(24) and 146 of the 1867 Act. The *Rupert's Land Transfer* stated that the claims of the Indian tribes to compensation for lands required for purposes of settlement would be considered and settled in conformity with the equitable principles that had been used by the British Crown in its past dealings with the Aboriginal peoples. The *Indian Act* also seems to give Indians a measure of self-government, which implies that they are sovereign. Finally, the *Constitution Act, 1982,* the Universal Declaration of Human Rights, and the Declaration Regarding Non Self-Governing Territories (of which Canada is a signatory) provide some basis for concluding that Indians have sovereignty.

In addition to the various statutes or acts that have been part of our history, the Canadian and British courts have made rulings that would seem to recognize the inherent sovereignty of the Aboriginal people. In the early *Mohegan Indians* v. *Connecticut* (1769) case, the Privy Council made explicit recognition of tribal sovereignty. This view was reinforced in a series of judgments in the United States (1810–1832). In the *Worchester* v. *Georgia* (1832) case, the Court affirmed that Indian nations are recognized as having rights of self-government. The courts also upheld the *Royal Proclamation* of 1763 as confirming the inherent sovereignty of Indian Nations. Canadian court cases that concur with the above include the *R.* v. *White and Bob* (1964); *Calder* v. *Attorney General of British Columbia* (1973); and *The Queen* v. *The Secretary of State for Foreign and Commonwealth Affairs* (1982). The Canadian case *Hamlet of Baker Lake* v. *Minister of Indian Affairs and Northern Development* (1980) illustrates that the courts recognize the existence of Aboriginal land-use rights and that these rights belong to the Aboriginal collectivity. Thus, if the collectivity has rights, it must be able to determine (as a collectivity) how it will exercise and dispose of those rights (Schwartz, 1986; Nammack, 1969).

Two additional sources of support for Indian sovereignty have been customary law and the trust responsibility in Section 91(24) of the *Constitution Act, 1867*. In the first case, the question is whether or not Indians had laws that were distinct from Canadian law. If they actually had laws and their laws were different, then those laws could be continued and could provide a basis for claiming nationhood. In the second case, the question is whether or not the federal government has a "trust responsibility" for Indian nations (Jhappan, 1993), i.e., to what extent the federal government is responsible for Indian people.

With the above evidence in hand, The Royal Commission on Aboriginal Peoples argues that the Canadian Constitution protects Aboriginal peoples' inherent rights of self-government and the *Charter of Rights and Freedoms* allows for the exercise of this right. Thus there is no need to amend the Constitution to ensure that Aboriginal groups have the right to exercise self-government. Wilkins (1999) agrees with the above and claims that, on the basis of evidence presented over the past century, there are sufficient grounds to support the claim that traditional Aboriginal collectivities have unextinguished Aboriginal rights to govern themselves. Nevertheless, the courts have not embraced such a conclusion. In fact, when given the opportunity, most courts have evaded answering the question. Why? Wilkins (1999) suggests that the courts have a concern as to the impact such a decision would have on the lives of both Aboriginal and non-Aboriginal residents in Canada. As Binnie (1990) points out, a decision acknowledging Aboriginal self-government would "leave the courts with inadequate mechanism to regulate the overlapping interests of communities occupying contiguous territory" (p. 217).

While the cases cited above seem to suggest that Indians are indeed First Nations and have sovereignty, several arguments have been used by the Crown to refute these claims. First, the Crown cites the doctrine of continuity, which states that in the case of conquest or cession, the rights of a "civilized" original people and their laws remain intact until the colonial government changes them through an act of its own parliament. This, they argue, has occurred over time with the introduction of British law. They also argue that since the Aboriginal peoples were not "civilized" at the time of European entry, the laws of the colonizing country took immediate effect. A second argument put forth by the federal government is that, depending on how the *Royal Proclamation* of 1763 is interpreted, sovereignty does or does not exist for Indians. The government has interpreted a key phrase of the Proclamation in a way that suggests that Indians *do not* have sovereignty. This phrase states that restrictions on settlements into Indian country were to be in place "for the present or until our future pleasure be made known." The courts have interpreted this to mean that Indian tenure under the *Royal Proclamation* of 1763 was a personal usufructuary right dependent upon the good will of the sovereign. This ruling was made explicit in the *St. Catherines Milling* case and has set a precedent for all later decisions. In some cases it has allowed the courts to set aside the issue of the doctrine of continuity when trying to make a decision on Indian sovereignty.

Finally, the courts (and the government using these court decisions) have argued that treaties with the Indians were not international treaties. The courts have ruled (with no explanation) that while the agreements with the Indians are known as treaties, they are not treaties in the sense of public international law; that is, they are not treaties between sovereign nations. Moreover, judges have argued that where treaties were entered into with Aboriginal peoples, they involved a commitment by Indians to obey the sovereign. Finally, no continuing right to self-government (if it existed prior to the signing of the treaty) is mentioned in any treaty (Henderson et al., 2000).

Today the issue remains as unclear as it was a century ago. No statute, court decision, or political statement has been provided by which the issue might be resolved. Aboriginal people still argue that they have sovereignty; the government says they don't. The issue has recently moved out of the judicial context and into the political arena. Today the government is trying to address the issues of Aboriginal rights and self-government—two crucial concerns that pertain to the sovereignty issue. It is unlikely that the courts or the government will ever find Aboriginal peoples to have sovereignty. This statement reflects both past judicial decisions handed down on Aboriginal issues and practical concerns. Politically speaking, Aboriginal self-government would not be a palatable solution to most Canadians. Pragmatically, it would mean that a substantial realignment of our parliamentary democratic system would need to be undertaken (Jhappan, 1990).

In an attempt to address this issue without actually confronting the specific concern of sovereignty, the federal government has chosen to discuss two matters that flow from the sovereignty issue—Aboriginal rights and self-government. Aboriginal rights were dealt with in the *Constitution Act, 1982,* and are still being discussed in an attempt to define and implement them. Self-government, the second concern, was addressed by the government's *Penner Report* and is now (under a variety of guises) being implemented. In the end, the federal government hopes that negotiations toward the resolution of these two areas will pose solutions that are acceptable to both groups so that sovereignty will no longer be an issue of concern to Aboriginal people.

Aboriginal Rights

With the passing of the Constitution in 1982, Aboriginal peoples have had their Aboriginal and treaty rights recognized and affirmed. Section 32 of the Constitution explicitly states that all laws and policies in Canada must be consistent with these rights. While the federal government has accepted these guidelines in principle, in practice it continues to develop policy and programs that run counter to the Constitution. This is most clearly seen in the area of land rights. Aboriginal people feel that their land rights should be recognized and that actions should be taken to reaffirm those rights. On the other hand, the government has taken the position that it wants to extinguish the "burden" of Aboriginal rights (ONWA, 1983).

Needless to say, the government's position was found wanting by Aboriginal people and was finally called into question by the courts with the 1973 *Calder* v. *Attorney General of British Columbia* and the 1974 *Cardinal* v. *The Queen* rulings. Ten years later *Nowegijick* v. *The Queen* (1983) and *Guerin* v. *The Queen* (1984) would reaffirm these earlier decisions and fundamentally alter the relationship between Aboriginal people and the government (both federal and provincial). Since these rulings, both parties have continued the process of trying to resolve the question of rights and responsibilities; however, today the assumptions have changed (Anaya et al., 1995).

During the past decade, because of international pressure and domestic concern, the Canadian government has tried to grapple with the issue of Aboriginal rights. Specifically, the patriation of the Constitution led to a sense of urgency in resolving the problem. In the end, the government entrenched Aboriginal rights in the Constitution without knowing or specifying what they entailed. The inclusion of the phrase "existing rights" has done little to clarify the meaning of the concept, although as Flanagan (1983a, 1985) points out, it may provide a legitimate basis for excluding Métis Aboriginal rights claims.

There are two opposed opinions about the existence of Aboriginal rights in Canada. On the one hand, there are number of academics, historians, and some legal advisors who are convinced of their existence (Wilkins, 1999; Davies, 1985). When one considers case law, however, it appears that many of the judges are not of the same opinion. Past and current court decisions suggest that if Aboriginal rights do exist, they take the form of personal usufruct—the right of an individual to occupy and use a piece of land—not collective, group rights. The *Baker Lake* decision (1980) is one notable exception to this rule.

The *Hamlet of Baker Lake* v. *Minister of Indian Affairs and Northern Development* decision arose out of a dispute between the Inuit around Baker Lake and the private corporations that were attempting to exploit the mineral potential in the area. In this case, Justice Mahoney ruled that the original Inuit had an organized society. He stated that they did not have a very elaborate system of institutions but that theirs was a society organized to exploit the resources available in the area. He also recognized the existence of Aboriginal land use rights *and* that these rights belonged to the Aboriginal collectivity. It follows that, if the collectivity has rights, it must also have the right to determine how it will exercise those rights.

An Aboriginal tribe, however, has no status as a legal entity under international law. It is generally accepted that, even though Indians were "sovereign and independent" societies before Europeans entered North America, this status was lost through the operation of European international law. The British and American claims tribunals have stated that an Indian tribe is not subject to international law and is a legal unit only insofar as the law of the country in which it lives recognizes it as such (Bennett, 1978; Gibbins, 1986b; Anaya, 2000).

International law has a more direct influence on how Canada deals with its Aboriginal people through the international treaties that have been signed and ratified by Canada. Breach of these treaties could bring international censure, judgment by the International Court of Justice, or an arbitration tribunal. Again, however, one must remember that Indians have no international standing and thus cannot sue Canada for breach of its obligations toward them. It should also be noted that Canada is not legally bound by many international treaties because it has not signed them. The rationale for not signing them has two bases: (1) many of the matters involved are not under federal competence but provincial, and (2) a concept of written codes of human rights seems to be contrary to common law and to the doctrine of parliamentary sovereignty (Culhane, 1998).

The Concept of Right

The word "right" seems to mean that one person has an affirmative claim against another—that is, the other person has a legal duty to respect that right. Thus, the concepts of right and duty seem to go hand in hand. However, the concept of right is not to be confused with that of privilege. The difference seems to lie in the fact that it is the absence of duty that identifies a privilege. Thus, the privilege to do a certain act arises where the privileged person has no duty to refrain from doing the privileged act. When people assert that they have a right, it means that they are confirming that they have a legal interest in an object, such as land. But whether or not someone else can change the nature of that legal interest depends on the powers and the immunities associated with that object. Powers are created by statute and involve the ability to change the nature of the interest. Anyone who tries to deny another's interest in an object but does not have the power to do so can be accused of acting *ultra vires*—that is, beyond the scope of the powers granted them by law (Henderson, 1978; Barsh and Henderson, 1982; Dupuis and McNeil, 1995).

In the end, the best we can offer for a definition of Aboriginal rights is the one suggested by Cumming (1973b): "Those property rights which Aboriginal people retain as a result of their original use and occupancy of lands" (p. 238). This is not to suggest that this is an official or even legal definition used by litigants or governments. It is simply a definition that seems to capture the essence of Aboriginal rights (Weaver, 1985).

What legal or political conditions would be necessary for Natives to convince others that they have Aboriginal rights? Elliott (1991) has noted three ways in which it could be argued that such rights exist. One of the most easily recognized ways is through reference to royal prerogatives. These are statements made by a government with regard to some issue; if local governments have not been established, they have the force of statutes. In Canada, the *Royal Proclamation* (1763) is an example of a royal prerogative. The *Royal Proclamation* was issued by King George III of Britain, and one section of it deals with Indian people. It suggests that Indians had a pre-existing title to lands. Some would argue, therefore, that it supports Aboriginal claims to Aboriginal rights. The section that deals with Indian people has never been repealed and thus still remains part of our legal system (Henderson, 1985).

A second way in which the existence of Aboriginal rights can be argued in Canada is by reference to the decisions of the courts—that is, common law. As Elliott (1991) points out, two conflicting notions about Aboriginal rights have emerged out of common law. One was that the *Royal Proclamation* of 1763 gave Indians Aboriginal title, and the other was that Aboriginal title was derived from their use and occupancy of the land from time immemorial.

The courts' interpretation that Aboriginal title derives from royal prerogative was based on one of the few court cases dealing with Aboriginal rights. This case, *St. Catherines Milling and Lumber Company* v. *The Queen, 1885,* influenced the court's interpretations of Aboriginal rights for nearly 100 years. The key component of the decision, handed down by the Privy Council, was the recognition of the existence in law of an Indian interest in the land in question, and the Council attributed the interest solely to the provisions of the *Royal Proclamation* of 1763 (Elliott, 1991).

In 1973, Canadian common law on the issue of Aboriginal rights would change from an exclusive basis in royal prerogative to include a possible basis in use and occupancy. This new interpretation was based on the *Calder* v. *Attorney General of British Columbia* (1973) case. In this case, the Nisga'a Indians (represented by Calder) lost their land claims but won judicial recognition of the crucial issue that their claim to the land was based on their ancestors' occupation and use of it from time immemorial (Gibbins and Ponting, 1986).

Today, both arguments are used to support Aboriginal claims of Aboriginal rights. However, the question remains as to whether the *Calder* case stands as a general legal recognition of the validity of occupancy-based claims. The answer, unfortunately, is both yes and no. Some courts have recognized and accepted this argument, while others have not. A review of court decisions would suggest that lower Canadian courts have accepted occupancy-based title as a legitimate argument, while higher courts have not yet given clear legal recognition to occupancy-based Aboriginal title (Elliott, 1991: 81; Federation of Saskatchewan Indian Nations, 1985; Green, 1983).

The third support for Aboriginal rights comes from the constitutional framework of a country (Henderson, et al., 2000). While there has been no general legislation passed by the Canadian Parliament that explicitly recognizes Aboriginal title, there are some pieces of legislation that implicitly apply to Aboriginal rights—for example, the *Manitoba Act,*

1870; the *Dominion Lands Act,* from 1872 to 1908; land cession treaties; and, more recently, Sections 35 and 37(1) and (2) of the *Constitution Act, 1982.*

As noted above, Aboriginal title, until lately, was interpreted as resting solely upon royal prerogative. More recently, occupancy-based arguments are being re-evaluated and put forward. Finally, issues emerging out of the patriated Canadian Constitution are beginning to come to the foreground. However, because our court system continues to approach law from a positivist framework, there is little chance that the courts will change their interpretation. Henderson (1983) and Elliott (1991) have noted that the Canadian courts have looked at the legal system as a closed system, and have evaluated the laws on procedural or technical issues rather than undertaking a comprehensive examination of Aboriginal rights.

The second issue arising from the concept of Aboriginal rights is the question of content. In other words, assuming that Aboriginal rights exist, what do they entail? How long do they exist and under what restrictions? Elliott (1991) looks at land rights and provides us with a concrete example. He begins his analysis of these rights by setting fee simple interest in land as a base line. Fee simple, he points out, gives the owner an unlimited right to use and occupy the land for an indefinite period of time. In addition, there are no restrictions on owners who want to alienate the land. Using fee simple as a comparative construct, we can see the variations that are possible. For example, do Aboriginal peoples hold title to the land? How can Indians alienate their land? Although a few of these concerns have been dealt with by lower courts, previous experience suggests that higher courts tend to reverse these decisions. Finally, the very fact that so few cases have come before the courts has also created uncertainty as to the content of Aboriginal rights.

We now move to the issue of changing or extinguishing Aboriginal rights. Here the question is whether or not these rights can be legally terminated or otherwise changed so that they are not as comprehensive as previously thought. The law has provided for this. Again, using Elliott's example of land title, one can point to treaties that were negotiated for the express purpose of obtaining land rights from Indians. The issue becomes more problematic, however, when actions taken by the government seem to extinguish Aboriginal rights (land title) while not explicitly saying so. This was one of the reasons why the Supreme Court justices differed in their decisions with regard to the Nisga'a in the *Calder* case.

Finally, we address the question of compensation for Aboriginal rights. As Elliott (1991) has noted, although many statutes provide for compensation when property is expropriated, there is no constitutional right to compensation. Even though the Canadian *Charter of Rights and Freedoms* provides for the right of the individual to life, liberty, security of person, enjoyment of property, and the right not to be deprived of any of these except by due process of law, it does not deal with compensation. In other words, if private property is expropriated, there is no legal statute that forces the government to compensate one for it (but see Mainville 2001).

Regardless of the tentativeness, vagueness, and lack of clarity of the above issues, the *Constitution Act, 1982* recognizes and affirms the *existing* Aboriginal rights. What these rights are is now the subject of debate. Aboriginal people argue that they include a number of general concerns—e.g., education, self-government, and housing. But others feel that the list needs to be more specific. The task now before the courts and politicians is to define and outline exactly what Aboriginal rights entail.

Noteworthy court cases have supported interpretations long held by Aboriginal people but which are reluctantly accepted by government officials. For example, the landmark decision of the Supreme Court in 1973 in the Nisga'a land claim case forced Canadians to change their views about Aboriginal land claims. The Supreme Court decision in 1990 (*Sparrow* v. *The Queen*) ruled that Indian rights could only be removed if there were explicit legislation. Thus, unless specific legislation was passed to divest Aboriginal people of their land claims and right of self-government, the rights remain theirs. The prerogative legislation that confirmed Aboriginal self-government has never been repealed, and thus one has to conclude that other rights also exist.[3] This has become more compelling since the inclusion of the statement that "existing Aboriginal and treaty rights of the Aboriginal peoples of Canada are hereby recognized and affirmed," in Section 35 of the *Constitution Act, 1982*. This means that if these rights existed prior to 1982, it is not possible, unless the Constitution is changed, to do away with Aboriginal rights—e.g., land and self-government.

If the evidence overwhelmingly points to the existence of Aboriginal rights, why have these not been acted upon? First, for a number of years government officials simply refused to acknowledge that Aboriginal people had specific claims or rights beyond that of ordinary Canadian citizens. Government officials acted in a unilateral fashion to suspend certain rights through a variety of procedures. For example, it would not be until the second half of the 20th century that Aboriginal persons had federal voting rights. In other cases, historical documents were not released or were ignored as not relevant to the case at hand. Still other procedures were implemented to keep Aboriginal groups from pursuing various claims— e.g., preventing lawyers from accepting monies to act on behalf of Indian peoples. The end result was that Aboriginal claims, whatever they were, were defined by Canadians as not of sufficient importance for federal or provincial officials to pursue; Aboriginal claims were considered to be a myth perpetuated by Aboriginal people.

After the 1973 Supreme Court decision, both levels of government had to face the legitimacy of Aboriginal claims. The government's initial reaction was to claim that these rights had been repealed or rendered inoperative. Still others claimed that Aboriginal rights had been "superseded" by federal and/or provincial legislation. As Clark (1994: 149) points out, this might have been appropriate if Aboriginal self-government had been constituted as domestic common law instead of being confirmed by imperial legislation. In other cases, provincial governments claimed that the 1763 *Royal Proclamation* did not apply to them; others suggested that the *Quebec Act, 1774* repealed the *Royal Proclamation* and, thus, it was not operative. Whatever the basis, they argued that Aboriginal claims had been extinguished, or at least derogated, from the constitutional character of the protection identified by the *Royal Proclamation.* However, a decade later it would become clear that the number of court rulings in favour of Aboriginal peoples' claims supported the Aboriginal position. As a result of these court decisions and a concurrent change in the public's attitude toward the rights of Aboriginal people, the federal government began to embark upon a new policy for Indian affairs.

One might also ask why Aboriginal people have not pursued their claim of Aboriginal rights more vigorously. In other words, if the case is clear that Aboriginal people have certain rights (e.g., land and self-government), why have they not directly challenged the federal government? The answer lies in the practical realities of implementing these rights. The federal government envisions the many administrative and financial costs involved in attempting to implement many different Aboriginal governments; for example, assuming that each band achieved self-government, there would be over 600 different Aboriginal governments (Ponting and Gibbins, 1980). Government officials are concerned with the cost of operating such a structure. Finally, there would be the cost of reparation to

Aboriginal peoples by government—that is, if the federal government accepted the inherent right to self-government, under the rulings outlined in recent court cases compensation would have to be made to those bands who expressed a desire to achieve self-government in the past but were thwarted by the federal government. As a result, government officials have steadfastly rejected the idea of Aboriginal rights, irrespective of the court decisions. Nevertheless, as legal decisions have reinforced Aboriginal claims—e.g., claims to self-government, to land, and to the government's fiduciary responsibility to Aboriginal people—the federal government has been forced to deal publicly with these ideals, without fundamentally changing its ideology.

The question still remains as to why Aboriginal people have not "forced the hand" of government to recognize their specific claims. First of all, this would mean pursuing additional court cases and running the risk of not having their case upheld. A recent case in British Columbia (*Delgamuukw* v. *British Columbia*), for example, supports their suspicions. And, even though that decision was reversed by a higher court, the claims of Aboriginal groups remain in suspension until a higher court rules. Second, Aboriginal people have always viewed the courts as foreign institutions that they do not fully understand. But perhaps even more important is the issue of money. It is all very well to force the government, through the courts, to admit to the existence of such rights as self-government. However, even if such rights were publicly recognized, the government is not obligated to bear the cost of resulting administrative structures—it would be a pyrrhic victory for Aboriginal people.

As a consequence of the above scenario, both the Aboriginal people and the federal government have tried to establish a common ground for dealing with Aboriginal rights claims from which a compromise acceptable to both parties would result. The federal government developed its first strategy to deal with this problem in the 1973 Indian Affairs Policy Statement. This document noted that the government was determined to find the most effective way of giving Aboriginal peoples control over their affairs. It clearly stated that the government was aware of the problem of Aboriginal claims and was prepared to do something about it. However, the statement was equally clear in developing a policy that preserved the government's view of reality. For example, while the federal government acknowledges the Aboriginal right of self-government, the only form of self-government defined as acceptable seems to be the delegated-municipal style. This position was buttressed by the federal government's concurrent policy that self-government would be dealt with in all comprehensive land claims. This strategy for enticing Aboriginal people to accept self-government under these conditions focused on providing Aboriginal people with funds if they were willing participants in the process of negotiating their claims, whatever they were. The acceptance of negotiations as a mode of decision making meant that the government would not have to relinquish decision making to an independent third party—e.g., the courts. And, by not allowing the courts the right to make decisions, the government avoided the possibility of any (in its view) unacceptable decision confirming Aboriginal rights—e.g., inherent traditional self-government. Aboriginal people caught between the confirmation of rights and the lack of funds to implement them sought to enter the negotiation process in the belief that they could achieve both goals. They did so on the basis of past actions they had undertaken with regard to the federal government and the belief that they could replicate the results. For example, the gains Quebec Cree achieved when they dropped their court case—guaranteed annual income, a land base, and funds to operate Aboriginal businesses—gave some support to this view. In other cases, bands were able to negotiate specific claims that they felt were in their favour, instead of taking the long, expensive route through the courts.

After this period of unprecedented development, the leadership of major Aboriginal organizations became further removed from Aboriginal communities—a trend that has continued since then, unfortunately. For example, the National Indian Brotherhood began to act in much the same manner as any other large political organization that is funded by an outside agency and thus no longer feels responsible to the people it ostensibly represents. Most Aboriginal organizations were established in large urban areas where few of the people they represented resided. It was difficult to maintain communications, especially when representatives of Aboriginal organizations began to sound like the federal bureaucrats with whom Aboriginal people had dealt for so many years. Aboriginal staff placed in departments that dealt with Aboriginal people (e.g., Indian and Northern Affairs) were subject to the constraints of federal policy. As a result, they found themselves to be ineffectual, and they were increasingly disregarded as agents of change. At this time, the federal government also began to cut back on funding. A call for a decentralization of Aboriginal organizations led to the creation of the Assembly of First Nations and the phasing out of the National Indian Brotherhood. However, by this time the effectiveness of the NIB had been substantially reduced; first by the funding cuts implemented by the federal government, and then by the Aboriginal perception of the organization as ineffective. The inability of Aboriginal people either to thwart or to change the content of the *Constitution Act, 1982* further weakened their effectiveness. The end result was that by the mid-1980s Aboriginal organizations were disorganized, demoralized, and without effective leadership. It was at this time that the federal government publicly revealed its new policy regarding Aboriginal rights.

THE CONCEPT OF SELF-GOVERNMENT

Until the late 1970s, the federal and provincial governments' response to demands for Indian self-government was an adamant "no." They took the position that they could not recognize Indian sovereignty because the only sovereignty that existed in Canada was vested in the Crown. Therefore, if any group claimed sovereignty on any other basis—such as use and occupancy from time immemorial—governments were not prepared to discuss or even consider it. It has only been since the constitutional debate of the early 1980s and the first ministers' conferences that the federal government has agreed to act on the issue. The Supreme Court's ruling in the *Musqueam* case (1985) has also persuaded the two levels of government to rethink their position. In that case, the Supreme Court recognized that Indian sovereignty and Indian rights are *independent and apart from the Crown.* The Court ruled that these rights flowed from Indian title and Indian occupation (Cardinal, 1986). Nevertheless, provincial governments remain highly skeptical of such a change, although they have not overtly contested further discussion of the issue. Their concerns about Aboriginal self-government and their willingness to discuss the issues today emerge out of their growing recognition of the increased role they might play in Aboriginal affairs. They are also acutely aware of the federal government's thinking on this issue. For example, Indian Affairs published its *Directional Plan of the 1980s,* in which it argued that Indians, instead of using so many federal programs and resources, should take advantage of more provincial programs and resources. Other federal documents, such as the *Nielsen Study Team Report* (1986) and the *Indian and Native Sector* (1986), reiterated these strategies (Harvey, 1996).

Although these federal policies have only selectively been implemented, they have certainly influenced the provinces' perception of how the federal government plans to act in the future and have forced them to develop strategies to deal with the possible changes in policy. Because there are significant differences in political philosophies among provinces there are both constitutional and practical implications to consider. As a result, there are several different stances taken by the individual provinces: Alberta insists that Indians are a federal responsibility, while Quebec's position is more ambiguous (Calder, 1986; Gadacz and McBlane, 1999).

From the other side, there has never been a single position among Aboriginal groups as to what self-government means or how it is to be implemented (Cardinal, 1986). Indians have insisted that their inherent sovereignty defines and formalizes them as a fourth level of government. Inuit, on the other hand, prefer to develop a provincial-type government because they occupy a large land area and make up nearly all of the population of that area. Finally, the non-status Indians and Métis have publicly accepted the fact that any government for them will have to be delegated by either the provincial or the federal government. It is clear that, because of different historical experiences, the evolution of Aboriginal–non-Aboriginal relationships has not been the same for the three major Aboriginal groups (Hawkes, 1985).

Nevertheless, there is some agreement on what is embodied in the concept of self-government. In general terms, Aboriginal people agree that the concept of self-government (or autonomy) implies that for important national issues they will remain within the territorial jurisdiction of the provincial or federal government but that they will enjoy the freedom to regulate certain of their own affairs without interference from outside (Kulchynski, 1994; Hylton, 1994). While no list of issues has been drafted, it would seem that general principles of democracy, justice, and equality would be supported. Other rights such as freedom of speech, the right to be judged by one's peers, and equal access to educational and economic institutions would also be supported. By granting autonomy to Aboriginal peoples, the government would acknowledge that certain rights are to be given to a specific part of the state's population, which needs protection in view of the way that many of its characteristics differ from those of the majority of the population. Autonomy would also allow the people inhabiting an area to exercise direct control over important affairs of special concern to them, while allowing the larger entity, which retains certain powers over that area, to exercise those powers that are in the common interest of both Aboriginal and non-Aboriginal people (Umozurike, 1972). In order to preserve Aboriginal culture, language, and religion, Aboriginal people would prefer to have complete control over their own schools, and they are also interested in preventing the federal and provincial governments from interfering with their traditional way of life. Because they perceive that they are different from the majority of Canadians, they insist on different rights (Englestad and Bird, 1993).

Indian leaders would like to have a fourth order of government—one that fits into their notion of Indian sovereignty. Indians see self-government as a means of allowing them to achieve three central goals: (1) to increase local control and decision-making; (2) to recognize the diverse needs and cultures of Indians throughout Canada; and (3) to provide accountability to local electors rather than to a federal bureaucracy. This new order of government would have powers similar to those of the federal and provincial governments. It would, for example, have full jurisdiction over such areas as resources, education, social development, and taxation (McMahon and Martin, 1985).

In addition, the federal government has been contemplating an amendment to the *Indian Act* in order to establish a more solid legislative basis for Indian self-government. This response seems to be a result of the fact that Aboriginal spokespeople have never fully articulated what the concept of self-government ought to entail. While the concept has been discussed for several decades in a variety of contexts (Weaver, 1984), the full organizational structure and its implications continues to be worked out. Any federal government initiatives have consistently been challenged and criticized by First Nations. A case in point is *Bill C-7*, known as the *First Nations Governance Act*, which passed first reading in Parliament in October 2002. More than 50 amendments were subsequently recommended by the House of Commons Standing Committee on Aboriginal Affairs, Northern Development and Natural Resources. Criticized on a number of grounds by First Nations and non-Aboriginals alike, the Act proposed to remove sections of the existing *Indian Act* pertaining to elections, governance, and administration, and to replace them with a new set of rules. *Bill C-7* also proposed that First Nations communities become corporations and municipalities. At the time of this writing, the proposed Bill still remains to be passed by Parliament. So neither has it been defeated nor has it died on the order paper.

LEGAL AND POLITICAL ISSUES

Within our federal system we have different levels of government. As Rieber (1977) points out, each level of government relates directly to the immediately superior level, from which it receives its enabling organizational act. However, when Aboriginal government is introduced into the argument, a new structure emerges (see Figure 9.1). In this organizational structure, Aboriginal people would not only relate to the federal government (in its trust relationship) but also to lower levels of government.

The major problems confronting Aboriginal groups in attempting to establish self-government are diverse and extensive (see the papers in Hylton, 1994). For example, the issue of jurisdiction remains a basic problem. The issue of subrogation must also be resolved. This is the process whereby, as a consequence of a change of territorial sovereignty, there is a legal transfer of liabilities or of rights and duties arising from treaties and other international agreements. Added to this problem is the level of government that Aboriginal people have to deal with on any specific issues. For example, Aboriginal people are part of the tripartite (Aboriginal–federal–provincial) structure in which jurisdictional issues can arise in any one of the three relationships: Aboriginal–federal, Aboriginal–provincial, and provincial–federal. In some cases, issues fall clearly along one of the arms of this triangle. For example, reserves are clearly in the Aboriginal–federal arm of the triangle, except under certain circumstances. Other issues that have confronted Aboriginal people and that must be dealt with are domain (jurisdictional specification over property), fishing and hunting rights, law enforcement, financing, economic development, community development, and off-reserve Indian rights (Paton, 1982). We also find in the current situation that, according to the *Indian Act,* neither the band nor the band council can be incorporated for the purpose of establishing a band government. Since Aboriginal peoples are pressuring the federal government for local self-government, this problem must be

| FIGURE 9.1 | Different Levels of Government and Their Relationships |

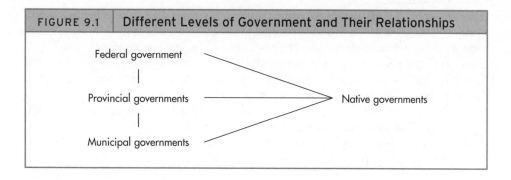

resolved. It must include both the legal and political issues at stake. For example, a municipal government can act in a fashion appropriate to the province, and it may act in a fashion appropriate to itself as a municipality. This means that, in part through social necessity, even though municipalities are created by the province they are able to control their own affairs. The federal government would like Aboriginal self-government to be modelled on municipal government. Aboriginal people, on the other hand, reject this proposal and wish to establish their own form of government that would not be dependent on the provincial governments for some issues and on the federal government for others (Cassidy and Bish, 1989; Ponting, 1997).

A Historical Backgrounder: The Federal Government's Early Response—Optional Indian Government Legislation

By 1986 Ottawa had introduced its community-based self-government policy and began negotiating with specific Aboriginal communities.[4] Aboriginal people have long argued that they require an authority base that would allow them, collectively, to advance their own interests. Furthermore, this authority had to derive from their Aboriginal title and not from Parliament (Tennant, 1984). They claim that they originally had a system of self-government that regulated their internal and external relations (Boldt et al., 1985). As Aboriginal organizations lobbied for self-government during the 1970s, DIAND developed a policy (without consulting Aboriginal people) to create band government. This devolutionary process was to lead to an entirely new relationship between Aboriginal people and the government. Each band would be given the opportunity to choose the form and structure of its self-government. This policy was rejected by Aboriginal people because it failed to recognize the Aboriginal source of authority (Tennant, 1984).

The rejection of DIAND's proposed self-government policy led to the creation of a special federal committee that was charged with reviewing all legal and related institutional factors affecting the status, development, and responsibilities of band government on Indian reserves (Task Force, 1982). Weaver (1984) goes on to show that the committee became a vehicle for articulating Indian interests to the public. After a cross-country hearing, the committee submitted its report in 1983.

The *Penner Report* listed 58 recommendations designed to integrate Indians into Canadian society. The most relevant for our purposes are the recommendations that Indian people should have self-government and that this should be recognized as an Aboriginal

right. As Tennant (1984) observed, the committee recommended that the Indian governments should derive their existence and legitimacy not from Parliament or legislation, nor
even from the Constitution, but from a pre-existing right. The committee proposed legislation that would have the federal and provincial governments recognize Indian governments, author federal–Indian agreements, and allow Indians to govern themselves
(Tennant, 1984). The committee also recommended that DIAND be phased out of existence as its functions were taken over by Indians. This particular recommendation is in line
with the average Canadian's thinking about DIAND.[5]

Finally, the committee recommended that the Indian band-government legislation proposed by DIAND be rejected and that new legislation be implemented to clear the way for
Indian self-government. It was felt that the proposed legislation simply involved a delegation of power rather than a recognition of the sovereignty of Indian First Nations.

The committee felt that Indian self-government could be implemented under the existing
constitutional structure, and many of its recommendations were set forth within this context.
However, committee members were also aware that other changes could take place outside
the constitutional structure. To this end, the committee recommended that the government
become involved in the creation of new legislation, increased funding, and administrative
arrangements. In summary, the *Penner Report* called for a new order of government to be
established in order to incorporate Aboriginal people into Canadian society. The primary unit
of self-government would be the band. Thus each Indian governing body would then be
related to the other two levels of government through the band government.

DIAND and the Assembly of First Nations (AFN) quickly responded to the recommendations of the committee. By the end of 1983 a draft policy, *Indian Nations
Recognition and Validating Act,* was completed by DIAND officials. This proposed act
formally recognized Indian First Nations and allowed each nation to enact legislation independently of Canada as long as it did not conflict with the laws of Parliament. The federal government responded in early 1984. It refused to accept self-government *as an
Aboriginal right.* Nevertheless, it agreed to drop the band-government legislation and
began investigating the possibility of implementing the spirit of the *Penner Report.*

The result was the creation of a new committee consisting of a number of people from
the constitutional unit of DIAND and the public-law unit of the Ministry of Justice. Their job
was to draft new legislation that would incorporate the recommendations of the *Penner
Report* but would also be palatable to Parliament. The first draft was rejected by the Priorities
and Planning Committee of the Cabinet. New officials were then added to the committee trying to draft the legislation. In June 1984, *Bill C-52, An Act Relating to Self-Government for
Indian Nations,* was introduced. While some of the recommendations of the *Penner Report*
were part of this bill, it was little more than a reformulation of the old band-government legislation. As Parliament dissolved, so did the bill and the policy alliance that had formed
between AFN and the government in the workings of the special committee. *Bill C-93* (discussed below), a revision of *C-52,* was then introduced and became the basis for establishing a negotiating stance with regard to self-government for Indians.

By proposing this legislation the federal government tried to (1) develop Aboriginal
self-reliance rather than dependency, (2) develop grassroots programs rather than Ottawa-
built programs, and (3) develop community control and participation. To achieve these
ends, more local control and decision making must be possible. The new policy must also
be flexible in order to deal with the diverse needs and cultures of Aboriginal people.

Finally, it is hoped that self-government will make Aboriginal officials more accountable to their own electors than to the federal government (Rawson, 1988). Structural changes in DIAND are also occurring in order to facilitate these program ends. For example, the department is being regionalized into four new sectors, and the Corporate Policy and Native Claims sectors have been dismantled and absorbed into the new organization.

Self-government for Aboriginal peoples means that they, as First Nations, will govern their own people and their own affairs, including land and its use. Self-government flows from Aboriginal rights, which provide for the right of a people's cultural survival and self-determination (Leonard, 1995). Specifically, this would exempt them (or at least protect them) from the application of laws of another jurisdiction (Ahenakew, 1985; Plain, 1985). The Aboriginal proposals for self-government call for a new order of government with powers similar to those of a province. In fact, some proposals have suggested that the Indian First Nations would have the right to sign international treaties and to issue valid passports (Dalon, 1985). These proposals have been summarily rejected by both levels of government. There is a great fear that until all the implications of self-government are clear, it cannot be entrenched in the Constitution or given even tentative support (Dalon, 1985; Long et al., 1983).

Nevertheless, the federal government's proposal does not suggest that each band's authority will come from its status as a sovereign entity. Rather, the authority is seen to exist because the federal government chose to delegate it to the band. Aboriginal people have objected vociferously to this stance. They are adamant that self-government is an inherent right. They point out that an all-party committee (the Special Committee on Indian Self-Government, 1983) endorsed their constituency's right to self-government. At the same time, as Dyck (1991) points out, there must be no illusions about the difficulties that will be encountered in trying to implement the process. Indians are more adept at resisting authority than they are at exercising it, and that will have to change if self-government is to succeed.

Indians wanted to entrench their rights in the Constitution by establishing a form of Indian government outside the framework of the *Indian Act* (Weaver, 1984, Tennant, 1984). In June 1984, legislation to allow for the recognition of Indian government was introduced in Parliament. The legislation was not meant to displace (or act as a substitute for) constitutional processes and initiatives. It was explicitly noted that it would not detract from existing Aboriginal and treaty rights affirmed in the Constitution (Long et al., 1982).

This proposed legislation (*Bill C-93*) was not what Indian people had in mind when they raised the matter of self-government. (See, for example, the Assembly of First Nations' Proposed 1985 Constitutional Accord Relating to the Aboriginal Peoples of Canada, First Ministers' Conference on Aboriginal Constitutional Matters, 1985.) Aboriginal peoples believe that in order to survive as a cultural entity they must have a land base and self-government. The government, although agreeing with the sentiment that self-government would be helpful, would first like to see the broad parameters as it maps out its response. For example, is it land-based? If so, this might be an appropriate model for Indians and Inuit but not necessarily for Métis. In addition, neither the provincial governments nor the federal government are prepared to include in the concept of self-government the notions of full independence or sovereignty. Although Aboriginal people do view self-government as an inherent right, they have always pictured its expression as taking place within the Canadian political system (Hawkes, 1985). They also believe that self-government could be attained even without a land base. This could be accomplished by guaranteed representation for Aboriginal peoples in the House of Commons, the provincial legislatures, and the Senate.

Indian Reaction

How did Aboriginal peoples react to this proposed early legislation dealing with Aboriginal self-government? In 1975, the National Indian Brotherhood passed a resolution that in part stated a need for a phased approach to revision of the *Indian Act.* It also put forth the principle of optional adoption by bands of any revised provisions of the Act (Hawkes, 1985). However, Indians today argue that because the political scene is radically different than in 1975, this resolution is no longer applicable and they consider it obsolete. They further argue that if the federal government had consulted with them, they would have long ago realized that this was no longer a viable position for Aboriginal people to hold.

The general principles of Indian government can be summarized as follows. These principles may not be fully endorsed by all Aboriginal people, but they would seem to be those that are most consistently advocated. Aboriginal people argue that *sovereignty exists in and of its own right.* It is a gift from their Creator, which has never been and can never be surrendered. In the past Aboriginal people formed a variety of political units, with their own government and other institutions. They claim that with colonization, their right to exercise their sovereignty was unjustly abrogated and ignored, and their political institutions were systematically dismantled. But, as in the past, they assert their sovereignty and the right to create their own unique institutions of self-government (DIAND, 1969).

In accordance with the principle of self-determination, Aboriginal people want to exercise their right to make and administer decisions on all matters pertaining to themselves and their lands. Aboriginal government is the expression of this inherent right of sovereign nations to self-determination. Aboriginal people anticipate a new order of government within Confederation, and they are renegotiating the terms of their relationship in the hope that the Constitution will recognize not only federal and provincial governments, but also Indian governments that will exercise full internal sovereignty.

First Nations claim to have exclusive legislative, executive, and administrative jurisdiction over Indian lands and resources and over the people within their territories. Indian territory will have three components: (1) territory as presently recognized; (2) territory to which there is a valid claim; and (3) those hunting, fishing, trapping, and gathering tracts not included in the first two components. Indian governments will have jurisdiction over all persons on Indian land and exclusive jurisdiction in determining Indian citizenship. They will be responsible for peace, order, and good government within Indian territory and for the maintenance and well-being of Indian people. Indian jurisdiction will not be limited to Indian territory when matters of social and cultural responsibility for its citizens extend beyond it (Hodgins et al., 1992). In point of fact, where First Nations have successfully negotiated comprehensive land claims agreements, there has also been the successful establishment of Aboriginal governments with wide-ranging jurisdictions and powers (see Chapter 8).

Indian people will continue to develop their own constitutions. They themselves will determine whether they choose to be single units or to amalgamate to pursue common goals as Indian nations. The actual form that these political units take will be based on the needs and aspirations of the Indian people involved. Aboriginal people feel that the rights confirmed by the *Royal Proclamation,* the *British North America Act,* the treaties, and the trust relationship between Indians and the federal government mean that the Government of Canada is responsible for providing the resources, including land, that will enable Aboriginal governments to attain their goal of economic self-sufficiency. This is a necessary complement to their goals of political and self-determination.

SELF-GOVERNMENT IN THE NEW MILLENNIUM

Despite significant progress, Aboriginal rights in Canadian law are still ill-defined, but several basic points are now clear. These rights are collective rights, which derive legal force from common law recognition of the legitimacy of the prior occupancy and use of certain territories. The essence of the common-law view of these rights is that they protect whatever it was that the organized society of Aboriginal peoples did before coming into contact with Europeans. To date this has focused Aboriginal concerns on land use and occupancy (usufruct), but, logically speaking, Aboriginal rights could include many other social activities, such as the determination of descent and family matters. And this, of course, is what is now being discussed under the rubric of self-government.

The *St. Catherines Milling* case, decided in the late 19th century, was regarded as the precedent-setting case with respect to Aboriginal rights until 1973. The general import of the decision was that the source of Indian rights in Canada was the *Royal Proclamation* of 1763. However, in 1973, the *Calder* case in British Columbia tentatively ruled that Indian rights were not dependent upon the *Royal Proclamation* but could be viewed as independent rights. However, it was not until 1984, with the *Guerin* case, that the Supreme Court ruled that Aboriginal rights were derived from the original possession of the North American continent—that is, that Indian interest in the land was a pre-existing legal right not created by the *Royal Proclamation,* by statute, or by executive order. This ruling set the stage for the federal government's willingness to begin discussions with Aboriginal people with regard to self-government (Canada, 1983).

The federal government's *Creating Opportunity: The Liberal Plan for Canada* (the Liberal Red Book, as it was called) outlined its commitment to act on the implementation of this fundamental right for Aboriginal peoples. In 1995, the federal government established a policy and a process by which it would be able to accept the principles of Aboriginal self-government. In developing the policy, the federal government consulted widely with Aboriginal people from across the country and included the provincial and territorial governments in the discussions. Today the government's position is that it recognizes the inherent right of self-government as an existing right within Section 35 of the *Constitution Act, 1982.* As such, it feels that negotiations with Aboriginal peoples are the preferred way to establish self-government, and litigation should be a last resort. In addition, because the form of self-government may take many different forms, the federal government feels that provincial governments are a necessary party to the negotiations. However, there are limits to the recognition of Aboriginal self-government: Aboriginal self-government does not include a right of sovereignty in the international law sense, nor will it result in sovereign independent Aboriginal nation states. As such, any agreement and form of self-government will have to provide that the *Charter of Rights and Freedoms* will apply to Aboriginal governments and institutions. Negotiations with Aboriginal groups will include a wide array of issues, including membership, marriage, education, social services, policing, property rights, taxation, hunting, housing, local

transportation, and a host of others. Any arrangement will have to harmonize with existing Canadian laws (Daugherty et al., 1980).

How will these agreements be implemented? There are a number of vehicles in which
these agreements could be put in place. Thus far, new treaties, parts of comprehensive land
claims, and addenda to existing treaties continue to be the favoured strategies. However,
other mechanisms have been identified by which self-government arrangements will be
implemented. These include legislation, contracts, and non-binding memoranda of understanding. There also is recognition that the form and process of achieving self-government
may be different for the various Aboriginal groups, and these have been identified. For
example, in the policy paper, there is an explicit recognition of the different groups—First
Nations; Inuit communities; Métis and Indian groups off a land base; Métis with a land
base; and Aboriginal groups in the western Northwest Territories. Finally the policy recognizes that Aboriginal self-government may have an impact upon third parties. As such,
the process of negotiating self-government has become public, and provinces, municipalities, and other interest groups will become party to the negotiations. The 1999 Sechelt
treaty is a good example of how the community was part of the overall process, but it is
not the only one. In July 2000, Westbank First Nation (WFN) in the central Okanagan concluded a self-government agreement with the federal government, the fifth self-government agreement for a Native community in Canada. The WFN agreement covers all
aspects of band management and accountability; introduces special land, resource, and
development codes; and opts the community out from the *Indian Act*. At the time of writing, this agreement awaits ratification (final approval) by the federal government; the
Westbank First Nation feels this will be but a formality.

The reader, having finished the material presented thus far, has probably found it very
difficult to ascertain the specifics of what is involved in the notion of Aboriginal self-
determination or Aboriginal rights. Our task now is to summarize what the central tenets
of self-government are from the perspective of Aboriginal peoples. We think that four factors constitute the overall Aboriginal thinking on self-government:

1. *Greater self-determination and social justice.* Protection of and control over one's own
   destiny, rather than subordination to political and bureaucratic authorities based outside the ethnic group.

2. *Economic development to end dependency, poverty, and unemployment.* Economic
   justice, in the sense of a fair distribution of wealth between the Aboriginal and non-
   Aboriginal populations.

3. *Protection and retention of Aboriginal culture.*

4. *Social vitality and development that will overcome such existing social problems as ill
   health, the housing crisis, irrelevant and demeaning education, and alienation.*

In order to achieve these aspirations, Aboriginal self-governments would need (1) political institutions that would be accountable to the Aboriginal electorate, (2) a territorial base,
(3) control over group membership, and (4) continuing fiscal support. This would mean
control over a number of areas that deal with or affect Aboriginal people—for example, citizenship, land, water, forestry, minerals, conservation, environment, economic development, education, health, cultural development, and law enforcement (Peters, 1987).

What is the scene today with regard to Aboriginal self-determination or Aboriginal
rights? There are several different forms of Aboriginal self-government that now exist in

Canadian society. All of these arrangements have focused on Aboriginal people with "status." Seven current strategies that have been established for achieving self-government for Aboriginal peoples are:

1. band government under the *Indian Act, 1876*;
2. the *Sechelt Indian Band Self-Government Act, 1986*;
3. community-based self-government;
4. the *Cree/Naskapi* (of Quebec) *Act,* Yukon First Nations Agreements;
5. the *Act Concerning Northern Villages and the Kativik Regional Government* (Inuit);
6. municipal style government; and
7. "regional" or "territorial" style government, which includes Nunavut (1999) and the 2003 Tlicho Agreement (Dogrib/Dene).

We will provide a brief discussion on four of these alternatives that illustrate the differences among them; the last, Nunavut, is discussed in detail in Chapter 10.

The *Indian Act*

Critics of band government under the *Indian Act* suggest that this is not a form of self-government but rather a form of self-administration. Nevertheless, under the *Indian Act,* band councils were created to implement the principles of democracy and to assure the existence of self-government. Under this form of government, a chief and band council are elected; the council has one chief, and one councillor is elected for every 100 band members. The powers held by the band council are wide-ranging—for example, providing for the health of band members, destroying and controlling noxious weeds, removing and punishing persons trespassing on the reserve, providing for entry permits to band lands, and regulating the residence of band members. Certain other bylaws can be passed if the government of Canada feels that the band has the ability to understand and implement the regulations. However, at the same time, the Minister of Indian and Northern Affairs can carry out activities on the reserve without band consent—for example, issuing permits for the use of reserve land and determining the location of roads on the reserve (DIAND, 1982c, 1982d).

Most provincial laws of a general nature are applied to Indian people. Under these regulations, a province, municipality, or corporation can expropriate reserve land for public use if it has the consent of the federal government. Certain federal laws take precedence over the *Indian Act,* although the exact relationship between laws in this respect is still under discussion. Each year bands receive money from Indian Affairs for the administration of their own and government programs. Today, over half of the budget allocated to Indians is controlled by band councils. These funding arrangements encompass areas such as education, housing, governance support, economic development, and other activities taking place on the reserve. In terms of actual dollars, First Nations now control well in excess of $4 billion each year. Other data show that Indians and Inuit now control 82 percent of the DIAND's Indian and Inuit Affairs Program expenditures through band councils, tribal councils, or other First Nations Aboriginal Organizations. These data confirm that First Nations' control of program expenditures has steadily increased over the past decade, within the operation of the *Indian Act* (Hylton, 1994).

The above brief summary illustrates that under the *Indian Act,* Aboriginal people do enjoy some elements of self-government. However, Aboriginal people argue that, under the *Indian Act,* almost all actions taken by band councils can be disallowed by the Minister. Furthermore, under these circumstances, Aboriginal people can only be reactive, not proactive. Finally, Aboriginal people argue that the present structural arrangements between them and the government are paternalistic and contribute to the continuing dependency of Aboriginal people (Fisher, 1977). Even the proposed First Nations Governance Act (*Bill C-7*, 2002–2003, mentioned above), proposed by the federal government to radically remake the *Indian Act*, has been criticized for its alleged effect of actually reinforcing the federal government's control of reserves and band governments.

The federal government's current thrust to strike a new relationship with the Aboriginal communities seems to always revolve around the *Indian Act.* There is a sense that if the content of the *Indian Act* can be further revised, amended, rewritten, and reconceptualized, a new partnership between Aboriginal peoples and the government can somehow be established. This assumption is being contested by First Nations.

The *Sechelt Act*

In an attempt to change the existing structural and institutional arrangements between Aboriginal people and the government, the *Sechelt Indian Band Self-Government Act* was passed in 1986. The Sechelt Indian band consists of 33 reserves located approximately 50 kilometres north of Vancouver along the coastline. Through this legislation, under which Indians are to assume the rights of self-government, the Sechelt band is established as a legal entity. A written band constitution is in place under the Act, and the band council becomes the governing body of the band. According to these legal conditions, the band may enter into contracts and agreements; acquire and hold property; and spend, borrow, and invest money. The council also has additional powers under the *Sechelt Act.* Not only does it enjoy all the powers identified under the *Indian Act,* it can also carry out actions that were previously entrusted to the Minister—for example, the construction of roads, the granting of access to and residence on Sechelt lands, and the zoning of land.

Currently, the organizational structure created under the *Sechelt Act* is contained within the confines of each of the reserves. However, the possibility exists that if the provincial government gives its approval for a referendum, the federal government could recognize a Sechelt Indian government district, which could then exercise jurisdiction over land outside the Sechelt reserves. If this were to happen, the Sechelt Indian government district council would be the political organization over the entire district. Under the *Sechelt Act,* both federal and provincial laws of general application would be in effect with regard to the band and its members, except those laws that are inconsistent with the *Indian Act* (Peters, 1987). The financing arrangements under the *Sechelt Act* are quite different from those of the *Indian Act.* Under the new Act, the band has powers to tax local residents and businesses for maintaining the local infrastructure. Furthermore, the band may seek external financing with regard to any projects they wish to take on. In addition, the band received a single lump sum of money to be held in trust for its own use.

In 1999, the Sechelt First Nation signed an agreement with the federal and provincial governments (a tripartite process) after five years of negotiation. This agreement is the first one signed by the B.C. Treaty Commission that is currently negotiating with 50 other Aboriginal groups. The new treaty will give the Sechelt $42 million in cash, 933 hectares of provincial Crown land, and an additional 288 hectares of non-Crown land. Other resources include commercial fishing licences, management of forest resources, and additional property within the coastal community. Band members will lose their tax-exempt status and will begin paying provincial and goods and services taxes eight years from now and income tax in twelve years. This new treaty incorporates self-government into the language and allows the communities to develop self-sufficiency.

Community-Based Self-Government

It was in 1978 that federal bureaucrats first proposed community-based government. This early "pre-policy," unannounced and invisible, was put into action as they forced Aboriginal peoples to separate land claims from self-government. While focusing on land claims, Aboriginal people were unaware that there was a new thrust. They were flushed with victory in winning new sources of funding and seemingly greater influence over the spending of monies earmarked for them. However, the economic recession of the early 1980s dealt a crippling blow to economic development and control by Aboriginal people. By the time the recession ended in the mid-1980s, Aboriginal people were once again economically dependent. And, by this time, government officials had firmly entrenched the policies and operating procedures for developing municipal-style self-government (Federation, 1977).

Early in 1982 the *Optional Indian Band Government Legislation* was introduced and, if accepted, would be incorporated into federal legislation. Those bands that did not want to participate (either then or in the future) could remain under the old *Indian Act.* However, the *Indian Act* would be revised and a new alternative funding arrangement would be implemented for those bands remaining under the jurisdiction of the Act. This new alternative would allow Aboriginal groups to apply to the federal government in order to assume greater control over various facets of reserve life; e.g., management of lands, monies, and definitions of who is a member of the band. If, at some future time, the "less advanced" bands wanted to further develop their own form of self-government, they would have the experience of exercising control over financial matters and other concerns (DIAND, 1982d).

In 1985 the federal Cabinet began to discuss constitutional and non-constitutional initiatives that would enable Aboriginal peoples to take on some form of self-government. In 1986 the federal government publicly announced its community-based self-government policy. This new policy was intended to circumvent parts of the *Indian Act.* Under this policy, a community can be individual bands, groups of bands, tribal councils, treaty groupings, or other regional entities. As a beginning, the government recognizes that not all bands are the same and that a great diversity of Aboriginal communities exists. As a result, the policy of self-government can be achieved through a number of avenues, each to be negotiated by the local community. After the 1987 First Ministers' Conference, Cabinet reaffirmed its commitment to constitutional process and continuation of a community self-government policy. One year later, Cabinet authorized up to 15 sets of self-government negotiations with individual bands.

The community-based self-government process is divided into four phases: (1) development: the building of community awareness and consensus with regard to goals; (2) framework: design of proposals that are more specific in terms of goals and structure of government; (3) substantive negotiations: negotiations of the two parties over specific issues proposed by the community; and (4) implementation: moving the proposal from paper to action in the community (DIAND, 1982h).

The policy guidelines delineated the boundaries of the demands the policy was designed to accommodate, as well as the contents of the negotiations. As noted by the policy:

- negotiations are to be conducted without prejudice to Aboriginal rights, existing or future land claims, or future constitutional developments;
- the extent and division of powers between the federal and provincial government will not be changed through self-government negotiations;
- there will be an attempt to accommodate Aboriginal governments within the existing constitutional framework;
- the resultant self-government structures must conform with the established principles, jurisdictions, and institutions of Canadian jurisprudence; and
- all financial arrangements will be consistent with the historic levels provided to that community.

There are many other issues that define the limits of what can be negotiated. For example, any area that the federal government refuses to negotiate with Aboriginal people—e.g., labour relations, immigration—is not on the bargaining table. Other provisions, such as the government's insistence that criteria for membership be established and retained, limit the nature and type of discussion. Each of the guidelines has been unilaterally established by the federal government with little consultation with Aboriginal people. Furthermore, thus far federal negotiators have adhered rigidly to the guidelines, arguing that Cabinet is the only body authorized to change them. At the same time, the government reserves the unilateral right to change the guidelines without prior notice or to introduce retroactive enclosures. Aboriginal people have pointed out that, in negotiations, federal agents have added guidelines that are not part of the written guidelines.

Nevertheless, once a community decides to pursue self-government, it must begin to put together a proposal that sets out, in as much detail as possible, the community's overall goals and aspirations in the area of self-government. The options range from exercising more of the authorities currently available under the *Indian Act* to new arrangements beyond the present limits of that Act. Different parts of the Department of Indian Affairs are responsible for assisting communities in a variety of areas. Hence, once a decision is made by the community to proceed, the proposal would be sent to the appropriate departmental officials for action. In point of fact, proposed agreements require virtually unanimous community agreement. Even the Westbank First Nation Agreement (2003), mentioned above, only passed on its third band ratification vote.

The federal government is very much aware of the control it can exert under this style of government. It is cognizant of the controls that go along with its brand of self-government; a form that makes Aboriginal decision-making processes more transparent and thus reviewable by the non-Aboriginal system. This, in turn, allows for a greater probability of subjecting Indian political and legal processes to the non-Aboriginal processes (Clark, 1994). Aboriginal people, on the other hand, prefer a more traditional form of government under which they could develop a measure of cultural and political autonomy.

Municipal Government

In recent times, a new form of self-government has been offered to Aboriginal people. This new form of self-government is similar to the existing municipal government. Under the policy, the unit (which could be a band, community, a number of reserves, etc.) would take on the political, economic, and social privileges and responsibilities as a normal municipal government in Canada. The unit would be able to establish residence lists, invoke taxation, create by-laws, own land, and carry out a relationship with the other two levels of government.

This new policy is enticing to Aboriginal people. It would, on the face of it, lead to greater self-control. It would also make Aboriginal leaders accountable to the local population they represent. And, acceptance of this controlled style of self-government would result in the financial support of the federal government. However, these new forms of municipal self-government are not a fourth level of government. The structure of the new forms of government also ensures that the local Aboriginal leaders would provide a buffer between individuals living on the reserves and the federal government. Concern and hostility would be deflected to local leadership, not Indian Affairs personnel. Finally, the acceptance of the municipal style of government by Aboriginal people would lead to acceptance of the dominant society's culture and values, thus ensuring the further assimilation of Aboriginal persons. The implications of this policy have not gone unnoticed by Aboriginal people; yet they are in a position in which they must make a decision.

Aboriginal people once again find themselves at the crossroads of their destiny. They are clearly cognizant that they will remain, for some time, economically dependent upon government for the implementation of various programs and services. At the same time, they are determined to develop greater self-control and self-reliance. Their task is to develop a workable system within the context of the Canadian federal system by which they can achieve this goal.

OBSTACLES TO PROGRESS

Given the relatively limited options that Aboriginal people have regarding self-government and the complexity of the process of applying for community-based self-government, few Aboriginal communities have progressed beyond the application stage. A considerable number of initial proposals are developed, but there is a noticeable decrease in the number as the process moves from the developmental stage to the framework-proposal stage. One million dollars was directly expended in the first year of operation in 1988, but since then, when bands began to develop their applications in earnest, this increased to almost six million annually. As the process continues and more bands make application, the cost increases.

The reader may wonder why so few arrangements have so far been carried out. If a few arrangements for developing self-government *have* been put in place, why are they not more numerous? Even though the gap between Aboriginal peoples and the government remains large, these few arrangements suggest that there have been some changes in the federal government's policy in this regard. Why not more? To document fully the reasons why more agreements have not been implemented is beyond the scope of this book. However, some major reasons will be identified and discussed.

First of all, there is a difference in approach with regard to how each of the Aboriginal groups—for example, Inuit, Métis, and Indian—seeks to realize Aboriginal self-government. These groups have diverse histories, languages, cultures, needs, and aspirations, and, therefore, they seek different solutions to the problem of self-government. On the other hand, the federal government wishes to provide one solution to the problem. Evidence today suggests that the government is moving away from this approach, but progress so far has been slow.

A second explanation for the lack of progress in the area of self-government is that Aboriginal peoples are approaching the problem from a different perspective than the federal and provincial governments. Aboriginal people are asking for constitutional recognition and protection of their rights (self-government) in terms of broad, undefined structures, with details to be worked out later. On the other hand, the governments are not willing to talk about rights in the abstract and want to know what the concepts mean before they are prepared to allow Aboriginal self-government. This impasse is referred to as the "empty versus full medicine chest" dilemma. Aboriginal people want to begin discussions assuming that the chest is full of rights, while the different levels of government want to assume that the chest is empty and then add to it. Related to this is the charge that neither the government nor the Aboriginal people have publicly articulated any clear, comprehensive policy in regard to the specifics of Aboriginal self-government (Denis, 1997).

A third reason for the slow progress is the Aboriginal suspicion of government initiatives and policies. The history of poor relations between the two parties has come to influence the interpretation of policies or programs set forth by either party. Aboriginal people argue that experiences over time in dealing with the governments have generally shown that any agreements struck worked to the detriment of Aboriginal people. They point to the way they were placed in a disadvantageous position by the signing of the treaties, by the 1969 White Paper, and, more recently, by the proposals in the *Nielsen Study Team Report on Native Programs*. As a result, Aboriginal people are very suspicious of any proposals set forth by the government.

A fourth factor that has contributed to the lack of arrangements for self-government has to do with the involvement (or lack of it) of the provinces. Status Indians feel that the issue of how they can achieve self-government concerns only the federal government. Once the agreement is in place, then the provincial governments will have to accept the arrangement. The provinces (and to a certain extent the federal government), the Métis, and the non-status Indians argue that, given the considerable presence of provincial programs and expenditures, the provinces will have to be involved if any meaningful progress is to be made.

Fifth, the financial implications of moving to self-government have also tended to draw out the negotiations between Aboriginal people and the government. Even when negotiations produce an agreement, the issue of financial responsibility creates major difficulties in implementing the program. If local bands are to provide a variety of services, how will they be operated and funded? Given that existing Aboriginal federal programs are already inferior to provincial programs, a considerable amount of additional monies will have to be injected into the programs to bring them up to provincial standards. Aboriginal people are aware of this, and linked to their general suspicion of the federal government is the feeling that the government's present movement toward allowing Aboriginal self-government might be little more than an attempt to abdicate its financial responsibility (DIAND, 1982e, 1982f, 1982g).

Finally, the federal government has changed its strategy and is now embracing municipal style governments. These forms of Aboriginal government would give greater control to the federal government while at the same time providing the optics that Aboriginal people have taken over. The courts have also recognized that Aboriginal rights are not absolute and may conflict with the legitimate interests of other Canadians. The municipal style self-government will allow Canadians to use existing relationships as a guideline to assess the newly acquired powers of Aboriginal communities.

CONCLUSION

The creation of many tribes has led to the use of tribalism as a tool for Aboriginal people negotiating with the federal government and with other special-interest groups. For example, being able to speak for a particular tribe gives leaders some credibility and enhances the leaders' ability to achieve specific goals. This has on occasion led to coalitions of several Aboriginal groups in their quest for a particular goal. However, the same structure also leads to inter-tribal conflict. As past experience has vividly shown, coalitions are notoriously unstable, and, as a result, they are usually unable to build long-lasting relationships. Rouch (1956) and Rohen (1967) discuss "super tribes" and the process of fission/fusion in attempting to illustrate this instability.

One would assume that, as Aboriginal Canadians continue their urbanization process, tribalism will lose some of its impact since they will be forced to live in a heterogeneous environment. This should weaken tribal identity. However, preliminary evidence suggests that this is not happening. Competition for political power and jobs in the urban areas has tended to increase rather than decrease the incidence of tribalism (Uchendu, 1970).

In their quest for self-government, Aboriginal people have created a fiction of statehood—a myth that they traditionally had hierarchically structured governments and a ruling elite. As Boldt and Long (1985b) note, these two factors have not been part of traditional Aboriginal society. The basis of Aboriginal social order, they maintain, was not built on hierarchical authority wielded by a central political organization. Their analysis of Aboriginal culture suggests that these values are irreconcilable with Indian history and experiences.

Nevertheless, Aboriginal people are claiming that they have always had some form of statehood and, thus, should also have self-government. The acceptance of this new-model form of European government by Aboriginal people has ushered in a new era with regard to Aboriginal and non-Aboriginal relationships. It also signifies a break with traditional Aboriginal culture and may mean that the forced assimilation employed by the Canadian government has been successful.

As Aboriginal people continue trying to obtain local control over their lives, they are increasingly using tribalism as a tool to achieve that end. This means that there will be continued inter-tribal conflicts over the important issues of the day. As each tribe seeks to preserve its own interests and obtain maximum power, conflict will become frequent.

The implementation of the municipal self-government policy, eventually to become the accepted norm, will require massive ideological and possibly structural changes in the Indian–Inuit Affairs Program. Historically, DIAND was an integrated agent–client organization. During the 1960s it changed to a highly differentiated, but also highly centralized, organizational structure with a number of divisions delivering programs or services to Indians and Inuit (Paton, 1982: 20). More recently, both the process of devolution (decentralization) and the concurrent implementation of the policy of band control have adjusted the program's focus. This is discussed in more detail in Chapter 12. The administrative and budgetary control held by INAC has remained highly centralized throughout its relationship with Canada's Aboriginal peoples.[6]

The different and varied approaches to Aboriginal self-government have been a response to dealing with the unwieldy and confused state of affairs that has prevailed in the Indian–Inuit Affairs Program for many decades (Paton, 1982: 34). This policy has given program authority to Aboriginal communities and established a system of funding that has placed bands in a position of direct responsibility to their constituencies.

NOTES

1. The unilateral imposition of *Bill C-31* by the federal government suggests that neither side has been able to establish a sympathetic relation with the other. *Bill C-31* changed the *Indian Act* with regard to band membership. Under this Bill, bands will control their own membership, and Indian women will no longer lose their status by marrying non-Indians. In addition, Indians who lost their status because of Section 12, 1(b) of the *Indian Act* can now be reinstated and allowed to return to their reserve (see Chapter 2).

2. When the concept of sovereignty is applied to a particular region or people, it suggests that a political state exists. As Nadeau (1979) points out, in order for a state to exist, three conditions have to be present: population, territory, and government. Indians argue that since they possess these three attributes, they should, in turn, have sovereignty.

3. As Clark (1994) points out, the concept of self-government must be distinguished from self-management/administration. These latter terms refer to managing or administering laws that have been created and put in place by other legal entities.

4. The information that follows is taken from published documents of DIAND, personal correspondence with DIAND officials, and from other internal documents produced by DIAND.

5. A series of national surveys showed that Canadians feel that the federal government has become too involved in Aboriginal affairs and that more and more responsibility should be taken over by the Aboriginal people themselves. The surveys also revealed that Canadians feel that Aboriginal people should become more involved in the national economy and that special rights should not exist for them.

6. Throughout the country there are wide variations in the organizational structure of DIAND programs. For example, in British Columbia the program and the budget are almost completely decentralized, while in Manitoba, Indian communities are taking over as DIAND is phasing itself out of existence.

WEBLINKS

www.ainc-inac.gc.ca/pr/agr/index_e.html

This Indian and Northern Affairs website is devoted to final agreements, treaties, comprehensive and specific claims, land governance agreements, status of claims, maps, implementation plans, and much more, including self-government agreements. An important related web link is **www.aboriginalcanada.gc.ca**, which is the Government of Canada's Aboriginal Canada Portal, a gateway to links to all major national Aboriginal organizations, economic development, self-government, language and heritage, health and social services, and more.

www.inac.gc.ca/ps/sg/index_e.html

The federal government has collected a number of documents relating to self-government issues at this website, including a statement of Ottawa's policy.

www.aaf.gov.bc.ca/aaf/treaty/nisgaa/docs/nisga_agreement.html

The B.C. treaty process led to the conclusion of the Nisga'a Final Agreement, which includes substantial self-government powers for the Nisga'a. The Agreement is the final settlement of the Nisga'a Aboriginal rights, title, and interest.

chapter ten

The Inuit of the North:
Nation Building in Practice

INTRODUCTION

Inuit inhabit vast areas of the Northwest Territories, the coast of Northern Labrador, and over one-quarter of Northern Quebec. The Inuit population has grown rapidly over the past decade and estimates suggest that, if the present trends continue, there will be nearly 100 000 Inuit in the North by 2016. Inuit origins in Canada go back nearly four millennia and, through their intimate knowledge of the land and its life forms, they have developed skills and technology uniquely adapted to one of the harshest and most demanding environments in Canada.

On April 1, 1999, Canadians witnessed a nation-building event when a new territory in Canada, Nunavut, was created. Nunavut, which means "Our Land" in Inuktitut, is the culmination of a dream held by Inuit for nearly half a century. It is an area in the Eastern Arctic region of Canada that is larger than the Atlantic provinces and Quebec combined. The spirit of Nunavut is characterized in its coat of arms. Beginning with the colours (blue and gold), it represents the riches of the land, sea, and sky. At the base of the shield, the Inuksuk symbolizes the stone monuments that guide the people of the land and the qulliq (stone lamp) represents light and warmth of the family and the community. At the top of the crest is the iglu, representing the traditional life of the people and the means of survival. Finally, on each side stand the tuku (caribou) and qilalugaq tugaalik (narwhal) that refer to the land and sea animals that are part of the rich natural heritage of the Nunavut. The flag chosen by the Inuit of Nunavut carries the same colours and has both an inuksuk and a star, representing the north star that has provided a guide for navigators.

At the same time, there are Inuit all across the northern region of Canada and they, like other ethnic groups, represent different cultures, languages, and people. Contact with the outside world came at different times and in different ways as one reviews the history of each of these groups. An analysis of Canada's Inuit provides a revealing look at such issues as class formation, assimilation, the sources and uses of power, community building, and intergenerational differences, just to mention a few. It also allows us to assess how Canadians have dealt with an ethnic group similar to but different from Indians.[1] Finally, it allows us to gain insights into the successes that Inuit have had in the past two decades over issues such as land claims—successes that Indian peoples have not had. We begin with a brief history of how contact came to be made with Inuit and then look at the social processes and change they have had to deal with. We also look at the issue of identity and how it has changed over time.

In Inuktitut, the word *Inuit* means "the people." It replaces the previous term, *Eskimo*, which is an Indian word used to identify these Arctic people. As Euro-Canadians entered the North they continued to use this term. It would not be until the 1970s that Inuit would ask others not to identify them as Eskimo. Nevertheless, today there are many Canadians who continue to call them Eskimo; and equally important, there are many residents of the Arctic who define themselves as Eskimos, continuing to use the labels attached to them more than a century ago. We also find that many Canadians view and treat Inuit as a homogeneous population and fail to recognize the different ethnic groupings of Inuit in the Arctic and the cultural differences between them (see Figure 10.1). There are many recognized Inuit communities, language groups, and delineated cultural areas. Thus, there is not one universal form of Inuit. Readers who are going on to specialize in Aboriginal Studies will see that the level of generality in this introductory text requires refinement and specificity as they begin to look at the micro structures of communities and individuals. For example, the Caribou Inuit traditions and interaction patterns are quite different from those of the Baffin Island Inuit, which in turn are different from those of the Netsilik. Nevertheless, it is possible to discuss some common and fundamental aspects of Inuit society in an introductory text. Hence, the more macro perspective will be adopted as we develop a portrait of Inuit in Canada.

A BRIEF HISTORY

Few Canadians realize that the Arctic has been the residence of many different peoples over the past centuries. It is estimated that approximately 10 000 years ago the people of the Small Knife entered the valleys and plateaus of Alaska and Yukon. They were replaced by the Long Spear People some 7000 years ago as they moved north into the lands vacated by the ice. This group was followed by the Denbigh People who, about 5000 years ago, moved into the east shore of the Bering Strait. A fourth prehistorical group in the North were the People of the Old Rock. These residents of Northern Quebec and Keewatin remained in the North until about 3000 years ago, when the climate grew colder and pushed the people southward. This group was replaced by the People of the Arrowhead (3000 years ago) and the Harpoon People, who entered the region approximately 2000 years ago (Crowe, 1974; Richardson, 1993).

Modern-day Inuit emerged from recent groups living in the North. In about 1000 B.C. the Dorset people moved to Baffin Island and spread rapidly across the Arctic. They moved down the Labrador coast and around the coast of Newfoundland by 500 A.D. Between 800 and 1300 A.D. new immigrants from the Western Arctic migrated to the East. The new immigrants were better organized and equipped than the Dorset, and with-

FIGURE 10.1	Approximate Location of Indian and Inuit Peoples in Northern Canada Before A.D. 1500, by Language and Dialect Groups

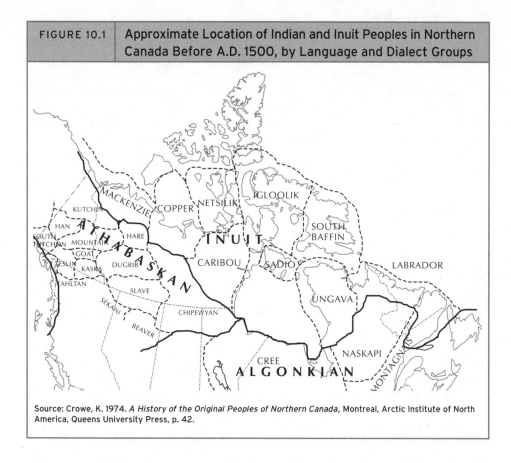

Source: Crowe, K. 1974. *A History of the Original Peoples of Northern Canada*, Montreal, Arctic Institute of North America, Queens University Press, p. 42.

in a few years the Dorset people disappeared. This new group (the Thule Inuit) are the direct ancestors of modern Canadian and other Arctic Inuit. It is thought that the original home of the Thule people was in Alaska. The Inuit of Northern Labrador are the most southerly and easterly of Canada's Inuit. They are descendants of Thule Eskimo and it is believed that they have lived in this area since the mid-15th century. They speak Inuktitut, but it is a unique dialect.

The contact period between Inuit and Europeans began around 1500 in the East and the late 1800s in the West. During the 1500s, various nations of Europe were exploring the world, wishing to conquer and spread the Christian faith to all. These European explorers first came into contact with Inuit on the eastern coast of Canada, and later in the Central Arctic as they made inroads into the archipelago. For example, the explorer Frobisher kidnapped Inuit both to confirm his landings in a new country and to set up exhibitions for Queen Elizabeth I. The extent of contact is evident by the fact that, during the 17th and 18th centuries, major conflicts between the English and the Inuit of Southern Labrador were taking place. In addition to the explorers, European ships began to hunt whales in the Eastern Arctic; most were Scottish and American, although ships from around the world came to these fertile grounds. In the beginning, the contacts between whalers and Inuit on the east coast were peaceful and symbiotic. The Inuit were able to trade for goods not otherwise available to them, and the ships' captains were able to obtain information about whales held only by the Inuit. There was a clear trade between information and material artifacts. By the early 20th century whaling ships were carrying on a brisk trade with the eastern Inuit. However, the influence of the Euro-Canadians went beyond the material and social artifacts brought by the whalers, who transmitted diseases that decimated many Inuit communities (e.g., scarlet fever and whooping cough) and introduced such goods as alcohol. Within a few years most of the Baleen whales in the Eastern Arctic had been harvested, and land animals—e.g., caribou and musk-ox—were close to extinction as a result of the hunting efforts of the whalers and Inuit.

Inuit and outsiders in the Western Arctic did not come in contact until later. American whalers entered the Western Arctic waters through the Bering Strait around the mid-19th century. Many whaling ships leaving San Francisco in the spring didn't arrive in the Arctic until the summer, and had to "winter over" in order to complete their catch. During this period they remained in the Western Arctic, bartering with local Inuit. Bartering was extensive, and the drawing power of the goods being offered by the whalers—e.g., guns and metal tools—was significant. The trade was so pervasive and lasted for so long that large numbers of Inuit migrated to the Beaufort Sea coast in order to participate in the exchange of goods.

The cultural impact of the American whalers was substantial, both in material artifacts and way of life. Over time, many of the species in the area were reduced to the point where they would not support human habitation. In addition, the introduction of influenza and other epidemics decimated the Inuvialuit population, forcing the whalers to bring in Alaskan Inupiat to help them. So great was the social impact that, when the whale market collapsed in the early 1900s, Inuit who were still alive were so integrated into the barter trade that they were unable to return to their former independent rural life.

Later, when the fur trade emerged, new agents of control from Southern Canada entered the Arctic. The fur traders, the missionaries, and the police would influence the lives of the Inuit across the Arctic for the next half-century (Crowe, 1974).[2] First were the French Compagnie du Nord and the free traders. These voyageurs were major influences on Inuit as they developed the fur trade. The establishment of forts along waterways and coastal areas as the centres of trade encouraged Inuit to engage in the fur trade and remain in localized areas. The voyageurs also established the beginning of an unequal trade relationship with the Inuit. Soon after, the Hudson's Bay Company began to dominate the fur trade and extend its sphere of influence into other domains of life.[3]

On the Labrador coast, the Moravian missionaries and traders began to have sustained contact with Inuit, which lasted for over 200 years. Other missionaries from various religious denominations were to enter the North and attempt to convert Inuit to Christianity.[4] Their impact on the social and cultural way of life of the Inuit was substantial. While their influence was directed toward religious activities, they struck at the basic norms and values of Inuit life. For example, religious groups destroyed the social solidarity of Inuit groups by insisting that sexual liaisons between men and women who were not married must stop.

The third group was the Royal Canadian Mounted Police. This group was sent into the North to establish a Canadian presence as well as to enforce Canadian law. Any behaviour by the Inuit that did not meet the minimum conditions of Canadian law was subject to immediate and harsh sanctions. As this triumvirate of Canadian institutions imposed its will it was able to influence every institutional sphere and network of the Inuit. By the mid-20th century, much of the traditional Inuit way of life had changed (McGhee, 1996).

The traditional way of life of Inuit in the Eastern Arctic underwent even more dramatic changes after World War II. As the fur trade collapsed there was a concurrent decline of caribou and fox, which led to a greater dependency on imported goods—e.g., clothes and food, from the South. The collapse of the fur trade also meant that the productive activities of Inuit—e.g., hunting and trapping—did not produce a wage or saleable goods. After World War II the federal government continued its centralization policy to "urbanize" the North with most of the Inuit population leaving the tundra, the sea, and the sea ice to live in small, serviced communities. At the same time, improved educational and medical facilities in the small towns of the Arctic attracted Inuit. There was also the possibility of wage jobs in these settlements. As a result, for the next two decades there was a steady migration of Inuit from the tundra to the settlements. This movement was supported by government bureaucrats, since it meant that their charges would be in easy reach at all times. Thus, permanent residence in the settlements began, and a social, economic, and transportation infrastructure was put in place in order to service the communities (Lu and Emerson, 1973).

For many years after Confederation the federal government's concern with the North and its people was solely directed toward establishing a physical presence and thus establishing sovereignty over the area. It was believed that if Canada were to lay claim to the Arctic, it would have to demonstrate to the world that it had permanent residents upon the soil it claimed as part of Canada. While the placement of Royal Canadian Mounted Police stations in various parts of the North went some way toward establishing sovereignty, there was also a belief that "other" Canadians would also have to be physically present. Moreover, there was a belief that the Canadian government would have to provide support to these residents. Thus, effective occupation was the initial and prime consideration for government officials as the 20th century emerged.[5] It was also incumbent upon the Canadian government to make sure that Canadians were living in the Arctic on a year-round basis. As such, relocation programs were invented in order to move Inuit to areas not previously inhabited. For example, families from Inukjuak would be relocated to the high Arctic such as Grise Fiord (in 1953), and later Inuit would be moved to Resolute Bay. Other Inuit relocations were put in place throughout the 1950s.[6] The placement of Inuit into permanent residences also demonstrates the push by government to urbanize the Arctic. Finally, the creation of communities in the Arctic was also justified on the basis that they would afford Inuit an opportunity to pursue their traditional lifestyle (Tester and Kulchynski, 1994).

When the potential of natural resource development emerged in the 1960s, Canadians once again looked to the North to solve their problems. By the end of the 1960s, Inuit were dominated economically, politically, and ideologically. The influence of the traders, missionaries, and police had been supplanted by the presence of the state and multinational corporations. Social programs were extended to Inuit, and housing and medical programs were expanded as the government took a lead in the economic and social development of the North. D'Anglure (1984) argues that the 1960s marked the end of the traditional culture of Inuit and the emergence of the modern economy in the North.

During the 1960s major economic development projects were carried out in the North. The underlying assumption in all these developments was that Southern Canada had needs that subordinated those of the indigenous population of the Arctic. There was also a belief that Inuit culture was inferior, and that the standard of living for Inuit needed to be enhanced. Nevertheless, the ambivalence of the federal government's policy toward Inuit showed through. On the one hand it was sure that Inuit culture was doomed, but at the same time it wanted to allow Inuit to "live off the land" if that was what Inuit wanted to do.[7] The result was a compromise: it was decided to create cooperatives as a tool that would allow Inuit integration into the economic structure of Canada, while at the same time allowing them to retain their traditional cultural patterns in other spheres of life. While there was no overall economic plan, there was a logic to the policy (Mitchell, 1996).

If there is a lesson to be learned from this short history of the Arctic, it is that the entry of Southern Canadians has always created a crisis for Inuit. As Moss (1995) points out, their presence has always been so intrusive that it displaced and disrupted Inuit culture. Thus, it should not come as a surprise that Inuit are less than enthusiastic about any plans that Southern Canadians have about the North, and that they wish to achieve some level of self-government that aligns with Inuit culture and cosmology.

It is important for the reader to understand the Inuit cosmology that guides their thinking and behaviour. While the following is a broad generalization for all Inuit, we believe the five central tenets of Inuit culture are:

1. the principle of communality (everyone must contribute)

2. the life principle (life may have to be sacrificed in order for others to survive)

3. every being contains its whole ancestry

4. there is no hierarchical classification of human and non-human creatures

5. each form contains multitudes (no form is stable) (Dybbroe, 1996.)

An example of the cultural disparity between Southern Canada and Nunavut can be seen in the reaction of Inuit to a plebiscite on sex parity. In early 1999, the residents of Nunavut elected 19 members to its first legislative assembly—18 men and one woman. The one successful female candidate had been a vocal opponent of a plebiscite defeated two years earlier that there be one male and one female from each political riding in the new Nunavut. The other 10 female candidates who did not speak out against the plebiscite were defeated. While this result surprised and amazed Southern bureaucrats who had devised the plan for gender equity, it was not surprising to residents of the North. And while Inuit recognize that their traditional conceptions of sex and leadership have changed, this externally imposed structure did not fit into their culture. As one Inuit spokesperson noted:

> No individual makes or enforces law. No group of individuals can speak on behalf of other individuals. No group of individuals constitutes an assembly or equivalent to government. The individualism of the culture is a barrier against any form of organized domination; the egalitarianism a barricade against competitive individualism. (Brody, 1987:121–122)

As Dybbroe (1996) points out, the impact of urbanization on gender relations may take more time to make itself felt. These relations take place within the confines of the family, which, although affected by urban life, as a private affair allows Inuit to maintain a semblance of control over their lives. Nevertheless, Inuit recognize that change is occurring and that they must adapt their beliefs and behaviours to the new way of life.

POPULATION AND SOCIO-DEMOGRAPHIC PROFILE

The total Inuit population at the 1996 Census was nearly 46 000. The national distribution of this population is seen in Table 10.1.[8] While this number is small relative to the total Canadian population, the distribution reveals a concentration in the Northern regions of Canada. (See Table 10.2 for an identification of the major Inuit communities in the North.) Perhaps what is even more important than the small numbers is the linkages that the Inuit have established with other Arctic groups—e.g., Chukotka (Russia), Alaska (United

TABLE 10.1	Inuit Population by Province, 2001	
	Number	Percent
Canada	45 070	100.0
Nunavut	22 560	50.0
Quebec	9 535	21.2
Newfoundland and Labrador	4 555	10.1
Northwest Territories	3 905	8.7
Ontario	1 380	3.1
Rest of Canada	3 145	7.0

Source: Table 1. "Population reporting an Inuit identity, Canada and selected provinces and territories, 2001," adapted from the Statistics Canada publication "Aboriginal Peoples of Canada, A demographic profile," Catalogue 96F0030, January 2003.

States), and Greenland (Denmark). These groups have formed an international alliance and have become politically active over the past quarter-century.

The age distribution (see Table 10.3) reveals that the Inuit population is very young, with nearly 40 percent under the age of 15. The birth rate for Inuit is estimated to be 4 percent, one of the highest in the world. If this rate were to continue, we could expect the population to double every 18 years. The high birth rate means that Inuit communities are "young" and will continue to exert pressure to integrate into the labour force for some years to come. Nevertheless, the Inuit life expectancy is the lowest in Canada, at 67.7 years for males and 70.2 years for females. Moreover, the infant mortality rate (15 deaths per 1000 live births) is three times the national rate. The mobility status of Inuit reveals a more stable pattern than for other Canadians, with 82 percent claiming that they had not moved in the previous year. Seventy-five percent of those claiming to be Inuit also claim Inuktitut as their mother tongue, with the remainder claiming English or French as their mother tongue. Eighty percent of Inuit are Protestant, with only 18 percent Catholic. The remainder are "other" or have no religious affiliation.

Unemployment is high in Inuit communities; unemployment rates of 60–80 percent are not uncommon. In the 1991 Census only slightly more than two-thirds of adults reported employment income.[9] The data from 1991 also show that, of the total adults, only 43 percent were employed, 14 percent were unemployed, and the remainder (42 percent) were not defined as part of the labour force. The depressed economy of the Arctic is the major structural reason for its high unemployment, and this is not likely to change in the near future. Even traditional occupations such as trapping and fishing are depressed as a result of the boycott of furs by Europeans; for example, in 1990 the total value of white fox pelts sold in the Northwest Territories was only $24 000. Nevertheless, nearly one-third of Inuit adults claim to engage in work activities to support themselves and their families for which they did not receive money.

Table 10.4 identifies Inuit placement in the occupational structure for 1991. The data show that most of the Inuit within the labour force are found in semi-skilled and manual labour types of jobs. There are some skilled craftspersons and semi-professionals, but these are limited. Even fewer are in positions of power and decision making. The data reveal that overall the health profession is the most popular field of choice, with 45 percent

TABLE 10.2	Village Population in Canadian Arctic, Percent Inuit and Language Competency, 1991 by Region						

Village	Total Pop.	% Inuit	Inuit Lang./ Pop.	Village	Total Pop.	% Inuit	Inuit Lang./ Pop.
Aklavik	763	51.1	18%	Broughton Island	439	95.7	96%
Inuvik	3,389	20.3	26%	Pangnirtung	1004	94.1	100%
Tuktoyaktuk	929	82.9	24%	Iqaluit	2947	62.6	92%
Sachs Harbour	158	85.4	30%	Lake Harbour	326	95.4	98%
Paulatuk	193	93.3	33%	Cape Dorset	872	93.5	99%
Total—Inuvik Region	**5432**	**39.9**	**25%**	Sanikiluaq	422	97.2	95%
Holman Island	303	97.4	61%	**Total—Baffin Region**	**9974**	**82.4**	**96%**
Kugluktuk	888	92.3	55%	**Total—N.W. Territories**	**24 129**	**75.1**	**83%**
Cambridge Bay	1002	70.0	50%				
Bathhurst/Baychimo	77	97.4	93%	Chisasibi	2375	2.1	20%
Others	45	44.4	50%	Kuujjuaraapik	410	47.6	100%
Gjoa Haven	650	96.1	93%	Umiujaq	235	95.7	100%
Spence Bay	488	94.3	90%	Inukjuak	778	93.8	100%
Pelly Bay	297	98.6	97%	Povungnituk	927	93.3	100%
Total—Kitikmeot Region	**3750**	**87.6**	**71%**	Akulivik	337	96.4	100%
				Ivujivik	208	96.1	100%
Repulse Bay	420	96.4	100%	Salluit	663	95.8	100%
Chesterfield	294	93.5	94%	Kangiqsujuaq	337	96.4	100%
Coral Harbour	477	95.4	99%	Quaqtaq	185	91.9	100%
Baker Lake	1009	93.6	94%	Kangirsuk	308	95.8	100%
Rankin Inlet	1374	76.4	93%	Aupaluk	110	86.4	100%
Whale Cove	210	90.4	100%	Tasiujaq	135	96.3	100%
Arviat	1189	96.9	96%	Kuujjuaq	1065	82.1	100%
Total—Keewatin Region	**4973**	**89.8**	**95%**	Kangiqsualujjuaq	383	97.9	100%
				Total—Quebec	**6131**	**89.5**	**99%**
Hall Beach	451	95.3	98%	Nan	1018	78.6	70%
Igloolik	857	95.7	100%	Davis Inlet	385	2.6	–
Resolute	184	73.4	85%	Hopedale	477	77.6	40%
Grise Fiord	114	93.1	100%	Makkovik	340	27.9	47%
Nanisivik	315	41.3	96%	Rigolet	317	15.8	40%
Arctic Bay	477	95.4	99%	Northwest River	526	12.4	23%
Pond Inlet	795	95.6	97%	Happy Valley	7248	3.7	28%
Clyde River	471	96.6	100%	**Total—Labrador**	**10 311**	**16.1**	**52%**
Others	300	60.0	81%				

Source: Louis-Jacques Dorais, "La situation linguistique dans l'Arctique," *Etudes/Inuit/Studies*, 1992, 16 (1-2), 246-248.

TABLE 10.3	Inuit Age Distribution 1996 and 2001			
	2001		1996	
	Number	Percent	Number	Percent
Age Group				
0-14	17 460	38.7	16 510	41.0
15-24	8 260	18.3	7 605	18.9
25-64	17 950	39.8	15 095	37.5
65 and over	1 405	3.1	1 015	2.5

Source: Table 1. "Population reporting an Inuit identity, and age groups, 1996 and 2001," adapted from the Statistics Canada publication "Aboriginal Peoples of Canada, A demographic profile," Catalogue 96F0030, January 2003.

of all Inuit employed in this area. However, it is more important for men, of whom nearly 70 percent are employed in some aspect of the health profession. This is followed by commerce. Again, there are gender differences, with only 8 percent of men and nearly 40 percent of Inuit women working in this field. Education also plays an important role in the Arctic. About 6 percent of the men in the labour force have gone into the field of education, and nearly one-quarter of the women (23 percent). It is also important to note that, regardless of the field, many of the jobs in the Arctic are in government (federal, territorial, and municipal) as opposed to the private sector.

While employment is related to income, the most recent data show that 17 percent of the Inuit adult population claimed no income during the 1991 year.[10] Ten percent made under $2000 per year, and another 30 percent made between $2000 and $10 000 per year. This

TABLE 10.4	Inuit Occupational Distribution by Sex (%), 1991 (Single response)	
	Male	Female
Total	7 005	5 805
Upper/middle level management	6.6	5.4
Prof./semi-prof.	10.8	21.2
Super/foreman	1.7	1.0
Clerical/sales	9.3	30.1
Skilled crafts.	12.3	1.0
Semiskilled	20.2	1.3
Manual labour	25.9	17.3
Other/not stated	13.2	22.7

Source: Statistics Canada, *Schooling, work and related activities, income, expenses and mobility.* 1991. Catalogue 89-534, September 1993, pp. 128-129.

means that well over half of the Inuit population made less than $10 000 per year. Twenty percent made between $10 000 and $20 000 while 16 percent made between $20 000 and $40 000 per year. Only 7 percent made more than $40 000 per year. When we look at those reporting employment income[11] we find that 20 percent of those in the labour force made under $2000 per year. One-third made between $2000 and $10 000, and 18 percent made between $10 000 and $20 000. Slightly more than one-fifth of the Inuit adult population made $20 000–$40 000 per year and only 8 percent made more than $40 000 per year. Overall, we find that males working full time had an average income of $29 999 while for females it was $24 441. Males working part time earned $9521 and females $6861.

As Inuit have become more involved in the wage economy, young people have redefined their involvement in subsistence activities. However, the change is not simple or straightforward. The cumulative changes have led to a reorientation of daily practices that has caused young Inuit to see subsistence activities as desirable and valuable but to see them as recreations and something to be enjoyed once other more important demands— e.g., waged labour-force participation—are met (Stern, 2000). Young people see the town they live in as the "place they work and live" and the land as a "place to get away from it all." In addition, participation in the labour force acts as both a barrier and facilitator for individuals to engage in "subsistence activities." For example, the additional cash allows those who have high status, high paying jobs to purchase snowmobiles and other pieces of equipment that facilitate their "back to the land" activities. However, those who are not able to afford this kind of equipment are not able to participate in subsistence activities.

Urbanization

Nearly one-fourth of the Inuit population live in large urban areas. The numbers below provides the reader with some sense of the size of Inuit populations in urban areas of Southern Canada. If Northern towns are added to the list, nearly 90 percent of the Inuit population live in nonrural areas.

Toronto	1900
Edmonton	850
Montreal	800
Ottawa–Hull	750
Calgary	650
Vancouver	600
Winnipeg	550

These numbers, when added to other urban areas across the country reveal that nearly 10 000 Inuit have their permanent residence outside the North. Kishigami (1999) found that Inuit living in the South comprised three major groupings: students, workers, and unemployed. She also found that many residents of Montreal had moved from the North in order to escape alcohol and drug problems, sexual and physical violence, and other problems of human relations in a small town. In short, she found that individuals' decision to move to an urban centre was not mainly a function of urban resources and opportunities available to them but was rather due to their desire to leave the North. Others, such as students once they completed their education, found they were able to expand their job opportunities and therefore postponed returning to the North. However, none of the Inuit living in the urban centres were able to develop or create an Inuit urban culture and identity. The lack of a strong social network and the paucity of Inuit in any one locale prevented the development of Inuit organizations, the continuation of the Inuit language, and the maintenance of Inuit culture.

Housing

The housing stock in the North is aging and of poor quality. It is estimated that today the Inuit of the Arctic need 3000 new homes, but the federal government has projected budgets for only about 300 per year. This requires that housing be provided through the income of Inuit and other sources. If the current population were to remain stable it would take a decade to provide the necessary housing units. However, by the end of the decade the population will have increased and older housing stock will have deteriorated even further. As a result, the housing crisis will continue. The average number of persons per dwelling is about 4.3, with the number of rooms per dwelling at 5.4. The number of persons per dwelling is substantially higher than the Canadian average and suggests that crowding is the usual condition for Inuit families. Nevertheless, the existing housing for Inuit is relatively new, with 40 percent having been built within the last decade.[12] An additional 30 percent is less than 20 years old. Because most of the housing is located in urban settings, nearly two-thirds are linked to a municipal water system. However, about one-quarter of the current dwellings obtain their water directly from surface water—e.g., streams or lakes.

Education

At the end of World War II only four schools existed in the Northwest Territories. Three were Catholic, and the other Anglican. When the federal government took over Northern education in 1947 it assumed that Inuit were illiterate and "backward" because they had not been exposed to the Southern Canadian educational system. Thus, without evaluating the type of educational system that the North required, the entire Southern educational structure was exported there. Two years later the government established a network of public schools for Inuit. However, because no Southern non-Inuit teachers could speak Inuktitut (or any of the dialects), the sole language of instruction was English.

By 1951 a system of residential schools was established, with students from remote areas being relocated to schools for up to 10 months a year. While the government covered the cost of education, the schools were run by religious institutions. These residential schools isolated children from their parents, whose socialization efforts were limited to short visits by the children. Parental control was replaced by the religious fervour exhibited by the Catholic or Anglican teachers who felt that students would do better once removed from the negative influences of home and parents.

Once communities grew to sufficient size, day schools were established. Nevertheless, the Southern, Euro-Canadian curriculum in Inuit schools continued to be taught by non-Inuit, Southern-trained teachers. It would not be until the 1960s that a curriculum was implemented that took into consideration Inuit language, culture, and values (Duffy, 1988). In 1970 administrative responsibility for Inuit schools was transferred to the government of the Northwest Territories. The Inuit Tapirisat's lobbying efforts were a major factor in the government's decision to change its educational methods in the Arctic. The Tapirisat proposed that courses be taught with a strong Northern orientation, and the Inuit

Cultural Institute was created to protect Inuit language and culture. In addition, the establishment of Nunavut and Aurora Arctic College has afforded the opportunity for Inuit students to obtain selected degrees while remaining in the North. As a result, many teachers in Inuit communities have bachelor's and master's degrees in education and have taken on some administrative responsibility in the schools.

Nevertheless, there has been and continues to be a high attrition rate of Inuit from the education system. Official data from Statistics Canada (1991) show that about one-third of Inuit children reach Grade 9, compared to over 80 percent for the Canadian population. Less than 15 percent graduate from high school and less than 1 percent go on to university. Today there are three post-secondary educational institutions in Nunavut–Iqualuit, Cambridge Bay, and Rankin Inlet. In other Nunavut communities, there are "community learning centres" that provide post-secondary courses. Focusing on the adult population[13] (ages 15–49), we find that 4 percent have no formal schooling and one-third have less than a Grade 8 education. Thirty-six percent claim to have a secondary education. Eleven percent claim some post-secondary education, with 14 percent having some form of certificate/diploma. Less than 1 percent have a university degree. When we look at the younger population (ages 5–14), we find that 99 percent are currently attending school, over three-quarters claiming to have an Aboriginal teacher. Eighty-one percent of the students claim that their teachers used English in the classroom. However, nearly three-quarters report that an Aboriginal language is also used in their classes. Grades 1–3 are taught in Inuktitut, even for non-Inuit students in the class. This suggests that today's classrooms are bilingual; perhaps equally important is the fact that Inuktitut is still a thriving language (Sarkadi, 1992).

Slightly less than two-thirds of children (ages 5–14) claim that they are able to speak Inuktitut.[14] A majority of students are taught by their parents and/or school teachers. Of those children who speak Inuktitut, about two-thirds claim to speak it in a variety of situations—at home, school, and other places. However, less than one-quarter of these children report reading Aboriginal language newspapers, newsletters, or magazines. Three-quarters of the adults claim to speak Inuktitut.[15] Three-quarters of these reported speaking Inuktitut in the home, while only one-third spoke it at work and only 10 percent in school. Two-thirds of the adults who claim to be Inuit are able to read Inuktitut, and nearly half of them claim to read Inuktitut newspapers and magazines. Sixty percent claim that they are able to write Inuktitut (Taqralik, 1984).

Health

Settlements with a population of over 200 usually have nursing stations, which are the backbone of the health care system of the North. They are staffed by registered nurses and are open 24 hours a day. Although health clinics have been established in the larger communities, the existence of hospitals in the North is not extensive. During the 1970s and 1980s the federal government carried out an evaluation of the efficiency and effectiveness of maintaining hospitals in the North. It concluded that, except in the major urban areas of the North, the existence of hospitals was inefficient, ineffective, and posed both staffing and financial hardships. For example, it found that while funds could be allocated to the construction of a hospital, staffing was most problematic. As such, even the best and most up-to-date equipment was useless if qualified staff were not in residence. In the end it was agreed that for serious medical cases, patients would be airlifted to nearby Northern hospitals or the nearest hospital in the South.[16] Nevertheless, many culturally relevant health services are provided in the existing hospitals—for example, in Iqaluit.

For the first half of the 20th century the most prevalent disease to afflict Inuit was tuberculosis. In 1944 the tuberculosis rate was 568 per 100 000. In an effort to deal with the disease the federal government promoted extensive relocation and regimentation of the Inuit population. Large Inuit communities were created in Southern Canada through the establishment of TB sanitariums, and it has been estimated that at one time the largest Inuit community was in Ontario. Ten years later the tuberculosis rate had dropped to 253, and by 1965 it was down to 90 per 100 000. Today the rate is less than 50 cases per 100 000, but this is still considerably higher than the overall Canadian rate.

Another health problem for Inuit is the infant mortality rate. In 1958 the rate for Inuit was the highest in the world, at 151 per 1000 live births (compared to 30 per 1000 for the rest of Canada). Again, due to improved health care, these figures have dropped dramatically over time. By the turn of the century, infant mortality rates were 15 per 1000 as compared to the national average of 5.7.

Inuit health has been influenced by ecological, social, and nutritional changes. For example, creating urban zones in permafrost areas has created major environmental and health problems for the residents. Poor nutrition has also contributed to a general lowering of health of Inuit in all areas of the North. Increasing consumption of imported foods with little or no nutritional value has characterized the Inuit's current eating habits. Over time Inuit came to rely more and more upon imported foods of whose nutritional content they were not aware.[17] Thus, the standard of health for Inuit has steadily deteriorated. Nevertheless, subjective indicators of health do not seem to match the assessment of nutritional experts. For example, during the 1991 Census, Inuit adults and children were asked to provide an indication of their health status. Nearly half of the children (under age 15) claimed to have excellent health. Only 3 percent felt that their health was "poor." However, when the adults were asked the same question the results were different. Only 27 percent claimed to have excellent health, with 13 percent claiming "fair" or "poor" health status. Moreover, nearly one-quarter of the adult Inuit population reported chronic health problems. In summary, while many economic strategies were developed to help the Inuit throughout the 1950s and 1960s, there has been no attempt to solve the nutritional problem facing Inuit people.

During the 1960s and 1970s, the death pattern and rate for Inuit changed dramatically. As tuberculosis decreased in importance, pneumonia became the leading cause of death. In the 1960s, pneumonia accounted for over one-fifth of the Inuit deaths. Today, "injuries, violence, and accidents" are the leading causes of death for Inuit. Specific events within this class are (in order of importance): suicides, drowning, crib death, gunshot wounds, asphyxia, motor vehicle accidents, and homicide. Drug and alcohol addictions have now become major problems facing Inuit people. In addition, new health hazards have appeared in the late 20th and early 21st centuries. Sexually transmitted diseases like gonorrhea and AIDS have attained near-crisis levels (Hobart, 1991).

As we assess the health of the Inuit people it is clear that several social and ecological factors have contributed to their decreasing quality of life, poor housing, nutrition, and poverty. The result is that the life expectancy of Inuit today is about 10 to 15 years less than that of a Canadian living in the South.

Law and Justice

As Canada began to impose its cultural and administrative structures on Northerners, the implementation of Southern law and justice prevailed. Today, most police services are provided by the RCMP with little input from Inuit residents. However, in some areas, such as Kativik, Quebec, a regional police force comprising many Inuit officers will operate in 14 Inuit communities (Secretariat aux affaires autochtones, 1988).

We also find that many Inuit are serving sentences in federal and territorial prisons. Faulkner (1992) carried out a study of over 50 Inuit men and women currently serving time in correctional institutions. She found that, with few exceptions, the major cause for imprisonment was substance abuse. She also found that in most federal jails workers are not sensitive to the cultural needs of Inuit prisoners. Although many correctional personnel have obtained cross-cultural training, much of it is geared to the cultural needs of Indians. In an attempt to deal with this concern, Corrections Canada is contracting out many of the activities dealing with Inuit inmates. Unfortunately, this means that it cannot control the quality of the work or the qualifications of the workers. Moreover, because the outsourced workers are not part of the Correctional Service of Canada they are not eligible to participate in government "managing diversity" programs.

Federal officials have also placed some Inuit in provincial facilities in an attempt to match the cultural programs and the needs of Inuit inmates. This also means that Inuit are closer to home and have some contact with family and friends, which they do not have when removed from the community and placed in Southern Canadian jails. However, it is unlikely that these provincial facilities have long-term programs and appropriate counselling services. One exception is the new "healing house" about to be constructed in Kagluktuk. Nevertheless, this Catch-22 situation has yet to be resolved (Faulkner, 1992).

ECONOMIC DEVELOPMENT

Under current arrangements, the North is completely dependent upon the federal government. With a current Gross Domestic Product of barely $1 billion, and a territorial budget of $730 million, Nunavut remains heavily dependent upon Ottawa. Over 90 percent of territorial government revenue is derived from federal transfer payments. All natural resource royalty payments in the North flow directly to the South. Government spending still accounts for about two-thirds of the territory's economy, and most of the best paying jobs are in the public sector.

When the federal government began to actively intervene in ongoing activities in the Northwest Territories during the 1950s, solutions to the economic plight of Inuit had a high priority. While co-ops in the rest of Canada were given lukewarm reception by the federal government, in the North they were supported and heavily subsidized. Although this was a departure from the usual stance taken by government it was felt that the end justified the means. The co-ops of the North were specifically ethnic and were not integrated into the mainstream co-op movement in Southern Canada. As such, they did not pose an economic threat to private industry. By 1966, 22 Arctic co-ops had been established, and by 1982 the annual level of business exceeded $30 million. Today there are over 40 active Inuit co-operatives, each belonging to one of two administrative bodies. There are 12 Arctic Quebec co-ops under the Montreal-based Fédération des Cooperatives du Nouveau-Québec, with the remainder being members of Arctic Cooperatives Limited (based in Winnipeg). Today the major activity of the co-ops has been in the production and marketing of handicrafts.

As noted above, co-ops were the federal government's economic structure of choice for integrating Inuit into Canadian society. But although there has been some success with these co-ops, particularly in the production of handicrafts, overall they have not allowed

Inuit to integrate economically and have not provided a linkage with other Canadian economic institutions. The inability of co-ops to increase their membership and assets meant
that Inuit were forced to look for new ways to develop sustainable economic ventures. But
with no large amounts of money, little human capital relevant to the industrial economy,
and limited backing by the federal government, this proved to be an impossible task.
However, the settlement of comprehensive land claims has provided some hope as new
forms of economic structures have emerged. When the new "development corporations"
were established, their first act was to hire qualified individuals. Because co-ops had provided a training ground for Inuit, they were the first place to look. And with offerings of
higher status and salaries, it was not difficult to produce "brain drain" in the co-op management. The impact of this action has been to further decrease the effectiveness of co-ops
as independent economic institutions.

Most of these new development corporations have focused their efforts on mega-
projects, requiring skilled workers and considerable "up-front, sunk costs." The end result
has been the hiring of large numbers of non-Inuit and a reliance on capital from outside the
region. For example, Makivik lost over $10 million in its first four years of operation. While
it is making a small profit today, many of the subsidiary companies are losing money or
have been terminated—e.g., Air Inuit and Kigiak Builders Inc. Nevertheless, other Inuit-
owned and operated businesses are slowly developing into sustainable operations.

A recent federal report on the "economic health" of Arctic communities shows that
only seven communities in the Northwest Territories were rated as being "developed,"
which means that they have good transportation systems, a significant private sector, and
the potential to provide residents with jobs. Six other communities had some "potential,"
but the majority were classified as "underdeveloped" and with no real economic potential.
However, when areas do have economic potential, Inuit involvement is challenged. For
example, the discovery of copper, cobalt, and nickel in Voisey's Bay (50 kilometres north
of Davis Inlet–Utshimassits) prompted the Inuit and Innu to more forcefully make their
land claim case, since Voisey's Bay is within the currently contested land area. However,
neither the federal nor provincial government has suggested that land rights might take
precedence over outside exploitation of natural resources. In a recent move, the province
of Newfoundland and Labrador has placed restrictions on the development of the potential nickel mine, and the developers have chosen to "shelve" their plans for the immediate
future and move their development efforts to other areas in the world that are "more
friendly" to the exploitation of natural resources.

Living in Arctic communities requires cash. And while new jobs have been created by
the establishment of Nunavut, many Northerners do not wish to work for government or
may not have the skills to participate. Many public service jobs created remain unfilled
because of the local population's lack of skills to fill them. This means that other employment opportunities will need to be created. During the late 1980s and early 1990s, non-
renewable resource development was touted as an alternative supply of work. However,
mining has never employed more than 1.5 percent of the Native labour force in the
Northwest Territories, and oil development has involved even fewer. Moreover, the boom
and bust nature of such activities creates a volatile and transient labour force. For example, after drilling levels in the Arctic Islands peaked at 37 wells in 1973, exploration
declined sharply, eventually coming to a halt in 1987. Nevertheless, there is some evidence
to suggest that part-time employment in the Arctic is preferred by Inuit in that it allows
them to participate in the traditional economy. Myers (2000) argues that the traditional

economy is an important component of local life and he points out that, in the 1980s, the average of $11 000 was an imputed value per Native household for country food and domestic production. He goes on to claim that more than 90 percent of Inuit households consume country food, and more than 70 percent hunt or fish.

In the mid-1990s, the Labour Force showed that Arctic communities continued their participation in hunting, fishing, trapping, and producing crafts. In the Baffin communities, between 34 and 76 percent of the labour force is involved in traditional economies. On the other hand, small businesses are increasing in the North, and Robinson et al. (1991) found that over half of the Northwest Territories' employment and 41 percent of the total payroll was made up of small businesses. Nevertheless, a combination of enterprises rooted in tradition (e.g., country food, commercial fishing, fur, leather, crafts, tourism), community based developments (e.g., renewable resources, retail, wholesale), and non-renewable resource development will be necessary. The North remains significantly unexplored, but there is considerable evidence that it is a rich storehouse of oil, gas, gold, copper, zinc, uranium, diamonds and other minerals. In 2001, mining was the largest sectoral contributor to the gross domestic product (20 percent). In that year, $90 million worth of mineral exploration activity was underway in Nunavut. Towns such as Yellowknife and Inuvik clearly have developed markets in the retail and wholesale business sector and could expand their scope. With regard to other communities such as Kugluktuk, Cape Dorset, and Norman Wells, these communities could expand their roles as regional supply centres and expand the local range of goods and services. Other smaller communities have potential for developing their arts and crafts and other forms of human and natural resource development. For example, one in five individuals in the Nunavut region sold crafts in 2002. The Waddington auction house that sells Inuit art sold more than $1.2 million of Inuit art in 2002. Regardless of the type of development undertaken in the North, it will have to be based more on the Inuit lifestyle, resources, and values.

The traditional economy of the Inuit is no longer the main support structure for the development of an Arctic economy. The existing structures remain isolated from both the Canadian and the global industrialized economies. Even the new development corporations that have been created are marginal in their ability to become "engines" of growth in the Arctic. As a result, there is a clear ethnic stratification in the Arctic that segregates Inuit from non-Inuit Southerners. This inequality is maintained through unequal access to jobs, services, and goods. Individual and structural discrimination has further divided the indigenous population from the remainder of the Arctic residents. For example, when the shrimp quota for Canada was increased because of new sources in the North, only 51 percent of the increase was allocated to Northern companies, with the remainder being allocated to Southern interests. In other cases where fish quotas have been increased—e.g., Nova Scotia—those provinces adjacent to the waters have received more than 80 percent of the increased quota. Nunavut and the Northwest Territories control one-quarter of the fisheries while Southern interests control the remainder. These kind of structural inequalities make it difficult for local businesses such as the Pangrirung Fisheries (which employs 100 people and processes 1.5 milion pounds of fish per year) to succeed.

Today there is a recognition that prior development of the North was Southern-driven, with variable benefits for Northern residents. As a result, the traditional-based economy has survived and reaffirmed the Inuit cultural and social values. Nevertheless, there is agreement that if the Inuit do not want to lose the young people of the North, they will need to develop and create community-based economic opportunities that meet the needs of Northern residents.

Inuit Corporate Structure: The Inuvialuit

In 1984 the federal government signed the Inuvialuit Final Agreement with the Committee for Original People's Entitlements, which represented the Inuvialuit of the Western Arctic. (See Figure 10.2 for the area encompassed under the agreement.) Under this agreement, the Inuvialuit relinquished their claim to lands in the Western Arctic in exchange for legal title to selected lands, financial compensation, and hunting, fishing, and trapping rights (Keeping, 1989: 2). When the Inuvialuit Western Agreement was signed a political and corporate structure was also created. The Inuvialuit Regional Corporation (successor to the Committee for Original People's Entitlement) is controlled by the six communities in the region. A number of subsidiary corporations were also established—e.g., the Inuvialuit Land Corporation, and Inuvialuit Development Corporation. The business activities of the Development Corporation are varied and extensive. They include ownership of an airline, a shipping company, a construction company (Koblunaq Construction), and the Inuvialuit Investment Corporation. The Development Corporation has not limited its investments to the northern region of Canada—e.g., Valgro Ltd. (industrial valve manufacturer for Western Canada) and Riverside Park Developments Inc. (real estate developer on Vancouver Island). Moreover, most of the money received by the Inuvialuit as compensation for relinquishing their rights to land has been used for developing new businesses, or has been invested in other financial portfolios.[18]

The settlement has brought the Inuvialuit new and growing prosperity. One of the achievements is the Inuvialuit Petroleum Corporation, an oil and gas exploration and production business owned by the Inuvialuit. With current assets of over $35 million, it has returned financial benefits to the community as well as providing training and opportunity for academic achievement. It has interests in over 100 oil wells and nearly as many gas wells.

These new economic structures have produced jobs for Inuit who otherwise would not have been able to enter the modern day labour force. However, a lack of education and technical skills has kept many of the Inuit from taking on these jobs. Professional positions such as lawyers and accountants have had to be given to non-Inuit, with the proviso that when Inuit became skilled they could take over these jobs (Duhaime, 1993).

As the Inuvialuit have tried to develop these new ethnic economic structures they have realized that they must develop links with other national and multinational companies. Thus, their primary activity today is to construct linkages that will provide them with the necessary capital and technology while at the same time allowing them to receive a fair return on their investment and keep the development within their scope of control. The Inuvialuit want their ventures to provide long-term opportunities for employment and training. Their overall goal is to nurture a more stable economy through recycling profits and wages, and to allow the Inuvialuit to contribute to, and gain from, the successful growth.

A TIME FOR CHANGE

As the Cold War intensified in the 1950s, the Distant Early Warning system was put in place throughout the Canadian Arctic.[19] These small, isolated military installations brought

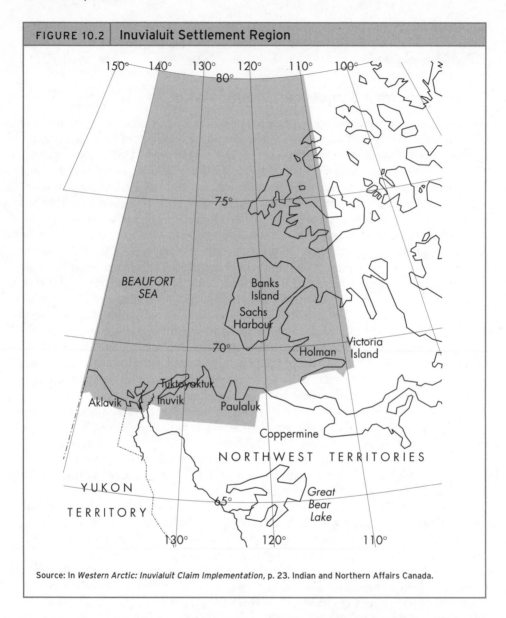

| FIGURE 10.2 | Inuvialuit Settlement Region |

Source: In *Western Arctic: Inuvialuit Claim Implementation*, p. 23. Indian and Northern Affairs Canada.

Southerners to the Arctic on a permanent basis. Infrastructures had to be put in place in order to ensure that these installations could be accessed at any time. It also meant that existing communities in the North had to be modernized so that they could act as a secondary stage to access these installations. In short, the modern industrial economy began to impact upon the Arctic. At the same time, social programs were made available to Inuit.

In the early 1960s the federal government implemented a policy to develop the natural resources of the North. By the end of the 1960s the government's "Roads for Resources" program, which gave direction to the development of the natural resources of the North, had introduced multinationals and their associated technology to the North. It was at this time that Inuit communities became more actively involved in policy and pro-grams directed toward the North, even though they were not able to participate in the programs due to a lack of educational and technical skills (Jull, 1982).

The Inuit have been interested in integrating into the larger economic institutional structures of Canada and concerned with Aboriginal rights for some time, but it has only been in the past few years that they have been able to forcefully act on those beliefs. They have been facilitated by external and internal forces. For example, environmental concerns, linkages with other national indigenous groups, land settlements in Alaska and Greenland, and less demand on developing petroleum resources in the North have reduced Southern intrusion into the Arctic and have given Inuit an opportunity to organize and clearly articulate their concerns as well as their goals as Canadians. At the same time, the participation by Inuit in domestic governmental structures (both federal and territorial) has produced an awareness of Inuit concerns and helped them to develop political and economic strategies to deal with those issues.

The process of decolonization has begun for Inuit as self-government negotiations have taken place in all four Arctic regions: Western Arctic (Inuvialuit), Nunavut (Eastern Arctic), Nunavik (Northern Quebec), and Northern Labrador. Inuit have always argued that they do not want to achieve self-determination through racially segregated structures or secession. They consider themselves Canadian, yet they want an explicit recognition of the place of Inuit in Canadian society.

POLITICAL DEVELOPMENTS

The question regarding the political structure of the North has been reviewed by the federal government many times in the past half-century. One of the first to investigate the issue of self-government was Fred Carrothers in the 1960s. His report (1967) concluded that the Northwest Territories should be self-governing and that Yellowknife should be its capital. More recently the *Drury Report* once again addressed the issue of self-government and division of the Northwest Territories. While the report did not reject the idea of division, it suggested that Inuit land claims and setting land aside for Inuit was a priority issue. The question of self-government and division could come later. The Inuit Tapirisat of Canada rejected this conclusion.

Ten years later, the Inuit Tapirisat of Canada presented a case for settlement of its land claim along with the creation of Nunavut. In 1979 the Inuit Tapirisat of Canada adopted the contents of the document entitled *Political Development in Nunavut.* By that time a Territorial Assembly had been put in place. The election that year brought about a change for the first time in the ethnic composition of the Assembly, a majority of whose members were of Aboriginal ancestry (Duhaime, 1992).

As Inuit continued to press their concerns the federal government agreed to hold a plebiscite. In 1982 the first plebiscite for division of the North was held, with 56 percent of those casting their ballots in favour. It was then agreed that two forums be established to discuss the separation issue: the Nunavut Constitutional Forum (in the Eastern Arctic) and the Western Constitutional Forum (in the Western North). By 1984 Inuvialuit of the Western Arctic independently signed an agreement with the federal government and settled their land claims. The activities of the Western Constitutional Forum were further supplanted by the Dene/Métis land claims negotiations. These negotiations continue, but no decision has been made regarding the fate of the Western MacKenzie Valley area of the North.

Since the 1970s, the federal and territorial governments have come to support the establishment of some form of self-government for Northerners. The creation of an Inuit government in Northern Quebec and in the Western Arctic, and more recently the creation of Nunavut, all suggest that the federal government is receptive to change in the North. All of these changes have involved land settlements that have given new direction to Inuit.

Provincial governments have their own constitutional existence without a formal reporting relationship to the federal government. Most of the provincial government structures are set through either constitutions or conventions. However, this is not the case for the territorial governments. Much of the power they wield is not provided for by statute, but is in place due to discussions between political leaders in the North and the federal minister. In some cases, this is given formal recognition in Letters of Instruction, while in others it is instituted through unwritten understandings between the federal and territorial governments (Indian and Northern Affairs Canada, 1993).

LAND CLAIMS

Aboriginal land claims are as old as Canada, and while many of the land claims were settled through treaty, there are virtually no treaties involving the North.[20] A review of government documents clearly demonstrates that the federal government did not want to treat Inuit as they did Indians. Federal officials were adamant that Inuit were not Indians (although the Supreme Court decided differently in 1939) and they therefore refused to establish treaties with the Inuit. As a result, until the 1970s, most of the land in the Yukon and Northwest Territories was under contested ownership. The *Alaska Native Claims Settlement Act* (1971) was the first modern Aboriginal land settlement in North America and became the precursor to modern Inuit land claims in Canada. It both set the stage and served as a model for Canadian settlements. However, it should be made clear that the impetus for settling land claims was not generated by Inuit but by the federal government. The government's interest in settling land claims emerged out of the potential difficulties it foresaw in developing the natural resources of the North. Land claims were entered into because the government saw them as a legal obstacle that needed to be dealt with as quickly as possible if development was to move forward (Mitchell, 1996). Today, two major Inuit land claims in the North have been settled while one, Nunavut, is nearly settled and the fourth, Labrador, is in the process of being negotiated.

James Bay

The first major, modern-day land claims settlement occurred in 1975 with the James Bay Cree and Inuit of Quebec, who reside north of the 55th parallel. It would not be until the James Bay Hydro development became an issue that anyone focused any concern on these people. Government interest was piqued only once the Inuit and Indians objected to the development and obtained a court injunction against it. The end result was the James Bay and Northern Quebec Agreement (1975) dealing with the Aboriginal land claims and compensation. In addition, the settlement provided Aboriginal people (both Inuit and Indians) with hunting rights, land rights, and an acceptance of Aboriginal rights. The Inuit communities of this region became public municipal governments under Quebec municipalities legislation (Purich, 1992).

When the James Bay settlement went into effect in 1975, both the Cree and Inuit in the region were awarded land ownership, land use, and financial compensation. This was the first modern Canadian land claims settlement and followed both the Alaska settlement and the *Calder* decision of the Supreme Court, which found that Aboriginal rights existed. The Kativik Regional government in Northern Quebec is the administrative structure now used to govern the region. This structure, like others advocated by Inuit, is not racially based. Because of their majority status the Inuit are able to control their regional government; however, their efforts are limited by their financial dependency on the federal government.[21]

Other organizational and administrative structures were also put in place. For example, under the James Bay Agreement the Makivik Corporation was created. Its role is to receive compensation and invest it in such a way that it will improve the quality of life of Inuit. The Kativik School Board was also established under the provisions of the James Bay Agreement.

Western Arctic

In the Western Arctic the Inuvialuit[22] formed the Committee for Original Peoples Entitlement and formed an alliance with Eastern Inuit. First proposed in 1976 by the Inuit Tapirisat of Canada, a proposal for establishing Nunavut was presented to the federal government. Later that year it was withdrawn and a new land claim was submitted a year later by the Committee for Original Peoples Entitlement, focusing only on the Western Arctic. The Inuvialuit Agreement was the second major land claims settlement reached in Canada since the federal land claims policy was put into effect in 1973. In 1984 the Inuvialuit Final Agreement was signed and provided a guarantee that Inuvialuit would not be treated any less favourably than any other group in the Western Arctic. Under this agreement, the Inuvialuit surrendered their rights to 344 000 square kilometres of land. In return they were guaranteed title to 91 000 square kilometres and mineral rights in one-seventh of that zone. In addition, they received $152 million compensation payable over a 13-year period. Several wildlife-management structures were also put into place, along with an income support program.

Labrador

As the Moravians entered the Eastern coast they were able to acquire land to base their operations. Labrador Inuit have been unsuccessfully trying to get their land back for some time. In 1974 the Labrador Inuit Association outlined its land claims against the federal government. However, it would take more than 10 years before a framework agreement to cover Labrador Inuit comprehensive claims negotiations was initialled by the interested parties. In 1978 the government accepted the claim by 3500 Inuit of Labrador. One year later the province of Newfoundland agreed to enter into the negotiations. It would not be until 1990 that the two governments signed a framework agreement outlining the scope, process, topics, and parameters for negotiation (Purich, 1992). It is important to note that these claims are on the "short list" of the federal government claims, meaning that they are a priority and have a high probability of being settled. Nevertheless, as we head into the 21st century, little progress has been made in settling the Labrador Inuit claim.

The Labrador Inuit Association is the regional organization that has spearheaded the struggle for recognition by the Inuit of Labrador. It represents about 5000 people and is recognized by the government of Canada and the province of Newfoundland and

Labrador. As Haysom (1992) points out, even though the Labrador Inuit Association has not been successful in negotiating specific claims, it has been influential outside the claims arena. Specifically, the Association has sponsored at least nine other organizations that are influential in the provision of social, health, and economic benefits to Inuit—e.g., the Torngat Regional Housing Association, Labrador Inuit Health Commission, Labrador Inuit Development Corporation, and the Labrador Inuit Alcohol and Drug Abuse Program.

Two factors have led to the attempts to settle the claims. First, there is great potential in the natural resources of the area; and second, the Department of National Defence wants to sign international military agreements. The civil disobedience carried out by the Innu (Indians) in Labrador over land claims suggests that Inuit may also "up the ante" in negotiating with the two levels of government as we head into the 21st century.

NEW FORMS OF GOVERNMENT

The existing government structure in the Northwest Territories consists of three levels: territorial, regional, and local. Local governments generally represent communities and are elected by local residents. Regional councils are made up of municipal officials chosen by local councils. Thus, they are responsible to local government councils. Regional councils are unique to the Northwest Territories and are funded by the territorial government. Most regional governments being proposed by Aboriginal people are not interested in obtaining the "law making" powers now held by the territorial Legislative Assembly. However, they are interested in obtaining more authority in running programs of the territorial government within their region. Without taking over ministerial responsibility, they want more program responsibility for setting policy and standards (Dickerson, 1993).

The existing structure of government in the Northwest Territories is highly centralized[23] and at the same time nonpartisan. Over the years, this has led to a population that is highly alienated from its government. While discussions of devolution have gone on for decades, there is little concrete evidence that local and regional councils have obtained additional powers. During the past decade the government of the Northwest Territories has sent out conflicting messages. On the one hand it has suggested that local governments need to take on "prime public authority" over services such as sewage, sidewalks, and fire protection. But at the same time there has been no attempt by the government of the Northwest Territories to spell out a division of powers between it and the local councils. As a result, there has been no change in the status quo (DIAND, 1982b).

If Inuit do not see the territorial government as legitimate, how are they to become integrated into Canadian society? Even though the government of the Northwest Territories has achieved some autonomy from the federal government, Inuit do not see the territorial government as supporting local and regional needs. There is a feeling that, as its actions become more pervasive, Inuit groups will be overwhelmed and lose any power to make decisions in their best interest. Inuit feel that political legitimacy will come only after devolution, which will involve some self-government powers (Dickerson, 1993).

The Quest for Self-Government

Language and cultural differences between Inuit and other Canadians have led Inuit to feel that they will never be able to achieve cultural security unless they have their own government. The legacy of outside control is perhaps the single most important issue that Inuit are fighting against. While resistance to outsiders has not always been successful, Inuit have been remarkably resistant to assimilation. Today, as Sambo (1992) points out, there continues to be an unwavering determination to identify both self and community as indigenous, despite major social, economic, and political change.

Nunavut (Our Land)

The push for Nunavut began in the 1960s, when international demand for energy products, mining, and hydroelectric resources was sparked by a global crisis. Canadians and other major resource users felt that new, stable sources of these commodities would need to be found if they were to ensure their access to these products. The North held vast amounts of these potential resources, and there was a rush to exploit them. As well, the Cold War was in full operation at this time and the Arctic and its strategic military importance was noted.

By the 1970s, the *Alaska Native Claims Settlement Act* (1971) had been passed by Congress and set the framework for other settlements that would follow. The Act also demonstrated to Canadians that agreements could be made that would simultaneously address the concerns of government, private industry, and indigenous people, while allowing for the development of natural resources. The international Copenhagen Conference in 1971 was also influential in giving legitimacy to the claims of indigenous peoples. It should be noted that one year after the concept of Nunavut was first proposed in 1976, it was withdrawn because it was a concept that people in the Arctic couldn't understand. It didn't express the realities of Inuit life and culture (Gombay, 2000). Dahl (1997) argues that the Aboriginal populations of the North exhibit a communitarian nationalism rather than regional nationalism, and their form of nationalism is not aligned with the politics of Canada. She goes on to argue that regional identities are superimposed on a people where no such identity has traditionally existed. As such, Inuit had a difficult time in attempting to accommodate self-government through public government.

Another global event having an impact on the claims laid by Inuit was the Danish Parliament's agreement to grant Home Rule for Greenland (1979). This agreement is unique in modern settlements in that it was the first to provide for wide-ranging Aboriginal self-government. Moreover, this agreement made no provisions for monetary compensation, nor did it require the Aboriginal people to give up their ancestral indigenous rights. Inuit involvement in constitutional reform has been well recognized since they first appeared before a special committee of the Senate and the House of Commons. Later they would be afforded observer status at the first ministers' conference on the Constitution. The Inuit Committee on National Issues was created in 1979 and, until it disbanded in 1987, this committee developed national positions on constitutional reform for the Inuit.

Through their various organizations (e.g., Inuit Tapirisat of Canada, the Nunavut Constitutional Forum, and the Tungavik Federation of Nunavut) the Inuit have struggled to achieve Inuit rights and the establishment of Nunavut.[24] The Inuit had wanted to create a Nunavut Territory out of the eastern half of the Northwest Territories for many years. It was first proposed in 1976,[25] supported through a referendum in the Northwest Territories in 1982, and eventually came into existence under the *Nunavut Act* (1993). This Act ensures their cultural survival through control of a non-racially based democratic government.

After the James Bay Cree and Inuit had settled with the federal and Quebec governments regarding land, resources, and control, the Inuvialuit settlement became the centre of concern for government, industry, and Aboriginal people. As a result of such support the Inuit began drafting proposals for a split of the Northwest Territories. To deal with the issue, the federal and government created the Western Constitutional Forum and the Nunavut Constitutional Forum in order to discuss the issues with their respective constituents.

Fenge (1992) points out that the Inuit used every method available to them through the 1980s in order to achieve the creation of Nunavut. Distance between Eastern communities and Yellowknife (the current capital of the Northwest Territories) was a prime argument presented to justify the existence of Nunavut. Other issues, such as the lack of east–west air traffic compared to north–south, revealed that the realities of the North were divided into two separate entities. Minority rights and group rights were also cited as important factors in the need to create Nunavut. For Inuit, self-government does not mean independence or secession from Canada, but rather that communities have the right to govern their own affairs. The forums established were a particularly suitable method for facilitating claim negotiations: environmental and social impact assessments of oil and gas development in the Arctic; national constitutional discussions; and advocacy by the Nunavut Constitutional Forum, an Inuit-dominated organization established for the specific purpose of achieving Nunavut.

In 1983 the Nunavut Constitutional Forum presented a proposal for how the government of the new territory would operate. The 1983 document, *Building Nunavut,* was widely circulated among Inuit communities. By 1985 the revised version, *Building Nunavut: Today and Tomorrow,* was required reading for all Inuit. When the Iqaluit Agreement was signed two years later with the federal government, the principles within this document were agreed upon by both the Western and Nunavut Constitutional Forums. In 1987 the Western Constitutional Forum agreed on the splitting of the Northwest Territories. By 1990 an agreement in principle was signed between government and the Inuit, giving support to the creation of a division of the existing Northwest Territories.

In 1991 the federal government released a comprehensive package of proposals for the Arctic, called *Shaping Canada's Future Together.* Both the federal government and the Inuit (through the Inuit Tapirisat of Canada) conducted hearings across the country; the results of these consultations formed the Pangnirtung Accord, which was adopted unanimously by the Inuit Assembly on the Constitution. The Inuit outlined three of their major concerns in this Accord. They wanted recognition of the inherent right of self-government, equal participation in the constitutional reform process, and recognition of Inuit as a distinct society with cultural and language rights. The Inuit Tapirisat of Canada presented a brief to the Minister of Constitutional Affairs, entitled *Inuit in Canada: Striving for Equality,* which expanded upon the three fundamental objectives of the Pangnirtung Accord. In 1992 a non-binding vote was held, establishing a boundary line that would separate Nunavut from the remainder of the Northwest Territories. Fifty-four percent voted in favour of the proposal.

Nunavut was created out of the central and eastern part of the Northwest Territories (see Figure 10.3). This comprehensive claim settled a long-standing land claim covering 2 million square kilometres in the centre and eastern region of the Northwest Territories. The Nunavut Territory came into existence in 1999 (see Figure 10.4). The Agreement gives Inuit title to more than 350 000 square kilometres of land, including nearly 40 000 square kilometres for which they have sole mineral rights. Like other Indian treaties, the Inuit agree to cede, release, and surrender all their Aboriginal rights and claims to the land and water.[26] An estimated 21 000 people (80 percent are Inuit[27]) live in this region. They are governed by a type of territorial government, with the goal of eventually becoming a province. There are about 30 communities in the new territory, most of which are Inuit, with the exception of Nanisivik (a mining community). The size of these communities ranges from a population of 3000 (Iqaluit) to very small villages (see Table 10.2). The Inuit have title to 350 000 square kilometres and access to other lands. Land can not be sold except to the state. The agreement allows for land titles to be held in two forms: fee simple including mineral rights, or fee simple excluding mineral rights. Finally, access to and across Inuit-owned lands is granted only with the consent of Inuit.

Compensation of $1.14 billion is to be paid over 14 years. Additional royalties from natural resource development will be paid to Inuit, a sharing of royalties that the government receives from natural resource development on Crown land. Specifically, Inuit will annually receive 50 percent of the first $2 million of resource royalties received by gov-

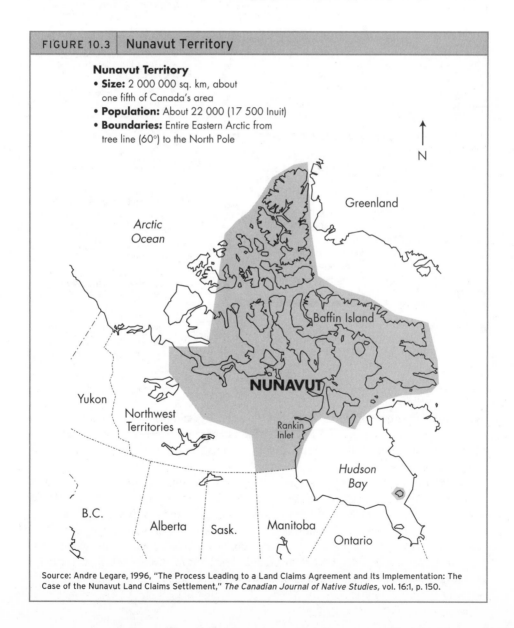

| FIGURE 10.3 | Nunavut Territory |

Nunavut Territory
- **Size:** 2 000 000 sq. km, about one fifth of Canada's area
- **Population:** About 22 000 (17 500 Inuit)
- **Boundaries:** Entire Eastern Arctic from tree line (60°) to the North Pole

Source: Andre Legare, 1996, "The Process Leading to a Land Claims Agreement and Its Implementation: The Case of the Nunavut Land Claims Settlement," *The Canadian Journal of Native Studies*, vol. 16:1, p. 150.

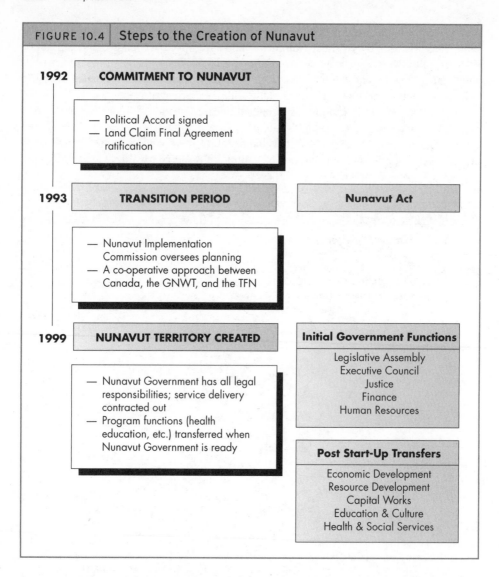

FIGURE 10.4 | Steps to the Creation of Nunavut

1992 COMMITMENT TO NUNAVUT

— Political Accord signed
— Land Claim Final Agreement ratification

1993 TRANSITION PERIOD   **Nunavut Act**

— Nunavut Implementation Commission oversees planning
— A co-operative approach between Canada, the GNWT, and the TFN

1999 NUNAVUT TERRITORY CREATED   **Initial Government Functions**

— Nunavut Government has all legal responsibilities; service delivery contracted out
— Program functions (health education, etc.) transferred when Nunavut Government is ready

Legislative Assembly
Executive Council
Justice
Finance
Human Resources

Post Start-Up Transfers

Economic Development
Resource Development
Capital Works
Education & Culture
Health & Social Services

ernment and 5 percent of additional resource royalties within the settlement area. In addition, a $13 million training trust fund has been established. There are also specific measures to increase Inuit employment within government in the Nunavut Settlement Area, and increased access to government contracts.

Nunavut will have three official languages: Inuktitut, English, and French. In anticipation of the split occurring, in mid-1990 the Inuit formed the Nunavut Wildlife Advisory Board in opposition to the existing territorial Wildlife Advisory Board. The Nunavut Tungavik Incorporation[28] will administer the land claim. This organization is responsible for making sure that the terms of the Nunavut Political Accord signed by the federal government are lived up to. Members of the organization meet in different Inuit villages to listen to the wishes of the people and to make decisions on implementing the content of the Nunavut Land Claims Agreement.

The Inuit also created a Nunavut Trust, an organization that receives the cash compensation under the land claims settlement. The Nunavut Agreement identifies five new institutions: a Nunavut Wildlife Management Board, a Nunavut Impact Review Board (which screens project proposals to determine whether there is a need for a review of environmental, social, or economic impacts), a Nunavut Planning Commission (which develops land use plans and monitors compliance with land use plans), a Nunavut Water Board, and a Surface Rights Tribunal. This last organization has jurisdiction across all of the Northwest Territories, whereas the others are limited to Nunavut. An advisory group called the Nunavut Implementation Commission was established to advise the government on the setting up of the government. Like Quebec, Nunavut is to be a "distinct" society, although it is structured so as to operate like any other province. Since 80 percent of the population are Inuit it is highly unlikely that the elected government would represent anything other than Inuit needs and goals. However, Nunavut does not hold title to any land or nonrenewable resources. The land is owned either by the Nunavut Tungavik Inc. or by the federal government.

Constitutionally, Nunavut has the same territorial powers afforded the Northwest Territories and Yukon. However, because of the Inuit majority, it is truly a form of self-government. As such, the Inuit will be in charge of education, health and social services, justice, and other social and economic programs. The legislative assembly (19 members) ran in the first election on a nonpartisan basis and operates in a consensus style.

As Legare (1996) points out, the dominant power structure in Nunavut is that of a coarchy (where all actors are in positions of power). However, he also notes that this mode is unstable and can be easily broken if a higher political status actor (policy maker) tries to impose its own solutions to Inuit demands. The question now remains as to whether or not Inuit can change the power structure to that of a stratarchy (where most, but not all, actors are in authority), which would allow them to take on positions of authority while other actors, e.g., transnational companies, have less power.

The realization of government in Nunavut has now been scaled back in terms of both funding and personnel. Ottawa reduced its financial commitment from $200 to $150 million for the creation of the new government. The new structure (called *Footprints 2*) has a smaller, more centralized, and less costly model of government than earlier planned. While the initial plan (*Footprints in New Snow*) called for 900 new jobs, it is now expected to have only 600, a majority being in the community of Iqaluit (the new capital of Nunavut). Nevertheless, the planned Nunavut government will have a premier, cabinet, legislature, and 10 ministries.

The Nunavut Agreement is not without its critics. Many believe that the Inuit gave away too much in return for the small amount of land, rights, and cash received. For example, the per capita cash payout is less than that received in the James Bay settlement. Others claim that there is no real power for the new territory. Still others feel that, since the Inuit owned all the land, they gave away much of what was really theirs to begin with. Moreover, there are many groups who opposed the creation of Nunavut. The Dene Nation vehemently opposed the proposed boundaries for Nunavut and called upon its members to vote against it. Likewise, Indians from Keewatin and the northern regions of Saskatchewan and Manitoba, as well as the Assembly of First Nations, were urged to vote against the proposal.

The issue of the western boundary between Nunavut and the remainder of the Northwest Territories has long been contentious. During the early years the Western and Nunavut Constitutional Forums, along with the Constitutional Alliance, met to negotiate the exact boundaries. Later, the Tungavik Federation of Nunavut and the Dene/Métis Joint

Negotiating Secretariat took over. After many years of negotiating, the two parties have not yet come to an agreement as to where the exact boundaries will be.

Residents of the Northwest Territories, and particularly those in the Mackenzie Valley, were given assurances that the federal government would provide additional funds to stabilize the level of services in the remainder of the Northwest Territories after the creation of Nunavut. Moreover, other residents of the Northwest Territories would not be asked to cover the cost of the establishment of Nunavut. A vote was taken over the boundary proposed by the proponents of Nunavut and passed (56–44 percent). The closeness of the vote reflects a divisiveness that stems from ethnic origin. Many Inuit communities voted 90 percent to accept the proposed split, while 90 percent of many Dene communities were against it.

Other critics argue that with 30 percent unemployment in the region, the Nunavut government will be unable to generate new jobs. Since most job creation activities are a result of the nonrenewable resources, negotiations will have to take place with major transnational corporations who have economic power. Inuit are well aware that one of their biggest challenges is to find a way out of the economic dependency that has become a debilitating legacy of colonial relations (Kulchynski, 1994). Moreover, critics argue, since most of the initial funding for the government is from the federal government, the Nunavut legislature will not have any autonomy.

RESISTANCE: CONFRONTATION AND POLITICAL ACTIONS

Inuit did not historically view themselves as a distinct ethnic group. It was only through contact with outsiders that a clear demarcation between "us" and "them" emerged. Mitchell (1996) claims that the birth of the pan-Inuit movement occurred with the development of co-ops. She goes on to argue that the 1980 co-op conference was referred to as the Pan-Arctic Conference, and that the relationship between Inuit and other Canadians was the central issue discussed. It was agreed by Inuit that co-ops would best serve their goal of achieving both economic and cultural independence.

Over the years Inuit have learned from other Aboriginal groups that ethnic organizations could become powerful tools in achieving community goals. The Inuit Tapirisat of Canada (created in 1971) grew out of a meeting of Inuit leaders in Coppermine, and has become the major organization speaking on behalf of Inuit in Canada. One of its first actions was to begin the preparation of what would become the 1976 proposal, *Nunavut*. The Labrador Inuit Association was established in 1973 as an affiliate member of the Inuit Tapirisat of Canada. In 1979 the latter created the Inuit Committee on National Issues, which was given sole responsibility to advance the Inuit case in constitutional negotiations. The Inuit Committee on National Issues has been active since the 1980s, when it formally stated that Canada had not respected Inuit nation status and had failed to recognize the constitutional status of Inuit people. Later, the Canadian Inuit would join forces with other international Inuit/Eskimo groups (Inuit Circumpolar Conference) and engage in political activities germane to the Arctic region. In 1992 the Inuit Circumpolar Conference asserted that Inuit are a distinct indigenous people that transcend existing political boundaries.

Mitchell (1996) argues that Inuit have used non-confrontational techniques in dealing with the dominant society. The total domination by the South did not mean that Inuit simply accepted each new value and artifact as it was introduced. Both passive and active resistance has been exhibited over time. Back to the land movements have been extensively used since the 1970s and have given Inuit the feeling of independence as well as lending credence to their traditional culture. Both elders and young Inuit have embraced this movement, which has also given legitimacy to the current land claims now being negotiated. Linked to this movement are the Inuit cultural associations that have sprung up over the past quarter-century. Language has been the focus of many of these associations, and is now viewed as an important indicator of cultural preservation. Other cultural associations (created in the 1970s) have taken on the larger task of revitalizing Inuit culture. For example, the Inuit Cultural Institute is obtaining knowledge from the elders in an attempt to preserve it as a basis for teaching new generations. The Inuit Tapirisat of Canada has created a Language Commission to standardize the two writing systems for Inuit: the roman orthography system developed by the Department of Indian and Northern Development and the syllabic system taught by the missionaries. Other organizations, such as the Torngasok Cultural Association in Labrador and the Avataq Cultural Institute (Northern Quebec), have similar objectives (Mitchell, 1996).

Other Inuit have taken on more direct confrontational strategies in dealing with social change. For example, in 1979 the Kitikmeot and Keewatin Inuit Association, along with other Aboriginal organizations, opposed the Polar Gas pipeline proposal. That same year the Inuit Tapirisat of Canada protested the International Whaling Commission's ban on beluga and narwhal hunting. More recently, the Quebec Inuit have presented a strong campaign for compensation for those Inuit who were forcibly relocated in the 1950s. However, on the whole, Inuit have not employed confrontational techniques. They have only reluctantly used them in an attempt to achieve their goals.

Inuit are using existing legitimate political organizations to express their concern about social change and the role that Southern Canadians play in the Arctic. Throughout the North, Inuit have supported members of their community in becoming elected as members of the Legislative Assembly of the Northwest Territories, as members of Parliament in Ottawa, or in their appointment to mainstream political bodies. Through participation in dominant, mainstream political organizations it is felt that Inuit can negotiate change and regulate intrusion by outsiders.

In the early 1970s Inuit from Alaska, Canada, and Greenland met in Copenhagen to discuss the "back to the land" movement. This unity movement was first tested in 1975 when the Alaska Eskimo were asked to support the Inuvialuit fight against the Canadian government's decision to allow offshore drilling in the Beaufort Sea. In 1977 Canadian Inuit joined forces with other Aboriginal peoples from Alaska, Greenland, and Russia. This pan-Eskimo movement has sponsored a yearly Inuit Circumpolar Conference at which issues common to all are discussed. In 1983 the Conference was accepted by the United Nations as a nongovernmental agency. It was also at this time that the Conference joined with the World Council of Indigenous Peoples, which established the Alaska Native Review Commission and which in turn hired Justice Thomas Berger as the commissioner. Its overall goal is to establish some control over the development of Arctic policy—e.g., natural resource, land, and environment. However, as Hamilton (1984) points out, this is not a radical movement that uses political rhetoric or public demonstrations but rather one that has carefully thought out the steps it will need to take if Inuit culture is to survive. Some have suggested that the Inuit's conciliatory stance is ineffective. Nevertheless, Inuit from around the world are now joining forces and developing linkages with other Aboriginal peoples who are realizing their mutual predicament.

The Inuit of today are caught in a complex web of institutional networks that hinders their attempts to overcome their marginality in Canadian society. First, they have been burdened with a history of exploitation and neglect. Second, the opportunities for economic development have not been extensive. Even marginal activities such as fur production have been devastated by European interest groups. Other forms of economic development—e.g., natural resource development—require large "up-front" and "sunk" capital that Inuit communities are unable to raise. Third, the ecology of the area makes it difficult for Inuit to develop cohesive organizational structures. Until recently, communication links were so tenuous that most Inuit communities acted in isolation. Fourth, the colonialization of the Arctic by Euro-Canadian Southerners has intruded into almost every institutional sphere of the Inuit.

The development of communication linkages among Inuit communities has provided the basis for organizational cohesion. Since television was introduced into the North in 1978 it has had both a positive and negative impact upon the culture of Inuit. It was not until 1982 that the Inuit Broadcasting Corporation aired its first program, and not until a decade later that it provided a dedicated channel. Its broadcasts are solely in Inuktitut and reach nearly 100 communities in the Northwest Territories, Yukon, Quebec, and Labrador.

Out of these linkages have come political and interest group organizations—e.g., the Inuit Tapirisat of Canada—which have provided the basis for political mobilization. As the organizations become more stable and influential, Inuit become better able to exert their sphere of influence upon the decisions that affect their lives. During the constitutional debate in 1992, Aboriginal people crashed the meeting at Harrington Lake. While the Inuit did not participate in this public display of confrontation, they did attempt to negotiate with other government (federal and provincial) officials to be included in the process.[29] Although the Inuit overwhelming supported the Charlottetown Accord, it was defeated in a national referendum.

Inuit of the North are facing the issue of modernity and identity like other colonialized areas. Inuit are slowly being incorporated into the contemporary mainstream society of Canada. As Dorais (1997) points out, this inclusion brought with it the economic, political, and cultural institutions developed by Western capitalist societies. In many respects, these values and organizations do not reflect Aboriginal values and attitudes. The forces of modernity, such as delinking space and time, are evident in Inuit communities, and the intrusion of individualism and specialization are seen in the behaviour of individuals as well as communities. These changes have brought about major changes in the way communities are organized, the way Inuit think about themselves, and the identity of the group. How Inuit will creatively deal with these forces and still remain Inuit is a major task set before them.

CONCLUSION

As the technocracy of the South invaded the Arctic, nothing was small or simple or readily apparent to the non-technical Inuit. Only experts from the South were capable of dealing with the large-scale public necessities. Within the Inuit communities, individual citizens were confronted by a bewildering bigness and complexity and had to defer on all matters to those who knew better. Indeed, it would have been a violation of Inuit reason to do otherwise. For years the technocracy of the Arctic grew without resistance, despite its failures. Moreover, those individuals working for the state did not see themselves as part of the political/industrial complex but rather as the conscientious managers of a social system that was inferior and needed to be replaced by a Southern social structure.[30] It has only been recently that this view of reality has come to be challenged by the Inuit.

From their earliest contacts, Canadians have defined Inuit as marginal both socially and economically. The federal government has relied upon its bureaucratic structure to develop strategies that would integrate Inuit into Canadian society. It promoted the Inuit traditional economy from the outset, believing that if Inuit were to remain in a relatively isolated condition it could avoid creating a dependent relationship and hence cost Canadian taxpayers less.

However, as the post-war period emerged, external events forced government officials to rethink this strategy. The new policy was to develop self-reliant Inuit who would become integrated into the capitalist mode of thought. Believing that the traditional economy could no longer support the Inuit, new settlements were created and smaller ones were expanded. As Tester and Kulchynski (1994) point out, bureaucrats wanted an infrastructure that would give Inuit a material security that had not been provided up to that time. In order to provide that security—e.g., housing, sanitation, and education, settlements had to be created that were accessible to Southern Canada. A new public service was sent to the North, which included teachers, social workers, and service officers. This new occupational layer was the force that would bring Inuit into the 20th century. In short, this new cadre of public employees was instrumental in ensuring that Inuit would begin to define the world in terms of economic or material logic rather than through their old perspective which emphasized kinship relations.

The creation of the urban settlement was crucial in implementing and carrying out such a strategy. Once Inuit were placed within a village context the new institutional structure would dominate their lives. They would be subjected to new forms of education, social welfare, justice, and economic relations that would totally encapsulate their existence.

Inuit are no longer nomadic hunters and gatherers, and their communal way of life, which balanced competition and cooperation, is no longer operable. Most of the subsistence activities carried out in the past are now in serious jeopardy. Even such mundane activities as the production of handicrafts are being challenged by their mass production in Southern Canada and elsewhere in the world. The production of furs through hunting and trapping has been curtailed by the lobbying forces of Europe. Only the industrial complex remains for Inuit to engage with. This process of incorporating capitalism, and the ideology that goes with it, is now unstoppable. As Mitchell (1996) points out, it is only belatedly and weakly that Inuit have resisted these forces.

As pointed out by many Northern researchers, subsistence activities by Inuit are no longer necessities of life. However, while not crucial to Inuit existence, they are considered important to them. Today the state, transnational corporations, Aboriginal organizations, and co-ops are the major employers of Inuit. The introduction of Southern educational practices has allowed young Inuit to be socialized into the dominant ideology and serves to neutralize their resistance to it. Yet Inuit remain uneducated and unskilled for the workforce. Under the present conditions they are of no use to industry (or very limited in demand). Handicraft is only one of a few marketable products emerging out of the North.[31] While collective hunting and distribution of goods remain, to some extent, an integral part of the Inuit community, Inuit sharing practices have broken down with the introduction of cash into the economy. Moreover, welfare and other state-sponsored programs have also weakened the old "sharing" traditions. Mitchell (1996) claims that the notion of private property and individualism is now an entrenched value within Inuit culture.

Through land settlements and mega-agreements with the federal government, Inuit are creating new capitalist, industrial organizations. These corporations have created a cash economy, become major employers in the region, and are taking on more political persuasion. Nevertheless, these new economic organizations are part of the larger transnational structure and must try to fit into a global network. Even though some linkages exist among Inuit organizations, external transnational organizations dominate these and set their agenda (Freeman, 1985).

The question remains as to how Inuit can become more self-sufficient and sustainable. How can they engage in productive activities within the North, using Northern capital and spending that capital in the North? Some Inuit organizations have chosen to forge alliances with existing external transnational companies—for example, through joint ventures. Unfortunately, on the basis of previous experience, the Inuit development corporations will allow only a few Inuit to become wealthy while the remainder take on wage jobs. Already there has been the creation of an indigenous ruling class that is convinced of the positive value of integration into Southern industrial forces. These individuals have taken on active and powerful roles within the Northwest Territories government. By involving these leaders in state politics, government has been able to control both the Inuit leaders and their constituents. Since most Inuit organizations and communication structures are funded by the federal government they must rely almost totally upon their support.

Southern Canadians, now seeing the influence of pan-Inuit groups, have become worried about the Inuit's potential power. For example, the sweeping powers that Inuit may wield over natural resource development mean that an ethnic–regional group of less than 50 000 people could control oil and gas development regardless of the needs of the 30 million-plus Southern Canadians. Some Canadians believe that Inuit have overstepped their boundaries of influence.

Inuit of today are well aware that they need an advanced education and social skills in order to integrate into the larger society while retaining their important cultural attributes. They also realize that if they are to survive as a people they will need to engage in more proactive strategies than they have utilized in the past. This means that more Inuit will need to become key players in the ongoing institutional structures of Arctic Canada. More Inuit will need to obtain the skills necessary to become community leaders and effectively network within the national and international sphere of power brokering. The early attempts by Inuit to adopt Western ways in the settlements were unsuccessful, and they became marginal people. Now they are trying to reverse this continuing trend of marginalization and exclusion. Their efforts have focused on self-government initiatives, promotion of Inuit culture, and the encouragement of sustainable development (Kuptana, 1992).

NOTES

1. Inuit experiences with non-Inuit are different from those of Indians in Canada. For example, Inuit do not fall under the jurisdiction of Section 91(24) of the *Constitution Act, 1982* and thus are not considered, legally, as Indians. This means that the *Indian Act* is not applicable to Inuit.

2. The Government of the Northwest Territories stopped using disc numbers in 1971 and substituted arbitrary surnames for them. This is now being resisted by Inuit.

3. After a time, the Hudson's Bay Company would be asked to act as a private agent for the government of Canada.

4. This group was also given the mandate to provide an education to Inuit.

5. The criteria for establishing sovereignty have changed over time. In the beginning, discovery or the issuance of Papal Bulls was considered sufficient for establishing sovereignty. However, by the 20th century, new criteria emerged.

6. The federal government has steadfastly argued that the relocation of Inuit was carried out on a humanitarian basis and was not intended to establish sovereignty. In fact, three separate reports have been commissioned by the federal government to address this issue. However, the work of Tester and Kulchynski (1994) throws considerable doubt on this argument. In the mid-1990s, after a decade-long campaign to force the federal government to accept its responsibility, 17 Inuit families finally reached a $10 million settlement.

7. Keeping Inuit "on the land" would not only reduce the financial commitment of the federal government but would also demonstrate Canada's sovereignty over the vast Arctic.

8. The statistics presented here are from the 1991 *Aboriginal Peoples Survey: Schooling, Work and Related Activities, Income, Expenses and Mobility; 1-Disability, 2-Housing; Language, Tradition, Health, Lifestyle and Social Issues;* and *Profile of Canada's Aboriginal Population.*

9. The overall participation rate in the labour force for Inuit was 57.2 percent in 1991, with an official unemployment rate of 25 percent.

10. Nearly one-fourth of the adult population reported having received social assistance during the past year.

11. Census Canada found that 76.3 percent of total income of Inuit was from employment, 21.6 percent from government transfers, and 2.1 percent from other sources.

12. In 1991 over half the dwellings required regular maintenance. One-quarter required minor repairs, while one-fifth of the current dwellings required major repairs.

13. If Inuit adults aged 50+ were included we would find that a majority of these individuals have no schooling or less than six years.

14. There are many different dialects spoken in the Arctic (Dorais, 1992).

15. About 2 percent of the adult population also reported being able to speak Cree and/or Montagnais–Naskapi.

16. The lack of a ground transportation infrastructure also influenced this decision.

17. The data show that in 1991, 87 percent of Inuit reported that they bought food to eat at home (excluding take-out). Forty percent claimed to have bought food from a restaurant or take-out.

18. Some dividends have been paid to elders in order to ensure that older Inuit will receive some short-term benefits from the Agreement.

19. This was the installation of a series of radar stations in the Arctic every four to five hundred kilometres, moving from the east to the west coast of Canada.

20. Treaty No. 11 is an exception and encompasses the Mackenzie Valley in the Northwest Territories. However, the terms of this treaty regarding land have never been implemented by the federal government.

21. The recent debate on Quebec secession has also produced tension between Inuit and Quebecers. In the 1996 referendum, Inuit were outspoken advocates of federalism and were almost unanimous in rejecting secession from Canada.

22. The Inuvialuit are descendants of Alaskan Eskimos. They live in the Western Arctic.

23. There is a belief by some government authorities that a more centralized system of constitutional authority is cheaper and more effective than a decentralized one (Government of Northwest Territories, 1990).

24. Pauktuutit (an Inuit women's association) clearly identified differences between Inuit and Qallunaat (persons with white faces) with regard to the use and priority placed upon formal institutions of government and written law (Moss, 1995).

25. It was actually the third version ("Political Development in Nunavut"), proposed by the Inuit Tapirisat in 1979, which became the starting point for an agreement in principle.

26. This agreement fully protects any Aboriginal or treaty right of adjacent Native groups who use lands in Nunavut. There are also special provisions that assure that their hunting and land use rights can continue in areas where their interests overlap the settlement area.

27. To be enrolled as an Inuit and benefit from the Agreement, a person must be recognized as an Inuk under Inuit custom or Inuit law, and be associated with a community or the Nunavut Settlement Area. One must also be a Canadian citizen and benefit in only one Canadian land claim agreement.

28. This organization succeeded the Tungavik Federation of Nunavut as the stakeholder representing the interests of the Inuit people of Nunavut.

29. The role Inuit played in this public demonstration was relegated to that of the Assembly of First Nations. It has been suggested that the role of Inuit was downplayed because the three chief negotiators for the Inuit were women.

30. Individual bureaucrats placed in the North had (and continue to have) very high turnover rates, and as a result their capacity for a longitudinal perspective on issues is limited.

31. A considerable amount of natural resources are exported from the North, but few Inuit participate in these extractive industries and few Inuit directly benefit from the few industrial activities currently in operation in the Arctic.

WEBLINKS

arcticcircle.uconn.edu

The Arctic Circle project examines Northern Aboriginal peoples in a number of Arctic Circle countries. The project's site includes excellent information about Canada's Inuit and Cree peoples.

npc.nunavut.ca/eng/index.html

The Nunavut Planning Commission website includes an overview of the Nunavut land claim, discussion of the territory's government and political structure, and more.

www.stats.gov.nu.ca

This Government of Nunavut website offers statistical information relating to the people of the Baffin, Keewatin, and Kitikmeot regions. Subject areas include Health, Economy, Justice, Education, Income, and Demography.

chapter eleven

Voices and Partners: Aboriginal Organizations in Canada

INTRODUCTION

The representation of indigenous knowledge as well as an indigenous worldview has come about through the efforts of Aboriginal organizations of many types. They have produced an awareness of the needs of Aboriginal people, including their need to be respected members of our society. The Aboriginal "movement," then, has had both a political and social impact on Canadian society. Aboriginal organizations have also instigated and supported legal challenges that have resolved conflicts and provided new opportunities for Aboriginal people. Many times they have been the centre of controversy in either the legal or the political field. Unfortunately, little has been written about these organizations and the role they have played in the development of Canada. In the 19th century several efforts were made by Aboriginal people to create regional and national political organizations. The demise of many of these organizations was generally the result of suppression by the federal government and of the internal discord among the Natives themselves that was created by government. These problems continued to plague Aboriginal political groups well into the 20th century. For example, the *Indian Act, 1927* prohibited the political organization of Aboriginal people beyond local levels of government (Whiteside, 1973b).

The short-lived and ineffectual structure of Aboriginal organizations has been the result of mistakes made by Aboriginal leadership, outside interference, and the inappropriateness of certain social structures within a larger social system. For example, the burgeoning number of Aboriginal organizations, all representing a myriad of goals and objectives, has prevented Aboriginal people from pursuing a cohesive and integrated set of objectives. Different tribal and linguistic groups have limited cohesive strategies from emerging.

The nature of the goals that the various organizations have set has also been problematic for Aboriginal people. Some groups have tried to pursue local objectives, while others have focused more on regional or national matters. Their goals have been political, social, religious, or economic, and this diffusion of focus has led to divisions among those pursuing the goals.

Early Aboriginal organizations were generally tied to specific concerns, such as particular land claims. These organizations had a single focus, were relatively simple in structure, and were limited to a particular area or group of Aboriginal people. Only since the mid-1950s have Aboriginal organizations become multifaceted, complex in structure, and representative of Aboriginal people from all across Canada (Patterson, 1972).

HISTORY OF ABORIGINAL ORGANIZATIONS

It has been suggested that the first Indian Association was established in about 1540, when the League of Iroquois was formed (Daugherty, 1982). This confederacy, composed of five Indian groups (Seneca, Mohawk, Onondaga, Oneida, and Cayuga), had a governing council to decide on important issues that affected all the tribes. In addition, the council acted as an arbitrator for inter-tribal disputes. This organization did not, however, deal with intra-tribal affairs, leaving each tribe to deal with its own internal affairs.

With the emergence of the fur trade the League began to exert its influence beyond the confines of the Five Nations. Their strategic location, relative political cohesion, and alliance with the Dutch and English permitted them to both influence the activities of the fur trade (Daugherty, 1982) and act as middlemen in that trade. This action led to a series of wars with the French and eventually caused the League to sign a treaty of neutrality with the French in 1701. This policy set the stage for relations between the Iroquois and the English after 1760. Furthermore, the League lost its key position as middleman in the fur trade. The encroachment of colonists and the success of the American Revolution brought about the final demise of the League.

In the late 1700s Joseph Brant (a Mohawk) tried to create a united Indian confederacy, but with little success. This interest was renewed by Tecumseh (a Shawnee), who also tried to organize the Indians of the Northwest into a united Indian Confederacy. In the early 1800s, however, his plan ended in his death. During the next 75 years various Indian leaders tried to unite Indians in an attempt to stop the westward and northward expansion of European civilization. Although great Indian leaders such as Crowfoot, Piapot, Peguis, and Big Bear made serious attempts to develop various organizational structures that would be effective in safeguarding Aboriginal interests, all of them were unsuccessful.

It was not until 1870 that the first Indian political organization in Canada was formed—the Grand General Indian Council of Ontario and Quebec. It was formed by both Iroquois and Ojibwa. Their major concern was with the government's implementation of Indian policy. A competing organization (League of Indians) was established in the late 19th century. The Council, faced with competition from the League coupled with a lack of operating funds, was forced to disband (Whiteside, 1980).

The League was based in the East, although its leaders thought of it as a national organization concerned with Indian rights. After several conferences, the League of Indians in Western Canada emerged, never to unite with its Eastern counterpart. This League split in 1933, and two branches (Alberta and Saskatchewan) were created. The Alberta branch renamed itself the Indian Association of Alberta in 1939, and remains active in political causes today. While other organizations such as the Catholic Indian League (1962) and the Calgary Urban Treaty Indian Alliance (1972) have existed in Alberta, they have been very narrowly focused and short-lived.

The Saskatchewan branch phased itself out in 1942, but in 1946 two new provincial organizations (the Protective Association for Indians and the Union of Saskatchewan Indians) united to form the Union of Saskatchewan Indians. By the late 1950s this group had changed its name to the Federation of Saskatchewan Indians. The Federation has taken an active role in promoting the social, political, and economic goals of both registered and non-registered Indians in Saskatchewan. More recently, the Saskatchewan Native Alliance (1970) was formed, and continues to be active today.

In British Columbia, the Nisga'a Indians formed the Nisga'a Land Committee in the latter part of the 19th century. This organization was the genesis of their concern with land claims, in particular the claim that would culminate with the 1973 Supreme Court decision and the subsequent development of the government's land claims policy. By 1915 a supporting organization, the Allied Tribes of British Columbia, was created to lobby for land claims. It was short-lived, and by the 1920s it had been dismantled. In 1931 the Native Brotherhood of British Columbia began and later amalgamated with the Pacific Coast Native Fishermen's Association, which gave it a broader base of both northern and southern coastal Indians. The Brotherhood, still in existence, did not focus on land claims; rather it was more concerned about social and economic issues.[1]

The members of the Brotherhood were all Protestants; in 1943, a rival Catholic organization, the North American Indian Brotherhood, was also established in British Columbia. Although the two groups did not clash overtly, ill feeling and discord between them prevented either from accomplishing much. The government seized on the contradictions between the two groups and used them as an excuse to ignore all the requests from both of them.

By the 1940s Indians from Eastern and Western Canada formed a new national organization, the Canadian Indian Brotherhood (later to be renamed the North American Indian Brotherhood). This organization had no religious bias and consisted solely of non-treaty Indians. In 1946 the Brotherhood attempted to form a coalition with treaty Indians from Saskatchewan. This proved fruitless, partly because of interference by Saskatchewan's CCF government. The NAIB remained active in national political affairs until it was phased out of existence in 1969. Aboriginal organizations in Manitoba did not emerge until the late 1940s when the Manitoba Indian Brotherhood was formed. Since then, the MIB has been disbanded and a new organization (the Four Nations Confederacy) has been formed. Attempts to merge status and non-status organizations have, at times, been successful. Nevertheless, a definite division continues to persist throughout Canada among non-treaty Indians, treaty Indians, and Métis.

In 1944, attempts were made to establish the North American Indian Brotherhood. The rather loose structure of this organization collapsed in 1950 due to internal discord. In 1954 the National Indian Council was formed, and in 1961 it became the official organization for both status and non-status Indians. By 1968 the NIC had split into two organizations: the National Indian Brotherhood for status Indians, and the Canadian Métis Society for non-status Natives. In 1970 the Métis Society became the Native Council of Canada. Also in 1970 the National Indian Council, composed of middle-class, urban Indians, formally dissolved; this was because of conflicts among its registered, non-registered, and Métis members.

Organizations in Eastern Canada, particularly since 1960, have not been as vociferous or as organized as their Western counterparts, but they do have a long history. In 1840 missionaries helped the Ojibwa of Ontario to form the General Council of the Ojibwa Nations of Indians; in 1846 this was renamed the General Council of Indian Chiefs. Although the Council originally included only Christians, in 1882 it expanded its base and became the General Council of Ontario. This organization lasted until 1938 and was the beginning of the present Union of Ontario Indians.

The Union of Ontario Indians was formed in 1946 and still actively concerns itself with contemporary Indian issues. Although Quebec's Indians are today without a major provincial organization, the Indians of Quebec Association was active during the 1960s and 1970s. Finally, in the Maritime provinces few Aboriginal organizations have been formed. While the Grand General Indian Council was active for a few years in the early 1940s, it would not be until 1967 that the Union of New Brunswick Indians was formed. It deals with Indians in both New Brunswick and Prince Edward Island. In 1969 the Union of Nova Scotia Indians was also formed (IRIW, 1978).

Even though more than a quarter of the Indians in Canada live in Ontario, they have not seriously attempted to link up with other provincial or national Aboriginal organizations. The independence and aggressiveness of the Iroquois on the Six Nations Reserve have given them a unique position among Indians in Canada.[2] This group was one of the first to develop agricultural practices and to establish semi-permanent villages. They were also advanced in their political structures, in that they developed powerful confederacies that had an impact on the region. This group became an important link in the trading networks that developed throughout the region. The pivotal role they have played historically has led them to preserve their traditions and culture, and this has placed them in direct conflict with the federal government. They have resisted the implementation of many policies of the government and have refused to be guided by the *Indian Act*. Other Aboriginal people, for example Métis in Eastern Canada, including those in Quebec, are considered non-Indians; as such, they are only nominally recognized by federal and provincial governments.

The emergence of a number of Indian organizations since the late 1960s reflects the impact of two events. First was the ill-fated federal White Paper on Aboriginal Policy in 1969. This policy statement evoked a strong response from Aboriginal people all over the country and acted as a catalyst for Aboriginal cooperation. It also allowed Indians to identify a clear-cut (at least from their perspective) event which plainly marked the federal government as the enemy. Secondly, changes in funding meant that Aboriginal organizations were eligible for federal funds, and these funds could come from sources other than DIAND. One example of the impact of the White Paper was the creation of the Association of Iroquois and Allied Indians to represent various bands when dealing with different levels of government (Daugherty, 1982). The Union of B.C. Indian Chiefs was also formed during this time (1969) as a result of the fusion of the Indian Homemakers Association of B.C., the Southern Vancouver Island Tribal Federation, and the North American Indian Brotherhood.

Many other Aboriginal organizations have been created or changed over the past century. The Council of Yukon Indians is the result of a merger between the Yukon Native Brotherhood (representing status Indians) and the Yukon Association of Non-Status Indians. Others have undergone some changes in structure; for example, the Indian Brotherhood of the Northwest Territories has emerged as the Dene Nation. Finally, more locally or regionally based Aboriginal organizations have developed because of their dealings with various levels of government—for example, Grand Council Treaty No. 9 and Grand Council Treaty No. 3.

The Métis have also seen a proliferation of organizations. While the first Métis political organization was established in 1937 (Métis of Saskatchewan), until the 1960s it was the only provincial Métis organization. Then, in rapid succession, Métis associations were formed in Alberta, Manitoba, and British Columbia; the National Canadian Métis Society also emerged. Métis were then represented at both the provincial and federal levels. In 1970 the Métis of the western provinces met and formed a new organization—the Native Council of Canada. Its goal is to promote Aboriginal rights, land claims, and various social and economic policies. The Native Council of Canada represents a wide spectrum of Aboriginal people, including some status Indians, Eastern Canadian Métis, and Aboriginal people without status under the *Indian Act.* The Council claims to represent 1.2 million Aboriginal people, while the federal government estimates the number to be about 100 000. Even though the Council has a diverse constituency and does not have a legal basis such as the *Indian Act,* the federal government has agreed to recognize it as a lobbying group, and even provided it with a seat at the first ministers' conference in 1982. The Métis National Council, a new organization that split from the Native Council of Canada,, was established in 1983, just before the first round of constitutional talks. Members of this new group felt that the Native Council of Canada did not reflect Métis aspirations for land and self-government.

After the split, the Native Council of Canada restyled itself the Congress of Aboriginal Peoples. Today the Métis National Council claims to represent only members of the Métis Nation. On the other hand, the Congress of Aboriginal Peoples represents anyone who claims "Métis status," including non-status Indians. The National Council has provincial affiliates in the three prairie provinces, although both organizations have provincial political affiliates in B.C. and Ontario. However, only the Congress has members who call themselves Métis in all the regions of Canada (Chartrand and Giokas, 2002). Today, we find that the Congress does not try to define the Métis people but rather views "Métis" as comprising a number of different groups and individuals. On the other hand, the National Council has tackled the definition of "Métis" and has clearly articulated its definition. Its membership consists of regional and provincial political representative organizations, not of Métis individuals. It includes organizations from across the country although the specific organizations may change over time. This shifting membership of the National Council demonstrates the dynamic character of many Aboriginal organizations.

The more than 50 000 Inuit have also become politically involved during the past two decades. The national organization, the Inuit Tapirisat of Canada, was created in 1970. Its first headquarters were in Edmonton, but by 1972 the organization had been reestablished in Ottawa. Its original goal was to preserve and promote Inuit culture as well as to negotiate land claims. But over the years it became evident that one single organization could not represent the diversity of Inuit. For this reason, six regional organizations have emerged: the Committee on Original Peoples Entitlement, or COPE (the Western Arctic); the Kitikmeot Inuit Association (the Central Arctic); the Keewatin Inuit Association (the Eastern Arctic); the Baffin Regional Association (Baffin Island); the Makivik Corporation (Quebec); and the Labrador Inuit Association. The Tungavik Federation of Nunavut, an umbrella organization, was created to represent the Inuit organizations east of the Mackenzie Delta. It has been through the TFN that the issue of Inuit land claims has been discussed.

COPE had its beginnings in the 1960s, when the political awareness of Aboriginal people was raised. Their political consciousness was first piqued in the late 1950s, when a group of Inuit whalers in the Tuktoyaktuk area arrived at an inland lake only to find all the fish dead from pollutants. Their resolve to establish local control came to fruition when, a decade later, COPE was officially formed (Frideres, 1974).

The Northern Quebec Inuit Association (NQIA) was also formed to deal with both local and national issues. The Association established two headquarters—one in Fort Chimo, the other in Montreal. Finally, the splinter Inuit group, Tungavinga Nunamimi, emerged in response to the James Bay Settlement set forth by the NQIA; as a result of their refusal to ratify the agreement, three settlements near Povungnituk created their own organization.

During the 1960s the concern for equal and just distribution of political power, national income, and collective socio-economic provisions grew (Delmar, 1986; Jamieson, 1979). Despite legal and political changes that supported the ideology of equality, inequality between men and women in society remained. The second international women's movement after the mid-1960s, therefore, focused on changing norms, values, and attitudes as they pertain to women's positions in society (Mitchell, 1986; Steinem, 1983). The movement not only provided new opportunities for women, but also redefined political issues, making them more pertinent to women in Canadian society (Smith et al., 1985). The women's movement had a significant impact on the awareness of Aboriginal women as well, and to a certain degree on the establishment of the Native Women's Association of Canada. It shaped a climate in which Aboriginal women could voice concerns and make them relevant to others (Fleming-Mathur, 1971; Krosenbrink-Gelissen, 1984). The emergence of an Aboriginal women's movement in Canada during the 1960s had been largely unnoticed by non-Aboriginal people, as well as by Aboriginal men (Bonney, 1976; Jamieson, 1979).

Prior to the creation of contemporary Aboriginal associations there were many tribal organizations. These were closely tied to the religious and cultural components of tribal life and were directed inward, toward members of the group, rather than outward toward society as a whole. Few tribal organizations presently exist, and their role for Aboriginal people is more symbolic than instrumental; however, in some areas there has been a resurgence of tribal groups, as in the case of pow-wows (Beaver, 1979).

Membership in the Aboriginal political organizations today has generally been determined by ascription: one is born into an organization, rather than choosing to join it. Legal factors also often determine membership; for example, membership in the National Indian Brotherhood was restricted to registered Indians. Table 11.1 illustrates the number of Aboriginal political associations that have been active since 1700. As the table shows, the total number of organizations has recently increased considerably although many fewer still exist. In a recent study, Newhouse (2003) found approximately 600 Aboriginal organizations in Canada at the end of the 20th century. Half were small for-profit organizations while the other half were not-for-profit organizations mostly located in urban areas. In 2004, there were an estimated 20 000 Aboriginal businesses focusing on economic developments in a number of areas. In a recent study of Western Canada, there were over 300 non-business Aboriginal organizations found in six Western Canadian cities, ranging from education to child care to cultural support (Newhouse, 2003).

Table 11.2 illustrates the primary function of a number of voluntary associations active at some point between 1800 and 1999. Many of these organizations emerged in crisis situations to serve a specific need at a specific time; hence, many of them have been very short-lived. However, in addition to solving a specific problem, other Aboriginal organizations have expanded their roles. For example, in urban centres, many of these organizations offer relief from the frustrations felt by Aboriginal people who have recently left the reserve. Aboriginal people with similar backgrounds, values, and experiences can meet to discuss ways of adapting to urban life and to find solutions to specific individual problems (Canada, 1988).

TABLE 11.1 — Major Aboriginal Political Voluntary Associations in Canada, by Date of Formation

	Prior to 1799	1800-99	1900-19	1920-29	1930-39	1940-49	1950-59	1960-69	1970-73	1974-80	1981-91	1992-97	TOTAL
National	2		1		2	1	1	4	5	2	2	0	20
Regional		2	1	4	1	1		1	1	4	3	2	20
National-Regional Total	2	2	2	4	3	2	1	5	6	6	5	2	40
Nfld.-Labrador								1	2	1	1	1	6
P.E.I.										1			1
New Brunswick								1	3	2	1	2	9
Nova Scotia						1		2	2	2	2	2	11
Quebec		1	1	2		1		3	5		3	1	17
Ontario		1	1	2		2	1	6	7	3	2	1	26
Manitoba					1		1	2	6	2	1	2	15
Saskatchewan				1	1	5	2	1	4	3	2	1	20
Alberta		1		1	2	1	1	4	3	3	3	3	22
B.C.		1	3	1	3	1	4	8	3	4	1	2	31
N.W.T.					1	1		3	3	4	1	3	15
Yukon								2	3	1	1	1	8
Provincial Total		4	5	7	7	12	9	33	41	26	18	21	183
Grand Total	4	8	9	15	13	16	11	43	54	38	28	23	262

Source: Don Whiteside, *Historical Development of Aboriginal Political Associations in Canada* (Ottawa: National Indian Brotherhood, 1973), 6. Additional data has been collected by the author since 1973.

TABLE 11.2	Reasons for the Formation of Aboriginal Canadian Associations by Time Periods							
	Specific: Treaty Rights, Land Rights, Social Issues		General Administrative Policies		Other General Protests		Total	
Year	No.	%	No.	%	No.	%	No.	%
I prior to 1849	4	100	–	–	–	–	4	100
II 1850-1939	10	31	19	59	3	9	32	100
III 1940-1965	4	14	18	62	7	24	29	100
IV 1966-1980	38	32	36	30	46	38	120	100
V 1981-1990	10	35	5	18	12	47	28	100
VI 1991-2000	12	34	6	8	17	58	35	100
Total	78	31	84	34	82	35	248	100

Note: For purposes of this analysis, all national, regional, and provincial associations were counted together. As a result, one could argue that nine "extra" provincial associations are included in the table (six in "specific protests," two in "administrative policies," and one in "general protests"). No cell, however, is changed by more than 3 percent because of the inclusion of associations that might be considered as "extras."

Source: Don Whiteside, *Historical Development of Aboriginal Political Associations in Canada* (Ottawa: National Indian Brotherhood, 1973), 10. Additional data has been collected by the author since 1973.

The contemporary organization structure has largely resulted from increased urbanization. Although the organizations function within an urban context, their members are generally rural in orientation and are concerned with rural issues. At present, there are few organizations run by Aboriginal people to address urban issues, e.g., Friendship Centres. Today's organizations are imbued with a sense of cultural nationalism, or what Smith (1981) calls "ethnic revival." The genesis of this lies in the emergence of Aboriginal intellectuals graduating from non-Aboriginal schools. These individuals were equipped to research and piece together an account of the past several centuries as seen from an Aboriginal perspective. And they were able to promote the historical legacy they discovered. This was reinforced when the National Indian Brotherhood reorganized itself under the rubric of the Assembly of First Nations. In addition, in their efforts to achieve their goals, Aboriginal organizations are beginning to use new tactics, such as confrontation, protest, demonstrations, and lobbying. As Tanner (1983) points out, Aboriginal people are also being taken seriously because they are (1) viewed as a threat to national security, and (2) now able to hire lawyers who have an expertise in Canadian law as it pertains to Aboriginal rights. Finally, the new tactics being employed have generated a great deal of publicity—Aboriginal issues now receive media attention and have entered everyday discourse. The result has been some additional pressure brought to bear on government officials to make some concessions (Gibbins, 1986a).

ABORIGINAL ORGANIZATIONAL STRUCTURE: A TYPOLOGY

There are three broad categories of Aboriginal organizations: band, local, and pan-Native. These three categories have been used to classify Aboriginal constituencies. For example, band organizations, which deal with the federal government, are based on historical precedents and have their authority vested in the *Indian Act*. Relations between Aboriginal people and government at this level are formal and regulated by the terms and conditions outlined in federal statutes. Local and pan-Aboriginal organizations, in contrast, have no statutory basis for their dealings with the government. Nevertheless, these two types of organizations have had extensive dealings with both government and non-government agencies over the years.

In a broad sense, the goals of these various Aboriginal organizations are similar. However, the individual groups pursue goals widely ranging from specific services to treaty rights to achieving changes in federal Indian policy. In the 1960s two events occurred simultaneously that had a tremendous effect on Aboriginal organizations. First, new programs were introduced into the reserves, which also brought substantial funds to an otherwise poor constituency. Second the urbanization of Indians meant that for the first time a large number of Aboriginal people would not be effectively served by a band organization. This meant that urban Aboriginal people had to develop their own organizations. However, neither the band nor the local organizations were able to achieve all their goals acting independently of one another, and this situation led to the emergence of pan-Aboriginal organizations.

The original Aboriginal urban organizations focused on economic and social welfare goals. The central goal of these organizations was to change Aboriginal–non-Aboriginal relations to accommodate urban Aboriginal communities and their interests (Cornell, 1988). The increase in the number of Aboriginal persons entering the urban areas resulted in a proliferation of organizations, reflecting the varied goals and objectives of each group. After a time of working at cross purposes, some of the organizations began to carry out cooperative efforts. After several successful ventures, new pan-Aboriginal organizations began to emerge. More recently, the pan-Aboriginal organizations have attempted to reduce federal control and increase their own control over band and tribal affairs (Aggamaway-Pierre, 1983).

Cornell (1988) has developed a typology of Aboriginal organizations that is based upon goals. The first distinction he makes is between reformative and transformative goals. A "reformative" organization focuses its efforts on changing the role of Aboriginal people without changing the structure of Aboriginal/non-Aboriginal relations. This approach is based on a belief that there must be a redistribution of social power/rewards to allow Aboriginal people their share, and that this can take place within the existing system. For example, they feel that more Aboriginal people should be hired by Indian Affairs, that more Aboriginal people should be in senior management positions, and that social services on the reserves need to be expanded. In summary, these organizations accept and endorse the existing structure of Canadian society and feel that only some changes are needed to make the existing system work better.

"Transformative" organizations agree that a redistribution of rewards and power needs to be undertaken, but not within the existing social structure. They feel that a fundamental change is required—for example, phasing out Indian Affairs, allowing Aboriginal people to establish their own legal system, reopening treaties. In summary, their goal is to change the existing structures that impinge upon Aboriginal people (Grand Council, 1998).

The second distinction Cornell makes among Aboriginal organizations is the degree to which each is integrative or segregative. This distinction reflects the degree of acceptance or rejection of dominant institutions. Organizations with an integrative perspective accept the appropriateness of the dominant culture and thus promote the dominant institutions as the way of maximizing Aboriginal interests. As a result of their general acceptance of the dominant institutions, they also believe that Aboriginal communities should be built on this model.

On the other hand, Aboriginal organizations with a segregative ideology argue against accepting the dominant institutional structure as a role model. These organizations promote goals and objectives that are fundamentally anti-assimilationist. This dichotomy is portrayed in Figure 11.1. When the two sets of distinctions are juxtaposed, we find that four basic types of Aboriginal organizations operate.

In Category 1 we find those Aboriginal organizations whose goals both accept the status quo (with some minor changes) and attempt to integrate into the dominant culture. Category 2 organizations attempt to fundamentally change existing Aboriginal/non-Aboriginal relations so that integration into the larger society can occur. Organizations in Category 3, while accepting current Aboriginal/non-Aboriginal relations, feel that Aboriginal people must develop their own institutions and culture. Category 4 represents those organizations that reject current Aboriginal/non-Aboriginal relations as well as the dominant institutional structure. Conflict is generally precipitated when organizations in this final category attempt to pursue their goals. Each of the four types of organization has had a substantial impact on Aboriginal/non-Aboriginal relations since the 1960s.

Reform-Integrate

Historically, organizations such as the National Indian Council and the Canadian Métis Society focused on helping Aboriginal people assimilate into the dominant society. More recently, friendship centres in large urban areas attempt to facilitate the adaptation and integrate Aboriginal people moving from reserves. Their goal is to integrate Aboriginal people into the dominant society with a minimum of stress. Friendship centres are designed to act both as drop-in centres and as counselling centres. Ideally, Aboriginal people who come to the city can use the facilities to help them adapt to urban life. However, a number of problems have plagued the centres since their formation. The federal government funds the centres only on a short-term, year-to-year basis; this prevents long-term planning and development. In addition, the amount of funding is not enough to allow the centres to play their role effectively and ease the process of urban adaptation (Minore and Hill, 1997).

Today the Métis Associations have taken a "reform-integrative" approach in that their goal is to right historical wrongs (through settling land claims), but once this has occurred, they are prepared to accept the basic structure of Canadian society (Daniels, 1981;

FIGURE 11.1	Types of Aboriginal Organizations		
		Aboriginal-White Relations	
		Reform	Transform
Orientation to institutions of dominant society	Integrate	1	2
	Segregate	3	4

Source: Based on S. Cornell, *The Return of the Native* (New York: Oxford, 1988), 154.

Flanagan, 1990; Barber, 1977). The Native Council of Canada's major interest was for individuals to be reinstated as Indians. No consideration was given to changing the status quo although in recent days, it would seem that the Métis National Council is moving toward an integrative-transformative organization (Grand Council Treaty, n.d.).

Integrate-Transform

Today, the Métis are attempting to entrench their rights in the Constitution by (1) adding a preamble that would reflect their historical contribution to Canadian society; (2) creating a charter of Aboriginal rights to entrench the collective rights of Métis; and (3) introducing an amending formula to guarantee Aboriginal participation in future constitutional conferences and amendments (Daniels, 1981: 19). They also are engaged in reviewing the existing federal and provincial legislation and policy that bear on Aboriginal issues. The United Treaty First Nations Council, representing 140 000 Aboriginal people, reflects their concern about the inability of AFN to deal with treaty issues. For example, they are concerned that the provinces are now involved in treaty negotiations, which they feel should involve only the federal government. However, after two years of intense lobbying, these groups have not produced structural changes to AFN, nor have they been able to attract other support.

The now defunct National Indian Brotherhood can also be placed in this category. Their mandate was to speak for registered Indians on a number of issues and to help them retain their Aboriginal values while operating within the larger Canadian context:

(a) to assist Indian people, and to work toward a solution of problems facing Indian people, including Indian culture and values;

(b) to operate as a national body to represent the Indian people, to act as a national spokesperson, and to disseminate information to the Indian people;

(c) to study, in conjunction with Indian representatives from the various parts of Canada, the problems confronting the Indians and to make representation to the government and other organizations on behalf of the Indians.

Its major concern was to assist local bands and regional organizations as well as to address the issue of Aboriginal rights (Ponting and Gibbins, 1980). However, before it moved to the next category, this organization closed and its successor, the Assembly of First Nations, emerged.

Another Aboriginal organization that would fit into this category is the Native Women's Association of Canada and the National Committee on Indian Rights for Indian Women. Its early focus was on ending the discriminatory aspects of the *Indian Act.* Its interest continues to be to end the sex-discriminatory status regulations in the *Indian Act.* In short, they want sexual equality. However, in pursuing this goal, it has found that Indian males are as much the problem as the *Indian Act.* Thus, those women who support these movements find themselves dealing with male Aboriginal leaders as Ottawa bureaucrats. A secondary goal is to provide a support base on which to develop Aboriginal women's self-confidence.

Segregate-Reform

In 1982, the Assembly of First Nations emerged as the primary national Aboriginal organization. It represents about 15 affiliated Indian associations and has recently concentrated its efforts on constitutional issues and self-government. In 1982, at the 3rd Annual

Assembly of First Nations held in Penticton, B.C., a new structure for an Assembly of First Nations was formally adopted by the Chiefs. This new organization was deliberately established outside the corporate structure defined by Canadian law. However, the original charter for the National Indian Brotherhood was maintained primarily as a legal vehicle for liability and funding purposes. As well, the NIB and its staff were to become the secretariat for the Assembly of First Nations. This change was the culmination of two years' work by the Interim Council of Chiefs.

In adopting an organizational structure (see Figure 11.2) for the Assembly of First Nations, the Chiefs were subject to a number of proposed amendments and additions. For example, provisions for an amendment clause, mechanisms for accountability, and a process for impeachment were to be included. These changes were to be developed by a subcommittee for presentation to the next Assembly of First Nations for review and acceptance by the Chiefs.

In 1982 a subcommittee called the Confederacy of Nations did meet to review a number of draft amendments that were prepared under its direction by staff of the AFN Secretariat. During its meeting the Confederacy of Nations adopted a number of items to be included and/or to replace or amend important elements of the Assembly of First Nations' organizational structure (Two-Axe Early et al., 1981).

The Confederacy of Nations is mandated to formulate policy and oversee the direction of the executive and secretariat between sessions of the Assembly. There is no direct comparison between the Assembly of First Nations and any body within government or, likely, within traditional First Nations structures. The intention of the Assembly of First Nations is to represent the needs and wishes of the several Indian nations. Each of these nations has territory and boundaries that reflect both its historical and contemporary geographical realities. Portfolios or standing councils, headed by a chairperson, are intended to develop policy to be recommended to the Confederacy and then to the Assembly and to oversee the implementation of policy laid down by the Assembly.

The Council of Elders develops the rules and procedures of the Assembly for ratification by the entire Assembly. This Council is a resource for the Assembly of First Nations and its constituents. The members of the Council are viewed as the custodians of the Assembly's rules and procedures, as they are for other traditional and customary laws. They have the authority to single out and admonish in public those whose behaviour is not in line with these customs and traditions. They educate those in the Assembly who are unfamiliar with their traditions and customs. They have responsibility for the development, implementation, and maintenance of a redress system that provides mechanisms for impeachment, discipline, and loss of membership. The Council of Elders also investigates and arbitrates any disputes within the Assembly. Finally, the Council selects and presents the Speaker of the Assembly to the Chiefs. It guides the Speaker in the exercise of his/her duties and in seeking consensus of the Assembly.

At the present time the ongoing political work of the Assembly is carried out by the Office of the National Chief. He is elected by the Chiefs in Assembly, and, for all intents and purposes, he represents the only body or person within the Assembly who can truly be held accountable by the Chiefs. Between Assemblies, the Confederacy tries to function as an Executive Committee and gives its own political mandates and direction to the Office of the National Chief.

Some Vice Chiefs in the past have carried portfolios. At present, all Vice Chiefs provide a means of communication between the National Chief and their regions. But in almost

FIGURE 11.2	Current AFN Organizational Structure

Assembly of First Nations
and Aboriginal People

Council of Elders

Confederacy of Nations

Executive Committee   Political Advisory
(National Chief & Vice Chiefs)   Council[1]

Priorities & Planning Committee[2]

Commission[3]   Commission[3]

Chairperson   Chairperson

Commissioners   Commissioners

Secretariat[4]

1. Political Advisory Council—This Council includes the Chairperson of each Commission or Committee. They have been appointed by the National Chief.

2. Priorities & Planning Committee—Set up by resolution of the Confederacy.

3. Commissions (15)
   • Chiefs' Committee on Education
   • Health and Social Well-Being Political Policy Committee
   • Social, Cultural and Spiritual Development (includes Youth Council)
   • Economic Development
   • First Nations Relations and Communications (includes Housing)
   • Constitutional Working Group (Task Force)
   • Treaty Unit
   • Parliamentary and Partisan Relations
   • Canadian Public Relations and Media
   • International
   • Indian Government Commission
   • Forestry Committee
   • Finance Committee
   • Commission on Structure
   • Federal Government Relations and DIAND

   There are few differences between a Commission and a Committee. Membership in both is informal. Selection of individuals is done on the basis of consultation with the National Chief and the Chairperson, regional input, and the person's willingness to be involved in a Commission or a Committee. Not all Commissions/Committees are set up by resolution; e.g., the Forestry Committee that came about as a reaction to government.

4. Secretariat—The National Chief is the administrative head of the Secretariat and is responsible for its day-to-day operation. All secretariat staff are responsible and accountable to the National Chief.

all cases, this function is secondary to their provincially or regionally held position, such as president of a provincial Indian association. And those whose vice-chief region is larger than the province or territory in which they hold another office frequently find that the task of reporting requires travel outside their primary territory, and this travel is in addition to their frequent trips to Ottawa and to the Confederacy meetings. The result is that many Indian leaders spend considerable time away from their constituencies. This frequent travel also produces "burnout" among leaders, and thus turnover in these positions is frequent.

The National Office has historically avoided running programs or providing services. At the same time, there is a desire to have the National Office valued and respected within the First Nations communities. Therefore, a role must be identified for the National Office—one that goes beyond support for the National Executive on major political issues (which have already been fairly well defined).

Since its creation the AFN has established several committees, commissions, and portfolios to address the concerns and direction of the First Nations. The current global organizational structure of the AFN is presented in Figure 11.2, and the Manpower Chart of the National Office and current list of salaried employees are described in the notes to that Figure.

The Assembly of First Nations was established by Chiefs to respect the sovereignty of First Nations. It can be described as an organization involved in a process of transition from the statutory origins of the National Indian Brotherhood toward a national political institution that derives its existence and direction exclusively and entirely from the First Nations. In some respects, it remains an organization that has not completely divorced itself from its statutory foundations (Final Report to Assembly of First Nations, February 18, 1985, mimeo).

The AFN takes the position that First Nations have the right to self-government, and that this right exists as an inherent Aboriginal right that has never been surrendered, relinquished, or diminished by any formal treaty or agreement, nor by the Constitution, legislation, or policies of non-Indian governments in Canada. One fundamental element of this right to self-government is the sovereignty of First Nations to freely determine their political, socio-economic, and cultural institutions, including the capacity to act in collectivities in the formation of regional or national institutions as forms of derivative governments. This power, although it exists, has yet to be exercised by the First Nations. Consequently, no contemporary national institutions exist as a derivative government of First Nations.

The AFN argues that any national institution established to represent or advance the interests of First Nations must reflect the sovereign jurisdiction of First Nations as the source of all that it does on behalf of the citizens of First Nations and, for that matter, on behalf of the governments of First Nations. Therefore, all powers, mandates, or responsibilities exercised on behalf of a First Nation are merely delegated, and the passage of time does not alter the nature and quality of the delegated power, mandate, or responsibility.

Delegation, according to the AFN, does not result in the transfer of sovereignty, nor does it diminish the jurisdiction of the First Nations. Furthermore, it can never result in the creation of an institution or body with inherent sovereignty that has a natural, independent right to act in all matters that concern the First Nations. As well, the AFN claims that all delegated power, mandate, or responsibility is a trust. Those individuals or institutions delegated with this trust have a sacred duty to implement or perform in strict compliance with the nature and quality of the delegation. Any variation to the delegated power, mandate, or responsibility that may arise as a result of the misinterpretation (deliberate or innocent) of the delegation, or that may derive from unilaterally or arbitrarily adding to, altering, or abridging the original delegation, is an affront to the First Nations and a usurpation of their sovereignty.

For the AFN, one of the inherent powers of First Nations is the capacity to create temporary or long-term institutions that will be expedient and necessary to accomplish the aspirations and destiny of First Nations. First Nations can:

(a) delegate responsibilities and duties and exact the fulfillment and performance of same;

(b) delegate power, authority or mandate and exact the fulfillment and performance of same;

(c) review, reconsider, alter, remove, transfer, amend or rescind at any time at their absolute discretion, any and all delegated responsibilities, powers, duties, authorities or mandates. (Assembly of First Nations' Report on Structure and Accountability, n.d., mimeo: 33)

In conclusion, the Assembly of First Nations is an organization composed of members from varying backgrounds, cultures, histories, and philosophies. Out of respect for diversity and for maintaining solidarity, the Assembly of First Nations is trying to develop some basic principles of organization that are acceptable to all the First Nations.

As stated earlier, the growth of Aboriginal organizations and movements is helping Aboriginal peoples to retain their culture and identity and is reinforcing links among them all over Canada. The pan-Indian movement emphasizes the values and beliefs central to the culture of Canadian Aboriginal people, regardless of local band differences.[3] Nevertheless, the development of pan-Indian organizations has been the first step in fostering a spirit of unity and brotherhood among Aboriginal people. This political activism also inspired a resurgent nationalism on the reserves, particularly in Eastern Canada. While some of the local or band goals were opposed to those of the pan-Indian movement, all were united in opposing Indian Affairs and developing greater self-determination. Pan-Indianism is largely an urban phenomenon. It not only promotes the traditional values of Aboriginal culture, but also tries to facilitate Aboriginal involvement in the business and professional life of the city. Its proponents feel that Aboriginal culture should be retained as a distinctive jewel in the cultural mosaic of Canadian society (Hertzberg, 1971).

Pan-Indian movements have many ties to the dominant culture. Their emergence has coincided with (although they are marginal to) the rise of conservation movements throughout North America. The leaders of pan-Indian movements have extensive contacts with the larger society, while retaining a strong affiliation to an Aboriginal tribe. Members of pan-Indian associations are generally bilingual, well-educated, and involved in typical Canadian occupations. Pan-Indianism presents a mixture of traditional Aboriginal and non-Aboriginal values. The emphasis on Aboriginal values is all-pervasive, and extends into the decision-making process. For example, Aboriginal people feel that, to be valid, resolution of an issue must be reached by consensus, not by majority vote.

Other cultural traits basic to pan-Indianism include an emphasis on sharing and an absence of emotional attachment to personal possessions. As historical potlatches show, considerable status can be achieved through the sharing of worldly goods; a refusal to share is interpreted as selfishness. Other Aboriginal characteristics that have received less attention from anthropologists include an acceptance of the behaviour of others and a deep respect for basic human rights. These attitudes often serve to alienate Aboriginal people from the self-serving, manipulative, dominant society that they find when they leave the reserve. As Lurie (1971) has shown, another Aboriginal cultural trait is withdrawal from situations that are anxiety-producing.

Although some Aboriginal and non-Aboriginal people see the reserve either as a prison or as a physical and psychological refuge, members of pan-Indian movements regard it as the basis for a viable community. They are not deterred by the fact that reserves are generally poverty-stricken, isolated, and lacking in essential services.

Over the years Aboriginal people have tried to build a pan-Indian movement, seeking to unite the various groups such as Métis and non-status Indians. Lussier (1984), however, claims that this movement is not working. He points out, for example, that the Métis, once they created their own organizations, set their own goals and objectives. To a certain extent, then, Aboriginal people are beginning to internalize the distinctions imposed on them by outsiders and to affirm the validity of these distinctions.

Segregate-Transform

Broadly speaking, Red Power organizations address the problem of Aboriginal people's inability either to separate from or to integrate with the rest of Canada (Franklin, 1969). While Red Power has so far failed to present a clear-cut program, its most important focus seems to be on the control of reserve lands (Fidler, 1970; Jack, 1970).

Red Power advocates are attempting to unite a number of other moderate and militant groups into a network across Canada. Although there are many important differences, some of their major ideological themes have been derived from the Black Power movements in the United States. In general, Red Power promotes self-supporting, self-directing, and commonly owned Aboriginal communities. Red Power members wish to create, develop, and carry out their own political, economic, and social programs. They also want to improve the Aboriginal's image on a personal level by changing both the negative stereotypes of Aboriginal people and their own negative thought patterns (Stewart, 1974).

Those Pan-American Indians (Indians who identify with South, Central, and North American Aboriginal people) who belong to the League of Nations are generally considered the most radical of the Red Power groups. The League is a very loose inter-tribal organization from which splinter groups, such as the National Alliance for Red Power (NARP), have emerged. Fewer and fewer militant youths are joining the League or one of its splinter groups. League members rally around the central issue of treaty and Aboriginal rights. They argue that Aboriginal tribes must be viewed as nations, and they want any litigation between Aboriginal peoples and the Canadian government to be referred to the United Nations. The militancy of these groups, exemplified by both peaceful and violent demonstrations since 1970, is continuing to grow (Lurie, 1971; Lambertus, 2004).

During the mid-1970s the American Indian Movement (AIM) gained some support in areas of Canada. AIM views itself as a grassroots organization in touch with the daily needs of Aboriginal people. Its general strategy is based on confrontational politics, coercive threats and, occasionally, violence. Its fluid membership and loose structure make it difficult to assess the number of its members. It is also difficult to determine the impact of this group on younger Aboriginal persons.

Boldt argues that the pan-Indian concept and the emergent political and cultural movement with which it is associated is serving to identify new boundaries and to create new over-arching Indian loyalties at the national level. It is a movement to enhance a sense of commonality and group consciousness which goes beyond mere political organizations to include recognition of a shared history of oppression, cultural attitudes, common interests, and hopes for the future (1980c: 4).

However, no more than 3 to 5 percent of today's Aboriginal people can be considered Red Power advocates. But this does not mean that militant organizations are not important. As research has shown, only a small percentage of a given population ever takes part in riots, revolutions, and urban guerrilla warfare. This small group, however, does need moral, economic, and physical support from the wider community—support that Aboriginal people seem increasingly willing to give to Red Power activists. It is not surprising that the RCMP has defined discontent among Aboriginal people as one of the most serious threats to Canadian unity.

Red Power supporters have shaken off the Canadian liberal humanism that views violence as the worst possible sin. They argue that violence is inevitable in the struggle to combat racism and achieve control over their lives. Although few non-Aboriginal people can agree, more and more Aboriginal people are beginning to do so. The recent activities of the Warrior Society at Oka and the supporting individuals who went to Oka or carried out militant activities elsewhere—e.g., the 1995 Gustafsen Lake standoff—suggest that while these organizations do not have a large membership, the potential number of recruits is high.

Other segregative-tranformative organizations take more contemporary forms of old traditional behaviour. The first of these is the pow-wow movement. The pow-wow is a planned inter-tribal affair usually held on neutral ground. There are dancing and social interactions, ritual healings, and serious discussions on the future of Aboriginal life. The young are encouraged to learn Aboriginal customs from their elders. It is hoped that, eventually, these pow-wows will build community solidarity among Aboriginal people everywhere.

As Corrigan (1970) points out, the pow-wow circuit acts as a communications network to promote the social and cultural integration of many Aboriginal groups. Other analysts, such as Howard (1951) and Lurie (1971), have also viewed the pow-wow as the current vehicle for achieving pan-Indianism. In an in-depth analysis, Dyck (1979) found that pow-wows constitute an autonomous achievement that summons a large community to celebrate the value and the excellence of Indianness in a manner that is both individually rewarding and collectively uncontroversial (p. 92–93). Furthermore, because pow-wows range over a large geographical area and provide continuity with the past, they can create a larger community out of various separate reserve communities.

The second form of segregative-transformative revitalization movement is the resurgence of prophet religions or religious pan-Indianism. Most Aboriginal religious movements have resisted assimilation efforts by the larger society. They have developed in the rural areas, and urge their followers to take up a style of life that is in harmony with nature. Humanity is viewed simply as one element of nature, always to be respected. A typical prophet religion was that led by Chief Robert Smallboy of Alberta.

There are other segregative-transformative organizations that do not take the conflict mode so characteristic of the Red Power organizations. Aboriginal people today are rediscovering their past and are attempting to sort out their identity. They are trying to develop a positive self-concept, and a group identity that can provide a reference point for them. They, like other minority groups, have developed myths that compensate for their subordinate status in Canadian society. These myths assert moral superiority of Aboriginal people over other Canadians; for example, they show Aboriginal people in harmony with nature, working to conserve the environment. These moral myths give Aboriginal people, oppressed for more than a century, a sense of positive self-esteem. In addition, the oppression experienced by them and their inability to fight back have produced a perpetual hostility in many of them. Moral superiority can also be one means of expressing their hostility (Fullwinder, 1969).

Today Aboriginal people are developing their sense of history and group identification. Ironically, it has been the Euro-Canadian–educated Aboriginal intelligentsia that has been instrumental in discovering, packaging, and promoting this sense of history and unification. Through a variety of techniques, they are trying to demonstrate their equality with other Canadians on three fronts: (1) through religious statements, (2) through the use of historical documents, and (3) through arguments that their culture is a product of the dominant culture's definition.

Because of the segregation and discrimination to which Aboriginal people are continually exposed, as well as their low position in the social and economic hierarchy of society, they are more or less suspended in a marginal position. As a result, within the Aboriginal communities a debate is taking place with regard to whether or not Aboriginal people should try to adapt to Canadian society. One sector of the community argues that the old traditional culture cannot provide Aboriginal people with the skills needed to survive in an urban industrial culture. Proponents of this view argue that Aboriginal culture has been assaulted by the dominant culture for so long and with such intensity that it cannot be salvaged. While the traditional cultural system may have been adaptive years ago, under today's conditions it no longer addresses the needs of Aboriginal people. It is useless, they argue, to continue to maintain a dying culture. Hence, their position is that Aboriginal people should take on the dominant industrial–urban culture and allow their traditional culture to fade into the past.

Other leaders argue that the dominant culture is not a moral one, nor is it relevant to their impoverished position in Canadian society. They feel that it cannot teach Aboriginal people how to cope with the kinds of situations that occur in their marginal position. This segment of the Aboriginal community argues that they must continue to develop their own culture and reject the dominant culture or any attempts to integrate (English, 1995).

The rejection of being dominated has been expressed by Aboriginal people in many different ways. Cornell (1988) identifies what he calls "lived" resistance movements in which Aboriginal communities tenaciously adhere to traditional Native values. These resistance movements are important in opposing social control efforts by the dominant group because they are not based on material interests but rather on a conceptualization of self and community. As a result, they challenge the values of the dominant society and of all of the assumptions held by those adhering to the dominant culture (Van Kirk, 1980).

These "passive" forms of resistance have given way, in more recent years, to more public forms of Aboriginal activism. The activist movement has resurged and increasing extra-institutional actions have been carried out—mass protests, civil disobedience, land seizures, occupying buildings, and taking up arms. Such forms of activism ensure that the issue under consideration is given a public forum. However, equally important is the symbolism of such actions. Active engagement in overt conflict signifies a fundamental rejection of the formalized, institutional procedures provided for dealing with their grievance (Katznelson, 1976).

A third segment of the community takes a different approach. They point out that oppression over the past century has produced a unique culture—one under siege. As a result, Aboriginal people experience numerous personality conflicts, have reduced self-esteem, and seek relief in the overuse of defence mechanisms. They argue that Aboriginal people must be able to resolve their inner conflicts and conquer the inner self. Freedom from within is the first step that Aboriginal people must take if they are to resolve their conflicts and remove the self-hatred that characterizes Aboriginal behaviour today. The next step is to gain self-knowledge by coming to grips with reality through education (Venne, 1998).

However, it is a unique type of education that is advocated. To take on a dominant education would be to ignore the fact that it prepares Aboriginal people for a world that is denied to them—that it bears, in other words, little relation to the Aboriginal individual's future experiences. Such an education would be neither functional nor adaptive for most Aboriginal people. On the other hand, to engage only in traditional education would also be maladaptive in an urban-industrial society. Leaders speaking from this third position argue that Aboriginal people's education has to be in the context of their marginal position. Aboriginal education must thus be provided at two levels (NWAC, 1985a, 1985b).

This short review of the different types of Aboriginal organizations has demonstrated several points. All of these organizations have become important vehicles for meeting the needs of Aboriginal peoples. They have all provided forums for the understanding and discussion of Aboriginal issues. Each of these organizations has also had to adapt its structure and objectives to existing conditions or face quickly losing its membership. Clearly, the use of formal organizations among Aboriginal people is likely to increase. They have discovered that formal organizations carry a sense of legitimacy that can be very effective in persuading governments to act in the interest of Aboriginal people (Fine, 1989). In addition, it should be noted that many Aboriginal organizations have elements of more than one ideology. Some may have combined ideological perspectives as the best way to achieve the goals and objectives they have set forth.

How have Aboriginal organizations and social movements improved the quality of Aboriginal life? Previously, the Aboriginal response to the dominant society has been to incorporate various aspects of that culture (Lurie, 1971). With the growth of various organizations and nationalist ideological movements, however, Aboriginal people are becoming more politically, socially, and economically aware. Formal organizations have allowed Aboriginal people to carry on discussions with the federal government on a legitimized basis. In the past, the government could reject Aboriginal claims and recommendations on the grounds that they were speaking as individuals, and thus any advice or recommendations that were conflicting or inconsistent could be ignored because they did not represent the demands of Aboriginal people as a whole. The creation of rational bureaucratic organizations reflects a collectively determined policy and allows for the presentation of cogent and coherent arguments on a variety of issues (Jamieson, 1978, 1979).

The impact of Aboriginal political organizations has been substantial, both on Aboriginal people and on government. These organizations have granted Aboriginal people input into the federal and provincial policies that affect them, thus providing them with instruments needed to bring about social change. But government has also found that dealing with an organization has many benefits. Because the bureaucracies within Aboriginal organizations are similar to those in government, both can now interact in an orderly, legitimate fashion. Government funding of most Aboriginal political organizations makes them more vulnerable to government control. As a consequence, Aboriginal leaders find themselves in the position of having to play by the government's rules in order to achieve their own goals—goals that may be at variance with those of the government. On the other hand, the government's power over Aboriginal organizations should not be overestimated. Governments also face a dilemma: without sufficient funds, Aboriginal organizations will not be able to negotiate; with too many funds, Aboriginal organizations will become too powerful (Krosenbrink-Gelissen, 1991). Weaver (1985) also notes that little evidence exists that demonstrates that the unequal power balance has compromised the positions held by national Aboriginal organizations on political issues.

LIMITS OF ABORIGINAL ORGANIZATIONS

The overall aim of many Aboriginal organizations is to gain input into the government decisions that affect them. In general, Aboriginal interest groups have found that appeals to MPs and MLAs are ineffective, except as a last resort. Rather, they have learned to focus on the bureaucratic organizations that affect them most directly, whether at the federal, provincial, or municipal level. Interest groups can also influence government in other ways, such as through annual submissions to Cabinet on aspects of federal policy. Local and provincial interest groups may deal directly with the government at any level, or may channel their appeal through whatever nationwide organizations they possess (Tanner, 1983).

The impact of an Aboriginal organization varies in direct proportion to its resources. By resources we mean group assets such as group solidarity, strong organizations, and money, which can be directed toward social action that enhances the capacity of the group to achieve its goals. During the first half of the 20th century Aboriginal resources were extremely limited; however, since the 1960s they have markedly increased. The nature and extent of these resources have varied over time. Depending on the action taken by Aboriginal people, those resources utilized are built up and remain part of the total resources available to them in future. The relative importance of different types of resources may vary from time to time and from situation to situation. For example, economic resources are important, but they may be subordinate to political or legal resources under certain conditions. Furthermore, some resources (primarily economic) are portable, or transferable, while others have limited application, e.g., legal.

Cornell (1988) argues that a useful classification of resources is by function. He identifies two types of resources: direct and mobilizational. Direct resources are those that directly influence the socio-political structure. Mobilization resources are those used in the process of bringing direct resources to bear on the issues under consideration.

One of the most common direct resources that organizations can use is the number of their members and/or supporters. However, because Aboriginal people have become both dispersed and factionalized, they have been unable to convert this resource into a force. Commodities that are held by an organization may also be a direct resource. However, the commodity must be one desired by others. In the case of Aboriginal people, such commodities are usually in the form of land, services, or some other special right. Land and natural resources commanded by various Aboriginal organizations have been and continue to be valued bargaining resources. Historically, military assets or, in the case of the fur trade, renewable resources, were desired. Over time many of these bargaining resources were lost, and thus Aboriginal power has decreased. A third type of direct resource is the extent to which an organization has allied itself with other organizations, particularly those with power. Aboriginal organizations' success in the past has been the result of linkages with other non-Aboriginal organizations—e.g., religious organizations, human rights groups, and conservation groups. Some of these organizations have the aid of Aboriginal people as a primary purpose; others have related political agendas and find the alliance with Aboriginal people useful for obtaining their own goals and objectives.

As noted above, direct resources may not be useful if they are not mobilized. Having alliances, money, and land is of little use if you cannot mobilize them at the time you need to exert power. An example of an organization with good mobilization is the Native Women's Association of Canada. There are some 400 local chapters spread over Canada with no less than 100 000 members. These informal groups foster networks, facilitate communications, and provide Aboriginal women with an opportunity to develop organizational skills. These local groups are linked to the provincial and national offices; this affords quick communications and the ability to spread information quickly (NWAC, 1981).

What are the resources that allow organizations to mobilize and direct their activities? First, if an organization is to engage in sustained, focused activities, it must maintain a structured organization and retain relationships with other organizations. A major explanation for a group's failure or success seems to lie in its basic organizational structure. In Table 11.3, Pross (1975) delineates differences between two types of interest groups. Institutional interest groups can be placed at one end of a structural spectrum, and issue-oriented groups at the other.

Because of their lack of organizational structure, issue-oriented groups are generally less effective in pursuing and achieving their goals. Moreover, their goals are restricted to a narrow focus and can only be pursued one at a time. The highly structured institutional groups, however, are free to pursue a number of broadly defined issues simultaneously. Issue-oriented groups have a small membership and a minimal, usually volunteer, staff to handle communications. Institutional groups, meanwhile, can bring extensive financial and human resources to bear on a variety of issues. Clearly, the Aboriginal organizations that are more institutional in nature have a greater chance of achieving their goals. Institutional organizations can choose from a variety of persuasive techniques, such as advertising, and can cultivate long-term formal and informal relations with government officials and senior civil servants (Wuttunee, 1972).

An organization with a strong network forms a basis for recruiting. And a sharing of recruits among organizations leads in turn to a sharing of some of the same ideas. Thus, the linkages of the network are continually strengthened. An institutional type of organization is also in a position to distribute many more ideas than can an issue-oriented one. Organizations within a network also find that decision making is facilitated and that coordinated action is more possible.

The ability of a group of Aboriginal people to achieve their goals is also a function of the social cohesiveness of the organization to which they belong. The more central membership in an organization becomes to an individual's self-concept (identity), the greater

TABLE 11.3	The Organizational Structure of Interest Groups	
Institutional	**Issue-oriented**
Possess organizational continuity and cohesion.	Have limited organization and cohesion.
Are knowledgeable about government sectors that affect them.	Possess poor information about government.
Have a stable membership.	Have a fluid membership.
Have concrete and immediate operational objectives.	Show an inability to formulate long-term goals.
See credibility of the organization as important.	See goal achievement as important.

Sources: Adapted from P. Pross, ed., *Pressure Group Behaviour in Canadian Politics*, (Toronto, McGraw-Hill, 1975); P. Pross, "Pressure Groups: Talking Chameleons," in M. Whittington and G. Williams, eds., *Canadian Politics in the 1980s*, (Toronto: Methuen, 1981).

the likelihood that the individual will act for the organization. The strength of the individual's identification with the organization also affects the nature and type of action he or she will take. Finally, leadership plays an important part in any organization's ability to carry out sustained social action. Any organization thus requires a pool of experienced, skilled individuals who are able to simultaneously deal with local community people as well as outsiders.

Certain factors associated with issue-oriented groups can reduce their effectiveness. For example, the emergence of divergent (or different) goals of various sub-interest groups leads to a decrease in ability to achieve goals as well as an increase in the amount of intergroup conflict. In addition, as the organization increases in scope and area, new sub-interest groups emerge—e.g., band affiliation, province, legal status, linguistics, and religion—that contribute to the multiple cleavages permeating Aboriginal organizations.

The internal leadership structure of an Aboriginal organization is also an important determinant of that organization's effectiveness in achieving its goals. Particularly important is the ability of Aboriginal leaders to exert strategic control over the goals and objectives of the organization. Organizational leaders must be adept at spanning boundaries at all times. They must monitor and control such factors as their clients' needs, funding opportunities, and reserve politics as they attempt to achieve their organization's goals. This requires leaders to be constantly vigilant in promoting their clients' interests, while at the same time maintaining their legitimacy in the eyes of external power groups (Howard, 1951).

As Pfeiffer and Salanchik (1978) point out, an organization survives when it is able to quickly adjust to external conditions and also cope with the environment in which it operates. For example, Aboriginal organizational leaders invest considerable time and effort in dealing with and attempting to influence such external agencies as DIAND, the Secretary of State, and various economic boards while also attending to the needs of their own constituents (Nielsen, 1991). The Native Women's Association of Canada was able to utilize the court rulings of the *Lavell* and *Bedard* cases as the basis for further lobbying efforts. They were able to identify "sex-equality" as the central issue of their organization and focus on that single goal (Cantryn, n.d.).

Nielsen and Silverman (1996) note that if an organization is dependent upon two sources for its resources then the task becomes even more difficult. An effort must be made to balance the relationships. Potential conflicts may arise in areas such as scope, priorities, and ideology. For example, funders of Aboriginal organizations may object to an organization expanding its services into areas that go beyond its usual range of activities. The funder may request that the organization withdraw that service (reduce its scope) or lose its funding. This may be more problematic if the constituency of the organization (Aboriginal people) is pressing the organization to continue its work in this area.

The organizational processes that have to be undertaken by Aboriginal organizations to survive are continuously in flux. Organizations with stable leadership and members are more likely to embark upon strategies that allow the organization to continue its existence. Oliver (1990) identifies several factors that push organizations into a "balancing" mode. Let us take each in turn. *Necessity* comes into play when the organization must take an action in order to meet some legal or regulatory requirement. Non-compliance with this requirement will lead to negative sanctions against the organization—e.g., loss of funding. Thus, when government officials require Aboriginal organizations to comply with certain legal standards, the organizations must put themselves into a balancing mode. Reciprocity *motivates* an organization when it attempts to collaborate or coordinate its activities with those of another in the hope that there will be a mutually beneficial outcome. There is an anticipation that the benefits of establishing a partnership will outweigh the disadvantages.

A third factor that makes it necessary for an organization's leadership to strive for balance is *efficiency*. All modern organizations are assessed in terms of their ratio of inputs to outputs. The cost–benefit ratios of Aboriginal organizations are continually being monitored. The establishment of a *stable* organization (resource flow and exchanges) is important if the Aboriginal organization is to remain in existence over time. Finally, the issue of *legitimacy* is significant to organization leaders. The image or reputation of the organization is important if it is to remain credible in the eyes of both its constituents and the broader society.

The evolution, survival, or phasing out of an organization is a function of both internal and external forces and how the organizational leadership deals with these forces. There is a need both to deal with the day-to-day issues and to attempt to predict where other organizations will be heading in the future. For if change is to take place and balance is to be achieved, the Aboriginal organization must integrate with, cooperate with, or support the goals and objectives evidenced by other organizations. If the disjunction between the Aboriginal organization and other organizations is too great, the Aboriginal organization will collapse for lack of support. Until recently, issued-oriented Aboriginal organizations have not attempted to achieve balance through cooperating with other organizations. They steadfastly retained their original goals and objectives and refused to change their strategies. The outcome has been a rapid demise of the organizations (Zlotkin, 1985).

As noted above, resources are not useful if they cannot be mobilized and brought to bear when needed. Aboriginal people have, in the past, mobilized some resources in the form of sporadic, incidental, collective action. However, this mobilization was not sustained and, within a short time, the resources were in disarray. Aboriginal people have lacked the structural organization necessary to carry out political action. An organizational structure, as noted by Cornell (1988), forms a basis for recruiting new members, linking members, and providing them with a vehicle to develop shared ideas and mutual respect. Thus, it helps develop a collective consciousness. Organizations also disseminate ideas that can be used to facilitate decisions and carry out concerted action.

To be sure, Aboriginal people have always had organizational structures. However, these structures were local (tribal) and focused around kinship. It has only been in recent years that pan-Indian and national Aboriginal organizations have emerged. Through this process various Aboriginal groups have become linked in their political action. However, while the organizational structures have emerged from the rural-based Aboriginal people, organizations are usually located in urban centres. Nor do they act on behalf of urban Aboriginal people.

Why haven't Aboriginal people become more involved in changing their lives? Why haven't they taken action in the past to provide themselves with the opportunities available to others? The answer seems to lie in their inability to amass the correct resources for the goals they want to achieve. As a rule, the greater the number and variety of resources held by a group, the greater their power. However, it is important to note that the importance of any resource is related to the issue being considered. As Cornell (1988) points out, not all resources are equally valuable, and their relative value depends on a variety of factors. For example, the size of a population is an important resource in a democracy but not in a dictatorship. Legal skills are important if decisions are made by a judiciary but are not as important if they are made through a political process. Resources can also be assessed in terms of their convertibility, reusability, and applicability. For example, education is convertible into jobs, income, and power. It also can be used over and over and has a wide applicability to a number of situations. On the other hand, legal skills have a limited applicability but can be used over and over.

Aboriginal organizational efforts are all limited by a relatively small population size, a lack of access to power, and a dependency on the federal government for funding and resources. Although Aboriginal organizations have been able to bring some pressure to bear on private companies and local government agencies, their dependency on the federal government is still the most significant limitation to their activities (Taylor, 1983).

Strategies are developed by opposing groups to discredit potentially powerful organizations. One tactic involves forcing the resignation of controversial leaders through sanctions. While this may solve problems in the short term, such government actions unwittingly contribute to the growth of Aboriginal nationalism. Nonetheless, the federal government continues to exert control over Aboriginal organizations by a variety of means. It can offer or withhold information that is essential for effective planning and operations. It can also co-opt the loyalties of Aboriginal leaders or define an organization as radical in order to reduce the chances of private financing and support.

Curtailing the access to communications is an effective way to reduce the creation and sustainability of networks. Table 11.4 shows the distribution of various Aboriginal publications in the eight regions of Canada. In the early 1990s there were less than 50 Aboriginal periodicals, compared to 37 in 1971. However, by the end of the millennium, the number of periodicals had dramatically increased. In addition, many single-issue magazines have been produced over the past five years.

Aboriginal periodicals tend to be rural in orientation, although over half are published in cities (Price, 1978). As Price (1972) points out, the growth of Aboriginal periodicals in

TABLE 11.4	Aboriginal Periodicals in Canada, 2001
Periodicals	Percent
Atlantic	8
Quebec	23
Ontario	29
Manitoba	13
Saskatchewan	24
Alberta	17
British Columbia	29
Territories	13
Total number	156

Note: Some periodicals are unilingual (French, English, Aboriginal), and others have some combination of languages.

Source: Based on Price, *Native Studies*, 1978, p. 186; Price, mimeo, 1985, p. 1. Author has collected additional information since 1985.

a city reflects the increasing development of other institutions. Periodicals provide information to many Aboriginal people throughout Canada and reinforce Aboriginal values. Most Aboriginal periodicals aim to develop political awareness and Aboriginal identity, as well as to promote action on particular issues. The Aboriginal press still remains in its infancy and faces an uncertain future. Finances are the major problem, and as Raudsepp (1997) points out, most Aboriginal presses have a tribal, rural, and scattered readership. This means that they are unable to build up a viable advertising base. Few papers have a combined advertising and circulation revenue exceeding 40 percent of their budgets. So if the presses are to survive, government funding will need to continue.

In addition to written media, radio and television play an important role in providing Aboriginal people with both general information about Canadian society and specific information about Aboriginal issues. Minore and Hill (1997) analyze the impact of the Northern Aboriginal Broadcast Access Program, which facilitates the production of regional television shows by Aboriginal communication societies in northern areas of seven provinces and in the territories. They demonstrate by case study how these programs have an empowering potential that is now being used by Aboriginal communities. Another example is the recently established television channel, APTV, which provides national coverage on a number of issues of relevance to Aboriginal people. As the producers of these programs gain experience and skill, they will become a major force in the presentation of the Aboriginal voice of Canada.

POLITICS AND NATIVE ORGANIZATIONS

After the federal government published its White Paper in 1969, a number of Aboriginal organizations began to play a leadership role in Aboriginal/non-Aboriginal relations. They abandoned their previous defensive positions and adopted offensive strategies. The White Paper produced a loose coalition of Aboriginal people who had previously belonged to separate groups with diverse goals.

Aboriginal organizations began their opposition to the White Paper with formal briefs presented to the federal government. These presentations were separate but similar in content; they included the Brown Paper by British Columbia Aboriginal people, the Red Paper (Citizens Plus) by Alberta Aboriginal people, and Wahbung by Manitoba Aboriginal people. Even those Aboriginal people who did not submit formal briefs appeared to be in basic agreement with those who did. The coalition that resulted from the White Paper was an important milestone in Aboriginal political organization. Aboriginal people had been unable to form strong coalitions against earlier bills, such as *Bill C-130* (1963), which provided for the disposition of Aboriginal claims.

The 1969 White Paper to some extent reflected the basic sentiments of the rest of Canada. It assumed that if Canadian Aboriginal people were to become fully integrated into Canadian society they would have to change radically. It argued that the separate legal status of Aboriginal people kept them from fully participating in the larger society. Therefore, the White Paper proposed to repeal the *Indian Act,* do away with the legal status of Indians, and phase out DIAND (Indian Policy, 1969: 6).

The opponents of the White Paper saw it as a disguised program of cultural extermination (Cardinal, 1969). Critics felt that Aboriginal people should remain legally, administratively, and socially separate if they so chose. The *Hawthorn Report* (1966–67), a sort of Royal Commission on the "Indian Problem," had just recommended that Aboriginal people be granted special status as "citizens plus" in order to ensure the preservation of their separate identity.[4]

In 1974, in response to the White Paper, a joint committee of the National Indian Brotherhood (NIB) and DIAND was created. Although it did not take the recommended form, a special Cabinet committee was created for the first time to deal specifically with Aboriginal concerns. The overall structure consisted of the NIB executive council and federal Cabinet ministers. Within this was also a joint subcommittee and a joint working group. However, in 1978 the NIB withdrew from the committee and it died a quiet death.

All the briefs submitted by Aboriginal organizations argued for immediate recognition of treaty and Aboriginal rights, and for the establishment of a commission to interpret the government's treaty obligations. They recommended that a claims commission be established through consultation with Aboriginal people and that it be able to make binding judgments. Others argued for a full-time minister of Indian Affairs and the creation of a permanent standing committee of the House of Commons and Senate to deal only with registered Indians. The Aboriginal briefs also urged Aboriginal control over reserve finances, taxation, reconciliation of injustices, housing, and health services.

The basic idea behind the White Paper was the elimination of the reserves. An examination of the reservation termination policy that was implemented in the United States sheds considerable light on this issue. Between 1953 and 1960 over 60 reserves were eliminated in the United States. By 1960 the results were clearly so disastrous that the scheme was halted. For example, in 1954 the Klamath Indian reservation of Oregon began to be phased out and, in 1958, termination was completed. Prior to termination, the Indians had developed a thriving business based on reserve forest products. From this resource alone, the average income for each person and the average family income was high. Many Indians worked at other jobs on and off the reserve, raising the average income per family and by 1954 standards, this placed the Indians in about the 90th percentile of income of the American population. Twenty years later, nearly one half the Klamaths were on welfare and their community had suffered as a result of extreme social disorganization. Family stability had decayed sharply, crimes of all kinds had risen acutely, and the community social network had broken down. Through termination, a thriving, self-sustaining community had deteriorated into a social disaster area.

Theoretically, the Klamaths should have succeeded in their transition. As Spencer and Jennings (1965) noted, the Klamaths were much more individualistic than other Indian tribes and, therefore, had more in common with the dominant society. If the results were so disastrous for the Klamaths, then they are bound to be worse for other Aboriginal people. Other terminations of American reserves have produced similar results. However, these findings are consistently ignored by those who favour the phasing out of reserves in Canada.

By the 1980s the federal government had decided not to implement the White Paper. However, new issues began to emerge that required the attention of Aboriginal people. The debate prior to passage of the *Constitution Act, 1982* required extensive allocation of Aboriginal resources in order to ensure that their interests were protected. As a result of their vigilant action, several constitutional amendments were adopted that recognize Aboriginal and treaty rights. These changes recognize and affirm "existing Aboriginal rights" (Section 35.1), which then had to be defined. Legal and financial resources had to be devoted to ensure that these rights would be properly defined and recognized. The subsequent first ministers' conferences (1983 to 1987) on Aboriginal affairs also required detailed attention. The introduction of a comprehensive land claims policy (1981), which was subsequently revised in 1986, also meant that Aboriginal people had to broaden their resource allocations. The *Penner Report* (1983) was a major all-party parliamentary report on Indian self-government, and while it reflected favourably on First Nations' quest for self-government, it meant that Aboriginal people would have to promote and lobby Canadians to establish what those rights were.

During the mid-1980s the *Nielsen Report* was made public. This report narrowly defined the government's legal obligation toward Aboriginal people and identified ways in which DIAND could trim its budget. A major campaign was undertaken by Aboriginal people to inform Canadians as to the federal government's legal and moral responsibility toward them. Legal challenges emerged, and the Supreme Court of Canada upheld the federal government's fiduciary responsibilities (*Guerin* v. *Regina,* 1985).

At the same time, the federal government reversed its century-long policy on enfranchisement and passed *Bill C-31.* This amendment to the *Indian Act* removed sex discrimination, and allowed for the reinstatement of persons who had lost their Indian status. Furthermore, bands would be given greater control over who was a member. All of these changes required extensive actions on the part of Aboriginal people. They also produced a great deal of internal factionalism within the Aboriginal community. The divisiveness created by this Bill still can be seen on many reserves and in numerous Aboriginal organizations (Ponting, 1991).

There were many other activities entered into by Aboriginal people during the 1980s that continued on into the 1990s. The policy review on land and trusts for Indians provoked considerable reaction by Indians. Economic changes also forced Aboriginal people to establish priorities as government extended fewer resources to combat social and health issues. Changing educational benefits and shifting health responsibilities onto the bands were just two ways in which government action forced Aboriginal people to reallocate their meagre resources.

Aboriginal people were required to respond to all of the above initiatives in substantial and meaningful ways. It meant that resources had to be properly allocated and actions had to be monitored over long periods of time. Because of the scarcity of many resources (e.g., money and legal expertise), alliances had to be established. While these linkages enhanced the ability of Aboriginal people to achieve their goals, they also made the process more complex and intricate. For example, instead of a dual interaction sequence, the introduction of a third party allowed for a triad to be established. This introduction of a third party allowed for coalitions to be formed, but it also meant that one of the coalitions could be against the Aboriginal people. The introduction of a fourth (or more) party simply made the process more complex.

An unlikely independent ally emerged in the 1980s—the courts. Traditionally, the legal system took a very positivistic position in interpreting the law, which generally meant legal rulings against Aboriginal people. However, toward the end of the 1980s, court decisions were supporting Aboriginal claims. The recent recognition of the Mi'kmaqs' and B.C. Indians' right to fish, the decision to hear the Manitoba Métis Federation's land claim, and the acknowledgement of Canada's fiduciary responsibility to Aboriginal peoples all gave both moral and legal support to the actions taken by them.

As a result of the actions taken by both the courts and Aboriginal organizations, there have been some federal and provincial policy changes regarding Aboriginal people. For example, the possibility of an independent claims commission is being discussed. Other legal changes are being contemplated by the federal government as Aboriginal organizations continue their relentless pursuit of justice in the moral and legal arena. Aboriginal peoples will continue to make their presence known. They are afraid that otherwise they will be ignored and forgotten by the larger society and the government of Canada. Rather than let that happen, they will continue to unite their forces to achieve their rightful position in Canadian society.

CHANGE THROUGH CONFLICT

Conflict permeates all aspects of our lives—in our homes, at work, and in our linkages with the community. As Black (1998) points out, conflict arises when one individual behaves in a manner that is defined by another as inappropriate and necessitating a response. Thus, conflict is a relational concept and involves the interaction of at least two groups. While some conflict causes deep and long-lasting physical and emotional impacts, other forms of conflict can produce a positive result (Law Commission of Canada, 1999). Moreover, the length and intensity of conflict can vary over time. This should alert the reader to the fact that conflict should not be seen as the other end of the continuum of order, nor should conflict always be viewed as harmful. Nevertheless, long-term conflict between groups within a society produces structural tensions that are difficult to change. Moreover, these conflicts can produce a context that becomes part of the culture of each group and defines future behaviour. How has conflict been managed? Aboriginal people have used the organizations they have created to challenge adversaries or those who seem to take advantage of the plight of Aboriginal people.

Conflict between Aboriginal and Euro-Canadian culture is not new; there have been numerous examples over time. While early conflict was widespread, it was sporadic and limited to the immediate locale. However, as we entered the 20th century, conflict became more endemic and widespread. Events occurring in British Columbia were quickly communicated across the country. Aboriginal peoples began to defend their way of life and reclaim resources they felt were theirs. Both political and legal negotiations were considered slow and cumbersome ways of solving problems (Richardson, 1993). Moreover, it seemed to Aboriginal people that the legal process was an inappropriate strategy to solve these conflict situations.

Resolving Conflicts: The Courts

When faced with resolving a conflict with Aboriginal people, the government has utilized the legal system. As such, courts have acted within a Euro-centric and positivistic model. Courts have operated on a logic that has not considered alternatives to Canadian principles. Sentencing circles, for example, were not considered until the 1980s, although the idea has been around for hundreds of years. Systematic implementation has only taken place in the Yukon. Medicine chests were considered to be small boxes containing local medicines and nothing more; any thought that they could be equated with health care premiums was unthinkable until recently. There have been some exceptions to the rule—e.g., the *Calder, Guerin,* and *Sparrow* decisions—but generally the courts have not been an ally of Aboriginal peoples. And as we have noted elsewhere, even when the courts do render decisions in favour of Aboriginal people, compensatory action by lower courts, governments, and private industries negates or limits the impact of these decisions. The 1988 *Eastmain* decision is characteristic of such court rulings.

In short, Aboriginal people generally have not looked to the courts to solve conflict situations involving them. Richardson (1993) points out that the law has shown itself to be a function of how an individual judge views Aboriginal society. In short, court cases involving Aboriginal people seem to reflect the attitude and perspective that an individual judge has about Aboriginal society and individual Aboriginal persons, as well as his or her conception about history. The contradictory decisions about Aboriginal peoples, and their claims over the past 50 years defy any coherent logic and have failed to produce an integrated body of law on Aboriginal rights. Aboriginal people feel that Canadian law ignores any Aboriginal conception of the world and is completely based upon European models of explanation. It is unthinkable that Canadian law would ever give serious consideration to the view that no one can own land or that a consensus model of society could exist. These differences in ethos have been reflected in conflicts over the past century.

In other legal cases, the behaviour of the courts and government is simply unfathomable. For example, when the Cree in Alberta submitted a land caveat to freeze development in the area where they live, the provincial government refused to accept the caveat and referred the matter to the provincial Supreme Court. At the same time, the government retroactively changed the law so that the Cree would lose their case when it came before the Court. In other cases, such as the *Delgamuukw et al.* v. *British Columbia* (1990), the Court not only rejected Aboriginal explanations about their society (as well as the explanations presented by expert witnesses such as anthropologists) but chastised them for wanting to continue a way of life that was different from the dominant Euro-Canadian culture. While this decision was appealed in 1993 and Aboriginal rights were once again accepted, the Appeal Court placed a narrow interpretation on their meaning.

From the perspective of the Aboriginal people, the courts have not listened to their concerns, have ignored their arguments, and have rendered decisions against their positions. At the same time, non-Aboriginal people view the courts as wielding too much influence in Aboriginal affairs and making decisions that do not reflect the will of the public. There is also a belief that the courts have sided with the Aboriginal people. These contrasting conceptions have emerged as the long-term conflicts between the two groups remain unresolved (Gamson, 1969).

COMPLIANCE IDEOLOGY

Each culture has its own system of shared values and beliefs that allows for its stable and efficient functioning. As such, each society has a collective orientation through which all members make decisions and resolve dilemmas. Members may not follow these orientations, but they are aware of the consequences if they do not. These orientations become embedded in the culture and take on moral and ethical values that govern people's behaviour. In other words, these rules inform people about what are appropriate goals and the appropriate ways in which these goals can be achieved. In short, the rules become guideposts that describe an individual's place in society, justify allegiance to that society, and prescribe the nature of participation in society (Wilson, 1992).

This compliance ideology (Wilson, 1992) serves its purpose by supporting the institutional arrangements and the behaviour of both individuals and organizations. Moreover, at the individual level, it allows people to carry out their behaviours with a minimum of transaction costs; i.e., each individual understands the rules of society as well as the consequences if they are violated. In the end, as Wilson (1992) points out, the compliance ideology provides an explanation and justification of the activities of institutions and individuals as well as their linkages. Laws are just one example of highly formalized compliance ideologies and are represented in highly codified forms. Other compliance ideologies may not be directly visible but represent the assumptions underlying most of our behaviour (Fletcher, 1992).

Aboriginal people older than 40 years of age have not been exposed to and socialized in the same compliance ideology as the younger generation. By and large they have remained outside mainstream Canadian culture, even though they have been exposed to the "new world order," and view the world very differently. Younger Aboriginal people have been exposed to the socializing efforts of mainstream society as well as to the compliance ideologies of their preceding generation; hence they have a bi-cultural orientation. But whatever their age, Aboriginal people are well aware of their inability to participate in the institutional spheres of mainstream society. Thus, there is a reluctance to "buy into" the mainstream compliance ideology.

Sources of Conflict

As we have noted elsewhere, there are many sources of conflict between Aboriginals and non-Aboriginals—e.g., religion, family life, and personal relations. However, one of the most important sources of conflict that has permeated Indian–non-Indian relations from the time of first contact has been that of land. From a European perspective, land is a central aspect of production in the triad of labour, capital, and land. Whereas Canadians believe that one cannot carry out economic activities unless all corners of the triad are achieved, Aboriginal people view land as a collective resource that is central to their identity (Armitage, 1995). The end result is that control over land continues to be of paramount importance for both parties—and lives are being lost from each side as the two groups attempt to grapple with the issue.

Dealing with the land issue during the 19th century involved establishing treaties with Aboriginal peoples. In return for extinguishing Aboriginal land rights, small parcels of land (reserves) were held for the exclusive use of Aboriginal peoples. Nevertheless, even these small parcels of land have proved to be an impediment and nuisance to Euro-Canadian development, and the test for land ownership still continues. Indians feel that the treaties were "once and for all" agreements, while non-Aboriginal people continue to chip away at the agreements made.

Armitage (1995) argues that in some respects the conflict over land is central to the relationship between Indians and non-Indians. Moreover, he argues that the relationship is defined on a racial basis and continues to remain a racial distinction. The continuous conflict over land has been frustrating for Aboriginal peoples and has been a major source of their anger and resentment toward non-Aboriginals. The clear demarcation between advantaged and disadvantaged is also always visible to Indians as they circulate among a non-Aboriginal population. Aboriginal people are clearly able to see that, while Canadians have prospered over the past half-century from economic development, they have not. They have been systematically excluded while other Canadians (native-born and immigrants) have been able to participate in the economic sphere that has enhanced their quality of life. Finally, the attitude of superiority (which manifests itself in the form of prejudice and discrimination) of non-Natives toward Natives is a continuous source of friction. Occasionally it takes the form of physical conflict. The question now remains whether or not this pent-up hostility will continue to be directed inward toward the self

(self-hate), toward other members of the Aboriginal community (in-group hostility), or toward the non-Aboriginal community (overt confrontation). As Justice Greenberg noted when he was sentencing Ronald "Lasagna" Cross for actions at the Oka conflict:

> I am satisfied that he was not motivated by greed or reasons of personal gain. He acted out a deep anger, rage, desperation and a sense of hopelessness, all the result of the systematic discrimination and racism against his people over several centuries.

He went on,

> For years, decades, even centuries, the aboriginal people of this country have endured, at best, indifference, neglect and unfairness and, at worst, open hostility, contempt, discrimination and racism. (Imai et al., 1993)

Over the past decade, conflict between Aboriginal and non-Aboriginal people has become a more common component of the interaction process. Recent examples, such as the Cardston blockade, the Oka resistance, and the Gustafson confrontation, confirm that Aboriginal peoples are not averse to engaging in overt physical conflict. Government officials have not been willing to act as partners with Aboriginal people in helping them, nor have they been willing to acknowledge wrongdoing and change their ways. Government continues to insist that it is helping Indians (as it has done for the past half-century), yet the objective evidence shows that it has done little to enhance the quality of Aboriginal life.

For example, the government claims that relocation schemes were used to solve problems being faced by Aboriginal communities. They have been used for over a century and continue today. The recent Royal Commission on Aboriginal Peoples (1996) grouped the relocation activities of government into two types: administrative and development. Administrative relocations were carried out to facilitate the operation of a government policy or to address the needs of Aboriginal people. For example, the Mi'kmaq of Nova Scotia were relocated to a central reserve in the 1940s in an attempt to reduce administrative costs (and to free up land for agricultural use by non-Aboriginal people). Twenty-five years later the GwaSala and Nakwaxdaxw Indians of British Columbia were relocated and amalgamated on a reserve in order to allow for more efficient delivery of government programs. At the same time the Innu of Labrador were moved to Davis Inlet, again for ease of government service delivery. After experiencing massive social problems for over nearly half a century, in 1994 the Innu agreed to a proposal to move from Davis Inlet to Little Sango Pond (back on the mainland), although a number of conditions still have to be met, including a long-term economic plan, site viability, and a formal ratification by Innu.

The second type of relocation also has a long tradition. Development relocation results from the implementation of an economic policy that involves tangible development activities—e.g., agriculture, hydro construction, or natural resource exploitation. The James Bay hydro development, which required thousands of Aboriginal people to relocate, is perhaps the best example. However, the massive oil/gas extraction activities as well as the logging efforts in the Lubicon Cree homeland in Alberta provides another example.

In either type of relocation, the movement of Aboriginal people has several consequences. First, the move severs people's relationships to the land and the immediate environs. Second, there is generally a loss of economic self-sufficiency. Third, there is generally a decline in health standards. Finally, the movement of people breaks bonds among them and produces changes in the social and political structures. (For a more detailed discussion of specific relocations, the reader should consult Volume 1—*Looking Forward, Looking Back*—of the Royal Commission on Aboriginal Peoples.)

If a people are resentful of and feel hatred toward their colonizers, why do they not speak up? Why don't they do something? Why don't they initiate overt conflict? It should be noted that Aboriginal people do respond to actions that they feel are discriminatory or that impact negatively on their community. However, unless these reactions are exceptional, the media generally do not report on them. As such, it will look, at first blush, like Aboriginal people are "doing nothing." Aboriginal people prefer (as a cultural attribute) to solve problems without resorting to direct confrontation or overt conflict. In other words, covert action may be the first step in dealing with a conflict situation. Their preference is to discuss the issue, evaluate a range of alternative solutions, and then attempt to achieve near consensus on the accepted solution. Sentencing circles are a good example of how this works (Linker, 1999). In the past, Aboriginal people used the courts as a primary way to solve conflict between Aboriginal and non-Aboriginal people in a variety of contexts— e.g., land rights, hunting rights, nonrenewable resource development, and social customs. However, in almost every case, Aboriginal people found that they have lost their preferred solution to the problem. Moreover, the courts force the actors to take an adversarial position, a stance Aboriginal people do not like to take. Finally, Aboriginal people have come to feel that there are no alternative solutions to their problems except to engage in direct confrontation such as blockades or sit-ins (Gibbins and Ponting, 1984; Slattery, 1985; Lambertus, 2004).

Aboriginal people have also begun to accept that conflict is an important element in the functioning of any society. While most people tend to see conflict as dysfunctional and detracting from the effective and efficient operation of society, it must be pointed out that conflict also has positive impacts. Aboriginal people have found that they can use conflict as a strategy to achieve their goals and objectives. For example, engaging in conflict forces the opposition parties to directly negotiate with the aggrieved parties. In doing so, dominant parties are forced to deal with the minorities as equals. In short, the dominant–subordinate relationship changes to one of equals. Second, the dominant party must communicate with the aggrieved party. Third, the nature of the complaint is made public and other interested parties may become involved in the negotiations. Finally, the dominant group may be forced to change its policies, attitudes, and behaviour toward the group initiating the conflict (Ponting and Symons, 1993).

CONCLUSION

Most non-Aboriginal Canadians do not see the logic of First Nations' holding the title of a "citizens plus" policy that grants special status to Aboriginal people, arguing instead that Aboriginals cannot be truly integrated into Euro-Canadian society unless special status is removed. Yet, as a charter group of Canada, British Canadians have always claimed special status, as have French Canadians with their entrenched language and religious rights.

Increasingly, Aboriginal people are viewed as a threat to the unity of Canada. Ottawa has learned well from its experiences with Quebec the problems that will arise if Aboriginal people gain power as a distinct cultural group. One solution is to refuse to recognize them as distinct, regardless of the problems they would face as a result of this policy. If Aboriginal people could be legally defined out of existence, the money now spent on them could be diverted to other, more cost-effective areas.

Removal of the legal status of Aboriginal people would not lessen discrimination against them. They would occupy the same depressed economic position as they do now, but without any group identification. They would become thoroughly marginal. Moreover, this marginality would not be wiped out in a generation; the stigma of Aboriginal birth is not only cultural, but physiological. Because intermarriage between Aboriginal and non-Aboriginal people is only slowly increasing in Canada, the marginal Aboriginal person will haunt Canadian society for many decades.[5]

Those who want to end the special status of Aboriginal people implicitly adhere to the myth of equality. This myth claims that, since everyone is equal, no one should be favoured or discriminated against. It is easy enough to stop the discrimination that favours Aboriginal people by eliminating economic incentives, affirmative action programs, educational advantages, and so on. However, out of political expediency and for other reasons, few efforts are made to stop discrimination against them. Aboriginal organizations have challenged this view and have used their collective powers to confront such a view.

In a nation that advocates cultural pluralism, suggestions that First Nations be eliminated seems incongruous. Nevertheless, the idea continues to be supported (as evidenced by the *Nielsen Report*) as a response to the recent growth of Aboriginal political and economic organizations. There is a recognition by the political elite that if these organizations are allowed to control reserve policies and funds, they will become formidable pressure groups in the 21st century. The harsh sanctions imposed by the Minister of Indian Affairs on the Indian Association of Alberta and the Assembly of First Nations reminds us all what Aboriginal organizations can expect if they continue to challenge Indian Affairs' authority.

At present, more than $1 million per year is provided to Aboriginal organizations, with limited results. One problem is simply that Aboriginal people are still in the process of developing the skills that most Euro-Canadians take for granted. Far more serious, however, is the fact that many Aboriginal organizations can only take action with federal approval. Only then will the funds be released. Moreover, the federal government seldom agrees with Aboriginal organizations on spending priorities. The government is constantly changing its long-range plans and shuffling its bureaucratic slots for allocating monies. Even when an allotment can be clearly perceived as unrealistic at the local level, it seldom can be changed. If INAC allocates several thousand dollars to be spent on a given project, then no amount of counter-argument by local Aboriginal organizations can divert this money into another project.

Although substantial amounts of money are given annually to Indian Affairs for Indians, very little of it is spent on meaningful programs that can activate long-range social change. For example, less than 15 percent of the funds given to Indian organizations over the past decade was used for developing economic projects, notwithstanding the federal government's stated claim that sustainable development strategies have the highest priority. Of the Indian and Northern Affairs Canada total budget, 43 percent is consumed by salaries and staff support for its non-Aboriginal bureaucrats and never reaches the reserve. If these salaries alone were given to reserve Indians, a sizeable capital base could be established to promote further economic development.

Political skills are vital to the survival of any group of people. In Canada, the cultural awakening of Aboriginal people has been preceded and outpaced by the growth of their political awareness. Aboriginal people are becoming increasingly sophisticated in their use of organizations to further their goals. This new knowledge will make itself felt more and more in Canada as we move into the 21st century.

NOTES

1. For a more complete discussion of the history of British Columbia Aboriginal organizations, the reader should consult Drucker (1958).

2. The Six Nations community is attempting to separate politically from Canada. This may account for their lack of militancy.

3. The term "pan-Indian" is not used by Indians but was invented and is used now by social scientists.

4. See, for example, the work of S. Weaver, *The Hidden Agenda: Indian Policy and the Trudeau Government,* University of Waterloo, Waterloo, Ontario, mimeo, 1980.

5. In 1961, the endogamous rate of Aboriginal marriages—Aboriginal persons marrying Aboriginal persons—was one of the highest in Canadian history. In fact, it increased from 91 percent in 1951 to over 93 percent in 1961. However, by 1971 the rate had decreased to 77 percent, and by 1981 a further decrease to 67 percent was evident.

WEBLINKS

www.aboriginalcanada.gc.ca/abdt/interface/interface2.nsf/engdoc/1.html

This website provides links to over 40 provincial, regional, and national Aboriginal organizations, associations, councils, foundations, institutes, and cooperatives, all listed by name.

The websites of several of Canada's major national Aboriginal organizations include:

www.afn.ca

(Assembly of First Nations),

www.abo-peoples.org/mainmenu.html

(Congress of Aboriginal Peoples),

www.metisnation.ca

(Métis National Council), and

www.nwac-hq.org

(Native Women's Association of Canada).

chapter twelve

The Department of Indian and Northern Affairs Canada

INTRODUCTION

One of the most important challenges to government is managing change successfully, to bring about political stability. In order to carry out change, agencies, departments, or bureaus are established to focus their activity to manage change. The British Indian Department, the first department set up by the Crown in America, was established in 1755 to deal with Indian issues. However, 1830 is considered the beginning of an ordered system of Indian administration in Canada. Thirty years later, responsibility for Indian affairs was transferred by the British government to the government of the Province of Canada. At the time of Confederation, the *British North American Act*, now called the *Constitution Act, 1867*, gave the new federal government legislative authority over "Indians and lands reserved for Indians." In 1939 a Supreme Court decision allowed this bureau also to deal with Inuit affairs even though they were not considered Indians as defined by the *Indian Act*. Over the years, Indian affairs have been under the control of many different government departments, such as Agriculture and Citizenship; it was not until the 1960s that the current structure was put in place.

The Department of Indian and Northern Affairs Canada (sometimes referred to by its previous name, the Department of Indian Affairs and Northern Development) comprises a complex number of programs, sectors, branches, directorates, and secretariats. Within the Department, the Indian and Inuit Affairs Program has four sectors that have been created to deal specifically with Aboriginal people. All of these organizations will be identified below to illustrate the size and complexity of the Program. And, it should be noted at the outset, the size and complexity of the organization's structure have certain implications in terms of how it operates. Furthermore, these branches, directorates, and secretariats are not the only federal agencies that deal with Aboriginal people. The Secretary of State, Justice, and the Medical Division all have units within their departments that have Aboriginal people as part of their mandate. In addition, there are many other branches of both the federal and provincial governments—e.g., Revenue Canada, Corporate Affairs—that deal with Aboriginal people. Hence, the scope and complexity of the structure of government involvement in Native life should be clear to the reader. The attendant problems of coordination and delivery are great indeed. It should come as no surprise, then, that there is a great deal of overlap, confusion, and tension among and between the many organizations that deal with Aboriginal people. Likewise, it should be clear that Aboriginal people find this complex web of uncoordinated organizations difficult to understand and to deal with. Finally, the utilitarianism of such a structure should be clear. It is almost impossible to lay blame to a specific individual or unit and unsuccessful change cannot be clearly traced to any single unit. In short, accountability is not possible under such a structure—a point that the Auditor General's office has made for many years.

The Department of Indian Affairs and Northern Development (since renamed) was created in 1966 and is responsible for all federal policy and programs concerning Canadian Indians and Inuit; it also administers the Northwest Territories and the Yukon. It administers over 50 separate acts, including the *Department of Indian Affairs and Northern Development Act*.[1] The Department's mission is to facilitate a better quality of life for First Nations, Inuit, and Northerners. In doing so, the Department must collaborate with other federal departments and provincial and territorial governments, and identify both short-term and long-term goals. The overall planning framework of Indian and Northern Affairs is to put in place programs and services that will improve the lives of Aboriginal people and increase their self-sufficiency. The Department's strategic directions are based on the federal government's action plan outlined in the document *Gathering Strength—Canada's Aboriginal Action Plan*. The actions to be taken by the Department are based on transforming relations with First Nations through supporting healthy and safe communities; closing the socio-economic gaps; improving management of land, environment, water, and natural resources; and honouring responsibilities and commitments. Specific actions will include: fulfilling the obligations of the federal government arising from treaties, the *Indian Act*, and other legislation; negotiating settlements in respect of claims to Aboriginal rights; supporting the economic development of the North and protecting the Northern environment, including Arctic seas; coordinating settlement implementation and continuing to promote self-reliance; establishing and implementing new funding arrangements with bands to facilitate Aboriginal education; and assessing existing program delivery mechanisms and related organizational structures to establish Indian control and community self-sufficiency.

This list does not imply any priorities of the Department, nor does it assess the importance of any one goal. The Department of Indian and Northern Affairs has been in an organizational flux over the past two decades and it continues to struggle over to how it will support Aboriginal communities. When it revised its mandate to "devolve" and support First Nations and Inuit in developing healthy, sustainable communities and in achieving their economic and social aspirations, the Department attempted to play a new role in the lives of Aboriginal people. This change to an "enabler" and an advocate for initiatives launched by Aboriginal people has been difficult to implement and is difficult for the

Department to accept. This new identity stands in stark contrast to the previously held role of controller and regulator of Indian issues. As Weaver (1991) points out,

> [I]n contrast to the historic role of DIAND as custodial administrator, new paradigm thinking proposes a smaller, more responsive and more development-oriented administrative role. Its job is to constructively support and advance First Nations political autonomy, and to service the negotiated agreements.... (pp. 14–15)

The reorganization was designed to achieve four goals that were identified after intensive meetings had gone on between the government and Aboriginal people. The four themes were self-government, economic development, quality of community life, and protection of the special relationship between the federal government and the Aboriginal people. In an attempt to achieve these goals, the department agreed that it would shift more decision making to Indian communities; remove barriers to economic growth; develop better housing, education, and social services in order to respond to local needs; achieve better management of Indian lands and monies; and protect the special relationship that exists between the federal government and the Indians and Inuit of Canada. In short, the Department is trying to strengthen Aboriginal governance, is reducing the socio-economic gap, and is encouraging healthy communities.

Central to the above is the desire to have status Indians and Inuit decide their own futures. The government's overriding objective is to nurture the socio-cultural and political development that will ultimately see Canada's first citizens realize their dreams. But this cannot be achieved without sound economic growth. Therefore, the federal government continues to contribute to economic development opportunities by bolstering Aboriginal participation in the educational system and commercially viable businesses and institutions.

As the reader will soon come to realize, Indian and Northern Affairs is not the only organization that funds activities related to Aboriginal people. For that reason, the Department has taken a broader perspective on how it deals with First Nations communities. Specifically, it has enacted a strategy of "Circles of Influence." The Department has certain activities and outputs that directly impinge upon Aboriginal people, for which it is solely responsible, and this "operational circle" represents activities that the Department has direct control over—e.g., funding, monitoring, policy. However, the Department is equally cognizant that because many other agencies—e.g., Health Canada—also have Aboriginals as part of their mandate, its members need to think more broadly. For this reason, it has introduced the notion of a "collaborative circle" of influence. This circle relies on partnerships to achieve the Department's goals. The collaborative-level results include adoption of practices that contribute to strategic outcomes by target communities and sectors, capacity enhancement, increased knowledge, and understanding of key requirements. These partnerships may be with other government departments/agencies, with First Nations, or with the private sector. Finally, the Department has taken an even broader perspective in adopting a "global circle" of influence. This describes both the existing conditions that affect strategic outcomes and desirable changes in those conditions. Although these conditions are beyond the Department's direct influence, it is still important to focus on activities that contribute to positive changes for First Nations in the long term (see Figure 12.1). For each goal identified in the accountability framework employed by the Department, decisions about programs and policies are to be made with this framework in mind. While this framework has only been in operation for a few years, the impact of such a strategy will be more clearly articulated in forthcoming years.

INDIAN AND INUIT AFFAIRS PROGRAM

In the early 1980s nearly 60 percent of the Indian and Inuit Affairs Program's expenditures were made through contribution arrangements to Indian bands or various Indian organizations. In turn, these groups provided the specific services as outlined in the contract or agreement. In 2000, Ontario and Manitoba were each allocated about 18 percent of the budget. In addition, 32 percent was equally divided between B.C. and Saskatchewan. Alberta received about 5 percent. The remaining portion of the budget was equally split among the Atlantic region, headquarters, and the territories. On a per capita basis, Ontario and Alberta have the lowest Indian Affairs Program expenditures. These low figures reflect the relatively high rate of employment in Ontario and the resource-rich bands in Alberta.

The Indian Affairs Program supports Aboriginals in their quest to preserve and develop their culture. Support is channelled through three streams. First, financial assistance is given to bands, councils, or non-profit corporations that support Aboriginal heritage. Second, a cultural development program supports Aboriginal artists. Third, the community social services provide advice and guidance to band councils, their staff, and community service organizations.

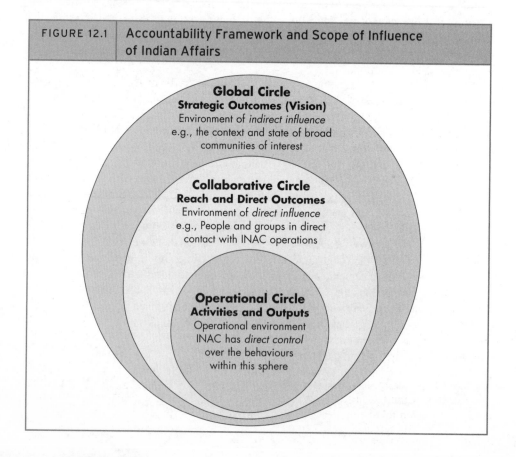

FIGURE 12.1 Accountability Framework and Scope of Influence of Indian Affairs

Global Circle
Strategic Outcomes (Vision)
Environment of *indirect influence*
e.g., the context and state of broad
communities of interest

Collaborative Circle
Reach and Direct Outcomes
Environment of *direct influence*
e.g., People and groups in direct
contact with INAC operations

Operational Circle
Activities and Outputs
Operational environment
INAC has *direct control*
over the behaviours
within this sphere

The Indian and Inuit Affairs Program traditionally has been highly centralized, with its headquarters in Ottawa. It is responsible for policy development, resource allocation, and planning for Indians and Inuit through a variety of methods—for example, direct service delivery, grants, and loans. However, since the late 1970s, when decentralization was introduced, the 10 regional offices—one in each territory, one for the Atlantic provinces, and one in each of the remaining provinces—have begun to develop their own programs. These programs emerge from the specific district structures (except in Manitoba). Thus, the districts have become influential, except in Alberta, where control is retained in the regional office.

Today we find that about 17 percent of the total number of employees of the Indian and Inuit Affairs Program are Aboriginals. However, Aboriginal workers in the Department have not yet gained access to policy-setting positions; only 4 percent of the Aboriginals employed by the Indian and Inuit Affairs Program are at the senior- and middle-management levels. The largest proportion—28 percent—is at the operational level, primarily involved in teaching. Less than 10 percent of its employees have been with the Indian and Inuit Affairs Program for more than 15 years. This latter group is generally called the "old guard" and has almost total control over policy development and implementation. Less than 1 percent of them are Aboriginals.

The Indian and Inuit Affairs Program's policies, objectives, priorities, and programs are established by senior executives and then passed down and back up the bureaucratic ladder.[2] Budgets must be developed for each program and approved by Parliament. Most of the budget of the Indian and Northern Affairs Program (74 percent) is nondiscretionary; that is, it is set aside for specific items and is non-transferable. However, as the year proceeds, the Indian Affairs Program often requests additional funds.

In 1967 the Indian and Inuit Affairs Program accounted for 1.06 percent of the government's total budget. This figure peaked at 1.74 percent in 1972–73 before it was reduced to 1.7 percent in 1980, and in 1987 it stood at about 1.6 percent. It has remained at this level for some time, although by 2003 the federal expenditures on Aboriginal programs represented 4.1 percent of the federal budget. In 1965, the Indian and Inuit Affairs Program was allocated about one-half of the total DIAND budget. This proportion increased to nearly 75 percent in 1969 and now constitutes 83 percent of the total Indian and Northern Affairs Canada budget.

Since 1960 considerable shifts have occurred in the distribution of funds among operating expenses, capital costs, and expenditures for grants and contributions. In the early 1960s over half of the budget was used to meet operating expenses, while the rest was evenly split between the other two categories. In 1980–81, however, operating expenditures accounted for only 37 percent of the budget, while capital expenditures on additions and betterments had decreased to 4 percent. Expenditures on grants and contributions had increased substantially and made up nearly 60 percent of the total budget (Annual Report, DIAND, 1980–81). This reallocation continues and suggests a wide-scale transfer of the administrative costs of Indian and Inuit Affairs programs to provincial governments.

The actual spending patterns of the Indian and Inuit Affairs Program also have substantially changed in recent years. In the early 1960s approximately 45 percent of the budget was spent on education. By 1978 this had decreased to 39 percent and by 1990 it was further reduced to 33 percent. Today it represents 26 percent. Other activities funded by the Indian and Inuit Affairs Program also show changes in fiscal priorities. Community affairs accounted for about 43.1 percent of the budget in 1970 and 1978, but decreased to slightly more than half that level in 1990. Economic development, previously a low priority for the Indian and Inuit Affairs Program, ranging from between 6 and 9 percent of the total budget, has been identified as a high priority for Indian Affairs as we enter the 21st century. However, the data show that in the 2003–04 planning estimates, it will account for less than 3 percent. In defence of Indian Affairs, they argue that funding in other areas such as capital facilities and social development will lead to an increase in economic development. Moreover, they note that with the introduction of new Aboriginal economic programs, private–public partnerships (P3s) will result, with greater leveraging abilities and thus greater economic impact.

STRUCTURE OF THE DEPARTMENT OF INDIAN AND NORTHERN AFFAIRS CANADA

The structure of Indian and Northern Affairs is outlined in Figure 12.2, with approximately 75 percent of its employees delivering more than 500 distinct services in 10 regions across the country.

The new organizational structure shows that there are nine major sectors in the Department: Economic Development and Special Initiatives, Policy and Strategic Direction, Lands and Trust Services, Claims and Indian Government, Northern Affairs, Corporate Services, Socio-Economic Policy and Programming, Legal Services Support, and Office of the Corporate Secretariat. This structure shows that each sector of the Department communicates directly to the Deputy Minister, while no formal linkages exist among the units. However, informal communication goes on among the various units on a daily basis in an attempt to keep each sector informed of other activities being carried out in the Department.

The Department administers the statutory requirements defined in the *Indian Act*, including the registration of Indian people, the deployment of reserve lands and other resources, and the regulation of band elections. It also attempts to ensure that the federal government's lawful obligations to Indians and Inuit under the *Indian Act* and the treaties are fulfilled. The Department provides a wide range of services of a federal, provincial, and municipal nature to Indians and Inuit. In meeting its responsibilities, the Indian and Inuit Affairs Program works closely with other federal departments and agencies such as National Health and Welfare and the Department of Justice. In keeping with the principle of self-development, the Department attempts to assist and support Aboriginals in achieving their cultural, educational, and social aspirations. In addition, the agency tries to promote the economic and community development needs of Aboriginals and to ensure that Canada's constitutional and statutory obligations and responsibilities to Aboriginals are fulfilled (Government of Canada, 1990).

There are three program/business lines in the Department. The first deals with Indian and Inuit Affairs, the second with Northern Affairs, and the third with administration. Indian and Inuit Affairs supports Aboriginals in achieving their self-government, economic, education, cultural, and community development needs and aspirations. It also helps to settle accepted Aboriginal claims through negotiations and to ensure fulfillment of Canada's constitutional and statutory obligations and responsibilities to Indian and Inuit people. The second program focuses on Northern Affairs and will not be discussed in this book. However, the goal of this sector is to promote the political, economic, scientific, and social development of Canada's North. This of course means it assists Northerners, including Aboriginal groups, to develop. The third component, administration, ensures that the bureaucracy established operates smoothly and efficiently to achieve the goals/objectives identified above. We now turn to a discussion of the major sectors within the Department.

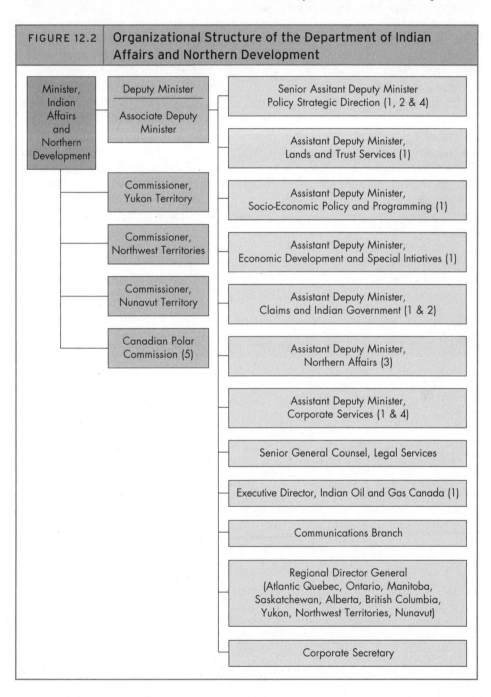

FIGURE 12.2   Organizational Structure of the Department of Indian Affairs and Northern Development

Economic Development

The Economic Development Sector is responsible for community planning, development, and access to resources. Two units (Socio-Economic Policy and Programs and Economic Development and Special Initiatives) have been created to deal with economic issues. The goal of this sector is to strengthen the economic base of First Nations communities, remove obstacles to economic development, and facilitate economic opportunities (see Figure 12.3). Most of the work of this sector is focused on developing and supporting the implementation of the Canadian Aboriginal Economic Development Strategy.

The government recently established the Canadian Aboriginal Economic Development Strategy, which is focused on helping Aboriginal peoples achieve their goal of economic self-reliance. This partnership among Indian and Northern Affairs, Industry, Science and Technology, and Employment and Immigration Canada has spent over $100 million over the past decade to ensure achievement of its goal. This approach is different from past attempts at providing economic development services directly to Aboriginal people. The new strategy offers support for Aboriginal economic development decision making, priority setting, and delivery of economic development services through community-based organizations and development.

In order to implement this program, the government has fostered linkages between Aboriginal communities, the private sector, and government (federal, provincial, and territorial) agencies in order to promote greater participation by Aboriginal people in the mainstream economy. The Canadian Aboriginal Economic Development Strategy

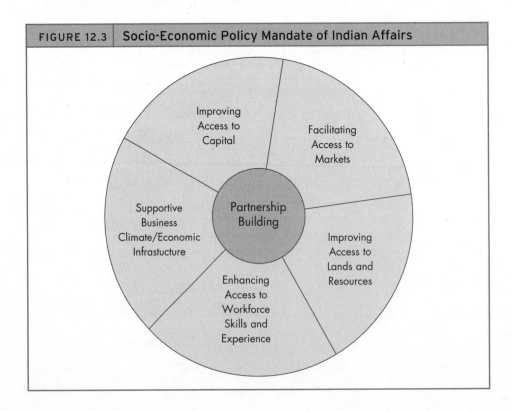

| FIGURE 12.3 | Socio-Economic Policy Mandate of Indian Affairs |

comprises eight programs: Business Development, Joint Ventures, Capital Corporations, Community Economic Planning and Development, Access to Resources, Urban Employment, Skills Development, and Research and Advocacy. These economic programs are the major activities that the federal government has undertaken to create economic development on the reserves and to help individual Aboriginals integrate into the mainstream economy.

The overall strategy employed by this group is to develop an Aboriginal economic development program for the long term, which will be designed to support control by Aboriginal communities—i.e., community-based decision making, priority setting, and delivery of services. Indian and Northern Affairs' community economic planning and development program has been the key component of this strategy. This component is designed to assist Aboriginals, through Community Economic Development organizations, to create, maintain, or strengthen local organizational, advisory, and development capacity, which will help Aboriginal community members more clearly define and achieve their economic goals.

The Commercial Development program handles the business development activities. Because of the creation of the Canada Aboriginal Economic Development Strategy, direct contributions to Aboriginal businesses will cease. In 2001–02, The Department budgeted nearly $140 million for economic development. An additional $900 million was set aside for capital facilities and maintenance. In addition to the above initiatives, Indian and Northern Affairs has created a number of other programs and strategies to enhance First Nations economic development. Programs such as the Resource Partnerships Program, Aboriginal Business Development Initiative, the Major Business Projects program, Procurement Strategy for Aboriginal Businesses, the Aboriginal Workforce Participation Initiative, and the Aboriginal Fisheries Strategy Allocation Transfer Program are just a few that add support to the economic development. For example, the Aboriginal Business Development initiative was launched in 1999, with $21 million designed to improve business development opportunities for Aboriginals. This initiative will strengthen the capacity of Aboriginal financial organizations (such as the Aboriginal Capital Corporations and Aboriginal Community Futures Development Corporations) to access capital and to network with other organizations, thus gaining access to new technologies, and it will expand the markets and outreach for Aboriginal entrepreneurs.

Policy and Strategic Direction

This unit oversees all of the other branches in the Department to ensure that policies from within Indian Affairs as well as from other Departments in the federal government that are developed for Indian people are consistent and aligned. It also develops long range goals and objectives for the Department of Indian Affairs. It carries out both internal and external environmental scans—e.g., population projections—to assess the political, legal, social, and technological changes that are taking place both within Canada and globally.

Lands and Trust Services

One of the more controversial sectors in the Indian and Inuit Affairs Program is the Lands and Trusts Services. This sector is supposed to administer the *Indian Act* and the Crown regulatory mechanisms that have been established over the years. It has recently been reshaped as a facilitator of change necessary for First Nations in order for them to take on greater responsibility and control over their lives. At the same time, it is a delivery agent of programs, services, and policies. From an operations perspective, it is divided into three inter-dependent branches that manage 21 business lines: the Registration, Revenues, and Band Governance Branch; the Lands and Environment Branch; and the Policy, Partnership, and Coordination Branch. The Registration, Revenues, and Band Governance Branch is responsible for elections, maintenance of Indian registration and lists, by-laws, Indian monies, estates, and transfer of control of membership, to mention just a few of their activities. The Indian Registry administers about 5 million hectares of land and processes some 100 000 transactions per year—e.g., birth and death certificates. The trust fund managed over $2.3 billion in 1997, with revenues of $1.4 billion and disbursements of well over $800 million.

The Lands and Environment Branch is responsible for First Nations land management initiatives, natural resources (forestry and minerals), land management, surveys, and land registration as well as all forms of environmental protection and remediation activities. This branch implemented the *Indian Lands Agreement Act* (1986), which was enacted into law in 1988. This Act permits bands in Ontario to negotiate with the province and the federal government to remove provincial interests in surrendered Indian lands and minerals. Over the past 10 years, this directorate has added 100 000 hectares of land to the total existing reserve land base in Canada (now at 2 786 996 hectares), an area roughly half the size of Nova Scotia. This branch also provides bands and Indian organizations with advisory, technical, and other support to deal with environmental problems. Finally, the Policy, Partnership and Coordination Branch acts as a facilitator of change necessary for First Nations to assume greater responsibility and control over their lands and governance systems. It also acts as a catalyst for legislative reform and an agent for change and devolution.

It should be noted that these three branches maintain linkages with other federal and arms-length organizations. In addition to the implementation of the Canada Aboriginal Economic Development Strategy, Lands and Trust Services also works in the area of Aboriginal taxation and in the administration of the *Indian Oil and Gas Act*. The Indian Oil and Gas Canada mandate is to identify, administer, and tender for permit or lease, Indian petroleum and natural gas rights on behalf of Indian bands. The Indian Taxation Advisory Board was created in the Economic Development Sector (as a result of *Bill C-115*, the 1988 amendment to the *Indian Act*) to consider new taxation bylaws. For example, the Board granted bands broad powers to tax interests in Indian lands. This group of 10 people (seven Indian leaders) also publishes reports on taxation, developed a model bylaw, and sponsors conferences on real property taxation. The Indian Taxation Advisory Board, which used to be part of Indian Affairs, is now an arms-length agency that deals with taxation-based issues in First Nations and maintains extensive linkages with the Lands and Trust Services. It also links with Indian Oil and Gas Canada to facilitate the development of fossil fuel–based resource harvesting

In its role of administering Indian land and money, this sector has been admonished over its role in administrating Indian funds. Recently the courts have awarded individuals and bands damages or other redress because Indian and Northern Affairs has not carried out proper administrative procedures. For example, in a landmark case, the Musquean band of British Columbia (*Guerin* v. *the Queen*, 1984) brought a breach of trust suit against the Crown. The federal government had not carried out the terms of a lease requested by the Indians and did not inform them of this breach. Almost a decade after the suit was launched, the Supreme Court ruled that a breach of trust had indeed occurred and found in favour of the Indians. This ruling overturned a federal Court of Appeal decision that had overturned the original judges' decision. The importance of the ruling lies in the judges' statement that the band had a "pre-existing right to its traditional lands" and that the Crown had "breached a fiduciary obligation to the band." This decision has forced the government to clarify its role when negotiating with third parties over Indian land, as well as to obtain informed consent from the band on whose behalf it is acting.

Claims and Indian Government

This sector manages the negotiations, settlement, and implementation of land claims agreements, as well as special claims settlements and self-government arrangements. Within this sector, four branches have been created: Comprehensive Claims, Specific Claims, Implementation, and Self-government.

The Comprehensive Claims Branch represents Canada in all negotiations of comprehensive land claims with Aboriginal groups. This branch (also known as the modern day treaties branch) has the responsibility to negotiate the settlement of land claims and to ensure that Aboriginal people are protected in the negotiated settlement. Its primary goal is to provide a clear and long-lasting definition of rights to lands and resources for Aboriginals and other Canadians. It is also responsible for ensuring that the settlement provides economic opportunities for Aboriginal groups, that the settlement respects the fundamental rights and freedoms of Canadians, and that the interests of the general public are respected.

Through the Specific Claims Branch, this sector undertakes the assessment of specific claims submitted by Indian bands and conducts negotiations on behalf of the government. The assessment process entails determining whether the federal government has breached legal obligations to a band and compensating the band if the government has breached this obligation.

The Implementation Branch monitors and manages the implementation of comprehensive land claims and self-government agreements. This branch also provides policy support and expertise where specific claims agreements are being settled. This branch ensures that what the parties agreed to is in fact carried out. There are two steps to this process. The first is the development of an implementation plan, while the second phase is the monitoring and management of actual implementation activities. Today, the parties to a land claims and/or self-government agreement must negotiate a plan, which becomes an integral part of the overall agreement. This plan identifies what must be done to put the agreement into effect, who will be responsible for which implementation activity, and how and when these activities will be undertaken.

The fourth branch of the sector is Self-government. Self-government agreements identify arrangements for Aboriginal groups to govern their internal affairs and assume greater responsibility and control over the decision making that affects their communities. Because Aboriginal groups have different needs, the federal government has recognized that there is no single model of self-government that will be used for all negotiations. As such, self-government arrangements will take many forms based on the diverse historical, cultural, political, and economic circumstances of the Aboriginal groups, regions, and communities involved.

Northern Affairs

The Northern Affairs sector assists the social, cultural, political, and economic development of the Yukon, Nunavut, and the Northwest Territories, and while not specifically directed toward Aboriginal people, it does place particular emphasis on the needs of Northern Aboriginals. The program operates directly, as well as indirectly, through the governments of the two territories. It also is responsible for the Polar Commission.

The Northern Affairs sector activities as they relate to Aboriginals focus on the settlement of land claims, establishing cooperative mechanisms to support economic development, and the enhancement of Arctic sovereignty and circumpolar cooperation. The Constitutional Development and Strategic Planning branch, Natural Resources and Economic Development branch, and Comprehensive Claims branch make up the focus of this program. The first branch's goal is to establish transfer programs resembling provincial programs to territorial governments, thus encouraging the development of Northern political institutions and diversification of the economy and reinforcing Canadians' sovereignty. The Natural Resources and Economic Development branch has a myriad of functions, ranging from the Biological Division—which focuses on the management of wildlife—to carrying out the responsibilities for the North American Air Defense Modernization Project.

Corporate Services and Legal Services focus on ensuring that operations within Indian and Northern Affairs are carried out effectively, efficiently, and legally. In addition, Legal Services Support oversees the various claims and grievances that are presented as well as ensures that all contracts between Indians and the government of Canada are appropriate.

THE COST OF THE DEPARTMENT OF INDIAN AND NORTHERN AFFAIRS

The government of Canada operates more than 100 programs that are directed in whole or in part toward Aboriginal people in Canada.[3] The direct cost of these programs is well in excess of $7 billion (see Table 12.1). The beneficiaries of these programs—Indians, Inuits, Métis, and non-status Indians—add up to almost one million people. However, as indicated previously, Indian and Inuit Affairs is not the only federal agency that provides services for Aboriginals.

Twelve federal departments offer programs for Aboriginal Canadians. Table 12.2 identifies the federal expenditures for Aboriginals over the past two decades. It shows that the overall annual budget has increased from $703 million to over $8 billion. During this time, the yearly growth rate in expenditures has varied from 3.2 percent to over 20 percent, with an average annual growth rate of 5.7 percent. Nearly two-thirds of the total budget is covered by Indian and Northern Affairs, with Health and Welfare Canada being the second largest contributor.

In 1975 the federal expenditures on Aboriginal programs represented 2.1 percent of overall federal expenditures (excluding expenditures on public debt). By 2003, this had increased to 4.6 percent of the federal budget. Overall, federal spending has now grown about 8 percent, while spending on Aboriginals is now increasing at about 11.2 percent annually.

Over the years the federal government has developed numerous programs for status Indians. Although we noted above that there are 12 major federal departments that deal with Aboriginals, nearly all federal expenditures flow through four main routes. Quasi-

TABLE 12.1	Approximate Federal Expenditures for Aboriginal Peoples[1]							
	Expenditures by Department[2] ($ Millions)				Federal Departments			
Year	INAC	NHW	EIC	CMHC	ISTC	SS	Other	Total
1975-76	587	74	–	3	26	13	–	703
1980-81	1134	155	57	58	44	23	4	1475
1985-86	1990	341	159	156	15	53	22	2736
1990-91	3081	578	152	199	85	45	22	4162
1991-92	3412	639	200	240	79	62	42	4674
1992-93	3647	706	200	272	76	51	89	5041
2003-04	5471	1682	337	307	40	69	1905	9811

Note:
1. Federal departments and agencies that have Aboriginal programs include Indian and Northern Affairs Canada; Health and Welfare Canada; Employment and Immigration Canada; Canada Mortgage and Housing Corporation; Industry, Science and Technology Canada; Secretary of State; Solicitor General; Fisheries and Oceans; Public Service Commission; Justice; and National Defence. Data are from annual reports of the respective departments.
2. 1991-92 and 1992-93 figures are from Main Estimates. Figures include spending on Aboriginal employment equity programs, but do not include spending on programs available to all Canadians, such as Old Age Security and Unemployment Insurance. Data are from annual reports of respective departments.

statutory programs receive 40 percent of the total budget. These programs are directed toward Indians living on reserves, and they reflect the legal obligations of Canada through the establishment of the *Indian Act, Constitution Act, 1982*, and other legal directives implemented over the past two centuries. Basic services (36 percent) include expenditures on schools, community infrastructures, health, housing, and local government. The third category of expenditures is claims. As noted previously, while this program only made up 3 percent of the total budget a decade ago, it has increased substantially over the next decade as the backlog of claims is settled (15 percent).

On a per capita basis the data show a steady increase over the past decade. In 1981, the per capita cost of operating Indian and Northern Affairs was $5 678. By 1993 it was well in excess of $12 000—a 54 percent increase, although it has subsequently decreased to just over $7000 in 2003. As noted earlier, the Department of Indian and Northern Affairs covers two-thirds of all Aboriginal expenditures. The actual programs and services delivered to Aboriginal people vary by group and location. Some are provided directly by the Indian and Inuit Affairs Program, while others come from territorial governments that are, in turn, reimbursed for their costs. Indians living on reserves deal directly with the federal government. On the other hand, off-reserve Indians face a complicated pattern of eligibility for government services (Government of Canada, 1985). The federal government takes the position that off-reserve Indians should avail themselves of provincial services, while the provinces argue that Indians are a federal responsibility. Sometimes proof of residence is required (e.g., proof of having lived 12 months off the reserve) before provinces consider Indians eligible for provincial services.

TABLE 12.2	Budgets for Federal Programs Directed to Aboriginal Peoples (millions)			
	1993–94	2003–04	% of INAC	% of Total
Indian and Northern Affairs Canada (INAC)				
Self-government	18.3	137	3	2
Claims	70.9	673	11	8
Economic Development	98	152	3	2
Lands, Revenues, and Trusts	140.3	119	2	1
Education	903.3	1431	23	16
Social Development	816.3	1194	19	13
Capital Facilities	665.1	1027	17	12
Band Management	269.4	377	6	4
Northern Affairs	572.4	133	2	2
Other	92.9	902	15	10
Subtotal	3647	6145	101	70
Other Government Departments/Agencies				
Health Canada	706.4	1682	–	19
Canadian Mortgage & Housing	271.8	307	–	3
Fisheries & Oceans	8.0	164	–	2
Solicitor General	44.7	84	–	1
Justice	9.7	13	–	–
National Defence	4.3	8	–	–
Secretary of State (Heritage)	51.3	69	–	1
Human Resources	200	337	–	4
Industry	76	40	–	–
Correctional Services	–	28	–	–
Indian Residential Schools and Resolution Canada	–	58	–	–
Natural Resources	–	17	–	–
Privy Council Office	–	15	–	–
Subtotal	1394.6	2820	–	30

FEDERAL EXPENDITURES: A COMPARISON

Courehene and Powell (1992) attempt to estimate the dollar value of federal spending on registered Indians living on the reserve. Overall, they find that on-reserve Indians receive about $9300 per capita per year. If administrative costs are added to this figure, the value increases to $10 100. If we compare this value with the total provincial expenditures per capita, we find that the overall expenditure for all Canadians is $10 500, although this value varies by province, with a low of $9700 in Newfoundland and Labrador and a high of $11 700 in Nova Scotia (Hory and Walker, 1991). This suggests that on a per capita basis Indians are receiving expenditures similar to other Canadians. While the numbers have changed in the past decade, the analysis of data today reveals that a similar pattern exists.

However, Indians argue that, because of their inferior position in Canadian society, the government needs to increase its expenditures. For confirmation of this view, the recent Royal Commission on Aboriginal Peoples recommends that additional expenditures be allocated to Aboriginal people in order for them to shed their low socio-economic status.

There has been considerable criticism of Indian and Northern Affairs with regard to its administrative expenditures, which amount to $1100 per person. Overall, this adds an additional $81 million per year to the total budget. However, the percentage of Indian and Northern Affairs' budget that is allocated to administrative overhead has declined throughout the past two decades. For example, in 1985 the Department's overhead was 6 percent of the total budget; by 2003 this had decreased to 3.2 percent. This reduction has come about through some loss of public employees, but much of it has come about through the process of devolution in which departmental activities have been turned over to First Nations.

It should be noted that services provided to Aboriginals far exceed the federal government's constitutional and legislative responsibility. Many programs and services have been implemented as a strategy to lessen Aboriginal poverty and distress. While some programs have produced positive results, most have been dismal failures—both in the short and the long term.

GOVERNMENT POLICY

Those who determine Indian and Inuit Affairs Program policies seldom, if ever, have direct experience with Aboriginal issues. Policies are developed by Indian and Inuit Affairs Program bureaucrats in headquarters and amended by bureaucrats from other government areas that are likely to be affected by the policies. As Weaver (1980) points out in her analysis of the 1960 White Paper, the Privy Council Office, the Prime Minister's Office, the Treasury Board, and the Cabinet wield the most direct influence on federal policy concerning Aboriginals. In the 1960s the Privy Council Office and Prime Minister's Office were restructured to assert the primacy of the prime minister and Cabinet in setting policy and monitoring programs. This restructuring has allowed the Privy Council Office, Prime Minister's Office, and Cabinet to maintain much closer control of Indian and Inuit Affairs Program activities and to evaluate those activities in the context of other government departments (Poss, 1975). The 1960s also saw a major restructuring of the system of standing committees in the House of Commons. This change has permitted members of Parliament to interact more directly with the staff of the Indian and Inuit Affairs Program and to expand their roles through a process of open discussion (Weaver, 1980).

These two changes removed policy development and implementation from the total control of particular departments and ensured that policies would be evaluated in the context of policies from other departments. Policy advisory councils were created to report to the Cabinet; in effect, these councils are one step above the Cabinet in power. Information from each department is now filtered through the Privy Council Office and Prime Minister's Office instead of passing directly from senior bureaucrats to Cabinet ministers (Ponting and Gibbins, 1980).[4]

These changes have had a direct effect on organized attempts by Aboriginals to influence policy and program development. There is now another entire set of bureaucrats that must be lobbied. Moreover, they can only be lobbied by an intermediary and within the confines of committees with legitimate powers of inquiry (Pross, 1975). As a result, Aboriginal groups have reorganized their efforts to influence the politics that affect them. They have also found new ways to counter the increasing input of the Privy Council Office and Prime Minister's Office into general policy recommendations (Preshus, 1974).

The federal government had previously maintained that, under Section 91(24) of the *British North America Act*, it had the constitutional obligation to provide funds and services to registered Indians on reserves. It argued that off-reserve Indians were a provincial responsibility. At present, there is ongoing debate between federal and provincial governments concerning which of them should finance and deliver services to Aboriginals both on and off the reserves.

The federal government acknowledges a special relationship between itself and Aboriginal Canadians. It agrees that registered Indians and Inuit possess special rights, privileges, and entitlements, whether they live on or off the reserves. But, although the federal government acknowledges its responsibility to on- and off-reserve Aboriginals, it claims that they should look to other levels of government for certain services. In addition, the federal government regards its responsibility for off-reserve services in a different light than that for on-reserve services. More specifically, under Section 91(24) of the *BNA Act* the government has accepted responsibility for on-reserve services in more program areas than for off-reserve services.

The federal government argues that as Aboriginals move off reserves they become citizens of a province; as such, they have a basic right to the same services provided by the province to all its other residents. Nevertheless, the federal government has a number of direct off-reserve support programs in such areas as housing and post-secondary education. In addition, it provides transfer and block payments to the provinces based on Aboriginal population figures under such programs as Established Program Financing and Equalization. These programs are intended to help provide the same services to Aboriginals as are provided to the general provincial population.

The federal government, then, maintains that each level of government has its respective responsibilities based on separate, distinct bonds with Aboriginal peoples. Aboriginals who live off reserves are residents of provinces and often contribute to provincial tax revenues; in addition, they have often provided indirectly many other resources now available to the provinces, and they are included in the calculation of transfer and block payments to the provinces. The provinces, on the other hand, take the position that Indians are a federal concern and not under the jurisdiction of provincial governments.

In early 1991 Ottawa decided to limit spending on social services for Indians. It decided that it would no longer pay social assistance to Indians for the first year after they leave a reserve. Provinces have reiterated their stance that Indians and the welfare of Indians, whether it be on-reserve or off-reserve, is a responsibility of the federal government. Indians likewise agree with the provinces' stand, and argue that the social services question is a federal responsibility and should not be transferred to the provinces. The projected costs and savings of such a move are also debated. Western provinces have argued that this policy change has cost each of them $15–$20 million per year. The federal government, while giving no specific figures, calculates the cost at much less. In addition, the federal government argues that the savings that accrue through this change will be reinvested in child and family services on the reserve. This program, they argue, will reduce long-term costs for Aboriginals and thus will save the provinces additional monies in the long term.

DEVOLUTION

The Indian and Inuit Affairs Program has been in the process of decentralization (decolonialization) since 1964. In 1969 the then Department of Indian Affairs and Northern Development simply stated in the White Paper that Aboriginals were to become a provincial responsibility. This policy was rejected by Aboriginal organizations and provincial governments alike. In the mid-1970s a new policy emerged involving the transfer of federal responsibility to Aboriginal bands rather than to the provinces. At the same time, administrative responsibilities were being shifted from Ottawa to the regional and district offices of DIAND. As a result, Aboriginals have gained a somewhat greater involvement in the policy formations of the Indian and Inuit Affairs Program (Ponting and Gibbins, 1980).

The devolution of responsibility for the delivery of services and programs from Indian and Northern Affairs to the direct control of First Nations began in earnest in the 1970s. This process is taking place through a range of mechanisms—funding contributions, alternative funding arrangements, grants, and flexible transfer payments. For example, in 1993 there were 110 signed alternative funding arrangements with 198 bands, totalling nearly $400 million. Today this figure has doubled. These alternative funding arrangements provide bands with the maximum level of authority available under existing legislation and policy. They also allow bands to redesign programs and re-allocate funds that meet community priorities.

From 1983 to 1993 the number of people working in the Indian and Inuit Program decreased by 42 percent. As a result of this strategy, Phase I of the Devolution Plan—which involves the transfers of community services such as social development and education—is now almost complete.

The shift of responsibility to band governments is taking place at three levels. First, funds for program management are being transferred from the Indian and Inuit Affairs Program to the direct control of the bands. This transfer began in 1968; by 1971, bands were managing about 14 percent of a $160 million budget and, by 1978–79, about 35 percent of a $659 million budget. Today they control over 70 percent of the budget exceeding $4 billion. Second, core funding grants are provided for the basic administrative costs of chiefs, councils, and band managers. In 1978–79, these grants represented 4 percent of the total DIAND budget; today this has nearly doubled to 7.5 percent. Third, band training and support services are supplied to encourage management skills and to provide technical support.

At present, the bands administer about 60 percent of the total capital and 80 percent of the school budgets. Approximately 90 percent of the bands are involved in the core funding program, but these figures show considerable regional disparity–e.g., Manitoba bands control a great deal of their operational expenditures, while the Yukon bands control very little. In addition to showing that over 80 percent of Indian and Inuit Affairs Program expenditures flow through Aboriginal governance structures, we also know that the number of full-time federal employees in the program has decreased by 51 percent from nearly 4000 in 1987 to less than half that number ten years later.

This policy of devolution was designed to promote the autonomy of Aboriginal bands and to support self-government. It marks a shift in federal policy from programs that promoted integration and assimilation to those that encourage tribal government and cultural self-sufficiency. Band councils are increasingly responsible for financial allocations. However, although the Indian and Inuit Affairs Program is relinquishing specific control over expenditures, it still retains control of the overall allocation of funds and demands an accounting of funds spent. In effect, this policy has shifted critical attention away from the Indian and Inuit Affairs Program to the local chief, council, and manager.

This policy also has meant that Aboriginals must be fully involved in discussions on a broad range of program-related and political issues. With the new band autonomy, certain programs can no longer be implemented without first consulting Aboriginals. Moreover, Aboriginal associations have been steadily putting pressure on the Indian and Inuit Affairs Program, requesting forums for discussion of a range of issues related to federal and provincial policies. Unfortunately, these consultations have not taken place. Or, in other cases, legitimately elected officials—e.g., Chiefs of the Assembly of First Nations—are bypassed, and discussions between Ottawa and individual members of the First Nations community are taking place.

Again, this attempt to provide a forum for Aboriginal participation reflects a shift in federal policy from a desire to assimilate Aboriginals toward an increasing emphasis on tribal government. The tripartite—i.e., federal/provincial/Aboriginal—discussion partly arose from a belief by Indian Affairs personnel that Aboriginals had developed enough political leadership skills to articulate their needs. In addition, the provinces became willing to discuss priority issues set forth by Aboriginals, largely to avoid being excluded from any far-reaching negotiations that might take place elsewhere in Canada. However, despite promises to the contrary, Aboriginals are still effectively excluded from much of the negotiation process. Currently, much of the discussion between federal and provincial officials circumvents involvement through the use of personal communications, confidential documents, and so on.

The origin of Indian and Northern Affairs' changing policy goes back to 1959, when Prime Minister John Diefenbaker was embarrassed during a foreign tour by strong criticism of Canada's Aboriginal policy. Upon his return, he established a joint committee of the Senate and the House of Commons to investigate and advise on the administration of Indian Affairs. The context was a favourable one for Aboriginal Canadians: Diefenbaker had just won a decisive victory in the 1958 election, and Gladstone—a Blood Indian from Alberta—had just been appointed to the Senate. Due to the joint committee's recommendations, the law was changed in 1960 to give Aboriginals the right to vote in federal elections. The committee also recommended that the Indian and Inuit Affairs Program should cease to provide special services to Aboriginals and instead should rely on and share the existing services of other agencies, including those of the provincial governments.

In 1976 a new mega-policy was introduced by the minister of Indian and Northern Affairs to promote "Indian identity within Canadian society." The definition and evolution of Aboriginal identity were to be treated as flexible and dynamic. In general, the policy continues to recognize Aboriginal status, treaty rights, and special privileges resulting from land claims settlements. Within Aboriginal band and reserve communities, local self-determination and control of Aboriginal affairs are to be encouraged. In addition, for the first time the policy noted that different needs, aspirations, and attitudes among Aboriginals in all parts of Canada rule out a single uniform strategy. As a result, the policy emphasizes joint participation in program development with organized Aboriginal leadership at all levels. Under the new policy, the federal government takes the initiative in defining the aims and general shape of strategies applied to Aboriginal issues. If the government chooses, this process can involve Aboriginal representatives at various levels. The major goal of the new policy is to transfer the administration of programs and resources to band governments. The rate of transfer is determined by the desire and ability of each to assume control of its own affairs, including the implementation of programs.

In general, policies at the Indian and Inuit Affairs Program are developed internally by middle-level administrative personnel who employ data collected by Indian Affairs and external consultants. Normally the Indian and Inuit Affairs Program hires 10 to 15 consultants per year to carry out specific research. Although policy development is continuous in the program, it tends to increase dramatically when a government has been defeated or when an election is in progress. This suggests that policy evaluation and development are not put in place as a result of "evidence based decision making" but rather as a political exercise (Ponting and Gibbins, 1980).

In today's environment, the government has tried to support strong, sustainable communities through such means as establishing government-to-government relations as well as enhancing the First Nations community's ability to establish proper governance structures. As an immediate activity, the Department has tried to empower First Nations constituents to hold their governments to account by providing First Nations with the tools to implement modern, effective governance regimes and practices. This has been supported by a number of legislative governance packages that have been introduced over the past two to three years—e.g., the *First Nations Governance Act*, the *Specific Claims Resolution Act*, the *First Nations Fiscal and Statistical Management Act*, and the *First Nations Land Management Act*. It is hoped that these pieces of legislation will allow First Nations communities to engage in activities such as leadership selection, administration, financial management, land resource management, citizen redress, and organization support. At the same time, the federal government will be able to decrease its involvement in the day-to-day operations of First Nations communities. Therefore, the capacity of First Nations to achieve self-sufficiency and develop their own public service will be enhanced.

THE LATENT FUNCTIONS OF THE INDIAN AND INUIT AFFAIRS PROGRAM

Like many other organizations, the Indian and Inuit Affairs Program is a highly structured, rational system that espouses specific policies and pursues specific goals. It has defined Aboriginal welfare as its sole concern; overtly, all its activities are geared to improving that welfare. Also like other organizations, however, the Indian and Inuit Affairs Program pursues certain latent goals that are quite independent of its stated formal goals. As Perrow (1980) and several others have observed, organizations often exist not only to serve their stated goals but to serve other interests as well. In fact, some would even argue that the stated policy and goals of an organization largely function only to legitimize its existence. An organization makes its stated goals explicit through its formal policy statements. Its latent goal structure, however, becomes apparent only through an examination of the services that it provides for interest groups other than those it manifestly serves.

The organizations dealing with Aboriginal people all possess a number of latent functions. For the past century, the Indian and Inuit Affairs Program and its forerunners have stated that their primary manifest goal is the ultimate participation of Aboriginals as equals in Canadian society. The latent goals of these organizations include such self-referential aims as cost-efficiency and freedom from conflict within their own structures. Another latent function is to provide resources for other organizations. Many other institutions make extensive use of the nearly $700 million and 3000 employees provided to the Indian and Inuit Affairs Program at public expense; examples range from Aboriginal organizations to educational institutions to businesses.

Although other latent functions could be documented here, none is so extensive as the latent attempt by federal administrators to control the lives of Aboriginals. Throughout its history, the major latent function of the Indian and Inuit Affairs Program has been the regulation of Aboriginal behaviour. Aboriginal people have been lured to cities where their dependent status forces them to conform, or they have been segregated on reserves, concealed from the view of middle-class Canadians. They have been arbitrarily dispersed throughout cities or forcibly bused out of town, back to the reserve. Often the control of Aboriginals has been achieved through the behavioural requirements attached to various social services. For example, the off-reserve housing program requires applicants to have steady full-time jobs before they are eligible for loans.

Regardless of the technique, the result is that Aboriginals are manipulated and restricted in their actions. To be sure, some Aboriginals are helped in the process and many have obtained educational benefits, training, counselling, and money, but only after conforming to middle-class behavioural criteria. Thus, control is the central goal of the majority of organizations dealing with Aboriginal people.

The insistence of the federal government upon control over its Aboriginal wards has characterized federal government–Aboriginal relations since Confederation. As Whiteside (1980) points out,

> Perhaps we should recall the various measures the bureaucrats introduced during this period to ensure "orderly administration": (1) the development of a single piece of legislation in 1876, to govern all the Indian Nations, regardless of varying traditions and history; (2) the systematic destruction of tribal governments and replacement of them with band councils which were really an extension of the Department's [Indian Affairs'] structure; (3) the systematic attempt to destroy Indian culture and the outlawing of Indian religious ceremonies; (4) the introduction of compulsory enfranchisement provisions to control bad Indians; (5) the systematic attempts to harness and discredit Indian leaders who attempt to develop or strengthen Indian political organization (p. 6).

On the reserve, the Indian and Inuit Affairs Program is a "total" institution in that it has a monopoly on the delivery of services to a captive clientele. Its organization is characterized by specialization, hierarchy, and regimentation, while its clients are relatively uneducated, unspecialized, and varied. By limiting the choices available to its Aboriginal clients, the Indian and Inuit Affairs Program shapes and standardizes Aboriginal behaviour at minimal cost and risk to itself.

The success of the Indian and Inuit Affairs Program is not assessed on the basis of the assistance it provides to Aboriginals but rather on the basis of how effectively it has kept Aboriginal behaviour under control. The brighter officials at the Indian and Inuit Affairs Program know perfectly well that they will not be fired, transferred, or demoted for failing to help Aboriginals receive decent education, find jobs, mend broken homes, and settle into life in the city. Rather, the officials' assessment will be based on the number of Aboriginals they handled, and at what cost per person. Programs that fail to meet their announced goals do not result in fired personnel or radical organizational changes. The upper management of the Indian and Inuit Affairs Program can simply blame failures on a need for organizational restructuring, a lack of adequately trained fieldworkers, a poorly allocated budget, and so on.

All this is not to suggest that the Indian and Inuit Affairs Program does not help Aboriginals. On the contrary, some Aboriginals get bursaries to go to university, some get loans to buy houses in the city, and others get vocational training. Nor is this analysis intended to suggest that Indian and Inuit Affairs Program officials deliberately neglect the needs of Aboriginal people. Rather, such neglect is the result of internal and structural forces that cause a reordering of goal priorities.

Certain internal forces acting upon the Indian and Inuit Affairs Program cause it to downplay its stated goal of improving the quality of Aboriginal life. First, government officials tend to become disproportionately concerned with the number of their employees, the size of their budgets, and the quantity, rather than the quality, of their programs. Because it is difficult, time-consuming, and speculative to assess the effectiveness of an organization, readily quantifiable criteria become the indicators of a successful program. Because these indicators measure cost efficiency rather than program effectiveness, they are simple to tabulate, highly visible, and extremely responsive to changes.

A second internal factor is the emphasis on stability within the Indian and Inuit Affairs Program. There is an implicit rule that conflict should not be evident in any federal department. If conflict does exist, it must remain an internal affair. The preoccupation of the Indian and Inuit Affairs Program with remaining conflict-free results, once again, in a downplaying of stated goals and objectives.

In all of the organizations that deal with Aboriginal issues, officials accept and promote the existing expectations, norms, and mores of a free-enterprise, class-based system. This places severe limitations on the programs offered to Aboriginal people. For example, not one organization has suggested that most of the Indian and Inuit Affairs Program's budget should be given directly to Aboriginal people or used to organize Aboriginals into an effective political force. Quite the contrary. One of the better-known attempts to organize Aboriginals politically in a Western urban centre resulted in the dissolution of one district office and substantial reassignment of personnel. A similar response ended the ill-fated Community Development Program, which was phased out within a few years of its inception.

Today's Aboriginal policy reflects the recent decisions of the courts as well as the recommendations of the Royal Commission on Aboriginal Peoples. Courts have become more intrusive in government–Indian relations and have clearly identified the rights and responsibilities of government and Indians. In addition, the Royal Commission identified key issues that needed to be addressed immediately if the mission of Indian and Northern Affairs is to be achieved. We now turn to a brief analysis of the Royal Commission.

THE ROYAL COMMISSION ON ABORIGINAL PEOPLES

The Royal Commission evolved out of the Oka crisis in 1990 and subsequent overt conflict that was erupting throughout the country as Aboriginals attempted to deal with legal and economic issues confronting them. An early version of the Commission's report was released in 1993, but it was not until late in 1996 that the Royal Commission tabled a six-volume, 5000 page document on the status of Aboriginal people in Canada. After four years and nearly $60 million, the most expensive federal inquiry in Canadian history laid out a 20-year plan to deal with Aboriginals. The report is based on 177 days of hearings, with 3500 witnesses and some internally commissioned research. The report concludes that Canada can no longer allow Aboriginals to remain dependent on the nation.

The report begins with a recap of historical events involving Indians, and demonstrates how they were made a dependent population. The Commission notes that Canada systematically denied Indians their nation status, violated most agreements made with Indians, and suppressed their culture and institutions. In short, the report claims that Canadians built a great liberal democracy, in part through the dispossession of Aboriginal people. As a result, Aboriginals exist in conditions of poverty and social upheaval. This reality has become a vicious circle of cause and effect. A key approach is not to allocate more money but to address the fractured historical relationship between Aboriginals and Canada. The roots of injustice lie in history–and it is there that the key to regeneration of Aboriginal society and a new and better relationship with the rest of Canada can be found.

Report Recommendations

The Commission was specific in its recommendations, and its major point was to encourage the federal government to move immediately and with major changes. Four themes made up the plan for political action that would take Aboriginal people to a better position in Canadian society. First, the Commission wanted the federal government to release a Royal Proclamation (and other related legislation) that would allow for the implementation of a new partnership between First Nations and the federal government. Second, it requested the federal government to begin to take action that would rebuild Aboriginal nations and help them re-establish their rightful place in Canadian society. This recognition of a new level of government would be introduced through a new piece of legislation called the *Aboriginal Nations Recognition and Government Act*. Third, the Commission recommended that various levels of government begin the process of negotiation as to how the new Aboriginal order of government in Canada would be established. Finally, the Commission recommended that new or renewed treaties between Aboriginal nations and other levels of government be undertaken.

The Commission also developed several principles upon which the government would be guided in formally recognizing the existence of Aboriginal nations, and established the criteria and process for recognition. The Commission wanted the government to accept these principles as important premises for negotiations between Aboriginals and the various levels of government. For example, one of the principles was that Aboriginal groups might assert their modern nationhood in a variety of ways. Another was that nationhood is linked to the principle of territoriality. There was an overarching belief by the Commission that a political relationship between Aboriginals and the federal government was a key factor in achieving the recommendations that the report outlined.

The report recommends that, over the next 20 years, the federal government spend an additional $38 billion on Aboriginals. The report notes that documents reveal that $2.5 billion per year is now spent to offset Aboriginal poverty ($50 billion over 20 years). It notes that about $1 billion is spent annually on social assistance on reserves, where unemployment hovers around 80 percent and Aboriginal communities endure Third World living conditions. But it notes that lost productivity, lost income, and lost potential taxes bring the total economic cost of the unhealthy relationship with Aboriginals to over $7 billion, equivalent to 1 percent of Canada's gross domestic product ($140 billion over the 20-year period). The report also notes that since over half of the Aboriginal population is under 25 years of age, if nothing is done the estimated cost for dealing with Aboriginals by the year 2016 will increase to $11 billion (see Table 12.3). The Commission forecasts that if monies were now invested the result would be a huge saving by 2016. Table 12.3 shows the specific cost of maintaining the status quo, as well as how government finances would change if the strategy were implemented.

The report proposes that the federal government increase its spending for Aboriginals to $1.5 billion for the next seven years and to $2 billion for 13 years. The logic of such a recommendation is that within 10 years there will be a fall in the remedial costs and a rise in government revenues as Aboriginal people become more productive and begin to make a net contribution to the economic development of Canada. For example, the expensive "front end" cost of addressing the housing crisis on reserves would cost nearly $3 billion. However, in 10 to 15 years the savings would be in excess of twice that value. The extra money would go toward building new health centres, stimulating the Aboriginal economy, upgrading the infrastructure on reserves, and dealing with crisis conditions now found in Aboriginal communities. Then a long-term program of training Aboriginals would be put in place. Later, monies would be used to settle land claims and to implement self-government.

The Commission also calls for an Aboriginal Parliament (The House of First Peoples) that would represent Aboriginals from across Canada and advise the federal government. This third level of government would represent First Nations. It is estimated that the more than 2000 reserves would coalesce into some 30 to 50 Aboriginal nations, such as the Cree or Algonquin. These nations would take on powers similar to that of the provinces with regard to Aboriginal people.

TABLE 12.3	Cost of the Status Quo	
	($ billions)	
	1996	2016
Cost to Aboriginal Peoples		
Earned income forgone	5.8	8.6
Income taxes forgone	-2.1	-3.1
Financial assistance from governments	-.8	-1.2
Net income loss of Aboriginal Peoples	**2.9**	**4.3**
Cost to Governments		
Expenditures on remedial programs	1.7	2.4
Financial assistance to Aboriginals	.8	1.2
Government revenue forgone	2.1	3.1
Total Cost to Governments	**4.6**	**6.7**
Total Cost of Status Quo	**7.5**	**11.0**

Note:
   The cost of the status quo is shown in italics. Other figures show how this cost is distributed.
   Most of the cost of forgone earned income ($5.8 billion in 1996) is borne by Aboriginal people in the form of lost income. The rest is borne by governments in the form of taxes forgone and various forms of assistance paid out. These costs to governments are not included in the amount given for Cost to Aboriginal People.

Source: Table 2.12: Present and Future Annual Cost of the Status Quo ($ billions), Changes in Government Finances under the Strategy ($ millions) from the Report of the Royal Commission on Aboriginal Peoples, Privy Council Office. Reproduced with the permission of the Minister of Public Works and Government Services Canada, 2004.

TABLE 12.4	Projected Results of the Royal Commission's Strategy	
	Additional allocation in the year	
	2001	2016
	($ millions)	($ millions)
Structural Measures		
Tribunal and treaty commissions	50	50
Nation rebuilding	50	0
Nation governments	50	425
Land claims settlements	0	1000
Total for Structural Measures	**150**	**1475**
Social and Economic Measures		
Healing, education, youth, and culture	300	150
Health care	100	(450)
Social services	100	(425)
Justice	25	(325)
Economic Opportunities and Living Conditions		
Economic development	350	225
Income transfers	0	(250)
Housing and infrastructure	400	350
Human resource development	150	425
Total for Social and Economic Measures	**1425**	**(300)**
Government Revenue Gains	–	(1550)
Overall Total	**1575**	**(375)**

Note:
  Positive entries (figures without parentheses) show the increase in spending by all governments needed to implement the strategy.
  Reductions are shown by numbers in parentheses in the second column. These relate to amounts saved as a result of the strategy (that is, amounts that would be spent if the status quo were to continue) and to additional revenues collected by governments.
  Figures are rounded to the nearest $25 million.

Source: Table 2.12: Present and Future Annual Cost of the Status Quo ($ billions), Changes in Government Finances under the Strategy ($ millions) from the Report of the Royal Commission on Aboriginal Peoples, Privy Council Office. Reproduced with the permission of the Minister of Public Works and Government Services Canada, 2004.

In the end, over 400 recommendations were put forth by the Commission. Specific recommendations ranged from the Queen and Parliament issuing a royal proclamation acknowledging mistakes of the past and committing governments to a new relationship to the availability of tax credits for investors in Aboriginal venture-capital corporations. Table 12.4 outlines the projected results of the Royal Commission's strategy.

Aboriginal Reaction

Aboriginal leaders were supportive of the Commission's report and felt that for the first time in many years they had something to look forward to. However, they also noted that if this report were not taken seriously Canadians should be prepared to face some serious social and economic consequences. As Mr. Erasmus (one of the members of the Commission) noted, "If the reality is that once more people's hopes have been dashed, and that this was all for nothing, then what we say is that people will resort to other things." The president of the Métis National Council also strongly supported the Commission's recognition of the Métis as an Aboriginal people who should have an adequate land base. In summary, most Aboriginal peoples responded favourably to the report and felt that positive outcomes would result.

Canadians' Reaction

An Insight Canada survey in 1997 found that only 18 percent of Canadians believed that the Royal Commission was the best way to arrive at a solution for Aboriginal people. A majority of Canadians had more confidence in Aboriginals themselves or their organizations. The survey also noted that Canadian attitudes toward Aboriginals are hardening. Nearly 40 percent of Canadians believed Aboriginals have themselves to blame for their problems, and almost half of the poll respondents believed that Aboriginals had an equal or better standard of living than the average. Fifty-eight percent of Canadians are not convinced that adequate measures are in place to ensure that money received from the government is managed responsibly by Aboriginals. In the end, it would seem that Indian issues are losing their importance for most Canadians as other concerns—e.g., jobs, health care, and education—are becoming more important items on the political agenda.

Government Reaction

The initial response by the government of the day was one of indifference and hostility. For some time, the federal government did not respond to the Commission's report. The Minister of Indian Affairs at the time noted that the report, because it was two years late in being submitted, had already been eclipsed by changes in the Department of Indian Affairs, claiming that changes in the Department had already addressed many of the issues raised in the report. Finally, the Minister noted that he would find it impossible to approach his Cabinet ministers for additional monies in this time of financial constraint. The Prime Minister also steered away from the report, and when invited to an all-chiefs conference at the time, declined to attend without offering an explanation. The federal government's sense of the negative political realities of providing more funding for Aboriginal communities, the lack of sensitivity or care for Aboriginal issues by the general population, and the emergence of other issues, all led to the downplaying of the Commission's recommendations.

However, the federal government's formal reaction to the Commission's report came on January 7, 1998, with the publication of the document *Gathering Strength—Canada's Aboriginal Action Plan*. This document, in tandem with another government document, *Sustainable Development Strategy*, outlines the goals of helping develop strong, healthy First Nations communities and setting up new relationships founded on mutual respect, with responsible, transparent, accountable, sustainable governance structures and institutions. It was an integrated, government-wide plan to address the major challenges facing Aboriginal people—structural reform of the federal government's Aboriginal programming to promote self-sufficiency and economic development, and the enhancement and strengthening of the capacity of Aboriginal governments and organizations to run accountable, responsive government systems. Some initial investments were made for "healing" and reconciliation, but these "one time" funds have since been exhausted and there has been no attempt to measure the impact of such a fund. However, the reader should be aware that the federal policy failed to endorse the national action plan recommended by the Royal Commission (Chartrand, 2002). Instead, the federal government has opted for its traditional strategy of trying for slow, incremental policy shifts. As Chartrand (2002) points out, the federal policy response seems to reflect the government's philosophy that incremental change is more politically manageable than the kind of fundamental change that was recommended by the Royal Commission.

On the other hand, each year, the Department of Indian and Northern Affairs has outlined its goals and objectives, and has provided a listing of the strategies it has taken (and plans to take for the next year) to achieve these goals. Finally, in its annual reports, the Department identifies targets and outcomes for each of the strategies and goals identified. For example, it was very clear in 1999 that it would be trying to enhance Aboriginal governance capacity. The recent introduction of *Bill C-31* (a newly proposed *Governance Act*) is clear evidence the Department has moved on this goal. However, how it arrived at this goal has been neither clear nor acceptable to a number of First Nations people. Other goals outlined by the federal government in 2000 have not been achieved at this time—e.g., to have 50–60 specific claims settled and to conclude up to 18 comprehensive claim settlement agreements-in-principle and up to 17 final agreements by 2003. Nevertheless, the accountability framework adopted by Indian and Northern Affairs allows one to track its progress in achieving goals (or lack thereof) over time. It also allows one to match resource investment with goals to assess if the allocation is appropriate and sufficient.

CONCLUSION

In summary, throughout Canada's history little attention has been paid to developing an Aboriginal policy that has had major Aboriginal input. Moreover, funding of Aboriginal programs has always been short-term, a pilot project, or underfunded. Once it became clear that Indians would accept their fate peacefully, the government was allowed to ignore Aboriginal issues for more pressing concerns, such as building the railroad and encouraging European settlement. In the history of Aboriginal–European relations, government has acted on Aboriginal issues only when forced to. And when government has acted, it has invariably done so in non-Aboriginal interests. Recently, the courts have become a major force in ensuring that government changes its perspective about Aboriginal issues. Judicial decisions since 1982, which form the basis of Aboriginal law in Canada, have grown increasingly more flexible and liberal in their interpretation of Aboriginal rights. As Isaac (2001) points out, restrictive, narrow views of these rights are being replaced by flexible and accommodating interpretations. These new interpretations have forced the federal government to make accommodations to existing programs and policies and to bring old attitudes and views about Aboriginal people in line with the courts' new decisions.

Our analysis of the Indian and Inuit Affairs Program has shown that its programs have changed considerably over the years, failing to reflect any long-term, consistent policy. In general, however, the Indian and Inuit Affairs Program has taken a wardship approach to Aboriginals. Its budget continues to grow in size, partly as a result of its increased bureaucratic structure; other government departments have also increased their budgets to deal with Aboriginal issues, but to little effect. Recently the federal government has tried to involve provincial governments in Aboriginal affairs. Generally, it has not had much success except in the area of treaty/land claims. Provincial governments, with much different agendas and priorities, have rejected the idea that they become directly involved in Aboriginal issues. They resist such involvement on the grounds that this is not their responsibility and that becoming involved would be the beginning of more involvement and associated costs.

For their part, Aboriginals have found out over the years that the government of Canada does not always favour Aboriginal interests when making decisions. Moreover, government departments do not live up to what they seem to have promised; nor do they implement the policies/programs that are expected by Aboriginal people. As a result, over the years, Aboriginal people have tended to distrust government in general. In particular, they are suspicious of the participation of provincial governments, fearing a lessening of federal responsibility. Aboriginal Canadians are convinced that the federal government must continue to honour its historical agreements with them, and that any transfer of these agreements is unlikely to be in their best interests. However, recently the federal government has undertaken a new strategy in approaching Aboriginal issues, by developing an Accountability Framework. This new strategy is designed to provide a clear articulation of the goals and objectives of Indian and Northern Affairs. Moreover, it should allow both the Department of Indian and Northern Affairs and Aboriginals an opportunity to see if the goals are being achieved.

NOTES

1. Legislation under Indian and Northern Affairs responsibility includes such Acts as the:

    Alberta Natural Resources Act
    Arctic Waters Pollution Prevention Act
    British Columbia Indian Cut-off Lands Settlement Act
    British Columbia Indian Lands Settlement Act
    British Columbia Treaty Commission Act
    Canada Petroleum Resources Act
    Caughnawaga Indian Reserve Act
    Condominium Ordinance Validation Act
    Cree-Naskapi (of Quebec) Act
    Dominion Water Power Act
    Indian Act
    Indian Lands Agreement (1986)
    Indian Lands, Settlement of Differences Act
    Indian Oil and Gas Act
    Indian (Soldier Settlement) Act
    James Bay and Northern Quebec Native Claims Settlement Act
    Land Titles Act
    Manitoba Natural Resources Act
    Nunavut Land Claims Agreement Act
    Northwest Territories Act
    Public Lands Grants Act
    Railway Belt Act
    St. Peter's Indian Reserve Act
    Sechelt Indian Band Self-Government Act
    Territorial Lands Act
    Waterton Glacier International Peace Park Act

Western Arctic (Inuvialuit) Claims Settlement Act
Yukon Act

2. The following descriptions of Indian and Northern Affairs and the summary of each sub-department's scope and mandate have been taken from the Department's website.

3. Much of the following discussion has been taken from the work of Ponting and Gibbins (1980).

4. Ponting and Gibbins (1980) indicate that "the resultant process is a complicated one which must be launched almost two years prior to the beginning (April 1) of the fiscal year for which the figures are being prepared."

WEBLINKS

www.ainc-inac.gc.ca

This site will allow you to click on a number of additional sites that will give you information about the mandate, role, and responsibilities of the Department. It will also provide answers to many questions that you might have about the Department, Aboriginal people, and how the two interface.

www.inac-ainc.gc.ca/pr/leg/index_e.html

This site will provide you with a complete list of legislation that is administered by the Department. It will allow you to review the legislation that the Department reviews and moderates each year.

www.tbs-sct.gc.ca/rma/database/aevedm_e.asp

This site will provide you with an evaluation of the Department by the Auditor General of Canada. It will also give you information about the Department's activities for the past year.

chapter thirteen

Aboriginal Economic Development: Local and Global Opportunities

INTRODUCTION

The development model used in the previous chapters incorporates the basic tenets of three major theoretical perspectives: internal colonialism, political economy, and settler society. The basic assumptions of internal colonialism have been fully articulated earlier in the book (Cumming, 1967; Carstens, 1971; Patterson, 1972). However, a more explicit statement regarding the other two perspectives will be useful for the reader (Stasiulis and Yuval-Davis, 1995; Clement and Williams, 1989; Dickinson and Bolaria, 1992). Satzewich and Wotherspoon (1993) have articulated the political economy of Aboriginal peoples, noting that their changing material circumstances shape, and are shaped by, their life experiences. Underlying the political economy approach is the understanding that the historical and current political economy is a recognition of Canada's historical domination by European and American influences. Beginning with a resource-based staples economy, they show how Canada entered the global economy with elements of technology showing through (Satzewich and Wotherspoon, 1993: 12). As Satzewich and Wotherspoon point out, at the centre of the political economy approach is the acceptance that people produce and reproduce the conditions for their existence. Their ability to do so (or change) is regulated by the conditions and context in which they find themselves. For example, ownership of property and resources significantly influences an individual's ability to engage in certain kinds of behaviour. Hence, it is important for social scientists to fully understand the historical and situational contexts in which groups of people find themselves as they participate in the political economy of any society. As such, it is imperative that the reader fully understand the position that Aboriginal people have held in Canadian society for the past two centuries.

The concept of "settler society" has been invoked to explain ethnic relations. These are societies that have been settled by Europeans, who have retained their political dominance over indigenous peoples. They are typified by colonialism where land, resources and labour were controlled by the sojourning group of European settlers (Stasiulis and Yuval-Davis, 1995). Settler societies generally have established social boundaries between the indigenous population and the European settlers. These boundaries, defined by the settlers, determine the actions defined as legitimate and legal for all members of society. In most settler societies, the dominant culture reflects the "mother" country's values and culture, and is constantly reinforced through immigration and importation of "mother" country institutions, values, ideologies, and economic practices. What worked in the mother country is reproduced in the colony.

These three perspectives have come to shape the explanation of why Aboriginal people have been excluded from the political and economic activities in today's society. Previously we have focused our discussion on the historical context in which Aboriginal–non-Aboriginal relationships emerged. However, to further explicate the contemporary scene, we need to investigate the political economy of Canadian society (Frank, 1967).

Since the turn of the century, Aboriginal people have been unable to participate fully in the Canadian economy. Even before our economy moved to an agricultural base and then on to one of modern technology, Aboriginal people were restricted in their involvement and, as a result, have fallen further behind in their ability to integrate. Aboriginal people find themselves operating in a subsistence or welfare economy parallel to that of the more modern economy. In other words, there are two economies in our society. This dual system emerged over time as changes in the institutional structure and technology took place. Aboriginal people were prevented from participating in the economy through a variety of policies and programs established by government. For example, Aboriginal people were prohibited from using resources in direct competition with non-Aboriginal users. Before the turn of the century, Aboriginal people were not allowed to take homestead lands, as these lands were available only to immigrants. Aboriginal people were refused licences to act as commercial big-game hunting outfitters in areas where non-Aboriginal people had established commercial enterprises. And when inland commercial fisheries were created in the Canadian Northwest, regulations were put in place so that Aboriginal people could not compete with non-Aboriginal people.

As Euro-Canadian society moved more quickly into an industrial–technological economy in the early twentieth century, Aboriginal people found themselves without the skills and resources necessary to participate. As a result, two almost separate economies emerged: a modern, dynamic sector (industrially and technologically based) and a traditional, land-based subsistence sector. The former creates change, which in turn promotes further change, while the latter resists change, clings to traditional ways, and sees little need to adopt new technology except when it is expedient to do so (Wien, 1986). Aboriginal people have discovered that, without the necessary skills, they will only be able to participate at the fringes of the industrial economy.

Initially, Aboriginal people were regarded as non-human savages to be exterminated or ignored. They were also regarded as lazy, filthy, uninhibited, and uncivilized. During the 19th century, Aboriginal people fell victim to conscious and unconscious genocide; the expansion of Western civilization that produced this result was viewed as a manifestation of Christianity. European settlers embodied the Protestant ethic of thrift and willingness to work hard. Because Aboriginal people did not share this ethic, they were rejected as pagan savages, with no claim to Christian charity (Hunt, 1940).

Eventually, through the proselytizing efforts of various churches, Aboriginal people became Christians (Trigger, 1965). As Christians, they came under the rubric of Christian ethics and could no longer be so blatantly exploited. Because prejudice and discrimination were by then solidly entrenched in Canadian society, an ideology of inherent European superiority was introduced to justify Euro-Canadian dominance and exploitation. European superiority and dominance were attributed to processes of natural selection, reflecting the Social Darwinism prevalent in the late 19th century.[1] By the laws of nature, then, European exploitation and westward expansion were inevitable. As Willhelm has argued:

> In the thoughts of the light-skinned people of early America, no White man ever commands because he "chooses" to do so; it is not by his choice, but by the will of God or the act of Nature that he rises to the fore at the expense of inferior races. To rule is really to submit, in the first instance, as an obedient believer of God's command and, in the second instance, as a helpless pawn abiding by Nature's laws governing the races of men. The White races, in the final analysis, never felt superior in an absolute sense since they yielded to the Christian Bible and to Nature's demand in commanding inferior races. (1969: 3–4)

The sciences, particularly biology, were perhaps unwitting contributors to racism in North America. Biologists in the late 19th century claimed that inferior species could be physiologically distinguished from superior species. Racial attributes were labelled and attributed to various groups in order to account for their behaviour. The scientists claimed, in fact, that the genetic, racial make-up of individuals caused their social behaviour; the evidence suggests that most Euro-Canadians believed them. This view extended to modernization theory—a theory of development articulated in the 1950s and 1960s—which suggested that adherence to traditional culture and beliefs stood in the way of progress, development, and civilization.

According to racist theory, no amount of effort by Aboriginal people or assistance from European settlers could therefore compensate for the Aboriginal people's natural inferiority. This conviction was evident in the government's decision to establish Aboriginal reservations. The reserves were to act as holding-pens for worthless people, inferior children, wards of the nation. In the treaties, when "concessions" were made to Aboriginal interests, they generally coincided with non-Aboriginal interests (J. Green, 1969). The Riel Rebellion of 1885, as well as the subsequent execution of Riel, were both the final extension and the climax of Aboriginal–non-Aboriginal relations in Canada in the 19th century, and established the pattern of subjugation that persists today.

Non-Aboriginal Canadians had a strategy in their relationship with Aboriginals prior to the patriation of the Constitution in 1982: the myth of equality (Willhelm, 1969). This myth's basic premise was that all humans were equal no matter how diverse they appeared to be. This, however, acted as a rationale for denying special privileges and affirmative action programs to various minority groups. The federal government's 1969 White Paper, which recommended that reserves be terminated and special status revoked, exemplified this myth. Current legislation somewhat continues to reflect this view of equality, though not as prominently. Proponents argue that the laws that express the equality of ethnic groups ought to be sufficient, regardless of the impact of centuries of entrenched discrimination.

An underlying assumption held perhaps by many Canadians is that Indians contribute little economic product to the Canadian economy. In addition, non-Aboriginal people feel that the larger dominant economy supports the Aboriginal economy through governmental subsidies and through the creation of and payment for a variety of health, economic, and social services. For example, many people point out that governmental transfers provide between 80 and 100 percent of Aboriginal salaries and non-earned income. If Aboriginal communities did not receive government subsidies, their local economies would collapse.

However, as Salisbury (1986) points out, this perspective and its underlying assumption represents a fundamental misunderstanding of the relation between Aboriginal people and the federal government (and, indeed, the people of Canada). For example, the flow of money stems specifically from a "contract" agreed upon by the two parties (the fiduciary relation between the Crown and the Aboriginal peoples) and cannot be revised or amended unilaterally over time. The contents of the agreement were agreed to by both parties at the time of signing and were in the best interests of both parties. The *Royal Proclamation* of 1763 is the best and earliest example of an agreement between the two parties that is still legally binding and recognized in the Canadian Constitution. Under this agreement, it was understood that in return for the Aboriginal peoples' recognition of the sovereignty of the monarch, the monarch would protect them and preserve the Aboriginal way of life. While some specifics of the agreement have been modified (in favour of the non-Aboriginal group), the federal government has accepted the spirit of the original agreement struck with Aboriginal peoples. Hence, the "subsidization" of services to Aboriginal people has been and continues to be paid for by Aboriginal people through their original transferring of land and allegiance in 1763.

THE EVOLUTION OF ABORIGINAL DEVELOPMENT

As the settler economy developed, Aboriginal economies were disrupted and put in disarray. Some of the more isolated reserves were less affected than those close to urban centres, but as external controls gradually became institutionalized, further indigenous community disruption occurred. While government wanted Aboriginal people to enter agricultural pursuits, these efforts were not successful because government did not provide sufficient resources such as land and capital (Carter, 1990). In fact, there is considerable evidence that the federal government of the time (late 19th century and early 20th century) purposely undermined Aboriginal successes and efforts in agriculture (Miller, 2000). Thus, the transition from a traditional to a modern economy was very difficult for many Aboriginal people, and their participation was marginal. Continuous debates as to whose responsibility Aboriginal people were further reduced their ability to secure support. As the Royal Commission on Aboriginal Peoples commented, prior to the 1960s, Aboriginal economic development was not a priority for the federal government, and as time went on Aboriginal dependency on federal assistance grew.

After World War II Aboriginal people began to shed their passivity and to demand a much more active role in Canadian society (Miller, 2000). The government (both provincial and federal), having experienced the atrocities of the war, began to implement policies that would forever change the ideological position of Aboriginal people. Human rights acts were passed, social assistance programs were put in place, and specific actions were taken regarding Aboriginal people—e.g., the *Indian Act* underwent its first major revision in almost a century. By the 1960s the federal government made public its report, *A Survey of the Contemporary Indians of Canada: Economic, Political, Educational Needs and Policies.* This report identified the poor quality of life experienced by Aboriginal people and concluded by suggesting extensive changes in government policy and programs. The government did act on the recommendation to set up programs for community development. (The most concrete program established was the Indian Revolving Fund, which became the major vehicle for funding Aboriginal communities.) The strategy was to follow two stages. First, the community would define its own problems and devise ways to achieve its goals. Then, the community would be given resources to implement the program. While Phase One was implemented, Phase Two was never sufficiently funded, and by the late 1960s the concept of community development died.

After refusing to give local communities the necessary resources to achieve their goals, Indian Affairs implemented the National Indian Advisory Board. However, its ineffectiveness led to its abandonment in the 1970s. By this time the federal government had settled on a more traditional and orthodox plan for integrating Aboriginal people into the economy—modernization. The new approach embodied the principle of assimilation, yet it was hidden behind more opaque beliefs. Modernization meant that if an individual wanted to enhance his or her quality of life, then he or she had to move from traditional beliefs, values, and behaviour to more modern ones. This meant that science would be the basis for action, creative rationality would be the underlying mode of operation, and new ways of thinking would be embraced. There was (and continues to be) a belief that change was inevitable and preferred. Furthermore, the direction of that change, along with its impact, could be controlled.

The federal government felt that Aboriginal people's traditional ways of life would have to end and a cultural replacement would have to be implemented. Specifically, individual values and goals needed to supersede those of groups or communities. Nevertheless, many Aboriginal groups rejected this approach. They began to suggest that economic integration of Aboriginal people would require more than the drive and motivation of each individual. They began to see the structure of our society as problematic in the poor quality of life for Aboriginal people. For example, the Métis Women's Association of Manitoba saw Aboriginal problems as a symptom of larger social and cultural problems, including patriarchy. It argued that, as long as development initiatives were handled solely by outsiders and men, the structural problems would remain.

The federal government, in its attempt to implement its modernization policy, established the Indian Economic Development Fund. This Fund continued the policy of funding only legal Indians. It provided direct loans, loan guarantees, and other forms of loans only to on-reserve projects. The National Indian Brotherhood publicly noted its objection to the way the fund was being operated by Ottawa. Aboriginal people felt that if economic development was to occur they must have control, and that this implied political autonomy (P. Elias, 1991).

In the mid-1970s the federal government began to develop community and regional plans for Aboriginal economic development. A joint effort of the National Indian Brotherhood and DIAND produced its first report in 1976. Nevertheless, this report made it clear that Aboriginal people were not prepared to sacrifice their culture, land, or identity in order to develop economically. They wanted to develop in such a way that the two structures were complementary. Aboriginal people felt that local self-government could be the structure wherein both economic development and cultural maintenance could coexist. It was under these conditions that Aboriginal organizations became involved in economic development. As P. Elias (1991) points out, by the late 1970s models of change advocated a more multidisciplinary approach. Social and cultural issues become more important and were sought to be integrated into these new models of social–economic change. The underlying assumption was that economic development included cultural revitalization as much as possible.

However, by the mid-1980s this integrated approach (which initially looked promising) had once more been set aside by Ottawa, and a more singular view of development took precedence—strict economic development. The multidisciplinary approach was ultimately abandoned by Aboriginal organizations, though more for practical reasons than ideological ones. Realizing how few resources they had, and the paucity of resources likely to be given to them by Ottawa, they believed that a multi-sector approach to development was doomed to failure. Nonetheless Aboriginal people realized that if full endorsement of the new federal policy was not forthcoming, even fewer funds would be available.

Thus, by the mid-1980s Aboriginal organizations accepted economic development, on a project-by-project basis, as the major thrust of advancement. At the same time, however, they tried to develop new ideologies through different channels. The ideas of self-government, sovereignty, and Indian rights began to surface and were pursued through other Canadian institutions—e.g., the courts. Nevertheless, they had now accepted a blended (Aboriginal/non-Aboriginal) course of action through which they would pursue their economic development. Meanwhile, the federal government continued to view its definition of development as the only acceptable one. The Indian Economic Development Fund (established in 1970) was replaced by the Canadian Aboriginal Economic Development Strategy, and in 1989 the Aboriginal Economic Development Strategy was created. All the development programs established in recent years by the federal government have been explicitly economic and favour individual entrepreneurship and enterprise over any strategies based on community control (P. Elias, 1991).

In 1989 the federal government earmarked nearly $900 million (over five years) for Aboriginal economic development. It also suggested that more Aboriginal control would be given with respect to financial resources and decision making. The design of the plan was such that Indian Affairs' role in program delivery would be phased out as local Aboriginal control took over. As Gadacz (1991) points out, DIAND's old focus on control, structure, rules, and procedures was to be replaced by collaboration, learning, networking, and innovation. In short, Indian Affairs would switch roles from a direct supplier of services to an assistant and facilitator for Aboriginal communities.

By the 1990s, funding policies once again began to change. An increased emphasis on providing training and education for all ages of Aboriginal people was the order of the day.

While community-based development became the overall paradigm used by government to encourage economic development in the 1960s (La Rusic, 1968), by the 1990s this perspective had disappeared and reappeared. However, its current appearance uses an integrated, holistic approach that includes such issues as governance, culture, spirituality, and education. In short, the economic strategy of today is to strengthen Aboriginal culture.

Today's philosophy recognizes that economic development is not solvable by a single approach, and that control over policy and programs must reflect community desires, needs, and control. There is also a belief that Aboriginal economic development cannot take place in isolation from the rest of the country. However, given the shortage of land and resource allocation for Aboriginal communities, this approach also recognizes the limitations of short-term economic development (Canada, 1978c).

ABORIGINAL DEVELOPMENT: THEORETICAL UNDERPINNINGS

In order to break the pattern of colonization, Aboriginal people must incorporate both the notions of individual entrepreneurship and community ownership with the goal of controlling reserve economies (Dubois, 1940; Royal Commission on Aboriginal Peoples, 1996b). The problems facing Aboriginal people can be addressed through the implementation of strategies that involve both individual and community-based resource development. First, Aboriginal people must be provided access to training and employment opportunities. Furthermore, the delivery and control of these opportunities must reside within the Aboriginal community. Aboriginal communities that have followed this strategy have emerged with some success, however modest. For example, in the 1980s and 1990s the Meadow Lake Tribal Council focused on economic development and provided 450 jobs directly, and another 240 indirectly, through a mixture of Indian government, tribal council, and band community–based enterprises. These economic ventures were kick-started with a $1.5 million loan from the federal government. Six years after they received the loan the community returned tax revenues to both the federal and provincial governments that total more than seven times the original loan. In addition, it saved Canadians money since over 200 people were removed from the welfare rolls.

A number of alternatives have been suggested as ways Aboriginal people could more fully integrate into the political economy of Canadian society. These recommendations and solutions for ending Aboriginal economic dependence have been around for three decades. For example, Heilbrun and Wellisz (1969) have suggested that the federal government provide funds for Aboriginal communities, as is done with the International Bank for Reconstruction and Development or the International Finance Corporation. These organizations make loans to underdeveloped countries based on long-term projects. These loans are not subject to an annual review, and thus financing is assured for five to seven years. Second, these projects could be reviewed and revised during the financing period so as to keep up with global changes. Finally, qualified staff would be attracted to projects because of the long-term stability and assured financing of the projects (Daugherty, 1978).

Koovos and Brown (1980) suggest that greater control over the goals and objectives of economic development, as well as its funding, needs to be placed within the Aboriginal community. Hatt (1969) agrees with MacGregor (1961), and states that control over various projects must originate in the Aboriginal community and not simply be subject to its control. Hatt goes on to argue that, if planning is not placed within the control of Aboriginal communities, the implementation of projects will not change the status quo.

Others, such as Sorenson and Wolfson (1969), suggest that in addition to long-term financing of economic projects in Aboriginal communities, other structural rearrangements need to be made. For example, they claim that the "unbalanced, single-industry" approach taken by government is unsustainable. In addition, they claim that secondary and tertiary industries must be planned for Aboriginal communities (Deprez and Sigurdson, 1969).

By the late 1990s the Royal Commission on Aboriginal Peoples came forward with recommendations that integrate the above arguments into more current philosophy and beliefs about the abilities of Aboriginal peoples. For too long, Aboriginal people have been forced by the federal government to spend inordinate amounts of time and energy trying to pick out the "correct" project—one that would succeed, if only marginally. As Cornell and Kalt (1992) note, instead of looking at the political and economic institutions and broader development strategies—e.g., sustainability—Aboriginal communities concerned themselves with picking a winner. As a result the degree of success was low, with the amount of time and resources allotted to the decision process being neither efficient nor cost effective (IRIW, 1978).

Cornell and Kalt (1992) and the Commission go on to say that economic development, at whatever level, is both complex and difficult. The specific situation and historical time period will profoundly influence the nature of the development, the extent of government support, and the probability of success of the project. For example, on the basis of many case studies they conclude that one of the most important factors in developing a success-ful economic project is to understand the political, economic, and geographic environment of the Aboriginal community. They identify eight major considerations in assessing the level of success of any project:

1. the degree to which Aboriginal people have the ability to make decisions;

2. the extent to which the project fills a unique economic niche or opportunity;

3. the degree to which the Aboriginal community has access to financial capital on a long-term basis;

4. the distance from the Aboriginal community to the market;

5. the amount of natural resources available to the community;

6. the level of human capital;

7. the organizational structure of the Aboriginal community; and

8. the level of integration of the Aboriginal community with the dominant society.

As Peters (1968) stated long ago, new industries and the upgrading of Aboriginal skills are the key to economic development. The creation of new jobs for Aboriginal people would also boost reserve profits, upgrade individual income standards, and provide invaluable work experience for the development of Aboriginal leaders in community and business affairs.

Several basic assumptions (which the federal government has been slow to accept) underline the need for community development and control. First, all people fundamen-tally desire to better themselves. When their attempts to do so are blocked, the social and psychological damage is considerable. Second, the major obstacle to improvement is a lack of such resources as funds, skills, equipment, and education. Third, given resources and opportunity, people find their own effective ways to meet their needs and improve their lives. In the past, Aboriginal people have been forced to try to solve problems through the solutions provided for them by government agencies; procedures not part of the dominant capitalist culture have been attacked and rejected. Fourth, a change in only one component of a group's behaviour seldom produces meaningful, lasting results. A simple influx of money does not solve very much given that the social behaviour of humanity has many facets; each component of behaviour stands in a relationship to other components. This interrelationship must be considered when attempts at change are made (Lagasse, 1962; Aberle, 1970).

Several structural changes need to take place. These changes will not happen overnight, nor will they occur without impact on Aboriginal people. The effects of indus-trialization on a population are well known and have been extensively documented. Industrialization has had a traumatic impact on people in virtually every society that has made the transition from agrarianism. The disruptions of social relationships and related customs and practices are particularly severe. These disruptions were evident when Aboriginal peoples changed from a nomadic to a sedentary society. For example, the tipi, which was well suited for nomadic people, provided shelter for Prairie Indians. However, when stationary houses were introduced (because of reserve living), the system of sanitation did not change accordingly. As a result, stationary homes became a fertile breeding ground for tuberculosis and other infectious diseases. In short, the transition to an industrial economy and a more sedentary lifestyle has always exacted a great deal in human suffering and demoralization from the people going through it. Hence, it should not be expected that Aboriginal people would somehow be exempt from this.

Nonetheless, it does not necessarily follow that Aboriginal people must experience the same level of disruption that others have had to undergo. Some structural changes can be introduced to bring about cultural and economic change with minimal impact. For example, movement into the city, a traditionally frustrating and tension-producing activity, can be facilitated through the proper institutional help. The removal of barriers to jobs can be implemented. The settlement of Aboriginal title, and the integration of development plans, can also be undertaken. In addition, development needs to proceed under local control— that is, only after plans have been developed that meet those local needs and priorities rather than those of the national or multinational companies. Finally, there must be more integration. Modern and traditional activities need to be developed together, rather than allowing one to develop at the expense of the other. The various institutional sectors of Aboriginal society also need to be integrated into the dominant society. For example, educational needs have to be integrated with economic needs, and health-care facilities need to be related to the work world (Wien, 1986).

This structural approach to social change necessitates an understanding of the institutional structures that influence Aboriginal life. Rather than focusing on the individual as the unit of analysis, such an approach examines the socio-economic role of internal Aboriginal institutions and their external relationships (Girvan, 1973). For too long, theorists have viewed Aboriginal–Euro-Canadian relations as an "Aboriginal problem" rather than as a "White problem," and have failed to take external factors into account (Skarlicki, n.d.).

Clearly, the "Aboriginal problem" has been created by the economic, cultural, and political structures of Canada. Contrary to previous explanations, the position of Aboriginal people in Canada is not the result of cultural isolation or particular psychological tendencies of Aboriginal people. Nor does individual racial and cultural discrimination provide a sufficient explanation for the low socio-economic position of Aboriginal people in Canada. While individual discrimination may have retarded socio-economic upward mobility, it has not eliminated it. Sunkel has shown that a totally marginal group is "deprived of all means of access to a source of income of reasonable level and stability" (1973: 141); clearly this is not the case for Aboriginal people in Canada.

The marginal position of Aboriginal people can only be explained when institutional and systemic discrimination against them are considered along with their limited sources of income and their lack of control over the means of production. The manner in which resources are deployed, whether human, capital, or technological, determines the level of employment, the extent of industrialization, and the distribution of income. As Mariategui (1934) pointed out in the early part of the last century, the roots of the Aboriginal problem are economic and lie in the system of land ownership. This clearly implies that the economy is not embedded in social relations, but rather that social relations are structures within society's economic institutions (Polanyi, 1974).

The federal government has argued against the creation of industries and jobs within the reserve. It steadfastly holds that the reserve is basically a residential area and cannot be converted to industrial or commercial use. For example, Recommendation 3 of the *Hawthorn Report* (1966–67) stated:

> The main emphasis on economic development should be on education, vocational training, and techniques of mobility to enable Indians to take employment in wage and salaried jobs. Development of locally available resources should be viewed as playing a secondary role for those who do not choose to seek outside employment.

On the basis of the above, it is clear that not all Aboriginal communities will benefit equally over time with similar types of development. Any proposed development should be tailor-made for a community and implemented only when internal and external conditions are appropriate. Economic development for Aboriginal peoples also means that they must regain control over decisions, both at the planning and the operational stages. This also means that developmental policies and programs must be designed and delivered by Aboriginal institutions. As the Royal Commission on Aboriginal Peoples notes, instead of Aboriginal communities having to adjust to the criteria and procedures of distant bureaucracies, the process needs to be reversed. The communities need to define priorities and the instruments best suited to meet them. As such, the transformation of Aboriginal economies is a large-scale undertaking that will require resources as well as concerted, comprehensive effort over an extended period (Royal Commission on Aboriginal Peoples, 1996a).

COMMUNITY SOCIO-ECONOMIC DEVELOPMENT FROM A FIRST NATIONS PERSPECTIVE: A CASE STUDY

In mid-1989 representatives of both the federal government and First Nations gathered near Calgary for the announcement of a new initiative in the area of Aboriginal economic development.[2] The Canadian Aboriginal Economic Development Strategy (CAEDS), was considered an important advance in Aboriginal economic programming over past initiatives, such as the 1983 Native Economic Development Program (which expired in 1989) and various other ongoing Indian and Northern Affairs development and financing programs. It promised to provide Native Indian peoples more flexibility, more money ($867 million over five years), and more control with respect to financial resources and decision making. The initiative also implied a definite change in the role of the federal government—particularly the Indian and Northern Affairs department—which, according to the initiative's scenario, has to remove itself even more from any direct involvement in program delivery than in the past (Government of Canada, 1989).

INAC's new role is to assist Indian/First Nations economic development organizations in developing and expanding the capacity to direct and deliver development programs and services themselves, things controlled in the past by INAC. The department's old focus on control, structure, rules and procedures will have to be replaced with an emphasis on collaboration, learning, networking, and innovation. CAEDS calls for INAC to change from being a direct supplier of services into an "assistant" for Aboriginal communities; the focus of economic development thus has to shift from being funder-oriented to being community-oriented.

For all intents and purposes the federal government's initiative has returned the responsibility for community economic development planning directly to the shoulders of

Aboriginal communities. This initiative was taken partly in recognition of the fact that increased funding is not always a solution to what is not always necessarily a funding shortage. The initiative was also taken in view of the fact that economic development policies originating from outside Aboriginal communities have seldom made the best use of locally available human and natural resources (Hanson, 1985: 62).

In response to CAEDS and the slow transformation of INAC, Aboriginal communities have become increasingly involved in the process of "capacity-building" to plan and formulate their own strategies for economic development. According to Hanson (1985: 41), "the strategy and programs to serve the needs of the Indian people/Native people... is relatively simple because most, if not all, elements are already in place." This is not to suggest that their implementation is simple, but rather that the attitudes and interests are, if Hanson's optimism is justified (and notwithstanding significant internal divisions of interest and concerns), "in place." Hanson suggests that, more than anything else, the needs of Aboriginal peoples are "for [an] opportunity to revitalize and strengthen the social, cultural and economic aspects of a way of life which are at the very core of their continuing existence as a collectivity" (p. 49).

Put simply, there is a need to revitalize the Aboriginal community, rather than to integrate Aboriginal society into mainstream society or to further intensify its dependency. The related ideas of decolonization and alternative economic development—"reversing the theft of human history," as it were—have been thoroughly explored in relation to Aboriginal as well as rural-based communities over the past several years (Puxley, 1977; Watkins, 1977; Blishen et al., 1979; Hanson, 1985; Ponting, 1986; Ross and Usher, 1986; Robinson and Ghostkeeper, 1987, 1988; Usher, 1989). The consensus is that there is indeed something there to revitalize.

Notwithstanding INAC's slow devolution and its gradual withdrawal from what is perceived by some as its more traditional role, in late 1989 and early 1990 Indian and Northern Affairs Canada initiated the Development Indicators Project. One of the purposes of the DIP as envisioned by the department was to develop a particular type of socio-economic planning tool—the socio-economic development indicator—that would support, but not interfere with, First Nations communities' capacity and ability to manage their own development and, in the process, to revitalize the social and cultural foundations of community life.

The overall significance of development indicators for First Nations communities is threefold. First, it might be suggested that the cornerstone for self-government is the gathering, processing, and use of timely information on development trends and conditions. Second, given the globalization of the economy, the necessary openness of Aboriginal communities towards the rest of the world, and the complexity of the interrelationships between communities and their environments, there is a need for a more sophisticated information system that serves to assess the internal and external forces that impact on a community's and a people's well-being. Third, and finally, economic development is really human development; socio-economic development indicators should therefore be Aboriginal value–based and should reflect a community's social and cultural life in a holistic sense.

The idea behind the Development Indicators Project was to develop a tool that First Nations communities could use in the process of managing their own socio-economic and cultural revitalization. Revitalization is defined in the dictionary as "to give new life or vigour to [something]," or to "revive" [something]; reference here can be made to the existing values, structures, organizations, and certain ways of doing things in the Aboriginal community. "Existing" might, optimistically, refer to traditional systems of governance, subsistence, dispute resolution, family and kinship life, spirituality, and so forth that might have survived culture contact and efforts at acculturation. "Existing" might, more realistically, refer to the structures that historically have been imposed on Aboriginal peoples and that are the outcome of an adaptive process that has taken place since contact times.

In the course of Aboriginal–Euro-Canadian relations, traditional systems have been replaced with foreign imposed ones, or they have been eroded to the point where they are in danger of being lost altogether. Aboriginal political structures, languages, and systems of religious beliefs and practices—including the family and kinship structure—have suffered oppression as well as transformations. Part of the revitalization process may involve reconstructing and reviving traditional ways of doing things, or at the very least, the process can involve gaining control over, modifying or imbuing existing imposed structures with a sense of local ownership and local values.

The key to successful revitalization/development lies in a unified (holistic) and dynamic approach that must take into account the social, cultural, political, and environmental/ecological aspects of Aboriginal community life—not just the "economic" aspect. One of the characteristics that distinguishes Aboriginal development from mainstream community development as the concept is usually defined in the literature is the equal significance of a non-market or subsistence orientation (Coffey and Polese, 1985; Hanson, 1985; Four Worlds Development Project, 1985; Robinson and Ghostkeeper, 1987, 1988; Usher, 1989). This unified approach thus includes local authority over economic decisions; the revival of traditional community structures; the creation of an economic mix that may include a combination of a subsistence, industrial, market, and retail orientation; cultural enrichment; and even the promotion of greater ecological harmony.

The idea of holistic development further includes all elements of human life that contribute to human welfare, such as nutrition, health, shelter, work and employment, the physical environment, and the socio-cultural environment. Participation in decision-making processes, a sense of human dignity, of belonging—anything pertaining to the "style" or pattern of development that is appropriate to Aboriginal people's values and circumstances—must likewise be part of a development strategy. In short, a holistic and unified approach to community development, or revitalization, calls for a renewed focus on people, not solely on the "product" or "project."

The rationale for generating Aboriginal-based socio-economic development indicators is based on the presumption that there are other kinds of development that are not based solely on the values and norms of an industrial society and on a market economy (see the essays in Watkins, 1977). There is a serious questioning of why an industrial and market-based economy that is the basis for development should entail environmental degradation, the squandering of non-renewable resources, the diminution of human dignity, and the alienation of the individual from social and cultural life among some of its consequences. Thomas Berger (1977, 1985), for example, has dealt in detail with the effects of industrial development on Aboriginal cultures with strong continuing ties to the land-based or bush economy. Berger (1977) argues that:

> It is self-deception to believe that large-scale industrial development would end unemployment and underemployment of Native people in the North. In the first place, we have always overestimated the extent to which Native people are unemployed and underemployed by under-stating their continued reliance on the land. Secondly, we have never fully recognized that industrial development has, in itself, contributed to social, economic, and geographic dislocation among Native people. (p. 123)

Despite the fact that Berger's arguments were developed in a Northern Canadian context, they are nevertheless applicable to other regions of the country that reflect a hinterland/metropolis or a dominant/subordinate dependency relationship. Berger (1985) continued developing ideas for the promotion of regional diversification by talking about strengthening the renewable resource sector. In the promotion of traditional strengths, Berger (1985: 55) wrote that the economy of subsistence lies at the heart of Aboriginal culture and "enables the Native peoples to feel at one with their ancestors, at home in the present, confident of the future."

Community revitalization/development could, realistically, be considered in the context of both a hinterland economic adaptation and a so-called multi-sectoral approach. In place of the dependency that accompanies external cash transfers to local Aboriginal (and even non-Aboriginal) economies, for example, options for development should be balanced, pragmatic, and locally controlled. One flexible and adaptable option may be a revitalized domestic economy, involving home or local production and household self-reliance, in combination with occupations that are based on the rhythm of a seasonal lifestyle. Unfortunately, "mainstream" socio-economic development has always regarded these factors as barriers, yet it might be precisely this option that could be the most viable for many Aboriginal communities in the face of their continued marginalization from metropolitan centres and relative geographical (and social) isolation (Usher, 1989).

Another option, in combination with the previous one, might be a mixed and multi-sectoral economic base. Such an economic base might consist of mixing primary resource extraction, cultural industries, light manufacturing, and service industries into one sustainable economy. Such a "mixture" would include the features of a subsistence/bush economy as well as an industrial/market-based economy. Going further, Robinson and Ghostkeeper (1987, 1988) have argued that there may even be emerging structural parallels between a traditional bush economy and a post-industrial, or "next," economy (one that focuses on information and services). Features shared by both types of economy might be exploited by Aboriginal entrepreneurs, and become the basis for community development that does not have to depend upon specialization, competition, hierarchy, or environmental degradation for success and viability (Indian Minerals Directorate, 1981a, 1981b).

Given the kinds of economic development that Aboriginal communities might opt for, conventional socio-economic indicators based solely on an industrial and market model need to be revised or, as appropriate, applied in a different way. There is clearly an absence of a framework suited to Aboriginal community needs. A new one may need to be created that will be more effective in the context of Aboriginal community life and that would fit with development choices based on local concerns.

INAC's Development Indicators Project has a number of goals: (1) to identify and generate a list of Aboriginal value–based indicators that could be used by First Nations peoples themselves to collect information on community life from a holistic perspective; (2) to test or validate this list of indicators in several communities (by way of workshops) in order to see if they adequately reflect the value systems of First Nations communities, as well as to look for consistent themes emerging across communities; and (3) to design a "template," or socio-economic indicator system, based on the findings and meaningful to community members, that could be used to describe a community's socio-economic profile. This template or indicator system would be used by economic development officers, band councillors, and others as a planning tool to gather and organize information that can support comprehensive community-based planning.

The process was begun, at the behest of INAC and with funding from INAC and other sources, when an organization in Edmonton called the First Nations Resource Council organized a symposium in the spring of 1990. Entitled "Socio-Economic/Quality of Life Indicators Symposium," the purpose was to talk about social and economic development from a quality of life perspective (First Nations Resource Council, 1990). The meeting was attended by Indian and Métis peoples, social scientists, community development practitioners, and several INAC officials. It was recognized by the participants that any sort of planning and development that is not imposed from the outside, but that comes from within, has ultimately to be guided by a people's values and vision of what they consider enabling (the strengths) and constraining (the weaknesses) in the community-building and development process.

The idea was to generate a list of community development indicators that could identify and somehow measure different aspects of a quality of life that would be meaningful in the context of First Nations communities. Efforts to measure community and First Nations development have often meant assessing social dependency or economic disparity. Symposium participants recognized that community development is an evolutionary, dynamic process that must be understood in both its quantitative and qualitative dimensions, something that "snapshot" statistics do not capture very well. The consensus that emerged from the meeting was that there is a need to extend measures of development beyond traditional (i.e., mainstream) indicators of disparity. As well, it was understood that the needs and specific requirements of any Aboriginal community mean that the tools traditionally used for monitoring community development may not suffice. Aboriginal development is a particular form of community development that requires its own unique framework of analysis and its own "social" or "development" indicators and set of measurement tools.

Social indicators are a combined, interpreted, and refined sets of statistics (Land, 1971; Land and Spilerman, 1975; Rossi and Gilmartin, 1980). This type of information can provide a glimpse of the "state" or condition of a community, region, country, etc., at a point in time (see Corporation for Enterprise Development, 1987; Lamontagne and Tremblay, 1989; Lane, 1989 for case studies of their application). Development indicators are statistics that measure socio-economic conditions and changes over time for various segments of a population, an entire community, a region or a country (Hicks et al., 1979). By socio-economic conditions is meant both the external ("objective," social, economic, physical) and the internal ("subjective," perceptual) contexts of human existence.

Indicators are also an important means by which information on the relative success or failure of individual development projects, programs, and policies can be gathered (Carley, 1981; Lane, 1989; Miles, 1985). The impact of development projects on the emotional, spiritual, and mental health of communities and their members can likewise be measured, assessed, and monitored by the use of socio-economic indicators (Campbell et al., 1976; Kennedy et al., 1978). Thus, the information that is collected can be used to plan, influence, and inform the decision-making process with regard to development planning even on a national scale (UNESCO, 1981, 1984). Still, information on the overall process of community revitalization, or holistic development, and resulting changes (both positive and negative) in a people's emotional, spiritual, and mental well-being is by no means easy to collect (see Brodhead, 1990: 4–15 for a useful review of the literature and methodology of development indicator research).

From the point of view of Aboriginal communities, however, many existing "mainstream" or non-Aboriginal indicators fall short of being effective data-gathering tools.

Mainstream indicators have often been developed in a predominantly urban and industrial context. Because they are externally created and imposed, they can be culturally biased. Quite often they are economic (disparity) indicators and so are very limited in their ability to help gather data related to the social, cultural, and spiritual aspects of community life. Many indicators may either not be valid in Aboriginal communities or may appeal to standards that are inappropriate (PJS Geach and Associates, 1985; Blishen et al., 1979). Blishen et al.'s (1979) study on socio-economic impact modelling suggests it is essential to ensure that the relevant variables of a model of Aboriginal development are selected rather than some "alien" criteria. Indeed, data such as the number of libraries, television sets, or telephones per household; crime rates; social assistance recipients; suicides; infant mortalities; unemployment and education levels; etc. per unit population, give, at best, a one-dimensional view of life.

As desirable as it may be to increase or decrease these numbers, such "typical" indicators do not always allow for a holistic measure or assessment of individual and/or community quality of life. Not only is it necessary to use these numbers in different ways, but the reasons underlying the statistics and the behaviours should themselves be identified and are information that should become a part of a quality of life assessment. Thus, like "appropriate technology," appropriate revitalization–development indicators, i.e., those that are Indian value-based, should be identified and validated at the community level and should, ideally, reflect both the underlying value system and the holistic nature of a particular community's social and cultural life (Lithman, 1983).

There exists a mutually reinforcing set of relationships between development, values, and a people's quality of life, or wellness. A framework, for example, based on the Plains Indian "medicine wheel" (or sacred hoop) may be appropriate for developing indicators (see Figure 13.1). Four areas of personal and community life can be defined, corresponding to the four quadrants of the medicine wheel (First Nations Resource Council, 1990: vi–viii) (see Table 13.1). To be meaningful for community development, ways of "measuring" each of the four areas, or quadrants of the medicine wheel, must be found. It is apparent that all of the four areas are very closely interrelated; it is unclear where one area ends and another begins (this, of course, highlights the holistic nature of the wheel and of life itself). While it was agreed that the four areas offered a holistic perspective of personal and community life, it was less clear—particularly in view of the extent of overlap between areas—which areas would yield the best kind of information that could be used in socio-economic planning and development. However, it is not at all clear that the data generated by any number of indicators are really a direct measure of something like "spirituality," "emotional well-being," or "self-determination." These areas (also referred to as "indices," in the parlance of indicator research) are very difficult to define, and it should be pointed out that indicators are by no means a replacement for definitions.

To begin to apply the framework, an important first step is to come up with some definitions of the four indices of personal and community life that correlate with the four quadrants of the "wheel." To ensure the validity of the indices, part of this crucial first step had to be the participation of First Nations communities and their members in the definition process itself. Accordingly, some of the definitions that were arrived at during workshops and discussions held in a number of First Nations communities in Alberta are shown in Table 13.2.

Many indicators were suggested that were thought to describe each of the four indices. They included the number of monogamous relationships, the levels of trust and sharing

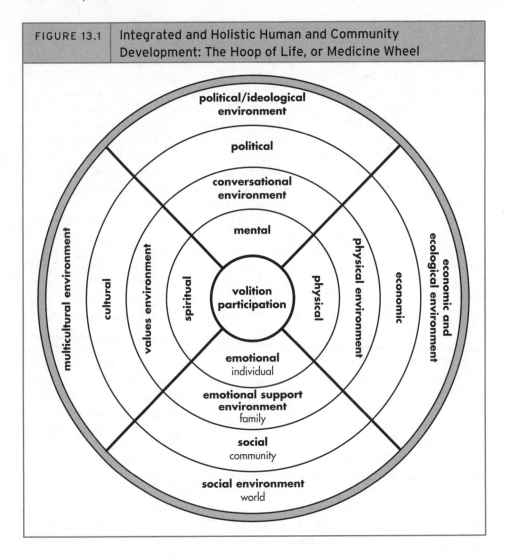

FIGURE 13.1   Integrated and Holistic Human and Community Development: The Hoop of Life, or Medicine Wheel

within and between families and community members, the number and kinds of clubs and associations, scholastic achievement levels, leisure activities, the number and kinds of cultural events, the extent and use of Indian languages, the role of elders, and so on. The difficulty that community participants faced, of course, was that any number of indicators they thought up seemed applicable across several indices, while at the same time the pool of indicators never seemed to be comprehensive enough. Thus, a more disciplined framework was still lacking whereby it would be possible to see how different aspects of social and community life would be affected—positively and negatively—by economic development. The question remained: What do designations like "the number of monogamous relationships" or "the extent and use of Indian languages" actually indicate or mean?

One of the outcomes of the community workshops was the proposal that it was best to identify a social indicator system that could be used to generate information that could gauge the extent to which economic development enhances or revitalizes each of the

TABLE 13.1	Four Areas of Human and Community Development Derived from the Medicine Wheel Concept
Four Areas of Personal and Community Life	**Four Quadrants of Medicine Wheel**
Family Stability/Community Support	Mental/Political Potentialities
Psychological/Emotional Well-Being	Emotional/Social Potentialities
Cultural/Spirituality	Cultural/Spiritual Potentialities
Economy/Self-Determination	Physical/Economic Potentialities

indices—e.g.,, family stability or spirituality—or whether development detracts from them. What is important, then, is not so much variables or indicators that define the indices, but rather how an organized system of variables and accompanying indicators could be used to somehow evaluate or anticipate the impact of development projects, programs, practices, and policies on each of the four indices of personal and community life from the point of view of individuals and from the perspective of the community (see Figure 13.2).

The logic of the proposed social indicator system would be as follows: How, as a result of an anticipated or actual economic development project or program, might family stability (one of four indices—the other three being emotional well-being, spirituality, and self-determination) be impacted upon by accompanying changes in such variables as demographics, work and employment, housing, etc., as measured by such indicators as male/female life expectancy, the presence of volunteer organizations, unemployment rates, levels of formal education, traditional learning opportunities, role of elders, persons per

TABLE 13.2	Community-Based Definitions of the Four Indices of Personal and Community Development	
Family Stability and Community Supports [Mental and Political]		**Culture/Spirituality [Cultural/Spiritual]**
Household integration		Pride in one's culture
Economic viability		Sense of identity
Member cohesion		Knowledge of tradition and of traditional values
Kinship loyalty		
Cross-kinship co-operation		
[Emotional/Social] Psychological/Emotional Well-being		**[Physical/Economic] Economic/Self-Determination**
General mental health		Control over one's own destiny and resources
Self-confidence		Creating/managing own opportunities
Self-esteem		Solving one's own problems
Positive self-image		Personal/community control

household, etc.? The same could be asked about psychological/emotional well-being: What kind of an effect will changes in community demographics, income and wealth distribution, or in the environment (or any other variable), as a result of an anticipated or actual development project, have on a person's mental health, self-confidence, or self-esteem? Would economic development enhance these or detract from them, and if so, in what ways?

That socio-economic development will have an effect, in one way or another, on community demographics, the health and nutrition of community members, housing and so forth, is obvious. Ideally, it should be possible for an Aboriginal community to plan and control the kinds of changes it desires—e.g., those that are compatible with the values of its people—by monitoring or anticipating change in the particular indicators believed to have an effect on the four aspects of individual and community life—namely, family stability, emotional well-being, spirituality, and self-determination. Community members themselves will determine, in whatever ways are appropriate and by whatever process they agree upon, those variables and related indicators that they feel are best associated with

---

FIGURE 13.2 | **A Proposed Social Indicator System**

INDICES

Family Stability/Community Supports
Culture/Spirituality
Psychological/Emotional Well-Being
Economy/Self-Determination

↑

VARIABLES

Demographics
Social and Cultural Groups
Learning Opportunities
Work and Employment
Income and Wealth Distribution
Health, Safety and Nutrition
Housing
Environment and Resources
Leisure, Culture and Use of Time
Conflict and Dispute Resolution

↑

INDICATORS

List of indicators associated with each variable above

↑

DEVELOPMENT PROJECTS AND PROGRAMS

promoting or contributing to the qualities they value most, such as family stability, emotional well-being, etc., in their own community setting.

The following is the list of 10 variables and their accompanying indicators:

1. **Demographics**
   male/female ratio
   age structure
   infant mortality
   male/female life expectancy
   death rate
   disability
   causes of death
   household type

2. **Social and Cultural Groups**
   clubs and associations
   interest groups
   degree of involvement in group
     (cross-kinship) activities
   daycare
   volunteer groups for the elderly
   youth groups
   organized sports/games

3. **Learning Opportunities**
   available education services
   level of mainstream education
   literacy rate
   school completion rate
   use of language
   role of elders
   availability of teachers
   mainstream vs. traditional learning
   availability of library/books

4. **Work and Employment**
   types of wage employment
   seasonal vs. regular work
   locally-owned shops and businesses
   creating/managing own employment
   employment of community members
   unemployment rate
   unemployment spell
   kinds of subsistence work

5. **Income & Wealth Distribution**
   income growth
   band taxation rate
   % social assistance recipients
   time spent on assistance
   loans/assets ratio
   investment income per capita
   transfer payment (amount/kind)
   earned income levels
   barter system?

6. **Health, Safety, and Nutrition**
   violent crimes
   number of suicides
   alcohol abuse
   levels and causes of disability
   accidents and causes
   food/water quality
   number of smokers
   children fully immunized?
   cases of cardiovascular disease
   cases of anxiety and depression
   prescription drug use
   incidence of hospitalizations

7. **Housing**
   # of homeless families
   dwelling standards
   availability of water/electricity
   # of owners vs. renters
   # of persons per house/household
   # of housing starts and finishes
   $$ spent on housing/renovations
   inside/outside toilets

8. **Environment and Resources**
   noise levels
   smells and odours
   levels of cleanliness
   sanitation facilities
   water quality
   waste management

9. Leisure, Culture, and Use of Time
use of language
ceremonies and cultural events
feelings of loneliness
role of elders
craft production for domestic
    use or for sale
cultural/recreational facilities

10. Conflict and Dispute Resolution
violent crimes
crime rate
incidence of vandalism
incidence of child/sexual abuse
# of incarcerations
kinds/levels of substance abuse
police or peacekeepers
dispute settlement forum or techniques
traditional modes of discipline
role of elders

As far as the indicators are concerned, they can be further disaggregated according to the kind of information that is sought and the use to which it might be put. Disaggregations can be as "coarse" or as "fine" in scale as circumstances allow or require. Age structure as an indicator within the variable "demographics," for example, can have as many or as few year-intervals as necessary. Household type (demographics), literacy rate (learning opportunities), types of employment (work and employment), etc., might be similarly disaggregated to fit local circumstances and to suit local needs. The number of indicators within each variable can of course be increased, decreased, prioritized, left out, and new ones added according to the goals, priorities, and requirements of community members. Many of the indicators listed above were actually suggested by participants at the First Nations community workshops. Both non-Aboriginal as well as "traditional" data items were included. Mainstream, or non-Aboriginal, indicators can of course be interpreted according to Aboriginal values, and so need not be accepted without question—nor be rejected simply because they are non-Aboriginal.

The 10 variables were adapted in part from social reporting or accounting systems used in both the United Kingdom and the United States (Carley, 1981: 114–120). In those systems, variables (or areas of social concern) are referred to as "programmatic divisions." The information generated by both systems is strictly descriptive and there are no attempts to explain how or why the conditions described came about; an argument can be made that they are therefore, by definition, not really social indicators. Their primary usefulness, however, lies in their attempt to delineate areas of social life that are of concern to citizens, interest groups, business people, educators, and elected officials/policymakers. In providing descriptive statistics they therefore provide background information for a social indicator system. By this is meant a "group of social indicators organized around component parts of the social system" (Carley, 1981: 47). According to Carley, the term usually implies consideration of a number of the diverse parts, or domains, that make up individual as well as community well-being.

The key, then, is that any given social indicator system must have a determined structure for the information derived from this system to be of any use. Social indicator systems can be organized along a number of different lines (Miles, 1985: 114). For example, a system can be organized programmatically on the basis of geography (national, regional, local); institutional arrangements of society (housing, health services, law, transportation, education); agency, program, or service type (welfare, housing, employment, education); and even on the basis of an individual's life-cycle (learning, working, retirement). None of these are necessarily mutually exclusive, of course (Gerber, 1990).

One method of structuring a social indicator system is to work from the general to the specific—that is, to identify community or social goals, refine them to generate more specific objectives, and eventually to arrive at some indicators of the achievement of that goal (e.g., called the "goal-to-indicator" system [UNESCO, 1981, 1984; Carley, 1981: 54], this method was also favoured by those community members who participated in the workshops). Here, there is an explicit internal logical consistency to the process of indicator development. The logical structure means that any particular indicator is related back to some goal or objective by the members of the community themselves. Making it "explicit" is clearly valuable for several reasons. First, it facilitates the building of some sort of causal models between goals and indicators. Secondly, and perhaps most importantly from the perspective of the Aboriginal community, it brings to the fore the value system of community members who themselves are actively structuring the system. It is a very good way of ensuring that the values of the community are articulated and reflected in the indicator system; it is also a good way of ensuring the participation of community members in this process.

It is suggested that the logical structure between the four indices, the ten variables, and their accompanying indicators as set out above qualifies as a social indicator system as defined by social indicator researchers—e.g., Rossi and Gilmartin, 1980. In contrast with existing socio-economic indicator models developed in the context of First Nations development planning—e.g., PJS Geach and Associates, 1985—however, the system advocated here is indeed "organized around component parts of the social system." Furthermore, a "goal-to-indicator" system can be used, based on the OECD model (Organization for Economic Co-operation and Development, 1973, 1974, 1976, 1982). The OECD, which comprises 24 Western (First World) member countries, developed a program intended to guide member governments in the preparation of social indicators. It was subsequently shown that the components of community well-being were similar across cultures as well as over time. Thus, the system of four indices and ten variables may be "universally" applicable across a range of communities dissimilar in economic prosperity, geography, and population size. Despite expected differences in the weighting and ordering of indicators within variables (reflecting different value orientations, priorities, etc.), the system of variables and indices themselves should therefore be applicable across different First Nations communities.

Despite some reservations about the applicability of the OECD model with respect to interpretation, comparability, and applicability in the context of Aboriginal development (Brodhead, 1990: 7), the authors of the OECD model make it clear that the identification and ranking of social concerns as well as their indicators has to be an ongoing process over time. What makes the structure of their model attractive is that the goal-to-indicator system has to be negotiated among the participants; this means that the selection of indicators reflects the participants' own value judgements on the components of individual and community well-being.

Thus, what would otherwise be a static exercise of collecting information now becomes an interactive as well as an interpretive process of collecting information with particular purposes in mind. One purpose may be to monitor and evaluate the effects of actual development projects on any number of variables (as reflected by their indicators) and, indirectly, on any of the four indices of personal and community life. How economic development may be perceived to affect family stability or spirituality, or, alternatively, how these may be enhanced by consciously choosing a particular development strategy, must necessarily be a process in which community members, chief-and-council, and/or those responsible for economic development are involved.

It is clear from the current thrust of federal government policy making and band/ tribal council development initiatives that the emphasis is increasingly being placed on self-reliance, self-government, and the use and development of local resources. On the one hand, INAC's openness towards the promotion of Aboriginal self-government may be seen as an implicit recognition of the need for a bottom-up approach to Aboriginal development. On the other hand, there is growing evidence that many First Nations communities are adopting a more entrepreneurial perspective on their common future. The creation, for example, of numerous Aboriginal-based development corporations and businesses is testimony to this trend—e.g., Canadian Indian Resource Corporation, 1990. Many communities, however, are still inclined to pursue more traditional paths of development.

An Aboriginal community's value system is part of the total resources of the community that must be considered during the actual course of economic revitalization and development. To generate a truly Aboriginal value–based list of indicators requires the identification of those aspects of the community and community life which residents desire to maintain, enhance, or even remove. Validating a list of indicators provides an opportunity to ascertain how ready community residents are for changes, which changes they feel are most desirable, urgent, or wholly unacceptable, and which values they anticipate might be compromised as a result of development.

This is not to suggest that a community's values be reduced to a checklist, but rather that people need to identify and discuss them in order to help them determine their development priorities. Community development clearly rests on a strong value foundation, and it must be a conscious, selective process. A development indicator system, while reflecting the value judgments and cultural views of those persons who construct and interpret them, is an essential tool. The system can be used to help collect and organize socio-economic data (including the values) in communities; a system gives those data shape and coherence. An indicator system, as a measure or description of community conditions in the broad sense, can aid in improving a community's planning capacity by making available information that planners can use.

The formulation and assessment of the effectiveness of holistic development strategies should be enhanced by the use of an indicator system described in this case study. Some "baseline" data are necessary in order to detect the effects of changes brought about by development in Aboriginal communities, and provide the foundation for helping the direction of that change. Indicators and an indicator system are a means of building this kind of a data base. Indeed, an indicator system—such as the one described above or a modified version of it—can be incorporated into more comprehensive First Nations development studies. The indicator system described in the case study and the case study itself has been utilized in a larger and more detailed study of First Nations socio-economic well-being (Armstrong and Rogers, 1996).

ECONOMIC DEVELOPMENT STRATEGIES AND APPROACHES

We will now discuss several ways in which Aboriginal people could develop their natural resource base: the concession, the joint venture, co-management, the service contract, the management agreement, the community development corporation, and local producers' cooperatives. Even though all these activities point to active participation by Aboriginal people in developing their mineral resources, the question of the extent of their involvement remains. How deeply do the bands want to be involved, for instance, in projects where the risk factor is high?

THE CONCESSION   This has been the traditional strategy whereby Indians (through the federal government) grant a company production rights. The company makes a direct equity investment for the sole purpose of extracting a resource (Bankes, 1983). As Asante (1979) points out, in many cases the concession amounted to a virtual assumption of sovereignty over the host country's resources by transnational corporations. Under these conditions, the corporation asserted ownership not only of the fixed assets but also of the natural resource itself (Bankes, 1983).

Under a concession agreement there is very little direct "up-front" cost for the band. Nor are there any operating costs. In addition, these agreements are easy to administer, since the need for supervision, auditing, and training is minimal. All of this is provided by the company that agrees to exploit the minerals. In short, the cost to the band is minimal, but the return is also minimal. Aboriginal people have also found that this type of agreement does not encourage the training of local residents in order to assume jobs in the industry, thereby introducing them into the wage economy (Meadow Lake, 1989).

THE JOINT VENTURE   This means that there are two (or more) parties that pool their money, technical expertise, and/or land in order to develop a project. There are two variations of this method. The first is one in which a separate legal entity is created that will be jointly owned by both parties, that is, the Aboriginal people and the development company. The second type does not involve the formation of a separate company, but instead the parties to the venture have a direct, undivided working interest in the project.

The joint venture type of agreement requires that Aboriginal people (1) have the technical expertise, and (2) have some "interest" that is considered valuable by the other party, such as land or mineral rights. There is both a direct and indirect cost with this type of development. The joint venture generally presents an opportunity for the local people to increase their control over the development. It can increase revenues to Aboriginal people and it allows for a flexible method of collecting revenues (Bankes, 1983; Asante, 1979).

THE CO-MANAGEMENT PARTNERSHIP   Partnerships involve two or more parties whereby Aboriginal people have a say in determining the rate and nature of development. Moreover, economic linkages with other organizations need to be evaluated and "costed out" as to the benefits and costs for Aboriginal communities. Aboriginal people have generally opted for co-management strategies when renewable resources are involved. Ownership of the resources is not necessary, but all parties must recognize that each party has a legitimate interest in them. Aboriginal people use co-management strategies based on the belief that the orderly use of resources will facilitate the survival and health of their environment. Pinkerton (1989) has argued that Aboriginal people will continue to prefer co-management between themselves and non-Aboriginal people. There are several reasons for this preference:

1. Co-management creates cooperation among individual workers.
2. Co-management creates a commitment among local workers to share both the costs and benefits of their efforts toward enhancement and conservation.

3. Co-management creates a higher degree of organization and mutual commitment among Aboriginal workers, which translates into a better bargaining relationship with external agents.

Co-management arrangements represent a transfer of decision-making power to Aboriginal people, and are therefore difficult to negotiate with non-Aboriginal people. However, the view that Aboriginal people have a legitimate interest in natural resources is one that is slowly being recognized by government and business. The 1990 *Sparrow* decision by the Supreme Court, which noted that Aboriginal people have a legal and legitimate interest in renewable resources, went far in alerting government and businesses to accept this perspective and consider co-management initiatives.

Examples of co-management can be seen in the Waterhen Moose and Wood Bison agreements between the Waterhen Anishinabe and the Manitoba government. The Teme-Augama Anishinabe in Ontario have used the courts for some time to resolve their land claims, after conflict between themselves and the government erupted in the late 1980s. In 1990 the two parties agreed to establish a co-management "stewardship agreement" over forest resources. A final example of co-management is the creation of the Porcupine Caribou Management Board, which is a massive undertaking involving the federal and both territorial governments as well as four Northern Aboriginal organizations.

THE SERVICE CONTRACT Under agreements of this type the status of Aboriginal ownership over the natural resource is reaffirmed. Thus, rather than transferring the title of the resource (as in a concession) to the developing company, the band simply hires the corporation as a contractor or business partner to perform a specific task for a specified amount of money. The disadvantage in using this type of strategy is that bands must have a substantial cash flow in order to pay for the up-front cost of the development, which can be quite high. Both Zakariya (1976) and Bankes (1983) point out that under this type of agreement the band would have no internal control over the project, and there would be few opportunities for Aboriginal people to gain employment or technical and administrative skills. Also, the project would have to be carefully monitored by the band to ensure that its members get the maximum benefits from it. The benefits of such an arrangement would include Aboriginal ownership and jurisdiction over the natural resource. In addition, other firms would supply the technology (and risk capital) to explore, develop, and market the resources.

THE MANAGEMENT AGREEMENT This is a strategy whereby Aboriginal people purchase expertise for a specified period of time. The contracted consultants can either act as advisors while the Aboriginal management retains sole control of the company, or the Aboriginal people can choose to relinquish control to the consultants.

THE COMMUNITY DEVELOPMENT CORPORATION A band or a First Nation can form a corporation and explore for minerals on its reserve. The corporation is granted permits and leases according to terms set by the federal government. These corporations are created to help plan and implement the business development goals of a community or region, and they can be involved either in risking capital or acting as an advisory body. A variation of this strategy is called a local producer's cartel, which involves the formation of a syndicate or trust that is able to take over a business venture from the original developer and carry on all negotiations with developers. In the mid-1960s, when 25 American Indian tribes created CERT (Council of Energy Resource Tribes) in order to control all mineral development on the reserves, they established a cartel.

Some bands and larger Aboriginal groups that have taken this course have chosen either to remain independent or to enter into joint ventures with other non-Aboriginal companies. Two major problems have beset those Aboriginal groups that have created corporations. First, the corporations tend to benefit from the development more than the band does, and may become more powerful than the band. This problem has been somewhat alleviated by making all members of the band (including newborns) members of the corporation. The second problem centres on the risk factor and the need for a considerable amount of money up front before the development starts. These difficulties are of course not insurmountable, as there have been numerous success stories throughout Canada. A notable one is Makivik Corporation, created in 1978 pursuant to the signing of the James Bay and Northern Québec Agreement (1975). The corporation, headquartered in Kuujjuaq (Nunavik, Quebec), has the mandate to implement the Agreement, and to administer the funds accorded to the Inuit.

THE LOCAL PRODUCERS' COOPERATIVE   These are usually voluntary, non-profit societies incorporated to run a business. The members of the cooperative own shares of the business and have one vote at each general meeting. A board of directors is elected to operate the business and carry out day-to-day activities. In effect, a cooperative is a business owned by its customers.

A history of the cooperatives shows that until the 1950s most of the Aboriginal trade in Canada (particularly in isolated regions) was carried out through the Hudson's Bay Company. In 1959 the government began to encourage and support a number of locally owned and operated cooperatives. This idea seemed to fit particularly well with one of the elements of Aboriginal culture—sharing. The first Aboriginal cooperatives were producer-oriented and involved such activities as art or fishing. Then consumer cooperatives emerged, where both importing and exporting activities were carried out. In many communities, cooperatives and other private enterprise businesses, such as the Hudson's Bay Company, exist side by side, selling and buying many of the same products.

In the past, Aboriginal cooperatives have encountered two major problems in their operations. First, they lacked skilled managers. Second, they found it difficult to engage in direct competition with integrated, multinational companies. Nevertheless, they have succeeded in providing employment for Aboriginal people. Today they are the largest employer of Aboriginal people in the North and elsewhere and register annual sales in excess of $30 million. There are currently well over 50 co-ops nationwide, employing more than 600 people and generating between $10 and $20 million in income. However, an infusion of government monies is still required for some co-ops to survive; to date, various government departments have contributed to the development of cooperatives. Much of this money is put towards training directors, managers, and staff. Additional federal monies are set aside to help with new production techniques and business marketing strategies.

Each of the strategies identified, including international ventures described in the box on page 402, point to the quest by Aboriginal people to gain control over their resources. The variety of strategies reflects the differing situations in which Aboriginal people find

Makivik Corporation

As the main engine of Nunavik's economic development, Makivik negotiates agreements with private- and public-sector partners. This includes ongoing negotiations with Hydro-Québec on existing and proposed James Bay hydroelectric projects, and the mining company Falconbridge Limited regarding the Raglan Nickel Mine project. Makivik, representing about 8500 Quebec Inuit and with offices in Quebec City, Montreal, and Ottawa, is also responsible for investing and managing funds obtained through these negotiations. Makivik is directly involved in economic development through its subsidiary companies, which include:

- Air Inuit: Nunavik's regional airline

- First Air: A major air carrier in Canada's eastern Arctic, with links to Greenland
- Seaku Fisheries: Exploits shrimp stocks and develops inshore projects with Inuit entrepreneurs
- Nunavik Arctic Foods Incorporated: Harvests and processes wild meats in four community processing centres and markets the products in Nunavik and southern markets.

These companies create jobs (and training) for the residents of Nunavik as well as providing essential services at competitive rates. The Corporation's portfolio size is in excess of $105 million and continues to grow.

Source: Information courtesy of Makivik Corporation, personal communication by R. Gadacz, 2003.

themselves. Yet the ultimate goal for Aboriginal people is to control their land and resources. Nevertheless, establishing the proper administrative structures is only the beginning. Once control has been established a structure will have to be devised in order to manage economic development and guarantee an enhancement of quality of life. This will require the necessary skills to operate businesses and to participate in what is increasingly a global economy.

The most widely employed development strategy used by Aboriginal people has probably been the concession. However, the joint venture has also become a more attractive alternative, and has been encouraged by the federal government's involvement. The government has loaned money to Aboriginal companies and has guaranteed its backing. But since they allow for no control or ownership of the natural resources, it is unlikely that these joint ventures will be a viable long-term economic strategy (Dyck and Waldram, 1993).

Each of the development strategies discussed above has benefits as well as costs. For this reason the type of agreement that an Aboriginal group might wish to make is ultimately determined by the group's goals. For example, if the Aboriginal group wanted to maintain a subsistence way of life, like the Cree of James Bay, and still allow development of natural resources, the concession type of agreement might be appropriate. On the other hand, if it wanted to become involved in the project, then a joint venture would seem more appropriate. For example, a joint venture called Shehtah Drilling was formed between Esso (50 percent), the Dene (25 percent), and the Métis (25 percent) development corporations in 1983 to conduct drilling and service-rig operations in the Northwest Territories.[3] The ATCO/EQUTAK drilling venture organized between Atco-Mustang Drilling and the

"Natives Talk Business in Nicaragua: Saskatchewan Group's Forestry Deal With Miskito Indians Reflects Entrepreneurial Trend"

By Erin Anderssen

The men from Meadow Lake Tribal Council motored down Nicaragua's Rio Coco in dugout canoes, stopping to talk business under the coconut trees in each community as they passed.

The group from Saskatchewan frequently spent the night, dining on fruits and beans, and sleeping on concrete. Often they would sit around a fire with the village elders and hear stories of children killing in war, and they would try to explain snow to people who have never known winter.

A few villages ahead, touching down in a helicopter, a group of Korean businessmen were making their pitch: Sell your trees to us, they'd promise, and we will build your village a baseball diamond.

The men from Meadow Lake promised nothing—except partnership. They made the same forestry-development offer to 72 Miskito Indian villages in the timber-rich land of Nicaragua's northern Atlantic coast. And not a single community said no.

"Those Koreans haven't moved a stick of wood for a year and a half," Meadow Lake chief executive Ray Ahenakew said with a chuckle.

The Meadow Lake forestry venture reflects a growing trend among Canada's aboriginal entrepreneurs, who are starting to see bright opportunities beyond the border. They are encouraged by a more pragmatic native leadership—most marked in Phil Fontaine, national chief of the Assembly of First Nations— which pushes economic development as key to self-government.

"Revitalizing first-nation economies should not be restricted to Canada," Mr. Fontaine said. "We go where there are opportunities. And we see the benefits in doing business with our brothers and sisters in other parts of the world. We're taking a page out of the Team Canada trade missions."

And Ottawa is happy to help— trade officials feel that Canada is missing the boat on development projects funded by international financial institutions such as the World Bank. The country's native bands, the logic goes, are ideally suited to helping other indigenous people set up culturally sensitive schools, build houses and hospitals in remote communities and develop their natural resources.

Deals like the Meadow Lake project could get much easier come 2005, the target date for a gigantic free-trade agreement with 34 countries in the hemisphere dubbed the Free Trade Area of the Americas. Negotiations start this week in Chile on the treaty, which would open up new markets in Central and South America. Leaders at the Santiago summit will also discuss the issue of poverty among indigenous people, a topic pushed onto the agenda by Canada.

Despite the opportunities (there is even talk of creating an indigenous-to-indigenous trademark), there are few aboriginal companies as established as Meadow Lake, which runs a forestry operation in northern Saskatchewan worth $60-million a year. Only about 50 aboriginal companies in Canada are considered export-ready, and fewer than a dozen have made progress signing international deals.

Makivik Corp., a company owned by the Inuit of Northern Quebec, is working on a lobster deal with the Miskito in Nicaragua. The Saskatoon Tribal Council is developing a coffee-packaging partnership with communities in Guatemala.

To help native bands make international links, the federal government appointed Blaine Favel, then head of the Saskatchewan Federation of Indian Nations, to a new post as counsellor on international indigenous issues in January. Since taking the job, Mr. Favel has travelled to Central America to meet Mayan and Miskito Indian leaders. "The stories are the same," he said. "So there's a great affinity. And trust is a large part of business."

At the Meadow Lake Tribal Council, work is underway to sell the deal to the wary central government of Nicaragua. The plan is to set up a small sawmill among the Miskito Indians and harvest a portion of the pine forest, splitting the initial profits in half.

Eventually, the Miskito Indians can buy out Meadow Lake completely, equipped and trained to run their own operation. Buyers, encouraged by the unanimous endorsement from the communities involved, are already calling from Texas, Mr. Ahenakew said.

"It's a good feeling," he said about his connection with the Miskito Indians. "But it's also the smartest way to do business."

Source: *The Globe and Mail*, April 13, 1998, page A4. Reproduced with permission.

Inuvialuit Development Corporation (with the assistance of Petro Canada); and the Beaufort Food Services, a joint venture between Beau-Tuk Marine and the Inuvialuit Development Corporation, are two other examples of joint ventures that have been relatively successful. Aboriginal international joint ventures of different kinds in this age of globalization and international capitalism are surely expected to increase in the decades to come.

Where successful agreements have been made to develop band natural resources, what do Aboriginal people do with their increased income? The number of cases is relatively small, but the Hobbema reserve in Alberta is one good example. There, the Samson Band's energy revenue exceeded $60 million even back in 1980. Besides appropriating one-half for individual band members, the band also built and operates a 283-hectare grain operation. But the band had also made investments beyond the agricultural domain. In the early 1980s, the Samson business manager bought the charter of the Edmonton Canadian Insurance Company for slightly more than $1 million. Other Samson Band investments now include rental properties in Edmonton, shares for subdivisions in three nearby towns, shares in a Vancouver condominium project, and shares in a housing development in Cold Lake, Alberta. Other oil-rich bands, like Samson, are also investing in land purchases, housing projects, and banks. One band is trying to work out a deal with a consortium that is seeking a national pay-television licence.

CONCLUSION

La Violette (1961) argues that for any ethnic group to survive it must be able to assert control over its fate. Essentially, the struggle for survival is a struggle for identity. The group must view its past positively and maintain strong links with traditional customs and beliefs. It must also achieve political equality and look forward to a promising future. These processes can be set in motion only at the grass-roots level. If Aboriginal people are going to control their destiny, they must implement some form of community control immediately. Aboriginal communities are slowly becoming involved in the process of capacity building, which allows them to plan and develop their own strategies for development. However, this development must revitalize and strengthen the social, cultural, and economic aspects of a way of life that is at the very core of being Aboriginal (Hanson, 1985). Over the years Aboriginal people have tried to develop community-based solutions to their economic plights.

At present, governments are encouraging Aboriginal people to develop small businesses on an individual basis. This ensures non-Aboriginal control in two ways: first, non-Aboriginal society wins the loyalties of the Aboriginal businesspeople, who are potentially important community leaders; and second, the visible ownership of local business by Aboriginal people defuses anti–non-Aboriginal feelings and reduces the likelihood of violent demonstrations. The community becomes more stable, the leadership potential of non-Aboriginal–affiliated Aboriginal businesspeople is enhanced, and the non-Aboriginal domination of the community economy, though less direct, remains intact. In addition, discontent is defused through acceptable channels (Tabb, 1970). Clearly, the strategy of individual entrepreneurship will not change the economic position of Aboriginal people substantially in the future.

Although community development must be encouraged, it must not be totally financed by the corporate sector of Canadian society. The federal government must not allow the corporate sector to interfere with or influence the development of Aboriginal communities, since economic development is not in the corporations' interests. So far, through close ties with the political elite, corporations have successfully blocked the federal financing that would permit Aboriginal development. For example, Saskatchewan First Nations hold $150 million in government-backed mortgages and pay almost $1 million a month to mortgage companies. If Aboriginal people started paying interest to their own institutions, the profit could be used to build up their own communities. If Aboriginal people are allowed to develop and control the reserves, they will eliminate corporate contracts for reserve projects and drain off the unskilled labour surplus for primary industries (Dyck, 1996).

If the corporate sector were allowed to initiate economic development on reserves, franchising would result. Under a franchise system, a corporation advances money to an individual Aboriginal person, who then manages a store that sells the corporation's product exclusively. The corporation also provides certain services and trains staff to ensure proper marketing techniques. In return for setting up the store, providing the loan, and training the staff, the company reaps several benefits, including a large percentage of the profits and access to the reserve and nearby communities. Franchising is an efficient and inexpensive way to guarantee non-Aboriginal corporate control of the reserve. Again, the presence of an Aboriginal staff defuses anti–non-Aboriginal sentiments and prevents the organization of a cohesive revolt. Moreover, the development of the reserve by outsiders allows for external control over the speed, extent, and nature of that development (Tabb, 1970: 58).

Although non-Aboriginal institutions are promoting individual entrepreneurship, many Aboriginal people have begun to recognize that the result of this policy will be continued subordination. Increasingly, cogent arguments like the following are put forward in support of Aboriginal community control and development:

To accomplish this task, four sets of recommendations are proposed: (i) The establishment of economically viable reserves controlled by the Indians with sufficient natural resources to ensure adequate incomes for the residents. The key element in this recommendation is that the natural resources of expanded Indian lands should be firmly placed in the control of the community and its representative leaders. (ii) The establishment of an Indian corporation which can receive direct grants and long-term low-interest loans to promote economic development on the reserve, to improve and initiate village services, and to in other ways enable Indians to better utilize their natural and economic resources. (iii) A major revamping of the educational system so as to reduce discontinuities in learning, sustain effective ties with parents, strengthen the student's self-image as Indian, and maintain his self-esteem, as well as prepare him to be economically and socially competent in dealing with the institutions of the larger Canadian society. (iv) The establishment of an Indian social development program, funded by the federal and/or provincial governments, which can assist in providing the mechanism for the emergence of new Indian leaders, increase communication with other Indian and non-Indian groups, and promote local and regional community, social, and political infra-structures. (Chance, 1970: 33–35)

As the process of Aboriginal development intensifies and expands, a balanced approach will be necessary in order to achieve the basic minimum needs of the community. Residents need to have basic educational qualifications, access to adequate health care facilities, basic housing, and experience in the labour force. Once these minimum balanced conditions have been achieved, an "unbalanced" approach to development must begin. In this approach, one central economic development is pursued. The decision as to what development should be fostered is dependent on the history of the community, its location, and the resources and skills available within it. As these factors are brought together, the central development will lead to other forms of development uniquely suited to the community. Once the key activity is established, money to support social programs will continue to rise without a need for additional specific long-range planning.[4]

Aboriginal people are also prepared to negotiate within the existing socio-legal system. In fact, both Aboriginal people and private industry as well as government are prepared to negotiate within certain boundaries. The boundaries generally determine the status quo, and all parties are accustomed to operating within it. However, Aboriginal people are pressing for change, and, thus, are posing demands that go beyond the status quo (Lightbody, 1969). As the critical point is approached in the negotiations, tension between the two negotiating parties emerges. Eventually, when Aboriginals force the issue beyond the critical point, tension changes to conflict. As Lightbody explains:

> [B]eyond [this critical point] the state must realign its institutional structures about a new ethnic configuration by either physically attempting to suppress the dissident elements into grudging assimilation into the culture, or through accepting the creation of the new.... (1969: 334)

Willingness to move beyond the critical point by either party varies with time and conditions, although the history of the negotiations is usually a good clue to whether or not conflict will emerge. For example, the Oldman River (Alberta) conflict, the Oka (Québec) conflict, and other Aboriginal–non-Aboriginal conflicts generally reflect a long history of Aboriginal peoples negotiating for social change that the other party is unwilling to accept. Constitutional talks and conferences since 1982 show that the government is slow to change the status quo when it deals with First Nations and Aboriginal peoples as a whole. While it is in favour of establishing conditions for a "distinct Québec society" in the Constitution, the government has been very slow to give Aboriginal peoples similar consideration.

Currently, Aboriginal people find themselves isolated from non-Aboriginal society and confronted by discrimination on a daily basis. To counter this position, they have recently begun the long, arduous task of defining their group identity and clarifying their future goals. The recent growth of Aboriginal organizations shows that Aboriginal people are strengthening their political and cultural position. And, as Boldt (1980b) has shown, they are increasingly willing to engage in "extra-legal" politics:

> Enlightened Indian leaders reject White society's comfortable notions of slow and steady progress toward the achievement of basic human rights for their people and most are inclined not only to approve of extra-legal activity as a justifiable means for achieving their conception of the "good society," but are also willing to participate and, if necessary, suffer the consequences of such actions for their cause. (p. 33)

Aboriginal people have learned over time that externally directed conflict tends to enhance group solidarity. Group boundaries come into sharp focus as in-group members are differentiated from out-group members. As conflict emerges, the group is also forced to explicitly define its aims and goals. As grievances are defined, adversaries emerge and are identified. In the case of Aboriginal groups, the adversaries are non-Aboriginal: relations between the two become a zero-sum game.

In a zero-sum game one player always gains precisely what the other player loses, and vice versa. In other words, relations between the two sides are always competitive and antagonistic. Identification with one's "side" pervades the daily life of each group member. Each participant finds a particular role in the collective action and receives internal and social rewards for behaviour that reinforces group aims. Identification with the group grows, as do linkages with other members. As Pettigrew describes:

> Recruits willingly and eagerly devote themselves to the group's goals. And they find themselves systematically rewarded [by the group].... They are expected to evince strong radical pride, to assert their full rights as citizens, to face jail and police brutality unhesitatingly for the cause. Note that these expected and rewarded actions all publicly commit the member to the group and its aim. (1964: 195–96)

And, as Himes states, out of organized group conflict grows a strong group identity:

> In the interactive process of organized group conflict, self-involvement is the opposite side of the coin of overt action. Actors become absorbed by ego and emotion into the group and the group is projected through their actions. This linkage of individual and group in ego and action is the substance of identity. (1966: 10)

With the emergence of a strong pan-Aboriginal identity, the sense of alienation experienced by many has been dispelled by a new sense of significance and purpose. The personal ethnic identity of Aboriginal people is stronger now than it has been for many decades, as leaders of national and provincial Aboriginal organizations have successfully developed a national cohesiveness. As Pitts (1974) points out, ethnic identity is a social product, a result of actions and interpretations in a social context. As Brown (1935) argued long ago:

> A race conscious group... is a social unit struggling for status in society. It is thus a conflict group and race consciousness itself is a result of conflict. The race of the group, though not intrinsically significant, becomes an identifying symbol, serving to intensify the sense of solidarity. (p. 572)

Aboriginal identification is a mixture of internal dynamics and external pressures. At present, that identification is being translated into what Enloe (1981) has called ethnic mobilization—the mobilization of an ethnic group's resources and manpower to better its position. Hopefully non-Aboriginal Canada will no longer respond with such demobilization techniques as the White Paper (1969) in order to remain in a controlling position. For, in response to such techniques, Aboriginal mobilization in turn would increase, and an accelerating spiral of conflict that could be set in motion would be counter-productive.

Even as we experience the first decade of the 21st century, more meaningful changes are still needed to enhance the political, socio-cultural, and economic position of Aboriginal people in Canada. As Canadians, we would be poorer as a nation if Aboriginal leaders and youth abandoned the legal and political means to effect those changes, or to direct their frustration and helplessness inwards. It is clear that we have a collective responsibility to ensure the prosperity and self-determination of this land's first inhabitants.

NOTES

1. In the middle of the 19th century Charles Darwin published his *On the Origin of Species*. His theoretical perspective centred on concepts such as evolution, natural selection, and survival of the fittest. It was an easy step for the layperson and the social scientist to apply these biological concepts as evidence that Europeans were somehow "more fit" than the groups they had defeated. Similarly, as long as a group continued to successfully exploit and win wars against other nations, it proved itself further evolved.

2. This case study is taken from Gadacz (1991), "Community Socio-Economic Development from a Plains Indian Perspective: A Proposed Social Indicator System and Planning Tool," *Native Studies Review*, Vol. 7 (1): 53–80. Used with permission.

3. The joint venture contract was worth $5 million. The majority of Shehtah drill crews are made up of skilled Aboriginal northerners (*Arctic Petroleum Operators' Association Review,* Vol. 6, 3, Winter 1983/84, Calgary, Alberta).

4. For a more thorough discussion on the relative merits of the "unbalanced" versus the "balanced" approach, see Rosenstein-Rodan, 1943; Nurkse, 1953; Scitovsky, 1954; Hirschmann, 1958; Lewis, 1956; Perroux, 1953; and Fellner, 1954. The first four authors advocate the balanced approach; the others support the unbalanced approach.

WEBLINKS

www.aboriginalcanada.gc.ca

The Aboriginal Canada Portal provides a link to the wider topic of economic development, with specific websites for business, finance, resources sector, tourism, trade, employment and more—all by province. This site also has internal links to several government departments involved with Aboriginal development, including Human Resources Development Canada (HRDC), Industry Canada, Natural Resources Canada, and Indian and Northern Affairs. In turn, each department provides links to Aboriginal businesses, cooperatives (including case studies), entrepreneurs, resource guides, and more.

www.dfait-maeci.gc.ca/aboriginalplanet/business/directory2002-en.asp

This website of the Department of Foreign Affairs and International Trade features a unique directory of Aboriginal exporters, listing individual links to such areas as fashion design, music and theatre, forestry and mining, telecommunications technology, industrial products, and more.

Bibliography

Aberle, D. 1970 "A Plan for Navaho Economic Development." In *American Indians: Facts and Future, Toward Economic Development for Native American Communities*, Joint Economic Committee. New York: Arno Press.

Ablon, Joan 1965 "American Indian Relocation: Problems of Dependency and Management in the City." *Phylon*, 26 (Winter 1965):362–371.

Adams, Howard 1975 *Prison of Grass*. Toronto: New Press.

Aggamaway-Pierre, M. 1983 Native Women and the State. In *Perspectives on Women in the 1980's*. Turner, J. and L. Emery (eds.), Winnipeg, The University of Manitoba Press, pp. 66–73.

Ahenakew, D. 1985 "Aboriginal Title and Aboriginal Rights. The Impossible and Unnecessary Task of Identification and Definition." In *The Quest for Justice*, M. Boldt, J. Long, and L. Little Bear (eds.). Toronto: The University of Toronto Press.

Alberta Federation of Métis Settlement Associations 1978 *The Métis People of Canada: A History*. Calgary: Gage Publishing Ltd.

Alberta, Government of 1991 *Report of the Task Force on the Criminal Justice System and Its Impact on the Indian and Métis People of Alberta*, Volume 1, Main Report, Edmonton.

Allan, D.J. 1943 "Indian Land Problems in Canada." In *The North American Indian Today*, C.T. Loram and T.F. McIlwraith (eds.). Toronto: University of Toronto Press.

Altman, J. and J. Nieuwenhuysen 1979 *The Economic Status of Australian Aborigines*. Cambridge: Cambridge University Press.

Anaya, S. James 2000 *Indigenous Peoples in International Law*. New York: Oxford University Press.

Anaya, S., R. Falk and D. Pharand 1995 *Canada's Fiduciary Obligation to Aboriginal Peoples in the Context of Accession to Sovereignty by Quebec*, Vol. 1, Ottawa, Minister of Supply and Services.

Anderson, A. 1978 "Linguistic Trends Among Saskatchewan Ethnic Groups." In *Ethnic Canadians*, M. Kovacs (ed.). Regina: University of Regina.

Anderson, C. and C. Denis 2003 "Urban Natives and the Nation: Before and After the Royal Commission on Aboriginal Peoples." *Canadian Review of Sociology and Anthropology*, 40, 4:373–390.

Anderson, David and Robert Wright 1971 *The Dark and Tangled Patch*. Boston: Houghton Mifflin Co.

Andrist, Ralph 1964 *The Long Death*. New York: Macmillan Publishing Co. Inc.

Antonowicz, D. H. and R. Ross 1994 "Essential Components of Successful Rehabilitation Programs for Offenders," *International Journal of Offender Therapy and Comparative Criminology*, 38, 2:97–104.

Armitage, A. 1995 *Comparing the Policy of Aboriginal Assimilation: Australia, Canada, and New Zealand*. Vancouver: University of British Columbia Press.

Armstrong, Robin and Tim Rogers 1996 *A First Nations Typology: Patterns of Socio-Economic Well-Being*. Research and Analysis Directorate, Policy and Strategic Direction, Department of Indian Affairs and Northern Development, Ottawa.

Asante, S. 1979 "Restructuring Transnational Mineral Agreements." *American Journal of International Law*, 73, 3:355–371.

Asch, Michael 1993 *Home and Native Land: Aboriginal Rights and the Canadian Constitution*. Vancouver: UBC Press.

_____ **1997** *Aboriginal and Treaty Rights in Canada: Essays on Law, Equality, and Respect for Difference*. UBC Press: Vancouver.

**Assembly of First Nations
1990a** Assembly of First
Nations' Critique of
Federal Government Land
Claims Policy, August 21,
Summerstown, Ontario.
_____ **1990b**
"Doublespeak of the 90s:
A Comparison of Federal
Government and First
Nation Perception of Land
Claims Process," August,
mimeo.

**Assembly of Manitoba
Chiefs/Indian and
Northern Affairs Canada
1994** *Towards First
Nations Governments in
Manitoba—Work Plan*.
November 22, 1994.

Bankes, N. 1983 *Resource
Leasing Options and the
Settlement of Aboriginal
Claims*. Ottawa: Canadian
Arctic Resources.
_____ **1986** "Indians'
Resource Rights and
Constitutional Enactments
in Western Canada
1871–1930." In *Essays in
Western Canadian Legal
History*, L. Knafla (ed.).
Toronto: Carswell:
29–164.

Barber, Lloyd 1977
*Commissioner of Indian
Claims: A Report:
Statements and
Submissions*. Ottawa:
Supply and Services
Canada.

Barkwell, L. J. 1988
Observations on discrimi-
nation and dehumanization
in the criminal justice system. Paper presented to
the *Aboriginal Justice
Inquiry: Inquiry
Proceedings*, December
15, 1988, Winnipeg: Four
Seasons Reporting
Services Ltd.

**Barkwell, L., N. Chartrand,
D. Gray, L. Longclaws,
and R. Richard 1989**

"Devalued People: The
Status of the Métis in the
Justice System," *The
Canadian Journal of
Native Studies*, 9.1,
121–150.

**Barman, J., Y. Hebert, and
D. McCaskill (eds.) 1987**
*Indian Education in
Canada*, Vol. II.
Vancouver: University of
British Columbia Press.

**Barsh, R. and J. Henderson
1982** "Aboriginal Rights,
Treaty Rights and Human
Rights: Tribe and
Constitutional Renewal."
*Journal of Canadian
Studies*, 2 (1982):55–81.

Bartlett, Richard 1980 *Indian
Act of Canada*. Saskatoon:
Native Law Centre,
University of
Saskatchewan.
_____ **1984** "Aboriginal
Land Claims at Common
Law." *Canadian Native
Law Reporter*, 1
(1984):1–63.

**Battiste, M. and J. Barman
(eds.) 1995** *First Nations
Education in Canada: The
Circle Unfolds*,
Vancouver, University of
British Columbia Press.

Beaver, J. 1979 *To Have What
Is One's Own*. Ottawa:
Department of Indian
Affairs and Northern
Development.

Bell, C. 1998 "New Directions
in the Law of Aboriginal
Rights," *Canadian Bar
Review*, 77,1 & 2:36–72.

Bell, Catherine 1991 "Who
Are the Métis in Section
35(2)?" *Alberta Law
Review*, Vol. 24, No.
2:351–381.

Bendix, R. 1964 *Native
Guilding and Citizenship*.
New York: John Wiley.

Benedict, R. 1950 *Patterns of
Culture*. New York:
Mentor Books.

Bennett, G. 1978 "Aboriginal
Title in the Common Law:
A Stoney Path Through
Feudal Doctrine." *Buffalo
Law Review*, 17 (1978):
601–623.

Berger, Thomas 1977
*Northern Frontier,
Northern Homeland—The
Report of the Mackenzie
Valley Pipeline Inquiry*,
Vol. 1. Ottawa: Minister
of Supply and Services
Canada.
_____ **1981** *Fragile
Freedoms: Human Rights
and Dissent in Canada*.
Toronto: Clarke, Irwin and
Co. Ltd.
_____ **1985** *Village
Journey*. New York: Hill
and Wang Co.

**Bherer, H., S. Gagnon,
J. Roberge 1990**
*Wampum and Letters
Patent*. Montreal: The
Institute for Research on
Public Policy.

**Bienvenue, Rita, and
A.H. Latif 1974** "Arrests,
Dispositions and
Recidivism: Comparison
of Indians and Whites."
*Canadian Journal of
Criminology and
Corrections*, 16
(1974):105–116.
_____ **1975** "The
Incidence of Arrests
Among Canadians of
Indian Ancestry." Paper
presented at Canadian
Sociology and
Anthropology meetings in
Kingston, Ontario.

Binnie, I. 1990 "The Sparrow
Doctrine: Beginning of the
End or End of the
Beginning?" *Queens Law
Journal*, 15:207–254.

Black, D. 1998 *The Social
Structure of Right and
Wrong*, 1998. San Diego,
California: Academic
Press.

Blais, Jean-Luc 1984 "Mineral Activities and Native Involvement on Indian Reserves." *Native Participation in Mineral Development Activities.* Queen's University, Kingston, Centre for Resource Studies.

Blauner, Robert 1969 "Internal Colonialism and Ghetto Revolt." *Social Problems*, 16 (Spring 1969):393–408.

Blishen, B., et al. 1979 *Socio-Economic Impact Model For Northern Development,* Volumes 1 and 2. Department of Indian and Northern Affairs, Canada.

Bobet, E. 1990 *The Inequalities in Health: A Comparison of Indian and Canadian Mortality Trends.* Ottawa: Health and Welfare Canada.

Bobet, E. 1997 *Diabetes Among First Nations People,* Statistics Canada, Ottawa, Medical Services Branch, Health Canada.

Bodley, J., 1988 *Tribal Peoples and Development Issues: A Global Overview.* Mountain View, CA: Mayfield Publishing Company. **Boe, R. 2000** "Aboriginal Inmates: Demographic Trends and Projections," *Forum*, 12, 1:7-9.

Boek, W.E., and J.K. Boek 1959 *The People of Indian Ancestry in Greater Winnipeg. Appendix 1: A Study of the Population of Indian Ancestry Living in Manitoba.* Winnipeg: Manitoba Department of Agriculture and Immigration.

Bolaria, S. 1979 "Self-Care and Lifestyles: Ideological and Policy Implications." In *Economy, Class and Social Reality,* J.A. Fry (ed.). Toronto: Butterworths, 350–363.

Boldt, M. 1973 "Indian Leaders in Canada: Attitudes Toward Equality, Identity, and Political Status." Ph.D. dissertation. New Haven: Yale University Press.

_____ **1980a** "Canadian Native Leadership: Context and Composition." *Canadian Ethnic Studies,* 12, 1 (1980a):15–33.

_____ **1980b** "Indian Leaders in Canada: Attitudes Toward Extra-Legal Action." *Journal of Ethnic Studies,* 8, 1 (1980b):71–83.

_____ **1980c** "Canadian Native Indian Leadership: Context and Composition." *Canadian Ethnic Studies Journal,* 12, 1 (1980c):71–83.

_____ **1981a** "Philosophy, Politics, and Extralegal Action: Native Indian Leaders in Canada." *Ethnic and Racial Studies,* 4, 2 (1981a):205–221.

_____ **1981b** "Social Correlates of Nationalism: A Study of Native Indian Leaders in a Canadian Internal Colony." *Comparative Political Studies,* 14, 2 (1981b): 205–231.

_____ **1981c** "Enlightenment Values, Romanticism and Attitudes Toward Political Status: A Study of Native Indian Leaders in Canada." *Canadian Review of Sociology and Anthropology,* 18, 4 (1981c):545–565.

_____ **1981d** "Social Correlates of Romanticism in an Internal Colony: A Study of Native Indian Leaders in Canada." *Ethnic Groups: An International Journal of Ethnic Studies,* 3, 4 (1981d):307–332.

_____ **1982** "Intellectual Orientations and Nationalism Among Leaders in an Internal Colony: A Theoretical and Comparative Perspective." *British Journal of Sociology,* 33, 4 (1982):484–510.

_____ **1993** *Surviving as Indians: The Challenge of Self Government.* Toronto: University of Toronto Press.

Boldt, M., and J. Long 1983 "Tribal Traditions and the Canadian Charter of Rights and Freedoms." Lethbridge, Alberta: University of Lethbridge. Mimeographed.

_____ **1985a** "Tribal Traditions and European–Western Political Ideologies: The Dilemma of Canada's Native Indians." In *The Quest for Justice,* M. Boldt, J. Long and L. Little Bear (eds.). Toronto: The University of Toronto Press.

_____ **1985b** "Tribal Philosophies and The Canadian Charter of Rights and Freedoms." In *The Quest for Justice,* M. Boldt, J. Long and L. Little Bear (eds.). Toronto: The University of Toronto Press.

Boldt, M., J.A. Long and L. Little Bear 1983a "The Concept of Sovereignty in the Political Thought of Canada's Native Indians." Mimeographed.

_____ **1985** (eds.). *The Quest for Justice.* Toronto: The University of Toronto Press.

Bonney, R. 1976 "The Role of Women in Indian Activism." In *The Western Canadian Journal of Anthropology*, 6, 3, pp. 243–248.

Bonta, J.U., S. Lipinski, and M. Martin 1992 "The Characteristics of Aboriginal Recidivists" *Canadian Journal of Criminology,* 34,3–4:517–521.

Bowles, R. 1979 "Charter Group or Capitalist Class: An Analysis of Faces Shaping Canadian Ethnic Structures." Mimeographed. Peterborough: Trent University.

Boxhill, Wally 1984 *1984 Census Data on the Native Peoples of Canada.* Ottawa: Statistics Canada.

Boyes, G.A. 1960 "New Goals for People of Indian Heritage." *Sixth Annual Conference on Indians and Métis.* Winnipeg: Welfare Council for Greater Winnipeg.

Braithwaite, J. 1990 *Crime, Shame and Reintegration.* Cambridge: Cambridge University Press.

_____ **1993** "Shame and Modernity," *British Journal of Criminology,* 33,1:54–68.

Braroe, N. 1975 *Indian and White: Self–Image and Interaction in a Canadian Plains Community.* Stanford: Stanford University Press.

Breton, Raymond, and Gail Grant Akian 1979 *Urban Institutions and People of Indian Ancestry.* Montreal: Institute for Research on Public Policy.

Brewster, H. 1971 "Economic Dependence." Mimeographed. London:

University of London, Institute of Commonwealth Studies.

British Columbia, Government of 1991 *The Report of the British Columbia Claims Task Force,* British Columbia Claims Task Force, Vancouver.

Brodhead, D., 1990 *Development Indicators in the Context of Aboriginal Development—An Overview.* Prepared for Indian and Northern Affairs Canada by E. T. Jackson and Associates Ltd., Ottawa. 42 pps.

Brody, Hugh 1971 *Indians on Skid Row: The Role of Alcohol and Community in the Adaptive Process of Indian and Urban Migrants.* Ottawa: Northern Science Research Group, Department of Indian Affairs and Northern Development. Information Canada.

_____ **1987** *Living Arctic.* Vancouver: Douglas and McIntyre Ltd.

Brown, Dee 1971 *Bury My Heart at Wounded Knee.* New York: Holt, Rinehart & Winston Inc.

_____ **1977** "Ultimate Respectability: Fur Trade Children in the 'Civilized World'." (Part One of Two Parts.) *The Beaver* (Winter 1977b):4–10.

_____ **1978** "Ultimate Respectability: Fur Trade Children in the 'Civilized World'." (Part Two of Two Parts.) *The Beaver* (Spring 1978):48–55.

_____ **1980a** "Linguistics, Solitudes, and Changing Social Categories." In *Old Trails and New Directions:*

Papers of the Third North American Fur Trade Conference, Carol M. Judd and Arthur J. Ray (eds.). Toronto: University of Toronto Press.

_____ **1980b** *Strangers in Blood.* Vancouver: University of British Columbia Press.

_____ **1996** *Reading Beyond Words: Context for Native History.* Peterborough: Broadview Press.

Brown, W.C. 1935 Racial Conflict Among South African Natives." *American Journal of Sociology*, 40 (1935):569–681.

Buckley, H. 1992 *From Wooden Ploughs to Welfare*, McGill-Queens University Press, Montreal and Kingston.

Burrell, G. and D. Sanders 1984 *Handbook of Case Law on the Indian Act.* Ottawa: DIAND.

Cairns, Alan C. 2000 *Citizens Plus: Aboriginal People and the Canadian State.* Vancouver: University of British Columbia Press.

Calder, W. 1986 "The Provinces and Indian Self Government in the Constitutional Forum." In *Indian–Provincial Government Relationship*, M. Boldt, J. Long, and L. Little Bear (eds.). Lethbridge: University of Lethbridge.

Caldwell, George 1967 *Indian Residential Schools.* Ottawa: Department of Indian Affairs and Northern Development.

Campbell, John and Alan Rew 1999 *Identity and Affect: Experiences of Identity in a Globalizing World.* London: Pluto Press.

Campbell, R. and L. Pal 1991
The Real Worlds of Canadian Politics.
Peterborough, Ontario:
Broadview Press.

Canada, Government of
1969a "Canadian
Committee on Corrections
Report" (Quimet Report).
Ottawa: Queen's Printer.

_____ **1969b** *Statement
of the Government of
Canada on Policy, 1969*
(White Paper). Ottawa:
Queen's Printer.

_____ **1966–70** *Annual
Reports: 1966–67;
1968–69; 1969–70.*
Department of Indian
Affairs and Northern
Development. Ottawa:
Queen's Printer, 1966–70.

_____ **1973** *Report of
Task Force: Policing on
Reserves.* Edmonton:
Department of Indian and
Northern Affairs.

_____ **1974** *Perspective
Canada I.* Ottawa:
Information Canada.

_____ **1977** *Perspective
Canada II.* Ottawa:
Statistics Canada, Supply
and Services.

_____ **1978a** *A
Recommended Plan for
Evaluation in Indian
Education.* Ottawa: IIAP,
Department of Indian
Affairs and Northern
Development, Program
Evaluation Branch.

_____ **1978b** "Evaluation
of the RCMP Indian
Special Constable Program
(Option 3B)." Ottawa:
IIAP, Evaluation Branch,
Department of Indian
Affairs and Northern
Development, March
1978b.

_____ **1978c** *Indian
Affairs and Northern
Development Business*
*Loan Fund: Indian
Economic Development
Direct Loan Order Policy
and Guidelines.* Ottawa:
Department of Indian
Affairs and Northern
Development, Loan Fund
Division.

_____ **1979a** *Perspective
Canada III.* Ottawa:
Statistics Canada, Supply
and Services.

_____ **1979b** *Social
Assistance and Related
Social Development
Programs of the
Department of Indian and
Northern Affairs.* Ottawa:
IIAP, Department of Indian
Affairs and Northern
Development.

_____ **1980** *Indian
Conditions, A Survey.*
Ottawa: Department of
Indian Affairs and
Northern Development.

_____ **1981** *In All
Fairness: A Native Claims
Policy.* Ottawa: Minister of
Supply and Services.

_____ **1982** *Population,
Repartition geographique—
Terre-Neuve.* Recensement
du Canada, 1981. Ottawa:
Statistique Canada
(Catalogue 93-901).

_____ **1983** *The Report
of the House of Commons
Special Committee on
Indian Self-Government*
(The Penner Report).
Ottawa: Minister of Supply
and Services Canada.

_____ **1984a** *Les
Autochtones au Canada.*
Ottawa: Statistique Canada
(Catalogue 99-937).

_____ **1984b** *Response of
the Government to the
Report of the Special
Committee on Indian Self-
Government* (reply to the
Penner Report). Ottawa.

_____ **1985a** *Living
Treaties: Lasting
Agreements.* Report of the
Task Force to Review
Comprehensive Claims
Policy. Ottawa: DIAND.

_____ **1985b** *Indian and
Native Programs.* A Study
Team Report to the Task
Force on Program Review.
Ottawa: Minister of Supply
and Services.

_____ **1988** *Census
Metropolitan Areas,
Dimensions,* Ottawa:
Supply and Services.

_____ **1989** *The
Canadian Aboriginal
Economic Development
Strategy.* Ottawa: Indian
and Northern Affairs
Canada.

_____ **1990** *Annual
Report, 1989–90,*
Department of Indian
Affairs and Northern
Development. Ottawa:
Minister of Supply and
Services.

_____ **1991** *Language,
Tradition, Health, Lifestyle
and Social Issues.* Ottawa:
Statistics Canada
(Catalogue 89-533),
(1991):52,102.

_____ **1996a** *Looking
Forward, Looking Back.
Royal Commission on
Aboriginal Peoples.*
Ottawa: Minister of Supply
and Services.

_____ **1996b**
*Restructuring the
Relationship.* Royal
Commission on Aboriginal
Peoples. Ottawa: Minister
of Supply and Services.

_____ **1996c** *Soliloquy
and Dialogue: Overview of
Major Trends in Public
Policy relating to
Aboriginal Peoples.* From
the series "Public Policy
and Aboriginal Peoples

1965–1992, Volume 1. Royal Commission on Aboriginal Peoples, Canada Communication Group: Ottawa.

_____ **1999a** *From Restorative Justice to Transformative Justice.* Ottawa: Law Commission of Canada.

_____**1999b** *A Second Diagnostic on the Health of First Nations and Inuit People in Canada*, November. Ottawa: Health Canada.

_____**2000** *Diabetes Among First Nations People.* Statistics Canada, Ottawa, Medical Services Branch, Health Canada.

_____**2003** *Registered Indian Population by Sex and Residence 2002.* Indian Affairs and Northern Development, Ottawa, Public Works and Government Services Canada.

_____ **n.d.** *Indian Claims in Canada/Revendications des Indiens au Canada.* Toronto: Clarke, Irwin and Co. Ltd.

Canadian Association in Support of the Native Peoples 1978 Bulletin on Native Women (special issue, 18,4), Ottawa: CASNP.

Canadian Indian Resource Corporation 1990 *Long Term Strategic Plan.* 34 pps.

Canadian Superintendent 1965 *The Education of Indian Children in Canada.* Toronto: Ryerson Press.

Cantryn, M. (n.d.) Evaluation—Native Women's Program, Ottawa: Secretary of State.

Cardinal, H. 1969 *The Unjust Society.* Edmonton: Hurtig Publishers

_____ **1977** *The Rebirth of Canada's Indians.* Edmonton: Hurtig Publishers.

_____ **1979** "Native Women and the Indian Act." In: Elliott, J. (ed.), *Two Nations, Many Cultures.* Scarborough: Prentice Hall Canada, pp. 44–50.

_____ **1986** "Constitutional Change and the Treaty 8 Renovation." In *Indian–Provincial Relations*, M. Boldt, J.A. Long and L. Little Bear (eds.). Lethbridge: The University of Lethbridge.

Carley, M., 1981 *Social Measurement and Social Indicators: Issues of Policy and Theory.* George Allen and Unwin, London.

Carpenter, Jock 1977 *Fifty Dollar Bride.* Sidney, B.C.: Gray's Publishing Ltd.

Carstens, Peter 1971 "Coercion and Change." In *Canadian Society*, Richard Ossenberg (ed.). Scarborough, Ontario: Prentice Hall Canada.

Carstens, P. 1991 *The Queen's People*, Toronto: University of Toronto Press.

Carter, S. 1990 *Lost Harvests*, Montreal and Kingston: McGill-Queen's University Press.

Cassidy, Frank and Robert Bish, 1989 *Indian Government: Its Meaning in Practice.* Halifax: Institute for Research on Public Policy.

Castellano, Marlene 1970 "Vocation or Identity: The Dilemma of Indian Youth." In *The Only Good Indian*, Waubageshig (ed.). Toronto: New Press.

Cawsey, Justice R. 1991 *Justice on Trial*, Vol. 1, Report of the Task Force on the Criminal Justice System and its Impact on the Indian and Métis People of Alberta, Edmonton: Attorney General of Alberta.

Chance, Norman 1970 *Development Change Among the Cree Indians of Quebec.* Ottawa: Summary Report, ARDA Project 34002 (Reprint 1970), Department of Regional Economic Expansion.

Chapman, L. 1972 Women's Rights and Special Status for Indians: Some Implications of the *Lavell* Case, Ottawa, Carleton University, n.p.

Charlebois, P. 1975 *The Life of Louis Riel.* Toronto: N.C. Press.

Chartier, C. 1988 *In the Best Interest of the Métis Child.* Saskatoon, Saskatchewan: Native Law Centre.

Chartrand, P. 1993 "Aboriginal Rights: The Dispossession of the Métis," *Osgoode Hall Law Journal*, 29:425–467.

Chartrand, P. (ed) 2002 *Who are Canada's Aboriginal Peoples?* Saskatoon, Purich Publishing Ltd.

Chase-Dunn, Christopher 1975 "The Effects of International Economic Dependence and Inequality: A Cross-National Study." *American Sociological Review*, 40 (1975):720–738.

Cheda, S. 1977 "Indian Women: An Historical Example and a Contemporary View." In Stephenson, M. (ed.), *Women in Canada.* Don Mills: General Publishing Co. Ltd., pp. 195–208.

Chrétien, J. 1969 "Indian Policy... Where Does It Stand?" Speech at Empire Club, Toronto, October 16, 1969.

Churchill, W. 1999 *Struggle for the Land*, Winnipeg, Arbeiter Ring.

Clark, M. 1999 *Tuberculosis in First Nations Communities*, 1999, Minister of Health, Ottawa, Public Works and Government Services Canada.

Clark, T. 1994 *Lonewolf vs. Hitchcock: Treaty Rights and Indian Law at the End of the Nineteenth Century*. Lincoln: University of Nebraska Press.

Clarke, Roger 1972 *In Them Days: The Breakdown of a Traditional Fishing Economy in an English Village on the Gaspé Coast*. Ph.D. dissertation. Montreal: McGill University Press.

Clatworthy, S. 2000 *Re-assessing the population Impacts of Bill C-31*, Ottawa: Research and Analysis Directorate, Indian and Northern Affairs Canada.

Clement, W. and G. Williams 1989 "Introduction." *The New Canadian Political Economy*, W. Clement and G. Williams (eds.). Kingston, Ontario: McGill-Queen's University Press.

Coates, K. 1991 *Best Left as Indians: Native–White Relations in the Yukon Territory, 1840–1973*. Montreal: McGill-Queen's University Press.

_____ **2000** *The Marshall Decision and Native Rights*. Montreal and Kingston: McGill-Queen's University Press.

Coates, K. and W. Morrison 1986 "More Than A Matter of Blood: The Federal Government, The Churches and the Mixed Blood Populations of the Yukon and the Mackenzie River Valley, 1890–1950." In *1885 and After*, F. Barron and J. Waldham (eds.). Regina: Canadian Plains Research Centre (1986):253–277.

Coffey, W. and M. Polese 1985 "Local Development: Conceptual Bases and Policy Implications." *Regional Studies* 19 (2): 85–93.

Cohen, F. 1947 "Original Indian Title." *Minnesota Law Review*, 32, 28 (1947):52–57.

Cole, C. 1939 *Colbert and a Century of French Mercantilism*. 2 Vols., New York.

Colvin, E. 1981 "Legal Process and the Resolution of Indian Claims." *Studies in Aboriginal Rights*, #3. Saskatoon: Native Law Centre, University of Saskatchewan.

Comeau, P. and A. Santin 1990 *The First Canadians: A Profile of Canada's Native People Today*. Toronto: Lorimer.

Cook, Curtis, and Juan Lindau (eds.) 2000 *Aboriginal Rights and Self-Government*. Montreal and Kingston: McGill-Queen's University Press.

Cornell, S. 1988 *The Return of the Native*. New York: Oxford University Press.

Cornell, S. and J. Kalt 1992 "Reloading the Dice: Improving the Economic Development on American Indian Reservations." *What Can Tribes Do? Structure and Institutions in American Indian Economic Development*, S. Cornell and J. Kalt (eds.). Los Angeles: American Indian Studies Center, University of California.

Corporation for Enterprise Development 1987 *Making the Grade: The Development Report Card for the States*. Washington, D.C.

Corrigan, S. 1970 "The Plains Indian Pow-wow: Cultural Integration in Manitoba and Saskatchewan." *Anthropologica*, 12, 2 (1970):253–271.

Coté, Françoise 1984 "Nunavut, la province qui veut naître." *L'actualité* (mars 1984):75–80.

Courchene, T. and L. Powell 1992 *A First Nations Province*, Kingston, Ontario, Queen's University Institute of Intergovernmental Relations.

Crowe, K. 1974 *A History of the Original Peoples of Northern Canada*. Arctic Institute of North America. Montreal: McGill-Queen's University Press.

Culhane, Dara 1998 *The Pleasure of the Crown: Anthropology, Law and First Nations*. Vancouver: Talonbooks.

Cultural Survival Quarterly *World Report on the Rights of Indigenous Peoples and Ethnic Minorities*. Cambridge, MA: Cultural Survival. [Volumes 1 – to date]

Cumming, G. Graham 1967 "The Health of the Original Canadians 1867–1967." *Medical Service Journal*, 13 (February 1967):115–166.

Cumming, P. 1967 "Public Lands, Native Land Claims

and Land Use." In *Canadian Public Land Use in Perspective*, J. Nelson, R. Scace, and R. Kouri (eds.). Proceedings of a symposium sponsored by the Social Science Research Council of Canada, Ottawa, (1967):206–238.

_____ 1969 "Indian Rights—A Century of Oppression." Mimeographed. Toronto: Indian–Eskimo Association of Canada, 1969.

_____ 1973a "Our Land—Our People: Native Rights, North of 60." In *Arctic Alternatives*, D. Pimlott, K. Vincent and C. McKnight (eds.). Ottawa: Canadian Arctic Resources Committee.

_____ 1973b "Native Rights and Law in an Age of Protest." *Alberta Law Review* (1973b):230–245.

Cumming, P., and N. Mickenberg 1972 *Native Rights in Canada*, 2nd ed. Toronto: Indian–Eskimo Association of Canada.

Dahl, J. 1997 "Gender Parity in Nunavut," *Indigenous Affairs*, 3-4:42-47.

Dahl, R. 1967 *Pluralist Democracy in the United States*. Chicago: Rand-McNally.

Dalon, R. 1985 "An Alberta Perspective on Aboriginal Peoples and The Constitution." In *The Quest for Justice*, M. Boldt, J.A. Long, and L. Little Bear (eds.). Toronto: University of Toronto Press.

D'Anglure, B. 1984 "Inuit of Quebec." *Handbook of North American Indians*, vol. 5 *Arctic*, D. Damas (ed.). Washington:
Smithsonian Institute, (1984):476–507.

Daniel, R. 1980 *A History of Native Claims Processes in Canada, 1867–1979.* Ottawa: Research Branch, Department of Indian Affairs and Northern Development.

Daniels, H. 1981 *Native People and the Constitution of Canada*. Ottawa: Mutual Press.

Darroch, A.G. 1980 "Another Look at Ethnicity, Stratification, and Social Mobility in Canada." In *Ethnicity and Ethnic Relations in Canada*, J. Goldstein and R. Bienvenue (eds.). Scarborough, Ontario: Butterworth and Co. (Canada) Ltd.

Daughery, W. 1978 *Discussion Report on Indian Taxation*. Ottawa: Department of Indian and Northern Affairs, Treaties and Historical Research Centre.

_____ 1982 *A Guide to Native Political Associations in Canada*. Treaties and Historical Research, Research Branch, Corporate Policy. Ottawa: Department of Indian and Northern Affairs.

Daugherty, Wayne, and Dennis Magill 1980 *Indian Government Under Indian Act Legislation, 1868–1951*. Ottawa: Research Branch, Department of Indian and Northern Affairs.

Davies, M. 1985 "Aspects of Aboriginal Rights in International Law." In *Aboriginal Peoples and the Law*. B. Morse (ed.). Ottawa: Carleton University Press, (1985):16–47.
Davis, Arthur K., Cecil L. French, William D. Knill, and Henry Zentner 1965 *A Northern Dilemma: Reference Papers*, Vol. 2. Calgary and Bellingham, WA.: Western Washington State College.

Delgamuukw* vs. *Her Majesty the Queen in Right of the Province of British Columbia. Supreme Court of Canada Decision, File No. 23799, December 11, 1997.

Delisle, H. and J. Ekoe 1993 "Prevalence of Non-Insulin Dependent Diabetes Mellitus and Impaired Glucose Tolerance in Two Algonquin Communities in Quebec." *Canadian Medical Association Journal*, 149:41-47.

Delmar, R. 1986 "What Is Feminism?" In Mitchell, J. and A. Oakley (eds.), *What Is Feminism?* Oxford: Basil Blackwell, pp. 8–33.

Deloria, V. and C. Lytle 1984 *The Nations Within: The Past and Future of American Indian Sovereignty*. New York: Pantheon Books.

Denis, Claude 1997 *We Are Not You: First Nations and Canadian Modernity.* Peterborough: Broadview Press.

Denton, T. 1972 "Migration from a Canadian Indian Reserve." *Journal of Canadian Studies*, 7 (1972):54–62.

Deprez, Paul, and Glen Sigurdson 1969 *Economic Status of the Canadian Indian: A Re-Examination.* Winnipeg: Centre for Settlement Studies, University of Manitoba.

DIAND 1969 *Statement of the Government of Canada on*

Indian Policy. Ottawa: Queen's Printer.

_____ **1978** *Native Claims: Policy, Processes and Perspectives*. Ottawa: Queen's Printer.

_____ **1980** *Indian Conditions. A Survey*. Ottawa: Minister of Supply and Services.

_____ **1981** *In All Fairness: A Native Claims Policy*. Ottawa: Queen's Printer.

_____ **1982a** *Outstanding Business: A Native Claims Policy*. Ottawa: Minister of Supply and Services.

_____ **1982b** *James Bay and Northern Quebec Agreement Implementation Review*. Ottawa: Minister of Supply and Services.

_____ **1982c** *Strengthening Indian Band Government in Canada*. Ottawa: Minister of Indian Affairs and Northern Development. Ottawa, c. 1982c.

_____ **1982d** *An Optional System of Indian Band Government*. Ottawa: Minister of Indian Affairs and Northern Development. Ottawa, d, 1982d.

_____ **1982e** "The Legislation Proposals." *Annex I*. Ottawa: Minister of Supply and Services, c. 1982e.

_____ **1982f** "Financial Considerations—The Funding System." *Annex II*. Ottawa: Minister of Supply and Services, c. 1982f.

_____ **1982g** "Appendix VI: Pick up of Provincial Program Costs." Ottawa: Mimeographed, c. 1982g.

_____ **1982h** *The Alternative of Optional Indian Band Government*

Legislation. Ottawa: Minister of Indian Affairs and Northern Development.

_____ **1984** House of Commons. Indian Self-Government in Canada: Report of the Special Committee, Ottawa.

_____ **1985** *Living Treaties: Lasting Agreements. Report of the Task Force to Review Comprehensive Claims Policy*. Ottawa: Department of Indian Affairs and Northern Development.

Dickason, D.P. 1992 *Canada's First Nations*, Toronto: McClelland and Stewart Ltd.

Dickason, Olive. 1984 *The Myth of the Savage and the Beginnings of French Colonialism in the Americas*. Edmonton, University of Alberta Press.

Dickason, Olive 1992 *Canada's First Nations: A History of Founding Peoples from Earliest Times*. Norman: University of Oklahoma Press.

Dickason, Olive. 2002 *Canada's First Nations*, Don Mills, Ontario, Oxford University Press.

Dickerson, M. 1993 *Whose North?* Calgary and Vancouver: The Arctic Institute of North America and the University of British Columbia Press.

Dickinson, H. and B. Bolaria 1992 "Expansion and Survival: Canadian Sociology and the Development of the Canadian Nation." *Handbook of Contemporary Developments in World Society*, 2nd ed., R. Mohan and D. Martindale (eds.).

New York: Greenwood Press.

Dobbin, Murray 1981 *The One-And-A-Half Men: The Story of Jim Brady and Malcolm Norris, Métis Patriots of the 20th Century*. Vancouver: New Star Books.

Doerr, A.D. 1974 "Indian Policy." In *Issues in Canadian Public Policy*. G.S. Doern and V.S. Wilson (eds.). Toronto: Macmillan.

Dorais, Louis-Jacques 1992 "La situation linguistique dans l'Arctique." *Etudes/Inuit/Studies*, 16, 1–2:237–255.

_____ **1997** *Quaqtaq: Modernity and Identity in an Inuit Community*. Toronto: University of Toronto Press.

Dosman, Edgar 1972 *Indians: The Urban Dilemma*. Toronto: McClelland and Stewart Ltd.

Driben, Paul 1975 *We Are Métis*. Ph.D. dissertation. Minneapolis: University of Minnesota.

_____ **1983** "The Nature of Métis Claims." *The Canadian Journal of Native Studies*, 3, 1(1983):183–196.

Drucker, P. 1958 *The Native Brotherhoods: Modern Intertribal Organizations on the Northwest Coast*. Bureau of American Ethnology, 168. Washington, D.C.: Smithsonian Institution.

Dubois, W. 1940 *Dusk of Dawn*. New York: Harcourt, Brace and Co.

Duclos, N. 1990 "Lessons of Difference: Feminist Theory on Cultural Diversity." In *Buffalo Law Review*, 38, 2, pp. 325–381.

Duff R. 1997 *The Indian History of British Columbia.* Rev. ed. Victoria: Royal British Columbia Museum.
_____ **1989** "The Limits of Judicial Independence," *Saskatchewan Law Review,* 61:247–275.

Duffy, R.Q. 1988 *The Road to Nunavut.* Kingston and Montreal: McGill-Queen's University Press.

Duhaime, G. 1992 "Le chasseur et le minotaure: Itineraire de l'autonomie politique au Nunavut," *Etudes/Inuit/Studies,* 16,1–2:149–177.
_____ **1993** *The Governing of Nunavut: Who Pays for What?,* Universite Laval, Groupe d'etudes Inuit et circumpolaires.

Dunning, R. 1972 "The Indian Situation: A Canadian Government Dilemma." *International Journal of Comparative Sociology,* 12 (June, 1972):128–134.
_____ **1976** "Some Speculations on the Canadian Indian Socio-Political Reality." In *The Patterns of 'Amerindian' Identity,* Marc-Adelard Tremblay (ed.). Quebec: Les Presses de l'Université Laval.

Dupuis, R. and K. McNeil 1995 *Canada's Fiduciary Obligation to Aboriginal Peoples in the Context of Accession to Sovereignty by Quebec,* Vol. 2, Ottawa, Minister of Supply and Services.

Dybbroe, S. 1996 "Questions of Identity and Issues of Self-Determination, *Etudes/Inuit/Studies,* 20,2: 39–53.

Dyck, Noel 1979 "Pow-wow and the Expression of Community in Western Canada." *Ethnos,* 1–2 (1979):78–79.
_____ **1980** "Indian, Métis, Native: Some Implications of Special Status." *Canadian Ethnic Studies,* 12, 1(1980): 34–36.
_____ **1981** "The Politics of Special Status: Indian Associations and the Administration of Indian Affairs." In *Ethnicity and Politics in Canada,* J. Dahlie and T. Fernando (eds.). Agincourt, Ontario: Methuen Publications.
_____ **1990** "Cultures, Communities and Claims: Anthropology and Native Studies in Canada, *Canadian Ethnic Studies,* Vol. 22, No. 3, pp. 40–55.
_____ **1991** *What Is the Indian "Problem"?* Memorial University of Newfoundland, Institute of Social and Economic Research.
_____ **1996** "Tutelage, Resistance and Co-optation in Canadian Indian Administration," *Canadian Review of Sociology and Anthropology,* 34, 3:333–348.

Dyck, Noel and James Waldram 1993 *Anthropology, Public Policy and Native Peoples in Canada.* Montreal: McGill-Queen's University Press.

Eberts, M. 1985 "The Use of Litigation Under the Canadian Charter of Rights and Freedoms as a Strategy for Achieving Change," In Nevitte, N. and A. Kornberg (eds.), *Minorities and the Canadian State.* Oakville: Mosaic Press, pp. 53–70.

Edmonton, City of 1976 *Native Adjustment to the Urban Environment: A Report on the Problems Encountered by Newly Arrived Natives in Edmonton.* Edmonton: Social Services Department, Social Planning Division.

Elias, D. 1976 "Indian Politics in the Canadian Political System." In *The Patterns of 'Amerindian' Identity,* Marc-Adelard Tremblay (ed.). Quebec: Les Presses de l'Université Laval (1976):35–64.

Elias, P. 1991 *Development of Aboriginal People's Communities,* York University, Captus Press.

Ellerby, L. 1995 "Community-Based Treatment of Aboriginal Sex Offenders: Facing Realities and Exploring Possibilities," *Forum on Corrections Research,* 6, 3:23–25.

Elliott, D. 1991 "Aboriginal Title." In *Aboriginal Peoples and the Law,* B. Morse (ed.). Ottawa: Carleton University Press, (1991):48–121.

Elliott, J.L. 1970 *Educational and Occupational Aspirations and Expectations: A Comparative Study of Indian and Non-Indian Youth.* Antigonish: St. Francis Xavier University.
_____ **1971** *Minority Canadians: Native Peoples.* Scarborough, Ontario: Prentice Hall Canada.
_____ **1980** "Native People, Power and Politics." *Multiculturalism,* 3, 3 (1980):10–74.

Englestad D. and J. Bird 1993 *Nation-To-Nation: Aboriginal Sovereignty and*

the Future of Canada.
Toronto: Anansi Press.

English, V. 1995 "Poverty and Native Women," in *Freedom Within the Margins*, C. Pizanias and J. Frideres (eds.). Calgary: Detselig Enterprises Ltd., pp. 111–118.

Enloe, C. 1981 "The Growth of the State and Ethnic Mobilization: The American Experience." *Ethnic and Racial Studies*, 4, 2 (1981):123–136.

Ens, Gerhard 1996 *Homeland to Hinterland: The Changing Worlds of the Red River Métis in the Nineteenth Century.* Toronto: University of Toronto Press.

Epprecht, N. 2000 "Programs for Aboriginal Offenders: A National Survey," *Forum*, 12,1:45–47.

Eschbach, K., K. Supple, and M. Snipp 1998 "Changes in Racial Identification and the Educational Attainment of American Indians, 1970–1990." *Demography,* 35,1:35–44.

Ewing Commission Report 1935 *Royal Commission on the Conditions of the Halfbreed Population of the Province of Alberta Report, 1935.* Sessional Paper No. 72.

Faulkner, C. 1992 "Inuit Offenders," in *Aboriginal Peoples and Canadian Criminal Justice*, by R. Silverman and M. Nielsen (eds.). Toronto: Butterworths.

Federation of Saskatchewan Indian Nations 1985 Memo from Chief Sol Sanderson re: Section 122 of the *BNA Act* and the Bilateral Process, Prince Albert, Saskatchewan.

Federation of Saskatchewan Indians 1977 *Indian Government: A Position Paper.* Prince Albert, Saskatchewan.

_____ **1978** "Off-Band Members in Saskatchewan." Mimeographed. Saskatoon.

Fellner, W. 1954 "Long-term Tendencies in Private Capital Formulation." *Long-Range Economic Projections*, Prince, National Bureau of Economic Research.

Fenge, T. 1992 "Political Development and Environmental Management in Northern Canada: The Case of the Nunavut Agreement." *Etudes/Inuit/Studies*, 16, 1–2:115–141.

Fernandez, Juan 1983 "La loi des Indiens: Un Instrument de gestion démo-graphique." Association Internationale des Démographes de Langue Française, *Démographie et gestion des sous-popula-tions*, 1 (1983):423–429.

Fidler, Dick 1970 *Red Power in Canada.* Toronto: Vanguard Publications.

Fields, D. and W. Stanbury 1975 *The Economic Impact of the Public Sector Upon the Indian of British Columbia.* Vancouver: University of British Columbia Press.

Fine, Sean 1989 "Near 1 in 4 Family Murders Among Natives, Study Says." *The Globe and Mail*, October 4. Toronto.

First Nations Resource Council 1990 *Socio-Economic/Quality of Life Indicators Symposium,* May 31 Report. 13 pps. Edmonton.

Fisher, A.D. 1969 "White Rites versus Indian Rights." *Transaction*, 7, November (1969):29–33.

Fisher, R. 1977 *Contact and Conflict: Indian–European Relations in British Columbia, 1774–1890.* Vancouver: University of British Columbia Press.

Flanagan, T. 1983a "The Case Against Métis Aboriginal Rights." *Canadian Public Policy*, 9 (1983):314–315.

_____ **1983b** *Riel and the Rebellion: 1885 Reconsidered*, Saskatoon: Western Producer Prairie Books.

_____ **1985** "Métis Aboriginal Rights: Some Historical and Contemporary Problems." In *The Quest for Justice*, M. Boldt, J. Long and L. Little Bear (eds.). Toronto: University of Toronto Press.

_____ **1990** "The History of Métis Aboriginal Rights: Politics, Principle and Policy," *Canadian Journal of Law and Society*, 5, pp. 71–94.

_____ **2000** *First Nations? Second Thoughts.* Montreal-Kingston: McGill-Queens University Press.

Fleming-Mathur, M. 1971 "Who Cares That a Woman's Work Is Never Done?" In *Indian Historian*, 4, 2, pp. 11–15.

Fleras, A. and J. L. Elliott 1992 *The Nations Within: Aboriginal–State Relations in Canada, United States, and New Zealand.* Don Mills, Ontario: Oxford University Press.

Fletcher, C. 1992 *Altered States? Federalism, Sovereignty and Self*

Government, No. 22. Australian National University, Federalism Research Centre.

Fontaine, P. 1998 "Aboriginal peoples making giant strides on long journey to better lives," *Canadian Speeches: Issues of the Day,* September, 32–34.

Foster, H. 1998–99 "Honoring the Queen: A Legal and Historical Perspective on the Nisga'a Treaty," *B.C. Studies,* 120:5–11.

Foster, John E. 1976 "Mixed Bloods in Western Canada: An Ecological Approach." "The Origins of the Mixed Bloods in the Canadian West." In *Essays on Western History,* Lewis H. Thomas (ed.). Edmonton: University of Alberta Press.

_____ 1978 "The Métis, the People and the Term." *Prairie Forum,* 3, 1 (Spring 1978):79–91.

Four Worlds Development Project 1985 *Developing Healthy Communities: Fundamental Strategies for Health Promotion.* Lethbridge: University of Lethbridge.

Four Worlds Development Project 1988 *Towards the Year 2000.* Lethbridge: University of Lethbridge.

Francis, D. 1983 *A History of the Native Peoples of Quebec, 1760–1867.* Ottawa: Indian Affairs and Northern Development.

Frank, André Gunder 1967 *Capitalism and Underdevelopment in Latin America.* New York: Monthly Review Press.

Franklin, Raymond 1969 "The Political Economy of Black Power." *Social Problems,* 16 (Winter 1969):286–301.

Freeman, M. 1985 "Traditional and Contemporary Roles of Inuit Women." In *Association of Canadian Universities for Northern Studies, Social Science in the North: Communicating Northern Values.* Ottawa: ACUNS, pp. 57–60.

French, B.F. 1851 *Historical Collections of Louisiana.* Dublin: Arbers Annals, 1851.

Frideres, J.S. 1972 "Indians and Education: A Canadian Failure." *Manitoba Journal of Education,* 7 (June 1972):27–30.

_____ 1974 *Canada's Indians: Contemporary Conflicts.* Scarborough, Ontario: Prentice Hall Canada.

_____ 1986 "Native Claims and Settlement in Yukon." In *Arduous Journey,* J.R. Ponting (ed.). Toronto: McClelland and Stewart (1986):284–301.

Frideres, J. and B. Robertson 1994 "Aboriginals and the Criminal Justice System: Australia and Canada." *International Journal of Contemporary Sociology,* 31,1:1–27.

Frideres, J. and J. Ryan 1980 *Program Evaluation of the Calgary Native Outreach Office.* Unpublished report. Calgary: University of Calgary.

Fuchs, Estelle 1970 "Time to Redeem an Old Promise." *Saturday Review* (January 24, 1970):53–58.

Fudge, S. 1983 "Too Weak to Win, Too Strong to Lose: Indians and Indian Policy in Canada." *B.C. Studies,* 57 (Spring 1983):137–145.

Fullwinder, S. 1969 *The Mind and Mood of Black America.* Homewood, Illinois: Dorsey Press.

Gadacz, René 1991 "Community Socio-Economic Development from a Plains Indian Perspective: A Proposed Social Indicator System and Planning Tool." *Native Studies Review,* 7, (1):53–80.

_____ 1999 "Aboriginal and Quebec Self-Determination under an MAI Regime." *Native Studies Review* 12 (2):93–110.

Gadacz, René and N. McBlane 1999 "Aboriginal Peoples and National Rights Issues in Quebec." Special Issue of the *Native Studies Review,* Volume 12, No. 2. University of Saskatchewan.

Gamson, W. 1969 *Power and Discontent.* Homewood, Illinois: Dorsey Press.

Gerber, L. 1977 "Community Characteristics and Out-Migration from Indian Communities: Regional Trends." Paper presented at Department of Indian Affairs and Northern Development, Ottawa, November 9, 1977.

_____ 1980 "The Development of Canadian Indian Communities: A Two-Dimensional Typology Reflecting Strategies of Adaptation to the Modern World." *The Canadian Review of Sociology and Anthropology,*16, 4 (1980):126–134.

Gerber, Linda M. 1990 "Multiple Jeopardy: A Socio-Economic Comparison of Men and Women Among the Indian,

Métis and Inuit Peoples of Canada," *Canadian Ethnic Studies*, Vol. 22, No. 3, pp. 69–84.

Gibbins, R. 1986a "Canadian Indians and the Canadian Constitution: A Difficult Passage Toward an Uncertain Destination." In *Arduous Journey*, J.R. Ponting (ed.). Toronto: McClelland and Stewart.

_____ **1986b** "Citizenship, Political and Intergovernmental Problems with Indian Self Government." In *Arduous Journey*, J.R. Ponting (ed.). Toronto: McClelland and Stewart.

Gibbins, R. and J.R. Ponting 1984 "Prairie Canadians' Orientations Towards Indians." *Prairie Forum*, 2, 1 (1984):57–81.

_____ **1986** "An Assessment of the Probable Impact of Aboriginal Self Government in Canada." In *The Politics of Gender, Ethnicity and Language in Canada*, A. Cairns and C. Williams (eds.). Vol. 34. Research Studies of the Royal Commission on the Economic Union and Development Prospects for Canada. Toronto: University of Toronto Press.

Gibson, G. 1998–99 "Comments on the Draft Nisga'a Treaty," *B.C. Studies,* 120:55–72.

Girvan, N. 1973 "The Development of Dependency Economics in the Caribbean and Latin America." *Social and Economic Studies*, 22 (1973):1–33.

Goikas, J and P. Chartrand 2002 "Who Are the Métis? A Review of the Law and Policy," in P. Chartrand (ed), *Who are Canada's Aboriginal People?*, Saskatoon, Purich Publishing Ltd.

Gombay, N. 2000 "The Politics of Culture: Gender Parity in the Legislative Assembly of Nunavut." *Etudes/Inuit/Studies*, 24,1:125–148.

Goodwill, J. 1971 "A New Horizon for Native Women in Canada." In Draper, J. (ed.), *Citizen Participation: Canada, A Book of Readings*. Toronto: Webb Offset Publications Ltd., pp. 362–370.

Gosnell, J. 1998/99 "Speech to the British Columbia Legislature, December 2, 1998." *B.C. Studies,* 120:5–11.

_____ **1999** "Nisga'a Treaty is a triumph for all Canadians." *Canadian Speeches: Issues of the Day,* 13,1:29–31

Grams, G., C. Herbert, C. Heffernan, B. Calam, M. Wilson, S. Grzybowski, D. Brown 1996 "Haida Perspectives on Living with Non-Insulin Dependent Diabetes." *Canadian Medical Association Journal,* 155:1563–1568.

Grand Council of the Crees 1998 *Never Without Consent: James Bay Crees' Stand Against Forcible Inclusion into an Independent Quebec.*

Grand Council Treaty No. 9 n.d. "A Declaration by the Ojibway–Cress Nation of Treaty No. 9 to the People of Canada."

Grant, A. 1996 *No End of Grief: Indian Residential Schools in Canada.* Winnipeg: Pemmican Publications Inc.

Green, C., J. Blanchard, A. Wajda, N. Depew, C. Cooke, L. Brazeau, S. Martel, C. Menard 1997 "Projecting Future Diabetes Prevalence in Manitoba First Nations," 4th International Conference on Diabetes and Aboriginal People, San Diego.

Green, Jerome 1969 "When Moral Prophecy Fails." *Catalyst*, 4 (Spring 1969):63–79.

Green, L. 1983 "Aboriginal Peoples, International Law and the Canadian Charter of Rights and Freedoms." In *The Canadian Bar Review*, 61, pp. 339–353.

Grescoe P. 1981 "A Nation's Disgrace." In *Health and Canadian Society,* D. Coburn, C. D'Arcy, P. New and G. Torrance (eds.). Markham: Fitzhenry & Whiteside, pp.127–140.

Guillemin, J. 1975 *Urban Renegades—The Cultural Strategy of American Indians*. New York: Columbia University Press.

Hagan, J. 1974 "Criminal Justice and Native People: A Study of Incarceration in a Canadian Province." *Canadian Review of Sociology and Anthropology*. Special issue (August 1974):220–236.

Hall, T. 1991 "Aboriginal Futures—Awakening Our Imagination." *Canadian Dimension*, July/August pp. 15–17.

Haman, Andrea 1992 "Periodical Publishing in Canada." *Canadian Social Trends*, Industry, Science and Technology, Supply and Services Canada, Statistics Canada, Ottawa, No. 25, Summer, pp. 29–31.

Hamilton, E. 1984 "Rosing Wins Second Term—Arctic Policy Delayed." *Inuit Today*, Special edition. Iqaluit: Inuit Circumpolar Conference, (February):6–7.

Hann R. and W. Harman 1993 "Predicting Release Risk for Aboriginal Penitentiary Inmates." Corrections Branch, Ministry of Solicitor General, User Report, 1993-21.

Hanselmann, C. 2001 *Urban Aboriginal People in Western Canada: Realities and Policies*. Calgary: Canada West Foundation.

Hanselmann, C. and R. Gibbins 2002 *Another Voice is Needed: Intergovernmentalism in the Urban Aboriginal Context*. Paper presented at the Reconfiguring Aboriginal–State Relations in Canada conference, Queens University, November.

Hanson, B., 1985 *Dual Realities—Dual Strategies: The Future Paths of the Aboriginal People's Development*. Saskatoon, privately printed.

Harper, A. 1947 "Canadian Indian Administration: The Treaty System." *America Indigena*, 7, 2 (1947):129–140.

Harris, S., J. Gittelsohn, A. Hanley, A. Barnie, T. Woleer, J. Gao, A. Logan, B. Zinman 1997 "The Prevalence of NIDDM and Associated Risk Factors in Native Canadians." *Diabetes Care*, 20:185-187.

Harrison, G.S. 1972 "The Alaska Native Claims Settlement Act: 1971." *Arctic*, 25, 3 (1972):232–233.

Harvey, S. 1996 "Two Models to Sovereignty: A Comparative History of the Mashantucket Pequot Tribal Nation and the Navajo Nation." *American Indian Culture and Research Journal*, 20,1:147–194.

Hatt, Fred K. 1969 "The Métis and Community Development in Northeastern Alberta." In *Perspectives on Regions and Regionalism and Other Papers*, B.Y. Card (ed.). Edmonton: University of Alberta, (1969):111–119.

_____ **1972** "The Canadian Métis: Recent Interpretations." *Canadian Ethnic Studies*, 3, 1 (1972):23–26.

_____ **1982** "On Hold: A Review of 'In All Fairness: A Native Claims Policy.'" *The Canadian Journal of Native Studies*, 2, 2 (1982):352–355.

_____ **1983** "The Northwest Scrip Commissions as Federal Policy—Some Initial Findings." *The Canadian Journal of Native Studies*, 3, 1 (1983):117–130.

Hawkes, D. 1985 *Aboriginal Self-Government*. Kingston, Ontario: Queen's University, Institute of Intergovernmental Relations.

Hawkes, David C. and Evelyn J. Peters 1987 *Issues in Entrenching Aboriginal Self-Government*. Kingston, Ontario: Queen's University, Institute of Intergovernmental Relations.

Hawley, D. 1990 *1990 Indian Act*, Toronto: Carswell.

Hawthorn, H.B. 1966–67 *A Survey of the Contemporary Indians of Canada*, 2 Vols. Indian Affairs Branch. Ottawa: Queen's Printer, 1966–67. Excerpts reproduced by permission of Information Canada.

Haysom, V. 1992 "The Struggle for Recognition: Labrador Inuit Negotiations for Land Rights and Self-Government." *Etudes/Inuit/Studies*, 16, 1–2:179–197.

Hedican, E. 1991 "On the Ethno-Politics of Canadian Native Leadership and Identity." *Ethnic Groups*, 9:1–15.

_____ **1995** *Applied Anthropology in Canada: Understanding Aboriginal Issues.* Toronto: University of Toronto Press.

Heilbrun, James, and Stanislaw Wellisz 1969 "An Economic Program for the Ghetto." In *Urban Riots*, Robert Conner (ed.). New York: Random House Inc.

Henderson, J., M. Benson and I. Findlay 2000 *Aboriginal Tenure in the Constitution of Canada.* Scarborough, ON: Carswell.

Henderson, J.Y. 1985 "The Doctrine of Aboriginal Rights in Western Legal Tradition." In *The Quest for Justice*, M. Boldt, J. Long and L. Little Bear (eds.). Toronto: University of Toronto Press.

Henderson, W. 1983 "Canadian Legal and Judicial Philosophies on the Doctrine of Aboriginal Rights." In *Aboriginal Rights: Toward an Understanding*, J. Long, M. Boldt and L. Little Bear, (eds.). Lethbridge, Alberta: University of Lethbridge.

Henderson, W.B. 1978 *Land Tenure in Indian Reserves*. Ottawa: DIAND.
_____ 1980 "Canada's Indian Reserves: The Usufruct in our Constitution." *Ottawa Law Review*, 12 (1980):160–187.

Hermann, J. and K. O'Connor 1996 "American Indians and the Berger Court." *Social Science Quarterly*, 17, 1:127–144.

Hertzberg, Hazel 1971 *Search for an American Indian Identity: Modern Pan-Indian Movements*. Syracuse, N.Y.: Syracuse University Press.

Himes, J. 1966 "The Functions of Racial Conflict." *Social Forces*, 45 (1966):1–10.

Hirschmann, Alberta 1971 *The Strategy of Economic Development*. New Haven: Yale University Press.

Hobart, C. 1991 "The Impact of Resource Development on the Health of Native People in the Northwest Territories." *Readings in Aboriginal Studies, Human Services*, Vol. 1, S. Corrigan (ed.). Brandon, Manitoba: Bearpaw Publishing, (1991):82–100.

Hodgins, B., S. Heard and J. Milloy 1992 *Co-Existence? Studies in Ontario–First Nations Relations*, Trent University, Peterborough, Ontario, Frost Centre for Canadian Heritage and Development Studies.

Holmes, J. 1987 *Bill C-31, Equality or Disparity? The Effects of the New Indian Act on Native Women*. Ottawa: CACSW.

Honigman, John 1967 *Personality in Culture*. New York: Harper and Row Inc.

House of Commons 1982 Minutes of Proceedings and Evidence of the Sub-Committee on Indian Women and the *Indian Act*, Issue No. 2, Ottawa: Minister of Supply and Services Canada.

Howard, J. 1951 "Notes on the Dakota Grass Dance." *Southwestern Journal of Anthropology*, 7 (1951):82–85.

Howard, John Kinsey 1952 *Strange Empire*. Toronto: Swan Publishing Co.Ltd.

Hughes, Ken 1991 *The Summer of 1990*. Fifth Report of the Standing Committee on Aboriginal Affairs, Ottawa.

Hunt, George 1940 *The Wars of the Iroquois: A Study in Intertribal Trade Relations*. Madison: University of Wisconsin Press.

Hutchins, P., C. Hilling and D. Schulze 1999 "The Aboriginal Right to Self-Government and the Canadian Constitution: The Ghost in the Machine," *U.B.C. Law Review,* 29, 2:251–287.

Hylton, John ed., 1994 *Aboriginal Self-Government in Canada: Current Trends and Issues.* Saskatoon: Purich Publishers.

Hylton, John 1981 "The Native Offender in Saskatchewan, Some Implications for Crime Prevention Planning." In *Selected Papers of the Canadian Congress for the Prevention of Crime*. Winnipeg: Canadian Association for the Prevention of Crime.

Imai, Shin 1999 *Indian Act and Aboriginal Constitutional Provisions*. Scarborough: Carswell.

Imai, Shin and Donna Hawley 1995 *The Annotated Indian Act*. Toronto: Carswell.

Imai, S., K. Logan and G. Stein 1993 *Aboriginal Law Handbook*. Toronto: Carswell.

INAC 1977 *Arctic Women's Workshop*. Ottawa: DIAND.
_____ 1982 *The Elimination of Sex Discrimination from the Indian Act*. Ottawa: DIAND.
_____ 1983 *A Demographic Profile of Registered Indian Women*. Ottawa: DIAND.
_____ 1988 *Basic Departmental Data*. Ottawa: Minister of Supply and Services.

Indian Association of Alberta 1971 *The Native People*. Edmonton.

Indian Claims Commission 1975 *Indian Claims in Canada: An Essay and Bibliography*. Ottawa: Supply and Services.

Indian Minerals Directorate 1981a Personal Communication, Reserves and Trust Branch, Department of Indian and Northern Development, Ottawa.
_____ 1981b Minerals Inventory, Reserve and Trust Branch, Department of Indian and Northern Development, Ottawa.

Indian Tribes of Manitoba 1972 *Wahbung (Our Tomorrows)*. Winnipeg: Manitoba Indian Brotherhood.

Innis, Harold A. 1970 *The Fur Trade in Canada*. Toronto and Buffalo: University of Toronto Press.

IRIW, n.d. Alberta Committee, The Arbitrary Enfranchisement of Indian Women, Edmonton: IRIW.

_____ **1978** Research Workshop: Resolutions, Edmonton, IRIW, n.p.

_____ **1979** A Study on the Emotional Impact of Arbitrary Enfranchisement on Native Women and on Their Families in Canada, Edmonton: IRIW.

Irwin, A. 1968 "Management Policy for Indian Owned Minerals: Possible Application to Northern Resources." *Proceedings of a Symposium on the Implications of Northern Mineral Resources Management for Human Development*, No. 5, Edmonton: Boreal Institute, University of Alberta.

Isaac, T. 1995 *Aboriginal Law: Cases, Materials, and Commentary*. Saskatoon: Purich Publishing.

Iverson, P. 1990 "Plains Indians and Australian Aborigines in the Twentieth Century." In P. Olson (ed.), *The Struggle for the Land*. Lincoln, Nebraska: University of Nebraska Press, pp. 171–188.

Jack, Henry 1970 "Native Alliance for Red Power." In *The Only Good Indian*, Waubageshig (ed.). Toronto: New Press.

Jackson, M. 1992 "In Search of the Pathways to Justice: Alternative Dispute Resolution in Aboriginal Communities." *U.B.C. Law Review,* 26: 139–152.

Jaenen, C. 1986 "French Sovereignty and Native Nationhood during the French Regime." Native Studies Review, 2:83–113.

Jamieson, K. 1978 *Indian Women and the Law in Canada: A Citizens Minus*. Ottawa: Minister of Supply and Services Canada.

_____ **1979** "Multiple Jeopardy: The Evolution of a Native Women's Movement." In *Atlantis* (part 2), 4, 2, pp. 157–178.

Jamieson, M. 1989 "Aboriginal Women— Barriers to Economic Development," mimeo.

Jantzen, L. 2002 "Reporting Métis in Urban Centres on the 1996 Census," *Canadian Ethnic Studies*, 35,1:149–170.

Jarvis, G and T. Heaton 1989 "Language Shift Among Those of Aboriginal Mother Tongue in Canada." *Canadian Studies in Population*, vol. 16(1), pp. 25–42.

Jefferson, C. 1978 *Conquest by Law*, Solicitor General Canada. Ottawa: Supply and Services Canada.

Jenness, Diamond n.d. *The Indian Background of Canadian History*. Bulletin No. 86, Anthropological Series No. 21. Ottawa: Department of Mines and Resources.

_____ **1967** *Indians of Canada*, 7th ed. Ottawa: Queen's Printer.

Jhappan, R. 1993 "Inherency, 'Three Nations' and Collective Rights: The Evolution of Aboriginal Constitutional Discourse from 1982 to the Charlottetown Accord." *International Journal of Canadian Studies*, 7–8:225–259.

Jhappan, C. Radha 1990 "Indian Symbolic Politics: The Double-Edged Sword of Publicity," *Canadian*

Ethnic Studies, Vol. 22, No. 3, pp. 19–39.

Johnson, S. 1976 *Migrating Native Peoples Program*. Ottawa: National Association of Friendship Centres.

Johnston, J. 1997 Aboriginal Offender Survey: Case Files and Interview Sample, Ottawa, Correctional Service Canada.

Joseph, S. 1991 "Assimilation Tools: Then and Now." In *In Celebration of Our Survival*, D. Jensen and C. Brooks (eds.), Vancouver, University of British Columbia Press, pp 65–79.

Jull, Peter 1982 "Nunavut." *Northern Perspectives*, 10, 2.

Junger-Tas, J. 1994 "Alternative Sanctions: Myth and Reality." *European Journal of Criminal Policy and Research,* Consistency in Sentencing Issue, Kugler Publication, 2,1:44–66.

Kardiner, Abraham and Lionel Ovesey 1951 *The Mark of Oppression*. New York: W.W. Norton and Co.

Katznelson, I. 1976 "The Crisis of the Capitalist City: Urban Politics and Social Control." In W. Hawley and M. Lipsky (eds.), *Theoretical Perspectives in Urban Politics*, Englewood Cliffs: Prentice Hall.

Kaye, L. 1981 "I think I'm Indian... But others aren't sure." In *Ontario Indian*, 4, 5, p.8, p. 34.

Keeping, J. 1989 *The Inuvialuit Final Agreement*. Calgary, Alberta: The Canadian Institute of Resources Law, The University of Calgary.

Kennedy, L., et al. 1978
"Subjective Evaluation of
Well-Being: Problems and
Prospects." *Social
Indicators Research* 5:
457–474.

Kennedy, Raymond 1945 The
Colonial Crisis and the
Future." In *The Science of
Man in the World Crisis.*
Ralph Linton (ed.). New
York: Columbia University
Press.

Kerr, S. 1975 *Women's Rights
and Two National Native
Organizations: The Native
Council of Canada and the
National Indian
Brotherhood.* Ottawa:
Carleton University, n.p.

King, Cecil 1972 "Sociological
Implications of the
Jeannette Corbiere Lavell
Case." *The Northian*, 8
(March 1972): 44–45.

Kishigami, N. 1999 "Why do
Inuit Move to Montreal? A
Research Note on Urban
Inuit." *Etudes/Inuit/Studies*,
23,1:221-227.

Knight, D. 1985 "A Study of
Learning Style and its
Implication for Education
of Indian People." Mimeo.

Knight, Rolf 1978 *Indians at
Work. An Informal History
of Native Indian Labour in
British Columbia,
1858–1930.* Vancouver:
New Star Books.

**Koovos, A. and E. Brown
1980** "The Implications of
the International Energy
Markets for Indian
Resources." *The Journal of
Energy and Development*,
5, (1980):252–257.

Kreager, P. 1997 "Population
and Identity." In D. Kertzer
and T. Fricke (eds.),
*Anthropological
Demography: Toward a
New Synthesis.* Chicago:
University of Chicago
Press.

**Krosenbrink-Gelissen, L.
1983** *Native Women of
Manitoba, Canada:
Feminism or Ethnicity?*
Nijmegen: Catholic
University of Nijmegen, n.p.

_____ **1984a** "De
Canadese Indian Act en de
gevolgen daarvan voor
Indiaanse vrouwen." In *De
Kiva*, 21, 3, pp. 44–45.

_____ **1984b** *No Indian
Women, No Indian Nation:
Canadian Native Women in
Search of Their Identity.*
Nijmegen: Catholic Univ.
of Nijmegen, n.p.

_____ **1989** "The Métis
National Council:
Continuity and Change
Among the Canadian
Métis." *Native American
Studies*, 3:1, pp. 33–41.

_____ **1991** *Sexual
Equality as an Aboriginal
Right.* Saarbrucken,
Germany:
Verlagbreitenbach.

Kulchynski, P. (ed.) 1994
*Unjust Relations:
Aboriginal Rights in
Canadian Courts.* Toronto:
Oxford University Press.

Kuptana, R. 1992 "The
Canadian Inuit and the
Renewal of Canada."
Etudes/Inuit/Studies, 16,
1–2:39–42.

**Lachance-Brulotte, Ginette
1984** "La nuptialité des
Indiens du Canada." In *Les
populations amerindiennes
et inuit du Canada, Aperçu
démographique.*
Normandeau L. et V. Piche
(eds.). Montréal: Les
Presses de l'Université de
Montréal.

Laing, A. 1967 *Indians and the
Law.* Ottawa: Queen's
Printer.

Lambertus, Sandra 2004
*Wartime Images,
Peacetime Wounds: The
Media and the Gustafsen
Lake Standoff.* Vancouver:
UBC Press.

**Lamontagne, F. and
C. Tremblay 1989**
*Development Indices: A
Quebec Regional
Comparison.* Local
Development Paper No.
14, Economic Council of
Canada. 70. pps.

Land, K. 1971 "On the
Definition of Social
Indicators." *The American
Sociologist* 6:322–325.

**Land, K. and S. Spilerman
1975** *Social Indicator
Models.* Russell Sage
Foundation, New York.

Lane, B. 1989 *Canadian
Healthy Communities
Project: A Conceptual
Model for Winnipeg.*
Health and the Community
1. Winnipeg: Institute of
Urban Studies.

Lang, O. 1974 "Politics of
Land Claims Settlements."
Muskox, 14.

LaPrairie, C. 1996 *Examining
Aboriginal Corrections in
Canada.* Solicitor General
of Canada, Ottawa, Supply
and Services of Canada.

_____ **1998** "The 'New'
Justice: Some Implications
for Aboriginal
Communities." *Canadian
Journal of Criminology*,
40:60–78.

**LaPrairie, Carol and
J. Roberts 1997** "Circle
Sentencing, Restorative
Justice and the Role of the
Community." *Canadian
Journal of Criminology*,
34:40–52.

La Rusic, Ignatius 1968
Hunter to Proletarian.
Research paper for Cree
Development Change
Project.

Laselva, S. 1998–99
"Aboriginal Self-
Government and the
Foundations of Canadian

Nationhood." *B.C. Studies,* 120:41–55.

Laslett, P. 1963 "The Face-to-Face Society." In *Philosophy, Politics and Society*, P. Laslett (ed.). Oxford: Basil Blackwell.

Latulippe-Skamoto, Claudette 1971 *Estimation de la mortalité des Indiens du Canada 1900–1968.* Mémoire de maîtrise, Département de sociologie, Université d'Ottawa.

La Violette, F.E. 1961 *The Struggle for Survival.* Toronto: University of Toronto Press.

Le Devoir 1985 *16 000 femmes et 46 000 enfants pouront recouvrer leur statu d'Indien* (1 mars, 1985):4.

Legare, A. 1996 "The Process Leading to a Land Claims Agreement and its Implementation: The Case of Nunavut Land Claims Settlement." *Canadian Journal of Native Studies,* 16,1:139–163.

Legare, Jacques 1981 *La mortalité infantile des Inuit dans l'après-guerre.* Montréal: Université de Montréal, Departement de démographie.

Leonard, D. 1995 "Indigenous Nature of Water." *The DLA Financial,* 2,3:15–27.

Leslie, J. and R. Maguire 1978 *The Historical Development of the Indian Act, Treaties, and Historical Research Centres.* Ottawa: Department of Indian Affairs and Northern Development, PRE Group.

Levesque, C. 2003 "The Presence of Aboriginal Peoples in Quebec's Cities: Multiple Movements, Diverse Issues," in *Not Strangers in These Parts,*

D. Newhouse and E. Peters (eds.), Ottawa, Policy Research Institute, pp. 23–34.

Levine, S. 1970 "The Survival of Indian Identity." In *The American Indian Today*, S. Levine and N. Lurie (eds.). Hardmondsworth: Pelican.

Lewis, W. 1956 "Economic Development with Unlimited Supplies of Labour." *Manchester School of Economic and Social Studies,* 23 (May 1956):153–160.

Lightbody, J. 1969 "A Note on the Theory of Nationalism as a Function of Ethnic Demands." *Canadian Journal of Political Science,* 2 (1969):327–337.

Lindesmith, A., and S. Strauss 1968 *Social Psychology.* New York: Holt, Rinehart and Winston.

Linker, M. 1999 "Sentencing Circles and the Dilemma of Difference." *Criminal Law Quarterly,* 42,1:116–128.

_____ 1983 *The Practice of Underdevelopment and the Theory of Development. The Canadian Indian Case.* Stockholm: Department of Social Anthropology, University of Stockholm.

Long, J.A., M. Boldt, and L. Little Bear 1982 "Federal Indian Policy and Indian Self-Government in Canada: An Analysis of a Current Proposal." *Canadian Public Policy,* 8, 2 (1982):189–199.

_____ 1983 (eds.). *Aboriginal Rights: Toward an Understanding.* Lethbridge: Law Foundation.

Longboat, D. 1987 "First Nations Control of Education: The Path to Our

Survival as Nations." In *Indian Education in Canada*, J. Barman, Y. Hebert and D. McCaskill (eds.), Vol. 2. Vancouver: University of British Columbia Press.

Lower, A. 1957 *Colony to Nation: A History of Canada.* Toronto: Longman, Green & Co.

Lu, Chang-Mei, et Emerson Mathurin 1973 *Projections démographiques des Territoires du Nord-Ouest jusqu'en 1981.* Ottawa: Affairs Indiennes et du Nord, au nord du 60.

Lurie, N. 1971 "The Contemporary American Indian Scene." In *North American Indians in Historical Perspective*, E. Leacock and N. Lurie (eds.). New York: Random House Inc.

Lussier, A. 1979 *Louis Riel and the Métis: Riel Mini Conference Papers.* Winnipeg: Pemmican Publisher.

_____ 1984 *The Métis and Non-Status Indians 1967–1984, and the Métis and the Indians 1960–1984.* Ottawa: Treaties and Historical Research Centre, Department of Indian Affairs and Northern Development.

Lussier, Antoine S. and D. Bruce Sealey (eds.) 1978 *The Other Natives— Les Métis.* Winnipeg: Manitoba Métis Federation Press.

Lyon, L., J. Friesen, W.R. Unruh, and R. Hertoz 1970 *Intercultural Education.* Calgary: Faculty of Education, University of Calgary.

Lyon, N. 1985 "Constitutional Issues in Native Law." In *Aboriginal Peoples and the Law*, B. Morse (ed.). Ottawa: Carleton University Press.

MacGregor R. 1961 *Racial and Ethnic Relations in America*. Boston: Allyn and Bacon.

Macklem, Patrick 2001 *Indigenous Differences and the Constitution of Canada*. Toronto: University of Toronto Press.

Mainville, Robert 2001 *An Overview of Aboriginal and Treaty Rights and Compensation for Their Breach*. Saskatoon: Purich Publishers.

Mallea, R. 1994 *Aboriginal Law: Apartheid in Canada*, Brandon, Manitoba, Bearpaw Publishing.

Manitoba Indian Brotherhood 1971 *Wahbung: Our Tomorrows*. Winnipeg: October, 1971.

Manitoba Métis Federation Justice Committee 1989 *Research and Analysis of the Impact of the Justice System on the Métis: Report to the Aboriginal Justice Inquiry*, November 22, 1989. Winnipeg: Manitoba Métis Federation Inc.

Manuel, G. and M. Poslums 1974 *The Fourth World: An Indian Reality*. Toronto: Collier-Macmillan Canada Ltd.

Mariategui, J.C. 1934 *Siete ensayos de interpretación de la sealidad peruana*, 2nd ed. Lima: Editorial Librariá Peruana.

Marshall, Donald, vs. Her Majesty the Queen, Supreme Court of Canada Decision, File No. 26014, September 17 1999.

Marule, M.S. 1977 "The Canadian Government's Termination Policy: From 1969 to the Present Day." In *One Century Later*, J. Getty and D. Smith (eds.). Vancouver: University of British Columbia Press.

Mathias, Chief Joe and G. Yabsley 1991 "Conspiracy of Legislation: The Supression of Indian Rights in Canada." In *In Celebration of Our Survival*, D. Jensen and C. Brooks (eds.), University of British Columbia Press, Vancouver, pp. 34–47.

Maxim, P. and J. White 2003 "Toward an Index of Community Capacity: Predicting Community Potential for Successful Program Transfer." In *Aboriginal Conditions*, J. White, P. Maxim and D. Beavon (eds.), Vancouver, UBC Press, pp. 248–263.

Maybury-Lewis, David 1997 *Indigenous Peoples, Ethnic Groups, and the State.* Cultural Survival Studies in Ethnicity and Change, Volume 1. Boston: Allyn and Bacon.

McCaskill, D. 1981 "The Urbanization of Indians in Winnipeg, Toronto, Edmonton, and Vancouver: A Comparative Analysis." *Culture*, 1 (1981):82–89.

_____ **1985** *Patterns of Criminality and Corrections Among Native Offenders in Manitoba: A Longitudinal Analysis,* Ottawa, Correctional Service Canada.

McCullum, H. and K. McCullum 1975 *This Land Is Not for Sale.* Toronto: Anglican Book Centre.

McGhee, R. 1996 *Ancient People of the Arctic*. Vancouver: University of British Columbia Press.

McInnis, E. 1959 *Canada: A Political and Social History*. New York: Holt, Rinehart and Winston Inc.

McMahon, D. and F. Martin 1995 *Aboriginal Self-Government: Legal and Constitutional Issues,* Ottawa, Minister of Supply and Services.

McNab, David 1999 *Circles of Time: Aboriginal Land Rights and Resistance in Ontario*. Waterloo: Wilfred Laurier University Press.

Meadow Lake Tribal Council 1989 A Position Paper on Indian Labour Force Development, submitted to the Canadian Labour Market and Productivity Centre, October.

Meadows, M. 1981 *Adaptation to Urban Life by Native Women.* Calgary: University of Calgary Department. of Sociology.

Melville, B. 1981 *Indian Reserves and Indian Treaty Problems in Northeastern B.C.* Vancouver: B.C. Hydro and Power Authority.

Mendelson, M. and K. Battle 1999 *Aboriginal People in Canada's Labour Market*. Ottawa: Caledon Institute of Social Policy, June.

Mendes, E. and P. Bendin n.d. "The New Canadian Charter of Rights and International Law and Aboriginal Self-Determination: A Proposal for a New Direction." Mimeographed, Saskatoon, Saskatchewan.

Mensah, J. 1996 "Treaty Negotiations in British Columbia: The Utility of Geographic Information Management Techniques." *The Canadian Journal of Native Studies*, 16,1:1–14.

Métis National Council 1983 *A Brief to the Standing Senate Committee on Legal and Constitutional Affairs*, Ottawa, September 8.

_____ 1984 *The Métis Natives*. Toronto: Métis National Council.

Métis and Non-Status Indian Crime and Justice Commission 1977 *Report*. Serpent River Reserve, Cutler, Ontario: Woodland Studio.

Mickenberg, Neil 1971 "Aboriginal Rights in Canada and the United States." *Osgoode Hall Law Journal*, 9 (1971):154.

Miles, I. 1985 *Social Indicators for Human Development*. London: Frances Pinter (Publishers).

Miller, J.R. 1991 *Sweet Promises*. Toronto: University of Toronto Press.

_____ 2000 *Skyscrapers Hide the Heavens: A History of Indian–White Relations in Canada*. Toronto: University of Toronto Press.

Minore, J. and M. Hill 1997 "Native Language Broadcasting: An Experiment in Empowerment." In *The Mass Media and Canadian Diversity*, S. Nancoo and R. Nancoo (eds.), Mississauga, Canadian Educators' Press, pp. 162–186.

Mitchell, M. 1996 *From Talking Chiefs to a Native Corporate Elite*. Montreal and Kingston: McGill-Queen's University Press.

Mitchell, J. 1986 "Reflections on Twenty Years of Feminism." In *What Is Feminism?* Mitchell, J. and A. Oakley (eds.), Oxford: Basil Blackwell, pp. 34–48.

Moore, R. 1978 *The Historical Development of the Indian Act*. Draft Manuscript. Ottawa: Department of Indian Affairs and Northern Development.

Morris, Alexander 1880 *The Treaties of Canada with the Indians of Manitoba and the North West Territories*. Toronto: Belfords, Clark & Co.

Morrison, Bruce and Rod Wilson 1995 *Native Peoples: The Canadian Experience*. Toronto: McClelland & Stewart.

Morse, B. (ed.) 1991 *Aboriginal Peoples and the Law: Indian, Métis and Inuit Rights in Canada*. Ottawa: Carleton University Press.

Morton, W.L. 1963 *The Kingdom of Canada: A General History from Earliest Times*. Toronto: McClelland and Stewart.

_____ 1981 "The Historical Phenomenon of Minorities: The Canadian Experience." *Canadian Ethnic Studies*, 13, 3 (1981):1–39.

Moss, W. 1990 "Indigenous Self-Government in Canada and Sexual Equality under the Indian Act: Resolving Conflicts Between Collective and Individual Rights," *Queen's Law Journal*, 15,2:267–295.

_____ 1995 "Inuit Perspectives on Treaty Rights and Governance Issues." *Aboriginal Self-Government*, P. Macklem, et al (eds.). Ottawa: Royal Commission on Aboriginal Peoples, (1995):55–139.

Moss, W. and P. Niemczak 1991 *Aboriginal Land Claims Issues*. Ottawa, Library of Parliament.

Motiuk, L, and M. Nafekh 2000 "Aboriginal Offenders in Federal Corrections: A Profile." *Forum*, 12,1:10–14.

Mount Pleasant-Jette, M 1993 *Creating a Climate of Confidence: Providing Services Within Aboriginal Communities*. In National Round Table on Economic Issues and Resources, Ottawa, Royal Commission on Aboriginal Issues, April 27.

Murray, G. to J. Kempt 1834 "Correspondence and Other Papers Relating to Aboriginal Tribes in British Possessions." January 25, 1830, *British Parliamentary Papers*, No. 617, 88.

Myers, H. 2001 "Options for Appropriate Development in Nunavut Communities." *Etudes/Inuit/Studies*, 24,1:25–40.

Nadeau, Ron 1979 *Indian Local Government*. Ottawa: Department of Indian Affairs and Northern Development. Policy Research and Evaluation.

Nagey N., C. Larocque, and C. McBride 1989 Highlights of Aboriginal Conditions, 1981–2001. Ottawa: Indian and Northern Affairs, Minister of Supply and Services.

Nagler, Mark 1971 *Indians in the City*. Ottawa: Canadian Research Centre for Anthropology, St. Paul University.

Nammack, Georgina 1969
Fraud, Politics, and the Dispossession of the Indians. Norman, Oklahoma: University of Oklahoma Press.

National Indian Brotherhood 1977 *Proposed Revisions of the Indian Act.* Ottawa: NIB.

Neils, Elaine 1971
Reservations to City. Chicago: University of Chicago Press.

Neilsen, Marianne O. 1990
"Canadian Correctional Policy and Native Inmates: The Control of Social Dynamite." *Canadian Ethnic Studies*, Vol. 22, No. 3, pp. 110–121.

Newhouse, D. 2003 "The Invisible Infrastructure: Urban Aboriginal Institutions and Organizations." In *Not Strangers in these Parts*, D. Newhouse and E. Peters (eds.), Ottawa, Policy Research Institute, pp. 243–254.

Newhouse, D. and E. Peters (eds). 2003 *Not Strangers in These Parts: Urban Aboriginal Peoples*. Ottawa, Policy Research Initiative.

Nichols, R. 1998 *Indians in the United States and Canada.* Lincoln and London: University of Nebraska Press.

Nielsen, M. 1991 "Balance and Strategy: Native Criminal Justice Organizations, Native Communities and the Canadian State." Kingston: Paper presented at the Annual Meeting of the Canadian Sociology and Anthropology Association.

Nielsen, M. and R. Silverman (eds.) 1996 *Native Americans, Crime and Justice*. Boulder, Colorado: Westview Press.

Niezen, Ronald 1998
Defending the Land: Sovereignty and Forest Life in James Bay Cree Society. Boston: Allyn and Bacon.

Nisga'a Final Agreement. Initialled August 4, 1998, Queen's Printer, Cat. No. 842364.

_____ **1990** *Political and Constitutional Development in the Northwest Territories.* Yellowknife, Northwest Territories.

Norris, M.J. 1998 "Canada's Aboriginal Languages." *Canadian Social Trends*, Winter, pp. 8–16.

Norris, M.J., M. Cooke, and S. Clatworthy 2002 "Aboriginal Mobility and Migration Patterns and Policy Implications." In *Population Mobility and Indigenous Peoples in Australasia and North America*, J. Taylor and M. Bell (eds.), London, Routledge Press.

Nuffield, Joan 1998 *Issues in Urban Corrections for Aboriginal People*. Solicitor General of Canada, Ottawa, Ministry of the Solicitor General.

Nurkse, Ragnar 1953
Problems of Capital Formation in Underdeveloped Countries. New York: Oxford University Press.

Nuttall R. 1982 "The Development of Indian Boards of Health in Alberta," *Canadian Journal of Public Health,* 73:300–303.

NWAC 1981 "Statement by NWAC on Native Women's Rights." In *Women and the Constitution in Canada.* Doerr, A. and M. Carrier (eds.) Ottawa: CACSW, PP. 64–73.

_____ **1985a** *First Nation Citizenship: A Discussion Paper.* Ottawa: NWAC.

_____ **1985b** *A Voice of Many Nations: Native Women.* Ottawa: NWAC.

O'Callaghan, E. (ed.) 1856–57 *Documents Relative to the Colonial History of the State of New York: 1856–1857*, Albany, New York.

O'Conner, R. 1976 Letter to Joyceville Penitentiary to the Symposium on Natives and the Criminal Justice System, Ottawa, Carleton University, October 21, 1976.

Oliver, C. 1990 "Determinants of Interorganizational Relationships: Integrative and Future Directions." *Academy of Management Review*, Vol. 15, No. 2, pp. 241–265.

Ombudsman of Manitoba 1989 *Nineteenth Annual Report of the Ombudsman*. Winnipeg: Queen's Printer for the Province of Manitoba.

O'Meara, S. and D. West 1996 *From Our Eyes: Learning from Indigenous Peoples*. Toronto: Garamond Press.

ONWA 1983 *Nations Within a Nation: An Aboriginal Right?* A Report of the Conference Proceedings, November 12, 13 and 14, 1982, Thunder Bay: ONWA.

Organization for Economic Co-Operation and Development (OECD) 1973 *List of Social Concerns Common to Most OECD Countries.* The OECD Social Indicator Development Program, 1. Paris.

_____ 1974 *Subjective Elements of Well-Being.* The OECD Social Indicator Development Program, 2. Paris.

_____ 1976 *Measuring Social Well-Being.* The OECD Social Indicator Development Program, 3. Paris.

_____ 1982 *The OECD List of Social Indicators.* The OECD Social Development Program, 5. Paris.

Ossenberg, R. (ed.) 1980 *Power and Change in Canada.* Toronto: McClelland and Stewart.

Paige, J. 1971 "Political Orientation and Riot Participation." *American Sociological Review,* 36 (1971):810–819.

Paquette, Lyne, et Jeannine Perreault 1984 "Un demi-million d'Indiens inscrits au Canada en l'an 2000?" *Cahiers québécois de démographie,* 13, 1 (1984):101–115.

Pask, R. and J. Scott 1971 "Learning Strategies and Individual Competence." *International Journal of Man–Machine Studies,* 4 (1971):217–253.

Paton, R. 1982 *New Policies and Old Organizations: Can Indian Affairs Change?* Centre for Policy and Program Assessment, School of Public Administration. Ottawa: Carleton University.

Patterson, E. Palmer 1972 *The Canadian Indians: A History Since 1500.* Toronto: Collier-MacMillan Canada Ltd.

Paul, P. 1990 *Bill C-31: The Trojan Horse: An Analysis of the Social, Economic and Political Reaction of First Nation People as a Result of Bill C-31.* A Thesis, The University of New Brunswick.

Pelletier, Emile 1974 *A Social History of the Manitoba Métis.* Winnipeg: Manitoba Métis Federation Press.

_____ 1975 *Exploitation of Métis Lands.* Winnipeg: Manitoba Métis Federation Press.

Pelletier, W. 1970 *Two Articles.* Toronto: Neewin Publishing Co., 1970.

Pennekeok, F. 1976 "The Anglican Church and the Disintegration of Red River Society, 1818–1870." In *The West and the Nation,* C. Berger and R. Cook (eds.). Toronto: McClelland and Stewart.

Penner, K., chairman (Penner Report) 1983 *Indian Self-Government in Canada: Report of the Special Committee.* Ottawa: Minister of Supply and Services.

Perreault, Jeannine, Lyne Paquette, et M.V. George 1985 *Projections de la population indienne inscrite, 1982–1996.* Ottawa: Affaires indiennes et du Nord Canada.

Perroux, F. 1953 "Note sur la notion de 'pole de crois-sance.'" *Économic appliquée,* 8, (janvier 1953):307–320.

Perry, Richard 1996 *From Time Immemorial:*

Indigenous Peoples and State Systems. Austin: University of Texas Press.

Peters, E. 1987 *Aboriginal Self Government Arrangements in Canada: An Overview.* Kingston, Ontario: Queen's University, Institute of Intergovernmental Relations.

Peters, E., M. Rosenberg and G. Halseth 1989 "The Ontario Métis: A People Without an Identity." Mimeo.Peters, E., 2002 "Our City Indians: Negotiating the Meaning of First Nations Urbanization in Canada, 1945–1975." *Historical Geography,* 30:69–84.

Peters, Omar 1968 "Canada's Indians and Eskimos and Human Rights." Paper presented to the Thinkers' Conference on Cultural Rights. Mimeographed.

Peterson, Jacqueline and Jennifer S.H. Brown (eds.) 1985 *The New Peoples: Being and Becoming Métis in North America.* Winnipeg: The University of Manitoba Press.

Pettigrew, T. 1964 *A Profile of the Negro American.* Princeton: D. Van Nostrand Co.

Pfeiffer, J. and G. Salanchik 1978 *The External Control of Organizations: A Resource Dependence Perspective.* New York: Harper and Row.

Piche, Victor, and M.V. George 1973 "Estimates of vital rates for the Canadian Indians, 1960–1970." *Demography,* 10(1973):367–382.

Pinkerton, E. 1989 *Co-opera-tive Management of Local Fisheries: New Directions* *for Improved Management and Community Development*, Vancouver: University of British Columbia Press.

Pitts, J. 1974 "The Study of Race Consciousness: Comments on New Directions." *American Journal of Sociology*, 80 (1974):665–687.

PJS Geach and Associates 1985 *Band Planning Handbook on the Use of Socio-Economic Indicators.* Prepared for Department of Indian Affairs and Northern Development, B.C. Region.

Plain, F. 1985 "A Treaty on the Rights of the Aboriginal Peoples of the Continent of North America." In *The Quest for Justice*, M. Boldt, J. Long, and L. Little Bear (eds.). Toronto: The University of Toronto Press.

Polanyi, Karl 1974 *The Great Transformation.* Boston: Beacon Press Inc.

_____ **1987** *Profiles of Public Opinion on Canadian Natives and Native Issues: Special Status and Self Government.* Calgary: Research Unit for Public Policy Studies, The University of Calgary.

_____ **1991** "An Indian Policy for Canada in the 21st Century." In C. Remie and J. Lacroix (eds.), *Canada on the Threshold of the 21st Century*, Amsterdam: John Benjamins Pub. Co.

_____ **1997** *First Nations in Canada: Perspectives on Opportunity, Empowerment, and Self-Determination.* Toronto: McGraw-Hill Ryerson Limited.

Ponting, J.R. 1986 *Arduous Journey: Canadian Indians and Decolonization.* Toronto: McClelland and Stewart.

Ponting, J.R. and R. Gibbins 1980 *Out of Irrelevance: A Socio-Political Introduction to Indian Affairs of Canada.* Toronto: Butterworth & Co. (Canada) Ltd.

Ponting, J. Rick and G. Symons 1993 "Environmental Geo-Politics and the New World Order: Grande Baleine, the Crees and Hydro-Quebec" Paper presented at the International Conference Geopolitics of the Environment and the New World Order: Limits, Conficts, Insecurity?" Chantilly, France, January 5–9.

Price, J. 1972 "U.S. and Canadian Indian Periodicals." *Canadian Review of Sociology and Anthropology*, 9, May (1972):150–162.

_____ **1978** *Native Studies.* Toronto: McGraw-Hill Ryerson Ltd.

_____ **1979** *Indians of Canada: Cultural Dynamics.* Scarborough, Ontario; Prentice Hall Canada.

_____ **1981** "The Viability of Indian Languages in Canada." *Canadian Journal of Native Studies*, 1, 2 (1981): 349–361.

_____ **1982** "Historical Theory and the Applied Anthropology of U.S. and Canadian Indians." *Human Organization*, 41, 2 (1982):42–53.

Price, R. (ed.) 1979 *The Spirit of the Alberta Indian Treaties.* Montreal: Institute for Research on Public Policy.

Priest, G. 1984 *Aboriginal Languages in Canada.* Ottawa: Minister of Supply and Services.

Pross, P. 1975 *Pressure Group Behaviour in Canadian Politics.* Scarborough, Ontario: McGraw-Hill Ryerson Inc.

Pryor, E. 1984 *Profile of Native Women: 1981 Census of Canada.* Ottawa: Minister of Supply and Services Canada.

Public Affairs, Employment and Immigration and Aboriginal Employment and Training Group 1990 "Pathways to Success: Aboriginal Employment and Training Strategy." Mimeo.

Purich, D. 1988 *The Métis.* Toronto: James Lorimer and Co.

_____ **1992** *The Inuit and Their Land.* Toronto: James Lorimer & Company, Pub.

The Quill, **Brandon University Newspaper**, 22/10/82, p. 12: "Native women in Canada: The least members of society."

Ram, Ball et A. Romaniuc 1984 *Fertility Projections of Registered Indians.* Ottawa: Statistique Canada (in edit.).

Raudsepp, E. 1997 "Emergent Media: The Native Press in Canada." In *The Mass Media and Canadian Diversity*, S. Nancoo and R. Nancoo (eds.), Mississauga, Canadian Educators' Press, pp. 187–206.

Raunet, D. 1984 *Without Surrender Without Consent.* Vancouver: Douglas & McIntyre.

Rawson B. 1988 "Federal Perspectives on Indian–Provincial Relations." In *Governments in Conflict?* J.A. Long and Menno Boldt (eds.). Toronto: University of Toronto Press, pp. 147–154.

Ray, Arthur J. 1974 *Indians in the Fur Trade*. Toronto and Buffalo: University of Toronto Press.

_____ **1996** *I Have Lived Here Since the World Began*. Toronto: Key Porter Books.

Rea, K. 1976 *The Political Economy Northern Development, No. 36*. Ottawa: Science Council of Canada Background Study, Information Canada.

Reeves, W. and J. Frideres 1981 "Government Policy and Indian Urbanization: The Alberta Case." *Canadian Public Policy*, 7, 4 (Autumn 1981):584–595.

Reitz, J. 1974 "Language and Ethnic Community Survival;" *The Canadian Review of Sociology and Anthropology*, Special Issue, pp. 104–122.

Report of the Affairs of the Indians in Canada 1844 "History of the Relations between the Government and the Indians." *Journals*, Section 1. Ottawa: Queen's Printer, 1844.

Richardson, B. 1972 *James Bay*. San Francisco: Sierra Club.

_____ **1993** *People of Terra Nullius*. Vancouver: Douglas & McIntyre.

Rieber, J. 1977 *Fundamental Concerns Regarding Indian Local Government: A Discussion Paper of Potential Problem and Research Areas*. Ottawa: Department of Indian Affairs and Northern Development.

Robertson, Eleanor 1988 *Native Women in Conflict with the Law*. Winnipeg: Unpublished.

Robinson, M., M. Dickerson, M. Pretes 1991 "Sustainable Development in Small Northern Communities: A Micro Perspective." In *Old Pathways and New Directions: Towards a Sustainable Future*, Calgary, Arctic Institute of North America.

Robinson, M. and E. Ghostkeeper 1987 "Native and Local Economies: A Consideration of Economic Evolution and the Next Economy." *Arctic* 40 (2): 138-144.

_____ **1988** "Implementing the Next Economy in a Unified Context: A Case Study of the Paddle Prairie Mall Corporation." *Arctic* 41 (3):173–182.

Robitaille, Norbert et Robert Coiniere 1984 *Aperçu de la situation démographique et socio- économique des Inuit du Canada*. Ottawa: Direction de la recherche, Orientations générales, Affaires indiennes et du Nord Canada.

Rohen, D. 1967 *The Quest for Self-Determination*. New York: Yale University Press.

Romaniuk, A. and V. Piche 1972 "Natality Estimates for the Canadian Indians by Stable Population Models, 1900–1969." *The Canadian Review of Sociology and Anthropology*, 9, 1 (1972):1–20.

Romanow, R. 1985 "Aboriginal Rights in the Constitutional Process," in M. Boldt and J. Long (eds.), *The Quest for Justice: Aboriginal Peoples and Aboriginal Rights*, Toronto: University of Toronto Press, pp. 23–82.

Roosens, E. 1986 *Micronationalisme; een antropologie van het etnische reveil*. Leuven: Uitgeverij Acco.

Rosenstein-Rodan, P.N. 1943 "Problems of Industrialization of Eastern and South-eastern Europe." *Economic Journal*, 53 (June September 1943): 128–156.

Ross, Alexander 1972 *The Red River Settlement*. Edmonton: Hurtig Publishers.

Ross, R. 1996 *Returning to the Teachings*. Saskatoon, University of Saskatchewan.

Ross, D. and P. Usher, 1986 *From the Roots Up: Economic Development as if Community Mattered*. Toronto: James Lorimer.

Rossi, R. and K. Gilmartin, 1980 *The Handbook of Social Indicators*. New York: Garland Press.

Rotman, Leonard I. 1996 *Parallel Paths: Fiduciary Doctrine and the Crown–Native Relationship in Canada*. Toronto: University of Toronto Press.

_____ **1997** "Symposium on Aboriginal Legal Issues." Special Issue of *Alberta Law Review*, 36 (1). University of Alberta.

Rouch, J. 1956 "Migration au Ghana." Fo. de la Société des Africanistus, 17, 1956.

Rowe, G. et M. J. Norris 1984 *Mortality Projections for Registered Indians*. Ottawa: Statistique Canada (inedit.).

Ryan, J. 1978 *Wall of Words: The Betrayal of the Urban Indian*. Toronto: Peter Martin Associates.

Salisbury, R. 1986 *A Homeland for the Cree*. Kingston and Montreal: McGill-Queen's University Press.

Sambo, D. 1992 "Indigenous Human Rights: The Role of Inuit at the United Nations Working Group on Indigenous Peoples." *Etudes/Inuit/Studies*, 16, 1–2:27–32.

Sanders, D. 1975 "Indian Women: A Brief History of Their Roles and Rights," *McGill Law Journal*, 21, 4, pp. 656–672.

_____ 1983a "The Rights of the Aboriginal Peoples of Canada." *Canadian Bar Review*, 6, 1 (1983):314–338.

_____ 1983b "Prior Claims: Aboriginal People in the Constitution of Canada." In *Canada and the New Constitution: The Unfinished Business*, S. Beck and I. Bernier (eds.). Montreal: Institute for Research on Public Policy.

_____ 1983c "The Indian Lobby." In *And No One Cheered*, K. Banting and R. Simeon (eds.). Toronto: Methuen.

_____ 1985a "The Indian Lobby and the Canadian Constitution, 1978–1982," In *Indigenous Peoples and the Nation-State: 'Fourth World' Politics in Canada, Australia and Norway*, Dyck, N. (ed.), St. John's: Memorial University of Newfoundland, Institute of Social and Economic Research, pp. 151–189.

_____ 1985b "Aboriginal Rights: The Search for Recognition in International Law." In *The Quest for Justice*, M. Boldt, J. Long, and L. Little Bear (eds.). Toronto: University of Toronto Press.

_____ 1990 "The Supreme Court of Canada and the 'Legal and Political Struggle' Over Indigenous Rights." *Canadian Ethnic Studies*, Vol. 22, No. 3, pp. 122–129.

Sarkadi, L. 1992 "Nunavut: Carving Out a New Territory in the North." *Calgary Herald*, January 4, A5.

Satzewich V. and T. Wotherspoon 1993 *First Nations: Race, Class and Gender Relations*. Scarborough, Ontario: Nelson Canada.

Sawchuk, Joe 1978 *The Métis of Manitoba: Reformulation of an Ethnic Identity*. Toronto: Peter Martin Associates.

_____ 1998 *The Dynamics of Native Politics: The Alberta Métis Experience*. Saskatoon: Purich Publishing.

Sawchuk, J., P. Sawchuk and T. Ferguson 1981 *Métis Land Rights in Alberta: A Political History*. Edmonton: The Métis Association of Alberta.

Schissel, B. and T. Wotherspoon 2003 *The Legacy of School for Aboriginal People*. Toronto: Oxford University Press.

Schmeiser, D. 1974 *The Native Offender and the Law*. Ottawa: Information Canada.

Schouls, T. 2004 *Shifting Boundaries: Aboriginal Identity, Pluralist Theory, and the Politics of Self Government*. Vancouver; UBC Press.

Schwartz, B. 1985 *First Principle: Constitutional Reform with Respect to the Aboriginal Peoples of Canada, 1982–84*. Kingston: Institute of Intergovernmental Relations, Queen's University.

Scitovsky, T. 1954 "Two Concepts of External Economics." *Journal of Political Economy*, 62 (April 1954):143–152.

Sealey, D. Bruce 1975 "One Plus One Equals One." In *The Other Natives: the Métis*. Antoine S. Lussier and D. Bruce Sealey (eds.). Winnipeg: Manitoba Métis Federation Press.

Sealey, D. Bruce, and Antoine S. Lussier 1975 *The Métis—Canada's Forgotten People*. Winnipeg: Manitoba Métis Federation Press.

Secretariat aux affaires autochtones 1988 *Les Autochtones au Quebec*. Quebec: Les Publications du Quebec.

Shaw, T. 1985 "Ethnicity as the resilient paradigm: From 1960s to the 1980s." Mimeographed, Dalhousie University, Halifax, Nova Scotia.

Shea, I.G. 1879 *Charlevoix's History of New France*. New York: Colonial Documents, Vol. 2, 1879.

Shewell, H. 2004 *"Enough to KeepThem Alive": Indian Social Welfare in Canada, 1873–1965*. Toronto:

University of Toronto Press.

Shkilnyk, A. 1985 *A Poison Stronger Than Love: The Destruction of an Ojibwa Community.* New Haven and London: Yale University Press.

Siggner, A. 1980 "A Socio-demographic Profile of Indians in Canada." In *Out of Irrelevance*, J.R. Ponting and R. Gibbins (eds.). Toronto: Butterworth and Co. (Canada) Ltd.

_____ **1986** "The Socio-demographic Conditions of Registered Indians." *Canadian Social Trends* (Winter 1986):2–9.

_____ **1998** *Aboriginal Population Characteristics: Fifteen Years of Data, What Have We Learned?* Research paper #15, The University of Calgary, Calgary, Alberta.

Siggner, A. 2003 "Urban Aboriginal Populations: An Update Using the 2001 Census Results." In *Not Strangers in These Parts: Urban Aboriginal Peoples*, D. Newhouse and E. Peters (eds.). Ottawa, Policy Research Initiative.

Siggner, A. and C. Locatelli 1980 *Regional Population Projections by Age, Sex, and Residence for Canada's Registered Indian Population, 1976–1991.* Ottawa: Research Branch, Department of Indian Affairs and Northern Development.

Silman, J. 1987 *Enough is Enough: Aboriginal Women Speak Out.* Toronto: The Women's Press.

Skarlicki, D., n.d. *Socio-Economic Planning Model: Tools for Native Community Economic Planning.* Edmonton: First Nations Resource Council.

Skea, W. 1993–94 "The Canadian Newspaper Industry's Portrayal of the Oka Crisis." *Native Studies Review*, 9,1:15–31.

Slattery, B. 1985 "The Hidden Constitution: Aboriginal Rights in Canada." In *The Quest for Justice*, M. Boldt, J. Long, and L. Little Bear (eds.). Toronto: The University of Toronto Press.

Smith, A. 1981 *The Ethnic Revival.* New York: Cambridge University Press.

Smith, D. 1993 *The Seventh Fire.* Toronto, Key Porter Books.

Smith, J. et al. 1985 "The Changing Political Situation of Women in Canada." In *Minorities and the Canadian State*, Nevitte, N. and A. Kornberg (eds.). Oakville: Mosaic Press, pp. 221–238.

Solicitor General of Canada 1985 *Native and Non-Native Admissions to Federal, Provincial and Territorial Correctional Institutions.* Ottawa: Solicitor General of Canada.

_____ **1989** *Task Force on Aboriginal Peoples in Federal Corrections: Final Report.* Ottawa: Solicitor General of Canada.

Sorenson, Gary and Murray Wolfson 1969 "Black Economic Independence: Some Preliminary Thoughts." *The Annals of Regional Science*, 3 (December 1969):168–178.

Special Senate Committee Hearing on Poverty 1970 *Proceedings*, Vols. 13–14. Ottawa: Supply and Services Canada.

Speck, D. C. 1989 "The Indian Health Transfer Policy: A Step in the Right Direction, A Revenge of the Hidden Policy?" *Native Studies Review*, Vol. 5, No. 1, pp. 187–214.

Spencer, R. and J. Jennings 1965 *The Native Americans.* New York: Harper and Row.

Sprenger, G. Herman 1972 "The Métis Nation: Buffalo Hunting versus Agriculture in the Red River Settlement." *Western Canadian Journal of Anthropology*, 3, 1 (1972):158–178.

Stanbury and Fields 1975 *Success and Failure: Indians in Urban Society.* Vancouver: University of British Columbia Press.

Stanley, George 1952 "The Indian Background of Canadian History." *Canadian Historical Association Annual Report.* Canadian Historical Society.

_____ **1961** *The Birth of Western Canada: A History of the Riel Rebellions.* New York: Longman, Green and Co.

Starblanket, N. 1979 *On the Rights of Indian Women and Children Under the Indian Act.* Ottawa: NIB.

Stasiulis, D. and N. Yuval-Davis (eds.) 1995 *Unsettling Settler Societies*, Vol. 11, London, Sage Publications.

Statistics Canada 1989 *Canadian Social Trends: Violence in the Family.* Ottawa: Statistics Canada.

Steinem, G. 1983 "Perspectives on Women in the 1980s: The Baird Poskanzer Memorial Lecture." In *Perspectives on Women in the 1980s*, Turner, J. and L. Emery (eds.). Winnipeg: The University of Manitoba Press, pp. 14–27.

Stern, P. 2000 "Subsistence: Work and Leisure." *Etudes/Inuit/Studies*, 24,1:9–24.

Sterritt, N. 1998–99 "The Nisga'a Treaty: Competing Claims Ignored!" *B.C. Studies,* 120:73–98.

Stewart, Walter. 1974 "Red Power." In *Canada's Indians: Contemporary Conflicts*, J.S. Frideres (ed.). Scarborough, Ontario: Prentice Hall Canada.

Stymeist, David H. 1975 *Ethnics and Indians: Social Relations in a Northwestern Ontario Town*. Toronto: Peter Martin Associates.

Sunkel, Oswaldo 1973 "Transitional Capitalism and National Disintegration in Latin America." *Social and Economic Studies*, 22 (1973):132–176.

Surtees, R.J. 1969 "The Development of an Indian Reserve Policy in Canada." *Ontario History*, LCI, 2 (June 1969):87–98.

Swain, H. 1988 "Comprehensive Claims." *Transition*, 1, 6 (December 1988):7–9.

Symons, T.H.B. 1970 "The Obligations of History: A Review of Native Rights in Canada." *Indian–Eskimo Association of Canada Bulletin*, 2, 3 (1970):5–7.

Tabb, William 1970 *The Political Economy of the Black Ghetto*. New York: W.W. Norton and Co.

Tanner, A. (ed.) 1983 *The Politics of Indianness*. Institute of Social and Economic Research, Memorial University of Newfoundland, St. John's, Newfoundland.

Taqralik 1984 "Native Women's Association Offers Help to Inuit Women." Mimeo.

Taylor, J. 1983 "An Historical Introduction to Métis Claims in Canada." *The Canadian Journal of Native Studies*, 3 (1983):151–181.

Tennant, P. 1984 "Indian Self Government: Progress or Stalemate." *Canadian Public Policy*, 10, 2 (1984):211–215.

_____ **1985** "Aboriginal Rights and the Penner Report on Indian Self Government." In *The Quest for Justice*, M. Boldt, J. Long, and L. Little Bear (eds.). Toronto: The University of Toronto Press.

Tester, F. and P. Kulchyski 1994 *Tammarniit (Mistakes): Inuit Relocation in the Eastern Arctic, 1939–63*. Vancouver: University of British Columbia Press.

Thomas, D.H. 1972 "Western Shoshoni Ecology Settlement Patterns and Beyond." In *Great Basin Cultural Ecology: A Symposium*. D.D. Fowler (ed.). Desert Research Institute, Publications in the Social Sciences, 8.

Thomas, Robert K. 1985 "Afterward." In *The New Peoples: Being and Becoming Métis in North America*, Jacqueline Peterson and Jennifer S.H. Brown (eds.). Winnipeg: The University of Manitoba Press (1985):243–251.

Thompson, R. 1982 "Aboriginal Title and Mining Legislation in the Northwest Territories." *Studies in Aboriginal Rights No. 6*. Saskatoon, Saskatchewan: University of Saskatchewan Native Law Centre.

Titley, B. 1983 "W.M. Graham: Indian Agent Extraordinaire." *Prairie Forum*, 8, (1983):26–28.

_____ **1986** *A Narrow Vision*. Vancouver: University of British Columbia Press.

Tjepkema, M. 2001 "The Health of the Off-Reserve Aboriginal Population." *Supplement to Health Reports*, vol. 13, Ottawa, Statistics Canada, Cat. No. 82-003.

Tobias, J. 1976 "Protection, Civilization, Assimilation: An Outline of Canada's Indian Policy." *Western Canadian Journal of Anthropology*, 6, 2 (1976):13–30.

Treaty 7 Elders and Tribal Council, 1996 *The True Spirit and Original Intent of Treaty*. Montreal and Kingston: McGill-Queen's University Press.

Trigger, B. 1965 "The Jesuits and the Fur Trade." *Ethnohistory*, 12 (Winter 1965):30–53.

_____ **1985** *Natives and Newcomers*. Kingston and Montreal: McGill-Queen's University Press.

Trudel, Marcel and Genevieve Jain 1970 "Canadian History Textbooks." *Studies of the Royal Commission on*

Bilingualism and Biculturalism, No. 5. Ottawa: Queen's Printer.

Turpel, Mary 1990 "Aboriginal Peoples and the Canadian Charter: Interpretive Monopolies, Cultural Differences." *Canadian Human Rights Year Book*, Ottawa: University of Ottawa, Human Rights Research and Education Centre, 1989–90, pp. 3–45.

Two-Axe Early, M. et al. 1981 "Ethnicity and Femininity as Determinants of Life Experience." *Canadian Ethnic Studies*, 13, 1, pp. 37–42.

Uchendu, U. 1970 "The Passing of Tribal Man: A West African Experience." In *The Passing of Tribal Man in Africa*, P. Gutlaind (ed.). Leiden: E.J. Brill (1970):51–56.

Umorzurike, U. 1972 *Self-Determination in International Law*. Hamden, Ct.: Anchor Books.

United Nations Educational, Scientific and Cultural Organization (UNESCO) 1981 "Socio-Economic Indicators for Planning: Methodological Aspects and Selected Examples." *Socio-Economic Studies* 2. Paris.

_____ **1984** "Applicability of Indicators of Socio-Economic Change for Development Planning." *Socio-Economic Studies* 7. Paris.

Usher, P. 1989 *Towards a Strategy for Supporting the Domestic Economy of the Northwest Territories*. Ottawa.

Vachon, R. 1982 "Traditional Legal Ways of Native Peoples and the Struggle for Native Rights." *Inter-Culture*, 15 (1982):1–18.

Vanderburgh, R. 1968 *The Canadian Indians in Ontario's School Texts: A Study of Social Studies Textbooks, Grades 1 through 8*. Report prepared for the University Women's Club of Port Credit, Ontario.

Van Kirk, Sylvia 1980 *Many Tender Ties*. Winnipeg: Watson & Dwyer Publishing.

Venne, Sharon Helen 1998 *Our Elders Understand Our Rights: Evolving International Law Regarding Indigenous Peoples*. Penticton, BC: Theytus Books.

Vick-Westgate, A. 2002 *Nunavik*. Calgary: University of Calgary Press.

Vincent, David 1970 *An Evaluation of the Indian–Métis Urban Problem*. Winnipeg: University of Winnipeg Press.

Waddell, Jack and O.M. Watson 1971 *The American Indian in Urban Society*. Boston: Little, Brown and Co.

Walker, James 1971 "The Indians in Canadian Historical Writing." Paper delivered at Canadian Historical Association Meetings.

Walsh, Gerald 1971 *Indians in Transition*. Toronto: McClelland and Stewart.

Ward, M. 1988 *Indian Education in Canada*. MA Thesis, College of Education, University of Saskatchewan, Saskatoon.

Washburn, Wilcomb 1965 "Indian Removal Policy: Administrative, Historical, and Moral Criteria for Judging Its Success or Failure." *Ethno-History*, 12 (Winter 1965):274–278.

Watkins, M. 1977 *Dene Nation: The Colony Within*. Toronto: University of Toronto Press.

Watson, G. 1979 "On Getting Nothing Back: Managing the Meaning of Ethnicity in Canada's Northwest Territories." *Ethnos*, 1–2 (1979):99–118.

_____ **1981** "The Reification of Ethnicity and its Political Consequences in the North." *Canadian Review of Sociology and Anthropology*, 18, 40 (1981):453–469.

Waubageshig 1970 *The Only Good Indian*. Toronto: New Press.

Weaver, S. 1978 *Indian Women, Marriage and Legal Status*. Waterloo: University of Waterloo, n.p.

_____ **1981** *Making Canadian Indian Policy: The Hidden Agenda 1968–1970*. Toronto: University of Toronto Press.

_____ **1983** "Federal Difficulties with Aboriginal Rights Demands." In *Aboriginal Rights: Towards an Understanding*, J.A. Long, M. Boldt, and L. Little Bear (eds.). Lethbridge: University of Lethbridge.

_____ **1984** "A Commentary on the Penner Report," *Canadian Public Policy*, 10, 2 (1984):215–221.

_____ **1985** "Political Representivity and Indigenous Minorities in Canada and Australia." In N. Dyck (ed.), *Indigenous*

Peoples and the Nation State: 'Fourth World' Politics in Canada, Australia and Norway, St. John's: Memorial University of Newfoundland.

_____ **1986** "Indian Policy in the New Conservative Government, Part II: The Nielsen Task Force in the Context of Recent Policy Initiatives." *Native Studies Review*, 2, 2 (1986):1–47.

Weitz, J. **1971** *Cultural Change and Field Dependence in Two Native Canadian Linguistic Families*. Unpublished Ph.D. dissertation, University of Ottawa, 1971.

Welsh, A. **2000** "Aboriginal Offenders and Full Parole: A Profile," *Forum*, 12,1:61–64.

Wertman, P. **1983** "Planning and Development After the James Bay Agreement." *The Canadian Journal of Native Studies*, 2, 3 (1983):48–56.

Werett, J. and D. Brown **1994** *Models of Aboriginal Government in Urban Areas, Policy and Strategic Direction.* Ottawa, Department of Indian Affairs and Northern Development.

White, Jerry P., Paul Maxim, Dan Beavon **2003** *Aboriginal Conditions: Research as a Foundation for Public Policy.* Vancouver: University of British Columbia Press.

White, P. **1985** *Native Women: A Statistical Overview*. Ottawa: SOS.

Whitehead, S., B. Henning, J. Johnston, A. Devlin **1996** *Developing an Injury Morbidity and Mortality Profile in the Sioux Lookout Zone: 1992–1995.* Canadian Hospitals Injury Reporting and Prevention Program, Ottawa.

Whiteside, D. **1972** "A Good Blanket Has Four Corners: An Initial Comparison of the Colonial Administration of Aboriginals in Canada and the United States." Paper presented at the Western Association of Sociology and Anthropology, Calgary.

_____ **1973a** *Historical Development of Aboriginal Political Associations in Canada*. Ottawa: NIB.

_____ **1973b** "Historical Development of Aboriginal Associations in Canada: Documentation." Ottawa: National Indian Brotherhood.

_____ **1980** "Bullets, Bibles, Bureaucrats, and Businessmen: Indian Administration in Upper Canada, 1746–1980." Address to the Indian Historical Conference, Walpole Island Reserve, November 15, 1980.

Wien, F. **1986** *Rebuilding the Economic Base of Indian Communities: The MicMac in Nova Scotia*. Montreal: Institute for Research on Public Policy.

Wildsmith, B. **1985** "Pre Confederation Treaties." In *Aboriginal Peoples and the Law*, B. Morse (ed.). Ottawa: Carleton University Press, pp.122–271.

Wilkins **1999** "... But We Need the Eggs: The Royal Commission, the Charter of Rights and the Inherent Right of Aboriginal Self-Government." *University of Toronto Law Journal,* XLIV, 1:53–121.

Willhelm, Sidney M. **1969** "Red Man, Black Man, and White America: The Constitutional Approach to Genocide." *Catalyst*, 4 (Spring 1969):3–4.

Wilson, Richard W. **1992** *Compliance Ideologies: Rethinking Political Culture*, Cambridge University Press.

Wong, D. **2002** *Cities at the Crossroads: Addressing Intergovernmental Structures for Western Canada's Cities*. Calgary, August, Canada West Foundation.

Woodward, J. **1989** *Native Law*. Toronto: Carswell.

Wotherspoon, T. **2003** "Prospects for a New Middle Class Among Urban Aboriginal People" In *Not Strangers in these Parts*, D. Newhouse and E. Peters (eds.), Ottawa, Policy Research Institute, pp. 147–166.

Wright, C. **1995** "Diversions are a Bright Light." *Native Issues Monthly*, special issue, 61–63.

Wuttunee, W. **1972** *Ruffled Feathers*. Calgary: Bell Books Ltd.

Yerxa, J. **1990** *Report on the Survey of the First Nations of Alberta.* Edmonton: John Yerxa Research Incorporated.

Young, K. **1984** "Indian Health Services in Canada: A Sociohistorical Perspective." *Social Science and Medicine*, Vol. 18, No. 3, pp. 257–264.

Young, T. J. O'Neill, B. Elias **1999** *Chronic Diseases, First Nations and Inuit Regional Health Survey.* First Nations and Inuit Regional Health Survey, National Steering Committee, Ottawa.

Young, T., J. O'Neill,
   B. Elias, J. Readin,
   G. McDonald 1998 (First
National and Inuit
Regional Health Survey
National Steering
Committees and Technical
Committees), "Chronic
Diseases Among Aboriginal
People in Canada."
Conference of the National
Aboriginal Information and
Research, Ottawa.

Zakariya, H. 1976 "New
Directions in the Search for
and Development of
Petroleum Resources in the
Developing Countries."
*Vanderbilt Journal of
Transnational Law*, 9
(Summer 1976):545–577.

Zlotkin, N. 1983 *Unfinished
Business: Aboriginal
Peoples and The 1983
Constitutional Conference*.
Kingston: Institute of
Intergovernmental
Relations, Queen's
University.

_____ 1985 "Post-
Confederation Treaties." In
*Aboriginal Peoples and the
Law*, B. Morse (ed.).
Ottawa: Carleton
University Press.

Index